ROMANESQUE PATRONS AND PROCESSES

The twenty-five papers in this volume arise from a conference jointly organised by the British Archaeological Association and the Museu Nacional d'Art de Catalunya in Barcelona. They explore the making of art and architecture in Latin Europe and the Mediterranean between *c.* 1000 and *c.* 1250, with a particular focus on questions of patronage, design and instrumentality.

No previous studies of patterns of artistic production during the Romanesque period rival the breadth of coverage encompassed by this volume – both in terms of geographical origin and media, and in terms of historical approach. Topics range from case studies on Santiago de Compostela, the Armenian Cathedral in Jerusalem and the Winchester Bible to reflections on textuality and donor literacy, the culture of abbatial patronage at Saint-Michel de Cuxa and the re-invention of slab relief sculpture around 1100. The volume also includes papers that attempt to recover the procedures that coloured interaction between artists and patrons – a serious theme in a collection that opens with 'Function, condition and process in eleventh-century Anglo-Norman church architecture' and ends with a consideration of 'The death of the patron'.

Jordi Camps is Chief Curator of the Medieval Department of the Museu Nacional d'Art de Catalunya (MNAC) in Barcelona, where he has curated a number of exhibitions. He is one of the principal scientific coordinators of the *Enciclopedia del Románico en Cataluña* and is a member of the project Magistri Cataloniae. His personal research interests revolve around sculpture between the 11th and 13th centuries, and the history and historiography of the Romanesque collections at MNAC.

Manuel Castiñeiras is Associate Professor of Medieval Art History at the Universitat Autònoma de Barcelona (UAB), where he acted as the Head of the Department of Art and Musicology from 2014–17. His research focuses on Romanesque art and medieval panel painting, though he has also worked widely on pilgrimage and the question of artistic exchange in the Mediterranean. He is currently the 2017–18 Samuel H. Kress Senior Fellow at the Center for Advanced Study in the Visual Arts-National Gallery of Art, in Washington DC.

John McNeill teaches at Oxford University's Department of Continuing Education and is Honorary Secretary of the British Archaeological Association, for whom he has edited and contributed to volumes on Anjou, King's Lynn and the Fens, the medieval cloister and English medieval chantries. He was instrumental in establishing the BAA's International Romanesque conference series and has a particular interest in the design of medieval monastic precincts.

Richard Plant has taught at a number of institutions and worked for many years at Christie's Education in London, where he was Deputy Academic Director. His research interests lie in the buildings of the Anglo-Norman realm and the Holy Roman Empire, in particular architectural iconography. He is Publicity Officer for the British Archaeological Association and co-edited the first volume in this series, *Romanesque and the Past*.

ROMANESQUE PATRONS AND PROCESSES
Design and Instrumentality in the Art and Architecture of Romanesque Europe

Edited by
Jordi Camps, Manuel Castiñeiras,
John McNeill and Richard Plant

BRITISH ARCHAEOLOGICAL ASSOCIATION
2018

LONDON AND NEW YORK

First published 2018
by Routledge
2 Park Square, Milton Park, Abingdon, Oxon OX14 4RN

and by Routledge
711 Third Avenue, New York, NY 10017

Routledge is an imprint of the Taylor & Francis Group, an informa business

© 2018 British Archaeological Association

The right of Jordi Camps, Manuel Castiñeiras, John McNeill, and Richard Plant to be identified as the authors of the editorial material, and of the authors for their individual chapters, has been asserted in accordance with sections 77 and 78 of the Copyright, Designs and Patents Act 1988.

All rights reserved. No part of this book may be reprinted or reproduced or utilised in any form or by any electronic, mechanical, or other means, now known or hereafter invented, including photocopying and recording, or in any information storage or retrieval system, without permission in writing from the publishers.

Trademark notice: Product or corporate names may be trademarks or registered trademarks, and are used only for identification and explanation without intent to infringe.

Disclaimer Statements in the volume reflect the views of the authors, and not necessarily those of the Association, editors or publisher.

British Library Cataloguing-in-Publication Data
A catalogue record for this book is available from the British Library

Library of Congress Cataloging-in-Publication Data
A catalog record for this book has been requested

ISBN: 978-1-138-47704-9 (hbk)
ISBN: 978-1-138-47703-2 (pbk)
ISBN: 978-1-351-10560-6 (ebk)

Typeset in Times New Roman
by Apex CoVantage, LLC

CONTENTS

Advisory panel	vii
Notes on contributors	viii
Preface	xii
Chapter abstracts	xiii
Colour plates	xxi

Function, condition and process in eleventh-century Anglo-Norman church architecture
Richard Gem — 1

Matilda and the cities of the Gregorian Reform
Arturo Carlo Quintavalle — 15

Romanesque Cathedrals in Northern Italy – building processes between bishop and commune
Bruno Klein — 31

Episcopal patronage in the reform of Catalan Cathedral canonries during the first Romanesque period: A new approach
Eduardo Carrero Santamaria — 39

The role of kings and bishops in the introduction of Romanesque art in Navarre and Aragon
Javier Martínez de Aguirre — 47

From Peláez to Gelmírez: the problem of art patronage at the Romanesque Cathedral of Santiago de Compostela
Jens Rueffer — 63

Patronage, Romanesque architecture and the Languedoc
Eric Fernie — 73

The Armenian Cathedral of Saints James in Jerusalem: Melisende and the question of exchange between East And West
Armen Kazaryan — 83

Grandmont and the English Kings: An example of patronage in the context of an ascetic architectural trend
Claude Andrault-Schmitt — 93

The Hospital, England and Sigena: A footnote
Neil Stratford — 109

Henry of Blois, St Hugh and Henry II: The Winchester Bible reconsidered
Christopher Norton — 117

Patrons, institutions and public in the making of Catalan Romanesque art during the Comital period (1000–1137)
Manuel Castiñeiras — 143

The artistic patronage of Abbot Gregorius at Cuixà: Models and tributes
Anna Orriols — 159

A Limousin ciborium in medieval Catalonia
Joan Duran-Porta — 175

The Jaca ivories: Towards a revaluation of eleventh-century female artistic patronage in the Kingdom of Aragon
Verónica C. Abenza Soria — 183

The Aemilian casket reliquary: A product of institutional patronage
Melanie Hanan — 195

Patronage at the Cathedral of Tarragona: Cult and residential space
Esther Lozano-López & Marta Serrano-Coll — 205

An Anglo-Norman at Terrassa? Augustinian Canons and Thomas Becket at the end of the twelfth century
Carles Sánchez Márquez — 219

Agency and the re-invention of slab relief sculpture at San Isidoro de León *c*. 1100
Rose Walker — 235

Patron and liturgy: The liturgical setting of the Cathedral Church of San Martino in Lucca after 1070 and the Gregorian Reform
Carlotta Taddei — 251

The 'Literate' lay donor: Textuality and the Romanesque patron
Robert A. Maxwell — 259

Remarks on patron inscriptions with restricted presence
Wilfried E. Keil — 279

The twelfth-century patrons of the Bridekirk font
Hugh Doherty — 291

The scope of competence of the painter and the patron in mural painting in the Romanesque period
Anne Leturque — 313

The death of the patron: Agency, style and the making of the *Liber Feudorum Maior* of Barcelona
Shannon L. Wearing — 327

Index — 337

ADVISORY PANEL

Dr. Elizabeth Valdez del Alamo: Montclair University, New Jersey
Prof. Claude Andrault Schmidt: CESCM, Université de Poitiers
Prof. Michele Bacci: Universität Freiburg
Prof. Giovanni Coppola: Università degli Studi Suor Orsola Benincasa, Napoli
Prof. Maria Monica Donato (†): Scuola Normale Superiore di Pisa
Dr. Ute Engel: Ludwig-Maximilians-Universität München
Prof. Peter Fergusson: Wellesley College
Prof. Eric Fernie: Courtauld Institute, London
Prof. Peter Klein, Eberhard-Karls- Universität-Tübingen
Prof. John Lowden: Courtauld Institute, London
Dr. Gerhard Lutz: Dom-Museum, Hildesheim
Dr. Therese Martin, CSIC, Madrid
Dr. Tom Nixon: Courtauld Insititue, London
Prof. Roger Stalley: Trinity College, Dublin
Neil Stratford: Keeper Emeritus, British Museum
Dr. Béla Zsolt Szakács: Central European University, Budapest
Prof. Eliane Vergnolle: Université de Franche-Comté

BRITISH ARCHAEOLOGICAL ASSOCIATION STEERING GROUP

Dr. Rosa Bacile: Tate Gallery, London
Dr. Jordi Camps i Soria: Museu Nacional d'Art de Catalunya, Barcelona
Prof. Manuel Castiñeiras: Universitat Autònoma de Barcelona
Professor Lindy Grant: President, BAA
John McNeill: Hon. Secretary, BAA
Dr. Richard Plant: Hon. Publicity Officer, BAA
Gemma Ylla-Català: Museu Nacional d'Art de Catalunya, Barcelona

NOTES ON CONTRIBUTORS

Verónica C. Abenza Soria joined the Department of Art and Musicology at the Universitat Autònoma de Barcelona in 2013 as a research fellow. She held a Spanish MICINN Predoctoral fellowship in support of her thesis research on female artistic patronage in Aragon, Navarre and Catalonia (11th–13th centuries) (2013–2017) and held the Fondazione di Studi di Storia dell'Arte Roberto Longhi (Florence, Italy) fellowship in support of her research on the frescoes of the Chapterhouse of Santa María de Sigena (Aragon, Spain) and the frescoes of the church of San Michele degli Scalzi (Pisa, Italy) (2016–2017). She is currently part of the Spanish MICINN research project *Mobility and Artistic Transfer in the Medieval Mediterranean (1187-1388): artists, objects and models-Magistri Mediterranei*.

Javier Martínez de Aguirre is Professor of Medieval Art History at the Complutense University of Madrid. His research areas are Iberian Romanesque and Gothic art, and medieval heraldry. His publications include *Roncesvalles: Hospital y santuario en el Camino de Santiago*, *Torres del Río: Iglesia del Santo Sepulcro*, *El escudo de armas de Navarra*, *Emblemas heráldicos en el arte medieval navarro* and *Arte y monarquía en Navarra 1328–1425*. He edited the *Enciclopedia del Románico en Zaragoza* (2010, 2 vols) and the *Enciclopedia del Románico en Navarra* (2008, 3 vols).

Claude Andrault-Schmitt is Emeritus Professor of Medieval Art History at the *Centre d'études supérieures de civilisation médiévale* (University of Poitiers). She works on monastic architecture in the 12th and 13th centuries, as well as the early Gothic architecture of Aquitaine and the Loire Valley. She has written or directed monographs on Notre-Dame-la-Grande at Poitiers, St-Martial at Limoges, the Cathedral of Tours, canonial life and culture at St-Yrieix and, above all, on Poitiers Cathedral. Besides more synthetic papers for various journals, she has published a number of short monographs for the Société française d'archéologie in its annual *Congrès archéologique*. She is President of the *Societé des Antiquaires de l'Ouest*.

Jordi Camps i Sòria is Chief Curator of the Medieval Department of the Museu Nacional d'Art de Catalunya (MNAC) in Barcelona, where he has curated a number of exhibitions. He is one of the principal scientific coordinators of the *Enciclopedia del Románico en Cataluña* and is a member of the research project *Magistri Cataloniae*. His personal research interests revolve around sculpture between the eleventh to thirteenth centuries, and the history and historiography of the Romanesque Collections at MNAC.

Eduardo Carrero Santamaria is Lecturer in the Medieval History of Art at the Universitat Autònoma de Barcelona. His most recent research deals with the relationship between architecture and ritual, grounded in an understanding of architectural space as a performative place. All his research is united by a methodological focus on the interaction between architecture and liturgy, exploring the possibilities, limitations and perspectives that the liturgy offers in the study of architectural history. His many publications include the coordination of a volume on the relationships between architecture and liturgy in the cathedrals of the Crown of Aragón (2014), a monograph on the Medieval Cathedrals of Galicia (2005) and a synthesis of new proposals on the problematic Cathedral of Oviedo (2003).

Manuel Antonio Castiñeiras González is currently Associate Professor in the Medieval Art History at the Universitat Autònoma de Barcelona (UAB), where he has acted as the Head of the Department of Art and Musicology from 2014–2017. Previously he was Chief Curator of the Romanesque Collection at the *Museu Nacional d'Art de Catalunya* (MNAC, Barcelona) (2005–2010) and Associate Professor in the University of Santiago de Compostela (Spain) (1997–2005). His research focuses on Romanesque art and medieval panel painting. He has also worked widely on medieval Pilgrimage and the question of artistic exchange in the Mediterranean between the 11th and 15th centuries. He is currently developing a wide-ranging project on artistic encounters with Byzantium during the Mediterranean expansion of the Crown of Aragon as the 2017–2018 Samuel H. Kress Senior Fellow at the Center for Advanced Study in the Visual Arts-National Gallery of Art, in Washington D.C.

Hugh Doherty is a Lecturer in Medieval History at the University of East Anglia. He is interested in Late Antiquity, the early medieval period and the Romanesque world.

Joan Duran-Porta holds a Ph.D in art history from the Universitat Autònoma de Barcelona, where he is currently Assistant Professor in the department of Art and Musicology. He also teaches at the Universitat de Lleida and at the Universitat Oberta de Catalunya. Between 2007 and 2011 he was assistant curator in the Museu Nacional d'Art de Catalunya (Barcelona). He specialised in medieval metalwork, particularly of the Romanesque period. He uses a multifocal approach based on the analysis of production, patronage, import and social uses of sumptuary goods. His secondary research interests include First Romanesque architecture in southern Europe, and women as artists and patrons in medieval art.

Eric Fernie has taught at the universities of Witwatersrand, East Anglia, Edinburgh and London, where he was Director of the Courtauld Institute. He is a fellow of the British Academy, the Royal Society of Edinburgh, the Society of Antiquaries of London (of which he has been President) and the Society of Antiquaries of Scotland. His books include *The Architecture of the Anglo-Saxons* (1983), *An Architectural History of Norwich Cathedral* (1993), *Art History and its Methods* (1995), *The Architecture of Norman England* (2000) and *Romanesque Architecture: The First Style of the European Age* (2014).

Richard Gem is a graduate of Cambridge University with an M.A. in archaeology and Ph.D in the history of art. He is the former Secretary of the Cathedrals Fabric Commission for England (the body responsible for control over, and advice to, England's historic cathedrals regarding their fabric and contents). He has held research fellowships at the Institute of Archaeology and the Courtauld Institute in the University of London. He has published widely on early medieval and Romanesque architecture, including two volumes of collected papers in 2004, and some fifteen subsequent papers on Late-Antique, Anglo-Saxon, Romanesque and early Irish architecture.

Melanie Hanan is a lecturer at Fordham University and The Cloisters, The Metropolitan Museum of Art, in New York City. Her research focuses on Romanesque metalwork, especially reliquaries in relation to medieval liturgy. She is currently working on a monograph entitled *House of God on the Altar*, which explores the use of casket – or box-shaped – reliquaries in the Middle Ages. This monograph is based on her doctoral dissertation and research completed in 2016 and 2017 thanks to a Kress Research Grant from the ICMA and a fellowship at the Center for Medieval Studies at Fordham University. Dr. Hanan received her Ph.D from the Institute of Fine Arts at NYU, and her M.A. from the Courtauld Institute of Art.

Armen Kazaryan is Vice-Director of the State Institute for Art Studies at the Russian Federation's Ministry of Culture. He is also a Vice-Director of the Research Institute for the Theory and History of Architecture and Town-Planning (Moscow). He is the author of around 200 publications, as well as having acted as a consultant on several architectural restoration projects. His four-volume study 'Church Architecture of the Seventh Century in Transcaucasian Countries: The Formation and Development of the Tradition' (Moscow, 2012–2013, written and published in Russian) was honoured with the Europa Nostra Award (2014) and with the Toros Toramanian Award (2016). He is currently working on a large-scale study of the architecture of Ani, the medieval capital of Armenia. He has cooperated with the World Monuments Fund and Turkish restorers in the conservation of monuments of Armenian architecture in eastern Turkey.

Wilfried E. Keil studied Film and TV business administration in Dortmund, and Art History, Philosophy and Classical Archaeology in Munich before receiving his Ph.D in 2011 at the Ruprecht-Karls-University Heidelberg with a thesis on Romanesque beast-columns (publication: Romanische Bestiensäulen, Berlin 2018). He has participated in several research initiatives concerned with building archaeology, inventory and excavations at the Institute for European Art History at Heidelberg University. Since July 2011 he has worked as a postdoctoral researcher concerned with script and character on a major project entitled 'Material Text Cultures. Materiality and Presence of Writing in Non-Typographic Societies'. His research interests are Medieval Architecture and Sculpture, Renaissance Sculpture, Animal Iconography, Inscriptions and Film. He has written a number of scholarly articles and is currently writing a monograph about the presence and restricted presence of inscriptions in medieval architecture and sculpture.

Bruno Klein studied art history in Berlin, Paris, Cologne and Bonn. In 1983 he received a doctorate from the Free University of Berlin with a dissertation on the beginnings of French High Gothic architecture. He was a scholar at the German Institute of Art History in Florence and an academic assistant in Göttingen, where he habilitated in 1991 with a paper on Italian Romanesque architecture and sculpture. Bruno Klein is now Professor in History of Art at Technische Universität Dresden and a member of the Saxonian Academy of Sciences. In 2015/16 he was Richard-Krautheimer Gastprofessor at the Bibliotheca Hertziana, Rome. His research focusses on Medieval art and the history of architecture from Antiquity to the present day. In particular, Bruno Klein highlights the role of communication in both the conception and creation of artworks as well as in their medial distribution. He was editor and/or author of several books, among them *Die Kirche als Baustelle* (*The church as a building site*) (2013), *Gothic: Visual Art of the Middle Ages 1140–1500* (*2012*) and *Geschichte der bildenden Kunst in Deutschland* (*A History of Visual Art in Germany – Gothic*) (2017).

Anne Leturque holds a doctorate in the history of medieval art, having been jointly supervised by Professors Manuel Castiñeiras and Géraldine Mallet in Barcelona and Montpellier respectively. She organised and coordinated the *factura* research programme, which has now developed into a collaborative platform [http://factura-recherche.org] and curated the exhibition: *Du fragment à l'ensemble: les peintures murales de Casesnoves*. She also co-directed with Géraldine Mallet a publication entitled *Arts picturaux en territoires catalans (XIIe–XIVe siècle: approches matérielles, techniques et comparatives* (Montpellier 2015). Anne Leturque has been a lecturer at Paul-Valéry University Montpellier since 2012 and is a researcher and associate member of the Montpellier Centre for Medieval Studies [http://cemm.upv.

univ-montp3.fr/equipe/membres-associes/anne-leturque], a member of the scientific and cultural project at the Maison aux Images de Lagrasse (Aude) [http://rcppm.org/blog/] and the research programme *Magistri Mediterranei* [www.magistrimediterranei.org/en/project/].

Esther Lozano-López (Ph.D 2003) has held teaching and research positions at the University of Girona (2007–10), at the Universitat Autònoma in Barcelona (2010–11) at the Universitat Rovira i Vigili in Tarragona (2011–12), and at the School of New Interactive Technologies; ENTI-Universitat of Barcelona (2017). She has also lectured at the Spanish National University of Distance Education (UNED) from 2009. Her research is concerned with medieval iconography and its social and cultural contexts, with how iconographical programmes in turn relate to architectural space (particularly in cathedrals and monasteries), and, above all, to Romanesque sculpture in the Iberian Peninsula. She has also published in the field of ecclesiastical patronage, memory, visual discourse and epigraphy.

John McNeill teaches at Oxford University's Department of Continuing Education, and is Honorary Secretary of the British Archaeological Association, for whom he has edited and contributed to volumes on Anjou, King's Lynn and the Fens, the medieval cloister and English medieval chantries. He was instrumental in establishing the BAA's International Romanesque Conference Series and has a particular interest in the design of medieval monastic precincts.

Robert A. Maxwell (Sherman Fairchild Associate Professor of Fine Arts, Institute of Fine Arts, New York University) has published on sculpture, illumination, and medieval urbanism. He is editor, with K. Ambrose, of *Current Directions in Eleventh- and Twelfth-Century Sculpture Studies* (2011) and of *Representing History, 900–1300: Art, Music, History* (2010). Recent essays include 'Le livre-objet entre oralité et 'literacy': la memoria du medium dans le monde juridique' (2017) and 'Pictura como Figura': autenticidad artística y duplicidad en Raluy' (2015). He is currently completing a book on illuminated historical and legal texts (cartularies, chronicles) of the central Middle Ages.

Christopher Norton is Emeritus Professor of Medieval Art and Architecture in the Department of History of Art and the Centre for Medieval Studies at the University of York. He has published widely on aspects of medieval art and architecture.

Anna Orriols is Associate Professor of Art History at the Universitat Autònoma de Barcelona (UAB). Her research focuses on Catalan medieval art, specifically on the iconographical programmes found in Romanesque wall painting, on manuscript illumination (in particular the *scriptoria* of Girona and Cuixà and manuscript copies of Beatus of Liébana's *Commentary on the Apocalypse*), hagiographical programmes and episcopal imagery and patronage. Her current interests explore the relationship between the various arts in Catalan Romanesque, the representation of patrons and artists on works of art, and the depiction of the wonderful, magical and miraculous in medieval art, along with objects and jewels believed to have magical properties, a subject about which she is co-organizing a symposium to be held in Barcelona in October 2018 (Imago & Mirabilia). Anna Orriols is part of the research group (GdR) *Magistri Cataloniae* at the Universitat Autònoma de Barcelona (Departament d'Art i Musicologia). Most of her publications are to be found on academia.edu.

Richard Plant has taught at a number of institutions and worked for many years at Christie's Education in London, where he was deputy academic director. His research interests lie in the buildings of the Anglo-Norman realm and the Holy Roman Empire, in particular in architectural iconography. He is Publicity Officer for the British Archaeological Association and co-edited the first volume in this series, *Romanesque and the Past*.

Arturo Carlo Quintavalle was appointed Professor of the History of Art at the Università di Parma in 1965, where he also presided over the Faculty of Letters. He was responsible for the *Convegni internazionali su temi dell'arte medieval*, which he organised for 14 successive years in Parma, and whose transactions he edited. He has curated exhibitions on *Wiligelmo e Matilde* (Mantova 1991), *Benedetto Antelami* (Parma 1990) and *Il medioevo delle cattedrali* (Parma 2006) and has published extensively on the medieval art and architecture of central and northern Italy, both on specific buildings – *Il Duomo di Modena* (Modena 1964), *La cattedrale di Parma* (Parma 1974), *Il Duomo di Cremona* (1973 and 2010) – and on more wide-ranging medieval themes – *La strada Romea* (Milano 1975), *Vie dei pellegrini nell'Emilia occidentale* (Roma 1977) and *Romanico padano civiltà d'occidente* (Firenze 1969). He has a particular interest in the use of architecture and imagery during the period of the Gregorian Reform, the work of Master Niccolo and the importance of the Antique during the 11th and 12th centuries. Professor Quintavalle is a member of the Accademia dei Lincei.

Jens Rueffer received his Ph.D from Humboldt-University (Berlin) in 1998 with a thesis on Cistercian aesthetic culture and habilitated at the University of Bern in 2010 with a thesis on manufacturing and the perception of medieval sculpture (*Werkprozess – Wahrnehmung – Interpretation*, Berlin 2014). From 2007–10 he worked within a larger project on the building history of the cathedral of St. James in Santiago de Compostela focusing on the medieval sources (*Die Kathedrale von Santigo de Compostela 1075–1211. Eine Quellenstudie.* Freiburg 2010). As an independent scholar he has taught as a visiting professor at the Universities of Bern, Freiburg, Darmstadt, Graz and Vienna. His research concentrates on various aspects of medieval architecture and sculpture as well as on the art and architecture of monastic orders with a special focus on the Cistercians.

Carles Sánchez Márquez wrote his Ph.D on the *Organisation of Romanesque cathedral workshops in Spain* at the Universitat Autònoma de Barcelona, where he now works as a lecturer in medieval art history. His researches interests focus on Romanesque artists, sculpture (particularly portals) and mural painting, as well as on Pilgrimage and the spread of the cult of St Nicholas in the Iberian Peninsula. He has presented the results of his research at conferences at the Scuola Normale Superiore in Pisa (*Index Magistri Cataloniae. Artisti tra anonimato e firma nella Catalogna e nel bacino Mediterraneo*), Perpignan (*L'anonymat et la signature des artistes dans la Catalogne et le bassin méditerranéen*) and Barcelona. He has also published articles in academic journals such as Iconographica, Ad Limina, Codex Aquilarensis and Cahiers de Saint-Michel de Cuxa. Carles Sanchez is a member of the research group *Magistri Cataloniae* and the research project *Magistri Mediterranei* at the Universitat Autònoma de Barcelona (UAB).

Marta Serrano Coll is currently Associate Professor in the department of History and History of Art at the Universitat Rovira i Virgili in Tarragona (URV) where she has taught since 2006. She is a member of the international research group TEMPLA whose work is concerned with Romanesque cathedrals and their environmental contexts in Catalonia. She is also interested in images of power in the art of the Middle Ages and the extent to which art functioned as an advertisement to proclaim and promote the monarchical institutions of the Iberian Peninsula. Her recent publications include studies on Romanesque sculpture and hagiography.

Neil Stratford is Emeritus Keeper of Medieval and Later Antiquities at The British Museum and, in addition to having held a number of teaching posts in London and the United States, was Professor of medieval art and archaeology at L'Ecole nationale des Chartes in Paris. He is the director and principle author of the *Corpus de la sculpture de Cluny, I. Les parties orientales de la Grande Eglise Cluny III*, associé étranger de l'Académie des Inscriptions et Belles-Lettres (Institut de France) and was awarded the grand prix de La Société Française d'Archéologie in 2011.

Carlotta Taddei is an independent researcher in Medieval Art History. After completing her Ph.D on 12th-century sculpture in Lucca she worked for the department of Cultural Heritage at the University of Parma. She was a member of the organizing committee for all fourteen international conferences of the Italian Association of Medieval Art Historians (AISAME) that were held in Parma between 1998 and 2012. She also helped with the exhibition *Il Medioevo delle Cattedrali* (Parma 2006) and collaborated in the publication of the proceedings and catalogue. She obtained the National Scientific Qualification in 2012. She is currently teaching at the European School in Parma and at the University of Modena and Reggio Emilia. Her research interests are rooted in the Romanesque and Gothic architecture and sculpture of Northern Italy, and the liturgical setting of the medieval church and town. Recent publications are 'Le ventre de la cathédrale', in G. Boto & C. García de Castro Valdés (eds.), *Material and Action in European Cathedrals. Building, decorating, celebrating* (2017) and 'Costruire lo spazio sacro fuori dalla Cattedrale. La liturgia stazionale" in G. Boto, A. Garcìa Aviles & H. Kessler (eds.), *Construir lo sagrado en la Europa romànica. Reliquia, espacio, imagen y rito* (2017).

Rose Walker is a specialist in the art and architecture of medieval Spain. She was Academic Registrar and Deputy Secretary of The Courtauld Institute of Art, before deciding to pursue a second career as an art historian. She has published two books: *Views of Transition. Liturgy and Illumination in Medieval Spain* (1998) and *Art of Spain and Portugal from the Romans to the Early Middle Ages* (2016), as well as a range of articles on manuscripts, sculpture, wall-paintings and the sumptuary arts.

Shannon L. Wearing received her Ph.D at the Institute of Fine Arts, New York University, in 2015. She specialises in the art and architecture of medieval Spain, with an emphasis on illuminated manuscripts of the 12th and 13th centuries. At present she serves as the Assistant Editor of the journal *Res: Anthropology and Aesthetics*, and is an invited Affiliate of the UCLA Center for Medieval and Renaissance Studies. She has taught at the University of California, Irvine; New York University; and The City College of New York. Her most recent article is 'Holy Donors, Mighty Queens: Imaging Women in the Spanish Cathedral Cartularies of the Long Twelfth Century', published in the *Journal of Medieval History* in 2016. Her current book project focuses on royal artistic patronage and courtly culture in and around Barcelona at the turn of the 13th century.

PREFACE

The twenty-five essays in this volume are the result of the third in the British Archeological Association's biennial series of International Romanesque Conferences – organised in collaboration with the Museu Nacional d'Art de Catalunya and the research project *Artistas, patronos y público: Cataluña y el Mediterráneo (siglos XI-XV) – Magistri Cataloniae (MICINN HAR2011–23015)*. The conference was held over three days from 7–9 April 2014 in the lecture theatre of the Museu Nacional d'Art de Catalunya in Barcelona. For 2014 we settled on the theme *ROMANESQUE PATRONS AND PROCESSES*, and the aim was to examine patronage, design and instrumentality in their broadest senses across Latin Europe between *c.* 1000 and *c.* 1200. Thus, in addition to papers on individual patrons (both clerical and lay), the initial call for papers encouraged submissions which dealt with institutional patronage. Did institutional patronage differ from individual patronage, and was it understood by contemporaries as being different? To what extent is the individual by whom an artefact was apparently commissioned acting as an individual? The conference also addressed the people and processes involved in commissioning buildings or works of art – the mechanics of design – authorship – intermediaries and agents – and the extent to which patrons are designers. Changes in the patterns of patronage are fundamental to understanding the procedures involved in the development of a work of art, crystallised in how long-running commissions cope with changes of patron, or other types of alteration: decisions to move site, changes of plan, simplification, failure or abandonment, in addition to changes of use. What are the limits to patronal influence?

Such was the promise of the conference, helped by what we saw as the innate potential in bringing scholars together to discuss these themes surrounded by the collections of the Museu Nacional d'Art de Catalunya. The papers that were finally delivered in Barcelona were hearteningly varied in subject and approach, touching on the Kingdom of Jerusalem, Italy, France, Germany and Spain, while ranging across media to include discussions of artistic techniques, patronal emulation, textuality, liturgical models, regional identity and the deployment of materials. This geographical variety was also reflected in the 90 people who attended the conference and made their way to Catalonia from the UK, Spain, Italy, France, Germany, Switzerland, Hungary, Norway, Russia, US and Japan, twelve of them postgraduate students to whom the British Archaeological Association awarded scholarships covering the cost of the conference, visits and accommodation. The discussion did not end with the final conference dinner. As most scholars had travelled considerable distances to attend the conference, there were two additional days of visits on the 10–11 April, enabling the majority of those who attended the conference to spend further time together and visit a variety of Romanesque monuments at Sant Pere de Rodes, Girona, Tarragona and Santes Creus.

For their help in making the conference possible and illuminating its progress we would particularly like to thank the director of the Museu Nacional d'Art de Catalunya, Pepe Serra, who was supportive through the planning stage of the conference and was generous to a fault in all he provided at the conference itself. Above all, we would like to extend heartfelt thanks to Gemma Ylla-Català, who effectively combined the roles of conference secretary and chief orchestrator of logistics, and remained unflappable and superbly effective throughout. Grateful thanks are due to the Conference team and steering group, namely Manuel Castiñeiras and Jordi Camps as convenors, and Rosa Maria Bacile, Lindy Grant, John McNeill and Richard Plant as the London end of the steering group. We are also immensely grateful to those who gave site presentations during the Thursday and Friday visits, namely Manuel Castiñeiras, Jordi Camps, John McNeill, Veronica Abenza Soria, Laura Bartolomé, Rose Walker, Gerardo Boto, Marta Serrano Coll, Esther Lozano, Elizabeth Valdez del Alamo and Tom Nickson. Twenty-five out of the thirty papers and poster presentations given at the conference are published here, and though not all the papers were specifically intended for publication enough were for this volume to reflect the character of the conference.

Bringing out this set of conference transactions has taken longer than it should, and in the course of it the editors have incurred innumerable debts. Many of these relate to the conference itself, and the editors would like to express their gratitude to the small Steering Group which ultimately brought the conference into being, to the Advisory Panel (see p. vii) and, of course, to the contributors. Grateful thanks are also due to Tony Carr for the extraordinary elan he has again brought to the task of providing an index, and to Autumn Spalding for seeing this volume through production with exemplary speed, professionalism and good humour. Finally, without the resourcefulness, patience and keen generosity of John Osborn there would be no International Conference series. The editors, the British Archaeological Association, and the wider world of Romanesque scholarship are profoundly in his debt.

John McNeill and Richard Plant

CHAPTER ABSTRACTS

FUNCTION, CONDITION AND PROCESS IN ELEVENTH-CENTURY ANGLO-NORMAN CHURCH ARCHITECTURE

Richard Gem

This chapter sets out a general model for how the creation of Romanesque architecture in England in the late-eleventh-century was determined by three factors: the intended functions of the building; the prevailing conditions limiting the possibilities of its realisation; and the practical processes surrounding its actual construction. The model is then illustrated by three major churches for which we have a reasonable body of documentary source material, and for which we have substantial surviving fabric or, at least, good archaeological evidence for their appearance: the Cathedral and St Augustine's Abbey at Canterbury, and St Albans Abbey. The diverse available sources throw light on the buildings: first on their liturgical usage, symbolic expression and projection of status; then on the financial resources to fund them; and finally on the procedures for administering the construction and the craftsmen employed.

MATILDA AND THE CITIES OF THE GREGORIAN REFORM

Arturo Carlo Quintavalle

The power and patronage of Matilda of Canossa extended over a vast area: while traditional scholarship has emphasised her influence over rural monasteries, the evidence from cities under her sway, particularly Modena, Cremona and Piacenza, is no less revealing. This chapter lays out the evidence for a relationship between a change in narrative models and a change in the structure of power in the different towns, reinforcing a geography of power for the pro-papal faction, linked to burial and a closely-related set of workshops.

ROMANESQUE CATHEDRALS IN NORTHERN ITALY – BUILDING PROCESSES BETWEEN BISHOP AND COMMUNE

Bruno Klein

Cathedral-building in the Middle Ages was a process which engaged a number of different people, groups and institutions. Bishops and Chapters are the first to be mentioned, although the laity – whether noble or not – may also have contributed. In eleventh and twelfth century Northern Italy a particular set of circumstances seems to have emerged: on the one hand, the role of bishops was weakened as a result of the reform of the Church, on the other, we begin to encounter more self-conscious citizens, who increasingly organised themselves into communes.

The reconstruction of several cathedrals in northern Italy opened as these new circumstances began to bite, during an interregnum, in the period between bishops. This indicates that the construction of a cathedral was increasingly regarded as the task of the commune in its proper sense: a commune that embraced all its members – clergy and laity – as equal patrons. The process of building also created an opportunity to redefine the role of, and the relationship between, the major ecclesiastical and secular institutions. Finally, it facilitated and perhaps even encouraged the establishment of new institutions such as the communes themselves, or the incorporation of some of their members into specialist organisations, like guilds. The construction of the well-known cathedrals of Modena and Piacenza will be reconsidered in light of the above.

EPISCOPAL PATRONAGE IN THE REFORM OF CATALAN CATHEDRAL CANONRIES DURING THE FIRST ROMANESQUE PERIOD: A NEW APPROACH

Eduardo Carrero Santamaria

Catalan cathedral canonries underwent significant architectural redevelopment during the eleventh century; redevelopment that coincided with a period of cultural prosperity and political stability. These changes developed from existing traditions that can be traced back to the sixth century, but which survive only in the documentary record, or can be seen in an exceptional architectural ensemble such as Terrassa (which lost its episcopal status in the 8th century). This chapter emphasizes the importance of this early medieval substrate, which predates the eleventh-century reforms, as well as innovations that were developed as a part of the reforms themselves. At the same time, I argue that the reconstruction of Catalan cathedral complexes was not due to the agency of a single man - the celebrated Bishop Oliba of Vic. Rather, these architectural changes must be attributed to a group of bishops, all of whom participated in a programme of cultural renewal. From a material point of view, I will consider a series of 'church complexes' known from documents, which, with the exception of Seu d'Urgell, share the tendency, common in European Romanesque architecture, to bring together separate cult spaces into a single building.

THE ROLE OF KINGS AND BISHOPS IN THE INTRODUCTION OF ROMANESQUE ART IN NAVARRE AND ARAGON

Javier Martínez de Aguirre

This chapter examines the role that kings and bishops played in three fundamental works of Romanesque architecture in Navarre and Aragon: the monastery of Leire and the cathedrals of Jaca and Pamplona. Both the documentary evidence and the historical context show that royal intervention was limited to promotion and funding, and to the churches' monumental character. The role of the bishops was significantly more direct and determining. It is very likely that Sancho, abbot-bishop of Leire, visited Cluny, where he befriended Abbot Odilo; and that Pedro de Rodez, bishop of Pamplona, had been a monk at Conques and later visited Toulouse and Santiago de Compostela. In all three cases, it is clear that construction was intended as a monumental manifesto for the new direction taken by their respective institutions under the banner of ecclesiastical reform. As regards Jaca Cathedral, the author proposes certain new considerations that help us understand the overall configuration of the building. The two portal programmes, and the more legible and intentional facets of the building's architecture, were probably conceived by Bishop Pedro (1086–99), a former monk of San Juan de la Peña. They reflect a spirituality with monastic roots, enhanced by political allegories that might have been addressed to King Sancho Ramírez.

FROM PELÁEZ TO GELMÍREZ: THE PROBLEM OF ART PATRONAGE AT THE ROMANESQUE CATHEDRAL OF SANTIAGO DE COMPOSTELA

Jens Rueffer

This chapter aims to point up the conflicts, changing interests and alliances among different protagonists as patrons. By focusing on the object, and the period from c. 1075 to c. 1140, the question of who supported the cathedral of Santiago de Compostela will be posed, along with its opposite - who refused – sometimes only temporarily – to support the enterprise for special reasons. This chapter is based on a rereading of three important historical sources, the Concordia de Antealtares, the Liber Sancti Jacobi, and the Historia Compostelana, as well as the new archaeological investigation undertaken by a research group from the University of Cottbus under the direction of Professor Klaus Rheidt. In analysing these texts, I would like to stress those interests that can be related to artistic patronage, as well as the ambiguities and omissions in the texts. The result is a vivid mosaic of claims, interests and expectations, different to that which would emerge if one focused on the patronage of a single person.

PATRONAGE, ROMANESQUE ARCHITECTURE AND THE LANGUEDOC

Eric Fernie

The March of Gothia is not widely referred to in the literature on the architectural history of France in the eleventh century. The chapter offers an assessment of its relevance to the First Romanesque architecture of what is now known as lower Languedoc. It examines the political history of the area from the Romans to the eleventh century, the route by which the style was introduced (via Provence or via Catalonia), and the relationships of the buildings to others, especially those of Catalonia.

THE ARMENIAN CATHEDRAL OF SAINTS JAMES IN JERUSALEM: MELISENDE AND THE QUESTION OF EXCHANGE BETWEEN EAST AND WEST

Armen Kazaryan

This chapter is devoted to a great monument of Mediterranean culture – the Armenian cathedral of Saints James in Jerusalem – specifically to its patronage and to the origins of its architecture. Sources for the cathedral can be found in Armenian and Eastern Christian buildings, while several motifs that are used belong squarely within a Latin tradition. It has been suggested that Melisende, Queen of Jerusalem (1131–61) and Armenian on her mother's side, was instrumental in commissioning the cathedral and that her role was instrumental in facilitating facilitated a process of cultural exchange. The study concludes that Melisende was important, though not so much in ensuring the inclusion of significant Armenian national features in the building, but by effectively inserting an Armenian cathedral into the wider panoply of Latin and pan-European art. It also seems clear that the cathedral architect's method of combining different architectural ideas came about as the result of instructions from the patron.

GRANDMONT AND THE ENGLISH KINGS: AN EXAMPLE OF PATRONAGE IN THE CONTEXT OF AN ASCETIC ARCHITECTURAL TREND

Claude Andrault-Schmitt

Although the documentary records for the Limousin abbey of Grandmont are awash with forgeries and dubious legends, they are nonetheless accurate in attributing the role of patrons of the abbey to Kings Henry II, Richard and John. Pipe Rolls record the despatch of lead for the roof from Newcastle in 1175–77, and interest in Grandmont was shown by the kings' seneschals between 1192 and 1214. Unfortunately the abbey buildings no longer survive and the recent excavations were complicated by numerous reconstructions. However, we can at least be confident that the monastic church had a long and narrow aisleless nave and a large apse. This chapter will argue that the church was not built in a specifically 'Angevin' manner, but was related to both local and international ascetic trends. Two other buildings within the diocese of Limoges will be discussed: the mother-church of the Order of L'Artige and the Cistercian abbey church of Bonlieu. In its turn, Grandmont is said to have provided a model for the smaller houses of the Order, all of which resemble one another, whether they are in England or in Languedoc. Built at the beginning of the 13th century, they represent a type of 'tardorromanico' – the term here not intended pejoratively.

THE HOSPITAL, ENGLAND AND SIGENA: A FOOTNOTE

Neil Stratford

The female Hospitallers' convent at Sigena and its famous chapter-house (where the wall-paintings were largely destroyed in 1936) are discussed from the point of view of the Hospital's leaders in the 1180s. The European mission of Heraclius, patriarch of Jerusalem, in 1184/5 and the role of the knights in the mission are also discussed. Various candidates are mentioned as possible intermediaries in relation to the painter or painters who, as is well known, figure among the later artists of the Winchester Bible. The personal and political connections between England and the Hospital could explain the presence of a leading 'English' painter in Aragon in the 1180s.

HENRY OF BLOIS, ST HUGH AND HENRY II: THE WINCHESTER BIBLE RECONSIDERED

Christopher Norton

The desire to link anonymous masterpieces with famous names, whether of artists or of patrons, is deep-rooted, as can be seen with the number of works of art which cluster around such names as Nicholas of Verdun and Abbot Suger. The magnificent illuminated bible at Winchester Cathedral has long been associated with one of the most celebrated art patrons of the age, Henry of Blois, bishop of Winchester from 1129 to 1171. Indeed, the bible has been associated with three of the outstanding personalities of the age. Not only has Henry of Blois been credited with its inception, but St Hugh of Lincoln and King Henry II have also been connected to it, at a later stage in its production. Current scholarly opinion tends to accept Henry of Blois' involvement, while questioning the bible's association with St Hugh and Henry II. In this chapter I propose to re-examine the evidence for both claims.

PATRONS, INSTITUTIONS AND PUBLIC IN THE MAKING OF CATALAN ROMANESQUE ART DURING THE COMITAL PERIOD (1000–1137)

Manuel Castiñeiras

Until the middle of the twelfth century, Catalonia was not a centre but a periphery. Being outside the orbit of the major royal powers, and therefore without a courtly art, the former Marca Hispanica remained distant from the artistic foci of

Carolingian and Post-Carolingian art. Besides, it was without a metropolitan see until the conquest of Tarragona. Hence, from the very outset the local Church, together with the lay magnates, exerted artistic agency in an attempt to shore up their ecclesiastical and political status, based on their alliance with the Papacy. In this regard, Oliba, abbot of Ripoll and Cuixà and bishop of Vic, along with his comital family, were leaders in what many authors have defined as the Catalan mini-renaissance of the eleventh century, while Saint Ot of La Seu d'Urgell and his relatives, the counts of Pallars, were a driving force in the transformation of the monumental arts during the late eleventh and early twelfth centuries. The distinctive role of aristocratic women in the promotion of the minor arts (metalwork and embroidery) during the comital period is also a topic that deserves detailed analysis.

THE ARTISTIC PATRONAGE OF ABBOT GREGORIUS AT CUIXÀ: MODELS AND TRIBUTES

Anna Orriols

Sant Miquel de Cuixà was an outstanding Catalan monastery. Founded in the 9th century and closely associated with the counts of Cerdanya, it enjoyed successive moments of splendour before starting to fade in the late twelfth century. This chapter is concerned with the work that can be associated with two abbots – Oliba (1008–46) and Gregorius (c. 1120–1146) – and argues for an unusual sensitivity shown in the patronage of one for the other.

A LIMOUSIN CIBORIUM IN MEDIEVAL CATALONIA

Joan Duran-Porta

This chapter studies the background of the patronage of the Limousin ciborium found in the region of la Cerdanya in Catalonia and presently preserved in Barcelona, in the collection at the Museu Nacional d'Art de Catalunya. Formal analysis of the ciborium's style confirms the traditionally established links with the famous Maître Alpais ciborium, yet it also enables us to relate it to a series of Limousin works produced for the Order of Grandmont. Contacts between the Catalan royals and the aforementioned order, which held important priories in the Languedoc (at that time controlled by Catalans), provide support to the hypothesis regarding specific Catalan patronage of this ciborium, which may have been commissioned by an individual who most likely had close ties to the court, and later imported into Catalan lands.

THE JACA IVORIES: TOWARDS A REVALUATION OF ELEVENTH-CENTURY FEMALE ARTISTIC PATRONAGE IN THE KINGDOM OF ARAGON

Verónica C. Abenza Soria

The marriage, around 1071, between Sancho Ramírez, King of Aragon, and Felicia of Roucy, with the acquiescence of the Papacy, highlighted his aspirations to bind his reign to the ideology of the Gregorian Reform. In this context, Felicia de Roucy's commission of the Jaca ivories is evidence of her intellectual efforts to reinforce her husband's political outlook. It also operates as a mirror that reflects the mutability of medieval women's identity in their interaction with elite society. The link between Felicia and the female convent of Santa Maria de Santa Cruz de la Serós, for whom the work was commissioned, could have epitomized the spirit that moved her husband in the construction of Jaca Cathedral. A critical review of the acquisition, manufacture and reuse of the ivories and their arrangement as a memento allows us to reconsider the concept of the copy, the use of formal vocabularies from both Byzantine and Romanesque traditions, the functional ambiguity of these works, and a wider dialogue among the arts.

THE AEMILIAN CASKET RELIQUARY: A PRODUCT OF INSTITUTIONAL PATRONAGE

Melanie Hanan

Scholars have typically studied the eleventh-century Aemilian reliquary from the Spanish monastery San Millán de la Cogolla in order to reconstruct its original appearance and to compare its imagery to historical sources. This article uses these studies in conjunction with medieval liturgical evidence to compare the form and iconography of the reliquary with contemporary religious practices. In doing so it demonstrates that the Aemilian reliquary was designed to resonate visually with the devotions of a range of worshippers under different circumstances, from the monks themselves to the laity. As a result, this object stands as the first extant example of a type of reliquary that became popular at monasteries throughout Europe given the diverse ways in which it could be used.

PATRONAGE AT THE CATHEDRAL OF TARRAGONA: CULT AND RESIDENTIAL SPACE

Esther Lozano-López and Marta Serrano-Coll

The aim of this study is to analyse the extent to which patrons were important in the construction of the cathedral of Tarragona. Rather than concentrating solely on the archbishops, until now the focus of most research, we will use the material evidence available (epigraphs, iconography, texts) to analyse the role of other key players in the building's design. In this respect, members of the clergy are shown to have been active participants in the construction of the cathedral, irrespective of their standing within the community. Consequently, the first part of this article focuses on determining the precise role that they played in this process. At the same time, the fact that we are also investigating the heraldic emblems carved on certain imposts in the cloister means that we can trace its complex and extended chronology in much greater detail. In general, despite the biased and confusing documentary sources, we aim to provide an analysis that brings together the prosopographical sources to determine the role of the patrons in terms of their economic, political, social and religious status, both within and without the cathedral. Only then can we understand the singularities of this exceptional building as a setting for the manifestation of power.

AN ANGLO-NORMAN AT TERRASSA? AUGUSTINIAN CANONS AND THOMAS BECKET AT THE END OF THE TWELFTH CENTURY

Carles Sánchez Márquez

During the second half of the twelfth century, Augustinian houses attached to the congregation of Saint-Ruf at Avignon held a significant number of manuscripts (Vitae, Passio and Miracula) and liturgical texts that refer to the sainted archbishop of Canterbury, Thomas Becket. This important corpus demonstrates that the cult of Becket spread quickly through the congregation of Saint-Ruf. The means whereby devotion to Becket was disseminated around the Mediterranean more generally has yet to be determined satisfactorily – and it may be that there were several different agencies. This chapter examines one example, and argues that the presence of an Anglo-Norman canon – Arveus or Harveus (Harvey) – could have been the driving force behind the Romanesque paintings depicting the martyrdom of Thomas Becket in the church of Sta Maria at Terrassa, and therefore of the adoption of the cult of Becket in at least one Augustinian house. Harvey played an important role in the house of canons regular at Terrassa, in as much as he was a scribe and signed documents during the second half of the twelfth century.

AGENCY AND THE RE-INVENTION OF SLAB RELIEF SCULPTURE AT SAN ISIDORO DE LEÓN C. 1100

Rose Walker

This chapter considers one particular medium of Romanesque art, slab relief sculpture, by focussing on the Portal of the Lamb at San Isidoro in León. Through this case study it reviews several aspects of process: an 'umbrella' level of direction from the papacy, the involvement of multiple 'patrons', the use of Roman sarcophagi as archetypes and the agency of artists.

PATRON AND LITURGY: THE LITURGICAL SETTING OF THE CATHEDRAL CHURCH OF SAN MARTINO IN LUCCA AFTER 1070 AND THE GREGORIAN REFORM

Carlotta Taddei

Anselmo da Baggio became bishop of Lucca in 1057 and remained bishop even after he was elected Pope, taking the title Alexander II (1061–73). The Tuscan city thus experienced a condition normally unique to Rome during his pontificate. Written sources celebrate Anselmo da Baggio as the patron of the Romanesque Cathedral and speak of his intention to extend the Gregorian reform across the city. Anselmo/Alexander II also effected important changes in Lucca's liturgy. The liturgy is revealed to have been the principal vehicle whereby the role of the church of San Martino was enhanced, emerging as a single, integrated and reformed cathedral church.

THE 'LITERATE' LAY DONOR: TEXTUALITY AND THE ROMANESQUE PATRON

Robert A. Maxwell

Romanesque images of patronage commonly show a donor offering or transferring a miniature model of a gift. A relatively novel type of image, however, emerged in the eleventh and twelfth centuries where text played an unprecedented role. This chapter proposes to view that new iconography in relation to transformative quality of the written word in those centuries. Diplomatics especially – with its attendant notarial formulas and language, seals and sealing, rituals and performances – brought new consequences for the relationship of the donor to his or her donation. Significantly, this development extended to lay, including non-royal, individuals, and this chapter argues that imagery increasingly portrayed the laity as having agency in the diplomatic handling of their donations. Some images show patrons in the act of preparing a charter of donation themselves, while others show them as readers of their gift's diplomatic record, and still others position lay donors as diplomatic authorities managing written records. The imagery points to donors' growing implication as actors in the specifically textual culture of diplomatics, positing the patron as a 'literate' agent of that culture. It also presents an unexpected picture of how claims to the power of 'literacy' gradually became part of a visual language of donation.

REMARKS ON PATRON INSCRIPTIONS WITH RESTRICTED PRESENCE

Wilfried E. Keil

Patron inscriptions are usually clearly visible, meaning that they are present to viewers. Some patron inscriptions, however, are of limited visibility, a patron inscription of so-called restricted presence. In this article the Juliana-relief in the eastern sanctuary of Worms Cathedral is used as the major example of this second type. It is directed towards the altar and is not visible to church visitors. The patron inscription ADELBRAHT MONETARIVS is one of three inscriptions on this relief. Its placement raises several questions concerning its function. Why did Adelbraht have his name placed in a position that afforded limited visibility? There could be several reasons: the inscription might have functioned as a legal document; or the patron could have thereby taken care of his own memoria, since the priest is able to see the inscription before the Mass; finally, the process of inscription could be connected with the inscribing of his name in the 'Book of Life'. There is also the question of the level of importance given to proximity to the altar or to the tomb or relic of a saint. This could be analogous to the tradition to being buried as close as possible to the bodies of saints.

THE TWELFTH-CENTURY PATRONS OF THE BRIDEKIRK FONT

Hugh Doherty

This chapter uses long-neglected evidence – two twelfth-century deeds from the archive of St Brigit's church, Bridekirk, printed by William Dugdale in 1673 – to examine the circumstances which resulted in the building of the first stone church on the site and the carving of the magnificent font. This evidence reveals the combined contribution of two leading laymen of Cumberland, the small body of priests serving the church of St Brigit and the mason, Rikard, and his team of workmen. The result is a study of the interplay of authority, devotion and artistic craftsmanship in one corner of the twelfth-century West.

THE SCOPE OF COMPETENCE OF THE PAINTER AND THE PATRON IN MURAL PAINTING IN THE ROMANESQUE PERIOD

Anne Leturque

This chapter proposes a review of the roles of the artist and the patron in the design and execution of a mural in the Romanesque period. The direct written and figurative evidence we have on this subject is unfortunately very limited. Nevertheless, the importance of the patron's role in medieval creation is the focus of numerous studies, to the detriment of that of the painter, often regarded as a mere executor. By drawing on alternative sources, such as treatises on artistic technology, it is possible to reconsider the approach to these issues. Thus, the purpose of this article is to focus on the role of the painter, as the holder of knowledge, tools and skills essential in the design and execution of a wall painting cycle. In the pictorial project, the result of a dialogue between the different actors, one cannot deny the influence of the habits and requirements of artistic practice on intellectual projection and the achievement of a painted work. The painter is no longer merely a passive executor but a co-author. The mastery of drawing is of prime importance in this enterprise.

THE DEATH OF THE PATRON: AGENCY, STYLE AND THE MAKING OF THE *LIBER FEUDORUM MAIOR* OF BARCELONA

Shannon L. Wearing

This essay takes as its focus the frontispiece of the Liber Feudorum Maior, an illuminated cartulary commissioned by Alfonso II, King of Aragon and Count of Barcelona (r. 1162–96). This miniature – iconographically unique in the history of medieval art – constructs an image of the patronage of the manuscript itself, with an emphasis on the active roles played by King Alfonso as its patron, and Ramon de Caldes, Dean of Barcelona Cathedral and head of the royal chancery, as its compiler. I contextualise this image in relation to unresolved questions surrounding the manuscript's chronology and patronal history. At the heart of this mystery is the book's incorporation of two stylistically divergent sets of illuminations – one in keeping with Romanesque pictorial traditions in Catalonia, the other embracing a more naturalistic approach associated with the so-called Channel Style or Year 1200 Style. While various scholars have suggested that this latter group of illustrations should be dated c. 1220, long after the deaths of both Alfonso and Ramon, I argue that the full spectrum of stylistic, iconographic and patronal evidence makes an earlier date more likely. Beyond addressing a simple dating controversy, this essay demonstrates that Alfonso's cartulary represents an ideal case study for examining the complexities of royal patronage; it also considers the investigation of patronage as an art historical methodology more broadly.

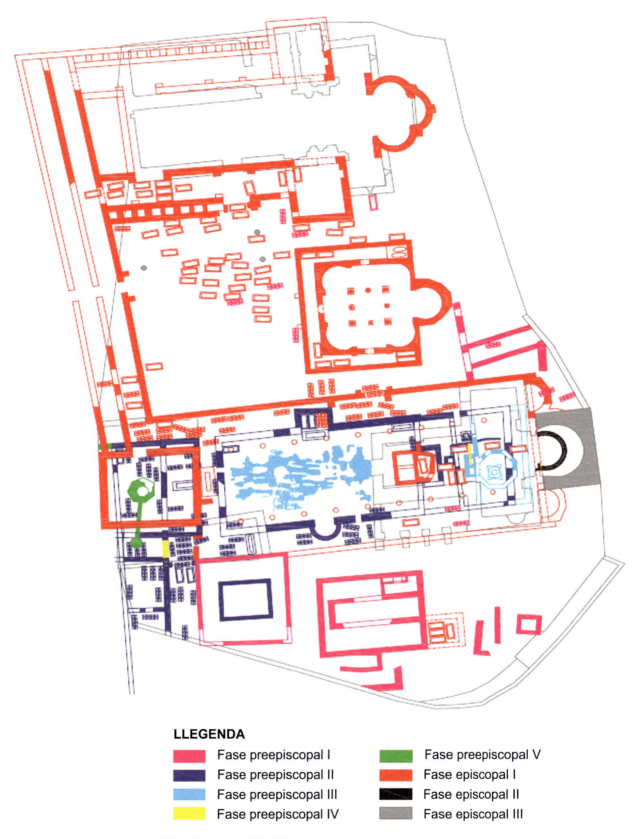

PLATE I *Terrassa, Group of Churches (after ERAUB).*

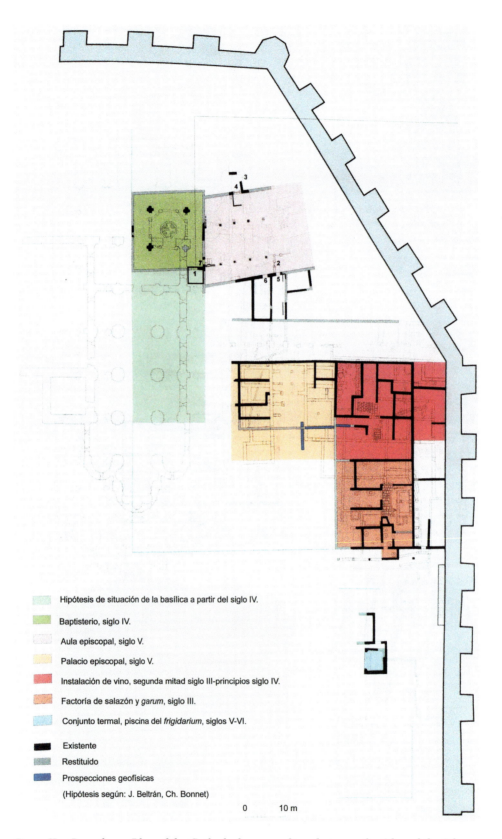

PLATE II *Barcelona. Plan of the Cathedral surroundings between the 6th and the 7th centuries (after MUHBA).*

PLATE III *Monastery of Khtskonk: Church of Surb Sargis (1024). (A. Kazaryan)*

PLATE IV *Winchester Bible, f. 120v. The start of IV Kings. Text by the first scribe, decorative lettering by the second rubricator, initial by the Master of the Leaping Figures (John Crook)*

PLATE V *Winchester Bible, f. 131. The start of the Book of Isaiah written on a replacement bifolium by the second scribe. Decorative lettering by the second rubricator, initial by the Master of the Gothic Majesty (John Crook)*

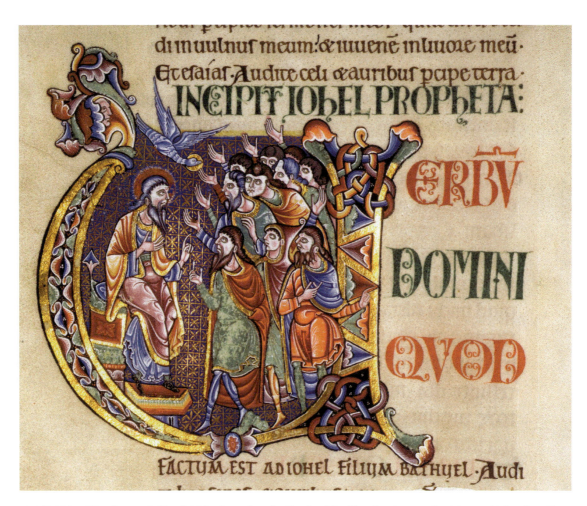

PLATE VI (TOP)   *Winchester Bible, f. 200v. Initial to the Book of Joel by the Apocrypha Master (John Crook)*

PLATE VI (BOTTOM)   *Winchester Bible, f. 3. Initial to St Jerome's Letter to Damasus. Decorative lettering by the first rubricator (John Crook)*

PLATE VII (TOP)   *Winchester Bible, f. 246. Unfinished double initial to Psalm 101, painted by the Morgan Master over a drawing by the Master of the Leaping Figures.* © *The Dean and Chapter of Winchester*

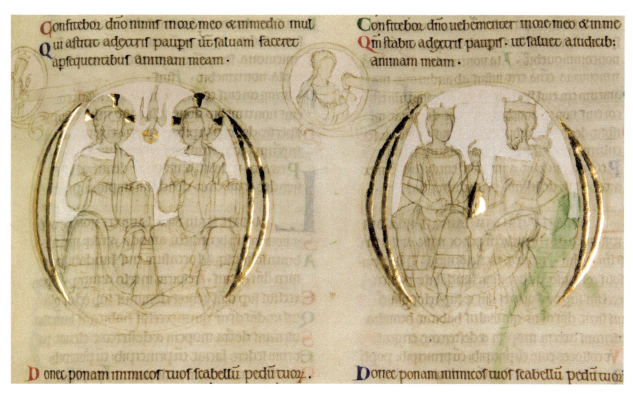

PLATE VII (BOTTOM)   *Winchester Bible, f. 250. Unfinished double initial to Psalm 109 by the Master of the Gothic Majesty (John Crook)*

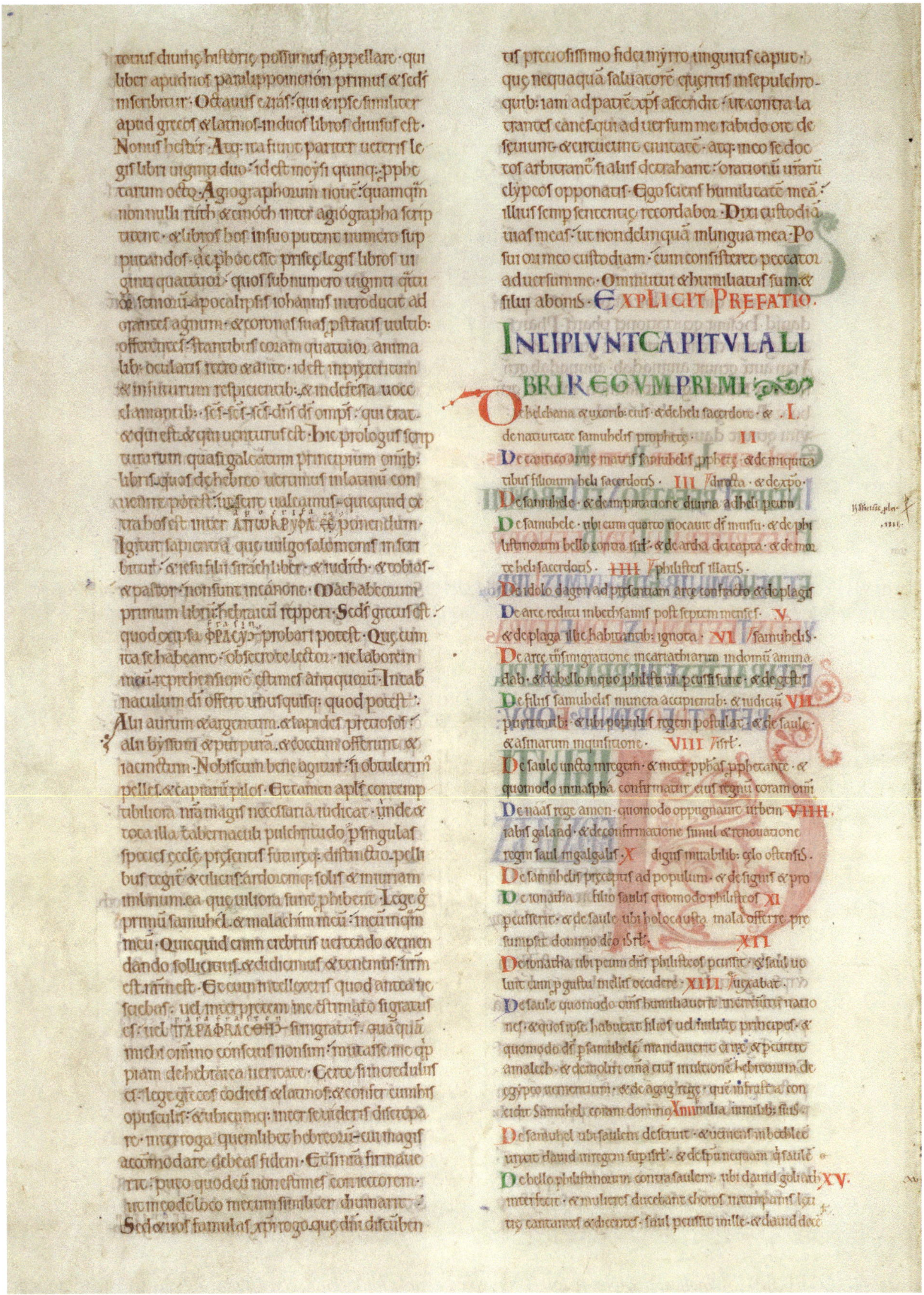

PLATE VIII *Winchester Bible, f. 87v. The conclusion to the preface to 1 Kings and the start of the capitula (© The Dean and Chapter of Winchester)*

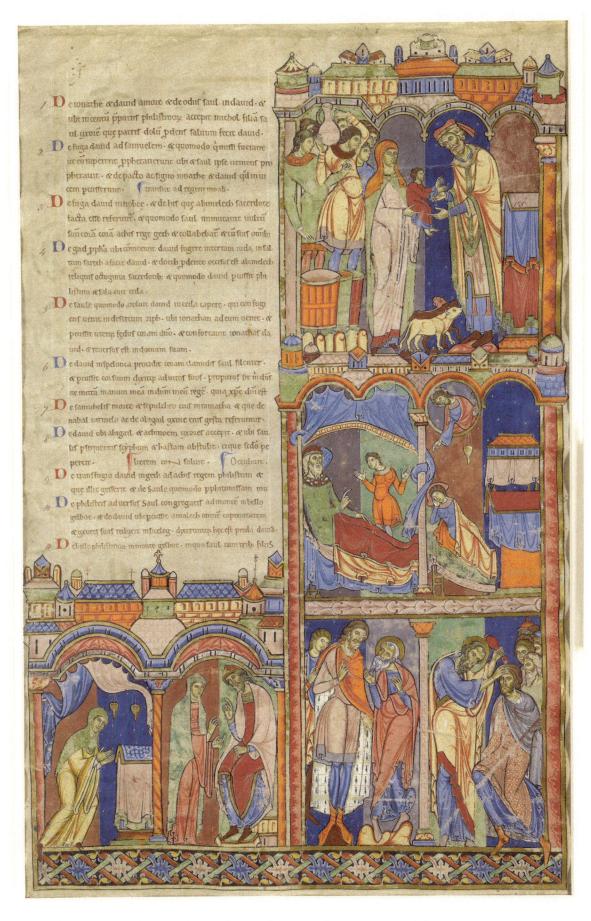

PLATE IX *The Morgan Leaf, recto. The conclusion of the capitula to 1 Kings, and the story of Samuel and Saul, designed and partly painted by the Apocrypha Master, completed by the Morgan Master (© The Mogan Library and Museum)*

PLATE X *The Morgan Leaf, verso. The story of David, designed and partly painted by the Apocrypha Master, completed by the Morgan Master (© The Mogan Library and Museum)*

PLATE XI *Winchester Bible, f. 88. The conclusion of the capitula and the start of the text of 1 Kings. Text by the first scribe, decorative lettering by the first rubricator, initial designed by the Apocrypha Master and painted by the Morgan Master (© The Dean and Chapter of Winchester)*

PLATE XII *Rome, Biblioteca Apostolica Vaticana, MS Lat. 5729, fol. 95v (Ripoll Bible): Temple of Solomon (1027-32). (© Biblioteca Apotolica Vaticana)*

PLATE XIII *Girona Cathedral Treasury:* Creation Tapestry *(c. 1097). (© Capitol Catedral de Girona)*

PLATE XIV *Mural paintings from the central apse of Sant Pere del Burgal (c. 1097–1106): funerary portrait of Lucy, countess of Pallars, bearing a candle. (Barcelona MNAC, 113138 © Museu Nacional d'Art de Catalunya. Foto: Calveras/Mérida/Sagristà)*

PLATE XV (TOP) *Rodes Bible. Paris, Bibliothèque Nationale de France, MS lat. 6, vol. II, fol. 130v.* (© Bibliothèque nationale de France)

PLATE XV (BOTTOM) *Sant Quirze de Pedret: Central apse showing the souls of the martyrs under the altar (Solsona, Museu Diocesà i Comarcal)* © *Museu Diocesà i Comarcal de Solsona*

PLATE XVI *Barcelona: MNAC. Limousin Ciborium – general view* (© *Museu Nacional d'Art de Catalunya. Foto: Calveras/Mérida/Sagristà*)

PLATE XVII *New York: Metropolitan Museum of Art. Jaca panel (Accession N. 17.190.33). © The Metropolitan Museum of Art*

PLATE XVIII *New York: Metropolitan Museum of Art. Jaca panel (Accession N. 17.190.33).* © *The Metropolitan Museum of Art*

PLATE XIX (TOP)   Santa Maria de Terrassa: wall paintings: *Apse semidome*

PLATE XIX (BOTTOM)   Santa Maria de Terrassa: wall paintings: *Murder of Thomas Becket*

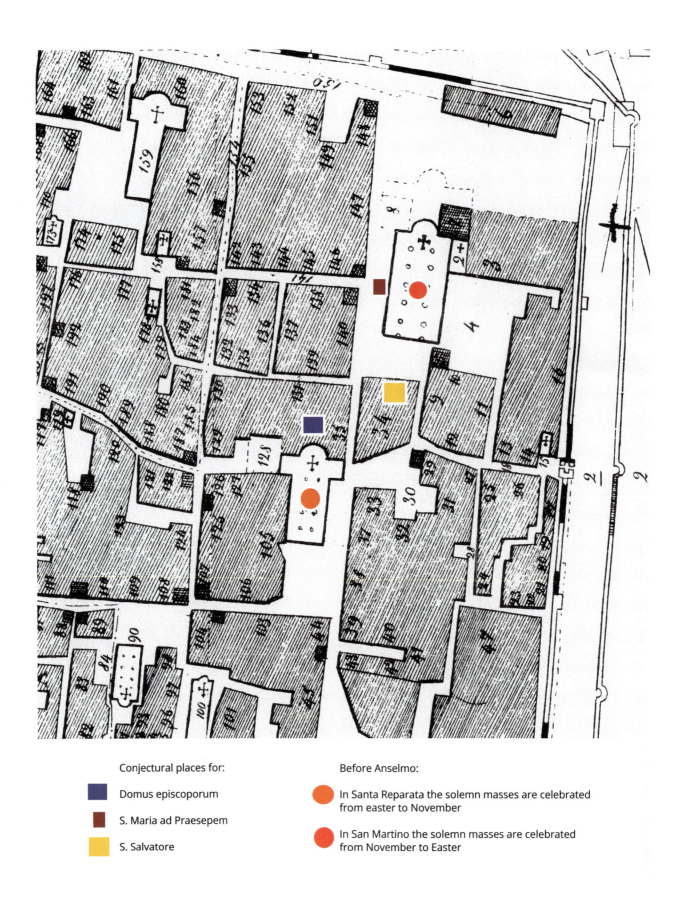

PLATE XX *Plan of Lucca c.1200, after Matraia – detail of the curtis.*

PLATE XXI (TOP)   *Saint-Martin de Fenollar: General view of the chancel (Christian Bachelier)*

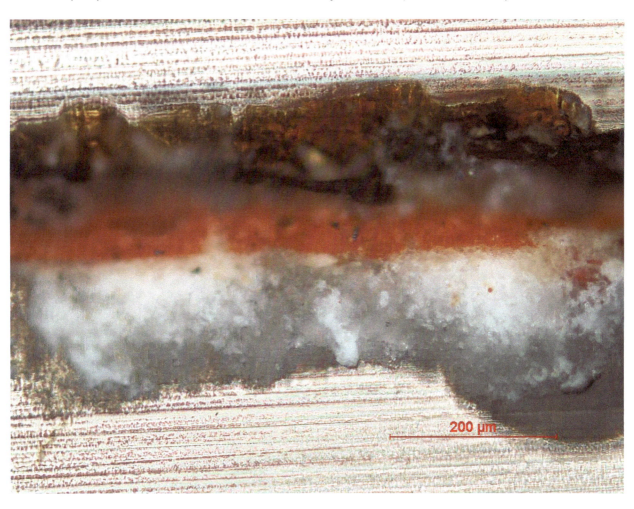

PLATE XXI (BOTTOM)   *Santa Maria de Terrassa: cross-section of a sample taken from the candlesticks showing the use of tinfoil (Petula Stagni). Photo: CRBMC (Ricardo Suárez). In the image four different layers can be observed. The top layer is a brown translucid organic coat (lacqueror resin), the second layer is the metallic sheet shown in grey. The third layer in red colour corresponds to the pictorial layer (background colour of its sampling location). Finally, the white forth stratum is the preparation layer.*

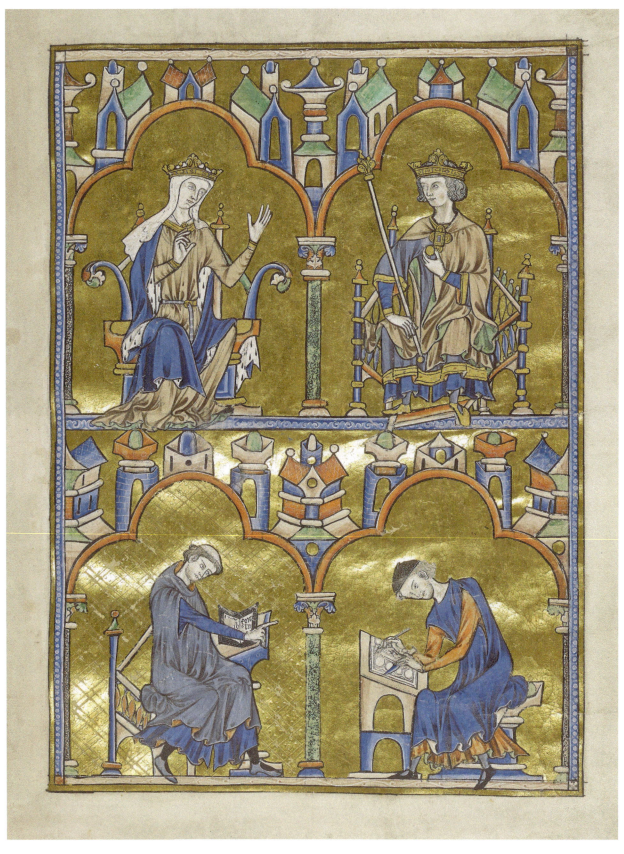

PLATE XXII *Toledo Bible moralisée, New York, Pierpont Morgan Library, MS M.240, fol. 8r.*

FUNCTION, CONDITION AND PROCESS IN ELEVENTH-CENTURY ANGLO-NORMAN CHURCH ARCHITECTURE

Richard Gem

INTRODUCTION

Any building project starts with the patron responsible for commissioning and funding the work, whether the patron is an individual or a community. The patron thus stands at the point of origin of the ensuing process that delivers the final building: but that process and the patron's engagement with it are multifaceted. This paper seeks to explore this interrelationship by considering three aspects: the intended function of a building; the limitations conditioning its realization; and the actual practical delivery of the project. These will be evaluated against four major projects of the late 11th century at Canterbury and St Albans.

A GENERAL MODEL

1. Intended functions

Under the heading 'intended functions' a number of considerations are included. The first of these is the **practical** function to which a building is to be put together with the facilities necessary to support that function. Thus, in considering a church, its practical function is a matter of **religious usage**. That is, its central and most important function would be to provide a setting appropriate to the celebration of the liturgy by clergy and people, together with accommodation of the clerical personnel necessary to perform that liturgy.[1] At the core of this were the daily office and the mass, along with the other sacraments. But alongside these a church might also have to provide for para-liturgical activities. Most notably, where the church housed the shrine of a saint, pilgrimage could generate large crowds at certain times.

The second aspect of function is that of **symbolic expression**. Such symbolism may exist at a general level, where the aesthetic qualities of a building are designed to be appropriate to its function. One form this might take would be where the overall splendour of a church was intended to make it an offering worthy of the glory of God. Another was where the church was envisaged as a type of the heavenly temple or city, and this approach could find its justification in New Testament texts, such as the *Letter to the Hebrews* and the *Revelation of St John*.[2]

A more concrete form of symbolism or iconography may be instantiated where a building was designed with reference to specific concepts, or to particular places. Thus, for example, a church might be designed with reference to the symbolism of the Holy Cross, or to one of the holy places of the Christian world, such as Rome or Jerusalem.

The third aspect of function is where the building is conceived as a **projection of status** by the patron – essentially of his socio-economic status. Thus, a church building might project the power of a prelate as a magnate of the Church or the realm, rather more than as a pastor of his flock. Or, rather differently, it might project the power of the saint whose relics lay there, forming the focus of a spiritual and territorial estate. The function of buildings in projecting the socio-economic status of their patrons is a consideration that currently enjoys a degree of prominence in art-historical dialogue, reflecting a more general trend of reading the past primarily in terms of social and economic history. But, while such factors certainly deserve their appropriate place, they should not be privileged to the exclusion of others. Buildings were generally more than the expression of the power and wealth of their patrons, and we would be missing much of what they can tell us if we failed to look more widely.

2. Limiting conditions

Under the heading 'limiting conditions' may be considered the various practical conditions that both enabled and limited the implementation of a building project. Foremost among these was the availability of **resources**; that is, of funding, of materials and of labour.[3] To address this aspect a number of questions must be asked of the evidence. What funding did the patron have at his disposal? Was this generated from the endowments of his institution, or did he have to seek external financial assistance? Did the estates of the institution have available resources of materials, such as stone and timber, or did these have to be procured from elsewhere and, if so, at what distance? Again, did the institution have its own labour force, or did this have to be employed at the relevant rate of wages?

Even if all relevant resources were available in appropriate quantities, their effective deployment was dependent on **technical and design constraints**. If a patron had an ideal conception of the building he would like to commission, was it possible to access the professional skills necessary for its practical realisation? The patron himself or herself was seldom, if ever, a master of practical design, but would be dependent on the knowledge and skills of experts. However, exceptional design skills might not be so readily available, and the patron might be in competition with others to secure the best. And even then, did contemporary understanding of structural engineering permit the actual realisation of a complex design proposal?

3. Practical processes

Under the heading 'practical process' must be included the various strands necessary for the concrete realisation of a building, which would not have been very different from those involved in any modern project.

In the first place stands the **brief of the patron** or, in modern terms, the client. By a brief is meant the considered instructions of the patron, whether issued in writing or orally. This brief would have been developed on the basis of the patron's requirements for the function of the building and for its general character, both of which aspects would have been informed by his previous experience. But additionally, the patron's initial ideas would have been refined in consultation with the professional experts who had the practical skills to deliver his wishes. An agreed design brief, whether or not accompanied by drawings or a model, would then have formed the basis for the project.

However, the patron generally would not have wished to concern himself with the routine but necessary **administration of works**, and at this point relevant procedures would have needed to be put in place. These procedures had to provide for: the contracting of craftsmen and other workmen; the procurement of building materials; the supervision of works; and accounting for payments against the agreed budget. In modern times these tasks might be contracted to a specialist project manager; but in medieval times they would have to be assigned to someone with a more general administrative role in the patron's church community or wider circle.

A major logistical problem in any large building project was the **provision of materials** to the site. These materials included: stone for both ashlar work and rubble; sand and lime for mortar; timber for roofing, scaffolding and furnishing; lead for roofing; glass for windows; iron for various purposes; tiles for roofing and flooring; bronze for bell casting; ropes for pulleys – and so forth. Some of these materials might be available locally; while others might have to be sourced at a considerable distance and transport arranged over land and water by carriers. Transport of some materials was a difficult and potentially expensive operation, so that unnecessary burdens would be avoided by, for example, the preliminary preparation of stonework at the quarry, or the smelting of metal ores near the mines. In all, a considerable part of the budget might be consumed by the provision of materials before any of them were incorporated into the building.

The final stage of the process was the direction and **execution by craftsmen** of the actual construction work on site. This involved a wide range of specialists in different crafts together with more general labourers. Most important for the success of a project were the experts (*periti*) and the skilled craftsmen (*artifici*), among whom the masters (*magistri*) had a superior status. The overall master of the works (*magister operum*) had oversight of the whole building operation, and normally he would have been a specialist in masonry construction, a *caementarius*. But in addition other masters would have had responsibility for different specialist areas, including sculpture, painting, carpentry, glazing, metal working and so forth. The patron generally would have been responsible for the appointment of the *magister operum*; but often he may have had a particular interest also in securing the services of renowned craftsmen in other fields, such as a master painter or a master goldsmith. At a level below the masters and skilled craftsmen, the realisation of the project also required the assembling of a body of labourers (*operarii*). These might include travelling journeymen, but also persons permanently attached to the church for which the building was being constructed (such as the brethren of a monastery), and even sometimes enthusiastic volunteers motivated by religious fervour.

Instantiation of the model in Anglo-Norman architecture. The interaction between intended functions, limiting conditions and practical processes may help establish a model for the creation of major buildings in the Romanesque period. In what follows this will be tested against four interrelated building projects of the late 11th century, at Christ Church Cathedral and St Augustine's Abbey in Canterbury, and at St Albans Abbey, to see if the model actually elucidates the reality of commissioning and constructing such buildings in that particular time and place. The examples selected are ones for which we have a reasonable body of documentary source material, and for which we have substantial surviving fabric or, at least, good archaeological evidence for their appearance.

THE PATRONS AND THEIR PROJECTS

Canterbury, Christ Church Cathedral

The Anglo-Saxon cathedral of Christ Church in Canterbury had been destroyed by fire in 1067, and its rebuilding was undertaken under Archbishop Lanfranc (1070–89) immediately upon his arrival in his see.[4] Within seven years the new church was ready for use, and the whole was completed within Lanfranc's lifetime, together with enlarged domestic offices for the monks and his own curia.[5]

Lanfranc had a varied career before arriving in Canterbury.[6] He had been born c. 1015 in Pavia and trained initially in the law, before moving to France c. 1030 and becoming a teacher of the arts at Avranches. Then c. 1042 he converted to the monastic life and entered the abbey of Le Bec-Hellouin. There he continued teaching before soon becoming prior, and c. 1060 he started rebuilding the church. However, in 1063 he was transferred by Duke William to become abbot of his newly-founded monastery of Saint-Etienne in Caen. At Caen he would have had overall responsibility for the construction of the new church and offices, but these had barely got off the ground before he was transferred again in 1070 to Canterbury, where he was faced once more with the need for a major building project. Lanfranc as an intellectual figure was an important scholar, biblical and patristic commentator, and theological protagonist; while he was also a capable ecclesiastical administrator and politician: but for his views on the visual arts there is little direct evidence apart from his works themselves.

Lanfranc's successor Archbishop Anselm (1093–1109) undertook a great enlargement of the cathedral to the east of its central tower, and this work was begun c. 1093x1096. Eadmer, a member of Anselm's household and reliable witness, says that the work took place with the archbishop 'providing for, disposing and beginning' the work.[7] This can be interpreted as meaning that as patron he provided for the financing of the project, that he set out the brief and that he put the actual construction in hand. The project was completed under Anselm's successors Ralf d'Escures (1114–22) and William of Corbeil (1123–36), but its character had already been determined. A preliminary dedication may have taken place in 1114, while the final dedication was in 1130.[8]

Anselm's background was rather similar to Lanfranc's.[9] Born in 1033 of a noble family in Aosta, he moved to Normandy c. 1060 to study at Bec under Lanfranc. There he became prior and in 1078 abbot. Following Lanfranc's death in 1089, Anselm was chosen as his successor by the clergy, but his appointment was not ratified until 1093 by the king; twice subsequently he withdrew into exile, from 1097 to 1100 and from 1103 to 1106/7. Anselm is well known as the leading intellectual figure of his day in Europe. Also, he is revealed in his writings as having a deep interest in the arts, both as theorist and patron.[10]

Canterbury, St Augustine's Abbey

The second great religious house in Canterbury was St Augustine's Abbey, where a remodelling of the ancient buildings had been started in 1049 but was left abandoned following 1061. A complete rebuilding of the church and monastic offices was begun subsequently by Abbot Scolland (1070–87).[11] Arriving in Canterbury as abbot elect in 1070, and especially after his formal installation in 1072, Scolland showed himself 'most ardent in the building of the august monastery'; and when in Rome he even consulted Pope Alexander II about the project.[12] However, the new church was only completed under his successors: Wido (1087–c. 1093), whose imposition by Lanfranc caused a rebellion among the monks; and then Hugh de Flori (1108–26), a monk of Bec, whose appointment was again contested and his formal blessing as abbot long delayed.

Scolland had a more restricted background than Lanfranc or Anselm. Before his appointment to the abbacy of St Augustine's he had been a monk of the Norman monastery of Le Mont-Saint-Michel, which had been reformed under William of Volpiano at the beginning of the 11th century. Rebuilding of the abbey church had been begun in 1023 but continued into the period when Scolland was a monk at Mont-Saint-Michel. As a monk he had worked in the scriptorium, and he is named in a colophon to one manuscript, in which he is described as 'shining pre-eminently with all sacred doctrine'.[13]

St Alban's Abbey

The church at St Albans went back in origin to late antiquity and had emerged as a monastic house in the Anglo-Saxon period. Following the Norman Conquest, Abbot Paul (1077–93) undertook the complete rebuilding of the church and monastic offices over a period of eleven years; this work was completed by his successor, Abbot Richard, and the new church was dedicated in 1115.[14]

Paul was a nephew of Archbishop Lanfranc and presumably, therefore, of similar north Italian origin. He had been a monk of the abbey of Saint-Etienne in Caen before his election to the abbacy of St Alban's in 1077, which he then held for just over sixteen years until his death in 1093. Richard d'Aubigny, Paul's successor, was from a noble Norman family and had been a monk at Lessay before his appointment.

INTENDED FUNCTIONS

Religious usage

All three of the churches under consideration were served by monastic communities; a primary function, therefore, was to provide a setting for the monastic liturgy in the church, together with domestic offices for the accommodation of the monks.

Canterbury Cathedral had been served by a monastic community since well before the Norman Conquest so that, as a priority following the fire, Archbishop Lanfranc needed to provide a new setting for the monastic choir where the cursus of the daily office might be celebrated, and also to provide a place for his throne when he presided over the liturgy. His detailed interest in the monastic liturgy is demonstrated by the monastic customary that he drew up for Christ Church, based mainly on the Cluniac *Liber Tramitis* and Bernard of Cluny but also with Bec influences.[15] The customary did not lay down any blueprint for the form of the church; but, since it was written only after the construction of the new church had been undertaken, if not completed, the liturgy that it prescribed must have been conformable to the building.[16]

A certain amount of archaeological evidence and extant fabric, when combined with the detailed architectural description of the parts of Lanfranc's church surviving in the late 12th century written by the monk Gervase, gives an overall picture of the liturgical arrangements.[17] To the east of the crossing was a short presbytery containing the high altar, raised up over a crypt and flanked by side chapels. The monks' choir must have been located in the east bays of the nave and perhaps extended into the crossing.[18] The flanking transepts contained galleries, one of which supported a pipe organ; while to the east of the transepts were deep two-storied chapels. The chapel of the Virgin Mary occupied the north aisle of the nave, flanking the choir.

In support of the liturgical function of the cathedral, and of its religious life more generally, Lanfranc greatly increased the size of the monastic community by 100, to a total of 140 or 150 monks.[19] For this enlarged community he provided suitable new domestic buildings, including the cloister, cellarium, refectory and dormitory.[20] Parts of these survive, and the huge scale of the dormitory is an index of the increased size of the community.

Anselm's subsequent extension of Lanfranc's church entailed a radical reconfiguration of the liturgical space, with the main vessel of the building being doubled in length and the monks' choir being transferred to east of the crossing. Beyond this choir, a greatly extended presbytery led up to the repositioned high altar; while the surrounding aisles and ambulatory gave access to a substantially increased number of subsidiary chapels. Eadmer referred to the extension as an *oratorium*, meaning (as in the Rule of St Benedict) the place of prayer for the monks.[21] Perhaps one reason for this radical reorganisation of the building was to allow a spatial separation between the monastic liturgy and other functions taking place in the nave. But it also enabled the choir to be placed on the same level as the presbytery, rather than having a change in floor level interposed between the two.

At St Augustine's Abbey, a previous remodelling scheme had been abandoned in the 1060s and was characterised by Goscelin of Saint-Bertin (who was a monk at St Augustine's) as having been 'unsuitable for monastic usage', although he blamed the craftsmen for this rather than the patron: the new buildings, he must have intended to imply, remedied this defect.[22] As at the cathedral, the monastic choir was now set in the crossing and east bays of the nave. But it was flanked by only simple transept arms with single-storied chapels. To the east of the choir the presbytery was raised over a crypt, constituting two liturgical spaces, dedicated respectively to the Apostles Peter and Paul above and the Virgin Mary below: these corresponded to two previously separate churches, axially aligned, which the new building replaced.[23]

At St Albans, Lanfranc is said to have given to Abbot Paul a copy of his monastic customary, written in his own hand; and so it may be assumed that the liturgy at St Alban's during his abbacy was very similar to that at Canterbury Cathedral.[24] Unsurprisingly, therefore, the liturgical planning of the building was rather similar to Christ Church. The high altar and presbytery occupied an extended eastern arm, separated by solid side walls from flanking chapels; while the monks' choir was placed in the crossing and east bays of the nave. The transepts, however, were devoid of galleries, but provided with twin eastern chapels.

These churches had to provide not only for the liturgical arrangements for the monastic liturgy; but in all three cases they also held custody of the shrines of important saints. At Christ Church, before the Norman Conquest there were two principle cults, those of the former archbishops St Dunstan (died 988) and St Ælfheah (martyred 1012); in addition to which there were many other relics.[25] Lanfranc transferred the remains of earlier archbishops into his new church, and, although there is no direct evidence, he probably relocated Dunstan and Ælfheah in the presbytery, providing them with new tombs and monuments; other archiepiscopal remains were placed in wooden chests on the gallery in the north transept.[26] Subsequently, Anselm relocated St Dunstan and St Ælfheah into his new presbytery, near the high altar.[27] The 'Instructions for Novices' at Canterbury, contained in a later document, direct the young monk on entering the choir to prostrate first before the high altar steps, then to bow before the altars of St Ælfheah on his left and St Dunstan on his right.[28]

At St Augustine's the new church had to accommodate the tombs of a whole series of 7th-century archbishops of Canterbury and other saints, of which the abbey was the custodian, and whose significance was unquestioned. These were translated from the north *porticus* (side chapel) of the old church and relocated so as to surround the new presbytery, with some placed in the ambulatory and with the three principal shrines in the three radiating chapels. The resulting arrangement is shown in a unique 15th-century coloured sketch.[29]

Likewise at St Albans, the church had to provide a setting for the shrine of St Alban, who had been martyred and buried nearby during the Roman period, and around whose tomb the original church had been focussed. The story of Alban's martyrdom was included in Bede's *Historia Ecclesiastica* and would have been well known from that source, but there is no surviving evidence for a major cult or pilgrimage before the Norman Conquest. It would, therefore, have been a new departure if Abbot Paul made the shrine of the saint a focal point of the church, placing it in the apse behind the high altar, in an elongated presbytery arm.[30] In this position it differed from the two great churches in Canterbury, where the principle shrines were placed to either side of the high altar in Anselm's cathedral, and in the ambulatory in Scolland's abbey. In addition to the main shrine, the abbey possessed certain relics that were thought to have been deposited in St Alban's tomb by Bishop Germanus of Auxerre in the 5th century; for these Abbot Richard donated a new reliquary chest with gold images, and a second with gilding and ivory for other relics.[31]

Symbolic expression

When Canterbury cathedral had been founded by missionaries from Rome at the end of the 6th century, it had been dedicated to Christ the Saviour, clearly with reference to the *Basilica Salvatoris* at the Lateran, which was the cathedral church of the pope. Awareness of the Roman connections of Canterbury at its foundation was kept alive by Bede's *Historia Ecclesiastica* and would have been well known in the late 11th and early 12th centuries. Perhaps, then, it was not accidental that Anselm's extension of the cathedral, initiated around the 500th anniversary year of its original foundation, brought the internal length of the building up to a dimension corresponding with the length of St Peter's basilica in Rome.[32] A similar iconographic reference to St Peter's may have been intended in the case of St Albans, where the enormous length was a feature of the building from the start. Perhaps in this case the specific point being made was that, as St Peter was the proto-martyr of Rome, just so was St Alban of England.[33]

For the period under consideration, however, the element of symbolism at Canterbury Cathedral should be read rather more in its general aesthetic character as an expression of its function. In this respect the building displayed something of a contrast between the work of Lanfranc and that of Anselm. Lanfranc's building, which was closely related in its design to his former abbey of Saint-Etienne in Caen, was dignified but sober, not only because of the exigency of replacing quickly the fire-damaged building, but also perhaps expressing his mission to reform the English church and bring it back to a well-regulated norm.

On the other hand, the augmentation of the cathedral under Anselm and his successors was noted for its opulence. Thus Honorius Augustodunensis when he wrote his *Speculum Ecclesiae c.* 1100x1110 at the request of the monks of Christ Church, following his visit there, deployed an extended metaphor about the Church as the house of God borne up by the pillars of Scripture and adorned by the writings of the Fathers. In doing so, the picture in Honorius' mind would seem to have been Anselm's building, especially the programme of stained glass, painting and sculpture.[34] In the prologue, the Fathers were like skilled *pictores*, who 'adorned the house of the Lord with wondrous carvings and varied pictures'; while in the concluding 'Sermon for a Dedication' they were likened to a noble *pictor*, who 'girded the whole house with a varied adornment and distinguished it in a circuit as if with shining gems, and these remarkable things presented the whole house as if with an excellent picture in a circuit' – that is, a cycle of pictorial stained-glass windows.[35] A few years later, *c*. 1125, William of Malmesbury could say explicitly of Canterbury that Anselm 'rebuilt it so splendidly that nothing the like of it could be seen in England, in the light of the glass windows, in the brightness of the marble pavements, and in the multicoloured pictures <that lead the wondering eye to the heights of the panelled ceiling>'.[36] To these should be added the elaboration of its architectural articulation and intricacy of its sculptured capitals.

An appreciation of the aesthetic of the new Romanesque architecture was expressed also by the monk Goscelin, who settled at St Augustine's Abbey in the early 1090s. A decade earlier, in his *Liber Confortatorius*, he had opined that buildings should be 'glorious, magnificent, most lofty, most spacious, filled with light, and most beautiful'.[37] Although at the date he wrote this Goscelin may not yet have seen the new abbey church arising in Canterbury, it would equate well with the aesthetic of the building, as well as being concordant with William of Malmesbury's later description of Anselm's extended east arm at the cathedral.

The magnificence of these buildings was an appropriate expression of their function; but at the same time it could be more than this. As has been shown recently, the elaboration of the new east arm of Canterbury Cathedral was part of a profoundly conceived scheme drawn up by Anselm, aiming to make the new building, especially through the visual imagery of its programme of stained glass, an encapsulation of the spiritual truths of Christian belief in Christ as God-made-Man.[38] Artistic beauty and divine truth were closely linked.

Projecting status

From the moment of his appointment as archbishop of Canterbury, Lanfranc had developed an exalted conception of the status of his see, asserting that it was entitled to primatial jurisdiction not only over his province but over all of Britain.[39] This led to a strenuous conflict with the archbishop of York, who was wholly unwilling to concede the principle. The new cathedral at Canterbury should certainly be seen with this struggle in mind: although, projecting the unchallenged metropolitan status of the cathedral within its own province provided good enough reason in itself for the project.

Projecting the status of the see may again be seen as a factor behind the even greater ambition of the cathedral as extended by Anselm in the early 12th century. In the main apse a flight of steps led up behind the high altar to the throne, the 'seat of the patriarchate' (*cathedra patriarchatus*), where the archbishop would have appeared framed between the altar below and the gold and silver image of Christ in Majesty on the beam above it.[40] This arrangement dominated the east end visually, and clearly it was intended to make explicit the status of the archbishop as primate of all England. Perhaps also it reflected the reported description of Anselm by Pope Urban II as 'the apostolic [bishop] and patriarch' of insular Europe.[41]

At St Augustine's Abbey, on the eve of the Norman Conquest Abbot Æthelsige had obtained from Pope Alexander II the right to wear mitre and sandals.[42] This was followed up after the Conquest by the forgery of a series of pseudo papal and royal privileges claiming exemption from royal and episcopal jurisdiction, together with a status for the abbey as the mother of all English monasteries.[43] The construction of the new church was clearly intended as a projection of the importance of the abbey and at the same time, by making provision for the tombs of the early archbishops, it was an assertion of its institutional continuity going back to the apostolic mission of St Augustine himself: a continuity that placed it on a level footing with the cathedral.

At St Albans, the apparent prominence of the saint's shrine within the church raises a question as to why Alban's cult was of special interest to Abbot Paul, and to his patron Archbishop Lanfranc. The archbishop's primatial see had been founded on the authority of Pope Gregory I and his emissary Augustine. But perhaps, we may speculate, Lanfranc felt that the status of Canterbury could be enhanced by promoting the Church of Augustine and Gregory as a re-affirmation of an older tradition, according to which this country was not a new-comer to the Christian Church in the 6th century, but could compare in antiquity with the other churches of the West. By promoting the cult of Alban at a monastery that had no claim to episcopal status, and which was under his patronage, such an evocation of antiquity could be created without any infringement of Canterbury's status. This evocation was underlined by the very act of constructing a church with redeployed Roman materials (albeit the majority of these would have been concealed under the rendered surface finish).

LIMITING CONDITIONS

Financial resources

The archbishopric of Canterbury appears in Domesday Book as endowed with extensive estates, divided nominally between those assigned to the archbishop and those to the monks; though in practice all were under the control of the archbishop.[44] In principle, then, there may have been no shortage of resources available for Lanfranc to draw upon in financing the rebuilding of the cathedral; but, the exact disposable income from the cathedral estates is difficult to calculate from Domesday Book alone, while the latter survey takes no account of spiritual revenues.[45]

For the funding of Anselm's ambitious building programme there is rather more evidence. Looking back on the archbishop's achievements, Eadmer says that Anselm 'devoted from his own [resources] a great quantity of money to the enlargement of the house of God'; and that he made grants 'from those things that he possessed in his lordship, and a half of the offerings at the high altar (the other half Father Lanfranc having granted), and certain estates pertaining from old times to the sustenance of the monks but later diverted to other purposes'.[46] Elsewhere more detail is recorded of some of these arrangements.

Eadmer relates that in 1096 King William II imposed a levy in order to pay for the support of his brother Duke Robert of Normandy on crusade. To meet his apportioned share, the archbishop took from the cathedral treasury gold and silver to the value of 200 marks of silver; while in compensation he granted to the monks for a seven-year term the revenues of the manor of Petham; 'and so for that period the church was put in possession of the vill, and the woodlands of the vill and all its revenues were consumed by the new work which stretched from the great tower towards the east, and which Father Anselm was worthy to have begun'.[47] Great Domesday records that in 1086 the archbishop's estate of Petham, reckoned in extent at 7 *sulungs* (around 1,680 acres, 680 hectares), was valued at £20.[48] The Canterbury 'Domesday Monachorum' of *c.* 1100 gives the same valuation; but it also records that renders were received *de firma* (food render, perhaps commuted for cash) and *de gablum* (rent).[49] More precisely, Eadmer states that the annual renders from the estate amounted to about *triginta librae denariorum*; that is, £30 by accounting unit of 240 pence to the *librum*.[50] Applied annually to the works over a period of seven years, this would have amounted to a total of £210 (315 marks). This sum was considerably more than the 200 marks (£133-6s-8d) taken by Anselm from the treasury in 1096:[51] so it seems that the transaction related not only to repaying the levy but also to the wider financing of the building project.

When Anselm went into exile in 1103, on account of his dispute with King Henry I, he wrote to Bishop Gundulf of Rochester urging him to intervene with the king to dissuade him from demanding money from the prior and monks of Christ Church who, he claimed, were in no position to pay. In this letter he says that the monks 'still are unable to have the half that I have assigned to the work begun on the church; and if they did have it, it is not appropriate for the king to demand anything from those who as monks have nothing themselves, nor does it fall upon them to give or lend what is not theirs'.[52] The 'half' was presumably the half share of offerings at the high altar. Later, on returning from exile in 1107, Anselm 'gave to the building works on the church the pennies that each year the parish churches were accustomed to pay to the mother church at Easter'.[53] What seems clear is that, in order to fund the enormous project, Anselm had to assemble money from a range of sources, including income from spiritualities as well as from church-owned estates.

The second great religious house in Canterbury, St Augustine's Abbey, was in the late-11th-century the sixth wealthiest monastery in England, with landed estates throughout the county of Kent producing a substantial income.[54] The abbey, therefore, was well placed to undertake an ambitious building project: but we know little in detail about how the financing of the project was arranged.

However, at St Alban's there seems a marked contrast between the modest scale of the landholdings of the abbey at the time of Domesday Book and the massive scale of the new church.[55] Compared with the approximate ratio between resources and scale of building at other contemporary cathedral and monastic churches in England, the mismatch at St Albans appears all the clearer. The church seems far too ambitious for what the abbey's resources should have allowed. One explanation may be provided by Matthew Paris' assertion that abbots Paul and Richard were assisted financially by archbishops Lanfranc and Anselm.[56] A figure of 1,000 marks contributed by Lanfranc is mentioned: that is, by accounting value £666-13s-4d.[57] This was more than three times the amount assigned to the work at Canterbury by Anselm from one estate over a seven-year period.

Assessing what recorded sums of money may mean in relation to expenditure on wages and materials for building works in this period is not straightforward. As to wages, different rates would have applied according to the skills of the employees, and whether or not they were provided with their food. The earliest regulated scale of wages in England dates only from the beginning of the 13th century and shows skilled craftsmen at 4d (4 silver pennies) a day without their food, and the less skilled at between 2d and 3d; but higher rates would have been necessary to retain the top masters, while labourers presumably received less.[58] Even if similar rates applied at a date a century earlier or more, the number of craftsmen and labourers employed on any particular 11th-century project is unknown and cannot be set against such rates.

Perhaps a general comparison may be made with Westminster Abbey as rebuilt by King Henry III in the middle of the 13th century, where initially 3,000 marks (£2,000) per annum were assigned from the royal treasury for the work, but this sum was not adequate in the event.[59] As to the proportion of this assigned to different purposes, a sample of the detailed accounts shows that, over a thirty-week period from April to the beginning of December in 1253, expenditure was more or less equally divided between wages and purchases; while an average of around 150 craftsmen in different trades were employed, and the same number again of labourers.[60]

The validity of making any comparison between an 11th-century building project and 13th-century Westminster has to be qualified by the very elaborate and notoriously costly character of the Westminster project. Furthermore, the balance of expenditure between wages and purchases may have varied, depending on the extent to which materials had to be purchased, as against being available from the estates owned by the commissioning church or provided by donors. Account must also be taken of possible inflation over the previous century and a half. Notwithstanding all these qualifications, for sake of illustration one might hazard a guess that if 100 craftsmen at 3d a day and 100 labourers at 1½d were employed at any one time on Anselm's project, then the costs in wages may have been approximately 844 marks per annum over a 50-week, 6-day-a-week year; which could be doubled to account for purchases of materials: amounting thus to 1,687 marks (£1,125) per annum. If this guess is even remotely near the actual figures involved, it may be concluded that the recorded sums at Canterbury and St Albans represent only a small part of the picture. Thus at St Albans, the 1,000 marks contributed by Lanfranc would be equivalent to only 91 marks per annum over each of the eleven years of the project. Alternatively, Lanfranc may have defrayed the costs over the first year in order to get the project under way.

Design and technical constraints

The projects under consideration represent an early stage in the introduction of the Romanesque style and its associated technology into England. Apart from the rebuilding of Westminster Abbey in the 1050s and 1060s, there was in the early years after the Norman Conquest no developed indigenous tradition of construction in the technology associated with the Romanesque style.[61] This meant that there were few masons who were trained in the new mode. It also meant that there was an under-developed quarrying industry, and hence a lack of capacity to supply the quantities of dressed ashlar required for buildings on a much larger scale than the traditional English norm. Equally, construction on a more massive scale, often involving masonry vaulting, would have raised engineering considerations that had not been experienced previously.

To meet these deficiencies, Archbishop Lanfranc, with his active involvement in the construction of the new abbey of Saint-Etienne in Caen, would have had little difficulty in drawing on relevant experience and personnel available in the workshop there, and transferring these skills from Normandy to his project at his cathedral in Canterbury. Similarly Abbot Paul, both from his own experience at Caen and from his relationship with Archbishop Lanfranc, was well placed to draw on the design experience gained in the workshops of Caen and Canterbury during the previous decade and a half. Despite this, the construction of the new building at St Alban's, with wall and pier facings of re-used brick, placed limitations on the architectural detailing that could be formed with this material, and in consequence the design was a rather pared-down version of the Caen and Canterbury Romanesque style.

Abbot Scolland's work at St Augustine's Abbey again drew in general on the Caen style, but the degree of departure from the Caen model in the planning of his church indicates that he was looking more widely to other sources to meet the particular requirements of his new church. Then, only a little later, Archbishop Anselm extended his horizons further again to undertake one of the most ambitious projects of its date in Europe, the sources for which suggest an international rather than purely Norman dimension.

PRACTICAL PROCESSES

Whereas the patrons' brief may be considered the point of departure for the implementation of any project, no direct evidence survives for the specific briefs in the cases under consideration. They can only be inferred in general terms from the personalities of the patrons and the nature of their different projects, as already discussed. It is necessary therefore to turn directly to the processes by which the briefs were put into practical effect.

Administration of works

As between Lanfranc's programme of works at Canterbury Cathedral and that initiated by Anselm, it is possible to see some adjustment in the system of administrative oversight. It is reasonably clear that it was Lanfranc himself who was the driving force behind the rapid rebuilding of the cathedral and monastic offices. However, while Lanfranc was still in Caen he had been assisted as coadjutor by the monk Gundulf, whom he then brought with him to Canterbury in 1070; and, 'since he was exceedingly diligent even in external affairs, he appointed him as manager of his household affairs'.[62] A few years later in 1077 he appointed Gundulf as his suffragan bishop at Rochester; and there he rebuilt the cathedral, assisted by contributions from Lanfranc. At some point, probably in the 1070s, Gundulf was appointed by King William I to 'preside over the works' of the Tower of London; he lodged at the time with a burgess of the city, Eadmer *Anhaende*, who in return asked to be made a *socius* of the church of Rochester.[63] Subsequently in 1089, King William II required Gundulf to build for him a castle in Rochester in consideration of the fact that Gundulf was 'very greatly knowledgeable and effective in the work of masons'; this was to be at the bishop's expense and cost him some £60.[64] It is reasonably clear that Gundulf's competence had nothing to do with any practical training as a mason, but with his administrative experience in managing building projects. Although he is not credited specifically with managing the project at Christ Church, there can be little doubt that this fell under the administrative responsibilities devolved upon him by Lanfranc.

Following Anselm's succession to the archbishopric, he again was the driving force behind the project for extending the cathedral. But upon his exile in 1103 he had to appoint his suffragan bishop, Gundulf, to take charge of his affairs in England, both domestic and external.[65] But Anselm also devolved greater responsibility for managing the monastery's affairs onto the priors of Christ Church.[66] This included responsibility for the fabric of the new eastern extension, to the degree that successive priors were accounted authors of the work, despite the fact that Anselm himself initiated it and had overall responsibility for it. Thus Prior Ernulf (*c.* 1096–1107), who had been a monk first at Saint-Simphorien in Beauvais, and later at Christ Church under Lanfranc, was credited by William of Malmesbury with responsibility for the splendour of the new east end.[67] Then, after Ernulf had been promoted to the abbacy of Peterborough, there was appointed in his place Conrad (1108/9–26), again a monk of the house and perhaps the sacrist, and it is to him that Gervase attributes the 'glorious completion' of the new choir.[68] This must mean that they were responsible for the immediate supervision and administration of the work, whereas responsibility for raising the necessary funding remained with Anselm and perhaps Gundulf.

By way of contrast, at St Augustine's it is clear that Abbot Scolland in person had an interest in the administration, as is shown by his involvement with the procurement of stone (see below). At St Albans nothing is recorded about the delegation of administrative arrangements, and again the impression is conveyed that Abbots Paul and Richard themselves took a direct interest in the works.

It may be that a distinction can be drawn here between cathedrals and abbeys. In the former, the bishop had clear overall control of affairs, with the authority to initiate a building campaign; but he was too busy to supervise the administration and delegated this to a coadjutor or to the prior. At an abbey, in this period at least, the abbot may have been less involved in external affairs and more able to give time to internal administrative matters, especially the important business of constructing a new church. But even so, any abbot no doubt delegated more routine matters to one or another of the obedientiaries of his monastery, such as the sacrist.

Provision of materials

The Canterbury region was devoid of good building stone and so, according to one source, Lanfranc had ready-prepared squared stones transported by sea from Caen.[69] This is borne out by the surviving parts of Lanfranc's building, which used stone from the quarries at Caen in Normandy, together with other material from quarries at Marquise in the Boulonnais and at Quarr in the Isle of Wight.[70] In making use of Caen stone, Lanfranc was continuing a practice with which he would have been familiar when the church of Saint-Etienne was being rebuilt during his abbacy. Subsequently the use of Caen stone as the major facing material continued in the eastward extension of the cathedral. The quarries at Caen lay on the ducal estate, and this raises a question as to whether William I may have provided stone for Christ Church as a donation, or whether Lanfranc had to purchase it at full cost. The answer to this is unknown, although it may be noted that the king did provide stone directly for the initial works at his own foundation of Battle Abbey.[71] Caen stone continued to be used under Anselm as the principal material for ashlar. As for timber, some of this was supplied from the estate at Petham, 4½ miles (12km) south of Canterbury which, as already noted, was given over by Anselm for supporting the works.[72]

For the procurement of stone for St Augustine's, Goscelin provides significant insights, and it is clear that Abbot Scolland himself took a close interest in the matter.[73] On one occasion the abbot personally, appraising someone as having the right skills, appointed him as master in charge of obtaining stone from the quarries at Marquise. The stone, according to its intended end-use, was shaped at the quarries before transport, thus reducing the burden that would have to be carried by ships on the dangerous voyage across the Channel to England.

Scolland also made arrangements for the procurement of stone through Vitalis, a Norman knight who held office as the royal superintendent (*exactor*) in charge of conveying stone from Caen for the Palace of Westminster. Vitalis was a lay member of the confraternity of St Augustine's Abbey, as well as a tenant of Archbishop Lanfranc, and he arranged to have a ship load of stone delivered to Canterbury. The ship master was contracted to supply the material at a set price, but only got paid on delivery; so losses at sea did not fall on the abbey. On presenting his letters of agreement to Abbot Scolland in person, the ship master received payment from him.

For the construction of the new abbey buildings at St Albans, materials were readily to hand in the form of bricks and ashlar stones, as well as flint rubble, salvaged from the site of the Roman town of Verulamium, at the foot of the hill on which the abbey lay. Considerable expenditure and labour on extraction, transport and preparation must have been saved thereby. Furthermore, it was said that some of these materials had already been stockpiled by Abbot Paul's predecessors.[74]

Execution by craftsmen

Masters of the works. It is extremely fortunate that Goscelin of Saint-Bertin preserved the name of the master of the works at St Augustine's Abbey, since this was one of the most significant buildings (alongside Christ Church) for sowing the seeds of the Romanesque style in England.[75] He was 'Blitherus, the most eminent master of the craftsmen and worthy designer of the church'.[76] The Latin name appears in the vernacular as Blittaere or Blutere, and in the hypocoristic form Blize; it is a Continental Germanic name and, therefore, he was a person of Continental origin, although from exactly where is uncertain. Nothing is recorded about the arrangements under which Blitherus was retained by St Augustine's as master of works.

Less fortunately, the name is unrecorded of the master of the works responsible for designing Lanfranc's new cathedral church at Canterbury; but the similarity of its design to that of Saint-Etienne in Caen would indicate that he came from that workshop. However, it is recorded that in 1086 Blize, the master of the works at St Augustine's Abbey, was retained also at Christ Church, from which he held one of the cathedral's estates, the small borough of Seasalter. In Great Domesday Seasalter is recorded as belonging to the archbishop's kitchen (perhaps a scribal error) and was held by Blize (Blitherus) from the monks; according to the Domesday Monachorum it belonged to the monks' kitchen.[77] The borough was valued at 100 shillings; but it is not known how much Blitherus received for himself from the returns of his holding, nor how much rent he paid to the monks. In view of the dissimilarities between Lanfranc's cathedral church and Scolland's abbey church, it may seem unlikely that they were designed by the same person. Blitherus, therefore, must have been responsible for some other project at Christ Church. What is significant, none the less, is to see one master working for the two great religious houses in Canterbury.

At St Alban's another name was preserved. According to Matthew Paris, Abbot Paul retained 'for his craftsmanship and labours Robert the mason (*caementarius*), who was capable beyond all the masons of his day'.[78] As to Robert's origins nothing is known, other than that he bore a name that was not English, but might have been found in Normandy or elsewhere on the Continent. For his services Robert and his heirs were granted by Abbot Paul a house in the town and the tenure of estates belonging to the abbey, at Sarratt and *Wanthone*; while later Abbot Richard made a further grant of an estate, at Sopwell, at an annual rent of 6s paid to the abbey.[79] Matthew Paris says that the Sarratt estate had previously been rented out at 60s a year, but that with it Abbot Paul was said 'to have paid in full for the work of Robert, at the agreed and assessed sum and without a burden on the church'.[80] Later, on his deathbed, Robert had handed back the estate freely to the prior and monks, renouncing any claims by himself or his heirs. If revenue worth 60s a year had been Robert's only payment it would represent a rate of only about 2 ½d per working day: but it must have been supplemented by income from his other estates, and by his house in the town. Apart from this, it is also recorded that Robert himself made an annual benefaction of 10s to the abbey.[81] The relationship between the master of the works and the abbey was therefore longstanding and reciprocal.

Other craftsmen. As to the other craftsmen working at Canterbury Cathedral, the brilliant glazing, multicoloured paintings and wonderful carvings referred to by William of Malmesbury and Honorius Augustodunensis are evidenced by surviving elements of their works, but the artists remain anonymous. The glass painters who executed Anselm's seemingly revolutionary programme for the glazing of the choir are represented by some surviving figures of prophets in the clearstory.[82] Wall-painting is represented by the scheme in St Gabriel's chapel, of a disputed date in the second quarter or second third of the 12th century.[83] Sculpture survives quite extensively with the magnificent series of late-11th-century capitals in the crypt and on the external walls of the aisles.[84] However, the craftsmen responsible for all these works remain anonymous.

The same anonymity hides the craftsmen and labourers engaged at St Augustine's. But a lone exception is provided by an *ex situ* sculptured capital that is inscribed ROBERTVS ME FECIT. This has been dated to *c.* 1100 on its style and compared with capitals in the crypt of the cathedral as well as with a manuscript from the abbey scriptorium.[85]

At St Albans the artist who was responsible for executing the painting (no longer extant) on the vault above or beyond the high altar is again anonymous.[86] However, we do know in some detail about the craftsman responsible a few years later for making a new shrine for the relics of St Alban. This was commissioned in 1123 by Abbot Geoffrey (1119–46), and the translation of the relics took place in 1129.[87] The craftsman responsible for the work was a monk of St Alban's named Anketil, who was an accomplished goldsmith; he was assisted by his young lay pupil Salamon.[88] At some point in his career Anketil had been summoned from England to work in Denmark for the king, and there for seven years he is said to have supervised (*praeerat*) the royal goldsmith's work and held the position of keeper of the mint and high treasurer. Then on returning to England he entered St Albans as a monk. The shrine was executed with gilded silver plates, worked with raised figures, and was adorned with gems, some of which were antique cameos and other stones from the abbey's treasury. The 'house-shaped' shrine in the form it had reached by the 13th century was depicted in a simplified way by Matthew Paris.[89] As to its detailed treatment, it may be asked whether, in view of Anketil's background, any non-figurative ornament possibly combined Romanesque and Scandinavian Urnes style elements.[90] Be that as it may, the story of Anketil illustrates well how master craftsmen had an important role in furnishing a church, as well as how such work might be undertaken by a monk with the relevant expertise.

CONCLUSIONS

By examining in detail the fragments of surviving and recorded information, and by comparing them against a theoretical model, a picture starts to emerge of the intentions, conditions and processes that lay behind the development of Romanesque architecture in England in the last third of the 11th century and at the beginning of the 12th century. Bishops and abbots coming to England from the Continent to take up office in cathedrals and abbeys brought with them experience and knowledge that differed from that of the English churchmen they were replacing: they had participated in intellectual and artistic currents that they now wished to introduce to their new churches. But to do so they had to reform the liturgy and observances of their religious communities, while expressing this in a new wave of architecture on a scale and pattern scarcely seen before in England. But the realisation of their vision was conditioned by the availability of resources, materials and skills. These were matters that bishops, with many other calls on their attention, had to delegate to others while maintaining in person the overall momentum of their vision; abbots, on the other hand, were better placed to remain personally involved. Just as a ballet dancer appears to the audience as an image of elegance and grace, while behind the image lies a reality of prolonged training, hard work and physical effort; so too behind the image of Romanesque architecture lie acquired skills, applied resources and practical actions that alone enabled the actual performance as material monument.

NOTES

[1] The centrality of the liturgy to understanding the cultural significance of a church is well emphasised by S. Boynton, *Shaping a Monastic Identity: Liturgy and History at the Imperial abbey of Farfa, 1000–1125* (Ithaca 2006).

[2] *Hebrews*, 8.1–5, where the Mosaic temple and rites are seen as the types and shadows (*exemplari et umbrae*) of the heavenly sanctuary where Christ ministers; *Revelation*, 21–22, where the construction of the new Jerusalem with precious materials is described.

[3] W. Vroom, *Financing Cathedral Building in the Middle Ages: the Generosity of the Faithful* (Amsterdam 2010), ch. 2, 'Sources of funding for building works', provides a useful overview of potential sources of funding; but this relates essentially to the period from the 12th century to the 14th and cannot be retrojected to the 11th century in the absence of specific evidence.

[4] On the Romanesque buildings under Lanfranc and Anselm see: R. Gem, 'The significance of the 11th-century rebuilding of Christ Church and St Augustine's, Canterbury, in the development of the Romanesque style', in *Medieval Art and Architecture at Canterbury Before 1200*, ed. N. Coldstream & P. Draper, British Archaeological Association Conference Transactions, v (Leeds 1982), 1–19; reprinted, R. Gem, *Studies in English Pre-Romanesque and Romanesque Architecture* (London 2004), II, 456–89; E. Fernie, 'St Anselm's crypt', in *Canterbury before 1200* (as above), 26–38; F. Woodman, *The Architectural History of Canterbury Cathedral* (London 1981); K. Blockley, M. Sparks & T. Tatton-Brown, *Canterbury Cathedral Nave: Archaeology, History and Architecture* (Canterbury 1997), 23–33, 111–23; E. Fernie, *The Architecture of Norman England* (Oxford 2000), 104–06, 140–44.

[5] Eadmer, *Historia Novorum in Anglia*, ed. M. Rule (Rolls Series 81, 1884), 13.

[6] On Lanfranc's career see M. Gibson, *Lanfranc of Bec* (Oxford 1978); H.E.J. Cowdrey, *Lanfranc: Scholar, Monk and Archbishop* (Oxford 2003).

[7] Eadmer, *Historia Novorum* (as n. 5), 219–220: *Ipsum oratorium quantum a maiore turri in orientem porrectum est, ipso patre Anselmo prouidente, disponente, incohante, auctum est.*

[8] 1114: Matthew Paris, *Chronica Maiora*, ed. H.R. Luard, 7 vols (Rolls Series 57, 1872–78), II, 141. 1130: multiple sources, including John of Worcester, ed. & trans. P. McGurk, *The Chronicle of John of Worcester*, III (Oxford Medieval Texts, Oxford 1998), 192–93.

[9] On Anselm's career see R.W. Southern, *St Anselm and his Biographers: a Study in Monastic Life and Thought 1095-c.1130* (Cambridge 1963); idem, *St Anselm: Portrait in a Landscape* (Cambridge 1990); S.N. Vaughan, *Archbishop Anselm 1093–1109: Bec Missionary, Canterbury Primate and Patriarch of Another World* (Farnham 2012).

[10] See the important reassessment by T.A. Heslop, 'St Anselm and the visual arts at Canterbury Cathedral, 1093–1109', in *Medieval Art, Architecture and Archaeology at Canterbury*, ed. A. Bovey, British Archaeological Association Conference Transactions, xxxv (Leeds 2013), 59–81.

[11] Gem, 'Christ Church and St Augustine's' (as n. 4); D. Sherlock & H. Woods, *St Augustine's Abbey: Report on Excavations, 1960–1978* (Maidstone 1988); T. Tatton-Brown, 'The buildings and topography of St Augustine's Abbey, Canterbury', *Journal of the British*

Archaeological Association, 144 (1991), 61–91; R. Gem (ed.), *St Augustine's Abbey Canterbury* (London 1997).

12. Goscelin's *De miraculis sancti Augustini*', cited R. Gem, 'Canterbury and the cushion capital: a commentary on passages from Goscelin's *De miraculis sancti Augustini*', in N. Stratford (ed.), *Romanesque and Gothic: Essays for George Zarnecki*, 2 vols. (Woodbridge 1989), 83–101; reprinted Gem, *Studies* (as n. 4), 518: . . . *abbas Scollandus in edificio augustalis monasterii ardentissimus.*

13. J.J.G. Alexander, *Norman Illumination at Mont St Michel* (Oxford 1970), 17–18, 40, 222: . . . SCOLLANDUS *que sacro prefulgens dogmate cuncto.*

14. The principle source is Matthew Paris, *Vitae . . . Viginti Trium Abbatum Sancti Albani*, ed. W. Wats, *Matthei Paris Historia Major &c* (London 1640), part II, 35–145, at 49–56; cp. 14th-century version by Thomas of Walsingham, *Gesta Abbatum Monasterii Sancti Albani*, ed. H.T. Riley, *Chronica Monasterii Sancti Albani*, 3 vols. (Rolls Series 28, 1867–69), I, 51–54.

15. *Decreta Lanfranci* ed. D. Knowles & C.N.L. Brooke, *The Monastic Constitutions of Lanfranc* (rev. ed. Oxford Medieval Texts, Oxford 2002), introduction xxxiv–xlii; Cowdrey, *Lanfranc* (as n. 6), 175–84. For Canterbury liturgy under Lanfranc see also: A.W. Klukas, 'The architectural implications of the *Decreta Lanfranci*', *Anglo-Norman Studies*, 6 (1983), 136–71; T.A. Heslop, 'The Canterbury calendars and the Norman conquest', in R. Eales & R. Sharpe (eds.), *Canterbury and the Norman Conquest: Churches, Saints and Scholars 1066–1109* (London 1995), 175–84; R.W. Pfaff, *The Liturgy in Medieval England: a History* (Cambridge & New York 2009), 106–10 et seq.; H. Gittos, 'Sources for the liturgy of Canterbury Cathedral in the central middle ages', in Bovey (ed.), *Medieval Art, Architecture and Archaeology at Canterbury* (as n. 10), 41–58.

16. The date of the Constitutions is uncertain, but the late 1070s seems most likely. See Knowles & Brooke, *Monastic Constitutions* (as n. 15), xxxiv–xlii; Cowdrey, *Lanfranc* (as n. 6), 154–60.

17. Gervase, *Tractatus de Combustione et Reparatione Cantuariensis Ecclesiae*, ed. W. Stubbs, *The Historical Works of Gervase of Canterbury*, 2 vols. (Rolls Series 73, 1879, 1880), I, 9–16.

18. M. Sparks, 'The liturgical use of the nave 1077–1540', in Blockley et al. *Canterbury Cathedral Nave* (as n. 4), at 121–23, suggests that the choir was located entirely in the nave because the area of the crossing was occupied by the steps rising up to the presbytery. However, for Lanfranc's building there is little actual archaeological evidence relating to the arrangement of steps providing access to the presbytery and crypt levels, since these were substantially remodelled in Anselm's building (Blockley, ibid, 26, 31–33, 114–15).

19. Gervase, *Acta Pontificum*, ed. Stubbs, *Historical Works* (as n. 17), II, 368.

20. Eadmer, *Historia Novorum* (as n. 5), 13; Lanfranc's *obit*, ed. M. Rule, *Lanfranc of Bec* (Oxford 1978), 228.

21. Eadmer, *Historia Novorum* (as n. 5), 219; cp. Rule of St Benedict, cap. 52, '*De oratorio monasterii*'.

22. Goscelin, *Historia Translationis Sancti Augustini Episcopi*, ed. Migne, *Patrologia Latina* 155 (Paris 1880), 33: . . . *quanquam monasticae habitationi incongruum fecisset artificum imperitia.*

23. Ibid., 39. The original dedication of the abbey to Sts Peter and Paul was later supplemented with the name of St Augustine, which then came to take priority. For the monastic customs at St Augustine's under Scolland there is little direct evidence: the earliest liturgical manuscript dates from *c*. 1093; that is, following Lanfranc's attempt to impose his authority on the monastery. See Pfaff, *Liturgy in Medieval England* (as n. 15), 113–18.

24. Matthew Paris, *Vitae Abbatum* (as n. 14), ed. Wats, II, 49, 61; *Gesta Abbatum* ed. Riley, I, 52, 61.

25. Eadmer, *De Reliquiis S. Audoeni*, ed. A. Wilmart, 'Edmeri Cantuarensis cantoris nova opuscula de sanctorum veneratione et obsecratione', *Revue des Sciences Religieuses*, 15 (1935), 362–67.

26. J. Crook, *English Medieval Shrines* (Woodbridge 2011), 121–25. The theory that Lanfranc demoted Sts Dunstan and Ælfheah in the early years of his episcopate is now doubted: see Knowles & Brooke, *Monastic Constitutions* (as n. 15), xxviii–xxxix; Cowdrey, *Lanfranc* (as n. 6), 175–184. Lanfranc, indeed, did question whether Ælfheah was to be culted as a martyr; but Anselm reassured him on this: Eadmer, *Vita Sancti Anselmi*, ed. & trans. R.W. Southern, *The Life of St Anselm by Eadmer* (Edinburgh 1962, rev. ed. Oxford 1972), 50–54.

27. Gervase, *Tractatus de Combustione* (as n. 17), 13; see also Crook, *English Medieval Shrines* (as n. 26), 137–38.

28. Appendix to Knowles & Brooke, *Monastic Constitutions* (as n. 15), 202, 206, 212, 228.

29. Published in Gem *St Augustine's Abbey* (as n. 11), colour plate 1. On the ceremonies accompanying the translation of the saints to their new shrines see R. Sharpe, 'The setting of St Augustine's translation, 1091' in Eales & Sharpe, *Canterbury and the Norman Conquest* (as n. 15), 1–13.

30. It is problematic that the sources do not recount a translation of St Alban into the new building under abbots Paul or Richard. Also to be noted is the claim made at Ely that, following the Norman Conquest, Abbot Ecgfrith had taken St Alban's relics there – *Liber Eliensis*, ed. E.O. Blake (Camden Society, 3rd ser., 92, London 1962), 176–77. This obscure episode is discussed by J. Crick, *Charters of St Albans Abbey* (British Academy Anglo-Saxon Charter ser., XII, Oxford 2007), 27–30. In connection with the provision of a new shrine in the 1120s (see below) there is no reference to any translation of St Alban's relics from one part of the church to another; furthermore the shrine was certainly in the apse behind and above the high altar by 1183 – Matthew Paris, *Vitae Abbatum* (as n. 13), ed. Wats, II, 92; *Gesta Abbatum* ed. Riley, I, 189. It seems most plausible that the shrine was in the apse from the late-11th-century onwards. For detailed discussions of the shrine and its history see: M Biddle, 'Remembering St Alban: the site of the shrine and discovery of the twelfth-century Purbeck marble shrine table', in *Alban and St Albans: Roman and Medieval Architecture, Art and Archaeology*, ed. M. Henig & P. Lindley, *British Archaeological Association Conference Transactions*, xxv (Leeds 2001), 124–61; Crook, *English Medieval Shrines* (as n. 26), 140–45, 204–08, 268–71.

31. Matthew Paris, *Vitae Abbatum* (as n. 13), ed. Wats, II, 55; *Gesta Abbatum* ed. Riley, I, 69–70. These relics later stood on an altar to the south side of St Alban's shrine – see E. Roberts, *The St William of York Mural and the Altar of the Relics in St. Albans Abbey* (Hertfordshire Local History Council, occasional paper 6, Chichester 1979).

32. R. Gem, 'St Peter's basilica in Rome *c*.1024–1159: a model for emulation?', in J. McNeill & R. Plant (eds.), *Romanesque and the Past: Retrospection in the Art and Architecture of Romanesque Europe* (Leeds 2013), 49–66, at 60–61.

33. Gem, 'St Peter's basilica in Rome' (as n. 32), 60–61.

34. As discussed by Heslop, 'St Anselm and the visual arts' (as n. 10), 65–66.

35. Honorius Augustodunensis, *Speculum Ecclesiae*, ed. Migne, *Patrologia Latina*, 172 (Paris 1895), cols. 807–1104. Prologue: *peritissimi pictores . . . mira caelatura et uaria pictura egregie ornauerunt domum Domini*; Sermon (cols. 1099–1104): *nobilis pictor . . . vario ornatu cinxit, ac totam domum in circuitu quasi praefulgidis gemmis distinxit, ac totam domum in circuitu quasi praestanti pictura insignes reddiderunt.*

36. William of Malmesbury, *De Gestis Pontificum Anglorum*, ed. N.E.S.A. Hamilton (Rolls Series 52, 1870), 138; ed. M. Winterbottom, 2 vols. (Oxford Medieval Texts, Oxford 2007), I, 220: . . . *adeo splendide reerexit ut nichil tale possit in Anglia uideri in uitrearum fenestrarum luce, in marmorei pauimenti nitore, in diuersicoloribus picturis <quae mirantes oculos trahunt ad fastigia lacunaris>.* In the manuscript the words shown here in < > brackets were struck through by William following his initial draft: his reason is unclear – not least since Gervase, *Tractatus de Combustione* (as n. 17), I, 13, refers to the existence over the east arm of 'a ceiling decorated with excellent painting' (*caelum egregia pictura decoratum*).

37. Goscelin, *Liber Confortatorius*, ed. C.H. Talbot, *Analecta Monastica* 3rd ser., *Studia Anselmiana* 37 (1955), 1–117, at 93: . . . *inclita, magnifica, precelsa, perampla, perlucida et perpulchra.* Cp. M. Otter, *Goscelin of Saint Bertin, The Book of Encouragement and Consolation* (Woodbridge 2004), 115–16.

38. Heslop, 'St Anselm and the visual arts' (as n. 10).

39. For a convenient summary of the dispute see F. Barlow, *The English Church 1066–1154* (London 1979), 29–47.

⁴⁰ Gervase, *Tractatus de Combustione* (as n. 17), I, 13.

⁴¹ Eadmer, *Vita Sancti Anselmi*, (as n. 26), 105: . . . *alterius orbis apostolicum et patriarchum*.

⁴² Goscelin, *Historia Translationis* (as n. 22), 33.

⁴³ Gibson, *Lanfranc* (as n. 6), 167–69, 235–36.

⁴⁴ Southern, *St Anselm and his Biographers* (as n. 9), 256–60. The estates of the monks were valued at £730 a year and were divided between providing for their food and their clothing.

⁴⁵ A. Williams & G.H. Martin, *Domesday Book: a Complete Translation* (London 1992). What the valuations in Domesday Book represent is a matter of debate. See e.g. D. Roffe, *Domesday: the Inquest and the Book* (Oxford 2000), 131–33, 230–42; idem, *Decoding Domesday* (Woodbridge 2007), 240–50. On his interpretation, valuations represent dues in cash for which an estate was liable; they were distinct from the renders in money and food generated from the productive activities of an estate.

⁴⁶ Eadmer, *Historia Novorum* (as n. 5), 220: . . . *plurimam pecuniae quantitatem in augmentum domus Dei conferente. Ex iis uero quae in dominio suo possidebat, et offerendae maioris altaris medietatem, aliam enim medietatem pater Lanfrancus contulerat, et quasdam terras ad subsidium monachorum antiquitus pertinentes, tunc autem alios usus distractas . . . concessit*.

⁴⁷ Eadmer, *Historia Novorum* (as n. 5), 74–75: *Et quidem eodem spatio ipsa ecclesia eadem uilla potita est, et siluae uillae et toti redditus eius in nouo opere quod a maiore turri in orientem tenditur, quodque ipse pater Anselmus incohasse dinoscitur, consumpta sunt*.

⁴⁸ Williams & Martin, *Domesday Book* (as n. 45), 11.

⁴⁹ D.C. Douglas, *The 'Domesday Monachorum' of Christ Church Canterbury* (London 1944), 83, 98. Petham conjointly with *Stursete* (the manor of Canterbury Westgate) returned £40 *de firma*, but it is not possible to separate out what came just from Petham. However, Petham on its own returned 106s-2¾d in *gablum*. In addition (p. 77), Petham paid 4s in *Romescot*; while the two churches of the manor, Petham and Waltham, paid 28d in Easter dues.

⁵⁰ On the complex issue of the relationship at this period between bullion weight, minted coin and accounting units see: S. Lyon, 'Silver weight and minted weight in England *c*.1000–1320, with a discussion of Domesday terminology, Edwardian farthings and the origin of English troy', *British Numismatic Journal* 76 (2006), 227–41; M. Allen, *Mints and Money in Medieval England* (Cambridge 2012), 134–42; idem, 'Mints and money in Norman England', *Anglo-Norman Studies* 34 (2012), 1–22, at 7–8.

⁵¹ In Domesday Book a *librum* as an accounting unit meant 240 pence; while a mark of silver meant 160 pence, or 13 shillings and 4 pence – Lyon, 'Silver weight and minted weight' (as n. 50), 237. But it is intriguing that the sum taken from the treasury by Anselm relates more closely to the Domesday valuation of the estate than to the actual renders from it (cp n. 45).

⁵² Anselm, *Epistolae*, 293, ed. F.S. Schmidt, *Anselmi Opera Omnia*, 6 vols. (Seckau & Edinburgh 1938–1961), IV, 213–14: *Ad opus etiam ecclesiae inceptum dimidium quod constitueram habere nequeunt; et si haberent, nec regem decet ab illis aliquid exigere, nec nihil nec se ipsos habent, sicut monachi, nec ad illos pertinet aliquid dare uel accommodare quod eorum non est*.

⁵³ *Ibid*.: *Dedit in opera ecclesiae denarios qui singulis annis de parochianis ecclesiis in Pascha matri ecclesiae peni solent*.

⁵⁴ A. Williams, 'The Anglo-Norman abbey', in Gem, *St Augustine's Abbey* (as n. 11), 50–66, at 56–59.

⁵⁵ On the apparent poverty of the pre-Conquest abbey see J. Crick, 'Offa, Ælfric and the refoundation of St Albans', in Henig & Lindley (as n. 30), 78–84; J. Crick, *Charters of St Albans Abbey* (as n. 30), 74–91.

⁵⁶ Matthew Paris, (as n. 14), *Vitae Abbatum* ed. Wats, II, 49, 50, 52; *Gesta Abbatum* ed. Riley, I, 52, 54, 61.

⁵⁷ Matthew Paris, (as n. 14), *Vitae Abbatum* ed. Wats, II, 50; *Gesta Abbatum* ed. Riley, I, 54: . . . *Lanfranco efficacitur adiuuante; qui, ut dicitur, mille marcas ad fabricam contulit faciendam*.

⁵⁸ L.F. Salzman, *Building in England Down to 1540: a Documentary History* (Oxford 1932), 68–70.

⁵⁹ R. Allen Brown, H.M. Colvin & A.J. Taylor, *The History of the King's Works*, I, *The Middle Ages*, 2 vols. (London 1963), I, 134.

⁶⁰ H.M. Colvin (ed.), *Building Accounts of King Henry III* (Oxford 1971), 248–85.

⁶¹ On Westminster see: R. Gem 'The Romanesque rebuilding of Westminster Abbey', *Anglo-Norman Studies* 3 (1980), 33–60; reprinted, Gem, (as n. 4), II, 417–53; E. Fernie, 'Reconstructing Edward's abbey at Westminster', in Stratford, *Romanesque and Gothic* (as n. 12), 63–67; E. Fernie, 'Edward the Confessor's Westminster Abbey', in R. Mortimer (ed.), *Edward the Confessor: the man and the Legend* (Woodbridge 2009), 138–50. On how some masons spanned the transition see, R. Gem, 'The English parish church in the 11th and early 12th centuries: a Great Rebuilding?', in J. Blair (ed.), *Minsters and Parish Churches: the Local Church in Transition 950–1200* (Oxford University Committee for Archaeology Monograph 17, 1988), 21–30.

⁶² *Vita Gundulfi*, ed. Migne, *Patrologia Latina* 159 (Paris 1854), 817–18: . . . *quia in rebus etiam exterioribus industrius ualde erat, rei familiaris sua procuratorem constituit*. On Gundulf's wider role see M. Bret, 'Gundulf and the cathedral communities of Canterbury and Rochester', in Eales & Sharpe, *Canterbury and the Norman Conquest* (as n. 29), 15–25.

⁶³ *Textus Roffensis*, ed. T. Hearne (Oxford 1720), 212; . . . *Gundulfus, ex paecepto regis Willelmi, praeesset operi magnae turris Londoniae*. See also E. Impey (ed.), *The White Tower* (New Haven & London 2008), ch. 2, R. Harris, 'The structural history of the White Tower', 29–93, especially 41–44.

⁶⁴ *Textus Roffensis* (as n. 52), 146; . . . *episcopus Gundulfus, quia in opere caementarii plurimum sciens et efficax erat*.

⁶⁵ Anselm, *Epistolae*, 299 (as n. 52), 219–21. See also D.E. Luscome, 'Bec, Christ Church and the correspondence of St Anselm', *Anglo-Norman Studies* 18 (1995), 1–17, at 10–12 for Anselm's correspondence with Gundulf.

⁶⁶ Eadmer, *Historia Novorum* (as n. 5), 219.

⁶⁷ William of Malmesbury, *Gesta Pontificum* (as n. 36), ed. Hamilton, 137–38; ed. Winterbottom, 220–21.

⁶⁸ Gervase, *Tractatus de Combustione* (as n. 17), 12. But the new work, as noted above, was not finally dedicated until 1130.

⁶⁹ Anonymous (attributed to Milo Crispin), *Vita Lanfanci*, ed. Migne, *Patrologia Latina* 150 (Paris 1880), 46.

⁷⁰ T.W.T. Tatton-Brown, 'La pierre de Caen en Angleterre', in M. Baylé (ed.), *L'Architecture Normande au Moyen Âge* (Caen 1977), 305–14; idem, 'Building stone in Canterbury *c*.1070–1525' in D. Parsons (ed.), *Stone Quarrying and Building in England AD 43–1525* (Chichester 1990), 70–82; Blockley et al., *Canterbury Cathedral Nave* (as n. 4), 23–25.

⁷¹ *Chronicon Monasterii de Bello*, ed. J.S. Brewer (Anglia Christiana Society, London 1846), 50: *delegauit etiam naues de proprio, quibus a Cadomensi uico lapidum copia ad opus propositum transueheretur*.

⁷² Cit. n. 47.

⁷³ On Goscelin's account of these matters see in detail R. Gem, 'Canterbury and the cushion capital' (as n. 12), 490–521.

⁷⁴ Matthew Paris, *Vitae Abbatum* (as n. 14), ed. Wats, II, 49; *Gesta Abbatum* ed. Riley, I, 52.

⁷⁵ Gem, 'Canterbury and the cushion capital' (as n. 12).

⁷⁶ Goscelin, *Historia Translationis* (as n. 22), 17: *praestantissimus artificum magister templique spectabilis dicator, Blitherus*.

⁷⁷ Williams & Martin, *Domesday Book* (as n. 45), 12; Douglas, *Domesday Monachorum* (as n. 49), 90.

⁷⁸ Matthew Paris, *Vitae Abbatum* (as n. 14), ed. Wats, II, 53; *Gesta Abbatum* ed. Riley, I, 63–64 : . . . *Roberto caementario . . . pro artificio suo et labore, quibus prae omnibus caementariis suo tempore pollebat*.

⁷⁹ Matthew Paris, *Vitae Abbatum* (as n. 14), ed. Wats, II, 53, 55; *Gesta Abbatum* ed. Riley, I, 63–64, 72.

⁸⁰ *Ibid*. *Abbas autem Paulus laborem eiusdem Roberti in pecunia pacta et taxata persoluisse, sine ecclesiae grauamine, tenebatur*.

⁸¹ *Liber de Benefactoribus*, ed. Riley, *Chronica* (as n. 14), III, 149.

⁸² M. Caviness, 'Romanesque 'belles verrières' in Canterbury', in Stratford, *Romanesque and Gothic* (as n. 12), 35–38.

⁸³ D. Park, 'The origins of Romanesque wall painting at Canterbury', unpublished lecture to British Archaeological Association conference, Canterbury, 18th July 2009.

[84] D. Kahn, *Canterbury Cathedral and its Romanesque Sculpture* (London and Austin, Texas 1991).

[85] G. Zarnecki, 'Sculpture', in exhibition catalogue *English Romanesque Art 1066–1200* (Hayward Gallery London 1984), cat. no. 107 (catalogue entry by D. Kahn).

[86] Paris, *Vitae Abbatum* (as n. 14), ed. Wats, II 52; *Gesta Abbatum* ed. Riley, I, 60.

[87] Henry of Huntingdon, *Historia Anglorum*, ed. D. Greenway (Oxford 1996), 625; Matthew Paris, *Vitae Abbatum* (as n. 14), ed. Wats, II, 58–60; *Gesta Abbatum* ed. Riley, I, 80–85. On the history of the shrine see Biddle, 'Remembering St Alban' (as n. 30).

[88] Paris, *Vitae Abbatum* (as n. 14), ed. Wats, II, 60; *Gesta Abbatum* ed. Riley, I, 87.

[89] British Library, Cotton MS, Nero D.i, fol. 22r, reproduced in Biddle, 'Remembering St Alban' (as n. 30), fig. 17.

[90] On the Urnes style in England and the Urnes-Romanesque style, with further references, see: J. Graham-Campbell, *Viking Art* (London 2013), 150–52, 187–90.

MATILDA AND THE CITIES OF THE GREGORIAN REFORM

Arturo Carlo Quintavalle

The image of the rule of Matilda of Canossa (1046–1115) that predominated in the historical studies of the first part of the last century, and indeed still does to some extent, is one of power over territories stretching from the river Po to the Apennines and into at least part of Tuscany, but not over the cities. In short, feudal lordship on the one hand and urban power with the growth of free communes on the other. I believe that this view, which is also often adopted by art historians, is in need of partial revision. It is true that we have many documents, particularly numerous in the case of San Benedetto Po (Polirone), attesting to Matilda's constant interest in that monument, not to mention the traditional attention to Frassinoro and the importance ascribed by Donizo in the *Vita Mathildis* to the monastery of Sant'Apollonio at Canossa.[1] Significance also attaches to the interest in Nonantola, where Matilda made major donations from 1091, having requisitioned and melted down the abbey's treasure in 1084 to pay her troops in the fighting against the Empire.

The most recent studies suggest that Matilda's policy was far more complex and should be interpreted at various levels.[2] First of all, she may have wished to continue with the plans of her father Boniface and to make Mantua the capital of a realm possibly encompassing the whole of northern Italy. It was indeed precisely in Mantua that Boniface had his *palatium* built. While the project fell through in 1091, when the city fell to the emperor, this happened after a long siege. A significant number of citizens supported Matilda and were finally to abandon the city. Secondly the Great Countess was unquestionably interested in the abbeys, but these remained for her strategic places in a precise geographical vision designed to counter any possible invasion. Thus Frassinoro defended the road of the Apennine passes, as did the system of fortified castles that Matilda maintained in the area between Modena and Reggio Emilia. The abbey of San Benedetto Po occupied a key location with respect to the old and new courses of the river Po and its tributary, the Lirone. The rich abbey of Nonantola was the focal point of the confrontation between the bishops of Modena and Bologna, and finally Canossa was only one of the many castles of Matilda's defence system on the Apennines, made famous by the clash between the pope and the emperor in 1077. It should not be forgotten that the abbeys were themselves places surrounded by walls, as in the case of Nonantola, and protecting an abbey therefore also meant maintaining a system of tutelage. The case of San Benedetto Po is different again, as it was affiliated to Cluny, a form of insurance, according to historians, with respect to the imperial authorities. Polirone was also important for the training of monks who were to fight, on being introduced into the secular clergy, on the side of the papacy for orthodoxy and against the empire.

The third point of Matilda's policy, as indicated – I repeat – by the most recent studies, was a vast plan of penetration into cities strongly marked by the presence of allied vassals, *capitanei*, nobles and feudatories. I shall give just a few examples. In Modena it was precisely these figures, in addition to the *cives* representing the mercantile and manufacturing middle class, that undertook the construction of the cathedral as from 1099 in Matilda's presence. In Parma she attempted to impose the bishop and papal legate Bernardo degli Uberti in 1101 and was forced to intervene in 1104 in order to free the prelate from imprisonment by supporters of the imperial party. It was not until 1106 that the bishop was finally able to establish himself in the city, and the resumption of building probably dates from then. In Cremona the existence of a power vacuum – like the absence of an orthodox bishop in Modena – enabled Matilda to intervene in connection with the rebuilding of the cathedral. These three examples are given in order to show how historians today also focus on the urban dimension of Matilda's policy. I shall now seek, albeit perhaps in overly schematic terms, to highlight the close connection between the Gregorian Reform, the introduction of new, orthodox, abbots and bishops, and the rebuilding of monasteries and cathedrals at the very moment when they transferred their allegiance from the emperor to the pope.

The abbey of Nonantola had pro-imperial abbots until 1073 and probably no abbot at all in the period 1074–75. As from 1086 the abbot was Damianus, a religious reformer and nephew of St Peter Damian. His period of office saw the rebuilding of the church, which probably began early in the next decade, as shown by the the most recent studies and the discovery of late-11th-century frescoes in the abbey's chapter house.[3] The Abbey church was severely altered as early as the end of the 12th century, and subsequently until

FIGURE 2.1

Abbey of Nonantola: tympanum (redeployed from a pulpit) (A.C. Quintavalle)

FIGURE 2.2

Abbey of Nonantola: tympanum, reverse showing Roman sculpture (A.C. Quintavalle)

FIGURE 2.3

Canossa castle: interior (A.C. Quintavalle)

the 18th, not to mention the wholesale restoration of the 19th and early 20th.[4] It still retains a sculpted portal of great interest, where the inscription on the architrave attests to the collapse of the upper sections of the building in 1117 and its rebuilding 'after four long years', therefore beginning in 1121.[5] The tympanum (Figure 2.1) was originally left open, the evangelist symbols were part of a pulpit and the Christ Pantocrator is from a screen, as the rear, which is part of a Roman frieze, must have been visible (Figure 2.2).[6] The monastery of Frassinoro was founded by Matilda's mother Beatrice in 1071 and its markedly ancient-style marble capitals suggest a connection with work beyond the Apennines.[7] While the monastery of Sant'Apollonio at Canossa, possibly founded between 1085 and 1090, is today certainly a ruin, as is the castle (Figure 2.3), there are still traces of Matilda's decision, attested by Donizo, to place her ancestors there in Roman sarcophagi between 1111 and 1112. Four sarcophagi remained intact until 1392, as confirmed by an epigraph transcribed by the humanist Nicola Fabrizio Ferrarini from Reggio Emilia (Figure 2.4).[8] The museum holds only some small fragments of ancient sarcophagi (Figure 2.5), the remains of those chosen by Matilda to bury her ancestors, as Donizo recalls in the prologue of his poem.[9]

The history of San Benedetto Po is complex. While nothing precise is known about Boniface's monastery, the most significant architectural works were carried out under the abbots Guglielmo (1080–99), the Cluniac Alberico (1099–*ante* 1123) and Enrico (1125–41). The question of chronology is still debated and the latest reconstructions suggest an early date for the church of Santa Maria, modelled on Cluny, perhaps in the 1090s.[10] This period may also have seen the start of work on rebuilding the major church, as is perhaps suggested by the evident misalignment of the plan. According to Piva, the scholar who has focussed most attention on the edifice, the layout with five radiating chapels is necessarily derived from Cluny III and therefore to be dated after the chapels of the ambulatory of that complex. The new abbey would therefore have been built under the abbot Alberico and related to Matilda's donation of 1101. It is also known that the chapter house was completed in 1109. Together with the surviving three Months (Figures 2.6 and 2.7) and a fragment of a Nativity (parts of a portal with the months depicted in the jambs and the infancy of Christ on the architrave as in Piacenza), all this suggests a date to the first decade of the 12th century, as does comparison of the sculptures with those of the Modena *Genesis*.

The history of Modena Cathedral is too well known, documented and debated to return to here.[11] Suffice it

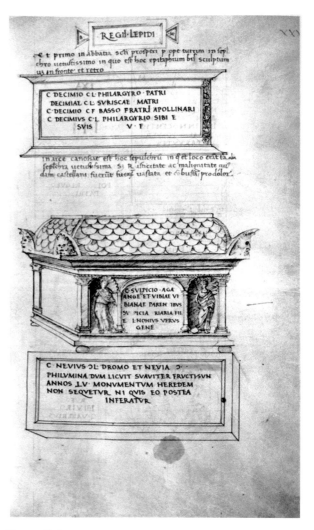

FIGURE 2.4

Drawing from the Antiquarium of Fabrizio Ferrarini (c. 1490), showing sarcophagus of S. Sulpicius Agatangelus, used for Matilda's ancestors

FIGURE 2.5

Canossa: Museo del castello; arcophagus fragment (A.C. Quintavalle)

to recall the documentary evidence: the slab now in the façade that gives the date of 1099 for its foundation (Figure 2.8); the slab in the apse that gives the date of 1106 for its papal consecration; and the *Relatio*, which illustrates how and when the new cathedral was built and emphasizes the decision taken by the architect Lanfranco to transfer the body of St Geminianus from the old church to the new apse because the old building was at an angle to the new one and obstructed work on the north side and the interior.[12] Importance also attaches to the two 'lives' of Geminianus in connection with the architrave of the side entrance known as the Porta dei Principi.[13] Further elements gleaned from the *Relatio* include the various actors involved: '*ordo clericorum . . . universus eiusdem ecclesie populus*', '*cives*' and '*ecclesiae milites*'. Matilda was present '*cum suo exercitu*'. The translation of the relics was delayed for the arrival of Pope Paschal II and the guardians of the tomb comprised six '*de ordine militum*' and twelve '*de civibus*'. Matilda therefore had her own men and took part in every phase of the translation, as she had earlier in the act of foundation and the opening of the sarcophagus. The problem that arises at this point is the relationship between Matilda and the city, which is also made evident by the presence of Bonsignore, bishop of Reggio Emilia, accompanied by Dodone, later bishop of Modena, where the episcopal chair had previously remained vacant.

Let us, however, consider another moment of Matilda's relations with cities, this time Cremona, where the bishop Arnolfo da Velate (1068–78), appointed by the Emperor Henry IV, was excommunicated in 1078 by Pope Gregory VII. He was succeeded by the reformer Gualtiero

FIGURE 2.6

San Benedetto Po, museum: fragments from the portal of the months: October (A.C. Quintavalle)

FIGURE 2.7

San Benedetto Po, museum: fragments from the portal of the months: November and December (A.C. Quintavalle)

(1086–87), after which the see was left vacant. Matilda formed an anti-imperial alliance with the cities of Milan, Lodi, Piacenza and Cremona in 1093. In 1097 she entered into negotiations with the *capitanei* as it appears that Cremona had had no bishop for about two decades and the pro-imperial Ugo da Noceto (1110–17) may never have been consecrated. The situation was therefore similar to the one in Modena. Giordano da Clivio, the pro-papal archbishop of Milan, deposed Ugo and installed Oberto da Dovara (1118–62) in Cremona. Matilda's presence therefore appears to have been significant in the city for many years. In 1097, with a document drawn up in Piadena on 26 December, she yielded the important *insula Fulcherii* to Cremona in exchange for a political and military alliance.[14] The agreement was entered into by the *capitanei*, *valvassori* and *cives*, the first two being feudal orders but not the third. In short, Matilda was deeply involved in events inside the city also in periods when the episcopal see was vacant. Work on the building of Cremona's cathedral started in 1107, as attested by a slab held by the prophets Enoch and Elijah, now in the sacristy (Figure. 2.9). A partial collapse in 1117 was followed by rebuilding after an interval of time because the relics of St Himerius of Cremona remained 'for a long time' beneath the rubble, presumably at the end of the edifice where the crypt and saint's burial place were situated.[15]

The case of the cathedral of Piacenza is equally significant (Figure 2.10). The pro-imperial bishop Dionigi (1048–77) took part in the Council of Basel of 1061, at which Pietro Cadalo, bishop of Parma, was elected pope (the antipope Honorius II). Dionigi then returned to the fold, as attested in a letter of Gregory VII dated 27 November 1074. Another reformer was Bishop Bonizone of Piacenza (1088–89), the author of the important anti-heretical text *Liber ad amicum*, who was expelled from the city by supporters of the emperor. After a period of two years about which nothing is known, the pro-imperial Winrico (1091–93) was installed in his place. Piacenza soon returned to orthodoxy, however, as confirmed by the arrival of Pope Urban II, who convened the synod there of 1095. The see was then held by Aldo (1095–1121), who followed the First Crusade to the Holy Land, and Arduino (1121–47), who built the cathedral of Santa Giustina and Santa Maria. It should finally be recalled that in 1106, at the Council of Guastalla, Pope Paschal II, proclaimed the independence of the dioceses of Parma, Piacenza, Reggio Emilia, Modena and Bologna from Ravenna, the see until 1100 of the antipope Clement III.[16]

The case of Parma's cathedral is also important, the history of which I have already examined elsewhere. The strictly Lombard culture clearly visible in the apsidal section was transformed into a far more complex invention that also encompassed a vast presbytery enclosure attributable to Nicholaus and his assistants. I would regard this as connected with the city's transfer of allegiance from the empire to the papacy and acceptance, as we have seen, of Bernardo degli Uberti as bishop in 1106.[17]

It appears evident from this overly schematic outline that in the various cases where the Gregorian Reform was introduced – the abbeys of Nonantola and San Benedetto Po, the cathedrals of Modena, Cremona and Piacenza, but also many other examples in the territories under Matilda's control or influence – this was connected with the direct or indirect presence of the Great Countess, who granted prelates, unable to occupy their sees in cities like Modena and Parma, protection in her domains until it was possible to install them.

Let us now examine the locations of the new cathedrals, which are situated in all these cases – in Modena as in Cremona, Parma and Piacenza – outside the ancient Roman nucleus, thus making it possible to erect buildings of considerable size, though the growth of population is also a factor. This brings us to what connects not only these construction projects but also the monasteries of Nonantola and San Benedetto Po, namely the employment of a single

FIGURE 2.8

Modena Cathedral: façade, foundation inscription (A.C. Quintavalle)

FIGURE 2.9

Cremona, Cathedral, façade foundation inscription (Renzo Dionigi)

FIGURE 2.10

Piacenza Cathedral: façade (A.C. Quintavalle)

sculptor, first Wiligelmo and then Nicholaus, and their workshops. The architects, on the other hand, varied, Lanfranco in Modena and Nicholaus in Piacenza and perhaps Cremona.[18] The *Relatio* tells us the choice of Lanfranco as architect of Modena's cathedral was divinely inspired: *donante Dei misericordia vir quidam, nomine Lanfrancus mirabilis artifex mirificus edificator*. The great skill exhibited by this 'admirable artist and builder' is indicated further on: *erigitur itaque diversi operis machina; effodiuntur marmora insignia, sculpuntur ac poliuntur arte mirifica; sublevantur et construuntur magno cum labore et artificum astutia. Crescunt ergo parietes, crescit edifitium; laudatur et estollitur, summe Deus, tuum ineffabile benefitium*. It thus appears clear from this text, written shortly after 1106, that the relationship between sculpture and architecture was very close indeed. The machinery (hoists and other devices for lifting and scaffolding) are immediately noted because they are varied and required moreover to bear heavy weights, of stone and not only of bricks. Ancient marbles were, in fact, reworked and sometimes even carved. There are many pieces of Roman marble reused in the building, as shown by a recent study.[19] The construction thus grew not only in height but also in length. As stated in the *Relatio*, once the foundations had been dug, the walls were built above the level of the ground, and the building *in longum protenditur*.

Two miniatures of the *Relatio* appear to bear traces, as I have previously suggested, of a vision conceived as horizontal from the outset, and perhaps derived from a scheme painted on the walls of the Cathedral.[20] The proof, which escaped notice, is the continuity of the level of the terrain in the first three scenes, from the choice of the site to the digging of the foundations and the erection of brick quoins. The only space differently conceived is that of the *inventio* of the saint's body with Bonsignore, the bishop of Reggio Emilia, helping Lanfranco to raise the slab. Dodone, bishop of Modena, is on the right in the second row and Matilda on the left holding a piece of fabric, possibly to wrap the body. The guardians of the tomb, *cives* and *milites*, are shown at the bottom in front of the sarcophagus.

Let us now consider the information provided by the political history of the various cities and seek to connect it with the foregoing observations. With the stories carved in the jambs of the portal in the abbey's façade, Nonantola offers us a text by Wiligelmo's workshop that presents innovative elements. The left jamb shows the life of the saint, Aistulf, Anselm and Pope Hadrian III; in short, the history of the origins of the abbey and its relics. The right jamb instead shows the infancy of Christ, thus demonstrating how long the sculptor's book of drawings remained in use, as the same scenes are to be found in the north portal at Piacenza, dated around 1122 and

FIGURE 2.11

Piacenza Cathedral, façade lintel to north door (A.C. Quintavalle)

FIGURE 2.12

Abbey of Nonantola: Jamb showing the Virgin and the Magi (A.C. Quintavalle)

attributed to the same workshop[21] (Figures 2.11 and 2.12). In Nonantola and Piacenza alike, the first king in the Adoration of the Magi is kneeling whereas the three magi of the doors from Hildesheim and St. Maria im Kapitol in Cologne, for example, are standing. If the Virgin Mary was the symbol of the Church in the territories of the Gregorian Reform, kneeling before her, and hence the Church of Rome, takes on a precise political significance, and it is certainly no coincidence that this iconography was widespread throughout the west. The three surviving fragments of the portal with the Months, from San Benedetto Po. are connected, as we have seen, with those of Modena Cathedral and can be compared both with the panels of the Genesis and with the Prophets of the middle portal, and therefore assigned a date in the first decade of the 12th century. At this point, however, it becomes necessary to consider the chronology of the sculptures of the cathedral, which has recently been called into question once again. While most of the scholars from Porter on[22] regarded Wiligelmo as active up to 1110 at the latest, a chronology extending as far as 1130 has recently been put forward for the cathedral built by Lanfranco and hence indirectly also for Wiligelmo's sculpture.[23]

Apart from the difficulty of such a chronological span for a sculptor active from approximately 1107 to 1115 in Cremona, as we shall see, and documented at Nonantola around the beginning of the first decade of the century, we must ask what can have induced anyone to alter the chronology of the sculptures and so place Wiligelmo in the very different period of Nicholaus, a sculptor who was certainly his pupil but is markedly dissimilar in character. Some light may be shed by the long debate on the dating of the Porta della Pescheria, which was shifted by scholars like Émile Mâle to the mid 12th century.[24] More recent critics have distinguished two independent traditions for the Arthurian subject matter: the oral traditions related to the Modena archivolt and the written tradition of the poem *Historia regum Britanniae*. The thesis put forward in the art-critical literature of the first half of the 20th century, as developed by Geza de Francovich, instead suggests a Burgundian influence on the entrance as a whole, on 'Truth plucking out the tongue of falsehood', on the metopes and on many capitals on the north and south sides of Modena Cathedral.[25] While Roberto Salvini[26] also accepts this hypothesis, which entails marked shifts in chronology,[27] careful examination of the various pieces clearly shows that it is untenable and makes it possible to reassert the involvement of Wiligelmo in all the cases cited here. Comparison of the series of metopes – the two juxtaposed figures of the Antipodes, the figure with three arms and the Siren – with the images of Wiligelmo's Genesis on the façade – Eve and other figures – clearly shows the homogeneity of the group, allowances being made for the marked abrasion of these stone capitals exposed to the elements (Figures 2.13 and 2.14). The same homogeneity is indeed also to be found in another supposedly Burgundian piece, namely 'Truth plucking out the tongue of falsehood', the

FIGURE 2.13

Modena Cathedral: Eve (Wiligelmo) (A.C. Quintavalle)

FIGURE 2.14

Modena Cathedral: 'Metope' (A.C. Quintavalle)

anti-heretical meaning of which has recently been identified by Dorothy Glass.[28] This again displays marked similarities with the capitals of the half-columns outside the cathedral. The block of Genesis sculptures, the capitals on the façade attributed by practically all the scholars to Wiligelmo, like the one with the Sirens, the metopes, the two lateral portals and the Porta dei Principi with scenes in the life of St Geminianus therefore fit perfectly into Wiligelmo's period. The overall reading of the pieces of Modena Cathedral put forward by Frugoni, the reading of the metopes as images of the peoples of the earth[29] and the interpretation of the Genesis panels put forward by Gandolfo[30] all clearly demonstrate the anti-heretical character of the narrative. I shall not linger on this point.

Attention should, however, be drawn to the fact that the narrative system invented by Wiligelmo cannot have been confined to the exteriors of cathedrals or abbeys but must have extended to the interiors, which will entail a change in attribution. I suggested long ago[31] that the pulpit of Modena Cathedral, now shortened and placed at the top of the façade, should be attributed to Wiligelmo (Figures 2.15 and 2.16).[32] Despite its reduced state, that pulpit can be seen as the precise model of the pulpit of Cremona Cathedral, which is again incomplete; the Sagra of Carpi pulpit (Modena) (Figure. 2.17), which helps us

FIGURE 2.15

Modena Cathedral: façade sculptures from Wiligelmo's pulpit: Angel (A.C. Quintavalle)

FIGURE 2.16

Modena Cathedral, façade sculptures from Wiligelmo's pulpit: Lion (A.C. Quintavalle)

to understand how the slabs could have been arranged, as the front and the two sides are intact; the pulpit of Quarantoli, unfortunately reduced and fragmentary; and the pulpit now in Sant'Agata di Sorbara (Modena), of which only one animal remains, the lion of St Mark, unfortunately devoid of its original cornice. While preferring not to go on and list other pulpits that I have repeatedly discussed in the past, I must emphasize the importance of this internal furniture, first of all because it entails central access to the area of the presbytery, wherever there is a crypt, and confirms the significance attached by the Gregorian Reform to the Gospel and the reading of the Gospel. The pulpit also prompts reflection on the symbolic function of the books that constituted the cornerstones of the Reform, namely the Giant Bibles, which were exhibited on high at key moments of the religious rites, on the pulpit or on the altar dominating the nave.

The sculpture of Cremona Cathedral constitutes an imposing complex if we add, to the pieces remaining *in situ*, the remnants of the large vine of the middle portal, a small pediment, a telamon and other elements, all now in the Museo del Castello Sforzesco, Milan, but originally belonging to the cathedral.(Figure 2.18) The many pieces still in Cremona include the remains of two pulpits and there are evident traces of the involvement of the sculptor of the Porta della Pescheria (Figure 2.19) and the Porta dei Principi as well, in my view, as Wiligelmo for the central gate. The debate on whether Wiligelmo worked in Cremona and whether the prophets (Figure 2.20) are by him or a workshop, which has gone

FIGURE 2.17

Carpi: Santa Maria in Castello; pulpit (A.C. Quintavalle)

Figure 2.18

Milan: Museo del Castello, vine scroll (Wiligelmo) (A.C. Quintavalle)

Figure 2.20

Cremona Cathedral: façade, Prophet Isaiah (A.C. Quintavalle)

Figure 2.19

Modena Cathedral: Porta dei Pescheria (A.C. Quintavalle)

on since the days of Arthur Kingsley Porter, is quite irrelevant, as everything appears in any case to confirm the presence of the Modenese workshop in Cremona from 1107 and before the earthquake of 1117. Nicholaus, Wiligelmo's greatest pupil and continuer, may have worked in Cremona, possibly in a later phase. The portals of the façade of Piacenza Cathedral are attributed to the Cremonese workshop and the northern portal, as we have seen, to Wiligelmo, while the central and southern portals are the work of Nicholaus, who also produced some of the internal capitals, all dated between 1122 and 1132 or slightly later. In the end, the so-called School of Piacenza hypothesised by De Francovich[33] is simply Nicholaus and his assistants.[34]

A programme connected with the Gregorian Reform is certainly present in the codices produced in this period, as well as in the body of designs of Wiligelmo and his assistants who worked on the various buildings mentioned here – from Nonantola and Polirone to Modena, Cremona and Piacenza, while it was Nicholaus above all that worked in Parma within the more traditional framework of Lombard sculpture. In these workshop designs the revolution in meaning is evident and connected with new figures or ancient images subjected to semantic transformation. Anti-heretical functions are thus conferred on Enoch and Elijah, Samson and the lion, Genesis, Noah and the ark. The telamones represent the suffering of sinners and the lions either Christ or the Holy Roman Empire. Further images include the above mentioned Adoration of the Magi, the pilgrim to be found also – as I have shown – in the Joseph on his journey into Egypt, the armed pilgrimage of knights returning from Modena to Bari to Parma as a reference to the fight against the infidel, and the dominant figure of St Peter in half of the west.[35] In all the places where Wiligelmo and his assistants worked, we can discern a unified narrative that unquestionably derives from a precise project.

I shall now return to Matilda with some images from Donizo's *Vita Mathildis* (Vat. Lat. 4922), a Vatican codex from the early 12th century.[36] The first illustration (fol. 7v) shows Donizo presenting his poem to Matilda above the inscription *Mathildis lucens precor hoc cape cara volumen*. The elements comprise Matilda enthroned, a footrest, Donizo at a lectern to the left with the codex opened out, a red background signifying regal or imperial power, a mantle with a gold border, an aedicula and an armed figure on the right representing Matilda's *milites*. The well-known miniature fol. 49r. bears the inscription *Rex rogat abbatem mathildim supplicat atque*: 'the king implores the abbot and pleads with Matilda'.[37] We see Abbot Hugo of Cluny to the left,

FIGURE 2.21

Rome, Biblioteca apostolica Vaticana, Cod. Vat. Lat. 4922: Donizo, Vita Mathildis, fol 19r: Adalberto Atto receives relics of saints Vittore and Corona (above); and Bishop Goffredo of Brescia cuts the right arm of S. Apollonio

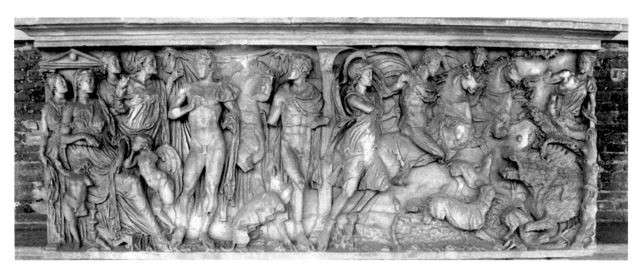

FIGURE 2.22

Pisa Camposanto: Sarcophagus of Phaedra re-used for Beatrice of Canossa (A.C. Quintavalle)

seated on a *sella plicabilis*, the Emperor Henry IV on his knees and Matilda enthroned beneath a ciborium turned towards the two figures with her arms outstretched to the right. Various events are recounted here and the only figure missing is Pope Gregory VII, who refused to receive the emperor. The abbot is speaking to Matilda, as indicated by the finger, she addresses both of them, and the emperor is kneeling, as he was outside Canossa. We thus have a combination of different moments. In short, the images are always strongly symbolic and closely related to the text.

In his poem, Donizo constructs a geography of power through burials: of Matilda buried in San Benedetto Po; of Beatrice in Pisa near the cathedral, inside or outside; of Boniface, treacherously slain, in Mantua; and finally of the ancestors at Canossa in at least four sarcophagi, some fragments of which still survive. The tombs of the ancestors are, however, like those of saints, the ones enclosing holy remains inside the cathedral or abbeys, and the images of Donizo's codex are therefore richly imbued with meaning. In fact, apart from Matilda's parents, all the ancestors represented in the miniatures were buried at Canossa. The author thus suggests their presence as symbols of the length of the dynasty but also as figures close to the sanctity of the precious relics held in the monastery of Sant'Apollonio at Canossa. The miniature fol. 19r thus shows Adalberto Atto obtaining the relics of Sts Victor and Corona and of St Apollonius (Figure 2.21). The two inscriptions above read as follows: *Corpora Sanctorum Rex Athoni dedit horum* and *Sancta Corona et Santus Victor. Membra secat Sancti Gotefredus dans ea patri*: Godfrey, bishop of Brescia, thus severed the right arm of St Apollonius and gave it to his father. Our interest focusses on the image in the lower panel, where we see, on the right, a sarcophagus with a vine shoot suggesting antiquity, like the ancient but very simple sarcophagus of St Geminianus, the ancient sarcophagusi of Matilda's ancestors, of Beatrice in Pisa (Figure 2.22) and perhaps of Boniface in Mantua.

In short, it is also burial in ancient sarcophagi that identifies the saints of the Gregorian Reform. Their relics alongside the tombs of the patrons and the geography of the burials is the geography of a political project that was to end with Matilda. It is a story in which holiness, feudal power and the astute politics of the lords of Canossa, of Boniface, Beatrice and Matilda, play an important part. The programmed image of the fight against the heresy of the antipopes and their bishops was conceived as a weapon of war not only in religious retreats but also within the opulent cities. Matilda was well aware of this, as were the intellectuals that worked alongside her, like Donizo in Canossa, and with them the cultured architects and sculptors Lanfranco, Wiligelmo and Nicholaus and their assistants.

NOTES

[1] Donizione, *Vita di Matilde di Canossa*, ed P. Golinelli, with an essay by V. Fumagalli (Milano 2008).

[2] See also: G. Fasoli, 'La realtà cittadina nei territori canossiani', in *Studi matildici*, Atti e memorie del III convegno, Reggio Emilia 7–9 ottobre 1977 (Modena 1978), 55–78; G. Sergi, 'I poteri dei Canossa, poteri delegati, poteri feudali, poteri signorili', in *I poteri dei Canossa da Reggio Emilia all'Europa*, Atti del convegno internazionale di studi, a cura di P. Golinelli, Reggio Emilia-Carpineti, 29–31 ottobre 1992 (Bologna 1994), 29–39; F. Menant, *Campagnes lombardes du Moyen Age: l'économie et la societé rurale nella regione de Bergame, de Cremone et de Brescia du Xe au XIIIe siècle* (Roma 1993); F. Menant, 'Cremona in età precomunale: il secolo XI', in *Storia di Cremona. I. Dall'alto medioevo all'età comunale*, ed G. Ardenna (Cremona 2004), 106–97; F. Menant, 'La prima età comunale (1097–1183)' in Ardenna (ed) *Storia di Cremona*, 198–281; A. Ricci, D. Romagnoli, 'Matilde e le città', in *Matilde e il tesoro dei Canossa tra castelli, monasteri e le città*, exh. cat., ed A. Calzona (Milano 2008) 153–63; U. Longo, 'I Canossa e le fondazioni monastiche', in Calzona (ed) *Matilde e il tesoro*, 117–39; G. Andenna, 'Il contesto generale, città e impero', in *Matilde di Canossa. Il papato l'impero, storia arte, cultura alle origini del romanico*, exh. cat. ed R. Salvarani and L. Castelfranchi (Milano 2008), 101–15; R. Salvarani, 'Mantova e i Canossa, fonti documentarie e problematiche aperte', in Salvarini and Castelfranchi (eds), *Matilde di Canossa*, 255–61.

³ F. Zuliani, C. Segre Montel, 'Il ritrovamento di un ciclo di pitture murali del tempo di Wiligelmo', in *Lanfranco e Wiligelmo. Il Duomo di Modena*, exh. cat. (Modena 1985), 659–83; C. Segre Montel, F. Zuliani, *La pittura nell'abbazia di Nonantola. Un refettorio affrescato di età romanica* (Nonantola 1991).

⁴ L. Serchia, P. Monari, C. Giudici, *Nonantola i restauri dell'Abbazia* (Modena 1984).

⁵ The inscription on the lintel reads: 'Silvestri celsi ceciderunt culmina templi/ mille redemptoris lapsis vertigine solis/ annis centenis septem nec non quoque denis/ quod refici magnos cepit post quattuor annos'. In *Romanico padano, civiltà d'occidente* (Firenze 1969), 33–47 I suggested the date of the portal to be around 1106–10; the renovated inscription after the earthquake of 1117 of the lintel with the infancy of Christ proves the re-employment of the sculptures. This dating, suggested in 1969, eliminates one of the supposed proofs of the late chronology of Wiligelmo in Modena. In many contributions I have proposed a dating of the portal and pulpit in Nonantola to around 1103 in connection with the chronology of the building as suggested by A. Calzona, 'Nonantola : L'abbazia "lombarda" e quella della "Riforma"', in *Lanfranco e Wiligelmo. Il Duomo di Modena*,(as n. 3). 701–32; for the sculptures see 733–37. See also; A.C. Quintavalle 'L'officina della Riforma: Wiligelmo, Lanfranco', in *Lanfranco e Wiligelmo. Il Duomo di Modena*,(as n. 3), 765–834.

⁶ The Pantocrator can be compared with the Genesis frieze in Modena Cathedral, confirming the dating of the sculptures at Nonantola to around 1103; D.F. Glass, *The Sculpture of Reform in North Italy, ca 1095–1130, History and Patronage of Romanesque Façades* (Farnham 2010) suggests a dating for the jambs of around 1095 and accepted my reconstruction of the pulpit.

⁷ See the catalogue entries by G. Bianchino on some of the capitals in the abbey in: A.C. Quintavalle and A Calzona (eds), *Wiligelmo e Matilde, l'officina romanica*, exh. cat. (Milano 1991) cat. 12 a-e, 357–61.

⁸ The date of the codex can be fixed around 1490; Nicola Fabrizio Ferrarini, *Antiquarium*, Reggio Emilia, Biblioteca Panizzi cod. C. 398 fol. 37: 'In arce Canossae est hoc sepulchrum, in quo etiam loco erant tria alia sepulchra vetustissima, sed rusticitate et malignitate cuiusdam castellani fuerunt vastata et combusta, pro dolorem'; in 1392 Canossa was sacked by Antonio Arrigoni; see the record by C. Franzoni in *Matilde e il tesoro* (as n. 2) 450–51.

⁹ Donizone, *Vita Mathildis* (as n. 1), 2: Donizo says he entered as a monk around 1086 andwrote the dedicatory letter to Matilda in 1114; when the settlement of roman sepulchers with Matilda's ancestor's bodies was finished: 'Cum ad clarorum principum mausoleum jam per quinque lustra nostra resideret humilitas, nullamque ex eis videret memoria quod apicum commendaret perpetuitas, accidit quando nuper vestri honoris sublimitas canossam deduci arcas iussit marmoreas ad tumulandum dignius eorum corpora. . . '. In Donizo's poem we can find many verses describing the princes' tombs; the dialogue between Canossa and Mantua for Bonifacio's body (verses 1128–37) or between Canossa and Pisa for Beatrice's (verses 1355–86). In the first book, we find the history of the other bodies in Canossa : 'quot marchiones sunt sepulti apud Canossam', verses 582–600. Matilda was to be buried in San Benedetto al Polirone; see also the catalogue of the exhibition: *L'abbazia di Matilde. Arte e storia in un grande monastero dell'Europa benedettina 1007–2007*, ed. Paolo Golinelli, San Benedetto Po, 31 agosto 2008–11 gennaio 2009 (Bologna 2008).

¹⁰ P. Piva, 'L'abbazia di Polirone nel XII secolo: architettura e vita monastica. Una lettura comparata della documentazione archeologica e scritta', in A.C. Quintavalle (ed.), *Arredi liturgici e architettura* (Milano, 2003) 53–85.

¹¹ Among the expanded bibliography, see: R. Salvini, *Wiligelmo e le origini della scultura romanica* (Milano 1956); A.C. Quintavalle, *La cattedrale di Modena*, intro by C.L. Ragghianti (Modena 1964–65); R. Salvini, *Il Duomo di Modena* (Modena 1966); *Il duomo di Modena. Atlante fotografico*, ed. M. Armandi, photographs by di Cesare Leonardi (Modena 1985); *Lanfranco e Wiligelmo. Il Duomo di Modena* (as n. 3).; C. Acidini Luchinat, L. Serchia, S. Piconi (eds), *I restauri del Duomo di Modena 1975–1984* (Modena 1984); C. Frugoni (ed) *Il Duomo di Modena*, Mirabilia Italiae 9 (Modena 1999).

¹² F. Gandolfo, 'Il cantiere dell'architetto Lanfranco e la cattedrale del vescovo Eriberto', *Arte medievale*, series 2, 3/1 (1989), 29–47.

¹³ P. Bortolotti, *Antiche vite di S. Geminiano vescovo e protettore di Modena* (Modena 1886)

¹⁴ See the document in: A. Ricci, D. Romagnoli, *Matilde e le città* (as n. 2), 160–61.

¹⁵ *Sicardi Episcopi Chronicon* records: 'Anno Domini MCXVI terraemotus magnus in Januario fuit, propter quem Ecclesia major Cremonensis corruit, et corpus Confessoris Himerii diu latuit sub ruina.' Rerum Italicarum Scriptores, 7, 594. Following Porter's analysis, see some other recent contributions: A.K. Porter, *Lombard Architecture* II (New Haven 1917), 371–93; A Puerari, *Il duomo di Cremona* (Milano 1971); F. Gandolfo, 'La cattedrale nel medioevo. I cicli scultorei', in *La cattedrale di Cremona. Affreschi e sculture*, ed. A. Tomei (Cinisello Balsamo 2001), 16–65; A.C. Quintavalle, 'La cattedrale di Cremona, Cluny, la scuola di Lanfranco e di Wiligelmo', in *Storia dell'arte*, 18 (1973) 117–72; A.C. Quintavalle, 'La cattedrale del 1107 e quelle del XIII secolo', in *Cattedrale di Cremona* (Parma 2007), 14–69; A. Calzona, *Il cantiere medievale della cattedrale di Cremona* (Milano 2009); A. Bonazzi (ed.) *Cattedrale di Cremona, i restauri degli ultimi vent'anni 1992–2011* (Milano 2012)

¹⁶ For the general historical framework for Piacenza, see: P. Racine (ed) *Storia della Diocesi di Piacenza, 5. Il Medioevo dalla riforma gregoriana alla vigilia della Riforma protestante* (Brescia 2009); B. Klein, *Die Kathedrale von Piacenza. Architektur und Skulptur der Romanik* (Worms 1995).

¹⁷ A.C. Quintavalle, *La cattedrale di Parma e il romanico europeo* (Parma 1974); M. Luchterhandt, *Die Kathedrale von Parma. Architektur und Skulptur im Zeitalter von Reichskirche und Kommunenbildung* (Munchen 2009).

¹⁸ A.C. Quintavalle, 'Niccolò architetto', in *Nicholaus e l'arte del suo tempo*, ed. A.M. Romanini, (Ferrara 1985), 167–256. The *Relatio* openly says that Nicholaus came from outside Matilda's dominions, but is difficult to say from where; some connections with monuments as S. Lorenzo in Verona could suggest a line of research, as I suggested in *La cattedrale di Modena* (as n. 11), 81.

¹⁹ E. Castelnuovo, 'Il cantiere, la scultura', in *Lanfranco e Wiligelmo. Il Duomo di Modena* (as n. 3) 294–97; M. Bertolani, U. Ferrari, 'Note sulla natura delle pietre usate nel duomo di Modena', in *Lanfranco e Wiligelmo. Il Duomo di Modena* (as n. 3) 298–304.

²⁰ A.C. Quintavalle, *La cattedrale di Modena* (as n. 11), 55 and 109–10, notes 29 and 30; I suggested the existence of a series of frescoes in the Cathedral celebrating the consecration, which may have been the models of these exceptional illuminated images.

²¹ On the abbey and its *scriptorium* see: M. Branchi, *Lo scriptorium e la biblioteca di Nonantola*, presentazione di G. Zanichelli, (Modena 2011).

²² A.K. Porter, *Lombard Architecture*(as n. 15); R. Salvini, *Wiligelmo e le origini della scultura romanica*(as n. 11).; A.C. Quintavalle, *La cattedrale di Modena* (as n. 11); R. Salvini, *Il Duomo di Modena* (as n. 11).

²³ A. Peroni, 'L'architetto Lanfranco e la struttura del Duomo', in *Lanfranco e Wiligelmo. Il Duomo di Modena* (as n. 3), 143–206. The late dating derives from a document of 13th of April 1137 subscribed by 'Magister Lanfrancus' as witness of an act of the Modena bishop Ribaldus.

²⁴ E. Mâle, *L'art religieux en France à l'époque romane* (Paris 1922), 268–69. Mâle compares the cycle to the 'Roman de Lancelot' of around 1160; other historians of art confirm this chronology on the basis of Geoffrey of Monmouth's poem *Historia regum Britanniae*, finished around 1136.

²⁵ G. de Francovich, 'Wiligelmo da Modena e gli inizi della scultura romanica europea', *Rivista del Regio Istituto di archeologia e storia dell'arte*, 7 (1940), 273.

²⁶ R. Salvini, *Wiligelmo e le origini della scultura romanica* (as n.11), pp. 160–61.

²⁷ In my book *La Cattedrale di Modena* (as n.11), I partially accepted these proposals; afterwords I changed my mind as in, for example, *Wiligelmo e Matilde, l'officina romanica* (as n. 7), in 'L'officina della Riforma: Wiligelmo, Lanfranco' (as n. 5).

[28] Glass, *Sculpture of Reform* (as n. 6), passim.

[29] C. Frugoni, *Le lastre veterotestamentarie e il programma della facciata*, in *Lanfranco e Wiligelmo. Il Duomo di Modena* (as n. 3), 422–31; C. Frugoni, 'Le metope, ipotesi di un loro significato', op.cit. 507–17

[30] F. Gandolfo, 'Note per una interpretazione iconologica delle storie del Genesi di Wiligelmo', in A.C. Quintavalle (ed.), *Romanico padano, romanico europeo*, Atti del Convegno internazionale di studi, a cura di, Modena-Parma, 26 ottobre-1 novembre 1977 (Parma 1982), 323–38; Glass, *Sculpture of Reform* (as n.6), passim.

[31] *Lanfranco e Wiligelmo. Il Duomo di Modena* (as n. 3) 770 and passim.

[32] Given by Roberto Salvini to the so called Maestro degli Evangelisti. R. Salvini, *Wiligelmo e le origini della scultura romanica* (as n. 11).

[33] G. De Francovich, *Benedetto Antelami architetto e scultore e l'arte del suo tempo* (Milano 1952)

[34] A.C. Quintavalle, 'Piacenza Cathedral, Lanfranco and the school of Wiligelmo', *Art Bulletin*, 55 (1972), 40–57; A.C. Quintavalle, 'NIccolò architetto e scultore' in A.M. Romanini (ed.), *NIcholaus e l'arte del suo tempo* (Ferrara 1985), 167–256; A.C.Quintavalle, 'Ritualità e strutture dell'arredo fra XI e XIII secolo: novità sull'officina di Niccolò a Fano, ad Ancona e su quella antelamica in Puglia', in A.C. Quintavalle (ed), *Medioevo i modelli*, (Milano 2002), 108–36.

[35] A.C. Quintavalle, 'San Pietro 'pellegrino' a Compostela', in A.C. Quintavalle (ed.), *Medioevo: l'Europa delle Cattedrali*, Atti del Convegno internazionale di studi, Parma 19–23 settembre 2006 (Milano 2007), 217–27.

[36] G.Z. Zanichelli, Vita Mathildis, cat 89 in *Il Medioevo delle Cattedrali. Chiesa e impero, la lotta delle immagini*, exh. cat. ed. A.C. Quintavalle (Milano 2005), 694–97.

[37] Donizone, *Vita di Matilde* (as n. 1); P. Golinelli, *Matilde e i Canossa* (Mursia 2004).

ROMANESQUE CATHEDRALS IN NORTHERN ITALY – BUILDING PROCESSES BETWEEN BISHOP AND COMMUNE

Bruno Klein

If we examine the role of patrons in the Middle Ages, we make an unconsciously clear distinction between institutional and individual patrons, but it is by no means so simple to draw the line. For example, if a bishop commissioned the rebuilding of a cathedral, then he may have been personally interested, and this special person was certainly someone of more active than passive temperament. Nevertheless, in this case he acted not as an individual person but as a representative of an institution, because, according to canon law, it was the duty of a bishop to ensure the existence of an adequate cathedral. If, however, a cathedral chapter cared for the building of a cathedral – which was generally the case – then conversely we should expect that some specific member was particularly engaged and involved. In fact, the chapter didn't manage the *fabrica* as a group, but it entrusted individual members with its management.[1] So it is not easy to distinguish individuals and institutions. And what about lay founders? Did they act as individuals, or as groups, or as members of an institution, a family and so on?

A second problem is that people and institutions are not and were not immutable. People change, just as institutions do, although institutionalisation actually has a goal in stabilisation. Medieval building processes often provided an opportunity to change the role of individuals and institutions as well as their relationships to each other.[2] A building process was even able to develop the role and the status of its patrons, not only in what concerned their position in relation to the building, but also in their social position in general.

Finally, institutions and individuals are notions that are only historically well defined. Neither institutions nor individuals have remained the same from the Middle Ages to the present day, nor stayed unaltered in such a very short period as the 12th century. A look at some very well-known buildings in northern Italy should help to exemplify such ideas about uncertainty, change and development during medieval building processes.

All these elements were relevant for the Romanesque cathedral of Modena (Figure 3.1).[3] Its construction began in 1099. The famous *Relatio corporis sancti Geminiani*,[4] the report on the events surrounding the construction of the new church, informs us that the ancient church was at this time too old, too small and threatened collapse, a situation that led the inhabitants of Modena to decide to build a new one. It is reported that in fact all the residents of the city shared this desire: the clerics, the knights and the citizens. All but one: at that moment Modena did not have a bishop, who was traditionally the lord of the city. The fact that the construction of the new building began at a time of *sede vacante*, is expressly mentioned by the *Relatio*. It would be very surprising if the people of Modena had, just in the period in which there was no bishop, noticed that their cathedral was too small and too ruinous, and then spontaneously began, even before a new bishop could be chosen, to start a new building. As mentioned, the commission and furnishing of a cathedral belonged to the rights and the duties of a bishop. So starting to rebuild a cathedral in the period of *sede vacante* was a very clear and mainly critical statement. The legal, but former, responsible institutional patron was replaced by a new one. And so the game became open, because at that moment the inhabitants of the city did not yet represent something comparable to a well-organised institution. Instead they were a very heterogeneous group of people with different interests and different statuses of self-organisation. An ancient institution – the bishop – was challenged by a new one – the city. The ancient institution was personally absent, and the new one still was not organised. The commune of Modena was only established some decades later. So we can observe a conflict between two institutions which were both at that very moment quite weak – but the first descending and the second ascending (Figure 3.2).

So it therefore cannot be surprising, that in the years after 1099 even the pope and the countess Matilda of Tuscany engaged themselves in the affairs of the rebuilding of Modena cathedral. They did it, both because the situation inside of the city of Modena was too unstable and needed external stabilisation – and, on the other hand, that unstable situation gave the opportunity for external forces to engage themselves, with the aim to profit from that uncertainty.

Regarding the further history of the building history of Modena cathedral, we can observe that the conflicts between the different parties continued: when, for example, it became necessary due to the building progress

FIGURE 3.1

Modena Cathedral: Exterior from south-east (after Giopie, Wikimedia)

to translate the relics of the patron saint of the city, San Geminiano, in 1106, it was extremely difficult to resolve the problem of how to manage that move, due to the extreme suspicion between the different parties. Each of them feared that the others would take possession of the relics. It is very surprising to see that in the end the new bishop and the architect of the building, named Lanfrancus, carried the relics together. It seems that the bishop became able to fulfill that very difficult task, because he had lost importance during the building process and was now able to act more freely. On the other hand, it is astonishing to see how an architect, hitherto nearly unknown as person or institution, could obtain such an important role. It seems that building processes were able to open and to set moving historically fairly closed constellations.

Unfortunately, we don't have any precise information about the circumstances of the building of the Romanesque cathedral of Cremona, which started in 1107. But there is no doubt, that in this year the bishop's throne of Cremona was empty.[5] (Figure 3.3) The famous inscription which reports the start of the construction in this very year, mentions only the bishop of Rome, Pope Paschal II, but the name of the local bishop is passed over in silence.

Historical information is a little bit better in the case of the construction of the Romanesque cathedral in Piacenza: here, building started most likely in 1122, as is reported by an inscription on the south porch. Although the inscription is actually modern, its literal correctness is well demonstrated by ancient documents.[6] Is it astonishing that 1122 was also the year in which Aldo, count-bishop

FIGURE 3.2

Modena, Archivio capitolare di Modena MS II.11, fol. 9r: Translation of the relics of S. Geminiano

FIGURE 3.3

Cremona Cathedral: Plaque recording the foundation of the Romanesque cathedral (Renzo Dionigi)

of Piacenza for nearly 25 years, died and his successor, named Arduino, was elected?[7] Only four years later, in 1126, the 'consuls' of the city were mentioned for the first time. This doesn't mean that the office of the 'consul' was created exactly at that moment, because consuls normally appeared in written records only some time after the installation of that office. But it is certain that the existence of consuls always indicates the achievement of a certain degree of autonomy of a commune. So it seems quite likely that there were connections between the change in the episcopate, the beginning of the construction of a new cathedral and the creation of the commune of Piacenza.[8] Here it is possible to observe social instability combined with a new political dynamic, and cathedral-building as a means in the struggle between old forces and new claims.

As in Modena, the commune of Piacenza wasn't yet able to act as a well-organised institution. In consequence, its engagement could hardly influence directly the form or the style of the monument, because there were no means to do so. Nevertheless, the new patrons weren't without any consequences on the layout of a new church: as we know from many cases of rebuilt churches in the Middle Ages, the clergy generally tried to maintain the ancient liturgical topography in the new building. Thus the special relationships between the altars, the liturgical choir and so on remained unchanged. When a new patron, or even an entire group of new patrons, engaged themselves in the building of a church, how could they find their place in the set of traditional holy places?

It is possible to observe some consequences of this shift at the cathedral of Piacenza. The building is clearly divided into different sections: There is a liturgical choir, situated over a very spacious crypt. Here, the reliquary of the saint patrons of the cathedral was exhibited, and according to the ancient book of ceremonies of the cathedral, the crypt served as the winter church for the chapter.[9] So it is quite evident that the eastern part of the cathedral was mainly reserved for the clergy, and that the clergy tried also to be in the possession of the cathedrals most important relics.

The laity had the nave and the transept, both quite spacious, with their own entrances and porches. In this part of the church, above the arcade of the central nave, there are reliefs of female saints and of prophets – the former on the south side, the latter on the north side (Figure 3.4). This is now a unique representation – not found in any other church – but such representations could also have been painted and are now lost. It is interesting to observe that the relics of saints were in the crypt, where the clergy was present, and the representations of saints in the nave, were the laity stayed. Who was responsible for the representation of the saints and prophets in the nave? And why were they shown? Because the laity wished to be among the saints? Or was it the wish of the clerics to show the supreme dominance of the saints in the entire cathedral?

Prophets are quite often to be found on the façades of Romanesque cathedrals in Northern Italy,[10] and sometimes, as in Cremona, they are holding long inscriptions, related probably to popular religious performances.[11] The female saints of Piacenza are the Virgin Mary and Saint Giustina, the two patrons of the cathedral, followed by Saint Candida and Saint Paolina. The relics of these two saints probably came to Piacenza only in 1120.[12] Finally there is Saint Margaret, one of the most popular saints of the time. In contrast to this inflation of female saints in the nave of the cathedral, there is a conspicuous lack of representation of male saints: images are lacking of the martyr San Antonino, patron of the former cathedral of Piacenza, or of the two holy bishops of the city, San Vittore und San Savino. In the absence of any written source to explain the phenomenon, it is only possible to state that in the nave of the cathedral there is a richer and even more innovative figurative decoration than in its eastern parts, choir and crypt.[13]

It is also only in those western parts of the cathedral that we find some other, very uncommon, reliefs of the 12th

Figure 3.4

Piacenza Cathedral: Nave reliefs of saints and prophets (Bruno Klein)

FIGURE 3.5

Piacenza Cathedral: Nave reliefs of lay patrons (Bruno Klein)

century (Figure 3.5). They are integrated in the pillars, and represent lay persons who without doubt contributed to the construction of the cathedral, because the reliefs are accompanied by inscriptions, saying that the columns were almost in the possession of those people: 'haec est columna – 'this is the column' of the represented person is the usual formulation of the inscriptions.[14] It is obvious that there must be some relation between the representations of the lay founders and the saints above them. Maybe, that those citizens were less interested in the representations of saint bishops, counterparts of the ecclesiastical lord of the city, than in images of more 'modern' and more 'popular' saints, which could not easily be claimed by one or another party of the society at Piacenza.

But that would only be pure speculation. It is more instructive to examine and to compare the reliefs which seem to show singular persons or groups of persons, responsible for the foundation of the respective pillar (Figure 3.6). There is only one pure verbal description without any pictorial representation, mentioning 'Ugo tinctor' and, as far as it is possible to read that inscription, 'Maria Bos', together as the patrons of that pillar. The Latin reads: 'Maria Bos et Vgo tinctor fecerunt fieri hanc colonam in templo d[omi]ni' – Maria Bos and Ugo Tinctor had made this column in the temple of the Lord. The same Ugo tinctor,

Hugh the dyer, is represented on another pillar as donor, but this time pictorially and as an individual person. On that relief, Ugo is shown as he is taking a cloth out of the vat. This is not the representation of any special action to underline the importance of Ugo for the social interaction in Piacenza, but it shows him as a wealthy individual, able and obviously willing to contribute to the construction of the city's cathedral. There is only one other relief showing such an individual person as patron of a pillar. It is the relief of 'Johannes caca in solario', John in his workshop, a wheelwright shown in action (Figure 3.6).

It is conspicuous that neither Ugo nor Johannes was explicitly mentioned as founder or patron of the column on which they are pictorially represented. So it seems that there was a certain restraint, avoiding an excessive highlighting of any individual person. On the other hand, the possessive inscriptions 'haec est colonna . . .' – this is the column of . . .', are exclusively reserved for groups with anonymous members. Among these we find two times the shoemakers, the tailors, the tanners and the bakers or oven owners. Clearly only groups of craftsmen or growing institutions had the right to declare a column as their own; individuals, however, had to be content with more modest hints. That indicates that there must have been a certain debate between individuals and groups, concerning their

FIGURE 3.6

Piacenza Cathedral: Nave reliefs of Ugo and Johannes (Bruno Klein)

respective roles in the construction of the Cathedral, and that problems of representation were solved by the diversity of representations and inscriptions.

The staging of individuality in the support of the construction of the cathedral was probably not desired or even highly regarded, because the aforementioned Ugo and Johannes hide themselves under the mantle of artisans, so as to appear similar to the other supporters. Individuals or not, the donors are all represented in action with their tools and their objects prominently placed and mostly large in scale (Figure 3.7). Comparing for example the shoes which the shoemakers are producing to the shoes on their feet, the disproportion is nearly grotesque. In consequence, it is necessary to distinguish two layers in the staging of the foundation of the cathedral. The first, and stronger, one was to be an active member in and for the city. The second was focussed on individual *memoria*, but its staging was absolutely overlaid by the first one.

It may be that the production of monuments of individual *memoria* was a very typical feature of the ancient nobility, and that modern communal burghers tried to distinguish themselves from that tradition – without being really able to ignore the attraction of that feature. So the only inscription mentioning a very individual sponsorship, 'Maria Bos et Vgo tinctor fecerunt fieri hanc colonnam', with the emblematic phrase 'fecerunt fieri', literally copied from a prominent deed of foundation, had to disappear into the shadows of a quite invisible part of the cathedral – and it is nearly impossible to find that inscription.

The reliefs seem to indicate that the guilds of Piacenza were the most important supporters of the construction of the cathedral. But there were not, as yet, any guilds in Piacenza in the second quarter of the 12th century, during the erection of those columns. So the reliefs give an insight into the formation of those institutions. More specifically, building and financing the cathedral contributed to the development and definition of those institutions, and generated differences between donations made by institutions and individuals as well as between the sponsorship of ecclesiastics and the laity.

Close examination and the reconstruction of quite different cases, mainly of Modena and Piacenza, not only gives some hint of the political and social situation in those cities at the end of the 11th and the beginning of the 12th century, but it also delivers information about the possibilities and representation of patronage in those cities. It is also possible to observe that unstable or critical relations between potential founders led to innovative solutions to represent their donations. If it is impossible to reconstruct the discussions about how to build and to patronize a cathedral building, the artistic effects of those discussions are perfectly visible. Finally: building a major city-church gave not only the possibility to redefine the role of different groups of founders, but it also offered the chance to claim and to establish new rights. There is no doubt that moments of political and social uncertainty were ideally suited to stage such claims. So the absence of an ancient force – the bishop – and the presence of a new one – the members of the commune – is no coincidence, but the condition for the creation of a new art. It would be interesting

FIGURE 3.7

Piacenza Cathedral: Reliefs of donors (Bruno Klein)

to analyse systematically when and where such situations arose, and to reconstruct the impact they had on this art.

NOTES

[1] W. Schöller, *Die rechtliche Organisation des Kirchenbaues im Mittelalter, vornehmlich des Kathedralbaues:Baulast, Bauherrenschaft, Baufinanzierung* (Köln 1989).

[2] B. Klein, 'Bauen bildet. Aspekte der gesellschaftliche Rolle von Bauprozessen mittelalterlicher Großbaustellen', in: *Kirche als Baustelle : große Sakralbauten des Mittelalters,* ed. K. Schröck, B. Klein and S. Bürger (Köln 2013), 11–22.

[3] The bibliography on Modena Cathedral is abundant, so I mention only some recent or classic studies: P. Bonacini, *La fabbrica di San Geminiano: regesto del codice capitolare O.II.11.* (Modena 2012); A. Peroni, 'La cripta del Duomo di Modena e l'avvio della costruzione dell'architetto Lanfranco', *Westfalen,* 87 (2009), 13–42; D. Glass, *The Sculpture of Reform in North Italy, ca. 1095–1130. History and Patronage of Romanesque Façades* (Farnham 2010); E. Castelnouvo and A. Peroni eds, *Wiligelmo e Lanfranco nell'Europa romanica* (Modena 1989).

[4] *Relatio translationis corporis sancti Geminiani, M.XC.IX-M.C.V,* ed. G. Bertoni, Raccolta degli Storici Italiani dal cinquecento al millecinquento, 4 (Citta di Castello 1907), (https://openlibrary.org/books/OL24983657M/Relatio_translationis_corporis_sancti_Geminiani_M.XC.IX-M.C.VI).

[5] Glass, *Sculpture of Reform* (as n. 3) 203–14; A. Calzona, *Il cantiere medievale della cattedrale di Cremona* (Cinisello Balsamo – Milano 2009); A. Puerari, *Il duomo di Cremona* (Milano 1971).

[6] B. Klein, *Die Kathedrale von Piacenza. Architektur und Skulptur der Romanik* (Worms 1995), 15, n. 18.

[7] D. Glass, *Sculpture of Reform* (as n. 3), 214–28, favours slightly different dates for the death of Aldo and the official start of his successor Grimerio. But I am in no doubt that the construction of the new cathedral began at about the time of the episcopal change.

[8] On the relations between bishop and commune, especially at Piacenza see: P. Racine: 'I vescovi e il governo comunale', *Il Medioevo. Dalle Riforma gregoriana alla vigilia della Riforme protestante,* Storia della Diocesi di Piacenza 2, P. Pierre Racine ed, (Brescia 2009), 96–123.

[9] B. Klein, *Piacenza* (as n. 6), 74.

[10] D. Glass, *Sculpture of Reform* (as n. 3), 175–81.

[11] D. Glass, *Sculpture of Reform* (as n. 3), 207–14.

[12] B. Klein, *Piacenza,* (as n. 6), 15, n. 18.

[13] In the eastern parts of the church there is only one figurative capital with scenes of Abraham's life, exactly between nave and choir. However, there are several figurative capitals in the nave: for example on the inner side of the façade with scenes of David and the stoning of Stephen, or in the North transept with Samson and the Lion.

[14] B: Klein, 'Die "Scuola di Piacenza"', in *Studien zur Geschichte der europäischen Skulptur im 12./13. Jahrhundert,* ed. H. Beck and K. Hengevoss-Dürkop (Frankfurt 1994), 1, 651–64.

EPISCOPAL PATRONAGE IN THE REFORM OF CATALAN CATHEDRAL CANONRIES DURING THE FIRST ROMANESQUE PERIOD: A NEW APPROACH

Eduardo Carrero Santamaria

INTRODUCTION

The beginning of the 11th century witnessed a renewal of interest in the apostolic life within cathedral chapters. In Old Catalonia, the restoration of diocesan jurisdiction that had been lost since the Muslim Conquest brought with it the revival of a communal life under a rule. These rules included not only the various versions of that approved by the Council of Aachen, but also miscellaneous rules drawn from a variety of patristic texts – known collectively as the Rules of the Holy Fathers – some of which have clear Iberian origins. Bishops Aeci of Barcelona (995–1010), Oliba of Vic (1017–46), Pere of Girona (1010–50) and Ermengol of Urgell (1010–35) attempted to restore communal life in their cathedrals.[1]

What prompted these peninsular bishops to reorganize the life of the cathedral community, in some cases stipulating for the first time that both canons and bishops should live communally? To my mind, the revitalisation of communal life that took place in Barcelona, Girona and Urgell was a direct response to the progressive relaxation in clerical lifestyle that had taken place in the ancient sees of Old Catalonia. This 11th-century reform initiated a cyclical pattern of rigour and relaxation that culminated in the definitive secularisation of cathedral chapters between the 13th and 16th centuries. In the immediate aftermath of reconquest, cathedral chapters were reorganised as part of a larger movement of urban replanning and renewal. By the start of the 11th century, the progressive relaxation of the customs of communal life prompted a structural reform of cathedral chapters. Between the 11th and 12th centuries, communal life decayed yet again, until, by the middle of the 12th century, we find the first references to cathedral chapters organised *secundum regulam Sancti Augustini*. This last coincided with the restoration of the sees of Lleida, Tortosa and Tarragona in southern Catalonia.

CATHEDRAL ARCHITECTURE AND THE REFORM OF CANONRIES

These institutional reforms had direct consequences for the physical fabric of cathedrals themselves. In Girona, the bishop and chapter decided in 1019 to build a *domus canonice*, destined for the regular life of the canons, referred to since the first half of the 11th century interchangeably as *clericis* or *canonicis* (Figure 4.1).[2] Bishop Aeci of Barcelona did the same in 1009, when the *claustra*, located next to the cathedral, and the buildings constructed within it, were given over to the canons' communal life. Meanwhile, in Seu d'Urgell, the sainted Bishop Ermengol restructured the cathedral chapter in 1010, thus continuing the reforms undertaken by his predecessor Salla, as is recorded in the surviving documentation.

All of these new architectural ensembles had their origins in much earlier structures, which we can date to around the 7th century thanks to documentary evidence that alludes to these cathedrals before their 11th-century reconstruction. Miquel dels Sants Gros has used the extant group of churches in Terrassa in order to reconstruct a series of buildings that no longer survive, but whose presence is attested in documentary sources. Thus, we can consider the cathedrals of Vic, Seu d'Urgell and Girona, together with the churches of Terrassa, within a larger European context. Working from later documentation that details the 10th-century restoration of the group of three churches in Terrassa, Gros has analysed the function of two, concluding that Sant Pere acted as a parish church, while Santa María served the clergy (colour plate I).[3]

The third church in this group poses problems. A centrally-planned church dedicated to St Michael, the lack of documentary sources or archaeological investigation of this site led the architect in charge of its restoration, Josep Puig i Cadafalch, to interpret the building as a baptistery.[4] This reinterpretation of the third church of Terrassa effectively brought the ecclesiastical complex into line with

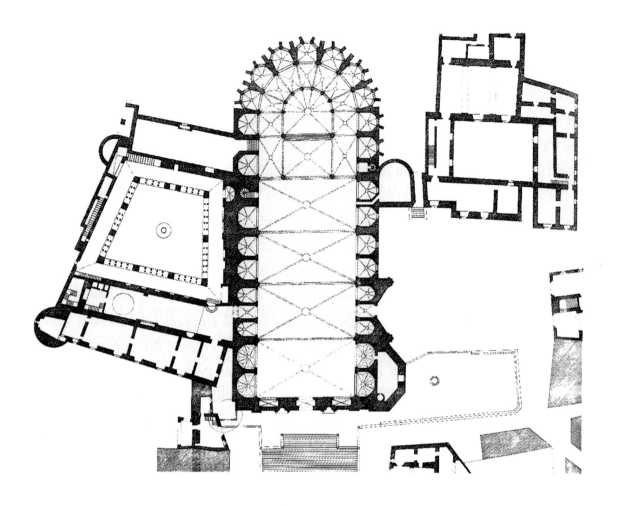

Figure 4.1

Cathedral of Girona. General plan (after J. A. Adell). On the East side of the Cloister, the remainings of the Domus Canonice transformed in a Gothic chapel.

other early medieval sites. Intense archaeological work at the end of the 20th century, however, has resulted in a radical revision of Puig i Cadafalch's baptistery.[5] In summary, there had been a basilica dedicated to the Virgin Mary on the site from the 5th century. This building was enlarged and given an adjoining baptistery. In the 6th century, two more churches were built to the north of the main basilica. The centrally-planned church of St Michael, decorated on three sides with a colonnaded porch, clearly had a funerary function, while the third church, dedicated to St Peter, functioned as the parish church. All three churches were connected by liturgical celebrations, and were enclosed by a common wall which encompassed their graveyards and the bishop's residential quarters at the southeastern corner of the complex. Finally, another funerary complex, interpreted as an episcopal chapel dedicated to Saints Justus and Pastor, has been identified along the southern flank of the church of Santa María.

From the 9th century, we have evidence of a group of four churches in the town of Elne, dedicated to saints Peter, Mary, Eulalia and Stephen, the last of which may have had a funerary function. The church of St Peter was long considered the first cathedral in the lower part of the town, before it was moved to the upper part at an unknown later date. St Eulalia took over the functions of the cathedral, and the church of St Stephen stood alongside the apse of St Eulalia until the 18th century.[6] The pre-11th-century cathedral of Vic offers an interesting puzzle. There is clear evidence of a cathedral complex dating from the 9th century, which consisted of three churches and two unique dedications. A donation by the Frankish king Eudes in 889 indicates that there was a church built in honour of the Virgin and St Peter.[7] The double dedication is unremarkable for this period, but in 947 we have a reference to construction works at the church of St Peter. A few years later in 952 and again in 981, two donations refer clearly to two separate churches in the city of Vic: one dedicated to St Peter and the other to the Virgin.[8] Moreover, the First Martyrology of the cathedral refers to the feast of the dedication of the church of Santa María in the 10th century.[9] The evidence thus complicates our ability to distinguish which of these two churches functioned as the cathedral church, and which functioned as the conventual church, perhaps for the exclusive use of the cathedral's lesser clergy. When the cathedral complex was rebuilt in the 11th century, both these functions were brought together in the church of St Peter, while the new church dedicated to the Virgin raises other issues, as we shall see. By the middle of the 11th century, there are no more documentary references to the double dedication to St Peter and the Virgin. From this moment on, documents refer to a sole foundation dedicated St Peter.

The third church in the ecclesiastical complex of Vic was dedicated to St Michael Archangel. The church of St Michael seems to have been located along the southern flank of St Peter, near the current location of the cloister. Its origins date back to the 10th-century episcopacy of Guadamir (948–57), and one of the cathedral martyrologies refers to the dedication of the church of St Michael during this time.[10] At the start of the 11th century, the church was still the beneficiary of a bequest *pro edificio suo*, and Bishop Borrell was buried in its crypt in 1017. But these three churches – St Peter, Santa María and St Michael – were not the only ones in the cathedral complex of Vic. A 985 donation refers to five separate foundations, including St Peter and four others that were 'subject' to it: the foundations of Santa María and St Michael that we just discussed, as well as two others dedicated to John the Baptist and St Felix.[11] Eduard Junyent has suggested that these dedications should be understood as references to spaces within the interior of the church of St Peter, perhaps as chapels associated with a hypothetical tripartite apse, consecrated on the 19th of May at some point in the middle of the 10th century.[12] But, what more can we say about these two dedications to John the Baptist and St Felix? Surviving documentation suggests that we are dealing in Vic with a possible baptistery dedicated to John the Baptist and a relic deposit dedicated to St Felix, both of which would have been located near the apse of Sant Peter. A parallel to this arrangement is the Visigothic cathedral of Valencia, which also had a baptistery and a *martyrium* dedicated to St Vincent, located on either side of the presbytery.[13] While the arrangement proposed for Vic is certainly plausible, for the moment we do not have enough archaeological evidence to be certain. Nevertheless, it is noteworthy that the chapels of the Romanesque transept were dedicated to John the Baptist and Paul (north), and Felix and Michael (south), thereby incorporating dedications from before the episcopacy of Oliba into the fabric of the cathedral.

In Girona, the Cathedral of Santa María had a space dedicated to St Michael, in which the cathedral clergy were supposed to pray in memory of Count Borrell II of Barcelona. Scholars have assumed this to be a separate space, independent of the old cathedral of Girona, even identifying it with archaeological remains uncovered in the northwestern corner of the cathedral cloister. I would like to counter this prevailing interpretation. Documentary sources are decidedly laconic with respect to the space dedicated to St Michael, *infra domum sancte Marie sedis Gerunde*. Not only do these sources fail to make clear whether or not we are dealing with an independent architectural space, they even suggest that we might interpret the dedication as that of an altar or chapel located in the interior of the main church, something which does, in fact, figure in later documentation.[14]

In Barcelona, mention of a cathedral dedicated to the Holy Cross and St Eulalia might lead us towards an interpretation similar to that which we have proposed for Girona (colour plate II). However, the translation of the body of St Eulalia in 878 from the church of Santa María into the cathedral tells us that the dedication to Eulalia involved not the ad hoc construction of a new building, but rather the installation of a new saint in the existing cathedral, and the subsequent rededication of the building. Similarly, Francesca Español has interpreted documentary references to a church of the Holy Sepulchre, located near the western façade of the cathedral, as indicating not an independent structure but rather a space associated with the western portion of the cathedral, as we find in Vic and Girona. The architectural form of this space was liturgically conditioned, and thus we see that the tower above the Holy Sepulchre in the Romanesque cathedral was also contemplated in the Gothic project for a monumental western ciborium. The organisation of space in Barcelona was therefore akin to that proposed by Carol Heitz for the Abbey of Centula, which had a similar structure located at the western 'foot' of the church, transformed during the late Gothic period into an antechamber with a central tower.[15] A curious cruciform church that has been identified among the chaotic remains of the northeastern part of the cathedral complex presents even more problems.[16] There is much that remains unknown about the form this building took, but tombs found in its vicinity suggest that the area around the putative church had a funerary function. What is clear is that the dedication to the Holy Sepulchre in Barcelona dates back to an early period. If documentary references to the structure in the western façade of the cathedral go back no earlier than the late 12th century, perhaps we are dealing with a process involving the integration of separate structures into the body of the cathedral, such as we have outlined in Vic. Finally, from the 10th century, there are references to churches dedicated to Mary and Peter, as well as a possible baptistery dedicated to John, in Seu d'Urgell. This complex of churches was radically reconfigured in the 11th century, as we shall see.

THE OFFICE OF BISHOP IN THE 11TH CENTURY

Returning to the 11th-century period of institutional and architectural renewal with which we began, we see that the figure of Bishop Oliba of Vic has traditionally been credited with a decisive role in the renewal that swept through the sees of Old Catalonia, as well as many of its monasteries. However, these renewals were not exclusively dependent on his individual agency, as the cases of Vic, Ripoll and Sant Pere de Rodes indicate.

Let us review each of these cases of reform. In Barcelona in the year 1009, Bishop Aeci granted his recently reformed chapter the *claustrum* situated between the cathedral and the episcopal palace. According to documentary descriptions, this *claustrum* was surrounded by a wall made of stones and lime, filled with fruit trees and a vineyard, within which was the refectory, still under construction in the early 11th century.[17] Matters are complex in Barcelona. The reinterpretation of the archaeological remains uncovered near the northern flank of the cathedral have led some to conclude that the palace of Barcelona's bishops was located here until the 12th century (colour plate II), even identifying the monumental late antique remains still visible beneath the floor of the city's museum as this episcopal palace. According to proponents of this view, the palace was moved to the southern side of the cathedral complex in the 12th century, but the earlier site remained episcopal property until the start of the 14th century, when the remains of the old building were granted by Bishop Pons de Gualba (1303–34) to King Jaime II in order to expand the neighbouring royal palace.[18] This hypothesis, suggested long ago by the classic historians of the see of Barcelona, has been taken up again by contemporary scholars. The details of the 14th century grant do not, however, support this interpretation. While the document describes how Bishop Pons de Gualba donated a house to the king so that he could expand the royal palace, the house in question was simply episcopal property, not the episcopal palace itself. Indeed, an earlier document of 1271 refers to the great possessions of the bishops next to the cathedral and the royal palace.[19] If we bear in mind that most of the houses that surrounded the cathedral were the property of the bishop and canons, the bishop's 14th-century donation becomes simply the sale of a house in his possession rather than the sale of his old palace. On the other hand, as the early eleventh-century document of Bishop Aeci suggests, the bishop of Barcelona's residence was already located near the south flank of the cathedral by 1009. The *claustrum* donated by Bishop Aeci to his chapter was the same space in which a cloister was subsequently built, and the episcopal palace appears in this document in the same location where it stands today.

Meanwhile, the construction of the Romanesque cathedral must have been carried out with full awareness of the important cult centred on the relics of St Eulalia. During the construction of the new Romanesque cathedral, St Eulalia's funerary monument was installed alongside the main altar of the Virgin Mary. Early sources tell us that the altar that accompanied the tomb monument was used for the celebration of the morning mass, the early office that, like Matins and other Marian and funerary offices, was carried out by those who could not attend the main mass owing to other obligations.[20] However, the surviving portions of the cathedral ordinary indicate that the morning mass was celebrated at the high altar, dedicated to the Holy Cross, which is exceptional in the context of cathedral liturgies more generally 'Non dicitur per ebdomadari missa in altari Sancte Eulalie . . . dicantur missa matutinalis in altari Sancte Crucis sub missa uoce cum diachono et subdiachono'.[21] Pope Clement VII (1523–34) granted indulgences to those who visited the tomb of St Eulalia for Saturday morning mass, along with the offices for the Virgin that were celebrated there, as well.[22] Although they refer to the Gothic cathedral, these later texts are valuable because they emphasize the close relationship between the matutinal altar, the nearby high altar and the presbytery. It is worth noting that it was common to find the matutinal altar immediately behind the high altar. This was an ideal space for the tombs of saints, creating a retro-chapel for the celebration of matutinal masses and the elaboration of the cult of important relics.[23] This appears to have been the model chosen for the Cathedral of Barcelona. In Barcelona, the apse was centred around two altars, the main altar dedicated to the Holy Cross and the matutinal altar dedicated to the Virgin Mary, while the tomb of St Eulalia occupied the area closest to the curve of the apse. On the south side was the seating area for the officiant and his ministers, next to the bishop's *cathedra*. In front of this area was the canons' choir, surrounding the altar, as we see in Vic, Girona, Roda de Isábena, Lleida and Zaragoza, among others.[24]

In Vic, the new Cathedral of Sant Pere was consecrated on 31 August 1038. Santa María, which may have functioned as a conventual church, was incorporated into the fabric of the new cathedral complex, taking the form of a large rotunda dedicated to a commemorative cult of the Virgin Mary (Figure 4.2). It is precisely this commemorative function, here to the Nativity in Bethlehem, that shapes the architectural form of the church of Santa María of Vic, which was reconstructed as a centrally-planned building alongside the western façade of the Cathedral of Sant Pere. Though the rotunda was destroyed in the 18th century, thanks to archaeological excavations we have a sense of the 11th-century situation of the building within the larger cathedral complex during the celebrated episcopacy of Oliba (1018–46).[25] Oliba's church of Santa María had a circular plan some ten and a half metres in diameter, and a western apse. This building was then reconstructed in the mid-12th-century, leaving a large circular church that was destroyed in the modern era.[26] The construction at Vic was contemporaneous with the extension of the monastic church of Sant Miquel de Cuixà, in particular its western rotunda. This architectural similarity makes even more sense when we bear in mind the close liturgical relationship between the principal cathedral church of Sant Pere and Santa María at Vic which, although documented in liturgical texts from the 13th century, can easily be pushed back in time to earlier centuries.[27] We may suppose that processions at Cuixà were similar.

In Seu d'Urgell, the capitular buildings were constructed in an L-shaped plan, to the south-east of the original cathedral. During the episcopacy of Ermengol, Seu d'Urgell became the most significant – and the most recently reconstructed – ecclesiastical complex for the old Catalan counts. Its reconstruction, dating from the early 11th century, maintained two main churches, to which was added the third church of Sant Miquel (conceived as a church for the minor canons) and two small churches dedicated to the Holy Sepulchre and to St Eulalia (Figure 4.3). As we see with St Michael at Fulda, the Holy

FIGURE 4.2

Cathedral of Vic. General plan, and the remains of the church of la Rodona (after Vila).

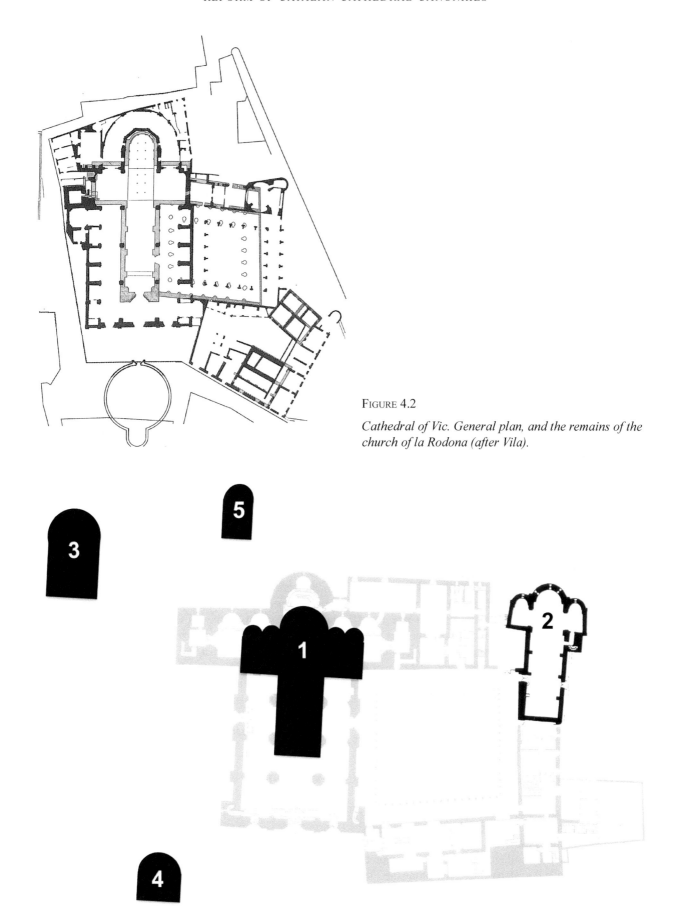

FIGURE 4.3

Cathedral of La Seu d'Urgell. 1. St Mary. 2. St Peter. 3. St Michael. 4. Holy Sepulchre. 5. St Eulalia.

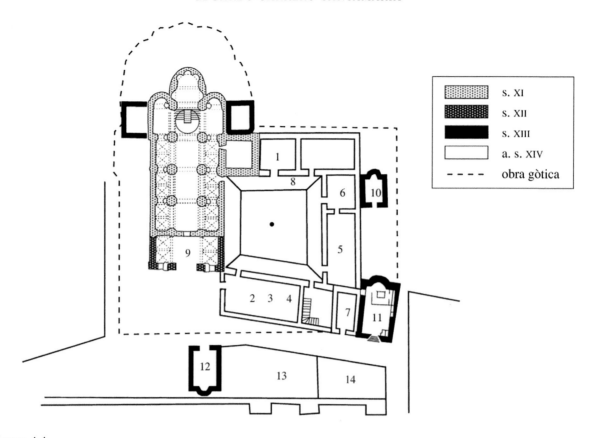

Figure 4.4

Cathedral of Barcelona. Topography during the 12th century (after Cristina Borau). 1. Chapter room. 2. Tithe Barn. 3. Dormitory. 4. New chapter room (after the secularisation, in the place of the old dormitory). 5. Refectory. 6. Kitchen. 7. Chaplaincy of St James. 8. Chapel of St Michael. 9. Galilea. 10. Chapel of the Corpus. 11. Chapel of the Virgins. 12. Chapel of St Blas and St Katherine. 13. Dean's House. 14. Archdeacon's House.

Sepulchres of Cambrai and Paderborn, or with St Maurice in Constance, the Holy Sepulchre at Seu d'Urgell was constructed at the initiative of a private individual (a certain Miró Viven) for his own personal funerary purposes. From this point on, the churches formed an integrated complex organised around spaces and dedications related to pilgrimage: St Peter's in Rome, the Holy Sepulchre in Jerusalem, St Eulalia in Barcelona and St Michael at Monte Gargano. The sites were all connected by liturgical routes to the main church dedicated to the Virgin Mary.[28]

In the cases of Seu d'Urgell and Vic, we encounter a phenomenon of reconstruction that seems to build upon a pre-existing arrangement of ecclesiastical buildings within the overall topography of a cathedral complex. This phenomenon is documented in all of the sees from an early date, while material testimony still survives in the old cathedral of Terrassa. The model followed for the reconstruction of these sees involved the integration into a single building of dedications that seem to have once been independent structures. Such is the case with the dedication to the Holy Sepulchre in Barcelona. Strangely, during the 13th and 14th centuries, the Cathedral of Barcelona underwent a process of fragmentation, whereby cult spaces metamorphosed into independent chapels surrounding the perimeter of the cathedral (Figure 4.4).[29] This process seems to have been born out of the communal life of the chapter and out of the need to bring into a single building several diverse functions. These included the needs of the chapter, and the parochial function of the bishop's church, as well as a variety of smaller funerary churches, baptisteries or commemorative buildings. As Carol Heitz has shown, the period before the 12th century saw the progressive integration into a single building of cult spaces that had previously been distributed throughout the cathedral complex. This brought with it the articulation of the interior space into areas reserved for the clergy and for the laity, the latter becoming the site for processions that before had connected the distinct architectural spaces of the cathedral precinct.[30]

CONCLUSION

In conclusion, let me leave you with a final thought. Only thirty years separate the reforms of the chapter of Barcelona from those at Seu d'Urgell. During this brief period, four bishops reorganised their chapters and reconstructed their cathedrals. We are clearly dealing with a time of widespread reform, and Oliba of Vic was far from the only protagonist in this story. Three other bishops participated in the reform process, and the documentary, art-historical and archaeological records reveal a monumental landscape far different from the fragmented geography of cult sites that we see in Terrassa or at other pre-reform sees. Only Seu d'Urgell seems to conserve a distribution of sacred sites more in accordance with earlier models of urban organisation, with a cathedral complex consisting of a central main church, Santa María, surrounded by four smaller churches. A glance at the dedications of this second complex of Urgell makes clear its dependence on and relationship to the most important cult and pilgrimage sites of medieval Europe. Along with the Cathedral dedication to the Virgin Mary, there is the church of Saints Peter, Paul and Andrew, a church dedicated to St Michael and the Archangels, another to St Eulalia of Barcelona, and finally a dedication to the Holy Sepulchre. Josep Guidiol's foundational study of Catalan pilgrimage to the holy places emphasizes the dedications we find at Seu d'Urgell: Jerusalem and its Holy Sepulchre, Rome – particularly the basilicas of St Peter and St Paul – St Michael on Monte Gargano.[31] When the tiny church of the Holy Sepulchre was founded in Seu d'Urgell, Jerusalem was still in Muslim hands. Was the construction of this Catalan version of the Holy Sepulchre, like so many other versions of this monument, a response to the difficulties of pilgrimage to the Holy Land? It would be remarkable if a visit to the churches of Urgell counted as a pilgrimage, as we see documented in papal bulls relating to the Christian recapture of the city of Tarragona (because the reconquest of the Iberian peninsula was also cast in terms of a crusade), or in the beautiful 1080 diploma of consecration for the church of Tolba. Visits to Tolba and donations of alms commuted the pilgrimage to the Holy Land, St Peter's in Rome, Santiago de Compostela, the Church of the Virgin Mary in Le Puy, *uel in aliam peregrinationem*.[32] Among the dedications to St Peter, St Michael and the Archangels, the Holy Sepulchre and St Eulalia, the absence of the dedication to Santiago among the churches of Urgell stands out. We do, however, have numerous testimonies of pilgrims to Santiago from Urgell, including Bishop Ermengol himself. At the same time, one of the altars in the Romanesque cathedral was dedicated to the Apostle James, while the meteoric rise of cult of Ermengol immediately following his death was also linked to the cult of St James. This connection to St James was made clear in both the topography of the cathedral, with its neighbouring altars, and in the iconography associated with the sainted bishop, replete with references to the legendary hagiography of James.[33]

Reflecting on the complex of dedications and their relationship to pilgrimage, early 11th-century Seu d'Urgell could be seen as a symbolic *mappa mundi* of the most important devotional centres of the time. If we again consider the question of atria, *terra ad cibarium*, and the urban landscape, we must imagine a principal church dedicated to the Virgin Mary set within a defined space, perhaps surrounded by a wall, around which were located four churches whose dedications are profoundly indicative of the contemporary religious imagination. At the same time that they demonstrate the desire to bring together the most important sacred spaces of the time. During this same period, another ecclesiastic, Bishop Oliba of Vic, was behind the creation of two of the most striking and evocative buildings of the age: the Marian rotundas at the west ends of the churches of St Michael in Cuixà and St Peter in Vic, both of them noteworthy for their commemorative function. Similarly, within a few years, chapels dedicated to the Holy Sepulchre were created for the upper story of the west ends of the cathedrals of Barcelona, Girona and Vic. In these circumstances is it so very difficult to imagine an urban topography of sacred spaces, focussed on the cathedral and its immediate vicinity at Seu d'Urgell? Most, though not all, the separate cult sites at Urgell were finally integrated into the main body of the cathedral during the 12th and 13th centuries, thereby vitiating the unique sacred topography of the 11th century. But whether accidental or not, the built environment of the Cathedral of the Virgin Mary in Seu d'Urgell consisted of an ensemble of churches dedicated to the Holy Places, linked via a complex stational liturgy which, although altered and transformed, survived until the beginning of the Early Modern period.

NOTES

[1] E. Carrero, '*Ecce quam bonum et quam iocundum habitare fratres in unum*. Vidas reglar y secular en las catedrales hispanas llegado el siglo XII', *Anuario de Estudios Medievales*, 30 (2000), 757–805 and E. Carrero, 'La *vita communis* en las catedrales peninsulares: Del registro diplomático a la evidencia arquitectónica', in *A Igreja e o Clero português no contexto europeu* (Lisbon 2005), 171–94.

[2] E. Carrero, 'El claustro de la *seu de Girona*. Orígenes arquitectónicos y modificaciones en su estructura y entorno', *Annals de l'Institut d'Estudis Gironins*, 45 (2004), 189–214, and M. Sureda Jubany, *Els precedents de la Catedral de Santa Maria de Girona* (Girona 2008).

[3] M. dels. S. Gros y Pujol, 'La funcionalitat litúrgica de les esglésies d'Ègara', in *Actes Simposi Internacional sobre les Esglésies de Sant Pere de Terrassa, 20, 21 i 22 de novembre de 1991* (Terrassa 1992,) 77–83.

[4] J. Puig i Cadafalch, *Notes arquitectòniques sobre les esglésies de Sant Pere de Terrassa* (Barcelona 1889) and idem, *La Seu Visigòtica d'Ègara* (Barcelona 1936), republished in J. Puig i Cadafalch, *Escrits d'arquitectura, art i política*, ed. X. Barral I Altet (Barcelona 2003), 397–427 and 429–51.

[5] M.G. García I Llinares, A. Moro García, and F. Tuset Bertrán, *La Seu episcopal d'Ègara: Arqueologia d'un conjunt cristià del segle IV al IX* (Tarragona 2009).

[6] P. Ponsich, 'Le groupe cathédral du vicus Helena et les origins de la ville épiscopale', in *Elne, ville et territoire-Elna, ciutat i territori: 2ème Recontres d'histoire et d'archéologie d'Elne, 1999* (Elne 2003), 131–39.

[7] E. Juyent i Subira, *Diplomatari de la catedral de Vic, segles IX–X*, 5 (Vich, 1980–96), I, doc. 12, 11–13.

[8] Juyent i Subira, *Diplomatari de la catedral de Vic* (as n.7), II, docs. 240 and 272, 203–04 and 228–29; IV, doc. 481, 405. Excavations in the area around the cathedral have been able to connect the twenty-seven remains exhumed from a necropolis with the cathedral. See C. Subiranas Fràbregas, 'L'excavació arqueològica a la plaça de la catedral de Vic (Osona): l'església de Santa Maria la Rodona', *Tribuna d'arqueologia*, 2004–2005 (2006), 313–40, especially 318–20.

[9] E. Juyent I Subira, *Diplomatari i escrits literaris de l'abat i bisbe Oliba*, ed. A.M. Mundó (Barcelona 1992), 389.

[10] Published in E. Flórez, *España Sagrada*, 29 vols (Madrid 1747–75), XXVIII, 322 and 326; J. Villanueva, *Viage literario a las Iglesias de España*, 22 vols (Madrid 1803–52), VI, 146.

[11] For an overview of the relevant sources, see E. Carrero, 'La arquitectura al servicio de las necesidades litúrgicas. Los conjuntos de iglesias', *I Anales de Historia del Arte*, extraordinary volume (2009) *Jornadas Complutenses de Arte Medieval*, 61–97.

[12] E. Juyent, 'La Catedral de Vich en el período de la Reconquista', *Ausa*, 5–50 (1964), 121–28; X. Barral I Altet, *La catedral romànica de Vic* (Barcelona 1979) 28; Juyent i Subira, *Diplomatari i escrits literaris* (as n. 9), 391.

[13] A.V. Riera i Lacomba, 'Origen i desenvolupament del nucli episcopal de València', in *VI reunió d'arqueologia cristiana hispànica. Les ciutats tardoantigues d'Hispania: Cristianització i topografia*, eds, J.M. Gurt and A. Riera (Barcelona 2005), 207–43.

[14] Sureda Jubany, *Els precedents* (as n. 2).

[15] C. Heitz, *Recherches sur les rapports entre architecture et liturgie à l'époque carolingienne* (Paris 1963), 28; F. Español, 'Massifs occidentaux dans l'architecture romane catalane', *Les Cahiers de Saint-Michel de Cuxa*, 27 (1996), 57–77, esp. 65–77.

[16] C. Bonnet and J. Beltrán de Heredia, 'Origen y evolución del grupo episcopal de Barcino: de los primeros tiempos cristianos a la época visigótica', *Barcino: de los primeros tiempos cristianos a la época visigótica*, ed. J. Beltrán de Heredia (Barcelona 2001), 73–93; Bonnet and Beltrán de Heredia, 'Nouveau regard sur le groupe épiscopal de Barcelone', *Rivista di Archeologia Cristiana*, 80 (2004), 137–58. See also the remarks of N. Duval, 'La cathédrale de paléochrétienne de Barcelone revisitée', *Bulletin Monumental*, 156 (1998), 403–10.

[17] S. Puig i Puig, *Episcopologio de la Sede barcinonense* (Barcelona 1929), doc. XXVIII, 368–69.

[18] Bonnet and Beltrán de Heredia, 'Nouveau regard sur le groupe épiscopal' (as n. 16).

[19] Puig i Puig, *Episcopologio* (as n. 17), doc. C, 451–55.

[20] E. Carrero Santamaría, 'El altar mayor y el altar matinal en el presbiterio de la catedral de Santiago de Compostela. La instalación litúrgica para el culto a un Apóstol', *Territorio, Sociedad y Poder*, 8 (2013), 19–52.

[21] Arxiu de la Catedral de Barcelona, cód. 77A, f. 237.

[22] Puig i Puig, *Episcopologio* (as n. 17), 269–70.

[23] E. Carrero Santamaría, 'Retrocapillas, trasaltares y girolas: liturgia, reliquias y enterramientos de prestigio en la arquitectura medieval', in *Imágenes del poder en la Edad Media. Estudios 'in memoriam' del Prof. Dr. Fernando Galván Freile*, 2 vols (León 2011), II, 63–81.

[24] On the choir of Jaca, see G. Fernández Somoza, 'Arquitectura y liturgia en la catedral de Jaca. Coro, claustro, reliquias y urbanismo', in *Arquitectura y liturgia. El contexto artístico de las consuetas catedralicias en la Corona de Aragón*, ed. E. Carrero (Palma de Mallorca 2014), 75–104. On the choir of Vic, see M. Sureda Jubany, 'Clero, espacios y liturgia en la Catedral de Vic: La iglesia de Sant Pere en los siglos XII y XIII', *Medievalia*, 17 (2014), 279–320.

[25] There is documentary evidence of construction taking place in 1039 in the Cathedral of Sant Pere in Vic. The will of a certain Guifré records his donation to the church and its construction project, while the eleventh-century Martyrology of Vic contains a notice of the festival celebrating its dedication in the presence of Bishop Oliba on 18 January. See Juyent, *Diplomatari i escrits literaris* (as n. 9), docs. 137 and 3, 233 and 389.

[26] See the important literature on the Rodona (Sta Maria) at Vic: E. Juyent, 'L'església de la Rodona', *Ausa*, 2 (1955–57), 447–53, republished in Juyent, *Monuments romànics d'Osona* (Vic 1987) 51–61, esp. 53; X. Barral i Altet, *La catedral romànica* (as n. 12), 107–12; J. Gudiol I Cunill, *Els claustres de la catedral de Vic* (Vic 1981), 67; Juyent, *Diplomatari i escrits literaris* (as n. 9), 389–90; C. Subiranas Fràbregas, 'L'església de Santa Maria la Rodona', *Arqueologia Medieval. Revista catalana d'arqueologia medieval*, 1 (2005), 8–31; Subiranas Fràbregas, 'L'excavació arqueològica a la plaça' (as n. 8), 320–30; Barral i Altet, 'Du Panthéon de Rome à Sainte-Marie la Rotonde de Vic: La transmission d'un modèle d'architecture mariale au début du XIe siècle et la politique "romaine" de l'abbé-évêque Oliba', *Les Cahiers de Saint-Michel de Cuxa*, 37 (2006), 63–75, esp. 64–65. On the demolition of the site and the conflict between the utilitarian intentions of the Bishop of Vic and the protectionist positions of the Royal Academy of Fine Arts, see, M. Mirambell i Abancó, 'La demolició de l'església de Santa Maria de la Rodona de Vic. Un exemple d'actuació sobre el patrimoni eclesiàstic al final del segle XVIII', in *Església, societat i poder a les terres de parla catalana. Actes del IV Congrés de la CCEPS, Vic, 20–21 febrer de 2004* (Valls 2005), 727–43.

[27] Carrero, "La arquitectura al servicio de las necesidades litúrgicas' (as n. 11).

[28] E. Carrero Santamaría, 'La Seu d'Urgell, el último conjunto de iglesias. Liturgia, paisaje urbano y arquitectura', *Anuario de Estudios Medievales*, 40 (2010), 251–91 and Carrero Santamaría, 'Las dos consuetas de La Seu d'Urgell', in *Arquitectura y liturgia. El contexto artístico de las consuetas catedralicias en la Corona de Aragón*, ed. E. Carrero (Palma de Mallorca 2014), 253–70.

[29] This process is documented in C. Borau, *Els promotors de capelles i retaules a la Barcelona del segle XIV* (Barcelona 2003), 298–344.

[30] J. Hubert, 'Les "cathédrales doubles" et l'historie de la liturgie', in *Atti del I Congresso Internazionale di Studi Longobardi, Spoleto, 27–30 settembre, 1951* (Spoleto 1951), 167–76 and C. Heitz, 'Architecture et liturgie processionnelle à l'époque préromane', *Revue de l'Art*, 24 (1974), 30–47. These scholars are followed in A. Erlande-Brandenburg, 'De la cathédrale double à la cathedrale unique', in *Saint-Pierre de Genève au fil des siècles*, ed. E. de Montmollin (Geneva 1991), 15–22. For a more recent consideration, see E. Carrero, 'La arquitectura al servicio de las necesidades litúrgicas (as n. 11), 61–97

[31] J. Gudiol, 'De peregrins i peregrinatges religiosos catalans', *Analecta sacra tarraconensia*, 3 (1927), 95–110.

[32] Gudiol, 'De peregrins i peregrinatges', 97–98. From a more general perspective, of particular relevance to this discussion, see R. Ousterhout, *'Loca Sancta* and the Architectural Response to Pilgrimage', in *The Blessings of Pilgrimage*, ed. R. Ousterhout (Urbana 1980), 108–24.

[33] Remains of wall paintings from the chapel in the apse have been identified as such by A. Orriols i Alsina, 'Un cicle de Sant Jaume i Sant Ermengol a la catedral de la Seu d'Urgell', in *El camí de Sant Jaume i Catalunya. Actes del Congrés Internacional celebrat a Barcelona, Cervera i Lleida, els diez 1, 17 i 18 d'octubre de 2003* (Abadia de Montserrat 2007), 409–17.

THE ROLE OF KINGS AND BISHOPS IN THE INTRODUCTION OF ROMANESQUE ART IN NAVARRE AND ARAGON

Javier Martínez de Aguirre

INTRODUCTION

The pre-Romanesque church of San Miguel de Villatuerta in Navarre is known for its relief carvings, which, according to currently accepted opinion, represent the ceremony of the blessing of troops marching into battle.[1] The *ordo* on which this is based dates from Visigothic times and underscores the principle of cooperation between bishops and kings in military ventures. The location of the reliefs seems to be related to the strategic importance of the site. It is halfway between Pamplona, the capital, and Nájera, the second city of the kingdom, near the ford where Abd-al-Rahman III's troops had attacked in the years 920 and 924. The inscription (Figure 5.1) extols the importance of Bishop Velasco, who governed the diocese of Pamplona in the decade around 970.[2] He is easily identified by his mitre and crosier and is mounted on a galloping horse. However, despite the mention of *Sancto re*, referring to Sancho Garcés II, King of Pamplona from 970 to 994, there is no equivalent representation among the roughly carved figures that can be identified with the monarch. It was the reliefs that saved this church from falling into oblivion. It wasn't noted for its architectural innovation or aspirations and, as far as we know, produced no imitators. The reliefs reflect the military vocation that predominated in the nascent kingdom of Pamplona and united the destinies of the crown and the mitre. The much greater size of the text referring to the bishop in the inscription and the greater prominence of the figure of the prelate suggest that it was he who was responsible for its construction. In this respect, Villatuerta sets a modest precedent for the joint presence of kings and bishops in architectural projects in Pyrenean lands.

The introduction of Romanesque architecture in the eleventh century similarly involved cooperation between kings and bishops on important buildings. I will analyse this in detail by focusing attention on three buildings of particular significance: the Abbey of Leire (Navarre) and the Cathedrals of Jaca (Aragon) and Pamplona (Navarre).

LEIRE: SANCHO THE KING AND SANCHO THE BISHOP

Our perspectives on the origins of Romanesque in the western Pyrenees are clouded by the relative importance of the Kingdoms of Aragon and Navarre in the later Middle Ages. Before the year 1000 there were no examples in these lands of Christian buildings that were greater than 25 m long or were vaulted throughout. Given that backdrop, the interest shown by Pamplonese sovereigns in enlarging the abbey church of San Salvador of Leire (Navarre) takes on a special significance, as exemplified in a document recording a donation by Sancho IV to the monastery on the occasion of the 1057 consecration of its church (Figure 5.2).[3] The young king, then just eighteen years old, had succeeded to the throne three years earlier, following the unexpected death of his father, García III while fighting Ferdinand I of Castile (García's brother). The donation commemorates the dead king and makes it known that the entire royal family was anxious to see the church finished.[4] Bear in mind, however, that Sancho IV did not attend the ceremony as patron but as a guest of the bishop, John.[5]

Knowledge of the historical context suggests the enlargement of the church was due to the grandfather of Sancho IV, the famous Sancho III the Great (1004–1035), and not his son, García III (1035–1054). There are no chronicles or documents to link these monarchs with the building, and the monastery itself instead acknowledges the figure of Sancho III's grandfather, Sancho II, who had probably been buried there. His imaginary coat of arms decorates a keystone of the Gothic vault.[6] However, there is no doubt Sancho III had the motive, opportunity and means to promote such an ambitious construction. This cannot be said of his successor, who was more interested in Santa María de Nájera. But, did Sancho III actually intervene? And, if so, in what way did he participate?

In early studies on the architecture of Leire, authors such as Madrazo, Bertaux, and Lampérez dated the Romanesque east end (Figure 5.3) to the time of Sancho

FIGURE 5.1

Inscription from San Miguel de Villatuerta (Navarre), Museo de Navarra, Pamplona © Museo de Navarra

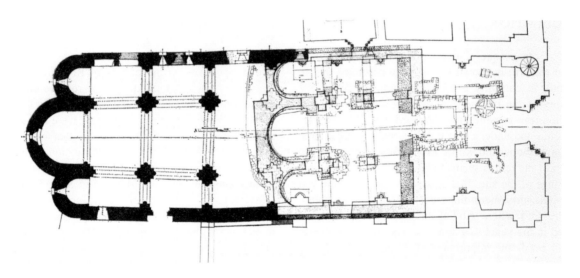

FIGURE 5.2

Plan of pre-Romanesque remains and Romanesque enlargement of Leire (Francisco Íñiguez Almech)

Ramírez (1064–1094), taking into consideration a second consecration documented in 1098.[7] Gómez Moreno accepted this date, although he was aware that the architecture of Leire would be decidedly '*retardataire*' for this chronology to work.[8] It was José María Lacarra, the great historian of medieval Navarre, who, in 1944, linked the enlargement of the Romanesque church to Sancho III.[9] His arguments included the character of the king, 'a pro-European reformist monarch', the important role played by the abbey in the kingdom of Pamplona at the beginning of the 11th century, and the 1057 consecration. Architectural renovation by Sancho III would have been 'in parallel with the monastic restoration and political resurgence of the first third of the eleventh century'.[10]

Lacarra's proposal was favourably received.[11] Although advances in historical studies have cast doubt on other actions attributed to Sancho III, such as the introduction of the Cluniac Reform to the peninsula or extensive investment in the Way of Saint James, perceptions of his role in the kingdom's architectural renewal have been enhanced, thanks to the detailed study of Leire's crypt and church published by Francisco Íñiguez in 1966 and subsequent 1970 article on the king's artistic patronage, studies which have achieved broad acceptance.[12]

Historical sources favour the hypothesis that the real driving force behind the enlargement was Abbot Sancho (1024–52), simultaneously abbot of Leire and bishop of Pamplona.[13] He was a singularly interesting character.[14] His life took a very different course from that of his predecessors, precisely because of the relationship he cultivated with Cluny, and he is the best candidate to be identified with the *Sancius Pampulanorum episcopus* mentioned by Odilo's biographer, Jotsaldo, who goes on to say that Bishop Sancho enjoyed a special friendship with the abbot of Cluny, to the extent that Odilo remembered him in instructions he left on his death.[15]

By the beginning of the 11th century, the monastery of Leire was already more than a century old. Its church consisted of a short aisled nave and a triple-apsed east end, straight on the exterior and semicircular inside in the Iberian early medieval manner. There is no record of any Moorish raid in the early years of the 11th century which might have affected the monastery.[16] Therefore, the 1057 ceremony will not have been the consecration of a church

FIGURE 5.3

East end, abbey church of Leire (Javier Martinez de Aguirre)

that had been burnt or defiled by enemies of the Christian faith. It will have marked the enlargement of a church that had become too small.

Sancho III will have been interested in Leire for two reasons. The first was a more general inclination towards monasticism: the Navarran texts of the *Roda Codex*, written shortly after his death, describe him as *desiderator et amator agmina monacorum*.[17] The second was because Leire had acted as the main burial church of the Pamplonese royal family since the 9th century. It is very likely that Sancho III's father and grandfather were buried there.[18] However, neither tradition, nor detailed study of the building provides any additional information as to Sancho's links with Leire, and involvement on the part of the monarch was probably limited to supporting the abbot's initiative to enlarge the church. The economic viability of new construction work can only have been sustained by donations to the abbey and the recovery of rents from the diocese of Pamplona. In this case, the king *did* intervene.[19] A telling example is found in an event that occurred in Zamarce, an enclave of ancient ecclesiastical land belonging to the cathedral, situated on the Roman road from Bordeaux to Astorga. According to a document dated 1031, the king convened the local elders to settle a dispute as to who owned the property. The meeting then decided in favour of the cathedral, vesting ownership in the bishop-abbot.[20]

Regardless of the arguments put forward by Íñiguez as to Sancho III's involvement in a number of building projects, the architectural ambition evident in the eastern parts of Leire is unquestionably greater than that of any other ecclesiastical projects: the crypt of San Antolín in Palencia, the lower church of San Juan de la Peña and the enlargement of San Millán de la Cogolla. As Janice Mann observed, if their monumental appearance had anything in common ('no single coherent formal language unites these monuments'), it was limited to their use of rounded arches and vaults, the fact they represent enlargements, and the respect they showed for existing buildings. That said, they share too few elements in common to be able to sustain the argument that they formed part of an architectural renewal consciously led by the monarch.[21]

The Leire enlargement was different. It signified a radical break with the previous modest architecture of the Kingdom of Pamplona because of its 'grandiose sobriety' (in the words of Georges Gaillard),[22] as evidenced by the use of large blocks of ashlar for walls and vaults, and the clumsy treatment of solutions derived from more refined architecture, such as alternating pillars and columns or the proliferation of archivolts on the doorways. Cabanot has compared the poor ornamentation of capitals, mouldings and corbels with works from the other side of the Pyrenees (Figure 5.4).[23] Could King Sancho III have seen buildings that inspired him to enlarge Leire? We have no record of this. His constant travels around the north of the Peninsula, from Ribagorza to León, did not take him to any church that we might recognise as a visual source for the monastic church. Nor, as far as we know, would he have seen a possible model on his celebrated 1010 trip to Saint Jean d'Angély.[24]

On the other hand, it does seem reasonable to attribute direct responsibility for the enlargement to Bishop-Abbot Sancho. Thanks to the co-operation of the king, who repeatedly referred to the prelate as 'my master' (perhaps also his chancellor), he managed economic resources far greater than those of his predecessors. His close relationship with Odilo, promoter of the monumental Cluny II, may explain his initiative for undertaking new work at Leire. This may necessitate a rethinking of the date at which work began, as a letter from Odilo to Abbot Paterno proves that Bishop-Abbot Sancho visited the Burgundian abbey after the death of Sancho III.[25]

The particularities of Leire's fabric can reasonably be explained by the circumstances surrounding its commission. Faced with a challenge without precedent in the immediate neighbourhood of Leire, the abbot would have contracted a master builder with limited training, entrusting him with a monumental building inspired by the refined architectural techniques the Abbot had seen elsewhere. A desire for ashlar masonry in the peninsular tradition and the hardness of the local stone made this work arduous. In developing an elevation out of a well-tried plan, the master builder either overlooked conventional proportional relationships between supports and arches, or simply disregarded them, as well as disregarding consistency of treatment, because he attached no importance to either. Through lack of experience, he improvised both the windowsills, which were recarved, and the points where different surfaces converged, in spite of which, he still managed to achieve an imposing building. The east end at Leire takes us back to a time when patrons and builders risked embarking on projects when they had no previous experience. This attitude

FIGURE 5.4

Crypt of Leire (C.J. Martínez Álava)

proved crucial for the rapid pace of architectural development at the beginning of the Romanesque period.

JACA: TWO BISHOPS AND ONE KING

Since Antonio Ubieto demonstrated the forgery of the three documents sustaining the attribution, hardly anyone now believes the old hypothesis that King Ramiro I of Aragon (1035–1064) was responsible for Jaca Cathedral.[26] Nevertheless, there are still historians who argue that Ramiro was responsible for an initial project which is conserved in the outline of the east end and the three lower courses of the northern apse.[27] In my opinion, examination of the apse shows that this initial 'Lombard' phase, supposedly interrupted soon after it was started, never existed (Figure 5.5). The lower courses are of the same size as others we find in various parts of the church, and their type is similar to that of the upper courses.[28]

For more than fifty years, scholarly opinion on Jaca has followed Ubieto, Moralejo, Durliat, and Simon, among others, in basing assessments of Jaca on the (genuine) documentation, its historical context, analysis of the architecture and the study of the sculpture.[29] All agree that the cathedral was begun during the reign of Sancho Ramírez, son of Ramiro I, some time after regional charters or *fueros* were granted to Jaca in 1077. It is perfectly conceivable that the church was finished during the reign of Pedro I (1094–1104), son of Sancho Ramírez. I therefore see no reason to conclude, as is frequently done, that the conquest of Huesca in 1096 caused a drastic interruption of the works. The refurbishment of the ancient mosque at Huesca in 1096, prior to its consecration as a Christian cathedral, lasted for no more than a few months. There is

FIGURE 5.5

North apse of Jaca Cathedral (Javier Martinez de Aguirre)

no obvious reason why it should have any consequences for construction at Jaca. There is also no evidence of a reduction in cathedral rents at Jaca, or a loss of interest in the city by its kings and bishops. The homogeneity of the sculptural decoration of the building, as shown by Gómez Moreno and Moralejo, supports the idea that a possible interruption – and a change of architect if there was one – would only have affected the upper parts of the central nave, built when the vaults of the east end and the transept were already finished.[30] In a recent examination, I detected an interruption in the masonry above the vaults on the south side of the nave, which then continues downwards with courses of different sizes. The masonry joint was situated at an ideal distance for the original walling to have acted as a temporary buttress for the transept vaults.[31]

After the assassination in 1076 of King Sancho IV, his cousin, Sancho Ramírez, came to the Pamplonese throne (Figure 5.6). Until then Sancho Ramírez had governed Aragon as count, without using the title 'king' (in a genuine document of 1072 his title was given as *gratia Dei aragonense* without the word *rex*). This had consequences at all levels. Ubieto and Cabanes affirm that Sancho Ramírez immediately called himself *gratia Dei rex Aragonensium et Pampilonensium*, in reference to his authority and royal power over both territories, now raised to the same level of dignity as sovereign kingdoms.[32] It is worth remembering that his father, Ramiro I, had paid homage and fealty to his own half-brother, the king of Pamplona, García III.[33]

Sancho Ramírez must have seen the advantage of having a city in the old Aragonese county, now raised to the status

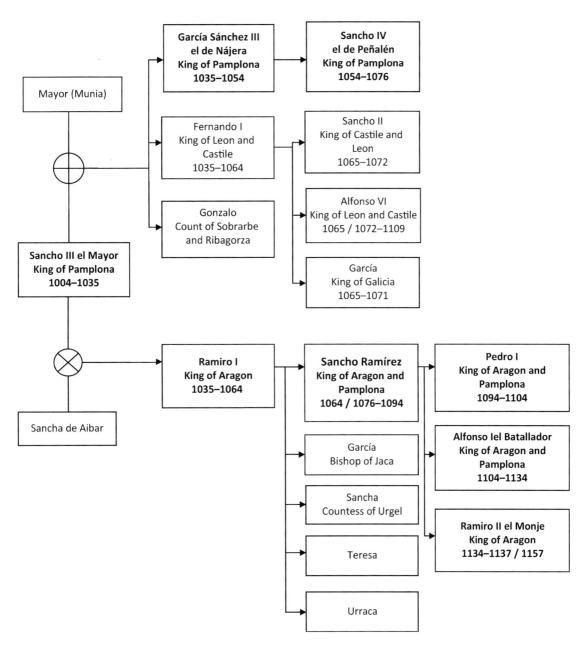

FIGURE 5.6

Family tree of the kings of Pamplona and Aragon 1004–1134

FIGURE 5.7

Corbel on the central apse of Jaca Cathedral (Javier Martinez de Aguirre)

of kingdom, as a seat for the bishopric of Aragon. Thus, he changed the legal status of Jaca from that of a free and independent *town* to that of *city*. The 1077 *fuero* expresses this with great solemnity: 'I, Sancho, by the grace of God King of the Aragonese and Pamplonese, hereby make it known to all men in the East, the West, the North and the South, that I wish to found a city in my town called Jaca.'[34] Jaca, by virtue of a palace already a royal seat, thus became an episcopal see. By this date, the Infante García, brother of Sancho Ramírez, had succeeded to the bishopric of Aragon.[35] García took another step towards the shaping of the cathedral see, in line with the winds of reform then prevailing in the Church. He established canonical life based on the Rule of Saint Augustine in a reform of the clergy responsible for San Pedro, the main church in Jaca. The change must have taken place between 1076 and 1079.[36] This could have been the moment that the idea of building a monumental church that departed from local tradition first took hold, though it wasn't until years later that we can be certain that work had started.

There is documentary proof that Santa Maria of Ujué (Navarre), whose architecture and sculpture indisputably derive from Jaca, was in building under the initiative of Sancho Ramírez in 1089.[37] This gives a *terminus ante quem* for the start of the cathedral of Jaca. Another significant landmark was the donation *ad labore* (sic) *de Sancti Petri de Iacha* contained in the disposal of assets made by the Infanta Urraca, sister of Sancho Ramírez, before the death of the king in 1094.[38] In this document the *infanta* refers to the bishop of Jaca as *meo magistro* and not as her or the king's brother, so this probably took place after the death of Bishop García in 1086. Consideration should also be given to one corbel of the east end (Figure 5.7), which Serafín Moralejo argued was carved by a member of the workshop of Bernardus Gilduinus at a time not too far removed from the consecration of the altar of Saint-Sernin in Toulouse in 1096.[39] Refining the chronology of the cathedral in more detail is no simple matter. It can be deduced that construction began in the 1080s, but we don't know whether this was before or after the death of Bishop-Infante in 1086. By way of conclusion, it is my opinion that the tower portico, which corresponds to a second project, was already standing before work began on San Pedro of Siresa in the 1110s.[40] As such, it is likely that the cathedral was planned and mostly built, during the bishoprics of the Infante García (1076–1086) and his successor, Pedro (1087–1099), the latter probably a former monk from San Juan de la Peña.[41]

A graphic recreation of Jaca cathedral around the year 1100 shows a highly distinctive church, characterised by a triple-apsed east end (Figure 5.8), a vaulted non-projecting transept, a ribbed crossing dome, and an aisled nave roofed in timber and reinforced by stone diaphragm arches (Figure 5.9), the remains of which have been recently discovered.[42] David Simon argued that the original interior was deliberately evocative of early Christian basilicas and suggested it may have been the outcome of a relationship that King Sancho Ramírez first established with the papacy on his journey to Rome in 1068 and which was re-established around 1087–1089.[43] In my opinion, Jaca is the Hispanic construction that best succeeds in recreating the architectural volumes and decoration of a Late Antique basilica and most strongly expresses the idea of the cathedral as a symbolic memorial to early Christian buildings – an association that Hélène Toubert, Valentino Pace and Arturo Carlo Quintavalle have applied to contemporary Italian buildings that were a product of Gregorian Reform.[44]

Nonetheless, the architecture is not the only key which might unlock the intentions behind the cathedral, nor reveal the identity of its principal patrons. Various scholars agree that the forms and themes of the sculpture at Jaca link it to royalty. The rich visual discourse represented by its tympana and capitals was organised in terms of political allegory. While not wishing to quote every author who has written on the subject, let us first remind ourselves that Dulce Ocón, Ruth Bartal, David Simon and Francisco de Asís García have all explored the relationships that link the Jaca chrismon (Figure 5.10) and Constantine's *Labarum* with respect to the warring vocation of the kings of Aragon.[45] Moralejo highlighted the donation that Sancho Ramírez made to Saint-Pons-de-Thomières in 1093, in which he compared himself to Abraham since he was also giving up his son Ramiro to God.[46] And Simon identified the presence of Moses on a capital on the west doorway (Figure 5.11) and related it to a papal bull addressed to Bishop García by Gregory VII, in which the pontiff called the king of Aragon a 'second Moses' for having introduced the Roman Rite (an act the Pope mistakenly attributed to Ramiro I).[47] Not only do I agree with this last identification, I would add that the side of the capital resembles the image of Gemini in San Isidoro of Leon.[48] Perhaps the capital was intended to draw attention to a parallel between the receipt of the Law by the brothers Moses and Aaron, and cooperation between the brothers, Sancho Ramírez and Bishop García, in introducing the *Lex Romana* and the rule of Saint Augustine to Jaca Cathedral.[49] Meanwhile, the choice of Abraham and Balaam as themes for the south doorway put Moralejo in mind of the descriptions of the Ishmaelites and Moabites used in the documentation of the time to refer, respectively, to the Moors and the Almoravids.[50] Finally, if we accept Moralejo's hypothesis

FIGURE 5.8

Hypothetical reconstruction of the east end of Jaca Cathedral (Marina and Javier Martínez de Aguirre)

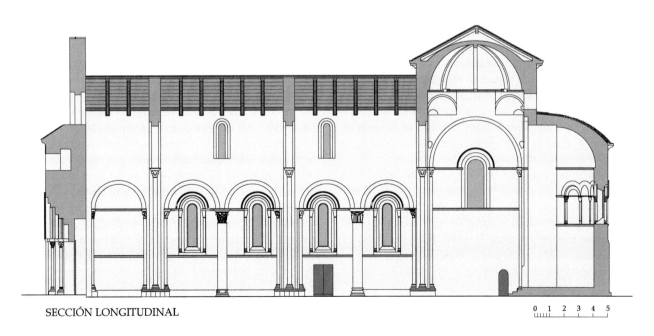

FIGURE 5.9

Hypothetical reconstruction of the section of Jaca Cathedral (Marina and Javier Martínez de Aguirre)

FIGURE 5.10

Tympanum of the west portal of Jaca Cathedral (Javier Martinez de Aguirre)

concerning another capital on the west doorway, which he identifies as Daniel and the Priests of Baal (Figure 5.12), we can see an allusion to the punishment of clerics who treat church assets as their own, a priestly vice that was explicitly condemned in the document describing the introduction of regular canonical life to Jaca.[51]

Thus, in contrast to Leire, Jaca encompasses a number of images that represent the king's thoughts on his role in the world, in both a military and a religious context. The signs and Old Testament scenes show in allegorical form what the king believed was his destiny as a vassal of God and the leader of a kingdom at war with the enemies of the faith. At first sight the emphasis on royal prerogatives and views would appear to relegate the bishop and the canons to a secondary role. In which case it would make no practical difference which prelate held the office of bishop, and the king's plans should not have been affected by conflict with his brother, Bishop García, in the years between 1080 and 1086.[52]

This said, the figurative programme of the cathedral is above all a religious one. Moreover, neither García nor Pedro always bent to the will of Sancho Ramírez, just as the king did not always uncomplainingly obey the pope. In a letter probably written in 1080, Richard, abbot of Saint-Victor of Marseille, one of Pope Gregory VII's legates, accused the king of seeking in his works the favour of men above the fear of God and salvation of souls.[53]

The inscriptions on the west tympanum unmistakably convey a religious intent. The chrismon that dominates this western entrance is not a sign of military victory – the *coeleste signum Dei* that, according to Lactantius, Constantine had put on the shields of his troops – but a Trinitarian sign of God: HAC IN SCULPTURA LECTOR SIC NOSCERE CVRA P PATER A GENITUS DUPLEX EST SPIRITUS ALMUS HII TRES IURE QUIDEM DOMINUS SUNT UNUS ET IDEM. Likewise, although their royal connotations cannot be denied, the lions that flank the chrismon here stand as the image of Jesus Christ: PARCERE STERNENTI LEO SCIT XPISTUSQUE PETENTI and IMPERIUM MORTIS CONCVLCANS EST LEO FORTIS. Taken as a whole, in accordance with the inscription underneath – VIVERE SI QUERIS QUI MORTIS LEGE TENERIS HVC SUPLICANDO VENI RENVENS FOMENTA VENENI COR VICIIS MUNDA PEREAS NE MORTE SECVNDA – the west doorway preaches Trinitarian dogma, the strength and mercy of Christ and the need for personal conversion for the salvation of the soul. It is a clerically formulated message destined for the faithful, one of whom was the monarch.

We are faced with a question of representation and connotation. The connotations relating to royalty are subordinate to the visual expression of the empire of God, and to the urgent task of establishing in society a life in keeping with the Gospel alongside the need for clerical reform, two of the ethical pillars of reformist popes and bishops. The religious connotations exist on a level with the monarchical ones. For example, episcopal authority can be seen in the relationship between the figure who prostrates himself at the feet of the lions and the ritual of public penitence, the episcopal prerogative practised in Aragonese dioceses up to the sixteenth century, as described by Antonio Durán Gudiol.[54] The figure who, according to this rite, stood in the position of the tympanum lion, with the penitent at his feet, was the bishop

FIGURE 5.11

Moses and Aaron, capital of the west portal of Jaca Cathedral (Javier Martinez de Aguirre)

FIGURE 5.12

Daniel holding the serpent Bel in front of Babylonian priests, capital of the west portal of Jaca Cathedral (Javier Martinez de Aguirre)

himself. Likewise, the virtue of humility is here exalted, as represented by the abasement of the prostrate figure. Simon reminds us that the serpent that this figure holds in his right hand also symbolises humility, manifest by its crawling and the constant shedding of its skin.[55]

The programme of the south doorway has attracted less attention, unsurprisingly given the drastic modification of the tympanum. However, Moralejo's reconstruction (Figure 5.13) is largely convincing, even though it is incomplete and his drawing does not entirely comply with what has been conserved.[56] The portal would have originally depicted a Christ in majesty, surrounded by symbols of the Evangelists. In order to support the lower semicircular stones, a trumeau would have been necessary, which, according to García, carried the David capital.[57] To either side are capitals dedicated to the sacrifice of Abraham and Balaam's Ass (Figures 5.14 and 5.15). In religious thinking, the doorway denotes the supreme sovereignty of Christ (greater than that of earthly kings), the transmission of doctrine through the Gospels, and the virtue of obedience. Abraham obeyed God when faced with an incomprehensible command. And the diviner, Balaam, sent by the king of the Moabites to curse the troops of Israel, that is, the troops of the Lord while they wandered through the desert, finally obeyed God, who sent his angel to stop the donkey. At the feet of Christ, David leads the song of praise to the Lord, accompanied by the Levites.

Christians are here seen as sons of Abraham because of their faith (as opposed to Muslims, known at the time as Ishmaelites, who were descended from the illegitimate lineage of Abraham), and Balaam as the diviner who ends up praising the Lord of the Israelites (the same Lord as for Christians) also correspond to the realm of political allegory. Indeed, the exaltation of humility exhibited at both doorways deserves a political interpretation. As Cowdrey pointed out, for Gregory VII obedience and humility were virtually synonymous. 'At his heart was obedience to the law and to the righteousness of God and to the admonitions of those upon earth who were his accredited spokesmen – especially to the Roman church and to the pope. (. . .) In Gregory's eyes, humility was, above all, the distinguishing virtue of a good king. (. . .) If King Saul was his exemplar of disobedience to the world of God (. . .) King David showed how humility won the favour of God. Another exemplar of humility was the Emperor Constantine'.[58]

The evident congruence of Jaca's programme and Gregory VII's views on the characteristic virtues of kings and emperors reveals the extent to which Jaca was imbued with reformist ideology. The abundance of scenes from the Old Testament is one of the repeating patterns found in programmes connected with the Gregorian

FIGURE 5.13

Hypothetical reconstruction of the south portal of Jaca Cathedral (Serafín Moralejo)

FIGURE 5.14

Sacrifice of Isaac, capital of the south portal of Jaca Cathedral (Javier Martinez de Aguirre)

FIGURE 5.15

Balaam, the donkey, and the angel, capital of the south portal of Jaca Cathedral (Javier Martinez de Aguirre)

Reform.[59] A Benedictine component is also visible. Chapter five of Benedict's Rule, the first to spell out the virtues of the monk, is dedicated to obedience. It begins by affirming that 'the first degree of humility is obedience without delay', while chapter seven defines humility, and is by far the longest chapter of the Rule.

The programme at Jaca is therefore the product of a cultivated mind that knew the Scriptures in depth, fought to defend papal and reformist principles, and may have had a Benedictine background. Would this profile fit the king or a member of his entourage, the bishop, or a member of the chapter? To deal with the king first, the actions of Sancho Ramírez with respect to the papacy and the Church cannot be described in terms of submission and the defence of reformist principles at any cost. Over the three decades of his reign, Sancho adapted to circumstances and attempted to benefit the kingdom and himself ahead of the Church, or at least achieve a mutual benefit for himself, the kingdom and the Church.[60] He was not a staunch defender of ecclesiastical independence with respect to temporal power, as was demonstrated in numerous episodes. One involves another Sancho, bishop of Aragon (1058–1075), who, according to a letter from Gregory VII, went to Rome to ask the pope to accept his resignation due to ill health. His resignation was refused because the two clerics that were proposed as replacements, both with the blessing of King Sancho Ramírez, were sons of concubines and did not fulfil the requisite canonical conditions.[61] It clearly mattered little to the king that he despatched his bishop with proposals that went against the spirit and letter of the reform. A second episode involved the bishopric of Pamplona. Following the death of Bishop Blasco Gardéliz in 1078, the king put first his brother and then his sister Sancha in charge of the bishopric.[62] This was completely at odds with the Church's independence with respect to civil power. We could continue with numerous examples of religious rents being exploited by the monarch himself, or by Aragonese nobles with the king's blessing. The above examples shed reasonable doubt on Sancho Ramírez's intervention in the design of a programme that mainly focused on the conversion of the faithful and was expressed in texts and images of a clearly ecclesiastical nature.

Little can be said about Jaca's chapter between 1080 and 1090 as we do not know the intellectual background of its members. Durán Gudiol cites a 12th-century memorial to the effect that after the death of the Bishop García 'the canons of Jaca (. . .) hoped to avoid a bishop-monk being imposed on them' which in the end was what happened.[63] In my opinion, this also rules them out as creators of a programme with so many reformist and monastic connotations.

As for Bishop García, his background would have attuned him to the king's objectives and royal image. He was appointed by the king, apparently without the blessing of the papal legate (which again casts doubt on the unswerving loyalty of both brothers to the reform movement). His main contribution to reform was to establish a communal life – *comunem vitam . . . secundum institucionem sancti patris nostri Augustini* – for the chapter at Jaca around 1076–1079.[64] But, as well as being a papal objective, chapter reform was part of the ecclesiastical policy of previous Hispanic monarchs, such as Ferdinand I, King of Castile and Leon and uncle of Sancho Ramírez. This had been agreed in the first canon of the Council of Coyanza in 1050, convened by Ferdinand *ad restaurationem nostrae Christianitatis*.[65] A final factor that weakens García's potential as a formative contributor to the cathedral, at least to its figurative programme, is the confrontation he had with his brother, King Sancho Ramírez. The first sign of disagreement can be traced back by to a letter from the papal legate Ricardo to Sancho Ramírez dated 1080 (although according to an account in a 12th-century memorial the events took place in 1082).[66] Durán contends that this confrontation reached a critical stage in 1083, when the king commanded his brother the bishop *cum magna conminatione* not to return to Alquézar if he 'valued the eyes in his head'. In 1085, at the siege of Zaragoza, Alfonso VI of Castile and Leon, Sancho Ramírez's adversary, even promised García the bishopric of Toledo, which, had it been accepted, would have entailed the bishop's departure from the kingdom of Aragon, along with his entourage. The brothers finally settled their disagreements in 1086, shortly before García's death.[67] After this, the papal legate, Frotardo, hastened to install Pedro as bishop in Jaca, where he occupied the cathedra until 1099.[68] In short, it is impossible to see Bishop García as a champion of reformist thinking as it was envisioned by Gregory VII between 1073 and 1085.

What we know of Bishop Pedro very much corresponds to the profile we have drawn out from the programme. There is no doubt that he supported the principles of the Gregorian Reform. He was directly appointed by the papal legate Frotardo, one of its fiercest proponents. It has also been suggested that Bishop Pedro was previously a monk from the Benedictine monastery of San Juan de la Peña, which was at the forefront of the reformist movement in Aragon. It was there that the Roman Liturgy had been introduced in 1071, liturgical unification being another objective of the reformist popes.[69] In 1084, Abbot Sancho sent an expedition to Almería to search for the relics of Saint Indalecius, one of seven 'apostles' who, according to legendary accounts known by Gregory VII, preached the Gospel in the Iberian Peninsula.[70] This initiative formed part of the reformist desire to return the Church to the times of Christ and his immediate successors; in a list of 12th-century relics from San Juan de la Peña, Saint Indalecius was identified as 'one of the sixty-two disciples of Jesus Christ'.[71] The capital with Daniel and Habakkuk from the enlargement of the church consecrated in 1094 demonstrates that San Juan de la Peña and Jaca cathedral shared sculptural forms and content in the late 1080s or early 1090s.[72]

If Bishop Pedro was the master iconographer and designer of the programme, then Sancho Ramírez's role in the figurative programme of Jaca Cathedral moves to the other side of the mirror. The tympana and capitals would not be political allegories proposed *by* the sovereign but *for* him. The monarch's documents were full of expressions of submission to God and the saints. As a good Christian, he was concerned for his final destiny. So, the proposed political allegories and images of humility and obedience would be well received, especially in the years in which the king renewed his vassalage to God and Saint Peter (around 1087–1089).[73] Moreover, Bishop Pedro was acting in the name of the legate, Frotardo, whose influence on Sancho Ramírez has been noted by Paul Kehr.[74] However, we cannot rule out the possibility that the king had previous knowledge of the programme and had given his blessing to it. A potentially harmonious relationship with Bishop Pedro and the cathedral clergy in everything that concerned religious worship in the cathedral could be the idea behind the south doorway capital of David and the Levites (Figure 5.16), for the Levites accompany the king on 'instruments which (the king) made for giving praise' (1 Chr 23, 5). One way or another, Sancho Ramírez probably did more than simply provide the financial means for finishing the great cathedral, something he yearned to do for 'his' city, Jaca, and his expanding kingdom.

To conclude, let us return to the arguments used to link the documents of Sancho Ramírez and Pedro I with the chrismon and with the capitals of Moses and Abraham. Could the texts have been the effect rather than the cause of the sculpture? The donation to Saint-Pons-de-Thomières, which compares the king to Abraham, dates from 1093, while the verbal equivalent of the tympanum of the chrismon can be found at the beginning of the endowment documents of San Juan de la Peña on the day of its consecration, the fourth of December, 1094.[75] Although the Trinitarian Invocation is a recurring theme in Aragonese and Pamplonese documentation in the 11th century, the 1094 consecration preamble glorifies in the mystery of the dogma like none other: *In nomine sancte et individue Trinitatis, inmensa et alma Trinitatis, qui est Pater et Filius et Spiritus Sanctus, una et coequalis esentia, sub divino imperioque Domini Nostri Ihesu Christi.* Both mentions open the way to speculation on the impact the Jaca doorways might have had on their contemporaries. At the same time, they raise a case – not a very solid one, I'll admit – for the building of the doorways at around this time. With respect to Gregory VII's comparison between the King of Aragon and Moses, let's remember that this is contained in a letter addressed to Garcia as Bishop of Jaca, not the king.[76] As it was kept in the cathedral archives, Bishop Pedro could have known about it and taken it into consideration when this part of the programme was designed.

PAMPLONA: KING PEDRO AND BISHOP PEDRO

Various reliable documents refer to the intervention of Kings Pedro I (1094–1104) and Alfonso I the Battler (1104–1134) in the construction of Pamplona Cathedral, in addition to Bishops Pedro de Rodez (1083–1115), Guillermo (1115–1122) and Sancho de Larrosa (1122–1142). These provide chronological milestones that mark the process and progress of building: a papal bull from Pope Urban II speaks of the new building project in 1097; the work was mentioned in a royal document in 1099; an inscription on a doorway alluded to the beginning of construction in 1100; the bishop made donations to the architect for his good service in 1101 and 1107; and Paschal II exhorted the king to help finish the cathedral in 1114.[77] Consecration of the cathedral took place in 1127.[78]

FIGURE 5.16

King David and his musicians, capital likely from the south portal of Jaca Cathedral (Javier Martinez de Aguirre)

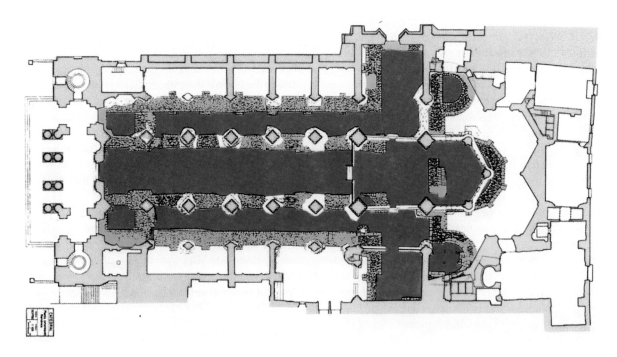

FIGURE 5.17

Foundations of the Romanesque church of Pamplona Cathedral (Mezquíriz and Tabar [1994])

FIGURE 5.18

Façade of the Romanesque canons' residence of Pamplona Cathedral (Javier Martinez de Aguirre)

There seems no doubt that direct and almost exclusive responsibility for the project was taken by Bishop Pedro de Rodez (Pierre d'Andouque). His name alone appears on the documents that mention the architect Esteban. Educated at Conques and Saint-Pons-de-Thomières, Pedro took the crusader vow at Clermont in November, 1095 and was present in Toulouse at the consecration of Saint-Sernin by Urban II in May, 1096. He therefore had first-hand experience of some of the great churches then under construction north of the Pyrenees, and he would later go to Santiago de Compostela where he consecrated one of the chapels of the ambulatory in 1105.[79] It is perhaps as a result of his wider knowledge of building that he embarked on a cathedral of such magnificent scale at Pamplona: more than 70 metres long and more than forty metres wide at the transepts (Figure 5.17).

As for King Pedro I, in addition to Urban II's 1097 missive, in which the king and his subjects were exhorted to help in the cathedral's construction, one reference seems to have been rather neglected in the recent literature. Pedro donated a piece of land by the river Salado for the purpose of building a mill 'for the construction of the said church of Santa María'.[80] Otherwise, according to Ubieto's itinerary, the king was in Pamplona just once after 1100, in December, 1103, which rather rules out the notion that he was closely involved in work on the building.[81]

Pedro de Rodez was the first bishop of Pamplona who is known to have come from outside Navarre, Aragon or La Rioja.[82] As at Jaca, the bishop reformed the chapter (in 1086, before he undertook the building of the new church). Another similarity is that he was appointed bishop in the time of Sancho Ramírez by the papal legate Frotardo, who had been his superior at Saint-Pons de Thomières. He was a supporter of the Gregorian Reform and was described by Urban II as 'a religious man of venerable life.'[83] Pedro began building at Pamplona with the construction of the canons' residence, a structure which has partially survived to this day.[84] This was finished in 1097 and it combined masonry typical of local stonemasons with portal sculpture reminiscent of Toulouse (Figure 5.18). He then began construction of the cathedral, a visual manifesto for a reform upon which the diocese had embarked – led by French clerics. José Goñi Gaztambide talks of the 'Frankish ecclesiastical invasion' when referring to Pamplona's chapter of canons in the time of Pedro de Rodez, when up to fifteen figures originating from the other side of the Pyrenees can be identified.[85]

Unlike the radically innovative character of Leire and Jaca, Pamplona Cathedral was a variation on architectural formulas that were spreading on both sides of the

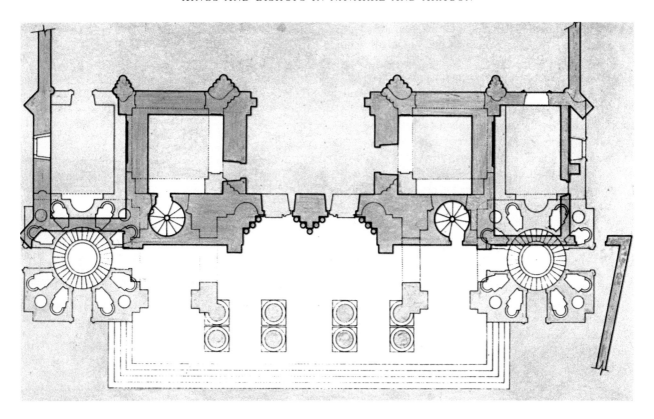

FIGURE 5.19

Project of Ventura Rodríguez for the façade of Pamplona Cathedral with the drawing of Romanesque west portal (Fernando Redón Huici)

Pyrenees at that time. The foundations were uncovered during excavations between 1990 and 1992.[86] The east end consisted of three separate apses. The lateral apses opened onto the centre of the respective arms of the transept, while the principal was polygonal on the exterior (with seven faces) and semicircular on the interior, in which we can recognise a variant of the design of the cathedral of Santiago de Compostela.[87] The west doorway consisted of two openings and eleven columns, as with the Portico de la Platerías at Santiago (Figure 5.19). The five capitals that have been conserved confirm the direct relationship with the Galician cathedral. The surviving sculpture is insufficient to determine whether the representational wealth and narrative complexity found on the portals at Santiago was imitated at Pamplona. Nevertheless, enough survives for us to conclude that the details of the project could reflect the architect's training, while the architectural ambition expressed on a broader scale could originate from guidelines laid down by the bishop.

How was the money needed for such a massive church acquired? It is not known how the monarchs responded to papal requests for help in its construction and there is hardly any record of extra rents offered by those holding power, except for a donation from Urraca de Zamora, daughter of Ferdinand I, in 1100.[88] Bishop Pedro knew how to collect large amounts made up of small contributions by the faithful, who, in return, were given the right to be buried in the cloister.[89] A noteworthy benefactor of the new church was the *confratria* or brotherhood, specifically mentioned in the papal exhortations of 1097 and 1114 as receiving the absolution and blessing of the pontiffs in return for helping to build the church.[90] This clearly doesn't refer to the chapter since the documents cite the canons by name (*clericorum regulariter uiuencium/canonicorum regulariter ibi uiuentium*), but refers instead to a group with open membership (*quicumque in prefati ecclesie confratria fuerint annotati*) whose collaboration was probably limited to the sphere of finance. Unfortunately, there are no further references in Pamplona to this medieval form of 'crowdfunding', possibly imported by Pedro de Rodez from building projects outside the kingdom of Navarre. Brotherhoods dedicated to the construction and maintenance of Romanesque churches are recorded somewhat later in other parts of Navarre, as at Roncesvalles, Estella and Eunate, which presumably followed the cathedral model.[91]

CONCLUSION

To summarise, with respect to the establishment of Romanesque architecture in the kingdoms of Aragon and Pamplona, there are three crucial buildings where one can see the interests of kings and bishops coming together. Given the mutual benefits implicit in the new constructions, interaction was close and continuous. However, the projects did not fully integrate crown and mitre because:

a) The kings did not play the prominent role that historiography would have us believe. Their ambition in the architectural field seems not to have been very specific and was primarily focussed on the external aspects of building, in other words, monumentality. Only Sancho Ramírez may have played a greater role as instigator – and even then as a recipient rather that of an ideologue – in the figurative programme of Jaca Cathedral.

b) The three buildings examined here are linked to bishops who either originated in more artistically advanced centres or had received training in environments favourable to innovation.

c) A determining factor in all cases was the intervention of prelates who supported ecclesiastical reform movements, with the result that the new constructions became monumental manifestos for the new paths taken by their respective institutions.

d) With regard to any distinction between the actions of laity and clergy, these three examples suggest that the effective promotion of church building, along with the design of figurative programmes, in the decades leading up to 1100 was a sphere of action led by clerics, at least in Navarre and Aragon – even in cases where we find political allegories linked to sovereigns.

ACKNOWLEDGEMENTS

The research published here formed part of the project 'Arte y reformas religiosas en la España medieval', financed by the Ministerio de Economía y Competitividad HAR2012–38037. I would like to express my gratitude to John McNeill for his careful consideration of my paper and for his many valuable remarks improving it.

NOTES

[1] J. Fontaine, *L'art préroman hispanique. L'art mozarabe* (La Pierre-qui-vire 1967), 255; S. de Silva y Verástegui, *Iconografía del siglo X en el Reino de Pamplona-Nájera* (Pamplona 1984), 158–61; J. Martínez de Aguirre, 'Creación de imágenes al servicio de la monarquía', in *Signos de identidad histórica para Navarra*, ed., A.J. Martín Duque (Pamplona 1996), 187–202; M. Poza Yagüe, 'El conjunto relivario de San Miguel de Villatuerta', in *Sancho el Mayor y sus herederos. El linaje que europeizó los reinos hispanos*, ed., I.G. Bango Torviso (Pamplona 2006), 609–13.

[2] IN DE . . . LO DNI SCI MIKAELI DNO SANCIO RE / INMNE DNI NSI IHV XPI / SCI MIKAEL DNO BLASCIO / DNO SANCIO ACTO NOMEN MAG / ESTR (. . .) FECIT. BELENGERES / ESCRIPSI. There are slightly different transcriptions in T. Biurrun, *El arte románico en Navarra* (Pamplona 1936), 37–39; J.M. Lacarra and J. Gudiol, 'El primer románico en Navarra', *Príncipe de Viana*, V (1944), 260; G. de Pamplona, 'La fecha de la construcción de San Miguel de Villatuerta, y las derivaciones de su nueva cronología', *Príncipe de Viana*, XV (1954), 221; and J.E. Uranga Galdiano and F. Íñiguez Almech, *Arte medieval navarro. Volumen Primero. Arte prerrománico* (Pamplona 1971), 115–16.

[3] A.J. Martín Duque, *Documentación Medieval de Leire (siglos IX a XII)* (Pamplona 1983), doc. 53.

[4] Ibid., 'Inter ea proles semper desiderans uidere illam dedicationem domus Sancti Salvatoris necnon sanctarum uirginum Nunilonis atque Elodiae.'

[5] Ibid., 'Deinde ego inuitatus domino meo Iohanne episcopo ac omni congregatione Legioris, accessi illuc per celebracionem illius sacracionis.'

[6] J. Martínez de Aguirre, 'La nave gótica de Leire: evidencias para una nueva cronología', *Archivo Español de Arte*, 253 (1991), 51–52; J. Martínez de Aguirre and F. Menéndez Pidal, *Emblemas heráldicos en el arte medieval navarro* (Pamplona 1996), 194.

[7] P. de Madrazo, 'San Salvador de Leyre, panteón de los reyes de Navarra', *Museo Español de Antigüedades*, V (1885), 207–33; E. Bertaux, 'La sculpture chrétienne en Espagne', in *Histoire de l'Art*, ed. A. Michel (Paris 1906), II, 256; V. Lampérez y Romea, *Historia de la arquitectura cristiana española en la Edad Media según el estudio de los elementos y los monumentos* (Madrid 1930), II, 222–26.

[8] M. Gómez Moreno, *El arte románico español. Esquema de un libro* (Madrid 1934), 150–52.

[9] J.M. Lacarra and J. Gudiol, 'El primer románico en Navarra', *Príncipe de Viana*, IV (1944), 221–72.

[10] Ibid., 230.

[11] J. Gudiol Ricart and J.A. Gaya Nuño, *Arquitectura y escultura románicas*, Ars Hispaniae, V (Madrid 1948), 121; G. Gaillard, 'La escultura del siglo XI en Navarra antes de las peregrinaciones', *Príncipe de Viana*, XVII (1956), 125; M. Durliat, *El arte románico en España* (Barcelona 1964), 70–71; L.M. de Lojendio, *Navarre romane* (La Pierre-qui-vire 1967), 71–73.

[12] F. Íñiguez Almech, 'El monasterio de San Salvador de Leyre', *Príncipe de Viana*, XXVII (1966), 189–220; idem, 'Las empresas constructivas de Sancho el Mayor. El castillo de Loarre', *Archivo Español de Arte*, XLIII (1970), 363–73; J.E. Uranga Galdiano and F. Íñiguez Almech, *Arte medieval navarro. Volumen Segundo. Arte románico* (Pamplona 1973), 41–51; J. Martínez de Aguirre, 'Hacia la monumentalización del reino', in *Signos de identidad histórica para Navarra*, ed., A.J. Martín Duque (Pamplona 1996), 281; J. Mann, 'A New Architecture for a New Order. The Building Projects of Sancho el Mayor (1004–1035)', in *The White Mantle of Churches. Architecture, Liturgy and Art around the Millenium*, ed., N. Hiscock (Turnhout 2003), 233–48; eadem, *Romanesque Architecture and Its Sculptural Decoration in Christian Spain: Exploring Frontiers and Defining Identities, 1000–1120* (Toronto 2009), 46–74.

[13] J. Martínez de Aguirre, 'L'art au temps de Sancho el Mayor: Leire', *Les Cahiers de Saint-Michel de Cuxa*, XL (2009), 237–50.

[14] J. Goñi Gaztambide, *Historia de los obispos de Pamplona I. Siglos IV–XIII* (Pamplona 1979), 160–87.

[15] 'Fuit etiam in remotis partibus occidentalium alter Sancius, Pampulanorum episcopus, qui ita sibi in amicitiis adhaesit et copiosis muneribus deservit, ut ad eum etiam de tam longinquis regionibus venire, et monachum se ab eo fieri decerneret. Quem intantum dulcis memoriae Odilo dilexit, ut etiam moriens de eo mentionem faceret, et post mortem suam ad eum visitandum, cum exuviis vestimentorum suorum duos fratres mitteret, qui illi finem vitae suae nuntiarent, et antiquam amicitiam sibi mortuo conciliarent, et rursum eandem a viventibus renovarent': J-P. Migne, *PL*, 142 (Paris 1853), 902.

[16] Íñiguez, *Leyre* (as n. 12), 193, supposes its destruction by Caliph's army, but as far as we know their attacks never damaged the monastery.

[17] J.M. Lacarra, 'Textos navarros del Códice de Roda', *Estudios de Edad Media de la Corona de Aragón*, 1 (Zaragoza 1945), 259.

[18] L.J. Fortún, 'Leire', *Sedes reales de Navarra* (Pamplona 1991), 275–95; idem, *Leyre, un señorío monástico en Navarra (siglos IX–XIX)* (Pamplona 1993), 86–89.

[19] J. Martínez de Aguirre, 'El primer intento de un románico monumental: Leire', *El arte románico en Navarra* (Pamplona 2002), 61–70; idem, 'Monasterio de San Salvador de Leire', *Enciclopedia del Románico en Navarra* (Aguilar de Campoo 2008), III, 1517.

[20] J. Goñi Gaztambide, *Colección diplomática de la Catedral de Pamplona. Tomo I (829–1243)* (Pamplona 1997), 34–35. On the Romanesque church of Zamarce, see J. Martínez de Aguirre, 'Ermita de Santa María de Zamarce / Zamartze', *Enciclopedia del Románico en Navarra* (Aguilar de Campoo 2008), II, 668–82.

[21] Mann, 'New Architecture' (as n. 12), 237.

[22] G. Gaillard, 'Escultura' (as n. 11), 123.

[23] J. Cabanot, 'Les débuts de la sculpture romane en Navarre : San Salvador de Leyre', *Les Cahiers de Saint-Michel de Cuxa*, 9 (1978), 21–50; idem, *Les débuts de la sculpture romane dans le Sud-Ouest de la France* (Paris 1987), 39–54.

²⁴ J.M. Lacarra, *Historia política del reino de Navarra desde sus orígenes hasta su incorporación a Castilla* (Pamplona 1972), I, 200–01.

²⁵ 'Rogamus praeterea ut hos missos, quos dominus Santius episcopus et nos mittimus, usque ad sanctum Joannem conducatis. Vult enim domnus episcopus sua omnia quae ibi dimisit, secum habere. Argentum, ut opus quod in nomine ipsius et in nomine regis defuncti super altare sancti Petri coepimus, ad perpetuum memoriale sui, et supra dicti regis perficiat': J-P. Migne, *PL*, 142 (Paris 1853), 942.

²⁶ A. Ubieto Arteta, 'La catedral románica de Jaca. Problemas de cronología', *Pirineos*, XVII–XVIII (1961–62), 125–37; idem, 'El románico de la catedral de Jaca y su cronología', *Príncipe de Viana*, XXV (1964), 187–200. The former attribution in R. de Huesca, *Teatro histórico de las Iglesias del Reyno de Aragón. Tomo VIII. De la Santa Iglesia de Jaca* (Pamplona 1802), 97; J.M. Quadrado, *Recuerdos y bellezas de España. Aragón* (Barcelona 1844), 175; Gómez Moreno, *Arte románico* (as n. 8), 66.

²⁷ J.F. Esteban Lorente, 'La metrología de la catedral de Jaca: 1', *Artigrama*, 14 (1999), 241–62; idem, 'La metrología de la catedral de Jaca: 2', *Artigrama*, 15 (2000), 231–58; idem., 'La metrología y sus consecuencias en las iglesias de la Alta Edad Media Española. IV. El románico del último tercio del siglo XI', *Artigrama*, 23 (2008), 388; F. Galtier Martí, 'La catedral de Jaca y el románico jaqués', in *Comarca de la Jacetania*, ed., J.L. Ona González y S. Sánchez Lanaspa (Zaragoza 2004), 138; B. Cabañero, 'Precedentes musulmanes y primer arte cristiano', in *Las Cinco Villas aragonesas en la Europa de los siglos XII y XIII: de la frontera natural a las fronteras políticas y socioeconómicas (foralidad y municipalidad)*, ed., E. Sarasa Sánchez (Zaragoza 2007), 231–32.

²⁸ J. Martínez de Aguirre, 'Arquitectura y soberanía. La catedral de Jaca y otras empresas constructivas de Sancho Ramírez', *Anales de Historia del Arte. Alfonso VI y el arte de su época. Vol. Extr., diciembre 2011*, 194–97.

²⁹ Ubieto, 'Románico' (as n. 26); S. Moralejo, 'La sculpture romane de la cathédrale de Jaca. État des questions', *Les Cahiers de Saint-Michel de Cuxa*, 10 (1979), 79–85; M. Durliat, *La sculpture romane de la route de Saint-Jacques. De Conques à Compostelle* (Dax 1990), 220–24; D.L. Simon, *La catedral de Jaca y su escultura. Ensayo* (Jaca 1997), 5–12; M.C. Lacarra Ducay, *Catedral y Museo Diocesano de Jaca* (Brussels 1993), 13–14.

³⁰ Gómez Moreno, *Arte románico* (as n. 8), 75; Moralejo, 'Sculpture' (as n. 29), 80.

³¹ Perhaps that masonry joint was simply part of the preparation for stopping building work over the winter, given that later a new master builder took over and introduced constructional changes.

³² A. Ubieto Arteta, *Orígenes de los reinos de Castilla y Aragón* (Zaragoza 1991), 176; M.D. Cabanes Pecourt, 'Diplomas y cancillería', in *Sancho Ramírez, rey de Aragón y su tiempo (1064–1094)*, ed., E. Sarasa Sánchez (Huesca 1994), 37.

³³ R. Jimeno Aranguren and A. Pescador Medrano, *Colección documental de Sancho Garcés III, el Mayor, rey de Pamplona (1004–1035)* (Pamplona 2003), doc. 78. Lacarra, *Historia* (as n. 24), I, 232–33.

³⁴ A. Ubieto Arteta, *Jaca: documentos municipales 971–1269* (Valencia 1975), 49.

³⁵ Garcia became bishop in 1076. J. Gavira Martín, *Episcopologios de sedes navarro-aragonesas durante los siglos XI y XII* (Madrid 1929), 44–48.

³⁶ A. Durán Gudiol, *La Iglesia de Aragón durante los reinados de Sancho Ramírez y Pedro I (1062?-1104)* (Rome 1962), 38–40. Augustine is mentioned four times in the earliest transcription of the charter, (Huesca, Archivo de la Catedral, 9–63), which dates from the beginning of 12th century. See below and note 64.

³⁷ A. Canellas López, *Colección Diplomática de Sancho Ramírez* (Zaragoza, 1993), 105–08; J. Martínez de Aguirre, 'Arquitectura medieval', in *Santa María de Ujué*, ed., M.R. Lazcano Martínez de Morentin (Pamplona 2011), 74.

³⁸ A. Ubieto Arteta, *Cartulario de Santa Cruz de la Serós* (Valencia 1966), 22–23.

³⁹ S. Moralejo, 'Une sculpture du style de Bernard Gilduin à Jaca', *Bull. mon.*, 131–131 (1973), 7–16.

⁴⁰ J. Martínez de Aguirre, E. Lozano López and Diana Lucía Gómez-Chacón, 'San Pedro de Siresa y Alfonso el Batallador', in *Monumentos singulares del románico. Nuevas lecturas sobre formas y usos*, ed., P.L. Huerta Huerta (Aguilar de Campoo 2012), 170.

⁴¹ Gavira, *Episcopologios* (as n. 35), 44–53; Durán, *Iglesia* (as n. 36), 51–52.

⁴² J. Martínez de Aguirre, 'The Architecture of Jaca Cathedral: The Project and its Impact', in *Cathedrals in Mediterranean Europe, Architecture, Ritual and Urban Context,* ed. G. Boto Varela (Turnhout 2016), 153–68.

⁴³ Simon, *Catedral* (as n. 29), 14–17.

⁴⁴ H. Toubert, *Un art dirigé. Réforme grégorienne et iconographie* (Paris 2007), 8; V. Pace, 'La Riforma e i suoi programmi figurativi: il caso romano, fra realtà storica e mito storiografico', in *Roma e la Riforma gregoriana. Tradizione e innovazioni artistiche (XI–XII secolo)*, ed. S. Romano and J. Enckell (Rome 2007), 50; A.C. Quintavalle, 'The Gregorian Reform and the Origins of Romanesque', in *Compostela and Europe: The Story of Diego Gelmírez*, ed., M. Castiñeiras (Milan 2010), 219–20.

⁴⁵ D. Ocón Alonso, 'Problemática del crismón trinitario', *Archivo Español de Arte*, LXI (1983), 260; eadem, 'El sello de Dios sobre la Iglesia: tímpanos con crismón en Navarra y Aragón', in *El tímpano románico. Imágenes, estructuras, audiencias*, ed. R. Sánchez Ameijeiras and J.L. Senra Gabriel y Galán (Santiago de Compostela 2003), 95–101; R. Bartal, 'The survival of early Christian symbols in 12th-Century Spain', *Príncipe de Viana*, XLVIII (1987) 299–315; D.L. Simon, 'El tímpano de la catedral de Jaca', *Congreso de Historia de la Corona de Aragón Jaca 1993. Actas t. III* (Zaragoza 1994), 417; ídem, *Catedral* (as n. 29) 20; F. de A. García García, 'Dogma, ritual y contienda: arte y frontera en el reino de Aragón a finales del siglo XI', in *Fronteras en discusión. La Península Ibérica en el siglo XII*, ed. J. Martos Quesada and M. Bueno Sánchez (Madrid 2012), 217–50.

⁴⁶ S. Moralejo, 'Le origini del programa iconografico dei portali nel Romanico spagnolo', *Atti del Convegno: Wiligelmo e Lanfranco nell'Europa romanica, Modena 24–27 ott. 1985* (Modena 1989), 37.

⁴⁷ D.L Simon, 'A Moses capital at Jaca', *Imágenes y promotores en el arte medieval. Miscelánea en homenaje a Joaquín Yarza Luaces*, ed. M.L. Melero (Bellaterra 2001), 209–19.

⁴⁸ Martínez de Aguirre, *Arquitectura y soberanía* (as n. 28), 225–27. Some damaged Zodiaque reliefs have been found recently in Jaca Cathedral: A. García Omedes 'El zodíaco de la catedral de Jaca', *Románico. Revista de arte de amigos del románico (AdR)*, 16 (2013), 32–39.

⁴⁹ The tympanum's inscription includes two words related to law: *iure* and *lege*: Martínez de Aguirre, 'Arquitectura y soberanía' (as n. 28), 224–25.

⁵⁰ Moralejo, 'Origini' (as n. 46), 38–39.

⁵¹ S. Moralejo, 'Aportaciones a la interpretación del programa iconográfico de la catedral de Jaca', in *Homenaje a don José María Lacarra de Miguel en su jubilación del profesorado. Estudios medievales* (Zaragoza 1977), 189–90.

⁵² If the west doorway had been built in the time of Bishop Pedro (1086–99), the programme would have had a retrospective component, and the capital showing Moses would have commemorated the time when Sancho Ramirez and García acted in step with each other for the benefit of the Church. P. Kehr, 'Cómo y cuándo se hizo Aragón feudatario de la Santa Sede. Estudio diplomático', *Estudios de Edad Media de la Corona de Aragón. Vol. 1* (Zaragoza, 1945), 311; D. Buesa Conde, *Sancho Ramírez, rey de aragoneses y pamploneses (1064–1094)* (Zaragoza 1996), 160–69.

⁵³ Durán, *Iglesia* (as n. 36), 41.

⁵⁴ Moralejo, 'Aportaciones' (as n. 51), 184–88; Moralejo, 'Sculpture' (as n. 29), 94–97. S.H. Caldwell, 'Penance, Baptism, Apocalypse: The Easter context of Jaca Cathedral's west tympanum', *Art History*, 3 (1980), 25–40. On public penitence in Aragon see, A. Durán Gudiol, 'La penitencia pública en la catedral de Huesca', *Argensola: Revista de Ciencias Sociales del Instituto de Estudios Altoaragoneses*, 12 (1952), 335–46.

⁵⁵ Simon, 'Tímpano' (as n. 45), 411–15.

⁵⁶ Moralejo, 'Sculpture' (as n. 29), 99–105.

⁵⁷ García, 'Dogma' (as n. 45), 234, n. 80. Gómez Moreno suggested the existence of a trumeau, which Moralejo consideró unnecessary: Gómez Moreno, *Arte románico* (as n. 8), 74; Moralejo, 'Sculpture' (as n. 29), 100.

⁵⁸ H.E.J. Cowdrey, *Pope Gregory VII 1073–1085* (Oxford 1998), 558.

⁵⁹ Toubert, *Art dirigé* (as n. 44), 187–88.

⁶⁰ L. García-Guijarro Ramos, 'El papado y el reino de Aragón en la segunda mitad del siglo XI', *Aragón en la Edad Media. XVIII* (Zaragoza 2004), 245–64.

⁶¹ P. Kehr, *Papsturkunden in Spanien. Vorarbeiten zur Hispania Pontificia II. Navarra und Aragon* (Berlin 1928), 265–67; A. Ubieto Arteta, 'La introducción del rito romano en Aragón y en Navarra', *Hispania Sacra*, 1 (1948), 311–13; F. Balaguer, 'Los límites del obispado de Aragón y el concilio de Jaca de 1063', *Estudios de Edad Media de la Corona de Aragón. 4* (Zaragoza 1950), 119–21; Durán, *Iglesia* (as n. 36), 30–32; Buesa, *Sancho Ramírez* (as n. 52), 152–54.

⁶² Goñi, *Obispos* (as n. 14), 224–27.

⁶³ Durán, *Iglesia* (as n. 36), 51.

⁶⁴ Durán, *Iglesia* (as n. 36), 38–40. The document (with a Spanish translation) was published by D. Sangorrín y Diest-Garcés, *El Libro de la Cadena del Concejo de Jaca. Documentos Reales, Episcopales y Municipales de los siglos X, XI, XII, XIII y XIV* (Zaragoza 1920), 63–73.

⁶⁵ A. García-Gallo de Diego, 'El Concilio de Coyanza. Contribución al estudio del Derecho Canónico español en la Alta Edad Media', *Anuario de Historia del Derecho español*, 20 (1950), 290.

⁶⁶ Buesa, *Sancho Ramírez* (as n. 52), 160. The memorial was published by P. Kehr, 'Cómo y cuándo' (as n. 52), 321–26.

⁶⁷ Durán, *Iglesia* (as n. 36), 45–51; Buesa, *Sancho Ramírez* (as n. 52), 158–64.

⁶⁸ Gavira, *Episcopologios* (as n. 41), 48–53; Durán, *Iglesia* (as n. 36), 51–52.

⁶⁹ C. Orcástegui Gros, *Crónica de San Juan de la Peña (Versión aragonesa). Edición crítica* (Zaragoza 1986), 36–37. Ubieto, 'Introducción' (as n. 61), 308–09.

⁷⁰ The pope referred to these seven bishops in a letter of 1074. A. Durán Gudiol, 'El traslado de las reliquias de san Indalecio a San Juan de la Peña', *Argensola: Revista de Ciencias Sociales del Instituto de Estudios Altoaragoneses*, 109 (1995), 13–24.

⁷¹ M.C. Díaz y Díaz, *Libros y librerías en La Rioja altomedieval* (Logroño 1979), 319–20. The reliquary was placed between the two main altars of the church.

⁷² D.L. Simon, 'Daniel and Habakkuk in Aragon', *Journal of the British Archaeological Association*, XXXVIII (1975), 50–55.

⁷³ Kehr, 'Cómo y cuándo' (as n. 52), 302–03 and 319.

⁷⁴ P. Kehr, 'El Papado y los reinos de Navarra y Aragón hasta mediados del siglo XII', *Estudios de Edad Media de la Corona de Aragón. Sección de Zaragoza. Vol. II* (Zaragoza 1946), 119.

⁷⁵ The donation to Saint-Pons de Thomières: A. Canellas López, *La colección diplomática de Sancho Ramírez* (Zaragoza 1993), doc. 136. The consecration of San Juan de la Peña: A. Ubieto Arteta, *Colección diplomática de Pedro I de Aragón y Navarra* (Zaragoza 1951), doc. 16.

⁷⁶ Kehr, 'Cómo y cuándo' (as n. 52), 314–17.

⁷⁷ Goñi, *Colección* (as n. 20), docs 67, 74, 94, 95, 114, and 125.

⁷⁸ J. Goñi Gaztambide, 'La fecha de construcción y consagración de la Catedral románica de Pamplona', *Príncipe de Viana*, X (1949), 385–95.

⁷⁹ Goñi, *Obispos* (as n. 14), 254–316; M. Soria, ' "Tolosae moritur, Pampilonae sepelitur": Pierre d'Andouque, un évêque malmené', in *La imagen del obispo hispano en la Edad Media*, ed. M. Aurell and A. García de la Borbolla García de Paredes (Pamplona 2004), 167–83.

⁸⁰ Goñi, *Colección* (as n. 20), docs 66 and 73. The rest of the donations, in 1095, 1097 and 1103, provide no other information regarding the construction: Ibid., docs 58, 65, and 101.

⁸¹ Ubieto, *Pedro I* (as n. 75), 203–08.

⁸² Goñi, *Obispos* (as n. 14).

⁸³ *Vite venerabilis vir ac religious*: C. Douais, *Cartulaire de l'abbaye de Saint Sernin de Toulouse* (Paris-Toulouse 1887), doc. 485.

⁸⁴ J. Martínez de Aguirre, 'Catedral de Santa María', *Enciclopedia del Románico en Navarra* (Aguilar de Campoo 2008), II, 1042–47.

⁸⁵ Goñi, *Obispos* (as n. 14), 297.

⁸⁶ M.A. Mezquíriz Irujo and M.I. Tabar Sarrías, 'Excavaciones arqueológicas en la catedral de Pamplona' *Trabajos de Arqueología Navarra*, 11 (1993–94), 310–11; eadem, *Los niveles del tiempo. Arqueología en la Catedral de Pamplona* (Pamplona 1993–94); M. Durliat, 'Le plan de la cathédrale romane de Pampelune', *Bull. mon.*, (1994), 227–28; E. Aragonés Estella, 'Época prerrománica y románica', *La Catedral de Pamplona 1394–1994* (Pamplona 1994), I, 136–40.

⁸⁷ J. Martínez de Aguirre, 'La iglesia catedral de Pamplona', *El arte románico en Navarra* (Pamplona 2002), 85–95; idem, 'Catedral' (as n. 84), 1038–49.

⁸⁸ Goñi, *Colección* (as in n. 20), doc. 85.

⁸⁹ Ibid., docs 89 (1100–15), 120 (c. 1110) and 121 (c. 1110).

⁹⁰ *Adiutorium ad edificandam ipsam ecclesiam / ad dictam ecclesiam construendam*: Ibid., docs 66 and 125.

⁹¹ For Roncesvalles see, M.I. Ostolaza, *Colección Diplomática de Santa María de Roncesvalles (1127–1300)* (Pamplona 1978), doc. 2. For Estella; 'cofradía de los sesenta': Goñi, *Colección* (as n. 20), doc. 345. For Santa María de Eunate, see J. Etayo, 'Información de los Prior Abbad y confres de Santa María de Onat sobre los artículos por su parte presentados contra el Rector e beneficiados de Muruçabal', *Boletín de la Comisión de Monumentos Históricos y Artísticos de Navarra*, 5 (1914), 65; J.M. Jimeno Jurío, 'Eunate y su cofradía. Ordenanzas antiguas', *Príncipe de Viana*, LVIII (1997), 87–118.

FROM PELÁEZ TO GELMÍREZ: THE PROBLEM OF ART PATRONAGE AT THE ROMANESQUE CATHEDRAL OF SANTIAGO DE COMPOSTELA

Jens Rueffer

The Romanesque cathedral of Santiago de Compostela was begun under the episcopacy of Diego I Peláez between 1075 and 1078 and brought to near completion under Archbishop Diego II Gelmírez.[1] The *Liber Sancti Jacobi* records the year 1122. The *Liber* reads, 'And since the first stone of its foundation was laid up to that in which the last was put in place there were forty-four years.'[2] But no consecration date from this period has been passed down. Gelmírez died in 1140. In 1168 Master Mateo was employed by King Fernando II to design and execute a significant modification of the western part of the cathedral.[3] The date in the inscription on the lintel of the *Pórtico de la Gloria* reads 1188.[4] Again, however, we do not know what the date means. Does it only relate to a single event – putting the lintel in its proper place – or does it refer to the architectural completion of the porch? According to a royal charter and the consecration crosses inside the church, the consecration occurred in 1211.[5] If we add all the years together, the cathedral appears to have been more or less a construction site for a period of 136 years. Within this time span eleven bishops governed the diocese, one queen and four kings ruled the country. With respect to the Romanesque cathedral, we may limit ourselves to the years between 1075/78 and the death of Archbishop Gelmírez in 1140. Within this span, many dignitaries and several institutions asserted different aims and interests regarding the cathedral: three bishops, Diego Peláez, Dalmacio and Diego Gelmírez; the dignitaries of the cathedral chapter; the convent of Antealtares; the kings and the queen of Castile-León Alfonso VI; his daughter Queen Urraca and her son King Alfonso VII; and not least the citizens of Santiago de Compostela.

I am approaching the question of patronage from a different angle, by focussing on the object and the period from 1075 to 1140, asking which persons supported the cathedral of Santiago de Compostela over that period of time or even refused – sometimes only temporarily – to support the enterprise for specific reasons. I wish to point out the conflicts, changing interests and alliances of the different protagonists as potential patrons in a broader sense. The result is a quite vivid mosaic of claims, interests and expectations that would not emerge if one would focus merely on one individual, like Diego II Gelmírez.

The following analysis is based on a re-examination of the three important historical sources, the *Concordia de Antealtares*,[6] the *Liber Sancti Jacobi*[7] and the *Historia Compostellana*,[8] in the light of the most recent archaeological investigation undertaken by a research group from the Technical University of Cottbus, Germany under the direction of Professor Klaus Rheidt.

For a better understanding of the historical development it is important to know the spatial situation around the years 1075/78 when, according to the story in the *Liber Sancti Jacobi*, the first foundation stone was laid.[9] It is of significance that the later town of Santiago de Compostela has its origin on the very same spot later called '*locus sanctus*' – the Holy Place (Figure 6.1).[10] The heart of the early settlement was not, as may often be observed in medieval history, a market-place or the crossing of trading routes, but a holy place, a spiritual site believed to be the burial place of St James. The old church from the end of the 9th century (Figure 6.2, no. 1) was of quite moderate size. The building was repaired after the pillage of Al Mansur in the early 11th century. The extent of the Romanesque cathedral is outlined with only a black line to illustrate what the new cathedral meant for the spatial situation of the buildings around the old church of St James. In front of the church towards the northwest, the *Crónicon Iriense* as well as *Historia Compostellana* mention a small building (Figure 6.2, no. 2) which was called the hospice.[11] It was founded by Bishop Sisnando I († 920) and established for the poor, men and woman alike. The *Crónicon Iriense* does not mention *expressis verbis* pilgrims. The building had to be razed to make room for the new Romanesque church. Strictly speaking, the hospice stood on the site upon which Gelmírez erected his new palace some time around 1120.[12] But no archaeological evidence of the hospice survives. Northeast of the old church of St James, situated between the church and the wall surrounding the *locus sanctus*, stood another church, *Santa María Corticela* (Figure 6.2, no. 3). The convent of *Santa María Corticela* was the

© British Archaeological Association 2018

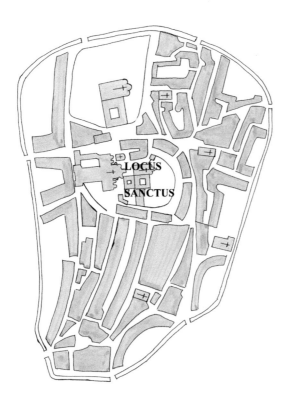

FIGURE 6.1

The town of Santiago de Compostela in the 12th century

predecessor of the monastery *San Martín Pinario*.[13] The church was founded in the early 10th century under Bishop Sisnando I. The narrow space did not allow for a cloister and claustral buildings. Thus, the convent received an area north of the wall, outside the *locus sanctus*, where the monks could erect the required monastic *officinae*. Bishop Mezonzo († 1003) gave permission to build a small oratory next to the claustral buildings outside the *locus sanctus*. The extension of the new cathedral, in particular its eastern portion, made it necessary to shorten the nave of the *Corticela* church. One can assume that it was only a question of time before the monks would demand a proper monastic oratory next to their cloister, and Bishop Diego II Gelmírez, who ruled between 1100 and 1140, dedicated this new monastic church in 1106.[14] The third institution, which is the oldest and the most significant, was located behind the eastern part of the old church of St James. It was the Benedictine monastery of Antealtares (Figure 6.2, no. 4). Whereas the other two institutions could very easily be relocated outside the *locus sanctus*, this was impossible in the case of the monastery of Antealtares. Antealtares affected the construction of the new church of St James mainly in two ways: firstly in spatial terms, and secondly in liturgical terms.

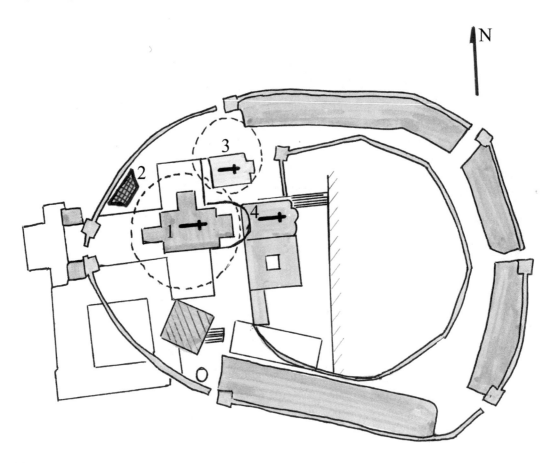

FIGURE 6.2

Santiago de Compostela: Schematic reconstruction of the Locus Sanctus around the year 1075 (After Fernando López Alsina)

BISHOP DIEGO PELÁEZ, KING ALFONSO VI AND ABBOT FAGILDO

The first important document shedding light on the beginning of the new building of the church of St James is the so called *Concordia de Antealtares*. The text has survived in a parchment copy from 1435, written by Fernán Eanes. This charter informs us about a controversy between Diego I Peláez, bishop of Iria Flavia, and Fagildo, abbot of the monastery of Antealtares. The document is an agreement settling a dispute between the bishop and the abbot. This agreement was achieved in the presence of Alfonso VI, king of Castile-León in 1077.[15] At this time the bishop still had his main residence in Iria Flavia, today's Padrón, a small town on the Atlantic coast, and the church of St James had not yet been elevated to the status of a cathedral. Furthermore, it was not the bishop and his chapter who held their daily

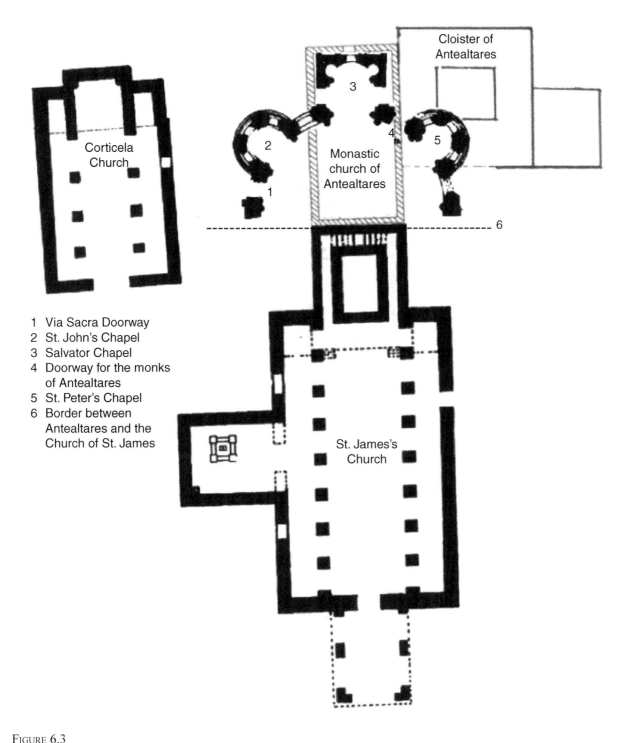

1 Via Sacra Doorway
2 St. John's Chapel
3 Salvator Chapel
4 Doorway for the monks of Antealtares
5 St. Peter's Chapel
6 Border between Antealtares and the Church of St. James

FIGURE 6.3

Situation c. 1077 showing the old church of St James, the monastic church of Antealtares, and the newly built eastern chapels of the new church of St James (After Victoriano Nodar Fernández)

liturgical services in the church of the apostle, but the monks of Antealtares.

According to the narrative part in the *Concordia de Antealtares* we are told that in the first half of the ninth century King Alfonso II gave the instruction to build the first church over the tomb of St James.[16] He also established a monastery adjacent to the east end of the mausoleum of the apostle. The main duty of the monks was to hold their liturgical services in the church and to tend to the tomb of the saint. The relation between the church of St James and the monastic church of Antealtares shown in Figure 6.3 illustrates only the information given in the *Concordia de Antealtares*. There is neither any archaeological evidence whatsoever for the size of the two buildings, nor do we know how closely the buildings were positioned in relation to each other. At the end of the 11th century, as the prestige of the saint increased, it also enhanced the reputation of the monastery of Antealtares. Performing the liturgical services at the altars was not only a question of reputation for the monks, but also a question of revenue, since the monks received a share of the income from the altars of the church of St James.[17]

The initiative of rebuilding the old church may have been launched by Bishop Diego I Peláez, with the approval of King Alfonso. But with regards to patronage, we must consider the term in a more general sense, that is: the bishop, the king *and* the convent of Antealtares. And this brings us back to the conflict already mentioned above. The *Concordia de Antealtares* states very explicitly that the space eastward of the mausoleum, separated in the image by a broken line (Figure 6.3, no. 6), belonged to the convent, and should still belong to the monks when the new east end of the Romanesque cathedral had been completed.[18] In other words, the chapels of St Peter, St John and the central Saviour chapel had been constructed on the grounds of the monastery. Furthermore, the convent was granted permission to build a door near the chapel of St John to serve as direct access for the monks to the new presbytery of the Romanesque cathedral. Finally, the convent was granted a fixed share of the income from the altar of St James.

The scale of the Romanesque cathedral made it necessary to raze the abbey church of Antealtares. We know from the *Concordia de Antealtares* that Abbot Fagildo, not the bishop, had a small church built at his own expense as an interim arrangement.[19] In 1077 the abbot still believed that he and his convent would be able to return to the church of St James. What we do not know are the promises made by the bishop to abbot and convent. Did the bishop intend to merge both churches, or did he promise the community a new monastic church, provided by him and his chapter? The two capitals on either side of the entrance of the central chapel of the new presbytery make it clear what future generations should believe. The capital on the north side shows Bishop Peláez between two angels (Figure 6.4). A similar composition was chosen for the capital on the opposite side, depicting the king of Castile-León, Alfonso VI (Figure 6.5). The inscription '*Tempore presulis Didaci inceptum hoc opus fuit*' tells us that the work was begun during the episcopacy of Diego. Diego Peláez, however, was displaced by

FIGURE 6.4

Santiago de Compostela: Church of St. James; capital at the entrance of the chapel of the Savious showing Bishop Diego Peláez (Jens Rueffer)

the king at the Council of Husillos in 1088 on charges of high treason and arrested. He died few years later.[20] The inscription for Alfonso – '*Regnante principe Adefonso constructum opus*' – informs us that the work was constructed during the reign of Alfonso VI, who died in 1109 and was buried in the Benedictine abbey at Sahagún.[21] The church was definitely not finished in 1109. We may safely assume that *opus* is to be interpreted as the presbytery only. More important to me seems the depiction of Alfonso and Diego. Neither the king nor the bishop wears typical royal or liturgical dress. They are depicted without *pontificalia* and the complete set of *regalia* respectively. Both are accompanied by angels who lift them up towards the Kingdom of Heaven. The two angels on either side of Diego as well as Alfonso seem to be an allusion to the ascension. While the body of Diego Peláez is only roughly indicated, King Alfonso wears a kind of diadem and a large cloak which is tied up in front of his chest like a key. In terms of medieval iconography the depiction of the bishop could be interpreted as his soul. This would mean that Peláez had already deceased when the capital was carved. But in the case of the king, who wears a diadem and a large cloak one may think of Elijah and Enoch. Both had the privilege to enter the

FIGURE 6.5

Santiago de Compostela: Church of St. James; capital at the entrance of the chapel of the Saviour showing King Alfonso VI (Jens Rueffer)

Kingdom of Heaven without dying. Thus, Alfonso is shown as a self-confident and powerful donor.[22] The *Concordia de Antealtares* and these figurative capitals are the first important signs in the process of expropriation and damnation of the convent of Antealtares. The *damnatio memoriae* of Antealtares is still perceivable in modern scholarship, as John Williams recently pointed out.[23]

With respect to the building history it is important to note that at the time the *Concordia de Antealtares* was sealed in 1077 the three easternmost chapels were already under construction.[24] Furthermore, we know from Klaus Rheidt's research that the bottom stone courses of the foundation of the northern tower of the later Romanesque west façade perfectly aligned with the old church of St James as well as with the central eastern Saviour chapel.[25] We do not know exactly when the foundations of the western towers were laid. But it is possible to date these building activities in close proximity to those of the eastern portions. If this proves true, we may assume that the design of the new church building was nearly complete from the very beginning, at least in its ground plan and its structural and spatial disposition (Figure 6.6): a three-aisled nave; a three-aisled transept with three chapels on the eastern side of each transept arm; a presbytery with ambulatory and five radiating chapels, with columns, piers, towers, staircases; and finally, the two-storey elevation with a circular gallery. Although there were changes to the design in the presbytery above the gallery level, one could suppose that even at this early stage a rough idea of the elevation of the transept and the nave had already been formed. The interior, despite later modifications or alterations, still displays a very homogeneous design (Figure 6.7). This feature is also emphasised in the

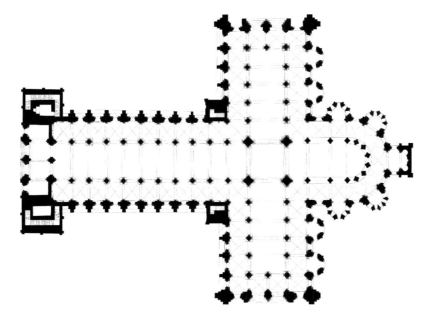

FIGURE 6.6

Santiago de Compostela: Ground-plan of the Romanesque church of St James (courtesy BTU Cottbus, Lehrstuhl für Baugeschichte)

FIGURE 6.7

Santiago the Compostela: Church of St James, looking east (Jens Rueffer)

Liber Sancti Jacobi: 'In truth, in this church no fissure or fault is found; it is admirably constructed, grand, spacious, bright, of proper magnitude, harmonious in width, length and height, of admirable and ineffable workmanship, built in two storeys, just like a royal palace.'[26]

The same *Codex*, compiled by an unknown cleric after 1140 and finished by 1165,[27] provides us with some information regarding the personnel involved in the enterprise: 'The master stonemasons who first constructed the basilica of the Blessed James were called Master Bernard the Elder, a marvellous master, and Robert, who, with about fifty other stonemasons, worked there actively when the most faithful lord Wicart and the lord canon of the chapter, Segeredo, and the lord abbot Gundesindo were in office, in the reign of Alfonso, King of Spain, and in the episcopacy of Dom Diego I, most valiant knight and generous man.'[28]

Apart from speculations that Bernard and Robert may have been French, we know absolutely nothing about the two master masons. The name Wicart poses a philological problem.[29] But the Prior or treasurer Segered and Abbot Gundesind – the latter was responsible for liturgical duties – are known through other sources.[30] Both died before 1111 and 1113 respectively. Bishop Diego is characterised as being a very generous man. This is an explicit reference to patronage, stressing above all the bishop's financial donations. The king is only mentioned because it happened during his reign, but not as an actual benefactor. All the workers were *ministrantibus fidelissimis*, which can be rendered as *faithful servants* [of the lords Segered and Gundesind]. This passage seems to suggest that Segered and Gundesind were a kind of *rector fabricae* while the bishop only guaranteed the fabric fund. Both were responsible for the building activities in a broader sense. The next paragraph in the *Liber Sancti Jacobi* states the time of completion previously mentioned. The building was begun in 1078 and completed after 44 years in 1122.[31] These dates are a topic of great debate, but the questions are not of interest here.[32] The real surprise is rather that there is no mention of Bishop Diego II Gelmírez whatsoever, although he is referred to a few paragraphs earlier as donor of the new silver antependium.[33] This is quite peculiar, because the construction period given in the *Liber Sancti Jacobi* from 1075/78 to 1122 clearly shows that of those years, Gelmírez governed almost 30 years as head of the diocese. Nevertheless, in the *Historia Compostellana* he is referred to as *sapiens architectus* acknowledging his rôle as builder.[34] One might also inquire why the author or the compiler of the *Liber Sancti Jacobi* only mentions people responsible for the construction until the end of the first decade of the 12th century.

THE INTERVENING PERIOD 1088 TO 1100

Bishop Peláez was, as has already been mentioned, deposed in 1088. He was not buried in the church. The seat of the see remained vacant until 1094, when Dalmacio, a former monk of Cluny, was elected bishop of Iria Flavia.[35] In his very short episcopacy – Dalmacio died in December 1095 – he achieved two important goals. At the council of Clermont-Ferrand in 1095 he was granted permission by Pope Urban II to transfer the see from Iria Flavia to Santiago de Compostela and to subject the bishopric only to the papacy.[36] After the death of Dalmacio, another vacancy of the see of nearly five years followed. In 1100 Diego Gelmírez became the first bishop to be elected bishop of Santiago de Compostela.

BISHOP GELMÍREZ, THE CATHEDRAL CHAPTER, QUEEN URRACA AND KING ALFONSO VII

Diego Gelmírez was in charge of the see as *vicarius* during both vacancies until he finally became bishop of Santiago de Compostela.[37] In 1120 he achieved a long desired aim: Pope Calixtus II elevated the bishopric of Santiago de Compostela to an archbishopric, as a first step temporarily and four years later permanently.[38] This seems to be Gelmírez's greatest triumph, one he worked towards for almost twenty years, spending a fortune in bribes and risking many conflicts with the cathedral chapter and the citizens of the town. As bishop, Gelmírez was unquestionably a patron in a general sense.³⁹ But his zeal for the church project can be illustrated by four incidents in particular. First, Gelmírez commanded the old sanctuary including the altar of St James be re-designed. This happened shortly after his election as bishop between 1102 and 1105 and – this seems significant – he did this against the resistance of the cathedral chapter.⁴⁰ Second, he stole important relics during his visit to Braga in 1102 in order to present those relics to the cathedral or to furnish the new altars in the new presbytery with these relics.⁴¹ Third, he donated the new antependium for the main altar;⁴² and finally, around the year 1120, he gave the order to construct a new monastic church for the convent of Antealtares.⁴³ This new monastic church received a new patron. It was now called San Pelayo. Pelagius was the hermit who, according to the legend, saw strange lights which led him to a certain tomb. He informed Bishop Teodemir of Iria Flavia, who recognised the tomb as that of St James.⁴⁴ With this new church, the monks of Antealtares lost not only their last direct connection to the cathedral but also their traditional rights on the altar and the tomb of St. James. Henceforth the archbishop and the chapter had the full authority over the church, the saint and his cult.

Gelmírez made an effort to win the royal dynasty of Castile-León as patrons of the saint and his church. This was a rather difficult enterprise and an enterprise without a happy end, but at the very beginning the idea seemed quite promising. The husband of the later Queen Urraca, Raymond of Burgundy, was buried in the cathedral in 1107.⁴⁵ Gelmírez served the count for some years as *publicus notarius, scriptor, cancellarius, secretarius et confessor*.⁴⁶ Raymond represents the first member of the royal dynasty to be buried in the cathedral, and his tomb constitutes the beginning of what decades later would be called the *Pantheon de los reyes*. When Raymond died, the bishop and the count of Traba became guardians of the infant Alfonso Raimundez, the later King Alfonso VII.⁴⁷ This was the next opportunity to bind the future king to the church of St James. Although Alfonso, on the initiative of Gelmírez, was crowned King of Galicia in 1111 and received the accolade in 1123 – both events took place in the cathedral – the relationship between the bishop and Alfonso remained strained, as did the relationship between Gelmírez and Alfonso's mother, Queen Urraca.⁴⁸ The queen, who died in 1126, was buried in San Isidoro in León, the monastery she had favoured with her support. Alfonso, who died in 1157, was buried in the cathedral of Toledo.

From the perspective of the royal family and their political interests, the main reason for their lack of interest in and support for the saint and his church may have been motivated by Santiago de Compostela's geographical location on the very edge of the realm, or as the *Liber Sancti Jacobi* called it, *finis terrae*. Santiago did not represent the heart of the realm, where one could establish a royal residence, a coronation church and a burial place for the memory of the dynasty. Royal patronage at the cathedral of Santiago de Compostela can be observed later, in the second half of the century when King Fernando II paid a lifelong salary to Master Matteo, responsible for rebuilding the western part of the cathedral from 1168 onwards. But this lies beyond the scope of this paper.

Gelmírez was not only the ecclesiastical sovereign over the church and the tomb of St James, but also the secular ruler of the town. While the pilgrims may have supported the building activities by donating money to the altar of Saint James, the citizens had a rather ambivalent relationship to the bishop. We know of two civil uprisings against the bishop and the cathedral. In 1116, Queen Urraca deliberately set parts of the regional nobility, parts of the cathedral chapter, and a part of the citizens against the bishop. The situation escalated, and in 1117 the mob set parts of the cathedral on fire.⁴⁹ In 1136 the situation was almost the same but with different alliances. But again, the citizens besieged the cathedral.⁵⁰ We do not know how great the damage was and what portions of the cathedral were affected.

Finally, we must briefly consider the canons of the cathedral chapter. As the *Liber Sancti Jacobi* proves, there was a kind of *magister fabricae* who administered the construction work on behalf of the bishop and the chapter. We know from both the *Liber Sancti Jacobi* and the *Historia Compostellana* that the treasurer Bernard donated money to build a new water supply and a well in front of the north transept façade for pilgrims.⁵¹ We have no information what the administration of the fabric meant regarding the design. What we do know from the *Historia Compostellana* is that Gelmírez spent far too much money on his political ambitions, thereby angering the cathedral chapter. The canons had to be patient many a time, before getting their new cloister and claustral buildings.⁵²

To make a long story very short, the Romanesque cathedral provides a good example for demonstrating how a wide range of protagonists played different roles when considering patronage in a broader sense. Bishop Diego Peláez and King Alfonso VI launched the project, but Alfonso preferred as burial place the abbey of Sahagún. Ambivalent too was the attitude of Queen Urraca and King Alfonso VII. Both supported Gelmírez as long as it corresponded to their interests, both opposed him when deemed useful. Both decided not to be buried in the church of St James. Gelmírez's interest in the new church building was rather an interest of convenience. He needed a large church to enhance the significance of the apostle and to accomplish his mission to become archbishop. The chapter supported the building activities only up to that point until they felt their own new buildings – the cloister and the claustral buildings – had been delayed indefinitely. The citizens had an ambivalent attitude, too, but the uprisings were not directed against the cathedral itself or against the apostle. These clashes were targeted against the bishop in his capacity as secular ruler over the town. And it was the latter who was the cause of the citizens' discontent. But the most interesting question for art historians, the question who exerted what influence on the architectural design, remains entirely speculative.

NOTES

[1] J. Rüffer, *Die Kathedrale von Santiago de Compostela (1075–1211). Eine Quellenstudie* (Freiburg i.Br. 2010). In the book I dealt with the sources in detail as well as discussed the secondary literature. In the following I have reduced references to a minimum.

[2] 'et ab anno quo primus lapis in fundamento eius ponitur, usque ad illum quo ultimus mittitur, xL.iiii. anni habentur': 'Liber Sancti Jacobi' IX, f 212r, P. Gerson, A. Shaver-Crandell, A. Stones, J. Krochalis (eds.), *The Pilgrim's Guide to Santiago the Compostela. Critical Edition*, vol. 2, The Text (London 1998), 84.

[3] Santiago de Compostela, Archivo de la Catedral, S 7a / 5; Rüffer, *Kathedrale* (as n. 1), 181–90.

[4] 'Anno ab incarnatione Domini M°C°LXXX°VIII° era IaCCaXXa-VI die kalendae aprilis superliminaria principalium portalium ecclesie beati Jacobi sunt collocata per magistrum Matheum qui a fundamentis ipsorum portalium gessit magisterium'. Rüffer, *Kathedrale* (as n. 1), 186, n. 301. The Spanish calculation of times 'Era' is the calculation of times 'Anno Domini' 38 years ahead.

[5] 'Facta carta Compostelle in die consecrationis ecclesie sci. iacobi XI. Kls. Maii. Era mccxlviiii' (= 21. April 1211). Santiago de Compostela, Archivo de la Catedral, Tumbo B, CF 33, f. 207r-207v, M.T. González Balasch, (ed.), *Tumbo B de la Catedral de Santiago* (Santiago de Compostela 2004), N° 261, 488–90. In one of the consecration crosses the inscription reads: ERA : MILLENA : NONA : VICIES : DVODENA : SVMMO : TEMPLA : DAVID : QVARTVS : PETRVS : ISTA DEDICAV[IT]. The year 'Era' 1249 corresponds to 1211 A.D. and Peter IV is Bishop Petrus Muñiz (1207–24), who dedicated the church.

[6] The original charter is lost, but a parchment copy from 1435 made by Fernán Eanes has survived (Santiago de Compostela, Arquivo Histórico Universitario: Fondo de la Universidad. Serie Histórica, legajo 81 – Santiago. Pinario. Escrituras en pergamino, pa. 46). There is still no critical edition. For the Latin text see: Rüffer, *Kathedrale* (as n. 1), 201–08.

[7] Editio princeps: *Liber Sancti Jacobi – Codex Calixtinus, Transcripción a partir del Códice original* ed. K. Herbers y M. Santos Noia (Santiago de Compostela 1999). For codicological descriptions and content see: M.C. Díaz y Díaz, *El Codice Calixtino de la cathedral de Santiago. Estudio codicológico y de contenido*, Monografías de Compostellanum, 2 (Santiago de Compostela 1988); P. Gerson, A. Shaver-Crandell, A. Stones, J. Krochalis (eds.), *The Pilgrim's Guide to Santiago the Compostela. Critical Edition*, vol. 1, The Manuscripts (London 1998); K. Herbers, *Der Jakobuskult des 12. Jahrhunderts und der 'Liber Sancti Jacobi'. Studien über das Verhältnis zwischen Religion und Gesellschaft im hohen Mittelalter* (Wiesbaden 1984).

[8] *Historia Compostellana*, Corpus christianorum continuatio mediaevalis, 70, cura et studio E. Falque Rey (Turnhout 1988); L. Vones, *Die 'Historia Compostellana' und die Kirchenpolitik des nordwestspanischen Raumes 1070–1130* (Köln, Wien 1980).

[9] 'Ecclesia autem fuit incepta, in era. Ia.Ca.XVI': Gerson, Shaver-Crandell, Stones, and Krochalis (eds), 'Liber Sancti Jacobi', IX (as n. 2), f. 212r, vol. 2, 84. For a brief discussion of the dates see note 32.

[10] For the history of the *locus sanctus* and the development of the medieval town of Santiago see: F. López Alsina, *La ciudad de Santiago de Compostela en la alta edad media* (Santiago de Compostela 1988); F. López Alsina, 'Santiago, eine Stadt für den Apostel', in *Santiago de Compostela. Pilgerwege*, ed. P. Gucci von Saucken (Augsburg 1995), 57–74; F. López Alsina, 'Die romanische Kathedrale von Santiago de Compostela in ihrem städtischen Umfeld', in *Die Kathedrale von Santiago de Compostela: das Ziel des Jakobsweges*, exhibition catalogue, ed. F.S. Lorenzo, J. Tejedor (Santiago de Compostela 1995), 37–56.

[11] '[. . .] sedes ad suscipiendos pauperes de familia, tam uiros quam feminas, inter turres, et de reditibus Ecclesie pro posse sustentabat eos'. *El Crónicon Iriense*, Memorial Histórico Español, 50, ed. M.R. García Álvarez (Madrid 1963), 1–240, quotation 113. The *Historia Compostellana* I, ii.3 (as n. 8), 11 reads: '[. . .] iuxta turrim principalis introitus huius ecclesie tam claudis quam cecis omnibusque debilibus sedes fecit constitui, hac uidelicet intentione, ut eorum helemosinis et oblationibus fidelium inopie sustentarentur'.

[12] The *Historia Compostellana* II, xxv (as n. 8), 268 mentions the building of the new episcopal palace at the request of bishop Gelmírez. While the old palace was situated on the south side of the church probably close to the Puerta de las Platerías, the new episcopal palace was erected with a private chapel for the archbishop on the north side of the new nave. The attribution of the location of the old episcopal palace is not based on archaeological evidence, but rather on the examination of written sources. F. López Alsina, 'Evolution urbaine de la Compostelle médiévale (IXe au XIIe siècle)', in *Santiago de Compostela 1000 Ans de Pèlerinage Européen*, exhibition catalogue (Gand 1985), 230–232; Rüffer, *Kathedrale* (as n. 1), 66–82; J.L. Senra Gabriel y Galán, 'The Episcopal Palace', in *St. James – The Hope*, exhibition catalogue (Santiago de Compostela 1999), 73–77.

[13] M.L. Álvarez, *El monasterio de San Martiño Pinario de Santiago de Compostela* (A Coruña 2003), 9–17. F. Fariña Busto, 'San Martiño Pinario in seiner Vergangenheit. Das Mittelalter', in *Galicia no tempo. Kloster San Martiño Pinario*, exhibition catalogue (Santiago de Compostela 1991), 61–67.

[14] *Historia Compostellana* I, xix.1 (as n. 8), 45.

[15] Rüffer, *Kathedrale* (as n. 1), 25–28.

[16] 'Qui prout erat affectu castimoniae diligens sanctitatem statim in honore eiusdem Apostoli fabricata ecclesia et circa eamdem alteram in honore beati baptistae Ioannis, [. . .]'. Rüffer, *Kathedrale* (as n. 1), 202.

[17] 'Demum episcopus, dum fabricaretur ecclesia, haberet beati Iacobi altaris pecuniam, unde prius monachi dimidiam possidebant. Et peracta / ecclesia abbas et monachi haberent partem tertiam et episcopus duas in perpetuum.' Rüffer, *Kathedrale* (as n. 1), 204–05.

[18] 'Et finite opera ecclesiae tertiam partem redditus ipsius beati Iacobi altaris vobis restituamus, servato semper vestro iure haereditatis per locum, ubi convenientiam karacterum scripturi et posituri sumus inter altare beati Iacobi et illa tria altaria continens huiusmodi signum D, id est A et D, posita linea ab eodem signo usque ad inferiorem angulum vestrae turris, quae in muro contineatur, et ab altero signo usque ad inferiorem angulum vestrae domus, qui / est circa cameram palatii; et deinceps per girum sicut in vestra dote regum Casti et Renamiri continetur.' Rüffer, *Kathedrale* (as n. 1), 206–07.

[19] 'Videns vero sanctissimus abbas ordinem monasticum, dum opus ecclesiae construeretur, ibi non perfecte observari posse, secum cogitans ecclesiam parvulam ad opus monachorum tria continentem altaria [. . .] construxit, ubi antiquitus pra[e]fatus Pelagius cellam habuit, et altare beati Pelagii martyris construxit.' Rüffer, *Kathedrale* (as n. 1), 203.

[20] Vones, *Die 'Historia Compostellana'* (as n. 8), 108–09.

[21] B.F. Reilly, *The Kingdom of León-Castilla Under King Alfonso VI, 1065–1109* (Princeton, NJ 1988), 363.

[22] S. Moralejo Álvarez, 'The *Codex Calixtinus* as an art-historical source', in *The Codex Calixtinus and the Shrine of St. James*, ed. J. Williams and A. Stones (Tübingen 1992), 207–23, esp. 213; Nodar Fernández, *Los inicios de la cathedral románica de Santiago: El ambicioso programa iconográfico de Diego Peláez* (Santiago de Compostela 2004), 84–93; M. Castiñeiras Gonzáles, 'La cathedral de Santiago de Compostela (1075–1122), obra maestra del románico europeo' in *Siete maravillas del románico español*, ed. P.L. Huerta (Aguilar de Campoo 2009), S. 227–89, esp. 232–41; J. Staebel, 'São Frutuoso de Montélios und die Salvatorkapelle der Kathedrale von Santiago de Compostela: Der Umbau unter Diego Gelmírez vor dem Hintergrund des *pium latrocinium*', in A. Arbeiter, C. Kothe, B. Marten (eds.), *Hispanies Norden im 11. Jahrhundert. Christliche Kunst im Umbruch – El Norte Hispánico en el siglo XI. Un cambio radical en el arte Cristiano* (Petersberg 2009), 141–50, esp. 146; S. Trinks, *Antike und Avantgarde. Skulptur am Jakobsweg im 11. Jahrhundert: Jaca – León – Santiago*, Actus et Imago, 4 (Berlin 2012), 225–27. Victoriano Nodar Fernández discusses the capitals at length. With respect to iconography he focusses on the depiction of King Alfonso and his relation to Bishop Diego Peláez. He regarded the key shaped cloak as a depiction of a real key while Stefan Trinks focusses on a special meaning of cloth in this context.

²³ J. Williams, 'The Tomb of St James: The View from the Other Side', in *Cross, Crescent and Conversion: Studies on the Medieval Spain and Christendom in Memory of Richard Fletcher*, The Medieval Mediterranean, Peoples, Economies and Cultures, 400–1500, 73, ed. by S. Barton, P. Linehan (Leiden 2008), 175–91.

²⁴ '[. . .] altare beati Petri apostolorum principis, quod modo construeretur infra ecclesiam beati Iacobi in sinistra parte ad exitum vestrae portae vestri capituli [. . .]'. Rüffer, *Kathedrale* (as n. 1), 205.

²⁵ K. Rheidt, 'Neue Forschungen zur Baugeschichte der Kathedrale von Santiago de Compostela – bauliche Entwicklungen und Bauphasen des Langhauses', in B. Nicolai, K. Rheidt (eds.), *Santiago de Compostela. Pilgerarchitektur und bildliche Repräsentation in neuer Perspektive* (Bern 2015), 99–129.

²⁶ 'In eadem uero aecclesia nulla scissura, uel corrupcio inuenitur; mirabiliter operator, magna, spaciosa, clara, magnitudine condecenti latitudine longitudine et altitudine congruenti, miro et ineffabili opera habetur, que etiam dupliciter uelut regale palacium operator.' Gerson, Shaver-Crandell, Stones, and Krochalis (eds), 'Liber Sancti Jacobi' (as n. 2), IX, f. 208r, vol. 2, 68, transl. 69.

²⁷ The date of the *Codex* is still a matter of debate. I have discussed the arguments at length in my Santiago book (Rüffer, *Kathedrale* [as n. 1], 91–95). Here, it may suffice to refer only to the problem of dating book five and the final compilation of the *Codex*. The *Codex* is a compilation of five books and a short appendix. One has therefore to distinguish between the dating of every single book and the dating of the whole compilation. Within book five the death of King Louis VI., who died in 1137, is mentioned. Therefore book five must have been finished after 1137, when precisely we do not know. In book one a reference is given to William, Patriarch of Jerusalem (1130–45), as well as to Diego Gelmírez as archbishop (1120–40). From this follows the earliest date of the compilation between 1137 and 1145. Furthermore it is known that the *Codex* was copied by a monk from Ripoll in 1173. He did not copy book five instead he gave a summary of its content. It is most likely that the monk used that copy that is still preserved in the cathedral archives. Finally, within the appendix a miracle is recorded which dates back to the year 1164. Thus, we may assume that the compilation was finished at the latest by 1165. This leaves a period of time between 1137/45 and 1165. The dating of individual events is much more complicated, because the author/compiler may have had access to older material, which, precisely, and to what extend we simply do not know.

²⁸ 'Didascali lapicide qui prius Beati Iacobi basilicam edificauerunt, nominabantur Domnus Bernardus senex, mirabilis magister, et Rotbertus cum ceteris lapicidibus circiter. L. qui ibi sedule operabantur, ministrantibus fidelissimis domnis. WICARTO et Domino Gundesindo, Regnante Ádefonso rege Yspaniarum, sub episcopo Domino Didaco primo et strenuissimo milite et generoso uiro'. Gerson, Shaver-Crandell, Stones, and Krochalis (eds), 'Liber Sancti Jacobi' (as n. 2), IX, f. 212r, vol. 2, 84, transl. 85.

²⁹ Rüffer, *Kathedrale* (as n. 1), 179, n. 289.

³⁰ Rüffer, *Kathedrale* (as n. 1), 178–79.

³¹ Gerson, Shaver-Crandell, Stones, and Krochalis (eds), 'Liber Sancti Jacobi' (as n. 2), IX, f. 212r, vol. 2, 84.

³² Apart from the precise date of the start, construction work should be considered as a process. Before the first building campaign can be started a building fund has to be set up, an administration has to be established, and a master builder be appointed. For church buildings, the laying of the foundation stone was often embedded into a liturgical ceremony which could be celebrated weeks, months or even years after the first work was done on the building site (G. Binding, S. Linscheid-Burdich, *Planen und Bauen im frühen und hohen Mittelalter* [Darmstadt 2002], 169–178). For the church of St James at Santiago de Compostela two dates are passed down: 1075 and 1078. The 'Liber Sancti Jacobi' V.9, f. 212r gives the year 1078 (ERA 1116), but the dates related to this event are dubious, because they yield 1073, 1074, and 1075 Gerson: Shaver-Crandell, Stones, and Krochalis (eds), 'Liber Sancti Jacobi' (as n. 2), vol.2, 84. Those three dates pose a philological problem, because the passage is written over an erasure. The *Historia Compostelana* I, lxxviii.2 (as n. 8), 121 mentions the 11th of Juli 1078 (Era Ia.C.XVI. V° Idus Iul.). An inscription on the jambs of the right entrance of the *Puerta de las Platerías* can be interpreted in two ways, either as ERA ICXLI / IDVS I[V]LII (11th of July 1103) or as ERA ICXVI (1078) as M. Schapiro convincingly argued. It depends how one wishes to suspend the engraved ligature, either with XL or with XV. The *Concordia de Antealtares*, as already mentioned, tells us that the three easternmost chapels were already under construction in 1077. Another heavily amended inscription referring to the consecration of the Saviours chapel reads according to Gómez Moreno: 'Consecra[ta. . .] nonasque trigeno anno [post dominice incarnationis milleno se]ptuageno quinto t[empore quo domus est fun]data iacobi]' (amendments are given in brackets). The chapel was consecrated thirty years after the house of St. James was founded in 1075. The consecration of the altars of the ambulatory is dated to 1105, this date is open to question. S. Moralejo, M. Castiñeiras, and H. Karge prefer the year 1075, whereas J.K. Conant opted for the year 1078 as J. d'Emilio still does. I would argue, as Whitehill did, that one should consider the beginning of building activities as a process rather than as a fixed date. The decision to rebuild the church could have been made even before 1075 and there is nothing to be said against the view that the ceremony of laying the foundation stone took place in 1078. K.J. Conant, *The Early Architectural History of the Cathedral of Santiago de Compostela* (Cambridge / Mass. 1926), 31; Á. del Castillo, 'Inscripciones inéditas de la catedral de Santiago', Boletín de la real Academia Gallega 15 (1926), 314–20, esp. 317–18; M. Gómez Moreno, *El arte románico español* (Madrid 1934), 113; W.M. Whitehill, 'The date of the beginning of the cathedral of Santiago de Compostela' *The Antiquaries Journal*, 15 (1935), 336–42; M. Schapiro, 'A note on an inscription of the cathedral of Santiago de Compostela' *Speculum*, 17 (1942), 261–62; F. Bouza Brey, 'El epígrafe fundacional de la Iglesia de Tomonde y el de la Puerta de las Platerías de la Catedral de Santiago', *Cuadernos de Estudios Gallegos* 17 (1962) 175–81; S. Moralejo, 'Santiago de Compostela. Die Errichtung eines romanischen Bauwerks', in *Die Baukunst im Mittelalter*, ed. R. Cassanelli (Düsseldorf 1995), 127–43, esp. 128–40; S. Moralejo Álvarez, 'The *Codex Calixtinus*' (as n. 22) 211–14; J. d'Emilio, 'Inscriptions and the Romanesque Church: Patrons, Prelates, and Craftsmen in Romanesque Galicia', in *Spanish Medieval Art: Recent Studies*, ed. C. Hourihane (Princeton, New Jersey 2007), S. 1–33, esp. 17–18; H. Karge, 'Die Kathedrale von Santiago de Compostela. Neue Forschungen zur Baugeschichte der romanischen Jakobuskirche', in *Hispaniens Norden im elften Jahrhundert – christliche Kunst im Umbruch*, Internationale Tagung, Göttingen, 27.-29. Februar 2004, ed. A. Arbeiter, C. Kothe, B. Marten (Petersberg 2009), 183–99, esp. 183–89; Castiñeiras González, 'La cathedral de Santiago de Compostela' (as n. 22), 232–41; C. Watson, *The Romanesque Cathedral of Santiago de Compostela: A Reassessment*, BAR International Series 1979, (Oxford 2009), 2–7; Rüffer, *Kathedrale* (as n. 1), 165–71; R. Horst, *Santiago de Compostela. Die Sakraltopographie der romanischen Jakobus-Kathedrale* (Korb 2012), S. 35–38.

³³ Gerson, Shaver-Crandell, Stones, and Krochalis (eds), 'Liber Sancti Jacobi' (as n. 2), IX, f. 211v, vol. 2, 80; S. Moralejo Álvarez, 'El patronazgo artístico del arzobispo Gelmírez (1100–1140): su reflejo en la obra e imagen de Santiago', in *Patrimonio artístico de Galicia y otros estudios. Homenaje al prof. Serafín Moralejo Álvarez*, dirección y coordinación Ángela Franco Mata, vol. 1 (Santiago de Compostela 2004), 289–99, esp. 298–99; S. Moralejo Álvarez, '*Ars sacra* et sculpture romane monumentale: le trésor et le chantier de Compostelle, *Les Cahiers de Saint-Michel de Cuxa*, 11 (1980), 189–238; M.A. Castiñeiras Gonzáles, 'Para una reconstrucción del altar mayor de Gelmirez: cien años después de López Ferreiro', *Compostellanum. Estudios Jacobeos*, 55 (2010), 575–640, esp. 607–21 with a virtual reconstruction of the main altar.

³⁴ *Historia Compostellana* I, lxxviii (as n. 8), 121; G. Binding, *Der früh- und hochmittelalterliche Bauherr als sapiens architectus*, second revised and extended edition (Darmstadt 1998).

³⁵ *Historia Compostellana* I, v-vi (as n. 8), 18–20.

³⁶ F. López Alsina, 'Urbano II y el traslado de la sede episcopal de Iria a Compostela', in *El Papado, la Iglesia Leonesa y la Basílica de Santiago a finales del siglo XI. El traslado de la Sede Episcopal de Iria a Compostela en 1095*, ed. by F. López Alsina (Santiago de Compostela 1999), 107–127.

³⁷ *Historia Compostellana* I, vii-ix.1 (as n. 8), 20–24.

³⁸ Vones, *Die 'Historia Compostellana'* (as n. 8), 365–473.

[39] K.R. Matthews, '"They wished to destroy the temple of God". Responses to Diego Gelmírez' Cathedral Construction in Santiago de Compostela, 1100–1140', PhD (University of Chicago 1995); B. Abou-El-Haj, 'Santiago in the Time of Diego Gelmírez', *Gesta* 36 (1997), 165–79; M.A. Castiñeiras Gonzáles, 'Didacus Gelmirius, Patron of the Arts. Compostela's long journey: from the periphery to the centre of Romanesque Art', in *Compostela and Europe. The Story of Diego Gelmírez*, exhibition catalogue (Milano 2010), 32–109.

[40] *Historia Compostellana* I, xviii (as n. 8), 43–44; Rüffer, *Kathedrale* (as n. 1), 44–51.

[41] *Historia Compostellana* I, x (as n. 8), 32–36, Rüffer, *Kathedrale* (as n. 1), 51–55.

[42] Gerson, Shaver-Crandell, Stones, and Krochalis (eds), 'Liber Sancti Jacobi' (as n. 2), IX, f. 211v, vol. 2, 80; S. Moralejo Álvarez, '*Ars sacra* et sculpture romane' (as n. 33), 204–10.

[43] *Historia Compostellana* II, i (as n. 8), 327.

[44] Rüffer, *Kathedrale* (as n. 1), 201–02; *Historia Compostellana* I, ii.1 (as n. 8), 9.

[45] *Historia Compostellana* I, xvii (as n. 8), 55; Rüffer, *Kathedrale* (as n. 1), 59–61.

[46] *Historia Compostellana*, Introduccíon, traduccíon, notas e índices de E. Falque Rey (Madrid 1994), 9; Vones, *Die 'Historia Compostellana'* (as n. 8), 115–16.

[47] Vones, *Die 'Historia Compostellana'* (as n. 8), 163–70.

[48] R.A. Fletcher, *Saint James's Catapult. The Life and Times of Diego Gelmírez of Santiago de Compostela*, (Oxford 1984), 129–162; Rüffer, *Kathedrale* (as n. 1), 61, 66–72, 82–87.

[49] *Historia Compostellana* I, cxiv.1–14 (as n. 8), 199–208; Rüffer, *Kathedrale* (as n. 1), 66–72.

[50] *Historia Compostellana* III, xlvii.1–3 (as n. 8), 508–10.

[51] Gerson, Shaver-Crandell, Stones, and Krochalis (eds), 'Liber Sancti Jacobi' (as n. 2), IX, f. 209r, vol. 2, 72; *Historia Compostellana* II, liv (as n. 8), 324–26.

[52] *Historia Compostellana* III, i (as n. 8), 420–21 and III, xxxvi, 483–84.

PATRONAGE, ROMANESQUE ARCHITECTURE AND THE LANGUEDOC

Eric Fernie

This paper is not so much a contribution to knowledge as a contribution to publicity. The object of the publicity is the March of Gothia, a political unit west of the Rhône on the Mediterranean coast of the Carolingian empire, which continued in existence to the middle of the 11th century and the era of First Romanesque architecture in the area (Figure 7.1). Mentions of it are non-existent or very restricted in prominent architectural studies, such as those of Robert de Lasteyrie, Josep Puig i Cadafalch, Kenneth Conant, Hans Kubach, Éliane Vergnolle and Xavier Barral i Altet.[1] What is normally used instead is the Languedoc, or more specifically lower Languedoc, as in the Zodiaque volume of 1978 (Figure 7.2).[2] The earliest use of the name Languedoc with reference to a political unit appears to be in the late 11th century, that is after the main period of building in the First Romanesque style.[3] I therefore thought it might be worth examining the March, to see if it had any relevance to the buildings and how their patrons saw themselves and their commissions.

The boundaries of the area remained remarkably consistent through centuries of violent change, reflected in a variety of names. Its origins are at least as old as the Roman empire, in the form of the province of *Gallia Narbonensis Prima*, which extended from the Rhône to the Pyrenees (Figure 7.3). By 476, when the area formed part of the Visigothic domains, it had come to be called Septimania (Figure 7.4). In 507 the Franks pushed the Visigoths out of Gaul, except, that is, for Septimania (Figure 7.5). Next, the Arabs invaded, traversing the Frankish kingdom up to the Loire, including Septimania, between 718 and 732. Between 732 and 740 the Franks pushed the Arabs back across the Pyrenees, except, once again, for Septimania (Figure 7.6), then in the 750s they completed the task and took that territory as well. Its exceptionalism can be partly explained by its geography, as mountains about 60 kms inland separate it from the interior to the north, while the Pyrenees are more traversable at the coast than further west. In the late 8th century, under Charlemagne, Septimania was made a duchy, no less.[4]

In the 9th and 10th centuries the Carolingian empire saw the establishing of a number of feudal entities north and south of the Pyrenees, including the counties of Toulouse, Barcelona and Roussillon, and the March of Gothia, the last replacing the Duchy of Septimania (Figure 7.7). The counties of Toulouse and Barcelona have reasonably clear historical outlines. Toulouse was in existence in the early 9th century, a new dynasty was started in 852 with Raymond I, and it became the centre of power in the south-eastern quarter of France until the 13th century. Barcelona was also established in the first half of the 9th century, and began a new sequence of rulers with Wilfred in 873, which ran into the 12th century, taking over the rest of the Spanish March, including Roussillon, after which it become part of the Principality of Catalonia.[5]

The March of Gothia is less clear. It was probably instituted in the middle of the 9th century, as Bernard of Septimania was executed in 844 and marquis Bernard of Gothia ruled from 865 to 878, while a papal bull of around 904 refers to a *monasterium sancti Petri in Gothia*. It is spoken of as ending with William I, duke of Aquitaine, in 918, but in a record of a gift to the abbey of Saint-Gilles in 961 the donor, Raymond, is called marquis of Gothia, it is referred to in the time of William Taillefer, who died in 1037, and Hugh, count of Rouergue, who died around 1054, was also known as the marquis of Gothia. Thereafter nothing is recorded as taking its place until the advent of Languedoc in the late 11th century.[6]

It has been suggested that Gothia was so named because of the high proportion of people of Visigothic descent living there. It might seem odd for the Carolingians, themselves Franks, to adopt, or allow to be adopted, the name of their erstwhile enemies, especially in preference to the existing, and Roman, name of Septimania. The answer to that might be that the Visigoths were not only no longer the enemy, those living in the Iberian peninsula under Arab rule were now allies, and seen as part of the Reconquista. Such an attitude would also explain the defining of Gothia as a march, one related to the Marca Hispanica as the Frankish frontier with the Arabs, with a corresponding status.

Turning to the architecture, very little is known of the area in the 9th and 10th centuries, though an Iberian character is indicated by the use of the horseshoe arch in the church of Saint-Martin-des-Puits of that date. It can be compared with churches in the peninsula such as those at Quintanilla de las Viñas and Baños de Cerrato, a type of building previously

© British Archaeological Association 2018

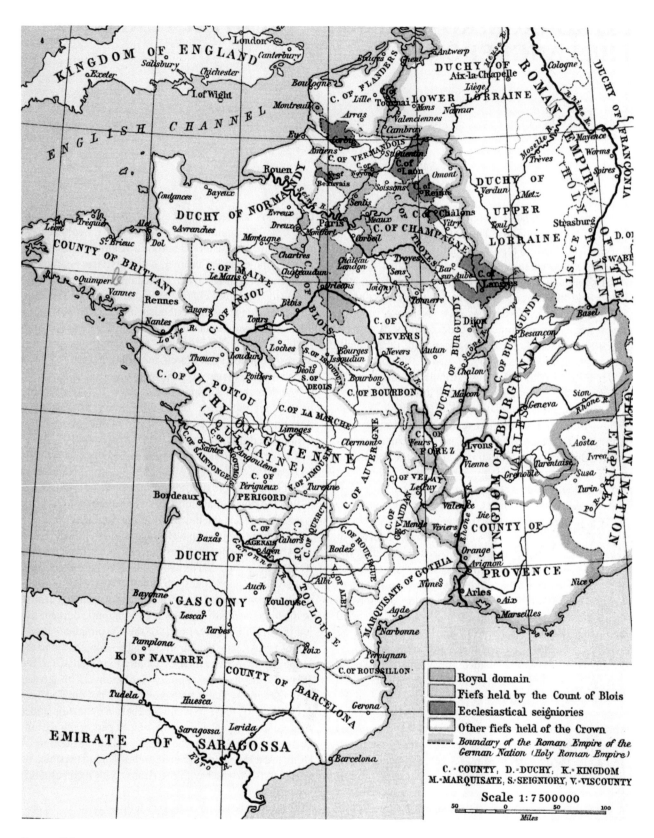

FIGURE 7.1

France in 1035 (from Shepherd's Historical Atlas, 1967)

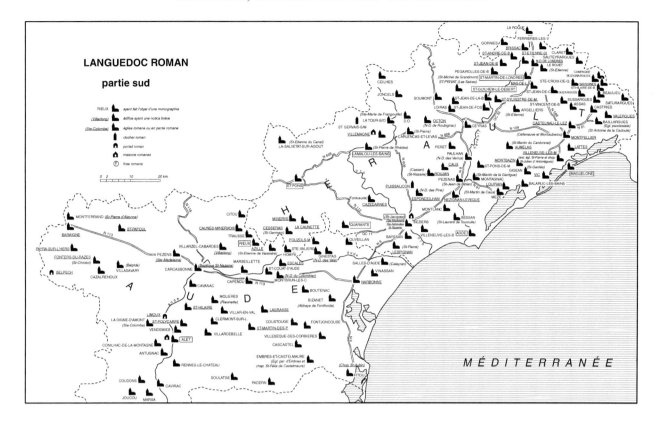

FIGURE 7.2

Lower Languedoc (Lugand, Nougaret and Saint-Jean)

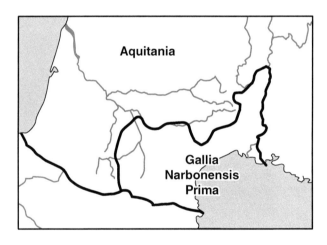

FIGURE 7.3

The Roman province of Gallia Narbonensis Prima (drawn by C. Kennish)

FIGURE 7.4

Visigothic territory in 476 (drawn by C. Kennish)

considered Visigothic but now dated on good grounds to the period of Arab rule in the 8th and 9th centuries.[7]

First Romanesque buildings in Gothia are clearly related to the First Romanesque buildings of Lombardy, where the style was formed. By what route was it introduced? The most direct is overland via Provence to Gothia and then to Catalonia (Figure 7.1). That is what appears to have happened in the regions to the north of Lombardy, towards Lake Geneva: people building interesting new buildings and neighbouring patrons then noting and emulating them. The same could have applied to Provence, through buildings such as the churches at Valdeblore, Levens, Saint-Pons and Sarrians, which have been tentatively dated to the first half of the 11th century.[8]

The alternative route is via Catalonia. This was Marcel Durliat's view, and there are good reasons for agreeing with him.[9] Three of these stand out. The first is the opening up of the sea route from northern Italy to Provence, Gothia and Catalonia in the 10th century. In the words of Christopher Hohler, 'If any single event can be thought

FIGURE 7.5
Visigothic territory after 507 (drawn by C. Kennish)

FIGURE 7.6
Arab territories in c. 740 (drawn by C. Kennish)

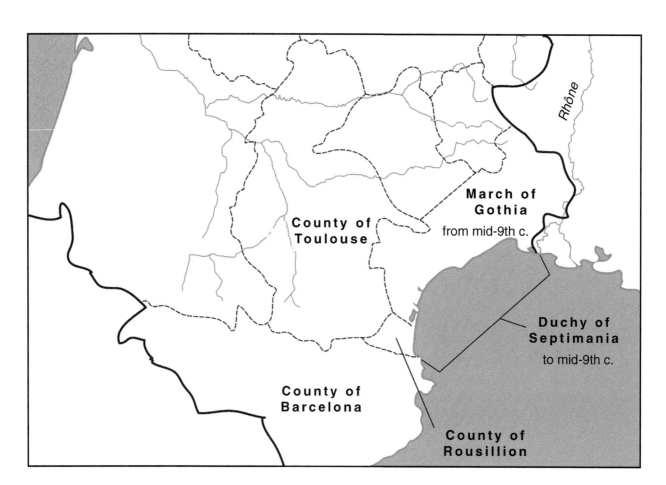

FIGURE 7.7
Carolingian political units (drawn by C. Kennish)

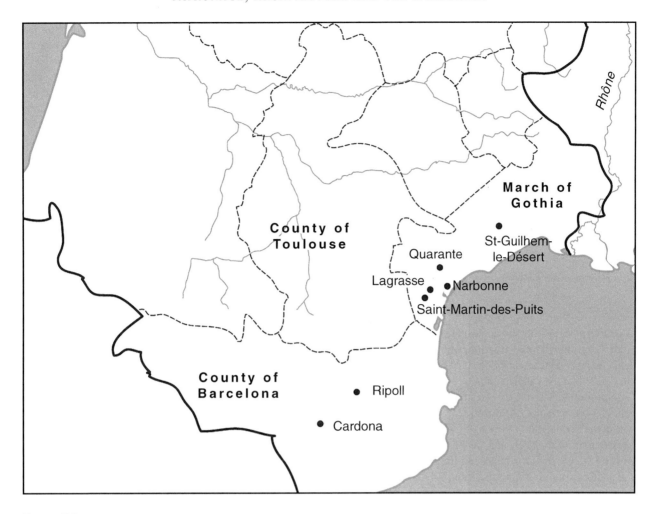

FIGURE 7.8

Catalonia, Gothia and Provence with sites mentioned in the text (drawn by C. Kennish)

to have touched off the economic revival of the 11th century it would seem to be the capture and holding to ransom of Maïeul, abbot of Cluny, by Saracen marauders in the summer of 972. He was returning to Burgundy from Rome, and his captors came from a pirate settlement near Fréjus which had successfully resisted all attempts to dislodge it for nearly a hundred years. St Maïeul's ransom was duly paid and he was released. But Cluny was the head of an influential congregation of monasteries, and they had been hurt in their pockets. A military coalition was at once assembled which, without delay or apparent difficulty, drove the Saracens at last and forever from the Riviera.'[10]

The second point supporting the sequence Lombardy, Catalonia, Gothia is the number of buildings in the style of the first third of the 11th century in Catalonia (earlier and more securely dated than equivalents in Provence), and the striking design of some of them.

The third is the character of the First Romanesque buildings in Gothia. These can be represented by three major monuments, namely the churches of the monasteries of Lagrasse, Quarante and Saint-Guilhem-le-Désert, datable to the second and third quarters of the 11th century (Figure 7.8).[11]

At Lagrasse the south arm of the transept with its three apses survives, the central one larger than the other two, while the vestiges of the north arm allow it to be reconstructed with the same form (Figure 7.9). The remains are undated.[12] The plan is very like the equivalent parts of Santa Maria at Ripoll in Catalonia of 1020 to 1032 (Figure 7.10), which has three apses on each arm of the transept. There are two things which suggest that Ripoll is earlier than Lagrasse. The first is that its plan can be directly related to that of its model, St Peter's in Rome (Figure 7.11), in having six units on the wall of the transept, and, as the apses at Ripoll are all the same size, the larger central apse in the set of three on the south arm at Lagrasse looks like a development out of Ripoll.[13] Second, the more finely cut masonry at Lagrasse also suggests a later date.[14] Neither of these observations constitutes proof, but they both support the same conclusion.

Quarante was consecrated in 1053 (Figures 7.12 and 7.13). It has a barrel-vaulted nave, east arm and transept arms, domes on squinches over the crossing and the south bay of the south transept and groins in the aisles. On the exterior, the main apse has eaves niches and the south apse paired arched corbel tables. These features make it very like Sant Vicenç at Cardona, which was built

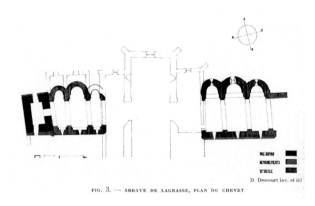

FIGURE 7.9

Monastery of Lagrasse (Aude); mid-11th-century church plan (Congrès Archéologique de France, 1973)

between 1019 and 1040 (Figures 7.14 and 7.15).[15] It is of course possible that the consecration of Quarante took place long after its construction, but accepting the evidence at face value again places the marcher building at a later date than the Catalan one.

Saint-Guilhem-le-Désert is more complicated as it contains the remains of three builds all broadly datable within the 11th century: the earliest church, of which two bays remain at the west end of the nave, then the main bays of the nave with a restricted transept and east end, and a later east end (Figures 7.16 and 7.17).[16] There was a

consecration in 1076. This has been related to each of the three periods of construction, but the majority view now has the nave belonging to the church consecrated in 1076 and the new east end built in the late 11th century. The aisled nave, restricted transept, barrel vaults, squinches and arched corbel tables of this middle build all relate Saint-Guilhem to Quarante, and via Quarante to Cardona, and, if the 1076 consecration date is accepted for this part of the church, then there can be little doubt that it is later than the Catalan building. Thus, all three of these churches are closely related to buildings in Catalonia, and are almost certainly later than them.

Institutional links do not prove or even suggest Catalan primacy, but they indicate the close connections between the two areas. Thus, Lagrasse was in receipt of donations from Catalans. It also had dependent monasteries in Catalonia, including Sant Pere del Burgal, as around 950 Sunyer, abbot of Lagrasse, returned land to the abbess of Burgal. In the middle of the 11th century the archbishop of Narbonne was a Catalan, son of the count of Cerdanya and nephew of Oliba of Ripoll, while the counts of Barcelona had an interest in the monastery of Corbières near Lagrasse.[17]

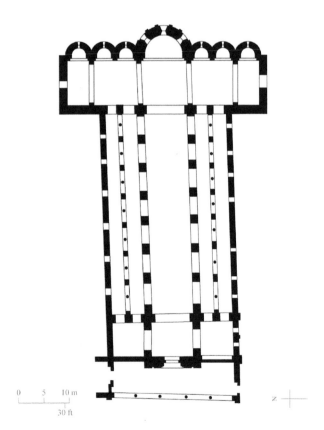

FIGURE 7.10

Monastery of Ripoll; Santa Maria (1020–32), plan

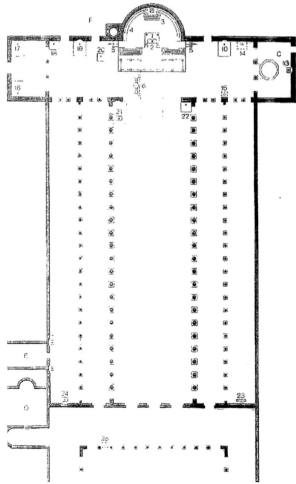

FIGURE 7.11

Rome, St Peter's, c. 320, plans: (Sible de Blaauw)

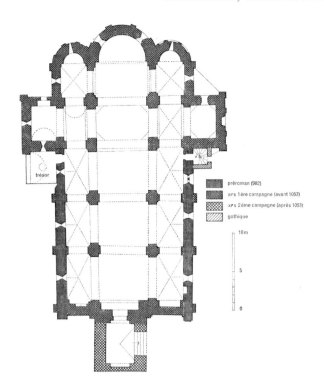

FIGURE 7.12

Monastery of Quarante (Hérault), church, consecrated 1053: plan (Congrès Archéologique de France, 1950)

FIGURE 7.13

Quarante: interior (Malcolm Thurlby)

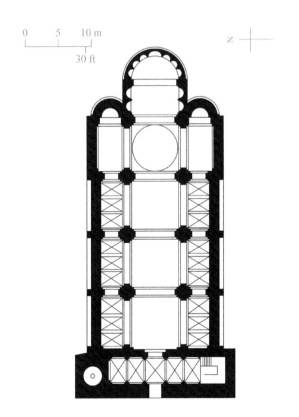

FIGURE 7.14

Sant Vicenç, Cardona, c. 1019–30: plan

FIGURE 7.15

Sant Vicenç, Cardona: interior

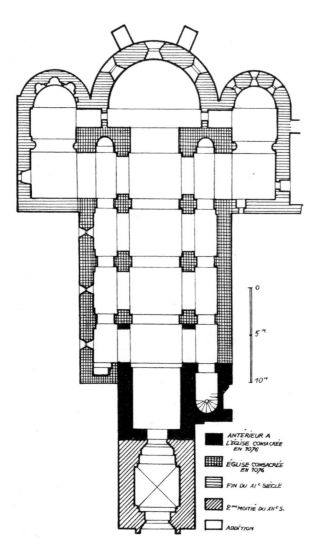

FIGURE 7.16

Saint-Guilhem-le-désert – plan of church consecrated in 1076 (Congrès Archéologique de France, 1950)

FIGURE 7.17

Saint-Guilhem-le-Désert: interior (Malcolm Thurlby)

If the preceding arguments and observations provide a reasonable case for the derivation of the First Romanesque architecture of Gothia from Catalonia, that immediately raises the question of motive: why should patrons, especially those who were natives of Gothia, wish to identify themselves with Catalonia? Perhaps the key issue is, where did people think they lived? The County of Toulouse, as the de facto centre of power, must be a possibility, but the paucity of architectural links tells against it.[18] If the identification was with the idea of Gothia, then the orientation would have been towards the Iberian peninsula, and therefore, most immediately, to Catalonia. An answer might also lie in the associations with the Visigoths. Should patrons have wanted to underline those associations in the sphere of architecture, might they not have selected the building types of the area of the Iberian peninsula most immediately available to them? It can only have helped that the leading structures of the period in Catalonia were among the most noteworthy anywhere in western Europe in the first third of the 11th century (and it has to be acknowledged that that could have been the main reason for emulating them). There could also be a negative possibility, namely that the First Romanesque style was adopted in Gothia in order to distinguish it from whatever was the current manner of the County of Toulouse. If this sounds far-fetched, then it is worth noting Sheila McTighe's suggestion that Catalonia adopted the First Romanesque style to differentiate itself from its Iberian neighbours to the west.[19]

In conclusion, I hope I have provided some basis for considering the March of Gothia a possible explanatory tool in the study of the First Romanesque architecture of its area, by reference to its name, the route by which the architectural style was introduced, the character of the buildings and surmises about the attitudes of their patrons.

ACKNOWLEDGEMENTS

I would like to record my thanks to the many people who have so generously helped me with this paper, including Euan McCartney Robson for information and arguments, Malcolm Thurlby for the same and photographs, Claude Andrault-Schmitt, Manuel Castiñeiras and Jordi Camps for bibliographical advice, Robert Boak for identifying a hiatus, Sible de Blaauw for his plan of St Peter's and Chris Kennish for his expert draughtsmanship.

NOTES

[1] R. de Lasteyrie, *L'architecture réligieuse en France á l'époque romane* (Paris 1912); J. Puig i Cadafalch, *Le premier art roman* (Paris 1928) (two references, but each in a political and not architectural context), and 'La place de la Catalogne dans la géographie générale et la chronologie du premier art roman', in his *La Catalogne a l'époque romane* (Paris 1932), 21–44; K.J. Conant, *Carolingian and Romanesque Architecture 800 to 1200* (Harmondsworth 1959) (two references, again not concerning architecture); H. Kubach, *Romanesque Architecture* (London 1988); É. Vergnolle, *L'art roman en France* (Paris 1994); and X. Barral i Altet, *Contre l'art roman? Essai sur un passé réinventé* (Paris 2006). P. Wolff, *Histoire du Languedoc* (Toulouse 1967), has no entry for Gothia in the index.

[2] J. Lugand, J. Nougaret, and R. Saint-Jean, *Languedoc roman: le Languedoc méditerranéen* (La-Pierre-qui-Vire 1975). M. Durliat, *Haut-Languedoc roman* (La-Pierre-qui-Vire 1978), covers the part of Languedoc centred on Toulouse. The three parts of Elisabeth Magnou-Nortier's 'La terre, la rente et le pouvoir dans les pays de Languedoc pendent le haut moyen age' (*Francia*, 9 (1981), 79–115; 10 (1982), 21–66; and 12 (1984), 53–118) provide a densely-referenced account of power in lower and upper Languedoc from the 9th century to the 11th, but there is no mention of Gothia, an indication of how recessive the March is in the documents.

[3] J.H. Hill and L.L. Hill, Raymond IV, Count of Toulouse (Westport, Conn. [1962] 1980), 7, 8 and 21, refer to 'charters of Languedoc', 'Raymond IV building his feudal state in 'Languedoc' in the late-11th-century, and his being able to 'weld Languedoc into the semblance of a state'. A.R. Lewis, 'The Dukes in the Regnum Francorum, A.D. 550–751', *Speculum*, 51 (1976), 381–410 at 409, accepts this evidence for 'the beginnings of a true principality of Languedoc in the late 11th century'.

[4] At this point it might appear that we are safe in deep history, but in 2005 Georges Frêche, president of Languedoc-Roussillon, founded in 1982, proposed changing the name of the region to Septimanie. To this he received a spirited reaction, on two fronts: from Narbonne, saying that by removing the name of Languedoc he would, *a un seul coup*, destroy 800 years of history, and from Catalonia, pointing out that removing the name Roussillon would hide the existence of the part of Catalonia which had existed north of the Pyrenees.

[5] Hill and Hill, *Count of Toulouse* (as n. 3); M. Aurell, *Les noces du comte: marriage et pouvoir en Catalogne, (785–1213)* (Paris 1995); J. Jarrett, *Rulers and Ruled in Frontier Catalonia, 880–1010: Pathways to Power* (Woodbridge 2010); H. Débax, 'Les réseaux aristocratiques autour de Lagrasse du IXe au XIe siècle. Contribution à l'histoire des origines de l'abbaye', in *L'abbaye de Lagrasse. Art, archéologie et histoire, Actes des journées d'études, 2012*, ed., S. Caucanas and N. Pousthomis (Archives départementales de l'Aude 2013), 35–48. These feudal entities have a very complicated history. Indeed, as Jarret puts it (135), events in this part of the world in the 9th and 10th centuries give a whole new meaning to the word anarchy, my favourite indication of which is the existence in one area of viscounts without the necessity for any counts.

The two names County of Barcelona and Catalonia offer a parallel to the March of Gothia and Languedoc, in that Catalonia is often (as in this paper) used for the territory in the period of the County, and the Spanish March. The parallel ends there, however. Whereas the name Languedoc has nothing to do with the label Gothia and covers a much larger area, the Principality of Catalonia is simply a later name for a similar area and political unit as the County of Barcelona and the Spanish March, and which, again unlike Languedoc, existed in a non-political form in the relevant centuries. M. Aurell, 'Aux origins de la Catalogne: le myth fondateur de la maison de Barcelone dans l'historiographie du XIIe siècle', *Académie des Inscriptions et Belles-Lettres, comptes rendus* (1998), 7–18.

[6] P. Bonnassie, *La Catalogne du milieu du Xe a la fin du XIe siècle: croissance et mutations d'une société* (Toulouse, 1975), 137; Jarrett, *Frontier Catalonia* (as n. 5), 8. Wolff (as n. 1), despite having no entry for Gothia in the index, mentions c. 872, 'Septimanie' ('que, de plus en plus, l'on appelait alors la Gothie')' (p. 131). For the bull of 904 and the gift of 961 see F. Mazel, 'Lieu sacré, aire de paix et seignurerie autour de l'abbaye de Saint-Gilles (fin IXe-debut XIIIe siècle)', in J. Théry, *Lieux sacrés et espace ecclésial (IXe–XVe siècle)* (Toulouse 2011), 229–76, 234 and 235 respectively. For the claim that William duke of Aquitaine was in the early 10th century the last Marquis of Gothia see J-J Domergue, *Essai sur le Gouvernement du Languedoc depuis les Romains jusqu'à notre siècle* (Paris 1773), 19; and for Hugh, count of Rouergue, see Hill and Hill (as n. 3), 2, who provide references to seven marquises of Gothia between the early 10th century and the middle of the 11th century.

[7] M. Durliat, 'L'église de Saint-Martin-des-Puits', *Congrès Archéologique de France: Pays de l'Aude*, 131 (1973), 140–47. M. de los Ángeles Utrero Agudo, 'Late Antique and Early Medieval Hispanic Churches and the Archaeology of Architecture: Revisions and Reinterpretations of Constructions, Chronologies and Contexts', *Medieval Archaeology*, 54 (2010), 1–33. Even if all the buildings previously identified as works of the Visigoths can be dated after their period, I would like to suggest that they might none the less have used the horseshoe arch. I say this because it was a Roman form, in use in the western parts of the empire, evident in examples in the Iberian peninsula such as the relief item 118 in Burgos museum and a stele in the Museu Sant Marc in León, and indeed as a prominent feature in no less Roman a building than the Pantheon, on the interior of the entrance arch.

[8] Puig i Cadafalch, *premier art roman* (as n. 1), 51: 'Il est probable qu'à travers la Provence, l'Italie se reliait aux Pyrénées pour constituer un vaste ensemble artistique. Malheureusement, les monuments anciennes antérieurs au XIe siècle sont assez rares en Provence.' On First Romanesque buildings in Provence see J. Thirion, 'L'influence lombarde dans les Alps française du Sud', *Bulletin Monumental*, 128 (1970), 7–40, J. Thirion, *Alpes romanes* (La-Pierre-qui-Vire 1980), and A. Hartmann-Virnich, 'Remarques sur l'architecture religieuse du premier âge roman en Provence (1030–1100)', *Hortus Artium Medievalium* (Journal of the International Research Centre for Late Antiquity and the Middle Ages, Zagreb-Motovan), 6 (2000), 35–64. Oddly, Lugand, Nougaret and Saint-Jean, *Languedoc méditerranéen* (as n. 2), 18, say of the First Romanesque that Provence 'ne l'a pas adoptée'.

[9] M. Durliat, 'L'art dans les pays de l'Aude', *Congrès Archéologique de France: Pays de l'Aude*, 131 (1973), 9–29 at 13.

[10] C. Hohler, 'A Bibliography for the Study of Romanesque and Early Gothic Art up to *c*. 1250', typescript, Courtauld Institute of Art, 1962, introduction. A sea route makes Narbonne a possible centre of distribution, but the case is difficult to prove or disprove because of the absence of First Romanesque buildings in the city. It might also appear that the Rhône would have facilitated the move of architectural ideas from the Mediterranean inland to Provence and Gothia, but this is unlikely to have been the case. It is a very fast-flowing river, so that travelling upstream is extremely difficult. This is clear from the statement that columns acquired by Odilo for Cluny were 'transported not without great labour by the headlong currents of the Durance and Rhône'. Even after the invention of steam, boats coming downstream seldom made the return journey. On the Rhône see Alan Borg, *Architectural Sculpture in Romanesque Provence* (Oxford 1972), 16, and for Odilo, Wolfgang Braunfels, *Monasteries of Western Europe: The Architecture of the Orders* (London 1972), 240: *ac per rapidissimos Durantiae Rhodanique cursus non sine magno labore advectis* (Jotsuald's Life of Odilo, Migne, *Patrologia Latina*, CXLII, col. 908).

[11] X. Barral i Altet, ed., *Le paysage monumental de la France, autour de l'an mil* (Paris 1987), 399–492: Languedoc-Roussillon.

[12] M. Durliat and D. Drocourt, 'L'abbaye de Lagrasse', *Congrès Archéologique de France: Pays de l'Aude*, 131 (1973), 104–22; and A. Hartmann-Virnich, 'Le monastère du Xe au milieu du XIIIe siècle d'après les indices archéologiques', in *abbaye de Lagrasse*, ed., Caucanas and Pousthomis (as n. 5), 73–83.

[13] For Ripoll see W.M. Whitehill, *Spanish Romanesque Architecture* (Oxford 1941), 35–44, and G. Gaillard, 'Ripoll', *Congrès*

Archéologique de France: Catalogne, 117 (1959), 117–59. Sible de Blaauw (*Cultus et Decor*, 2 vols (Vatican 1994), II, 451–756 and fig. 25) has demonstrated that the niches shown on Alfarano's plan of 1589 date from after the 11th century, and so could not have been the model for the six apses at Ripoll. Yet one possible explanation is that the niches were built to accommodate the five liturgical features (three in the south arm and two in the north) which were present in the transept before 1100, with the arrangement made symmetrical. For Catalan First Romanesque architecture as a whole see M. Castiñeiras, 'La cuestión lombarda en el primer románico catalan', in *Il medioevo delle cattedrali: chiesa e impero: la lotta delle imagini (secoli XI e XII)*, ed., A.C. Quintavalle, (Milan 2006), 345–55.

[14] Durliat and Drocourt, 'Lagrasse' (as n. 12), 112.

[15] J. Vallery-Radot, 'L'église Sainte-Marie de Quarante', *Congrès Archéologique de France: Pays de l'Aude*, 131 (1973), 307–22; Lugand, Nougaret and Saint-Jean, in *Languedoc méditerranéen* (as n. 2), 59–95; Vergnolle, *L'art roman* (as n. 1), 96–97. For Cardona see Whitehill, *Spanish Romanesque* (as n. 12), 45–51. Sarrians in western Provence is very like Quarante, with barrel-vaults, a bay between the apse and the crossing, and a crossing dome on squinches. See Hartmann-Virnich, 'Remarques' (as n. 8), 48–48.

[16] J. Vallery-Radot, 'Saint-Guilhem-le-Désert', *Congrès Archéologique de France: Montpellier*, 108 (1950), 156–80; Lugand, Nougaret and Saint-Jean, in *Languedoc méditerranéen* (as n. 2), 75–95.

[17] Puig i Cadafalch, *Premier Art Roman* (as n. 1), 43–47; Whitehill, *Spanish Romanesque* (as n. 12), 15; Durliat and Drocourt, 'Lagrasse' (as n. 12), 112; Lugand, Nougaret and Saint-Jean, *Languedoc méditerranéen* (as in n. 2), 18; Débax, 'réseaux aristocratiques' (as n. 5). Débax's concluding sentence (48) is highly relevant: 'Il pourrait être intéressant de chercher si cette proximité de l'abbaye avec les aristocraties du sud pendant deux siècles n'a pas eu aussi des conséquences en matière architecturale et stylistique.'

[18] Lugand, Nougaret and Saint-Jean, *le Languedoc méditerranéen* (as n. 2), 18, say of the First Romanesque style that 'le Haut-Languedoc toulousain . . . l'a toujours ignorée.' Yet it has to be acknowledged that there are First Romanesque buildings in upper Languedoc, such as the churches of the monasteries of Ambialet, founded between 1047 and 1060, and Lasplanques, probably of the late-11th-century. See Durliat, *Haut-Languedoc* (as n. 1), 231–36, figs 111–13, and 257–62, figs 115–17.

[19] As reported by J.D. Dodds, *Architecture and Ideology in Early Medieval Spain* (Pennsylvania University Park and London 1990), 169, n. 7.

THE ARMENIAN CATHEDRAL OF SAINTS JAMES IN JERUSALEM: MELISENDE AND THE QUESTION OF EXCHANGE BETWEEN EAST AND WEST

Armen Kazaryan

INTRODUCTION

The Cathedral of Saints James in Jerusalem (Սրբոց Յակոբեանց Վանք Հայոց in Armenian) belongs to the Armenian Church and is one of the most venerated churches in the Holy Land (Figure 8.1).[1] It is the principal church of the monastery of the same name, as well as acting as the cathedral of the Armenian Patriarch of Jerusalem. It occupies a significant part of the Armenian Quarter in the Old City of Jerusalem, and is bounded to its west by the street of the Armenian Orthodox Patriarchate (known in the middle ages as the street of Mount Sion), which in turn connects the Jaffa and Sion Gates. A monastery shares the cathedral precinct, along with the residence of the Armenian Patriarch of Jerusalem, a number of household buildings, a library and educational institutions.

According to tradition, the Cathedral of Saints James is the burial place of the 'brother of Christ', James the Just, and the place where the Apostle James the Great (son of Zebedee) was decapitated and where his head was buried – hence the plural Saints James of the dedication. The site also houses a tomb of Macarius, Bishop of Jerusalem (314–33).[2] The first actual building to have been created here is believed to be the Chapel of St Menas, adjacent to the cathedral on the north, founded by a patrician woman named Bassa in 444.[3] Also in the 5th century we hear that the dean of the cathedral was an Armenian priest, Andreas Melitenetsi.

The construction of the cathedral is not mentioned in surviving written sources, though there is an account of the then relatively new church given by the German pilgrim John of Würzburg (c. 1162–65): 'In the same place, not far from monastery of St Sabas . . . a large church [was] built in honour of St James the Great, where Armenian monks live and have a large hospital for bringing together the poor of their nation. There also the head of the same Apostle is held in great veneration: for he was decapitated by Herod, and his disciples took his body by divine providence to Galicia in the kingdom of Spain, having placed it on board of a ship in Jaffa, while his head remained in Palestine. The same head is still shown in that church to visiting pilgrims.'[4] Numerous later pilgrim accounts prove that the cathedral was always Armenian, in spite of arguments to the contrary by Greeks and Georgians. In the 18th century, especially, there were claims that the monastery of Saints James had originated with and initially belonged to the Georgian Church.[5]

To understand the current state of the cathedral, written sources on the extensive restoration of the church and monastery during the patriarchate of Gregory the Chain-Bearer (1715–49) are of great importance.[6] An inscription records repairs to the cupola in 1812, while work was also undertaken after the earthquake that struck Jerusalem on 23 May 1834.[7] For these later repairs there is an account by the Greek monk Neophytos of Cyprus: 'The Armenians surpassed [the Latins and the Greeks] in the question of building. They built on very solid foundations a new narthex to the church of St James and joined it to the Church; by other additions they made an enclosure for the women. The church was thereby greatly enlarged. The cupola of the Church was formerly open and covered with glass like the Baths, but now they finished it off in stone. The windows of the cupola were previously closed, like those of the Katholikon [in the Holy Sepulchre], and these were now opened. They painted the church and decorated it with many pictures.'[8]

A BRIEF HISTORIOGRAPHY AND OUTLINE OF THE STUDY

As Nurith Kenaan-Kedar remarked in her study of Armenian architecture in Jerusalem, the cathedral of Saints James 'has never been systematically studied as an individual architectural project'.[9] The following study doesn't materially change this, but it examines the building in relation to its probable patron and in the light of the importance of medieval Jerusalem as a meeting place of cultural traditions.[10]

A number of scholars have already suggested that the cathedral was constructed during the reign and with the

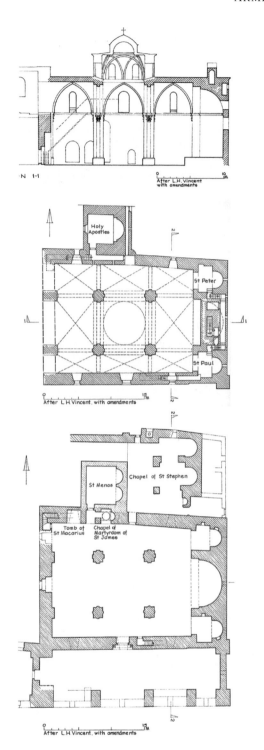

FIGURE 8.1

Jerusalem: Saints James Cathedral, plans and section (after Pringle)

encouragement of Melisende, Queen of Jerusalem (1131–61).[11] Claude Mutafian notes the warm reception given to the Armenian Catholicos Grigor III Pahlavuni in Jerusalem in April 1141.[12] For Denys Pringle this visit of the Armenian Catholicos to attend a synod held in the church of Mount Sion involving the Latin Patriarch, William I, the papal legate, Alberic, bishop of Ostia, William of Tyre and others, was probably the 'spur for the Armenian rebuilding of the cathedral church of St James, which must have been well advanced by the time that King Toros II visited King Amalric in Jerusalem around 1163'.[13] Folda felt that 'in the context of amicable relations and with the special interest of the queen [Melisende]', the church was erected in the 1140s, adding that as a patron of church construction in Jerusalem in the mid-12th-century, Melisende was in a position to persuade masons who had worked at the Holy Sepulchre into working on Saints James Cathedral.[14] Nurith Kenaan-Kedar also argued for Melisende as a donor to both Catholic and Armenian churches.[15]

If Melisende was the patron, what of the architecture? Kenaan-Kedar thought the masons like the architecture were Armenian, an opinion shared by Claude Mutafian, who saw the building as typically Armenian, and compared it to a number of 12th-century churches in Armenia.[16] However, as Denys Pringle has observed, the matter is not quite so straightforward. Pringle makes the important archaeological point that the piers and arches of the original 12th-century narthex 'bear the diagonal dressing and masonry marks typical of twelfth-century Frankish workmanship'.[17] Pringle concludes, 'While the layout of the building was evidently dictated by the requirements of the Armenian liturgy, the masonry marks on the south façade, the style of the capitals and south doorway, and the form of the vaulting all suggest a heavy involvement of Frankish masons in its construction.'[18]

I shall propose that earlier evaluations of Saints James Cathedral as a church that mixes Cilician (or wider West Armenian) and Romanesque architectural styles in a creative and purposeful manner well represents the building.[19] But what can we say about the role of Queen Melisende in its construction? There is no direct evidence for her participation. However, Mutafian's proposal that work on a new cathedral of Saints James could have been precipitated by the visit of the Catholicos Grigor III Pahlavuni to Jerusalem, and that both Melisende and he could be regarded as the primary patrons and initiators seems entirely plausible.[20] Such a magnificent church as St. James is unlikely to have been begun without the approval of the Catholicos, while the (probable) engagement of stonemasons from the Holy Sepulchre is unlikely to have been initiated without the Queen's support.

My conclusions are preliminary, in large part because study of the 12th-century fabric is compromised by the prevalence of late and post-medieval decoration (Figure 8.2). The lower parts of the walls are covered by ornamental glazed tiles (1727–37) from Kütahya in Asia Minor (a city famous for the production of painted faience).[21] Above this level, up to the level of the capitals, the walls are covered by two tiers of oil paintings on canvas, dating from the 18th and 19th centuries. The arches and vaults are plastered and white-washed. The mosaic floor dates to 1651. The altar has been moved to the space beneath the cupola and enclosed within an openwork grating where it supports an icon of Virgin and Child. The apse thus revealed is decorated in exquisite oriental style, though the lower section of the wall is covered by a blind arcade made up of carved marble slabs (1727–37), inside

FIGURE 8.2

Jerusalem: Saints James Cathedral, interior to east (S. Tarkhanova)

the frames of which are depicted bunches of flowers. Entrances to the chapels are through double-valve doors inlaid with wood and ivory of 1371. The altar zone and the space beneath the cupola, along with many of the lateral wall surfaces, are resplendent with numerous silver lamps, chandeliers and large porcelain eggs suspended from chains on which are painted figurative and ornamental designs along with dedicatory inscriptions. These are part of a larger tradition for the decoration of shrines, entirely typical for Armenians in Jerusalem.

As such, we cannot see the original internal surfaces of the building. This circumstance, taken with the absence of a full-scale archaeological study, has obviously hindered research.[22]

ARCHITECTURAL DESCRIPTION

The cathedral consists of a spacious, slightly elongated four-pillar hall with three apses to the east. It is fully vaulted, with a dome supported on four arches over the central bay, and groin vaults around this central core (Figure 8.3). Overall the church measures 28 m from east to west and between 18 and 20 m north to south (excluding the narthex). The central bay is a square with sides of 6.40 m.[23] The aisles are appreciably narrower than the central nave, and that to the north is irregular and tapers towards the east, narrowing by 1.20 metres from west to east.[24] The groin vaults over the nave bays are square while those over the aisle are approximately rectangular. The triapsidal east end (the altar zone) is contained within a solid masonry block, meaning the apses are square on the exterior and semi-circular on their inner surfaces. The block includes the principal apse, with a narrow *bema* flanked by two small apsidal *pastophoria*. Initially, these lateral chambers were open to the aisles, though the relatively low arches at the aisle ends allowed for small upper chapels to be created, reached through a narrow passage in the thickness of the south aisle wall that begins at a door in the central bay of the south aisle.[25] The principal entrance to the church was through a sculpted portal that brought one into the middle of the south aisle. This portal was sheltered within a narthex that ran the length of the church, originally open to the street through four arches, but in 1666 it was walled in to create the Etchmiadzin Chapel. Pringle speculated that, prior to the 17th century, there may have been an altar at the east end of the narthex, and that the space may have been used for baptisms from an early date.[26] If this were so, we would suggest that the baptismal niche to the left of the altar space also dates from the 12th century. Creating a baptismal niche in the northern wall of the church, close to the altar, is common in Armenian churches from as early as the 4th century.[27]

The most interesting and unusual feature of the building is the deployment of a type of dome, or cupola, set above an annular cornice that in turn sits over the pendentive crossing (Figure 8.4).[28] Fundamental to this composition are six arches that intersect to form a six-rayed star with a hexagon at its centre. A small dome appears over the hexagon, bounded by the intersecting arches. Given the way that the six arches intersect, twelve triangular severies are created outside the central hexagon, each one of which is covered by a flat ceiling (and roof). Those triangular compartments that are located in the points of the star (six in total) are decorated with ornamental cones in relief, perhaps intended to symbolise celestial bodies, while the shallower triangular compartments which sit between the points are left plain and open onto six large windows set into the drum. This whole complex composition is in turn contained within a drum, or *tholobate*, which rises to the height of the springing of the inner dome.

From the exterior, the drum is articulated by a blind arcade, divided into 24 parts. There is one smaller dome above this structure, corresponding to the inner cupola and topped by a modern roof. The windows of the drum are inscribed within six arches that are taller than the blind arcades and rise to an ogee head. However, the window arch mouldings differ from those of the blind arches, which they cut into just above springing level (Figure 8.5). The latter peculiarity makes it clear that the window heads post-date the blind arches. However, there is currently no consensus on the overall architectural evolution and date of the present drum and dome. Following Vincent and Abel, Pringle

FIGURE 8.3

Jerusalem: Saints James Cathedral, interior vaults of west bays (A. Kazaryan)

FIGURE 8.4

Jerusalem: Saints James Cathedral, interior of 'dome' (A. Kazaryan)

FIGURE 8.5

Jerusalem: Saints James Cathedral, exterior of 'dome' (M. Castiñeiras)

is disinclined to date the current internal arrangements to the time of the building of the church. He interprets a note on the renovation of the dome in 1812 as suggesting the intersecting arches were built at this date; at the same time, he hints at the possibility that the small inner dome was only added in the 1830s, after the earthquake. While noting that similarly elaborate cupolas can be found in medieval Armenian architecture, as well as in Spain, Pringle follows earlier European archaeologists in expressing doubt over the issue. 'If the dome of St James's could indeed be shown to be twelfth century, the latter [earlier Armenian vaults] would perhaps offer the most plausible source of inspiration, though it also seems possible that it is an antiquarian creation of the early modern period.'[29]

Taking the question of the date of the small inner dome first, it does indeed seem likely that this was created after the earthquake of 1834. That there was originally a single opening in some sort of tower-like central structure is mentioned in the accounts of numerous pilgrims. The earliest is that of John Poloner in the early-15th-century. 'In the middle, it [the Armenian church] has four square columns. It has no windows, except for a rounded glass one at its highest point, but has 300 or more lamps.'[30] And Anselm Adorno described the building as 'a most beautiful church having a tower carried at its highest point, rounded and with a broad aperture'.[31] Finally, the cathedral is undoubtedly represented in a manuscript of 1726 from Ottoman Galiopoli now in the Pushkin State Museum of Fine Arts in Moscow. Here one sees the cathedral's flat roof, with a blind arcade articulating the drum and an oculus marking its 'dome' (Figure 8.6).[32] Thus, it seems reasonably clear that the original upper oculus was closed after 1834 to be replaced by a dome, and that this is the most likely date at which six windows were cut into the drum. However, there is no reason to suppose that alterations were made to the intersecting arches at the same time. Although the drum can only be inspected at close quarters from the exterior, and the interior is anyway coated in post-medieval plaster and paint, our preliminary conclusion is that the internal arrangement of intersecting arches, together with the cylindrical drum and external blind arcading all date from the middle of the 12th century.

THE SOURCES OF THE ARCHITECTURE: THE MAIN SPACE

The plan of the cathedral draws on a type of four-columned cross-domed church that was well-established in the eastern Mediterranean and can be found in both Armenian and Byzantine traditions. The fact that the lateral *pastophoria* were open to the nave brings the building closer to Byzantine churches, but the existence of chapels above these and the use of compound piers rather than columns in the main elevation are entirely characteristic of medieval Armenian churches. In the 11th and 12th centuries churches in Armenia were aisleless, and employed compound responds (the only exception to this is Ani Cathedral of the last quarter of the 10th century). However, the plans of numerous, mostly ruined, Armenian churches in the Cilician Armenian kingdom, and cities to the east and south of it, differ from those of the Armenian Highlands. A now ruined and probably

example, are supported on pointed arches, carried on simplified Corinthian capitals of a sort widely used in Romanesque churches. And while at first sight the compound piers used at Jerusalem are not unlike those used in Greater Armenia more generally, as at Ani Cathedral (Figure 8.7), the particular form of the piers, as well as the type of hollow chamfer used for the imposts and continued as a stringcourse around the base of the apses, seems to belong to the Romanesque tradition. Among surviving churches of Jerusalem, similar forms can be found in the Holy Sepulchre and in the mid-12th-century church of St Anne by the pools of Bethesda.[33] The common springing point for both the arches and the groin vaults, excluding the central cupola bay, was also typical for the most part of Romanesque churches – both basilican and centrally-planned. Four-column churches built or reconstructed in Jerusalem under the Crusaders differed from Byzantine four-column churches. Beside the cathedral of Saints James, the chapel of St Helen in the Holy Sepulchre complex (which also now belongs to the Armenian Church) similarly springs groin vaults over the lateral bays from the same level as the pointed arches, and maintains a consistent height across the aisle bays.[34] Earlier four-pillar churches in the eastern Mediterranean had conceived the type as a centrally-planned

FIGURE 8.6

Illustration from the Armenian manuscript of 1726, Galiopoli (Pushkin State Museum of Fine Arts, Moscow)

12th-century church in Cilician Anazarva (Anavarza, Turkey) is a good example. This was aisled, with tall side apses open to the aisles and an overall plan firmly contained within a rectangular outline – all features found in the Armenian Cathedral of Saints James in Jerusalem. As with Anazarva, most surviving Armenian churches in Cilicia are striking in the way they adapt long-standing Armenian traditions into an essentially Byzantine context.

That is why, when one discusses the Armenian sources of the architecture of Saints James in Jerusalem, the Mediterranean-Armenian tradition is important. Links between the creative centres of Great Armenia and the architecture of the Cilician Armenian kingdom were weak, while the architecture of Armenian Cilicia was more or less completely integrated into the architectural culture of the Middle East. Comparisons of the imposts, cornices and archivolts of the Cathedral of Saints James with those of a Cilician Armenian church, such as that in the fortress of Anavarza, alongside 10th-to-13th-century monuments in the Armenian Highlands, reveals a much greater similarity between Jerusalem and Anavarza than to those of Highland Armenia.

If we then move away from the ground-plan and look instead at the upper levels of the cathedral, we are easily reminded of another cultural sphere – one much closer to a western European architectural environment – that of the Crusader Kingdom of Jerusalem. The vaults, for

FIGURE 8.7

Ani: Cathedral, interior (A. Kazaryan)

cross-domed church with four tall vaulted arms inside a square. Before moving on it may be worth pointing out that there is one type of building, represented by the probably late-11th-century church of San Vittore alle Chiuse (Marche, Italy).[35] That arguably sits between Byzantine cross-domed churches and the sort of basilican version of a four-pillar church that we see in Jerusalem. Only a more precise dating would enable us to understand whether buildings such as San Vittore, centrally-planned though with a cupola surrounded by eight consistently tall groin-vaulted bays, had been constructed in Europe before they appeared in Jerusalem.

Thus, the combination of a Byzantine or Armenian type of four-columned church with a 'western' system of arches and vaults can be seen in both the Chapel of Saint Helen and the Cathedral of Saints James. One minor point at issue which sits between the plan and the elevation is the status of the capitals. These are now effectively corbels at the top of the piers with their undersides visible (Figure 8.8). In 'classical' Romanesque architecture a capital would be supported by a half-column or pilaster. The unusual conformation at the Armenian Cathedral has led scholars to suppose that the supporting half-columns or pilasters were cut back in the late-18th-century, when painted canvasses were placed on the faces of the piers.[36] This view was endorsed by Denys Pringle: 'The capitals that support the pointed transverse arches defining the bays, however, indicate that the piers originally had a projecting pilaster or shaft on each face.'[37] It is impossible to check whether this is so today, since permission to remove any one canvas has not been forthcoming. But although the capitals obviously do project from the face of the piers, there is no sign of a corresponding projecting base. Thus, I would suggest the capitals were initially unsupported and simply corbelled out from the pier face. It is worth recalling that in the early 15th century John Poloner maintained the church 'had four square columns'.[38]

Notwithstanding the above, several architectural details – the slightly pointed arches, the Corinthianesque capitals, and the south portal – do point to a Romanesque tradition. Nurith Kenaan-Kedar has cast doubt on one aspect of this – the use of a type of radial voussoir with a convex face and soffit cut as a narrow rectangular ashlar block with rounded faces, which she terms a 'goudron frieze'. This, she believes, has antecedents in the 6th-century architecture of Greater Armenia, and to be an ultimately Armenian or north Syrian form whose use in Crusader Jerusalem was deliberately allusive.[39] My 30 years of study in the field of Armenian architecture has furnished me with few, if any, analogues for the shapes used in in the cathedral's south portal. The so-called 'goudron frieze' does not appear in Armenia, but it is typical of buildings in Crusader Jerusalem; most notably at the Holy Sepulchre, where it can be found on the western doorway to the Latin Patriarchate, as well as at the church of Saint Anne, both of them built in the mid-12th-century. The actual origins of the form remain uncertain. Its appearance on the Bab-al-Futuh in Cairo, completed in 1087, is probably significant, and may account for the popularity of the design in Sicily, where its first appearance was probably on the tower of the Martorana in Palermo. It is also used in the cloister at San Juan de Duero in Soria (Spain), and it is possible that the derivation is Mediterranean and the ultimate origin is Islamic Egypt. There is, however, a western French version – used in the same form as it is found in Jerusalem at Saint-Sulpice, Marignac (Charente-Maritime) of *c.* 1120, while tapered variations – conceived as truncated radial mouldings, can be traced back to the late-11th-century at Saint-Jouin-de-Marnes (Deux-Sèvres).[40]

Thus, the south portal at Saints James is typically Romanesque, like the Corinthianesque capitals and carved row of lambs on the west face of the north-east pier, lending support to Pringle's conclusion – a conclusion with which I agree – that Frankish masons were heavily involved in the construction of the church.[41]

THE ORIGIN OF THE UNUSUAL DOME – SANTA CRUZ IN TOLEDO AND SAINTS JAMES IN JERUSALEM

Even those specialists who think the intersecting arches and hexagonal opening are post-medieval cannot resist citing medieval analogues for the composition. Vincent and Abel mistakenly compared the cupola to work at the monastery at Haghpat (Armenia), thinking it was a

FIGURE 8.8

Jerusalem: Saints James Cathedral, interior capitals (A. Kazaryan)

building of the tenth century, whereas they, perhaps, meant the zhamatun of the church of Surb Nshan, though even here such roofing appeared only as a result of the renovation of 1209.[42] Following Arzumanyan, Pringle pointed to the dome of a church in the monastery of Khorakert (Armenia), which is indeed formally close, though without further comment, before moving on to discuss the cupola in front of the mihrab in the Great Mosque of Cordoba (961), along with 12th-century Spanish and French Christian derivatives of the Andalucian domes, as in the church of the Holy Sepulchre in Torres del Rio (Navarra).[43] While not neglecting the above examples, Kenaan-Kedar speculates that the form might be pre-Islamic, and traceable back to the architecture of 6th-century Great Armenia, though her argument remains unsubstantiated.[44]

The large group of Spanish and French Romanesque churches that deployed domes on intersecting arches has been investigated by Javier Martínez de Aguirre.[45] He sees the expansion of the composition in Europe as being related to perceptions of the Holy Sepulchre in Jerusalem, as the vault-type appears in buildings either dedicated to the Holy Sepulchre or designed in emulation of it. The vault-type is among their most interesting peculiarities, and appears at Torres del Rio (Rioja), Saint-Croix at Oloron-Sainte-Marie, L'Hôpital-Saint-Blaise (both Pyrénées-Atlantiques, and San-Miguel de Almazán (Castilla y Leon) in all of which it takes the form of an eight-pointed star.[46]

Though the earliest appearance of this kind of vault in Spain was in the great mosque at Córdoba, a similar pattern was used over the central section of the mosque of Bab-al-Mardum in Toledo, dated by inscription to 999. After the conquest of the city the mosque was given to the Knights of the Order of St John, who transformed it into the Chapel of the Holy Cross (*Ermita de la Santa Cruz*) and added the apse. Thus, the building was known as the church of the Holy Cross until 1186, when King Alfonso VIII took it from the knights. Martínez de Aguirre suggests that the conversion of the mosque created a link between the Islamic vault that was the centerpiece of the original building, and the recollection of the Holy Land in the imagination of the Hospitallers.[47]

As such, it was the central dome in the church of the Holy Cross in Toledo that inspired a number of interpretations of the form elsewhere in Spain and south-western France, all of which appeared after the construction of the Cathedral of Saints James in Jerusalem. Because all other Armenian examples of the form are also dated to a later period, we ought to consider whether a translation of the 'star-vault' idea from distant Spain to Jerusalem might have been possible. Given that the dedications of the relevant Spanish churches were connected to the Holy Land, and as pilgrimage from Spain to the Holy Land was significant and intertwined with the most venerated shrine in Spain as Santiago de Compostela, it may be worth recalling the legend of the discovery of the body of Saint James the Great in Spain, while his head was left in Jerusalem and buried on Mount Sion. According to the Historia Compostelana, the body of James has been transported to Compostela by his disciples from the place where it had been thrown outside the walls of Jerusalem.[48] As Spanish pilgrims and crusaders in Jerusalem had an obvious interest in the relic held in the Armenian cathedral, it is not impossible that a Spanish source could have informed the patron(s) or designer(s) of Saints James about the unusual form of the cupola of the church in Toledo.[49] They could have conveyed the idea that the dome rose above intersecting arches whose points were formed a star. Then, in a nod to Armenian tradition, where the six-pointed star was a venerated symbol, the design was transformed into a hexagon (Figure 8.9). In the 12th century, these stars were used at the base of Armenian stone crosses known as *khachkars*, where they were carved in relief on ornamental disks as a symbol of Golgotha.[50] If one accepts this, as a possibility at least, then Armenian tradition did have an impact on the dome, though only in the number of ribs.

However, looking back across the Mediterranean, it is noteworthy that no star-vaults, inherited from Moors, were constructed in Spain before the creation of the 'dome' at Saints James. Perhaps the construction of the Armenian Cathedral was the stimulus for these re-interpretations of the cupola at Toledo. It is also interesting that the rotunda in Torres del Rio was built on the Road of Santiago, the great pilgrimage route that connected the Holy Land with Santiago de Compostela – or, to put it another way, the road which connected the head of St James with his body. Can we be sure that the builders of Spanish and French star-vaults took them to refer to the Holy Sepulchre in Jerusalem and the Holy Sepulchre only? As we have seen, the 'quotation' was of an originally Islamic form used in mosques. Its meaning was transformed through the conversion of a mosque into the church of the Holy Cross. Could there have been other meanings – other impulses – behind the adoption of the form? And if so, could one of these have been an association with the cult of St James as it had been promoted in Jerusalem? In that case, the Armenian Cathedral of Saints James may have

FIGURE 8.9

Teghenyats: Monastery, relief-carved panel from altar support - first half of the 11th century (A. Kazaryan)

been the initiator of a tradition of star-vault construction across the whole of the Christian world.

IMITATION

If the intersecting star vaults of Spain are eight-sided, in Armenian churches they are always made hexagonal. The source for all other Armenian examples was, obviously, the cathedral of Saints James. The first example could be the dome of the church of the second half of the 12th century in Khorakert.[51] However, it was not the adoption of the form in Armenian churches that is striking. The composition flourished when it was translated into a type of building known as a *zhamatun* – that is a narthex that functioned as a mausoleum, or covered cemetery. This Armenian building type was seemingly first created at the monastery of Horomos (1038), and from the second half of the 12th century was actively developed. As early as Horomos, the type was associated with top lighting and was arranged as a type of tall stone tent with an upper oculus above a four-columned hall. I consider the form to be a citation of the Anastasis Rotunda in Jerusalem.[52] Later, regardless of the overall shape of the 'stone tent', the dome came to be articulated with edges or ribs to form a six-rayed star with an upper oculus, as in the monasteries of Khoranashat and Neghuts (Figure 8.10) – an obvious reference back to the cupola of the cathedral (and martyrium) of Saints James.

The 'dome' is the outstanding feature in the architecture of the cathedral of Saints James. And just as its interior treatment seems to have been carefully thought out and relates it to a larger architectural tradition, so with its exterior blind arcade. The 24 arches supported on paired columns looks directly to the dome of the Cathedral at Ani, the former capital of Armenia. The detailing of the paired columns at Jerusalem, their bases and capitals, leaves no doubt that they were intended to evoke forms that had been used in Armenia since the 7th century. The bulbous capitals and unmoulded abaci are unmistakeable, though even Ani does not have quite the elegance of Jerusalem (Figure 8.5 and colour plate III). That is why it is likely that Armenian masons will have worked alongside the Latins.

CONCLUSION

It is possible – even perhaps probable – that Melisende played a role in the construction of the cathedral of Saints

FIGURE 8.10

Neghuts: Monastery, vault of the zhamatun (A. Kazaryan)

James in Jerusalem. Her status as a ruler of a Crusader Kingdom in combination with her Armenian descent in some ways mirrors the architecture of the cathedral. This similarly combines Armenian and Eastern Christian sources and pulls them into a broadly occidental or Latin tradition, as is beautifully illustrated by the use of groin vaults around a central 'domed' square. The presence of relics of St James may also have been a factor in promoting a building that acted as a bridge between the architectural traditions of East and West. The importance of the building from an Armenian perspective is that it demonstrated how well-developed regional preferences for raised drums, bulbous capitals, four-pillar plans, *pastophoria* with upper chapels, and open oculi could be incorporated into a church that does not look out of place in the Mediterranean. We can only guess whether the impetus for this came directly from Melisende, or whether it was a decision of the senior clergy within the Armenian Church in Jerusalem. But there must have been close supervision for this sharing of forms from different architectural traditions to work – especially so given their execution by Frankish masons, and in all likelihood, masons who had worked at the Holy Sepulchre.

The Armenian cathedral helps us understand the 12th-century architecture of the Holy Land and its position with regard to the local traditions of the Mediterranean and the Middle East. Given its potential to shed light on a process of cultural exchange, a full-scale archeological study of the Armenian cathedral is much to be desired.

NOTES

[1] I want to express my gratitude to my colleagues; Manuel Castiñeiras, Javier Martínez de Aguirre and Mikael Arakelyan for useful discussions of issues related to the study.

[2] D. Pringle, *The Churches of Crusader Kingdom of Jerusalem: A Corpus*, vol. 3, *The City of Jerusalem*, (Cambridge 2007), 168–82; Բարսեղ Վրդ. Գալէմտէրեան, Երուսաղէմի Հայոց Սրբոց Յակոբեանց Մայր տաճարը դարերու ընթացքին – Very Rev. Parsegh Kalemderian, *The Armenian Cathedral of Sts. James Across the Ages*, (St. James Press 2007).

[3] Մ. Աղավնունի, Հայկական հին վանքեր եւ եկեղեցիներ Սուրբ Երկրի մէջ. ուսումնասիրութիւններ (M. Aghavnuni, *Armenian Old Monasteries and Churches in Holy Land*. . . (Jerusalem 1931), 251, 259–60; Շնորհք եպս., 'Նորոգութիւններ Ս. Մինասի մատրան մէջ' (Shnork, esp., 'Restorations in the chapel of St Minas', in Սիոն (Sion), 11–12 (1958), 289–93. Over the vaults of chapels and the church, there are three more chapels with narthexes: Surb Nshan (St Sign), Holy Apostles and Holy Resurrections.

[4] Pringle, *The City of Jerusalem* (as n. 2), 169.

[5] For a critical analysis see: C. Mutafian, 'Les reines arméniennes de Jérusalem et la fondation de la cathédrale des Saints-Jacques', in *La Méditerranée des Arméniens – XIIe – XVe siècle: Actes du colloque international sur le royaume arménien de Cilicie, tenu à Jérusalem en 2009*, ed., C. Mutafian (Paris 2014), 43–44. Part of the article can be found in a Russian translation: К. Мутафян, 'Королевы Иерусалима', in *Анив (Aniv)*, 1/10 (2007), 20–21.

[6] Pringle, *The City of Jerusalem* (as n. 2), 171.

[7] For the 1812 inscription see Pringle, *The City of Jerusalem* (as n. 2), 171. Kalemderian makes no mention of these inscriptions or repairs in his discussion of the recent history of the building. Kalemderian, *Armenian Cathedral* (as n. 2), 18.

[8] Pringle, *The City of Jerusalem* (as n. 2), 171–72.

[9] N. Kenaan-Kedar, 'Armenian Architecture in Twelfth-Century Crusader Jerusalem', in *Assaph Studies in Art History*, 3 (Tel Aviv 1998), 77.

[10] See M. Arakelyan and A. Kazaryan, 'Иаковов святых армянский монастырь в Иерусалиме' ('Saints James Monastery in Jerusalem'), *Православная энциклопедия (Orthodox Encyclopedia)*, vol. 20 (Moscow 2009), 576–80; A. Kazaryan 'Иерусалим: Архитектура И. эпохи крестоносцев' ('Jerusalem: Architecture of Jerusalem in the Epoch of the Crusaders') *Православная энциклопедия (Orthodox Encyclopedia)*, vol. 21 (Moscow 2009), 424–31.

[11] See, T.S.R. Boase, *Kingdoms and Strongholds of the Crusaders*, (London 1971), 103, Kenaan-Kedar, 'Armenian Architecture' (as n. 9), 77, and J. Folda, *The Art of the Crusaders in the Holy Land*, (Cambridge 2005), 247. Indeed, Folda comments, 'By virtue of her Armenian mother from Melitene, Morphia . . . the rebuilding of the Armenian church must have been of substantial importance to her.' For Melisende generally, see M. Tranovich, *Melisende of Jerusalem, The World of a Forgotten Crusader Queen*, (London 2011).

[12] Mutafian, 'Reines arméniennes' (as n. 5) 45.

[13] Pringle, *The City of Jerusalem* (as n. 2), 169; See also J. Prawer, 'The Armenians in Jerusalem under the Crusaders', in *Armenian and Biblical Studies*, ed. M.E. Stone, (Jerusalem 1976), 230–31; B. Narkiss, M.E. Stone and A.K. Sanjian, *Armenian Art Treasures of Jerusalem*, (New Rochelle 1979), 12.

[14] Folda, *Art of the Crusaders* (as n. 11), 247.

[15] Kenaan-Kedar, 'Armenian Architecture' (as n. 9), 85–86.

[16] Mutafian, 'Reines arméniennes' (as n. 5), 45.

[17] Pringle, *The City of Jerusalem* (as n. 2) 178, 181.

[18] Ibid, 181.

[19] This is the view taken by Fathers Vincent and Abel. See L.H. Vincent and F.M. Abel, *Jérusalem Nouvelle*, Jerusalem: Recherches de Topographie, d'Archeologie et d'Histoire, 2 (Paris 1914).

[20] Mutafian, 'Reines arméniennes' (as n. 5), 45.

[21] J. Carswell and C. Dowsett, *Kütahya Tiles and Pottery from the Armenian Cathedral of St. James, Jerusalem*, vol I (Oxford 1972), 8–9, 107–11.

[22] Local excavations were carried out in 1957 or 1958. See Շնորհք եպս., 'Սալարկում Ս. Հակոբրաց տաճարին և պատահական պեղումներ այդ առթիւ' (Shnork, esp., 'Paving of the St James Church and Casual Excavations in That End', in Սիոն (Sion), 7–8 (1958), 194–293; Kalemderian, *Armenian Cathedral* (as n. 2), 21–28.

[23] The irregular character of the plan, Pringle suggests, was due to the construction of the new church on the foundations of the walls of a first 5th- or 6th-century basilica church built against the chapel of Saint Menas; see: Pringle, *The City of Jerusalem* (as n. 2), 172 and 176.

[24] Vincent and Abel, *Jérusalem Nouvelle* (as n. 19), 533–34.

[25] See plan of the upper level of the church in Pringle, *The City of Jerusalem* (as n. 2), 174.

[26] Pringle, *The City of Jerusalem* (as n. 2), 178.

[27] A. Kazaryan, *Кафедральный собор Сурб Эчмиадзин и восточнохристианское зодчество IV – VII веков (The Cathedral of Holy Ejmiacin*. . .), (Moscow 2007), 62.

[28] The cornice is of 19th-century plaster. Its original forms are unknown.

[29] Pringle, *The City of Jerusalem* (as n. 2), 177. See also Vincent and Abel, *Jérusalem Nouvelle* (as n. 19), 536–37, 554–55, fig. 203–05, and Boase, *Kingdoms and Strongholds* (as n. 11), 94–95.

[30] Pringle, *The City of Jerusalem* (as n. 2), 170.

[31] Pringle, *The City of Jerusalem* (as n. 2), 170–71.

[32] M. Mseriants, *'Миниатюра армянской рукописи начала XVIII века'* ('The Miniatures of Armenian Manuscripts in the Early 18th Century'), in *Herald of the Social Sciences*, 4 (1968), 83–89, illustration 1 (See also: http://lraber.asj-oa.am/1260/1/83.pdf). The author doesn't connect the illustration with the Armenian Cathedral of Saints James, and instead compares the drawing to Armenian *zhamatuns*. This illustration from the manuscript by the miniaturist Khachko was ordered by vardapet Abraham Kretatsi (Pushkin State Museum, Moscow: No. 79938, p. 2b, 21.3 × 15.6 cm). It will be published by M. Arakelyan in his catalogue of the 9th – 19th-century Armenian manuscripts in Moscow's collections.

[33] Kazaryan, Jerusalem (as n. 10), 428–429.

34 A. Kazaryan, 'Четырехстолпные купольные храмы Иерусалима и Константинополя. Две архитектурные традиции XII – XIII веков' ('Four-column Domed Churches of Jerusalem of the 12th and 13th Centuries'), in *Всероссийская научная сессия византинистов (All-Russian Scientific Session of Byzantine Studies)*, (Moscow 2013), 119–20.

35 See P. Piva, *Marche Romaniche* (Milano 2003), 95–105.

36 Kalemderian notes that this group of pictures created in the late 18th and 19th centuries has not been studied; see: Kalemderian, *Armenian Cathedral* (as n. 2), 17.

37 Pringle, *The City of Jerusalem* (as n. 2), 174–75. See also Vincent and Abel, *Jerusalem nouvelle* (as n. 19), 534–35, figs 200–02. Pringle discusses the possible depths of potential pilasters or half-columns.

38 Pringle, *The City of Jerusalem* (as n. 2), 170.

39 Kenaan-Kedar. 'Armenian Architecture' (as n. 9), 85–86, and more recently, eadem, 'Decorative Architectural Sculpture in Crusader Jerusalem: The Eastern, Western and Armenian Sources of a Local Visual Culture', in *The Crusader World*, ed., A Boas (Abingdon 2016), 609–23.

40 Javier Martínez de Aguirre, 'San Juan de Duero y el Sepulcrum Domini de Jerusalén' in *Siete maravillas des románico español* (Aguilar de Campoo 2009), 141–43. A. Tcherikover, 'Romanesque Sculpted Archivolts in Western France: Forms and Techniques', *Arte Medievale*, 2nd series 3 (1989), 112–33. The term 'claveaux en dos de livre' is rather fittingly used to describe the form in France. I am very grateful to John McNeill for developing this discussion and adding important examples.

41 Pringle, *The City of Jerusalem* (as n. 2), 181.

42 Vincent and Abel, *Jérusalem Nouvelle* (as n. 19), 536–37, fig. 206. In this they were followed by Pringle, *The City of Jerusalem* (as n. 2), 176. For Surb Nshan, see O. Khalpakhchian, *Architectural Ensembles of Armenia*, (Moscow 1980), 192.

43 Pringle, *The City of Jerusalem* (as n. 2), 176–77.

44 Kenaan-Kedar. 'Armenian Architecture' (as n. 9), 81–83.

45 J. Martínez de Aguirre and L. Gil Cornet, *Torres del Río. Iglesia del Santo Sepulcro* (Pamplona 2004); Martínez de Aguirre, 'San Juan de Duero y el Sepulcrum Domini' (as n. 39), 109–48; Idem, 'Evocaciones de Jerusalén en la arquitectura del Camino de Santiago: el Santo Sepulcro y la Santa Cruz', in *VIII Congreso internacional de estudios Jacobeos* (2012), 195–223; Ibid, 'La Santa Cruz y el Santo Sepolcro: formas y espacios románicos', in *Monumentos singulares del románico. Nuevas lecturas sobre formas y usos* (Aguilar de Campoo 2012), 217–42.

46 Martínez de Aguirre, 'La Santa Cruz' (as n. 45), 227–33.

47 Martínez de Aguirre, 'La Santa Cruz' (as n. 45), 231.

48 Vincent and Abel *Jérusalem Nouvelle* (as n. 19), 528, text VI. Pringle, *The City of Jerusalem* (as n. 2), 168.

49 In the context of Spanish-Armenian contacts in the Orient, it is worth pointing out that there were communications between the kings of Aragon and Cilicia. And that although the testimony is late, there is a description of a pilgrimage by Martyros, the Armenian bishop of Erzinka (end of the 15th century) to Santiago de Compostela. See *Relation d'un voyage fait en Europe et dans l'Océan Atlantique, à la fin du XVe siècle sous le règne de Charles VIII*, ed. J. St-Martin (Paris 1827).

50 The design may also have recommended itself as it was based on the intersection of two triangles – another pattern popular within the Armenian church – whereas the eight-pointed designs favoured in Spanish churches were designed around squares.

51 Khalpakhchian dates the church to the late-12th or early-13th centuries, but alleges the dome was rebuilt in the mid-13th-century. See: Khalpakhchian, *Architectural Ensembles* (as n. 42), 297–99. However, there is no more reason to suppose the dome at Khorakert was reconstructed in the 13th century than there is to assume the cupola at Saints James in Jerusalem dates from the 13th century – which the author also alleges. See also B. Narkiss, M. Stone and A. Sanjian *Armenian Art Treasures of Jerusalem* (New Rochelle 1979). J.M. Thierry and P. Donabédian, *Armenian Art*, (New York 1989), 540–41, consider the date uncertain.

52 A. Kazaryan, 'The Zhamatun of Horomos: The Shaping of an Unprecedented Type of Fore-church Hall', in *kunsttexte.de, E-journal für Kunst- und Bildgeschichte* 3 (2014), sektion Funun, ed. P. Blessing. See http://edoc.hu-berlin.de/kunsttexte/2014-3/kazaryan-armen-4/PDF/kazaryan.pdf – accessed 14 March, 2017; A. Kazaryan, 'The Architecture of Horomos Monastery', in *Horomos Monastery: Art and History*, ed. E. Vardanyan (Paris 2015), 55–205, esp. 153–155.

GRANDMONT AND THE ENGLISH KINGS: AN EXAMPLE OF PATRONAGE IN THE CONTEXT OF AN ASCETIC ARCHITECTURAL TREND

Claude Andrault-Schmitt

'We have sent back your workmen,' the prior of Grandmont supposedly wrote to Henry II some time after the death of Thomas Becket.[1] One imagines English masons sailing across the Channel and riding through France in order to build a church in the harsh landscape of the Massif Central, a landscape that possibly evoked in the minds of the English the northern Marches of the Plantagenet Empire on the Anglo-Scottish borders.[2] Could there be a better example of direct patronage in the history of architecture? However, a careful reading of the Latin reveals that the traditional translation is incorrect. A fuller and more literal translation should read, 'We have sent back the workmen that your devotion had assigned to the church building' (*operarios remisimus devotionis vestrae aedificacantes ecclesiam domus tuae Grandimontis*).[3] Moreover, the letter that contains this sentence, supposedly written by Guillaume de Treignac, is probably a forgery. It is included in the French *Patrologia Latina* and in the English *Materials for the History of Thomas Becket* but not in the more exacting *Scriptores ordinis grandimontensis* published by Jean Becquet.[4] Scholars tend to overestimate Henry II's concern to found new religious houses as the result of Becket's murder. However, the purpose of this paper is neither to sift the sources, nor to reinterpret the architectural evidence. Instead, my intention is to set what is known of the medieval abbey buildings in the context of contemporary architecture in the region and in France. In the last four decades of the 12th century, a singular ascetic architectural trend developed that persisted in smaller and often much later Grandmontine churches. Whether these buildings should be categorised as Romanesque, however, is a question that exceeds the parameters of this short essay.

PATRONAGE AS FRIENDSHIP

Does the argument for Henry II's direct patronage entirely crumble as a result of a more critical reading of the texts? Not at all. Links between Henry II, his sons, Richard and John, and the priors of Grandmont did exist. At times the relationship was very warm, as can be seen in a letter by Prior Pierre Bernard, which invokes the king's love and reveals a strong personal friendship:

> *Praecellentissimo principi D. Henrico Dei gratia Anglorum regi, duci nostro Aquitanico, magnificentissimo pauperum Grandimontensium nutricio. . . . O si legere posses in corde meo, quod tibi de amore tuo, suo digito Deus inscribere dignatus est! Profecto cognosceres quod nulla lingua, licet erudite, sed nec stilus sufficiat exprimere quae* in tabulis cordis carnalibus, *Dei Spiritui placuit imprimere. Hanc pro uobis prosequemur obsecrationem in uestro Grandimonte, ab hoc primo electionis nostrae, ut latores praesentium notum facient . . .*[5]

Some of the facts and events that marked this friendship are well known. As early as 1159, during Henry's reign (*Henricus, nulli regum pietate secundus*),[6] several royal chronicles and courtly letters betray a striking appreciation of the Grandmontine brethren. Moreover, Grandmontine priors were trying to help Henry by encouraging Becket's return to England. According to his first will, the king's intention was to be buried at Grandmont. And Grandmont also received gifts of moral value, such as the famous Verneuil ordinance concerning debtors.[7] Henry stayed at Grandmont on several occasions:[8] some months after a consecration of the church in 1167;[9] possibly in 1173; again some four years later when he bought the county of La Marche for 6,000 marks; in March 1181 he reached an agreement with the bishop of Limoges at Grandmont; once more in May and June 1182; and possibly for the last time in 1183. Despite its remote location in rocky hills accessible along rough paths, Grandmont was a stage on the pilgrimage road to the Virgin of Rocamadour. The same road leading from Martel to Le Mans (via Grandmont?) and on to Rouen was also taken in June 1183 by the funeral cortège of Henry the Young King, *el jove rei englès*, whose death was lamented by the Limousin troubadour Bertran de Born as well as William Marshal.[10]

Above all, Henry II devoted both energy and resources to Grandmont, as is demonstrated by the gift of a piece of the True Cross brought from Jerusalem in 1174, by the grant of a papal bull for Grandmont, and above all

© British Archaeological Association 2018

by the negotiations he conducted with Pope Clement III to facilitate the canonisation of the Order's founder, Etienne de Muret.[11] The resulting *revelatio* or *elevatio* was attended by high ranking archbishops and bishops, and the saint's virtue manifested itself through healing and the working of miracles. The translation took place on 30 August 1189, two months after the king's death, as was accurately recorded in the narrative of the ceremony.

Richard I acted in charters for Grandmont as the Count of Poitiers and Duke of Aquitaine before 1189, and afterwards as king, when he is described as *Rex Angliae Ordinis Grandimondis Mecenas*.[12] He probably helped complete the buildings of Grandmont and commissioned some of its greatest *opus lemovicense* reliquaries. As for King John, it is likely that he paid greater attention to Grandmont than has been generally thought. He was concerned by a crisis among the brethren when he visited the monastery, arriving from La Rochelle in April 1214.[13] He created the potential for future English foundations in March 1203 at Rouen, when he declared the Grandmontines free of every toll or service. Significantly, it was the lords of his court – his marcher barons – who founded Grandmont's three English dependencies. These were Robert de Thurnham and his wife, Joan Fossard, who founded Eskdale-Grosmont in Yorkshire *c.* 1204; Walter de Lacy, who founded Craswall *c.* 1225; and Fulk Fitz Warin III, who founded Alberbury (Shropshire) between 1226 and 1234. The latter became an 'outlawed baron' after his death, while his funerary foundation in woods on the River Severn serves in what was to become the legend of Robin Hood.[14]

We can list various other grants from members of the Plantagenet family. Grandmont was supposedly left a large sum in the will of the Empress Matilda. Her son, Henry II, sent seven white bear furs in 1178 – a donation that is confirmed in the Pipe rolls.[15] According to Gervase, Henry's will of 1182 made provisions for 3000 silver marks to be given to Grandmont *(Domui et toti ordini grandimontis iii milia marcas argenti)*, more than to Fontevraud or to the Carthusians, and Grandmont is the only religious establishment in Aquitaine mentioned in the will.[16]

It is sometimes suggested that Richard made a donation towards the completion of the buildings when he visited the brethren in 1192, though the given date is impossible as he was then on crusade. More likely, he signed confirmations for the donations from Chinon after his return. His nephew Otho sent one thousand cuttlefishes a year from La Rochelle, and John was generous with charters between 1199 and 1214.[17] It is noteworthy that successive Plantagenet rulers continued to show generosity towards Grandmont, including Henry III, who was politically active in what remained of the Plantagenet domains in France.

None of the various gifts outlined above can be associated with the construction of Grandmont's buildings, unless they are clearly identified as such. Nevertheless, all sorts of alms (including food) would have helped the community in undertaking the construction of the monastery.[18] Alfonso's VI annual payments of Spanish gold to Cluny must similarly have helped the Burgundian monks build their new church.

THE LOCATION AND ITS BUILDINGS

The history of the abbey buildings and their later fate can be briefly summarised, picking out the few facts from the hagiography that has been built around them. The founder, and future saint, Etienne, set up his hermitage at Muret, near the village of Ambazac, where he died *c.* 1124. Thanks to the lord of Montcocu, his successors established a community of religious nearby, on the higher hills, in a 'priory' (Grandmont was not described as an 'abbey' until the 14th century). Around twenty years after Etienne's death, the lawmaker and fourth prior, Etienne de Liciac, composed a rule inspired by that of the regular canons. Misled by numerous later forgeries, some scholars have presumed an early diffusion of Grandmontine houses. However, the spread of the order in France (with more than 150 sites) is most likely to be contemporary with, or even subsequent to, the *elevatio* of Saint Etienne in 1189. The three English foundations fall exactly into this period, while the two Grandmontine houses in Spain, at Tudela and Estella, were founded later still, after 1265 and 1269, thanks to Thibaud de Champagne, King of Navarre (1253–70).

As far as the history of the mother house is concerned, disputes between the monks and the lay brothers troubled the papacy through much of the Middle Ages and began against the background of the Plantagenêt-Capetian wars.[19] Contrary to popular perception, this did not presage decline for the institution and, despite internal strife, the monastic buildings increased in size. An early church on the site was destroyed after 1733, when the then abbot decided to construct a shorter and more lavish church 'in the style of the Paris Pantheon'.[20] The new church was constructed to the north of the earlier church, in order to maintain the liturgy in the course of construction, though the subsequent building of a large new wing cut the medieval church in two. The new buildings, together with what remained of the medieval convent and its cemeteries, were destroyed after the Order was dissolved in 1772/1781. A cadastral map gives a good idea of the disposition in 1813 (Figure 9.1), though the

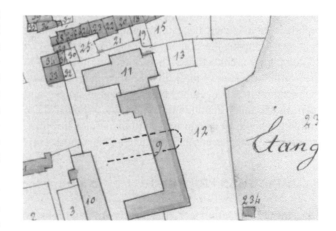

FIGURE 9.1

Grandmont (Haute-Vienne): Cadastral plan of 1813 showing the new church (11) and the east range which cut across the medieval church (9)

belated consequences of the French Revolution destroyed what was left, and even dried up some of the lakes and ponds, in spite of local resistance.

THE GRANT OF LEAD: GENUINE SOURCES AND MYTHIC NARRATIVES

Not all the sources reporting royal grants of lead to Grandmont are reliable. As we have already seen, the Limousin sources are to a large extent legendary. However, grants of lead are mentioned in a small number of charters and English diplomatic or financial records that are trustworthy. In some instances, such as the 1176 gift of lead, the pipe roll evidence confirms what is suggested in the legendary sources, thus supporting the historical veracity of the event. The *Great Roll of the Pipe for the Twenty-Second Year of the Reign of King Henry the Second* states briefly that a sum of £40 was paid for lead from the Carlisle mine 'for the house of God at Grandmont' *(Et pro plumbo at opus domus Dei de Grantmonte)*. Another line records: 'And for the location of two vessels to transport the lead that the king gives to the church of Grandmont, from Newcastle to La Rochelle' *(Et pro locandis. ij. navibus ad ducendum plumbum quod rex dedit ecclesie de Grosmunt a Novo Castello usque ad Rochell'. xj. l. et. ix. s. et. iiij. d. per breve Regis)*.[21] There is nothing surprising in this donation. The English kings had given lead tiles for church roofs to other institutions on several occasions. For example Henry I gave lead to Chartres and Richard I gave lead to Pontigny. Above all, between 1178 and 1188, Henry II arranged for lead for Clairvaux, to be transported initially from Newcastle to Rouen. It is important to note that in the gifts to Clairvaux a precise number of *carreatis plumbi* or *caretatas plumbi* is quoted ('a cart' should be understood as a 'cart load' and defines a measuring unit rather than referring to a type of vehicle).[22] Sometimes these cart loads waiting in the harbours had to be guarded, thus greatly increasing the cost. It would obviously be helpful to find precise references concerning the cost of lead sent to Grandmont, but there are none in the Pipe Rolls. This does not necessarily mean that there were no other donations. The lead for the roof of the cathedral at Le Mans, for example, is not included in the accounts, and similar gifts are very difficult to detect in Richard's time.[23] Besides, according to the Pipe Rolls, the Carlisle mines provided only three gifts of lead for continental buildings in Henry's time: Caen in 1169, Grandmont in 1175/6 and Clairvaux between 1178 and 1188. Moreover, among the three, the grant to Clairvaux was not strictly a gift but an exchange, because in return, and revealing a background in anti-heretical and diplomatic operations, the abbot sent to the king one of St Bernard's fingers.[24]

The history of the donations of lead left a strange legacy in Grandmontine and Limousin narratives. Jean Roudet, a 17th-century monk from Le Breuil-Bellay in Anjou, wrote a now-lost chronicle that mentioned an epic journey transporting a lot of carts of lead from La Rochelle. This was then inflated to 800 in some later copies. The arithmetic certainly suggests 60 cart loads for Grandmont could be more or less accurate.[25] Roudet's copiers went even further in developing the legend of the Grandmont lead. Each of the so called 'carts' was said to be driven by eight English horses, all of the same hair and colour. They were attended by the king's officers, who, amazingly, had decided that they were not rich enough to donate their own money, and left the abbey to the charity of the Plantagenet kings. The same secondary sources also suggest a failure of ambition to complete the building, and that the kings were persuaded to limit their largesse. Perhaps it was the modesty of the church that meant that no 17th-century commentator wanted to associate it with the patronage of princes.

Beyond this fairy tale, it is worth considering seriously the name given to the supposed driver of the lead carts and 'English horses' – a man called Brandin. Brandin is a historical figure. He was a mercenary who later became King John's seneschal in Gascony. Clearly, there is a confusion between the period in which the story is set, and the part played by the seneschals to Otho, Richard, Eleanor and John, who were either warriors from low extraction, like Pierre Bertin, or English knights.[26] None of them were active in 1175/6. They were still infants in the 1170s, but above all, they had no early interest in Grandmont because the county of La Marche had not yet been purchased by the Plantagenets. The keys to this historical confusion are the carved coats of arms, inscriptions and iron seals that were found at Grandmont, referring to Brandin as well as to magnates who were loyal to Richard but then made peace with John. These included Robert de Thurnham († 1211), seneschal of Anjou (1194–99); Poitou (1201) and Gascony (1207); and the Anglo-Irish (and Anglo-Welsh) Walter of Lacy, who was recalled from Ireland, landed at La Rochelle and then rode to Grandmont with King John on February 1214 (he was to be one of John's executors two years later).[27] These men were commemorated at Grandmont because of their gifts to the abbey.[28] In contrast to the monks' local aristocratic friends, Hugh Brun de Lusignan, who became count of La Marche after his enemies, the Plantagenet kings, had been deprived of their lands in northern Aquitaine, was commemorated but not buried at Grandmont. Grandmont served as a memorial and spiritual centre for the rulers of La Marche, from Henry II through to the later Lusignan counts, but none of them were buried there.

Whatever the truth may be, three points stand out. First, the lead roof is a recurrent feature in all descriptions of Grandmont. It was partially robbed in 1597, during the neglect that followed the Wars of Religion, then repaired, and replaced in 1702.[29] The old tiles were saved, however, and reused over the new church in the 18th century. The original lead roof could have been a source of local pride, shining bright among the dark hills, comparable to the effect of the roof of Saint-Martial in Limoges. Second, we should seriously consider the possibility that Henry II and Richard provided financial support for the construction of the monastic buildings, as well as for the church and its lead roofs. These monastic buildings included an enclosure wall with towers, an infirmary, a rectangular vaulted cloister with lead pipes and a lead pond, a chapter house and a refectory. This last is a reminder that the king liked 'to partake the brothers' meals in the refectory'.[30] We must also imagine at least two 'houses' for the English kings near the main door, perhaps connected to a double chapel – which explains the name *l'Angleterre* given to the northern terrace, regarded as an 'English land'. Third, it is clear that the period between *c*. 1190 and *c*. 1215 was as important for the institution as the reign of Henry II.

WHAT IS KNOWN ABOUT THE MEDIEVAL CHURCH

The official history

In October 1166 seven bishops led by the Archbishop of Bourges dedicated a church to the Virgin Mary at Grandmont, in which they placed relics of St Martial that had been borrowed from Limoges. Apart from the Archbishop of Bourges, the Norman Froger de Sées, a man close to King Henry II, was present, as well as the rival archbishop of Bordeaux, all the bishops of Aquitaine and several counts and knights. The translation of the founder's corpse was also celebrated, either several days earlier, or a few months later – the sources are unclear. The gift of lead was made ten years after this consecration as a contribution towards the construction – comparable with the seven years that elapsed between the consecration of Clairvaux (1174) and the reception of the first cart loads of lead there.

We also know the names of two masters of works. The first is described as *magistrum operis* Gerald, who was assisted by *caementari et alii operarri* in the time of Stephen de Liciac, that is to say before 1163. A legend connected with this Gerald informs us that after a terrible fall from the top of an arch, he recovered as the result of the intervention of the saint: *non est mortuus iste operarius sed dormit*.[31] Another name appears in the obituary: *Johannes Gastineus ecclesie nostre edificatory*.[32] This Jean Gâtine, whose name is French, died before 1170, when the obituary was written. He is probably the builder of the main part of the church, as it was consecrated in 1166.[33] The masonry work, especially the nave, is sometimes assigned to the lay brothers rather than to secular builders. Although the contribution of the lay brothers to monastic building work has become a commonplace, it was real enough at Grandmont, where the whole institution was sustained by the economic and political power of the lay brethren. The lay brothers' choir was situated in the western part of the nave.

The church was incomplete at the time of its consecration. Just before 1170, the prior, Pierre Bernard, is said to have vaulted the whole refectory, and to have finished the church from the chevet to the entrance of the brothers' choir. The church had been begun at the low (western) end.[34] In view of the sources, the dating of the church to *c*. 1160–75 seems reasonable, but does this date correspond to what can be adduced of the church in its late medieval state? The presbytery seems to have received attention after the primary build. In 1190, the Count of Champagne gave a rent for candles, later confirmed by Thibaud IV and Thibaud V. The setting of the reliquaries on the seven steps of the high altar is described in the treasury inventories and has been debated by J.R. Gaborit and G. Souchal.[35] After receiving a fragment of the True Cross, some relics of the Virgins of Cologne arrived in 1181 – the result of a celebrated journey by four Grandmontine brothers to Germany.[36] The main reliquaries were probably intended for the *elevatio* of the Saint in 1189, a few years after the treasury was robbed by Henry the Young King in order to pay his mercenaries. But the dating of the reliquaries is complicated: the enamels were clearly ordered at different periods. A dating to about 1189 or a few years later is generally accepted for the surviving big shrine, known as 'the Ambazac shrine' (Figure 9.2), although this contained a relic given in 1269 by Thibaud de Champagne. The apostles of the surviving antependium are dated *c*. 1230–40.[37] It is worth noting that the Grandmontines were famous for their enamel reliquaries, antependia or altarpieces. They survive from both the mother house and a number of smaller houses. Indeed, the most beautiful 'champlevé' enamel I know comes from Cherves near Cognac and is now in the Metropolitan Museum at New York. These objects deserve to be mentioned in the context of a discussion of the architecture for three reasons. First, because of the deliberate contrast they promote with an austere building. Second, because their disposition clearly cannot date from 1166. This suggests a subsequent reorganisation of the interior, and points to a continuity between Henry II and his successors as patrons of the abbey. Third, because the evidence suggests a liturgical setting that deployed metalwork on a huge scale. It is possible that this interior reorganisation was recognised in a new consecration in 1219 by the Archbishop of Bourges, although this consecration has been linked to a supposed renovation after the church had been damaged by excommunicated men.[38]

The ancient descriptions

Interpretation of the descriptive sources is marred by the contradictions and uncertainties surrounding the measurements, and by the terms used. Was a 'jambée' a leg, for instance? The first account was written by Pardoux de La Garde before 1591,[39] and a second by Jean Levesque in 1662.[40] A cost estimate from the 18th-century builder, Naurissart, is also very useful.[41] All three sources describe an aisleless church that was tall, very narrow and very long.[42] Two lateral chapels abutted this. A large and beautiful chapel on the north side was dedicated to St Peter and was later used as a sacristy. A smaller chapel to the south (the cloister side) was dedicated to St John the Baptist and St Bartholemew but also to the founder, because it was supposed to be on the site of the first humble church, and it sheltered the graves of the early priors, including Etienne. It was here in 1738, while digging the foundations for a new kitchen, that the tomb of Guillaume de Treignac

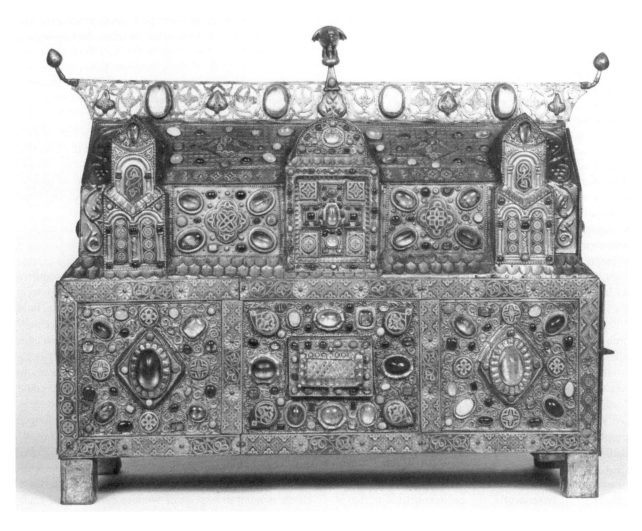

FIGURE 9.2

Ambazac (Haute-Vienne); shrine from Grandmont (C. Andrault-Schmitt)

was discovered. One author describes a northern chapel (which may be the same or another) belonging to the 'English cemetery', which was dedicated to St John the Baptist. He describes it as a double chapel, 'a vault upon a vault', with the upper chapel dedicated to St Michel.[43]

The church had twenty-two windows, probably eight for each wall of the nave. They must have been deeply splayed given the thickness of the lateral walls. But there were no bay divisions, properly speaking, because the transverse arches of the masonry vault sprang from corbels, or from projecting courses of ashlar – a point which surprised Pardoux when he saw a fallen stone of the vault, 'the size of a goose heart'. More amazement was produced by 'odd piers', used as liturgical markers (to borrow a term used by Eric Fernie):[44]

Cette église est belle par excellence pour la longueur qu'elle a. Et la voûte d'icelle n'est supportée d'aucuns piliers comme sont autres églises, fors de quatre piliers ou colonnes qui sont fort beaux et excellents qui sont aux quatre angles du grand autel joignant le premier degré d'icelle. Ces quatre piliers sont fort somptueux et admirables, faits en façon de colonne dorique alias ioniques et la façon d'iceux se nomme en latin stria, strae, ce sont comme gouttières engravées le long des colonnes de pierre ou chanfrein creux qu'on dit communément piliers cannelés lesquels soutiennent la voûte sur ledit autel.

(Pardoux de La Garde, with later manuscript rectifications)

Thus, the high altar was surrounded by four fluted columns with what resembled vertical channels or hollow chamfers. According to the description, the altar was crowned by a ribbed canopy, consisting of eight arches, thirty-two arch sections and golden medallions with flowers *('platines de cuivre doré')* – a kind of fan vaulting! We do not know, however, whether this was a vault made of ashlar and covered by ribs with liernes and tiercerons, or whether it was a canopy made of painted metal and wood serving as a ciborium. It may even have been a very late addition to the church.[45] I was once tempted to interpret the source as evidence for the original architectural disposition, and speculated that the ribs may have been formed by a fully-fledged rib vault – along the lines of the presbytery of the chapel of St-Julien at Petit-Quevilly, created by Henry II at Rouen. However, I suspect the altar complex as described by Pardoux was a late alteration. It could have been a metal ciborium, set upon four columns made of brass and enamel, similar to that commissioned by the bishop of Limoges from a local goldsmith between 1331 and 1333 for the collegiate church of La Chapelle-Taillefert.[46] It is important to note that there was in Pardoux's times a white linen canopy attached to the beautiful 'vault' by a metal chain, and that after Pardoux's time the apse was possibly reinforced and rebuilt (Naurissart saw brick vaults upon pillars and between stone ribs).

Be that as it may, some space was necessary for the daily mass at prime at the high altar, and although the church was wide enough, no description contains evidence of lateral bays, aisles or passageways leading into the apse, or of something that could be interpreted as lateral vaults. The reconstruction of the altar area is complicated by two questions concerning the entire church. First, the vault of the nave is sometimes said to have been a rib vault, but this interpretation is based on a misunderstanding of the word 'ogive' or 'ogif', which from the 13th to 19th centuries was used to designate a pointed arch (or its stones). Second, in order to understand the altar area, the reconstruction of the whole eastern apse needs to be considered. We know that the apse had five stained-glass windows, given by Hugh le Brun de Lusignan in 1208, just before his departure on crusade, ten years before the re-consecration.[47] They represented prophets and apostles, with a date, coats of arms and a dedication: *HUGO COMES MARCHIE. HANC FENESTRA VITREAM DEDIT BEATE MARIE*. This donation dates the stained glass windows, along with the (rebuilt?) apse walls. Consequently, we can reconstruct a chevet built on a semi-circular or a pentagonal plan – the latter remaining a possibility after the recent archaeological investigations.

Archaeology

Between 2013 and 2018, and for the first time, a programme of excavation was conducted under the direction of Philippe Racinet.[48] This is ongoing, but has already revealed an unexpectedly complex number of ground levels, a slope to the underlying granite bedrock and huge stone terraces built to support the later precinct.

As far as the church is concerned, the construction of the 18th-century buildings on the site of the former church is unfortunate, especially as they include a cellar that created a trench separating the apse from the nave. The southern wall of the nave has been completely destroyed. A solid stone buttress occupies the southern part of the apse, built as a reinforcement some decades before the 18th-century excavations (Figure 9.3). Moreover, the masonry includes reused mouldings (from shafts, ribs, cornices, bases, imposts, window embrasures and jambs) that seem to belong to the period *c.* 1190–1220. These mouldings could come from a monastic building that was demolished early, or from the cloister, and therefore may not have belonged to the first church. Indeed, several isolated capitals of the same period have been found that are too small to have been used in the church, and must have come from elsewhere (Figures 9.4 and 9.5). But, at the very least, these elements point to large-scale work to either side of 1200.

FIGURE 9.3

Grandmont: Excavation of the apse in 2014 (C. Andrault-Schmitt)

FIGURE 9.4

Grandmont, Capital reset in the front wall of a barn (C. Andrault-Schmitt)

FIGURE 9.5

Saint-Sylvestre (Haute-Vienne): cloister capital now in parish church (C. Andrault-Schmitt)

Late medieval material has also been uncovered, which could be the work of Guillaume de Fumel (1437–71), or might be from a restoration of around 1475? We know that shortly after this a beautiful tapestry and precious objects were given to the church. The main discovery for the Middle Ages is a tomb of a prelate in a privileged position, carved in the rock in the middle of the church.[49]

All that remains are the masonry courses of the lateral northern wall and the residue of a semicircular apse. The foundations are of very different depths, from east to west, and from north to south. In the nave, the early levels have all been dismantled but it seems that the pavement level was not very far above the natural substrate. The remains attest to the narrowness of the church (8.20 m *intra muros*) and the strength of the masonry (between 1.84 and 2.88 m thick), two features that are underlined in all the texts. They also prove that the apse was wider than the nave, as in all the smaller Grandmontine houses. Having found the remains of a wall in a house, archaeologists have also developed a hypothesis about the length of the church, which may have had an external length of 67.40 m (Figure 9.6). It is also likely that the church described by Pardoux, Levesque and Naurissard, preserved the same general perimeter as the 12th-13th-century church.

Three important questions remain for which there is currently no answer. First, the vaulting system in the eastern part of the church remains uncertain, and with it the nature of the presbytery (see above). Second, we are unsure as to the exact design of the chevet, partly because of later reconstruction, but also because it is possible to build pentagonal walls above semicircular foundations. Third, the shape and positioning of the lateral chapels remains uncertain. The northern structures that were discovered may correspond not to a lateral chapel, but to the strong buttress added *c.* 1643 (which may have been contemporary with the destruction of the chapels).

Whatever the details of the excavation teach us, conjectures as to a specifically 'Plantagenet' patronal influence on the design are clearly pointless.[50] However, it is possible to discern a distinctive aesthetic at work, evident in the use of crocket and water-leaf capitals and in the narrow aisleless nave – built without vertical wall articulation but seemingly barrel-vaulted and with high-level corbels.

UNDERSTANDING THE GRANDMONT CHURCH IN A LOCAL CONTEXT: THE 'ARROW-TYPE PLAN'

Notre-Dame at Grandmont is best understood as a building which reflects both a local and an international interest in ascetic expression, giving rise to an extremely distinctive plan, here described as 'arrow-type'. One source for the design may have been the historicist aisleless ground-plans that were used in churches related to the 11th-century Reform, as has been argued by Jill Franklin.[51] However, in Aquitaine, there were virtually no examples of long narrow naves before the middle of the 12th century. Therefore, it would be more profitable to look for comparisons among churches that were constructed by other ascetic orders within the larger region of western France, as and when their income enabled them to build stone churches. If the aisleless plan of Grandmont seems strange, it is only because we are used to the type of plan favoured by the Cistercians in Burgundy from the middle third of the 12th century, where the aisles served as a series of chapels. There are Cistercian churches that were originally aisleless, though these are, in fact, too early for my purpose. On the other hand, the female abbeys that were built with narrow and long naves are too late (Les Rosiers, Coyroux d'Obazine). Closer in date and more relevant are early Carthusian churches. Only a few are known, including what was possibly a lay church or 'correrie' at Witham (Somerset), and the main church and 'corroirie' at Le Liget, near Loches.[52] Both foundations were initiated

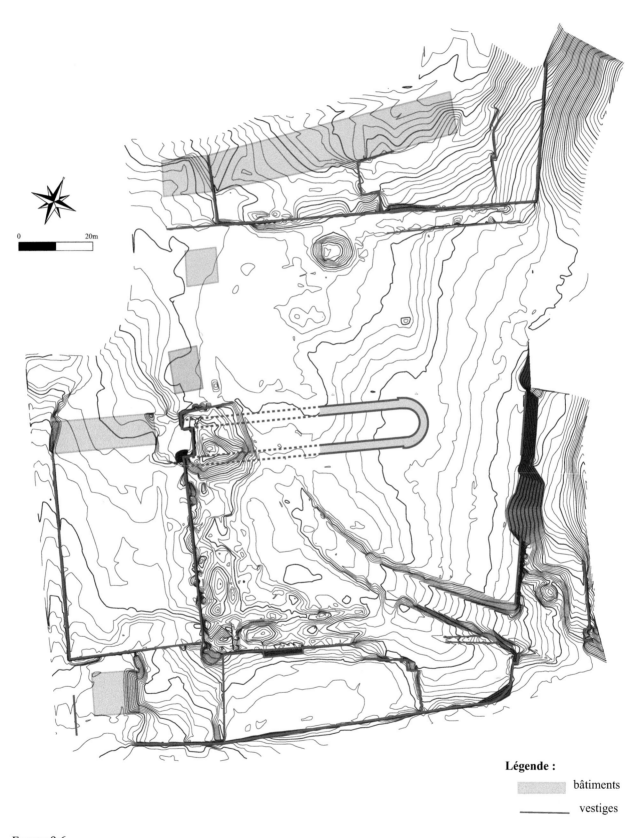

FIGURE 9.6

Grandmont: Plan showing the medieval church in its topographical setting (Philippe Racinet)

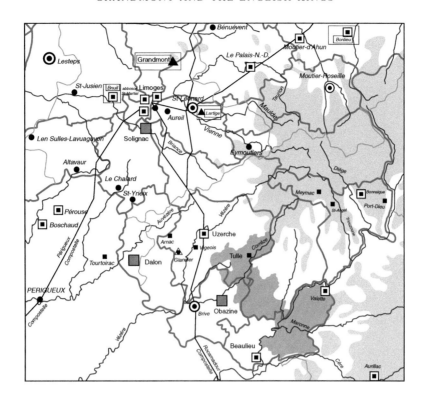

FIGURE 9.7

Map of the diocese of Limoges (from B. Barrière, Atlas du Limousin)

FIGURE 9.8

L'Artige (Haute-Vienne): East range of the cloister and southern chapel (C. Andrault-Schmitt)

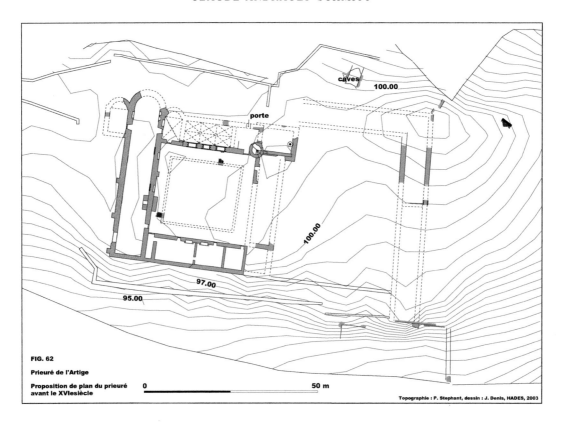

FIGURE 9.9A

L'Artige: Plan of Monastery (J. Denis, HADES)

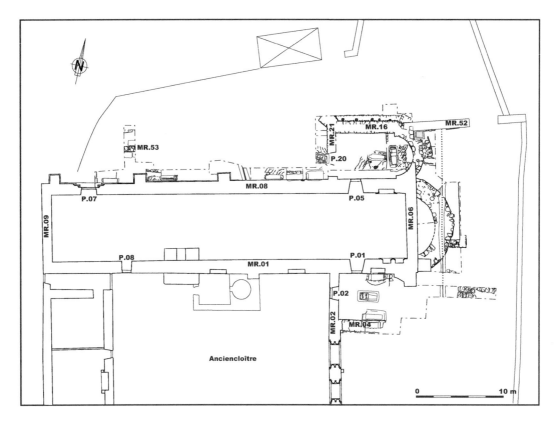

FIGURE 9.9B

L'Artige: Plan of church (J. Denis, HADES)

by Henry II *c.* 1178, and under Hugh of Avallon the community at Witham became important to the king. A long narrow nave is also known to have existed at Boschaud, a domically-vaulted Cistercian church which was a daughter-house of the Poitevin abbey of Les Châtelliers.[53]

Light can also be shed on the architectural model behind the church at Grandmont by looking at examples in the diocese of Limoges itself (Figure 9.7). The Benedictine church of Saint-Augustin in Limoges, the burial church of the bishops, was built between 1171 and 1180 and had a tall, barrel-vaulted, aisleless nave.[54] Above all, Grandmont is not far from L'Artige (near Saint-Léonard-de-Noblat), the mother house of a highly original ascetic order, founded by two penitent Venetian knights, Mark and his nephew Sebastian, both of whom are mentioned in the Grandmont obituary.[55] The house was established in a wild and uninhabited spot between 1174 and 1177. The date at which the priory is first described as 'L'Artige Neuve' is 1198, and is also the date of the dedication of the church and its main altar, some six decades before a new altar was installed in the presbytery.[56] The late-12th century-date is also confirmed by dendrochronology.[57] This, however, does not apply to the present church, which was heavily reconstructed (like Grandmont), but it does apply to the cloister. This has short and stocky columns, spur-bases, water-leaf or crocket capitals, and broad pointed arches with roll mouldings. Moreover, the remains of rib-vaults survive from the former chapter house (Figure 9.8). The first church is now best known thanks to excavations, with a short semicircular apse and thick walls – a design that compares closely to Grandmont's 'arrow plan'.[58] Two lateral chapels, originally barrel-vaulted like the nave, were virtually enclosed and included tombs (Figure 9.9). The north wall of the nave sustained a long gallery, which again sustained tombs, while he northern chapel still preserves its floor tiles. The southern chapel, *a parte claustri*, was dedicated to St Laurent, and was used for burial of the early priors and the commemoration of the founders.[59] As at Grandmont, the presbytery steps were reserved for the graves of high ranking brethren, often former bishops, who probably paid for this prestigious spot.[60] Thus, it is clear that different spaces were used for different types of burials. The chapels, where important saints were venerated, were reserved for the pious leaders of the community. High-ranking sinners, on the other hand, reliant on intercessionary prayer, were buried in the middle of the choir.

Grandmont lies between two Cistercian abbeys (there were eleven Cistercian monasteries in the diocese of Limoges), both belonging to the Dalon group and given to Pontigny in 1162. The abbey church of Beuil (Haute-Vienne) has entirely disappeared, but scholars suspect it was a simple single vessel with a large apse. The abbey church of Bonlieu (Creuse) is more interesting.[61] The east end might belong to a restoration campaign with groin (or rib) vaults, a pentagonal design and windows surrounded with high oculi. But the major part of the church, built between 1160 and 1180, had a transept and a long aisleless nave (Figure 9.10), once more of the 'arrow-type', with the same width as at Grandmont or L'Artige. The remaining bays of the nave (Figure 9.11) were covered by a barrel vault with transverse arches springing directly from the wall, and a series of curious putlog holes left over from the centering of the barrel vault.

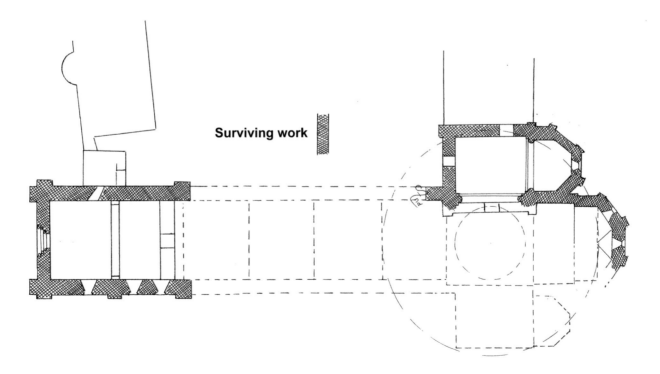

FIGURE 9.10

Bonlieu (Creuse): Plan of the Cistercian abbey (C. Andrault-Schmitt)

FIGURE 9.11

Bonlieu: Western bays of the abbey church (C. Andrault-Schmitt)

The location of the first occurrence of the aisleless or arrow-type church is unknown – Bonlieu, Grandmont, even L'Artige or Beuil. The question is unanswerable in the current state of research. It seems that faced with the constructions of the Burgundian Cistercians, an effort was made in the Limousin to create an alternative architectural image of asceticism at the time of Henry II. The lack of aisles can perhaps be explained by the fact that, as in female orders, nobody was supposed to walk around the liturgical choir. The narrow vessel could perfectly well accommodate the furnishings necessary for a choir. At Le Pin (near Poitiers), a Cistercian church with an aisleless nave that was built two or three decades before the community famously received grants from Richard I, a 17th-century witness saw 'stone seats' against the walls.[62] At Grandmont we know that there were two long choirs in the nave, together containing at least one hundred seats, one for the monks (with notable burial places in the middle) and a larger one for the lay brothers. L'Artige or Bonlieu have no connection with the English kings. Nonetheless, they may echo Grandmont, or perhaps it would be more accurate to state that all three are evidence of a similar artistic and liturgical programme.

THE CHURCH OF GRANDMONT AS A FOUNTAINHEAD FOR 'GRANDMONTINE ARCHITECTURE'

The expression 'Grandmontine-type' is generally used to describe smaller daughter houses, and not Grandmont itself. Although the notion of a 'plan-type' is anachronistic in relation to these houses, it is remarkable that – far more than is the case with Cistercian churches – all the lesser Grandmontine churches look alike, from Craswall in England to Languedoc, or from Normandy to Burgundy. They are defined by an aisleless and unarticulated nave, invariably barrel-vaulted, no transepts, and a semicircular or pentagonal chevet which is wider than the nave. The churches are small, but built of high quality masonry, as can be seen at Comberoumal near Millau, the best preserved and longest of them at 24 m (Figures 9.12 and 9.13). Some scholars have proposed that the explanation lies in canon 58 of the Order's *Institutio*. This specifies:

Quoniam omnis superfluitas a nostra religione prorsus debet esse aliena, ecclesia et cetera nostrae religionis aedificia plana sint et omni careant superfluitate. Omnis

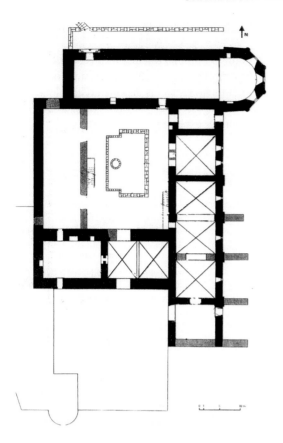

FIGURE 9.12

Comberoumal (Aveyron), the monastery (P. Bastide)

FIGURE 9.13

Comberoumal: Interior of church (C. Andrault-Schmitt)

FIGURE 9.14

Le Breuil-Bellay (Maine-et-Loire): Apse vault (C. Andrault-Schmitt)

pictura et omnis sculptura inutilis et superflua a nostris penitus absit aedificiis. Voutae quidem ecclesiarum sint tantum planae et simplicitati nostrae religionis congruae. Cum enim, testante ipsa Veritate, de omni uerbo otioso reddituri sumus rationem in die iudicii, multo magis de superfluis operibus.[63]

This badly written and redundant text is followed by a paraphrase from Matthew, 12, 36, saying that the men will be judged as much by their pointless words as by their useless works. The text is neither precise nor original enough to constitute a norm for building. The association between the French 'vouta' (a neologism) and the Latine 'plana' is also strange. The two words were obviously a description of the barrel vault covering the main space, even if some Grandmontine apses have ribs and liernes (Figure 9.14). The text selects a single feature, and suggests this suffices to constitute the imitation of a model. By this manner, it is possible that the builders of the church of Alberbury (Shropshire) believed that they were also imitating the mother church, although they chose an unvaulted square-ended nave, because they added a beautiful lateral chapel dedicated to St Stephen.[64]

The architecture of the smaller houses generally belongs to the late-12th-century or to the early-13th-century. Their churches are badly dated or dated very late, as we can see in western France: Breuil-Bellay (Maine-et-Loire) was consecrated in 1211, possibly two years after its foundation; Chassay-Grandmont (Vendée) is dated by dendrochronology to *c.* 1217/7; Bois-Rahier near Tours, a foundation of Henry II, was consecrated in 1254. I would suggest that the similarities among the buildings are because they all looked to Notre-Dame at Grandmont, even if we do not know how a medieval builder brother would see or imagine the mother house. This said, however, they represent loose adaptations rather than copies.

CONCLUSION

Patrons play only a very small part in architectural matters. Whoever is the patron, whoever the masters of works, and wherever they originate, an architectural design is always an alchemy, a mixing of international trends, local trends, local know-how and the special requirements of the building's specification. This is why, contrary to most opinion, Notre-Dame at Grandmont cannot be considered a one-off. All we can say is that Henry, Richard and John, with the consent of their administrators, supported several ascetic movements, and that these in turn promoted and were nourished by one of the great architectural trends of the 12th century. This movement lies behind architectural invention at Grandmont as it does with the architecture of the Carthusians or Templars. But without these three or four English kings, it is arguable that Grandmontine architecture would not exist. That is a lot for which to be remembered.

ACKNOWLEDGEMENTS

I am grateful to Philippe Racinet for his science and generosity in sharing with me the first results of his excavations, and to Julien Denis and the archaeologists from EVEHA (Limoges). Many thanks also to Alexandra Gajewski for her expert reading of this text.

NOTES

[1] See R. Graham, 'The Order of Grandmont and its Houses in England', *English Ecclesiastical Studies. Being Some Essays in Research in Medieval History* (London 1929), 209–46; then E. Hallam, 'Henry II, Richard I and the order of Grandmont', *Journal of Medieval History,* 1 (1975), 165–86.

[2] The wildness of the landscape became a literary commonplace as early as 1200. Thus the prior Gerard Itier: 'Grandmont is stern and very cold, unfertile and rocky, misty and exposed to the winds'. Graham, 'Order of Grandmont', (as n. 1), 211. For a fuller historiography and reappraisal, see C. Andrault-Schmitt, 'Un mémorial aristocratique: le monastère de Grandmont au comté de la Marche (1177–1307), *Cahiers de civilisation médiévale,* 59 (2016), 113–141.

[3] The erasing of the word *devotionis* is still common among contemporary scholars. The correct translation is given by L. Guibert, *Une page de l'histoire du clergé français au XVIIIe siècle. Destruction de l'ordre et de l'abbaye de Grandmont* (Paris-Limoges 1877), 48, or G. Bresson, 'Les trois églises de Grandmont', *Les Cahiers Grandmontains,* 22.

[4] J.-P. Migne, *Patrologia Latina,* 204; J.C. Robertson, Letter DC-CXLV, 448, 1171, in Rerum Britannicarum Medii Aevi Scriptores, VII (1885); J. Becquet ed., *Scriptores ordinis grandimontensis,* Corpus Christianorum VIII (Turnhout 1968).

[5] Letter from the Prior Pierre Bernard, *c.* 1163–1170, in Becquet, *Scriptores ordinis . . .,* 163–64. The words are those of Paul, in Cor., 3, 3: 'a letter not written on stone tablets, but on flesh tablets, on hearts'. About the power of friendship, see L. Moulinier-Brogi, 'Jean de Salisbury : un réseau d'amitiés continentales', *Culture politique des Plantagenêt (1154–1224),* ed., M. Aurell (Poitiers 2003), 341–59.

[6] From an inscription, after Bonaventure de Saint-Amable, *Histoire de Saint Martial* (1676), II, 15.

[7] '. . . *intuitu Divine amoris, et prece et petitione Bonorum Hominum de Grandi Monte motus'.* Howden, *Gesta regis,* ed. W. Stubbs, Rolls series (1867), 1, 194.

[8] R.W. Eyton, *Court, Household, and Itinerary of King Henry II* (London). But focusing from the charters and the Pipe Rolls is not sufficient. Eyton admits that the movements of the king's court are quite uncertain.

[9] W.L. Warren, *Henry II* (Los Angeles 1973), 105, after Robert de Torigni: 'the king of England spoke with the count of Toulouse at Grandmont'. For this year, Eyton unfortunately translates *Monte Grantem* by Mont-de-Marsan.

[10] With Henry the Young king's entrails being separately buried at Grandmont, this is the first royal burial that comes close to being dramatised. The cortège was described by the Limousin chronicler Geoffroy de Vigeois, as so often the only one to provide details of the event. The funeral falls into the last year recorded in his chronicle, and he describes numerous bishops waiting for the procession and the use of a white shroud, herbs and spices: P. Labbe, *Nova Bibliothecae* (Paris 1653), II, 338. The sermon of Thomas Agnelli, *De morte et sepultura Henrici Regis Junioris,* in Raoul de Coggeshall, does not mention the stop-over at Grandmont, but rather one at Saint-Savin: Raoul de Coggeshall, *Chronicon Anglicanum,* ed., J. Stevenson (Rolls Series, LXVI, 1875), 263–73. Roger de Howden says that a bishop tried to convince Henry the Young King that he should be buried at Grandmont, but he is unforthcoming about the cortège: *Gesta Regis Henrici Secundi,* ed., W. Stubbs (Rolls Series, XLIX, 1867) 2, 280. So is the *History of William Marshal* about the man who was in charge of the corpse: *Si com vers Roëm s'en alerent / Cil qui li giemble rei porterent, / Al Mans vindrend, si lor tolirent / Li*

chanoignie e grant feste en firent. The History of William Marshal, ed., A. Holden (London 2002), I, v. 7157–60.

11. Henry obtained the relic of the True Cross from King Amaury of Jerusalem, a relative. *Scriptores ordinis . . .*, VI, 215–16; *Bernard Itier. Chronique*, ed. J.-L. Lemaitre (Paris 1998), n°99.

12. Levesque, *Annales ordinis Grandimontis* (Troyes 1662), 188, about Richard's death.

13. 'Itinerary of King John', *Rotuli Litterarum patentium in Turri Londinensi*, 1, ed. Th. Duff Hardy (London 1835).

14. Alberbury, or Nova Abbacia, was first founded for regular canons. It served as a funerary monument for the founder Fulk (d. 1258) and, earlier, for his two successive wives. This patron is the hero of a novel (in French), originally a verse romance from the 13th century: R.J. Dean, *Anglo-norman literature. A Guide to Texts and Manuscripts* (London 1999), 92; G.S. Burgess, *Two Medieval Outlaws. Eustace the Monk and Fouke Fitz Waryn* (Cambridge 1997), 91–192. See the relevant entries in the *Oxford Dictionary of National Biography* for the above barons.

15. *The Great Rolls of the Pipe*, 28, p. 126. It is funny that J.T. Appleby compares the price of the furs and clothes to the gifts for building, concluding that the king's generosity is not so great: 'The ecclesiastical Foundations of Henry II', *The Catholic Historical Review*, 48 (1962), 205–15.

16. *The Historical Works of Gervase of Canterbury*, ed. W. Stubbs, (Rolls Series, LXXIII, 1879), I, 298–300.

17. This was confirmed by Eleanor in 1199. For all the gifts, A. Lecler, 'Histoire de l'abbaye de Grandmont', *Bulletin de la société archéologique et historique du Limousin*, 57/60 (1907–10) (sadly unreliable). For the various forms of Eleanor's devotion, see N. Vincent, 'Patronage, Politics and Piety in the Charters of Eleanor of Aquitaine', *Plantagenêts et Capétiens : confrontations et héritages*, éd. M. Aurell et N.-Y. Tonnerre (Turnhout 2006), 17–60.

18. Scholars have misinterpreted Grandmont because they have misunderstood the concept of poverty. The early periods of the monastery's history are legendary, but later the community's needs were exactly the same as those of other monastic establishments. They owned taxes, fishing rights, estates, ponds, mills, tithes, rents. See C. Andrault-Schmitt, 'Comberoumal (commune de Saint-Beauzély), maison grandmontaine', *Monuments de l'Aveyron. Congrès archéologique de France*, 166 (Paris 2011), 61–70.

19. The monks (supported by the Capetians) were pitted against the lay brethren, who in turn were supported by the Plantagenets. A bull of Clement III (1188) ordered a new election. But the crisis persisted for another century and more – until the 1317 reform.

20. L. Guibert, 'Destruction de l'ordre et de l'abbaye de Grandmont', *Bulletin de la société archéologique et historique du Limousin*, 25 (1877), 126.

21. *The Great Roll of the Pipe for the Twenty-Second Year of the Reign of King Henry II, vol. 25* (London 1904), 141, 137. See also Graham, 'The Order of Grandmont' (as n. 1), 217. Also R.F. Homer, 'Tin, Lead and Pewter', in *English Medieval Industries. Craftsmen, Techniques Products*, ed. by J. Blair and N. Ramsay (London 1991), 57–80. More recently by F. Madeline, 'Le don de plomb dans le patronage monastique d'Henri II Plantagenêt : usages et conditions de la production du plomb anglais dans la seconde moitié du XIIe siècle', *Archéologie médiévale*, 39 (2009), 31–52.

22. *The Great Roll of the Pipe for the Twenty-Fifth Year of the Reign of King Henry II, vol. 28* (London 1909), 30, and *The Great Roll of the Pipe for the Twenty-Seventh Year of the Reign of King Henry II, vol. 30* (London 1909), 47.

23. The *Nécrologe-obituaire de la cathédrale du Mans* thanks Henry II for such a gift in the middle of the 12th century: *'dedit etiam nobis plumbum ad operationdos parietes ecclesie nostre, quod et nobis nostro modico sumptu fecit afferri'. Nécrologe-obituaire de la cathédrale du Mans*, ed. G. Busson and A. Ledru (Le Mans 1906), 155–56. According to B. Fillion-Braguet, this gift is connected with the tomb of Geoffrey of Anjou, the king's father.

24. See the fundamental paper from J. Gillingham, 'Events and Opinions: Norman and English Views of Aquitaine c. 1152–1240', in M. Bull and C. Léglu, *The World of Eleanor of Aquitaine. Literature and Society in Southern France Between Eleventh and Thirteenth Centuries* (Woodbridge 2005), 57–82.

25. In 1178, the 66 livres for 100 carts for Clairvaux would correspond with 40 livres for 60 carts for Grandmont. See Andrault-Schmitt, 'Un mémorial' (as n. 2).

26. Pierre Bertin was seneschal of Poitou for Richard, Otho and Eleanor, and is said to have been a witness to a charter in 1192, He went on to play a leading part in the arbitration in favour of Grandmont c. 1197: A. Richard, *Histoire des comtes de Poitou*, 2 (Paris 1903) *passim*.

27. For King John's magnates and the 1214 campaign, see now Stephen Church, *King John and the Road to Magna Carta* (New York 2015), though this author does not mention a stay at Grandmont.

28. The gifts of lands, candles or incomes are often made simply 'to Grandmont', making it difficult to ascertain if 'Grandmont' designates the mother house or a small dependency.

29. G. Le Duc, 'Etat du clergé ou du diocèse de Limoges', *Bulletin de la société archéologique et historique du Limousin*, 46 (1898), 365.

30. Levesque, *Annales*, (as n. 12), 133.

31. *Vita*, in *Scriptores ordinis grandimontensis*, (as n. 4) III, 147: *Tempore domni Stephani Liciaco, uenerabilis quarti prioris Grandimontis, aedificabatur ecclesia in Grandimonte. Accidit autem quadam die cum operarii quondam lapidem magnum ac quadratum sursum in altum deferent, obuiam habuerunt Geraldum magistrum operis ipsius, quem inuiti et incaute ignorantes expulerunt a sommitate arcium, et corruit in terram, qui grauiter collisus occubuit, sanguis uero eius per oculos, per auros, per nares ac per os defluebat.*

32. J. Becquet, 'Le nécrologue primitif de Grandmont (Paris, BNF, MS lat. 1138)', *Etudes grandmontaines* (Ussel 1998), 9.

33. Bernard Itier (as n. 11), n°87. '*VII annis e demei jam expletis domus edificio*'.

34. *Gallia Christiana*, II (1720), 649, after Bernard Gui.

35. G. François-Souchal, 'Les émaux de Grandmont au XIIe siècle', *Bulletin monumental*, 120 (1962), 339–57, *Bulletin monumental*, 121 (1963), 41–64, 123–50, 219–35, 307–29, *Bulletin monumental*, 122 (1964), 7–35, 129–59; J.-R. Gaborit, 'L'autel majeur de Grandmont', *Cahiers de Civilisation médiévale*, 75 (1976), 231–46.

36. Two priests and two lay brothers: *Itinerarium a Guilelmo et Iberto Fratribus Grandimontis conscriptum*, ed. J. Becquet, *Scriptores* (as n. 4), 251–54.

37. Gaborit, 'L'autel majeur de Grandmont' (as n. 33). See the new reading for one of the inscriptions of an altarpiece: N'IGO LASERT. PARLA AM N'ETEVE DE MURET. The slab is dated after 1189 because of the nimbus.

38. Bernard Itier, (as n. 11), no. 139.

39. Limoges, Archives départementales. I SEM 81: in 1723 a hand wrote that some parts of the chronicle were burnt by the abbot who was unhappy with Pardoux.

40. Levesque's *Annales* were written 22 years after his departure from Grandmont (see n. 12).

41. Montpellier, Archives départementales. Hérault, 49 J 9, 1713/1737. The Naurissart estimate is published in the 2013 archaeological report.

42. Hallam, 'Henry II, Richard I and the order of Grandmont' (as n. 1), 169, imagines a church with aisles, which perhaps explains the mention of aisles in the otherwise excellent paper from L. Grant, 'Le patronage architectural d'Henri II et de son entourage', *Cahiers de Civilisation médiévale*, 37 (1994), 73–84. Some other interpretations are also surprising, as in J. Martin and L.E.M. Walker, 'At the feet of St Stephen Muret: Henry II and the order of Grandmont', *Journal of Medieval History*, 16 (1990), 1–12. The best reconstruction is that proposed by R. Graham and A.W. Clapham, 'The Order of Grandmont and its Houses in England', *Archaeologia*, 75 (1926), 159–210.

43. Guibert, *Une page de l'histoire* (as n. 3), 986.

44. E. Fernie, 'La fonction liturgique des piliers cantonnés dans la nef de la cathédrale de Laon', *Bulletin Monumental*, 145 (1987), 257–66.

45. Pardoux identified coats of arms as English roses (!), but they were perhaps decorative flowers. Souchal's (1963, 147–49) suggestion of a ciborium similar to that in S. Pietro ad Oratorium was dismissed by Gaborit, 'L'autel majeur', (as n.33), n. 11.

46. Despite Pardoux's statement citing 'stone columns', there is every chance that he misinterpreted the material evidence. La Chapelle (Creuse) is a funerary foundation, created by Cardinal Pierre de La Chapelle Taillefer: Limoges, Archives départementales, I SEM 58. My thanks to Robert Chanaud for this reference.

⁴⁷ The Limousin legend says that the Count de La Marche, Hugh IX, died at the Grandmontine house of Saint-Marc-l'Ecluse that he had founded nearby, and that he was buried at Grandmont. However, he actually died at Damiette in 1218/9.

⁴⁸ Philippe Racinet is a professor of archaeology at the University of Amiens. The programme is under the administrative supervision of the *Service régional de l'archéologie* (DRAC Limousin/Nouvelle Aquitaine).

⁴⁹ Several important bishops were buried in the church. The first seems to be Gerard III d'Escoraille, Bishop of Cahors (1151–99), a relative of a number of other French bishops, and an expert in Italian politics. Gerard was buried in the middle of the choir in 1209. His tomb was decorated with an effigy made from copper and enamel, showing the bishop in a reclining position and holding a crosier: Bernard Itier, (as n. 11), no.131. He was a great friend of Grandmont, present at both the 1166 and the 1189 ceremonies. We also know of the burial of an archbishop of Lyon in the monastic church.

⁵⁰ For reflections on the absence of evidence for a 'Plantagenet architecture' see, C. Andrault-Schmitt,'Le mécénat architectural en question: les chantiers de Saint-Yrieix, Grandmont et Le Pin à l'époque de Henri II' in *La cour Plantagenêt (1154–1204)* ed., M. Aurell (Poitiers 2000), 235–76. See also the conclusions from Philippe Bur, for *Culture politique des Plantagenêt,* and more recently C. Andrault-Schmitt, 'Fontevraud et Burgos: l'architecture reflète-t-elle une mémoire Plantagenêt in *Alfonso VIII y Leonor de Inglaterra: Confluencias artisticas en el entorno de 1200,* eds., M. Poza Yagüe and D. Olivares Martínez (Madrid 2017), 203–33.

⁵¹ J. Franklin, 'Iconic Architecture and the Medieval Reformation: Ambrose of Milan, Peter Damian, Stephen Harding and the Aisleless Cruciform Church', in *Romanesque and the Past*, ed., J. McNeill and R. Plant (Leeds 2013), 77–93.

⁵² For Witham Friary, see J. Orbach and N. Pevsner, *The Buildings of England. Somerset: South and West* (New Haven and London 2014 [1958, 341–42]. See also R. Wilson-North and S. Porter, 'Witham, Somerset: From Carthusian Monastery to Country House to Gothic Folly', *Architectural History,* 40 (1997), 81–97. For a global and recent view: G. Coppack and M. Aston, *Christ's Poor Men. The Carthusians in England* (2002).

⁵³ C. Andrault-Schmitt, 'L'abbaye de Boschaud', *Congrès archéologique de France: Périgord,* 155 (Paris 1999),107–17. See also C. Andrault-Schmitt, "L'expression architecturale chez les claravalliens de l'Aquitaine du nord: les abbatiales des Châtelliers, Boschaud et Valence", *Le temps long de Clairvaux. Nouvelles recherches, nouvelles perspectives,* A. Baudin et A. Grélois éd., Département de l'Aube, 2016, 261–82.

⁵⁴ See X. Lhermite, 'L'architecture religieuse à Limoges pendant le premier siècle de l'art gothique' (unpublished Ph. D thesis, University of Poitiers, 2007). The foundation stone was laid by Richard and Eleanor.

⁵⁵ J. Becquet, 'Aux origines du prieuré de L'Artige, chef d'ordre canonial en Limousin (XIIe et XIIIe siècles)', *Bulletin de la societé archéologique et historique du Limousin,* 90 (1963) 85–100 and 97 (1970), 83–142. The order was founded *longe a sancto Leonardo* c. 1100, admitted with a rule in 1158 (by papal bull from the English Adrian IV), and eventually numbered more than 50 houses. The papers by R. Crozet, in *Bulletin Monumental,* 115 (1957), 35–41, and C. Chabrely-Platon 'L'architecture artigienne', *Bulletin de la societé archéologique et historique du Limousin,* 112 (1985), 45–61, are now partly out of date. For the obituary, see Becquet, *Etudes grandmontaines* (as n. 32), 297.

⁵⁶ M.-M. Gauthier, 'La plaque de dédicace émaillée datée 1267 d'un autel jadis à L'Artige, aujourd'hui au musée national de Varsovie, et les autels de l'Artige', *Bulletin de la societé archéologique et historique du Limousin,* 87 (1960), 333–48.

⁵⁷ I am very grateful to Chr. Dormoy, of ARCHEOLABS, for his 2011 email, informing me that 5 reused pieces of wood can be dated between 1184 and 1191, and 17 others date to *c.* 1385 (unsurprising considering the reconstruction of the nave, and the stair-tower built astride the interior and exterior).

⁵⁸ J. Denis, for HADES, in *Bilan scientifique 2004,* DRAC Limousin, SRA, 74.

⁵⁹ Becquet, 'Aux origines du prieuré de L'Artige' (as n. 55), 95. The chapel of St Laurent received the grave of the 3rd and 4th priors.

⁶⁰ Becquet, 'Aux origines du prieuré de L'Artige' (as n. 55), 96: see also Hélie d'Ort, from Solignac, *ecclesiam construxit, dormitorium vetus atque refectorium qui sepultus est in ecclesia iuxta gradum presbyterii, ad pedes tumbe episcopalis.*

⁶¹ C. Andrault-Schmitt, 'La mise en œuvre des églises de granit en Limousin à la fin du XIIe siècle', in Y. Gallet éd., *Ex Quadris Lapidibus. La pierre et sa mise en œuvre dans l'art médiéval. Mélanges d'Histoire de l'art offerts à Eliane Vergnolle,* (Turnhout 2012), 81–92; and *eadem,* 'Loin de Clairvaux: trois enquêtes sur les filiations artistiques, de la Gartempe à la Galice', *Espace et territoire au Moyen Age. Hommages à Bernadette Barrière* (Bordeaux 2012), 63–83.

⁶² C. Andrault-Schmitt, 'Les églises cisterciennes du Poitou. L'invention architecturale et l'émergence d'un réseau européen (1129–1277)', *Revue historique du Centre-Ouest,* 1 (2004), 11–103.

⁶³ Some items were written a little before 1170, others at the beginning of the 13th century. Becquet, *Scriptores ordinis* (as n. 4), XIV, 524.

⁶⁴ J. Newman and N. Pevsner, *The Buildings of England. Shropshire* (New Haven and London 2006), 105. What remains is part of a farmhouse (White Abbey Farm); the square east end of the former church was pulled down in 1857 and the nave was excavated in 1925. However, the chapel of St Stephen survives. Fulk Fitz Warin III was originally buried in front of the main altar, before the presbytery steps.

THE HOSPITAL, ENGLAND AND SIGENA: A FOOTNOTE

Neil Stratford

The evidence presented in this paper is purely circumstantial.[1] I hope however that the historical context in which the chapter-house paintings at Sigena were created and the English connection of the paintings will be to some extent illuminated. The literature on the paintings rarely refers to the Hospital. It is the founders, Queen Sancha and King Alfonso II of Aragon, who are invoked to explain the chapter-house and its decoration, never the Hospital, which after all occupied the monastery from the middle years of the 12th century and received Sancha as a sister. It was also the Hospital that created a special Rule for the female Hospitallers at Sigena in 1188, the date of the official foundation of the new convent.[2] This convent was clearly conceived as the headquarters for the female Hospital in Aragon-Catalonia. By the official foundation date the Latin Kingdom was in crisis. Jerusalem was lost to Saladin in October 1187. The Prior of Saint-Gilles, the Hospital's European headquarters, gave Sigena in 1187 to Sancha, but it was made clear in the early charters of the convent that the Castellan of Amposta, the head of the Hospital in the kingdom of Aragon, had ultimate guardianship of the sisters of Sigena. A group of Hospitaller brothers *(fratres)* was resident at Sigena, which was a double community throughout its history, even if the prioress took decisions on behalf of the sisters.[3]

The events of August 1936, when anarchists set fire to the chapter-house, are well known, as is the remarkable series of photographs recording the room and its decoration taken by José Gudiol in May of that year and which provide so much of our knowledge of the room before calamity struck (Figure 10.1). A shadow of the chapter-house is presented today in the Museu Nacional d'Art de Catalunya in Barcelona (Figure 10.2). For over fifty years the chapter-house was abandoned and left without a roof (Figure 10.3), before it was restored in 1992 (Figure 10.4). I am taking for granted the generally accepted identity of the Sigena painter or painters with one or more of the later artists of the Winchester Bible, an identity first suggested by Otto Pächt and further elaborated by Walter

FIGURE 10.1

Sigena: Chapter-house in 1936 (Museu Nacional d'Art de Catalunya, Photo Arxiu Mas)

FIGURE 10.2

Sigena: Detail of chapter-house in the Museu Nacional d'Art de Catalunya (Museu Nacional d'Art de Catalunya, Photo Calveras/Mérida/Sagristà)

© British Archaeological Association 2018

FIGURE 10.3

Sigena: Chapter-house in 1973 (Jacques Lacoste)

FIGURE 10.4

Sigena: Chapter-house in 2013 (Jacques Lacoste)

FIGURE 10.5

Sigena: Chapter-house; Annunciation to the Shepherds (© Fundació Institut Amatller d'Art Hispànic. Foto Gudiol)

FIGURE 10.6

Winchester Bible; initial to Isaiah (John Crook)

Oakeshott (Figures 10.5 and 10.6).[4] I simply want to draw attention to certain events important to the history of the Hospital and which involve England and the English crown from the mid-1180s onwards. They may help to explain how some of the best painters of their time active in England came to work for the Hospital in Aragon.

Circa 1185 King Henry II founded the first house for women Hospitallers in England, among the first in Europe, at Buckland (Somerset).[5] In 1184, the Patriarch of Jerusalem, Heraclius, in a desperate bid for help to counter Muslim attack, mounted an embassy to the West, in which he was accompanied by prestigious relics, by the Master of the Temple, Arnaud de Torri Rubea (Arnau de Torroja), and by the Grand Master of the Hospital, Roger des Moulins (see map at Figure 10.7).[6] The party disembarked at Brindisi in December 1184 and proceeded north, probably via Rome. Following the death of the Master of the Temple in Verona, where Heraclius had no success in a meeting with Pope Lucius III and Emperor Frederick Barbarossa, the embassy travelled west across northern Italy into Gaul. Here they met an unsympathetic Philip Augustus in Paris, and Heraclius preached in Notre-Dame. The

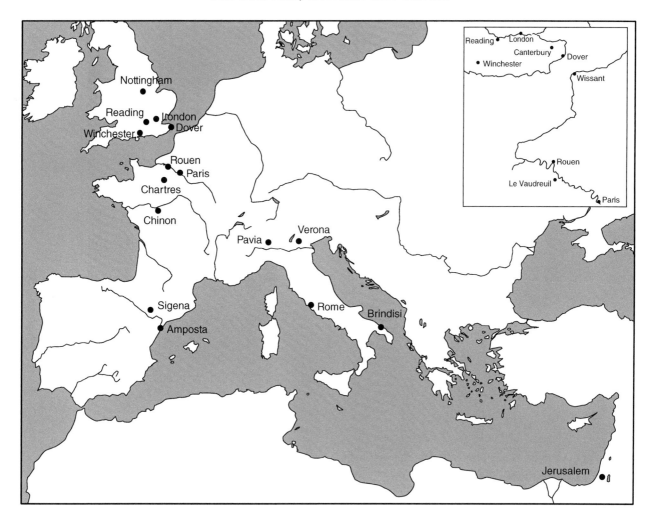

FIGURE 10.7

Map of the mission of 1184–85 (John McNeill)

Patriarch and the Master of the Hospital then crossed the Channel, arriving in Canterbury, according to the monk Gervase, on 29 January 1185, where they visited Becket's tomb-shrine in the cathedral crypt. King Henry II was heading north at the time, but turned back at Nottingham and seems to have met the Patriarch and the Master at Reading Abbey on 17 March, an event famous in English history. Two less reliable sources, including the Winchester annalist, place the meeting at Winchester and it is possible as Cartellieri suggested that there were two successive meetings, one of them at Winchester.[7] A week long council followed at Clerkenwell Hospital in London beginning on 18 March. It must have been on this occasion that the patriarch dedicated the church of the Hospitallers at Clerkenwell, whereas it was while he had previously passed through London on 10 February that he consecrated the Temple church (according to a lost inscription, which recorded the event).[8]

The king's reluctance to embark on crusade in spite of his vow to do so in 1170 led him to turn to the French king, Philip Augustus. Henry was at Dover on 10 April. With him on this occasion were, among others, Richard, bishop of Winchester; and John, prior of Winchester Cathedral priory; Roger des Moulins, the Grand Master of the Hospital; and Garnier de Nablous (or Neapolis), prior of the Hospital in England. Among the business transacted at Dover, presumably in the Castle, was the transfer of Holy Cross, Winchester, from the Hospital into the care of the bishop.[9] Henry's devotion to the Hospitallers has already been noted in connection with his foundation of Buckland; in his will of March 1182 the first bequests of 5000 marcs of silver are to the Masters of the Hospital and the Temple and a further 5000 marcs for the defence of the Holy Land. The sequel to the Dover meeting was embarkation for France (Henry landed at Wissant), Easter at Rouen, a fruitless meeting between kings Henry II and Philip Augustus at the castle of Le Vaudreuil and a disgruntled Heraclius. According to that scandal-monger, Giraldus Cambrensis, Heraclius warned Henry of divine retribution on three occasions, in London, at Dover and finally at Chinon, before he returned to the Holy Land at some time before the beginning of August.[10] The Master of the Hospital seems to have visited Chartres on this journey, while Heraclius visited

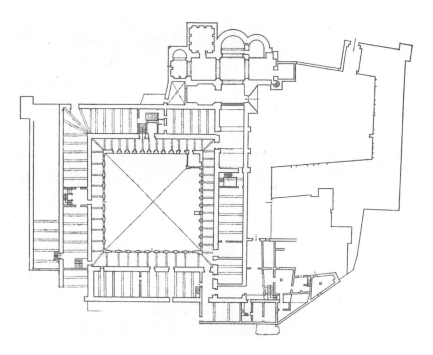

FIGURE 10.8

Sigena: Plan of monastery Iñiguez

Angers and Saumur. Heraclius' return journey was via Messina in Sicily. Roger des Moulins may have been in Pavia in November 1185 but he was certainly back in the east by the beginning of February 1186. It should be noted that this story of a journey by the Master of the Hospital involves Winchester and its bishop, Richard of Ilchester, King Henry II and the Hospital in England with its prior Garnier de Nablous.

Roger des Moulins was killed in battle some two months before Hattin in 1187. His interim successor was Ermengol de Aspa, and though according to Luttrell he was never elected Grand Master, he assumed control as *provisor* of the Order between May and October 1188.[11] He had become Castellan of Amposta, the frontier fortress near Tortosa, in 1180, and Sigena fell within the orbit of this Castellany from the time of its original creation in 1157. In 1182 Ermengol was appointed Prior of Saint-Gilles and general administrator of the Hospital in Provence and the Kingdom of Aragon. In Jonathan Riley-Smith's words, this effectively made him commander of much of France and Spain 'and probably in England as well'.[12] With two gaps (he was replaced in Saint-Gilles for a short time in 1185 and he assumed governance of the whole Order in 1188) he was Castellan of Amposta for most of the 1180s and was back in his post by 1190. It was Ermengol who confirmed the new Rule of Sigena while in the Holy Land as *provisor* of the Order in 1188. He was with Sancha the joint founder of the Sigena convent. He was thus uniquely well placed to introduce an 'international' artist to an important commission in Aragon through the Hospitaller movement. As for Garnier de Nablous, he probably arrived in England from the East

with the Patriarch and the Grand Master in 1185, and we left him as Prior of England at Dover in April 1185. His subsequent career was stellar. By June 1191 he had reached Syria from England and had become Grand Master of the Hospital, though he may have been elected as early as the second half of 1189. His interim movements included a visit to Paris still in his capacity as Prior of England in the first half of 1190, and he was in Messina with Richard I in October 1190. He played a prominent part in the Third Crusade and died in late 1192. But any or all of the other candidates mentioned above could have played a part in shaping the international career of 'The Morgan Master', for he is the most important artist linking the Winchester Bible and Sigena. I suggest that he could have been sent to Queen Sancha directly by Henry II before or soon after the king died in 1189. It should be remembered that at the death of Raymond Berengar IV of Aragon in 1162, Sancha's future husband, Alfonso II, was a minor and his territories were put under Henry's protection, a situation which at the least implies regular contacts between the two courts. Alternatively, he could have been sent to Sancha by the Prior of England, Garnier, in the late 1180s, with the knowledge and support of the Castellan, Ermengol de Aspa. The 'Morgan Master' may have become known to the Grand Master (Roger des Moulins) and the Prior of England (Garnier) at Winchester or Dover in early 1185.[13]

As to the date of the chapter-house paintings, they decorate a building which from its eccentric position on the plan of the convent (Figure 10.8) in relation to the church must have been built before the church was extended to the east in the early-13th-century.[14] It is intrinsically unlikely,

FIGURE 10.9

Sigena: 'Dormitory' to north (Jacques Lacoste)

FIGURE 10.10

Sigena: 'Dormitory' painted frieze (Jacques Lacoste)

though not impossible, that the paintings predate the 1188 foundation of the new convent. The great room is clearly more than a mere chapter-house and must have been conceived as an assembly room for the female Hospital in the kingdom of Aragon, where Queen Sancha could hold court with the Castellan of Amposta. Their seats would probably have been against the south wall, not facing the chapter-house entrance, which is the usual place for the president of chapter. The evidence for this unusual position is that the Crucifixion painting was in the centre of the south wall. A cross or its image was invariably placed above the president's seat in a chapter-house.[15]

A serious study of the monastic buildings is required, as many questions remain open. What was the original purpose of the huge room to the north of the chapter-house, for instance, which is always referred to as the dormitory (Figure 10.9)? It runs the entire length of the east and north ranges of the cloister at ground level. It would have housed a vast community, which, even allowing for the optimism of monastic founders, can never have been envisaged at Sigena. In 1207 the closed number (*numerus clausus*) of sisters was set at 30. Or did this room in part provide accommodation for the sick? Vestiges of paintings still on its walls (Figure 10.10) suggest that this vast space, architecturally similar to the chapter-house and clearly contemporary, was also decorated by the same team. The few decorative motifs which survive would not be out of place in the borders of the Winchester Bible. In which case the Morgan Master and his associates could have been active at Sigena for several years. For the time being, Karl Schuler's date for the paintings in the late 1180s or early 1190s seems entirely reasonable.[16] I would add that Queen Sancha took her vows in 1196, at the death of her husband Alfonso, and that she died and was buried at Sigena in 1208.

I will end by mentioning another building outside England, which may well reflect Henry II's patronage of the poor and sick. As mentioned above, following the meeting at Dover in April 1185, Henry crossed the channel and spent Easter at Rouen. The chapel of the leper hospital at Le Petit-Quevilly lies across the Seine from Rouen in the forest where Henry II had a residence and hunting lodge.[17] The leproserie is first mentioned in a charter datable between 1185 and 31 January 1188. Henry's only known stays at the Petit-Quevilly are in 1171 and 1174, but it would be surprising if he did not go there in 1185. Another pious hospital foundation of the king, its paintings survive (Figure 10.11). These are earlier than Sigena, probably of *c.* 1160–70, certainly paid for by the king and closely associated, like the Sigena chapter-house, with an insular artist – this time connected in style to the so-called Winchester Psalter (London, British Library, MS Cotton, Nero C IV). Henry II here disposed of the talents of a major 'English' painter within the lands of his Empire beyond the Channel. There is nothing surprising in this, just as there

Figure 10.11

Petit-Quevilly: Chapel of Saint Julien; detail of painting

is nothing surprising in the presence of a major 'English' painter working for the Hospital in Sigena.

NOTES

1. I would particularly like to thank Jacques Lacoste, who travelled with me to Sigena in 2013 and took many of the photographs of the chapter-house and monastery presented by me at the conference in Barcelona; especially valuable were his photographs taken in 1973 before the 1992 restoration. I would also like to thank John McNeill, who kindly prepared my PowerPoint presentation for the conference.

2. A. Ubieto, *Documentos de Sigena I*, Textos Medievales, 32 (Valencia 1972), numbers 5 and 6.

3. The various stages in the creation of the monastery of Santa Maria at Sigena are covered in A. Ubieto, *El Real Monasterio de Sigena (1188–1300)* (Valencia 1966). See also idem., *Documentos de Sigena* (as n. 2), nos 1–11.

4. O. Pächt, 'A cycle of English frescoes in Spain', *Burlington Magazine*, 103, (1961), 166–75. Walter Oakeshott, *Sigena. Romanesque Paintings in Spain and the Winchester Bible Artists* (London 1972).

5. W. Page, ed., *Victoria County History; Somerset, vol. II* (London 1911), 148–50.

6. For the historical sources which enable one to reconstruct the mission of 1184–85 see Appendix 1.

7. A. Cartellieri, *Philipp II. August König von Frankreich, Bd. II. Der Kreuzzug (1187–1191)*, (Leipzig and Paris 1906), 18–25.

8. For the text of the inscription and a reproduction of a drawing of the tympanum made in 1695, see R. Griffiths-Jones, "An Enrichment of Cherubims': Christopher Wren's Refurbishment of the Temple Church', in *The Temple Church in London: History, Architecture, Art*, ed., R. Griffiths-Jones and D. Park (Woodbridge 2010), 170 and plate 84.

9. J. Delaville le Roulx, *Cartulaire général de l'ordre des Hospitaliers de S. Jean de Jérusalem (1100–1310), tome I (1100–1200)*, (Paris 1894), no. 755.

10. For Giraldus Cambrensis, see Appendix.

11. A. Luttrell, 'Ermengol de Aspa, *Provisor* of the Hospital: 1188', *Crusades*, 4 (2005), 15–19.

12. J. Riley-Smith, *The Knights of St John in Jerusalem and Cyprus c.1050–1300* (London 1967), 106–07.

13. The suggestion of the possible recruitment of The Morgan Master and his team of painters in 1185 by the Hospital is remarkably consistent with the conclusions of Christopher Norton as to the date when the incomplete Winchester Bible was abandoned, conclusions published in this volume. Since the Barcelona conference, one of Christopher de Hamel's 2014 Panizzi lectures was devoted to the Winchester Bible (and will in due course be published by the British Library). The arguments advanced then as to the date and genesis of the Bible did not, in my opinion, carry conviction.

14. The plan of the monastery published here is after the plan made by Iñiguez before 1936 and published by del Arco in 1942. See R. del Arco y Garay, *Catalogo monumental de España: Huesca* (Madrid 1942), Vol. 1. It is deficient in certain respects, most notably in not showing the openings to the chapter-house, but it remains the most useful plan of the monastery published to date.

15. N. Stratford, 'Notes on the Norman Chapterhouse at Worcester', in *Medieval Art and Architecture at Worcester Cathedral*, ed. G. Popper, British Archaeological Association Conference Transactions, I (Leeds 1978), 55.

16. K.F. Schuler, 'Seeking institutional identity in the Chapterhouse at Sigena', in *Shaping Sacred Space and Institutional Identity in Romanesque Mural Painting. Essays in Honour of Otto Demus*, ed. T. Dale and J. Mitchell (London 2004), 245–56.

17. See N. Stratford, 'The wall-paintings of the Petit-Quevilly' in *Medieval Art, Architecture and Archaeology at Rouen*, ed. J. Stratford, British Archaeological Association Conference Transactions, XII (Leeds 1993), 51–59 and plates IX–XIV; idem, 'Le Petit-Quevilly, peintures murales de la chapelle Saint-Julien', *Congrès archéologique de France (Rouen et Pays de Caux)*, 161 (2005), 133–46.

APPENDIX

SELECT BIBLIOGRAPHY

[Excepting the final section listing the primary sources, the following bibliography is arranged chronologically and is intended historiographically]

Sigena

del Arco y Garay, R. *Catalogo monumental de España: Huesca*, 2 vols (Madrid 1942), 394–412 (vol. 1), figs 931–980 (vol. 2).

Pächt, O. 'A cycle of English frescoes in Spain', *Burlington Magazine*, 103 (1961), 166–175.

Ubieto Arteta, A. *Documentos de Sigena, I*, Textos Medievales, 32 (Valencia 1972), particularly numbers 1–11 on the foundation of the Convent.

Ubieto Arteta, A. *El Real Monasterio de Sigena (1188–1300)* (Valencia 1966).

Oakeshott, W. 'The Sigena paintings and the second style of rubrication in the Winchester Bible', in: *Kunsthistorische Forschungen Otto Pächt zu seinem 70. Geburtstag*, ed. A. Rosenauer, G. Weber (Salzburg 1972), 90–98.

Oakeshott, W. *Sigena. Romanesque paintings in Spain and the Winchester Bible artists* (London 1972).

Oakeshott, W. letter 'Sigena' to: *Times Literary Supplement*, 1 December, 1972.

Ayres, L. M. 'The work of the Morgan Master at Winchester and English painting of the Early Gothic period', *Art Bulletin*, LVI (1974), 201–223.

Gardelles, J. 'Le prieuré de Sigena aux XIIème et XIIIème siècles: étude architecturale', *Bulletin Monumental*, 133 (1975), 15–28.

Oakeshott, W. *The two Winchester Bibles* (Oxford 1981), 25, 71, 75–82, plates 15,78, 84, 99, 102, 105, 157, 160.

Schuler, K. F. *The Pictorial Program of the Chapterhouse of Sigena*, Ph.D thesis, New York University Institute of Fine Arts (1994), UMI Dissertation Services (Ann Arbor, Michigan), 1994.

Schuler, K. F. 'Seeking institutional identity in the Chapterhouse at Sigena', in *Shaping Sacred Space and Institutional Identity in Romanesque Mural Painting. Essays in honour of Otto Demus*, ed., T. Dale and J. Mitchell (London 2004), 245–256.

Ocón Alonso, D. 'Une salle capitulaire pour une reine: les peintures du chapitre de Sigena', *Les Cahiers de Saint-Michel de Cuxa*, XXXVIII (2007), 81–94.

Pagès i Paretas, M. *Pintura mural sagrada i profana,del romànic al primer gòtic* (Abadia di Montserrat 2012), 40–103, plats 4–36.

Pagès i Paretas, M. 'Un saltiri de Guillem II per a Monreale? Sobre els origens del Saltiri Anglocatalà de Paris', *Miscellània Litúrgica Catalana*, XX (2012), 287–308.

Ocón Alonso, D. 'The Paintings of the Chapter-House of Sigena and the Art of the Crusader Kingdoms', in *Romanesque and the Mediterranean*, ed., R. Bacile and J. McNeill (Leeds 2015), 277–295.

England and the hospital

The Rev. R. W. Eyton, *Court, Household and Itinerary of Henry II* (London 1878), II, 261–264 (1184/5 mission to England).

Delaville Le Roulx, J. *Cartulaire général de l'ordre des Hospitaliers de S. Jean de Jérusalem (1100–1310)*, Tome I (1100–1200), (Paris 1894), particularly 480–482 (no. 755) (the charter of 1185 at Dover).

Round, J.H. 'Garnier de Nablous, Prior of the Hospital in England, and Grand Master of the Order of St John of Jerusalem', *Archaeologia*, LVIII (1903), 383–390.

Cartellieri, A. *Philipp II. August König von Frankreich, Bd. II. Der Kreuzzug (1187–1191)* (Leipzig and Paris 1906), 18–25 (1184/5 mission).

Riley-Smith, J. *The knights of St John in Jerusalem and Cyprus c.1050–1310* (London 1967), 106–107 (Ermengol de Aspa).

Kedar, B. Z. 'The Patriarch Eraclius' in *Outremer. Studies in the history of the Crusading Kingdom of Jerusalem, presented to Joshua Prawer*, ed., B.Z. Kedar, H.E. Mayer, R.C. Smail (Jerusalem 1982), 177–204.

Mayer, H. E. 'Henry II of England and the Holy Land', *English Historical Review*, XCVII, 1982, 721–739.

Luttrell, A. 'Ermengol de Aspa, *Provisor* of the Hospital: 1188' *Crusades*, 4 (2005), 15–19.

Luttrell, A., Nicholson, H.J., 'Introduction: a Survey of Hospitaller Women in the Middle Ages', in *Hospitaller Women in the Middle Ages*, ed., A. Luttrell and H. Nicholson (Aldershot and Burlington, VT. 2006), particularly 29–41.

García-Guijarro Ramos, L. 'The Aragonese Hospitaller Monastery of Sigena: its early Stages, 1188-c. 1210' in *Hospitaller Women in the Middle Ages*, ed., A. Luttrell and H. Nicholson (Aldershot and Burlington, VT. 2006), 113–151.

Riley-Smith, J. 'King Henry II, Patriarch Heraclius and the English Templars and Hospitallers', in *Come l'orco della fiaba: Studi per Franco Cardini*, ed., M. Montesano (Florence 2010), 249–255.

Riley-Smith, J. *The Knights Hospitaller in the Levant, c. 1070–1309* (Basingstoke 2012), 38–41, 195–196 (Roger des Moulins and the 1184/5 mission).

Printed sources for the mission of 1184–1185

Benedict of Peterborough: *Gesta Regis Henrici Secundi*, ed. W. Stubbs (Rolls Series, XLIX/1, London, 1867), 331–333, 335–336, 337–338.

Chronicle of the Anonymous of Laon: *Chronicon universale anonymi Laudunensis*, ed. A. Cartellieri, W. Stechele (Leipzig and Paris 1909), 35–37.

Chronicle of Saint-Martin de Tours, ed. O. Holder-Egger, Monumenta Germaniae Historica, Scriptores Rerum Merovingicarum, XXVI (Hannover 1882), 450.

Continuator of William of Tyre, *L'estoire de Eracles Empereur et la Conqueste de la Terre d'Outremer*, in Recueil des Historiens des Croisades. Historiens occidentaux, (Paris 1859), Vol. 2, 2–3, 57–61.

Gerald of Wales: *Giraldi Cambrensis opera . . . De Principis Instructione*, ed. G. Warner (Rolls Series, XXI/8, London, 1891), 202–212; also his *De rebus a se gestis*, ed., J. Brewer (Rolls Series, XXI/1, London, 1861), 60–61; and his *Expugnatio hibernica*, ed. J. Dimock (Rolls Series, XXI/5, London, 1867), 360–364.

Gervase of Canterbury: *Gervasii Cantuariensis opera historica*, ed. W. Stubbs (Rolls Series, LXXIII/1, London, 1879), 325–326, cf. p. 298.

Herbert of Bosham: *Vita sancti Thomae. . ., auctore Herberto de Bosham*, in *Materials for the history of Thomas Becket, archbishop of Canterbury*, ed., J. Robertson (Rolls Series, LXVII/3, London, 1877), Vol. 3, 54–56.

Pipe Rolls: *The Great Roll of the Pipe for . . . 1184–1185* (London 1913), 45.

Ralph of Diceto: *Radulfi de Diceto Decani Lundoniensis Opera historica*, ed., W. Stubbs (Rolls Series, LXVIII/2, London, 1876), 27–34.

Ralph Niger: *Radulfus Niger. De re militari et triplici via peregrinationis Ierosolimitanae (1187/88)*, ed. L. Schmugge, Beiträge zur Geschichte und Quellenkunde des Mittelalters, Vol. 6 (Berlin and New York 1977), 186–187, cf.193–194.

Rigord: *Rigord, Histoire de Philippe Auguste (Gesta Philippi Augusti)*, ed. E. Carpentier, G. Pon and Y. Chauvin (Paris 2006), 178–183.

Robert of Saint-Marien, Auxerre: *Recueil des historiens des Gaules et de la France*, vol. 18, éd. M.-J.-J. Bruel and L. Delisle (Paris 1879), 252.

Roger of Howden: *Chronica magistri Rogeri de Houedene*, ed. W. Stubbs (Rolls Series, LI/2, London, 1869), 299–304.

Roger of Wendover: *Rogeri de Wendover Chronica, sive Flores Historiarum*, ed., H. Coxe (London 1841), Vol. 2, 415–418.

Royal Commission for Historical Monuments (England): *London, Vol. 4: The City* (London 1929), 137 (the lost inscription on the south door of the Temple church).

William of Andres: *Willelmi Chronica Andrensis*, ed., I. Heller, Monumenta Germaniae Historica, Scriptores Rerum Merovingicarum, XXIV (Hannover 1879), 716.

William of Newburgh: *Historia rerum anglicarum Willelmi Parvi, ordinis sancti Augustini canonici regularis in coenobio Beatae Mariae de Newburgh in agro eboracensi*, ed. H.C.Hamilton (London 1856), Vol. 1, 243–246.

Winchester annals: *Annales Monastici, Vol. II: Annales monasterii de Wintonia (AD. 519–1277)*, ed. H. Luard (Rolls Series, XXXVI, London, 1865), 62.

HENRY OF BLOIS, ST HUGH AND HENRY II: THE WINCHESTER BIBLE RECONSIDERED

Christopher Norton

The desire to link anonymous masterpieces with famous names, whether of artists or of patrons, is deep-rooted, as can be seen with the number of works of art which cluster around such names as Nicholas of Verdun and Abbot Suger. The magnificent illuminated bible at Winchester Cathedral has long been associated with one of the most celebrated art patrons of the age, Henry of Blois, bishop of Winchester from 1129 to 1171. Indeed, the bible has been associated with three of the outstanding personalities of the age. Not only has Henry of Blois been credited with its inception, but St Hugh of Lincoln and King Henry II have also been connected to it, at a later stage in its production. Current scholarly opinion tends to accept Henry of Blois' involvement, while questioning the bible's association with St Hugh and Henry II. In this paper I propose to re-examine the evidence for both claims.

The Winchester Bible needs little introduction.[1] Originally in two volumes, it contains no marks of provenance earlier than the 17th century, but it is generally assumed to have been at Winchester since the 12th century. The text was written by a single scribe in a superb, rounded script (colour plate IV) characterised by Neil Ker as typical of the middle decades of the 12th century, up to c. 1170.[2] Evidence from other giant bibles suggests that it would have taken a single scribe three or four years to copy the text.[3] In places, the original scribe corrected his own work, the corrections often standing out in darker ink. Subsequently, a second scribe made further corrections and emendations to the text of the Old Testament as far as the end of Psalm 71, a little way into the second volume of the manuscript as originally conceived. He also completed the text of Malachi at the very end of volume one which the first scribe had left incomplete, and he wrote a single bifolium (ff 131 and 134) at the start of the book of Isaiah, apparently to replace a damaged or lost original (colour plate V). The hand of the second scribe has also been identified in another great bible, known as the Auct Bible or the Bodleian Bible from its shelf-mark in the Bodleian Library (MS Auct. E. inf. 1–2). Close analysis of the two by Neil Ker demonstrated that the scribe corrected the texts of these two bibles together, so he must have had them both in the scriptorium at the same time. The second scribe wrote in a more angular script which is characteristic of the last decades of the 12th century, though he seems to have attempted to match his additions in the Winchester Bible to the style of the original scribe so as to minimise the visual differences between the two. Ker dated his work probably no earlier than 1170. The fact that the two replacement leaves at the start of Isaiah were inserted as a bifolium, not as separate folios, indicates that the manuscript was still unbound at this time, and this is corroborated by the fact that the quire signatures, used to ensure that the quires were bound in the correct order, are also in the hand of the second scribe (colour plate IV). The bible must have remained unbound in the scriptorium for a number of years.[4]

The illuminations tell a more complex story. Several artists of the highest calibre were employed, but even so, many of the illuminations were left unfinished. The seminal analysis by Walter Oakeshott published in 1945 has stood the test of time well, expanded and elaborated in later studies by Oakeshott himself and by other scholars. The precise relationships between the different artists have still not been fully elucidated, but it is generally accepted that the illuminators can be divided into an earlier and a later group. The first consists of the so-called Master of the Leaping Figures, who worked in a vigorous style using curvilinear damp-fold draperies characteristic of the middle decades of the twelfth century (colour plate IV), and another artist known as the Apocrypha Master, whose illuminations are in a distinct style which also finds parallels in the mid 12th century (colour plate VI top). Both of these artists left most of their illuminations unfinished (Figure 11.1), and many of them were completed by the four later artists to whom Oakeshott gave the names the Amalekite Master, the Morgan Master, the Master of the Genesis Initial and the Master of the Gothic Majesty. Between them, they completed all the initials in volume one (colour plates IV and VI, Figures 11.2 and 11.3), along with a handful at the start of volume two (colour plate VII). Their illuminations are characterised by figures (often set against a gold ground) which are less vigorous but more monumental in appearance, with facial types reminiscent of Byzantine or Byzantinising works of art. Their work is generally dated no earlier than 1170. The initial at the start of the book of Isaiah on the bifolium supplied by the second scribe (f. 131) is by the Master of

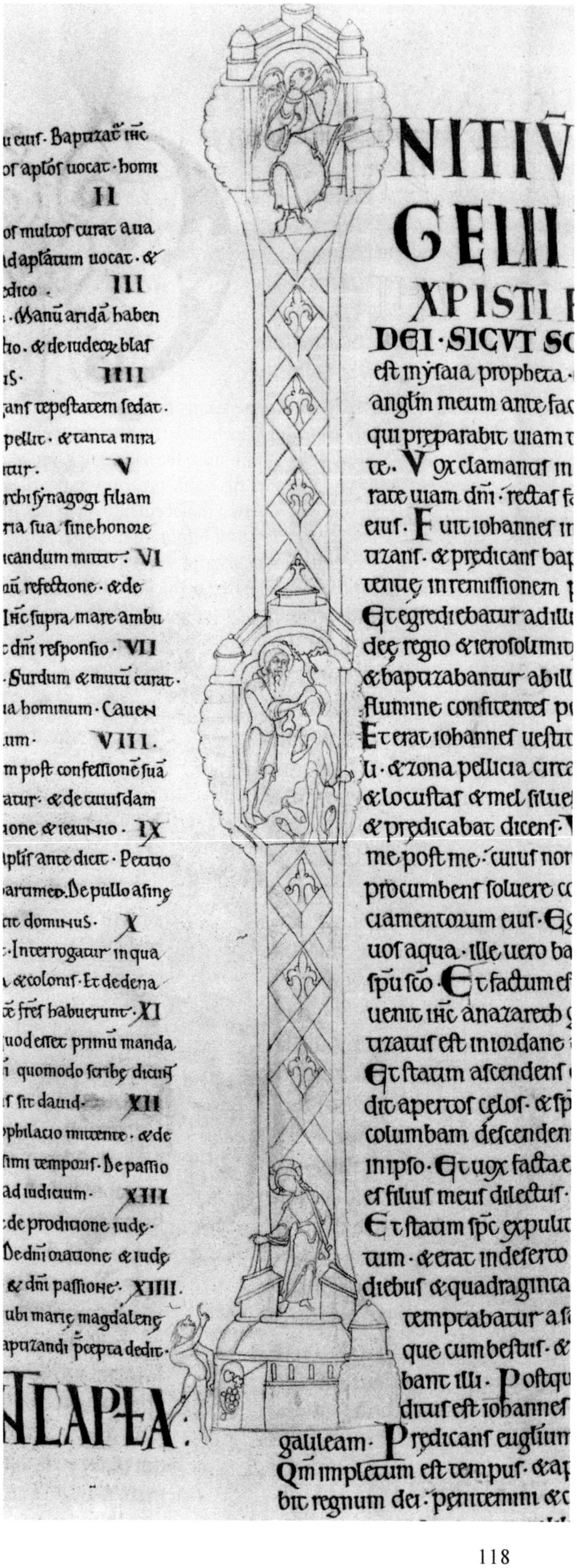

CHRISTOPHER NORTON

FIGURE 11.1

Winchester Bible, f. 387v. The start of the Gospel of St Mark. Text by the first scribe, decorative lettering by the first rubricator, drawing by the Master of the Leaping Figures. © The Dean and Chapter of Winchester

FIGURE 11.2

Winchester Bible, f. 169. The end of the text of the Lamentation of Jeremiah, followed by the illuminated initial to the Prayer of Jeremiah. Text by the first scribe, decorative lettering by the first rubricator, illuminated initial by the Morgan Master. (John Crook)

the Gothic Majesty, indicating that he at least was working with or after the second scribe (colour plate V). Oakeshott also identified two distinct types of rubrication. The earlier type, characterised by square capitals, is distributed across both volumes and is associated with the work of the first scribe and the first two artists (Figure 11.1). The later rubrics, which are found only in volume one, are characterised by rounded, uncial forms. In places these replace the work of the earlier rubricator, and it appears that the second rubricator worked in association with the second scribe and the second group of artists in bringing volume one to completion (colour plates IV and V).

The intricacies of the relationships between the two scribes, the two rubricators and the various illuminators are not our main concern, but the question of dating is important. On stylistic grounds the work by the Master of the Leaping Figures and the Apocrypha Master was originally placed by Oakeshott between 1140 and 1160, with the later initials extending in date as late as 1225.

In his later publications he placed the start of work on the Bible around 1160, and its abandonment no later than 1190.[5] The narrower dating has found widespread acceptance, and the project as a whole is now generally placed within the period *c*. 1155–90, still a broad enough timespan to allow different interpretations of the progress of the work and the relationships between the different elements in the bible. The initial campaign, including the work of the first scribe, the first rubricator, the Master of the Leaping Figures and the Apocrypha Master, is usually dated *c*. 1155–70. The four later artists along with the second scribe and the second rubricator are generally dated between 1170 and 1190. But it remains to some extent an open question whether there were two distinct phases of work, with a gap of some years in between; or whether the task of creating the bible continued gradually over a number of years with interruptions as new men were brought in to carry on the project. The illumination of the bible did not necessarily run *pari passu* with the work of the two scribes or the two rubricators. It should also be remembered that the dates quoted above carry all the provisos that need to be attached to stylistic dating, both palaeographical and art-historical. The same applies to the other manuscripts in which the hands of the Winchester Bible scribes and illuminators have been identified, none of which is precisely dated. An analysis of the relationships between these various manuscripts is beyond the scope of the present study, but some further discussion of the relationships between the different illuminators in the Winchester Bible is given in Appendix 1.

HENRY OF BLOIS

Henry of Blois is remembered for his munificent gifts of relics, vestments, jewels and precious liturgical fittings to Winchester Cathedral and elsewhere. The Henry of Blois enamelled plaques in the British Museum give an indication of the quality of the works commissioned by him. The great Tournai marble font in the cathedral is associated with Henry, as are some high-quality sculptural fragments. He is famously said to have purchased *veteres statuas* while in Rome and taken them back with him to Winchester, though quite what the expression refers to is debatable. Taken as a whole, the evidence shows Henry to have been, in Jeffrey West's words, 'a patron who sought to add to the spiritual wealth of the communities in his care by gifts of relics and the ornaments, objects and vestments necessary to the religious life and the celebration of the holy mysteries'. In this, he conformed to the pattern expected of wealthy senior ecclesiastics, albeit with greater largesse than most. He was the kind of man who might well have been involved in the production of a magnificent illuminated bible for his cathedral.[6]

Two pieces of evidence have been cited for Henry's involvement. In his 1981 monograph, Oakeshott wrote, 'When he died, he left an endowment for the scriptorium of St Swithun's [i.e. Winchester Cathedral]. . . . It would be hard to believe that Bishop Henry was not, in some way, even if that was only financial patronage, responsible for launching the project for a great bible.' Noting that the endowment was made early in the year of Henry's death, he added, 'It is perhaps not fanciful to read into this his anxiety that the bible should be completed.' The thrust of these remarks has implications both for the chronology and for the patronage of the bible. Other writers have made similar comments, but often without Oakeshott's caution, with the result that Henry's involvement is widely taken for granted, even sometimes stated as fact.[7]

Oakeshott cited Lehmann-Brockhaus, who printed a single clause from one of Henry of Blois' charters granting the church at Ellendon in Wiltshire to the prior and brothers of Winchester Cathedral for the writing of books and the maintenance of the organs.[8] A reading of the complete charter puts the matter in a rather different light. The clause in question comes from a lengthy charter dated 6 January 1171 *confirming* the rights and endowments of the cathedral priory. The potential for disputes between bishops and monastic cathedral chapters over the allocation of endowments is demonstrated by the case of Henry of Blois' erstwhile protégé, Hugh du Puiset, bishop of Durham between 1153 and 1195. He was involved in a long-drawn-out and bitter dispute with the monks of Durham which involved, *inter alia*, the forgery by the monks of charters designed to prove their case.[9] At Winchester there had been disputes between the bishops and the monks about the division of endowments earlier in the century. Henry of Blois' charter therefore provided an authoritative summary statement of the position at the end of his episcopate which could be referred to in the future should any disagreement arise. The grant of the church at Ellendon *ad libros conscribendos et organa reparanda* is merely a confirmation of a previous charter by Henry of Blois dated 1142x1143. This specifies that the church had been granted to the cantor (precentor) of the cathedral and to all of his successors in office *ad conscriptionem librorum et ad reparationem organorum et ad alia queque eidem monasterio necessarie supplenda*. It was, in fact, concerned not just with books (which were a standard responsibility of precentors), but with the provision of all the equipment necessary for the proper running of the liturgical life of the cathedral. Furthermore, in this earlier charter Henry of Blois was explicit that he was *restoring* the church at Ellendon to the cathedral for the purpose *ad quod antiquitus fuerat constitutum*. Two earlier charters survive from Henry's predecessor, William Giffard, dated 1107 and 1128x1129 respectively, both recording the grant of the church at Ellendon *ad libros faciendos*.[10] In short, the phrase in the 1171 charter is merely a confirmation of a long-standing arrangement designed to provide an endowment for the office of precentor in perpetuity. It is only tangentially relevant to the Winchester Bible.

More recently, it has been suggested that evidence for Henry's involvement can be found in the manuscript itself. The initial on f. 3, which accompanies St Jerome's letter to Pope Damasus, shows Jerome, on the left, presenting his work to the pope (colour plate VI bottom). It is attributed to the Genesis Master, and can almost certainly be dated after Henry of Blois' death.[11] Damasus is represented as a medieval bishop, in the guise (it has been suggested) of Bishop Henry, with the book beneath his arm representing the Winchester Bible itself. The black crosses on his vestments have been thought to refer to the Hospital of St Cross which Henry of Blois had founded in 1136.[12] However, the ecclesiastic on the right is not vested as a bishop. He is an *arch*bishop wearing a pallium, a thin strip of white cloth worn on top of the other vestments which was held in place by pins terminating in small crosses. The pallium was granted by the popes to archbishops as a sign of their rank, to distinguish them from bishops. Although he had ambitions to raise the see of Winchester to an archbishopric, Henry of Blois was never more than a bishop, and never wore the pallium. Prior to the introduction of the papal tiara, popes were regularly represented in art in archiepiscopal robes with a normal mitre. The figure on the right is Pope Damasus robed as an archbishop. A similar iconography can be found in other manuscripts of the period, such as the presentation miniature in the Helmarshausen Gospels of *c*. 1140, which shows Pope Damasus similarly attired.[13] The Winchester Bible initial is not an allusion to Henry of Blois.

The only discernible link between Henry of Blois and the bible is a coincidence of time and place. This is not to say that Henry of Blois had nothing to do with it. It is hardly credible that he would have been unaware of such a prestigious project being undertaken at the heart of his diocese during his lifetime. But the nature of any involvement requires further consideration. Having been an active protagonist during the civil war on the side of his brother, King Stephen, he went abroad at the start of Henry II's reign. After his return in 1158 he focussed his attention on ecclesiastical and episcopal affairs.[14] It could be that he commissioned the bible for his cathedral around this time. Or it may be that he commissioned it for his own use in the first instance, perhaps to be kept at the bishop's palace next door at Wolvesey, which he redeveloped on a grand scale.[15] In due course he could have given or bequeathed it (still unfinished) to the cathedral. A comparable case would be the Puiset Bible of *c.* 1180, which was given to Durham Cathedral by Bishop Hugh du Puiset.[16] Alternatively, the project could have been initiated by the monks of St Swithun, the monastic community at the cathedral. Not long before, the wealthy Benedictine monastery at Bury Saint Edmunds had commissioned the magnificent Bury Bible. The sacrist, called Hervey, covered all the costs of the bible for his brother Talbot, the prior;[17] but such an expensive undertaking could not have been carried out without the approval of the abbot, Anselm (1121–48). The mention of the sacrist is interesting. In Benedictine communities, responsibility for books within the monastery lay with the cantor (precentor). However, a few books fell within the purview of the sacrist. He was responsible for the high altar and any relics, treasures and ornaments associated with it. These would be kept securely in the sacristy when not required at the altar itself. Among them might be books which had assumed the status of relics through their antiquity or association with a particular saint, or which were categorised as treasures for the adornment of the high altar on account of their exceptional quality.[18] The sacrist's involvement suggests that the Bury

Bible was envisaged as just such a book. At Winchester, the head of the monastic community was the prior, and a commission of this kind could well have originated with him, or with the cantor, or with the sacrist.[19] On this hypothesis, Henry of Blois could have provided additional funding, or could have used his extensive contacts to find scribes and artists of the calibre required. But the cathedral priory could have had the resources to carry out the project on their own, in which case Henry's role may have been no more than to advise, support and encourage. Winchester was one of the very few cities in England in the mid-12th-century which had a community of resident artists and craftsmen with all the skills required for the production of illuminated manuscripts. The 1148 survey of Winchester, which was carried out for Henry of Blois, reveals in extraordinary detail the numbers, names and locations of property-holders within the city. Leatherworkers were comparatively numerous, and one man is described as a parchment-maker. There were four property-owning painters named Henry, Richard, Roger and William, who may have worked on manuscript illumination as well as monumental painting. Even if such men were not of the calibre of the Winchester Bible artists, they would have provided a potential source of supply for pigments and other painting materials. Gold for the illuminations could have come from the goldsmiths. There were an unusual number of these resident in Winchester, no doubt as a consequence of the fact that the royal treasury was based there. Another property-holder in 1148 was Gisulf the king's scribe, and there must have been many other scribes of one level of ability or another among the many clerks employed in the royal administration in Winchester (which was effectively the Angevin capital in England), quite apart from monastic scribes at the cathedral priory and in the other religious houses.[20] The picture which emerges is one of a sizeable community of artists, craftsmen and scribes living and working within a stone's throw of the cathedral. There must have been regular contacts between them and the monastic community. The enormous bible project must have been a regular topic of conversation not just among the monks but among interested parties in the wider community, including those who were employed by the king. Henry II himself may well have known about it.

So the bible emerged out of a context in mid-12th-century Winchester which was well-endowed materially, rich in artistic tradition, and able to draw on a wide range of contacts at the highest levels of society. If the name of Henry of Blois has tended to be attached to it in modern times, that is largely because of the reputation which he has gained as a patron of the arts. But in truth the extent of his involvement is quite uncertain. The commission could have emerged from various different sources, and its realisation over some decades must have been a collaborative affair. At this distance in time it is a hazardous business attempting to define the extent of Henry's involvement – if indeed he was involved at all. For it is not impossible that the bible was only begun after his death. The widely accepted pre-1170 date for the first phase of work is based on palaeographical and stylistic criteria. But there are few fixed points in the history of mid-12th-century manuscripts of this calibre; and while it is not so difficult to establish a date before which certain stylistic or palaeographical features do not appear, it is very difficult to determine when they went out of fashion. A project of such ambition and quality is likely to have been entrusted to experienced hands, and one cannot exclude the possibility that the scribe of the main text, the first rubricator and the first illuminators were mature men who had learned their trade in the middle decades of the century and continued to work in the same styles into the 1170s.[21] It would be as well to keep an open mind.

ST HUGH AND HENRY II

We come now to an incident from the 1180s which is recounted in the *Magna Vita* of St Hugh of Lincoln by Adam of Eynsham (Book II, Chapter XIII). It involves Henry II and the monks of Winchester Cathedral (St Swithun's Priory) as well as St Hugh, who at the time was prior of the Carthusian monastery at Witham in Somerset. Henry of Blois' successor as bishop of Winchester, Richard of Ilchester (1173–88), is not mentioned. The story was discussed by Oakeshott and has often been referred to by manuscript scholars, but it has never been subject to close analysis. To appreciate its nuances, it is necessary to read the whole story. The Latin text, printed in Appendix 2 to this paper, and the English translation which follows, are taken from the 1961–62 edition by Douie and Farmer. Some minor amendments to their translation are printed in italics, and an alternative translation of the passage between asterisks is given later.[22]

Chapter XIII

How he worked hard to obtain manuscripts of religious works, and concerning the Bible of the monks of Winchester which was given to the king and by him to Witham, which Hugh restored to its original owners, and the close friendship between these two religious communities.

'It is right to relate briefly one of the deeds of this man who was filled with a double love for God and his neighbour, since it shows so strikingly the intense charity which burned so brightly in him. When the buildings required by the customs of the order were almost finished and the number of brethren was complete, the good shepherd concentrated upon the training of the souls committed to his care in their holy profession. He devoted much labour to the making, purchase and acquisition by every possible means of manuscripts of religious works, since these were a great assistance in this task. It was a favourite saying of his that these were useful to all monks, but especially to those leading an eremitical life, for they provided riches and delight in times of tranquillity, weapons and armour in times of temptation, food for the hungry and medicine for the sick.

Once in private converse with the king, the lack of books happened to be mentioned. When he was advised to do his best to get them copied by professional scribes, he replied that he had no parchment. The king then said, 'How much money do you think I should give you to make up this defect?' He answered that *one* silver mark would be enough for a long time. At this the king smiled. 'What heavy demands you make on us,' he said, and immediately ordered ten marks to be given to the monk who was his companion. He also promised that he would send him a Bible containing the *entire corpus* of both Testaments.* The prior returned home, but the king did not forget his promise, and tried hard to find a really magnificent Bible for him. After an energetic search he was at last informed that the monks of St Swithun had recently made a fine and beautifully written Bible which (*it was said*) was to be used for reading in the refectory. He was greatly delighted by this discovery, and immediately summoned their prior, and asked that the gift he desired to make should be handed over to him, promising a handsome reward. His request was speedily granted. When the prior of Witham and his monks received and examined the Bible given to them by the king they were not a little delighted with it. The correctness of the text pleased them especially, even more than the delicacy of the penmanship and the general beauty of the manuscript.*

One of the monks of Winchester happened afterwards to come to Witham for the sake of edification. The prior, with his accustomed courtesy, entertained him, and gave him the spiritual counsels he had desired. His guest unexpectedly informed him how earnestly the lord king had deigned to ask his prior for the Bible. 'We are especially glad,' he said, 'that he should have given it to you, venerable father. If you are completely satisfied with it, all is well; but if not, and if it differs in any particular from your usage, we will, if you like, speedily make you a far *better* one, corresponding to your requirements in every detail. *For we* took considerable pains to make this *one* correspond to our own use *and customs.*' The prior was amazed, for he had not known before how the king had obtained it. He immediately said these words to the monk. 'Did the lord king indeed defraud your monastery of such an essential fruit of your labours? My dearest brother, your book shall be restored at once. I beg you most earnestly and humbly to ask your brethren to forgive us *for the fact that it was because of us, although we were unaware of it, that they lost their book.*' The monk, terrified at what he had heard, implored him in horrified tones *not to think or say such things*. It would be fatal to his own church that Hugh should on any pretext decline a royal gift which had so fortunately won for them the king's favour. This amused the prior, who answered: 'Is it true that you think that you are much more in his favour than usual, and do not regret that his goodwill towards you was purchased by this magnificent gift?' As he asserted that all his fellow monks were well content with the transaction, Hugh added, 'To make your satisfaction lasting the restitution of your precious masterpiece shall be kept secret by all of us. If you do not agree to receive this Bible secretly, I shall restore it to the man who sent it here, but if you take it away now, I shall never tell him.' There was no more argument. The monks received their book, as if it had been a newly acquired gift. They were delighted with the *book*, but still more with the courtesy and great generosity of the sender.

This action, as I have already said, demonstrated clearly the fervour of the twin loves which consumed the heart of this saintly man, since for his own advantage he would not deprive the monks of a masterpiece created for the glory of God, lest this might injure the divine honour even a little, or defraud those who had worked for it of what was profitable to them. His kindness and example were alike beneficial to his neighbours. From the reading of the book they received instruction, and were also inspired to imitate his brotherly charity, and both these things increased their devotion to their Creator. All his deeds, words and thoughts were directed to this very end, to assist his neighbour, and thus both of them should please God. *Nor in his pious and righteous intention was he deceived of his hope.* From this time onwards there grew up an especially warm friendship between both communities, the monks of Winchester and the hermits of Witham, which with God's help should long endure.'

The *Magna Vita* was written about ten years after Hugh's death (†1200) by Adam of Eynsham, a Benedictine monk who had been his chaplain for the last three years of his life. Adam's *Vita* is generally considered one of the most reliable of saints' lives, and to give an exceptionally vivid and accurate picture of St Hugh. In Book II Chapter XIV, immediately after the story of the bible, Adam says that he was urged to write the *Vita* by two senior former monks of Winchester, Robert, prior of St Swithun's from 1187 to 1191, and Ralph, the former sacrist. Both of them had transferred to Witham and become Carthusians.[23] They must have been privy to the story, both from the Winchester perspective and from the point of view of the Carthusians. Indeed, the implication is that it was one of them who negotiated with St Hugh for the bible's return. There is therefore no reason to doubt the essential veracity of the story; but equally it may not have been the whole story. The purpose of the *Vita* was to honour its subject and edify the reader, and Adam does not hesitate to point out the moral of the episode, namely St Hugh's intense love of God and neighbour. The fact that it concerns a manuscript is fortuitous, and the information provided about the bible is incidental. Much may be left unsaid. To avoid confusion, in the discussion which follows, the bible in the story will be referred to as the Witham Bible.

The story belongs to the period when Hugh was prior of Witham. He arrived there in the winter of 1179/80 and left in the summer of 1186, after his election to the see of Lincoln in May of that year. But it can be dated even more precisely. Witham had been founded by Henry II as part of his penance for the death of Becket. Book II of the *Vita* is constructed around three episodes in which Hugh goes to see the king and comes away with money for the fledgling community: first, to complete the purchase of the site and start building; second, to finish the buildings; and third, to acquire books – the incident with which we are concerned. Books were an essential part of the equipment of a new monastery and a legitimate call upon the resources of a founder. Now Henry II was in England on just three occasions in the relevant period, and the three episodes fit neatly with Henry's visits. The third of these took place between 10 June 1184 and 16 April 1185, and this must be the date of Henry's conversation with Hugh about manuscripts. On 10 April 1185, John, the prior of Winchester (†1187) and thus the *de facto* owner of the bible, was at Henry II's court at Dover. According to Eyton's painstaking analysis of the movements of the king and the members of his entourage, this was the *only* occasion when Prior John witnessed a royal charter, in spite of the fact that he must normally have been at Winchester when the king was in residence there. On 16 April Henry left for Normandy, and one wonders whether he might have summoned Prior John in order to wrap up the business of the bible before he left the country.[24] In any case, the final conversation between St Hugh and the Winchester monks must have taken place before Hugh left for Lincoln in summer 1186. So the episode recounted in the *Vita* took place between the summer of 1184 and the summer of 1186.

Establishing the date of this incident is relatively easy; discerning its implications for manuscript studies is a more delicate matter. It is not certain whether the Witham Bible was the one we know as the Winchester Bible. Oakeshott initially believed so, and was followed in this by a generation of manuscript scholars. Then, in his 1981 monograph, he changed his mind and argued that the Auct Bible was the one sent to St Hugh; and this seems to have become received wisdom. Like the Winchester Bible, the two-volume Auct Bible contains the complete text of the bible in a script datable to the middle decades of the twelfth century, and its earliest illuminated initials belong to the same period. These initials are of high quality, but not historiated. Whether the Auct Bible was written at Winchester or at some other centre, such as St Albans, has been disputed, but, as already noted, it definitely seems to have been at Winchester at an early date, when the second scribe of the Winchester Bible emended the texts of the two bibles together. Around the same time, further initials were added to the Auct Bible in a style similar to that of the Morgan Master.[25] So both bibles would potentially fit Adam of Eynsham's description of a bible which had been worked on recently, and which was characterised by the elegance of its script, its careful emendations and its overall beauty. Oakeshott states – and places great emphasis on this – that 'the story specifies (and also must, surely, imply, to make sense of it) that the book had been completed'. Since the textual corrections, the rubrications and the illuminations of the Winchester Bible were left unfinished, he argued that this ruled it out. The text of the Auct Bible, on the other hand, was corrected throughout.[26] However, Adam of Eynsham was neither an art historian nor a textual scholar, and he was writing not from the point of view of a cataloguer, but as a hagiographer. His readers (apart from a few elderly monks of Winchester and Witham) would not have been familiar with the Witham Bible, nor did they need to be. Adam states that Henry II offered to send a bible which contained the entire corpus of both Old and New Testaments. The *text* of the Winchester Bible is complete. As Larry Ayres pointed out long ago, this is surely what mattered most.[27] There is nothing in the text of the *Vita* that specifies that the Witham Bible was complete in Oakeshott's sense. The verb *conficere* used to describe the creation of the manuscript simply means 'make'. It is nowhere either stated or implied that the manuscript was complete in every respect. For that, *perficere* would have been more appropriate. The word *conficere* is used in two other places in Chapter XIII of Book II of the *Vita*, in each case simply referring to the creation of a new manuscript without any implication of total completion. First, at the start of the chapter, we are told that St Hugh devoted particular effort to making or purchasing manuscripts, or acquiring them by any other means (*sacris codicibus* conficiendis, *comparandis, et quibus posset modis acquirendis*). Second, during the conversation between St Hugh and the monks of Winchester, the latter offer to make him a replacement manuscript (*conficiemus*).[28] The Winchester Bible cannot be ruled out on the grounds of (supposed) incompleteness.

The *Vita* has often been cited as evidence that the great twelfth-century illuminated bibles could have been designed for use in the refectory.[29] This has always seemed improbable. A bible kept on a lectern on the floor of the refectory would have been exposed to physical damage, to spillages of food and drink, and to greasy fingers. On the other hand, if the refectory had a raised pulpitum built into the wall, as was often the case, the manuscript would have been invisible to all but the lector. Oakeshott thought (no doubt correctly) that the exceptional decoration of the Winchester Bible excluded such a mundane use for it – and this was another reason for his belief that it was the Auct Bible which was sent to Witham. But this is to miss the point of the story. Contrary to appearances, the *Vita* does *not* say that the Witham Bible was intended for use in the refectory. This is not a quibble about the absence of the word 'refectory': the phrase *in qua . . . debuisset* is a deliberate echo of the Rule of St Benedict, and the words *ad mensam edentium fratrum* unquestionably do refer to the refectory. The point is this: the text indicates that Henry II was *led to believe* that the Witham Bible was intended for use in the refectory. The key is in the verb, *debuisset*. The use of the subjunctive here means that it is reported speech, part of the message that was conveyed to the king. If its intended use in the refectory had been a simple statement of fact, the verb would be in the indicative. In English, this nuance can be conveyed by adding 'it was said' or some such phrase, as I have done in the translation above. In support of this reading, it may be noted that the main verb, *suggeritur*, is curiously oblique: not 'the king was told', but 'it was intimated (*or* suggested) to the king' that the bible was intended for use in the refectory. The difference is subtle, but substantial.

The 12th century was a time of intense discussion about the varieties of religious orders, about the differences between canons and monks, between Benedictines and Cistercians, about the roles of the military orders and of hermits. The Carthusians, with their special blend of the eremitical and coenobitic, had only just established themselves in England with the foundation of Witham, and their unique characteristics may not have been widely understood. The protagonists in the story, however, and many of Adam's readers would have been well versed in the differences between Benedictines and Carthusians and their implications. Against this background the story takes on a new significance. Henry II had set his mind on the Witham Bible. The Winchester monks were desperate to keep it, but did not dare oppose the king directly. Instead, they tried a diversionary tactic. They put it about that the bible was intended for use in the refectory. Why? Because Benedictines ate in the refectory every day and listened to readings while they ate; whereas the Carthusians had their meals separately, in their individual cells, in silence. Only on Sundays and major feast-days did they eat together in the refectory. On these occasions they did have readings, but the readings were integrated into a broader sequence of readings which extended across the daily offices in such a way as to ensure that the monks read the entire bible every year. Only a small minority were read in the refectory. This sequence was unique to the Carthusians, and they developed a distinct type of bible to match, marked up to show the cycle of readings. An early English Carthusian bible of the second quarter of the 13th century is annotated in this manner, with a few of the readings being marked *in refectorio*, because they were the exceptions. This bible must have come either from Witham or from nearby Hinton (founded in 1227), the only other Carthusian house in England at the time.[30] So the rationale of the response of the Winchester monks to Henry II was that the Witham Bible would have been an inappropriate gift for St Hugh. It was (they claimed) intended for use in the refectory; but the Carthusians seldom ate in their refectory, and on the few occasions when they did, they did not use a standard bible, but one which had been specially prepared for their own cycle of readings. The subterfuge failed to deflect the king. Perhaps he was oblivious to the differences between Benedictine and Carthusian practice; or perhaps he saw through the story and carried on regardless. Hugh, on the other hand, could use the subterfuge to his own ends. He must have known that the circumstances of the gift were questionable, that this was no mere off-the-shelf bible, but a magnificent manuscript that must have been years in the making. And in any case, it did not answer his need for books for everyday use. Both the Winchester and Auct Bibles are so massive and unwieldy that it is hard to see what practical use the Carthusians could have made of either.

The sub-text to the discussion with the Winchester monk (which should be read as Adam of Eynsham's literary dramatisation of some very delicate negotiations) is that both parties understood the situation implicitly and were tip-toeing their way around an unspoken but potentially explosive truth.[31] Great stress is laid on the question of whether the Witham Bible corresponded to Carthusian usage or not. If not, the Winchester community promised to make another one which did – presumably one that was customised for the Carthusians along the lines of the 13th-century manuscript from Witham or Hinton. That explains why the replacement bible would be 'better', i.e. much more useful to the Carthusians. The Latin is *longe meliorem*, 'far better', and not, as Oakeshott and the published translation would have it, 'far finer', or, as some have glossed it, 'even bigger', wrongly implying that Hugh would be impressed by an even grander or more beautiful manuscript. The dynamic of the story does not require that the Winchester monks should actually have supplied a replacement bible: nor is it said that they did. The discussion of monastic custom and usage was merely a way to find a form of words which would enable the Winchester monks to recover their manuscript without either being humiliated or offending the king. All the same, both parties realised that it would be prudent not to reveal that the Witham Bible had been returned to Winchester. So the whole business about the bible being intended for use in the refectory was merely a stratagem. While it failed to divert the king from his intention, it did provide Hugh with a means to solve a high-stakes version of a familiar problem: how to dispose of a valuable but unwanted gift without offending the giver.

So we should not be fooled into thinking that the Witham Bible was a refectory bible. On the contrary, the likely role of the sacrist in the bible's return points in a different direction: that it was the kind of book which would have adorned the high altar and would have been kept in the sacristy along with the church treasures.[32] After it was sent back to Winchester it must have been kept hidden at least until Henry II's death in 1189 and probably for some years thereafter. It would have been impossible to carry on working on it without word getting out. This is the key to identifying the Witham Bible. As is well known, the textual emendations and the illuminations of the Winchester Bible were never completed. The second scribe stopped emending the text at the end of Psalm 71. It is striking that the latest phase of illumination by the Byzantinising artists ceases at much the same place. The last work by the Genesis Master is to be found in the double Beatus initial of Psalm 1 on f. 218, where he painted over drawings by the Master of the Leaping Figures. The Morgan Master appears for the last time in the double initial to Psalm 101 on f. 246 (colour plate VII top), where his painting over the drawings by the Master of the Leaping Figures was left unfinished. Similarly, the final work by the Master of the Gothic Majesty was also left unfinished, namely the double initial to Psalm 109 (f. 250) (colour plate VII bottom) and the immediately following initial to Proverbs (f. 260), the latter once again over a drawing by the Master of the Leaping Figures.[33] The unfinished initials by the Morgan Master and the Master of the Gothic Majesty thus appear within a few folios of each other, shortly after the point where the second scribe abandoned his textual corrections. All of this suggests that the work on the Winchester Bible was interrupted suddenly, never to be resumed. The story of the Witham Bible provides a perfect explanation both for the interruption to the work on the Winchester Bible, and the failure to resume it subsequently. Had it been the Auct Bible which Henry II sent to St Hugh, the illumination of the Winchester Bible could have carried on to the end.[34] The opposite applies to the Auct Bible. Ker noted that there was a change in the process of emending the text of the Auct Bible at the end of Psalm 68 verse 8. Up to that point the emendations were first noted down in the margin, then the original text was corrected, and then the marginalia were erased. However, from this point onwards, the emendations in the margin were no longer erased. As Ker commented, 'It is remarkable that the corrections written in the margins of the "Auct" Bible have been erased only up to a point near to that at which corrections in the Winchester Bible cease.' It would seem that the correction of the Auct Bible was interrupted at the same point. However, unlike the Winchester Bible, the corrections in the Auct Bibile were completed, as were the illuminations.[35] It is hard to see how the work could have been completed had the Auct Bible been the Witham Bible. Oakeshott's original intuition was correct. It was the Winchester Bible which was sent to Witham.

The abandonment of work on the Winchester Bible can therefore be dated between June 1184 and the summer of 1186, perhaps around the time of Henry II's departure from England in April 1185. This falls within the period usually assigned on palaeographical and stylistic grounds to the latest contributions to the bible, and it gives us an unusually precise date for the individuals who were employed on it when the project came to a halt. These are, first, the second scribe, who was responsible for the bifolium at the start of the book of Isaiah (colour plate V) and the second set of textual emendations up to the middle of the book of Psalms. He also worked on the Auct Bible. Second, the second rubricator, who was responsible for the decorated lettering in the uncial style, which appears only in volume one (colour plates IV and V). And third, two at least of the illuminators, namely the Master of the Gothic Majesty and the Morgan Master, who both left initials unfinished. The Genesis Master left no initials unfinished. His work appears mostly in volume one, but he also completed the pair of Beatus initials at the start of the Psalms in volume two (f. 218) which had been begun by the Master of the Leaping Figures. It may just have been a coincidence that he left no unfinished initials. Alternatively, it may be that he stopped working a short while earlier. There would have been no difficulty having three or four individuals working on the Psalms at the same time, assuming that the manuscript was still unbound. Henry II's intervention would explain why the different contributors all apparently stopped work at about the same time. The book would then have had to be bound before being sent to Witham.

But why was the Winchester Bible chosen? Douie and Farmer translated the second paragraph of the story to mean that Henry II initially had no particular copy of the bible in mind, and only learnt about the Winchester Bible during the course of the search. Oakeshott translated the passage in a similar sense,[36] and this has been accepted in the subsequent literature. However, the Latin can be translated in a different way:

'The prior returned home. The king did not forget his promise. He made earnest enquiries about a very fine bible to give him. Eventually, as he kept asking insistently, it was indicated to him that the monks of St Swithun had made the outstanding bible recently with handsome workmanship to be read from while the brothers were eating at table. When he learned this, the king was very pleased. He summoned the prior of that church to come as quickly as possible, and asked for the gift which he desired to be given to him, promising generous compensation. His request was speedily granted. And so the prior and brothers of Witham received the book as a gift from the king. When they examined it, they too were greatly pleased with it, particularly appreciating the elegance of the script, as well as the overall beauty of the work, and its painstaking corrections.'

In many ways it would make much better sense if Henry had already set his mind on the Winchester Bible from the outset. As we have seen, he may well have known about it for some years. There would have been plenty of ordinary manuscripts of the bible in Winchester at the time, around the cathedral priory, at Hyde Abbey and the other religious houses, perhaps even in stock at the book-sellers. Any one of these would probably have been more useful for the Carthusians on a daily basis, and could have been acquired much more easily and cheaply. Even the Auct Bible, which is by any standards a magnificent manuscript, would have caused less resentment within the cathedral community.[37]

Whichever reading we prefer, why would Henry have insisted on such an extravagant and problematic gift? A clue is provided earlier on in Book II of the *Vita*. As well as business meetings to do with Witham, Hugh used to meet Henry individually for private conversations. He had an unusual rapport with the king, and Adam of Eynsham devotes part of Book II of the *Vita* to this theme.[38] He was the only person who could assuage Henry's anger when he was in a dark mood, sometimes even teasing him in public. On one celebrated occasion, arriving late for a meeting and finding the king in a fury, he disarmed him by reminding him of his descent from the bastard William the Conqueror. In private meetings he gave Henry personal advice and spiritual counsel, sometimes citing the examples of illustrious men of former times. Never was Henry more in need of it than following the rebellion and death of his son and heir, Henry the Young King, in 1183. The discussion about the manuscripts took place during Henry's first visit to England since the death of the Young King. It was probably just one of a number of conversations, of which no record does (or could) survive, in which Hugh sought to calm the king's anger and soften his grief. Or, as Adam of Eynsham puts it, 'At this time the king had often to face misfortunes of every kind, which he bore with more resignation owing to the consolations of this holy man.'

We perhaps have here a motive for Henry's determined generosity in the matter of the bible, whose gift went far beyond the normal obligations of a monastic founder.

Against this background, the iconography of the Morgan Leaf merits further scrutiny.[39] Inserted into the previously-written opening at the start of the First Book of Kings (*alias* I Samuel), it contains a sequence of images from the stories of Samuel and David (colour plates IX and X). The Old Testament contains numerous tales of the doings of the ancient kings of Israel and Judah, which provided precedents or parallels for the behaviour of medieval monarchs, and could be used to point a moral. The Books of Kings were a favourite place for historiated initials on the theme of kingship. There was also a tradition of narrative cycles from the life of David. However, this is the only narrative cycle of the story of Samuel and David in English 12th-century bibles; and the only other bible with an extant full-page illumination at this point, the Bury Bible, is completely different.[40] The individual scenes on the Morgan Leaf can be paralleled in continental manuscripts, but the selection of scenes is unique to the Winchester Bible; and it is this choice which may provide a clue to their significance. The essential narrative of the Morgan Leaf is not difficult to follow. The recto illustrates the story of Samuel. Starting at the bottom left with Hannah's prayers for a son, it continues down the right-hand column with scenes of Samuel's childhood in the Temple and his calling by God, concluding with his anointing of Saul to be the first king of Israel. The verso depicts scenes from the life of David. In the first register David confronts and kills Goliath and puts the Philistines to flight, watched by Saul and the army of the Israelites. David's triumph provoked Saul's jealousy, and in the second register Saul is shown trying to kill David with a spear while he plays the harp. This is followed by the anointing of David by Samuel in the presence of Jesse and his brothers. The bottom row starts with the death of Absalom, and the narrative concludes with David's grief on hearing the news, when he uttered his famous lamentation 'O my son Absalom, O Absalom my son'. The appositeness of this choice of scenes to Henry II is striking. He too succeeded to the throne as a young man after a period of conflict with the incumbent monarch, King Stephen, who, like Saul, had been properly anointed king but had fallen from favour. On the verso, Samuel's anointing of David is shown after the duel with Goliath and the final appearance of Saul, whereas in the Old Testament his anointing comes first. This may merely be a narrative device to simplify the story of David's succession; but it may also have been done in order to strengthen the parallel with Henry II, who was only anointed and crowned king after Stephen's death. Thus far the narrative is taken from the First Book of Kings. Of the many episodes from David's kingship recorded in the Second Book of Kings, the only one represented on the Morgan Leaf is the armed revolt of Absalom leading to his death and David's outpouring of grief.

So familiar is the Morgan Leaf that it is easy to overlook the fact that the image of David's grief at the death of Absalom which concludes the cycle is the first surviving representation of this scene in English art. Indeed, only a handful of earlier examples are recorded from western Europe. The story cannot fail to evoke the revolt and death of Henry II's own son, Henry the Young King. Having been anointed and crowned king in the presence of his father at Westminster in 1170, Henry the Young King became increasingly frustrated. As a crowned monarch, he could reasonably have expected to exercise royal functions, yet Henry II refused to relinquish any of his powers to his son. In 1173–74, the Young King, supported by his brothers, took up arms against his father. His campaign was not crowned with success, and he was forced to make accommodation with his father. However, ten years later, the Young King was in armed revolt against Henry II once more, this time dying on campaign in June 1183 before he had reached the age of thirty. Henry II was grief-stricken.[41]

The Young King's revolts were the most painful open sore to afflict Henry II in his later years, and caused profound disquiet across the Angevin Empire. Contemporaries were not slow to compare Henry the Young King to Absalom, and Henry II himself is said to have cited precedents in the Old Testament for kings who exacted terrible revenge on their enemies. Yet in the event, for all his grief, Henry II treated the Young King and his supporters with surprising leniency, and favourable comparisons were made with King David, who had shown no such clemency to Absalom's counsellors.[42] Against this background, it is hard not to read the Morgan Leaf in the light of contemporary events.

What passed between St Hugh and Henry II during their private conversations must forever remain a matter of speculation, but it is not fanciful to suppose that the biblical precedent of David and Absalom was discussed. Both Hugh and Henry used works of art to reflect on contemporary issues. Some years later, while at Fontevrault with the soon-to-be-crowned King John, Hugh gave him a sermon on the fate that awaited evil kings while standing in front of a sculpted tympanum of the Last Judgement at the entrance to the church. Hugh pointed out some crowned kings among the damned, and urged John to avoid a similar fate. In response, John pointed to some kings standing among the saved and said that he intended to be numbered among them. Adam of Eynsham concludes with a comment of St Hugh's about the purpose of Last Judgement sculptures: they were placed at the entrance to the church so that those who were about to enter should recognise the final fate which awaited them, pray for forgiveness, and thereby escape the torments of the damned and win everlasting joy. It is a rare contemporary statement of the didactic functions of portal sculptures, and gives an insight into the way in which Hugh envisaged works of art being employed to convey a spiritual message.[43] Henry II ordered an image of an eagle being mobbed by four of its young to be painted on the wall of one of the chambers of his palace at Winchester, as a permanent reminder of the rebellion of the Young King and his brothers.[44] The impact of the Morgan Leaf, when freshly painted by the Morgan Master in the early 1180s must have been immediate. Had Henry II seen it, he could hardly have ignored its relevance to his own

FIGURE 11.3

Winchester Bible, f. 99v. Initial to 2 Kings, painted by the Amalekite Master over a design by the Master of the Leaping Figures. (John Crook)

situation. Had he associated it with the words of spiritual consolation that he had received from St Hugh, this might explain why he was so determined to send him the Winchester Bible – the only manuscript in England, to our knowledge, to have contained an illuminated cycle which would have spoken so directly to his own predicament.

Whether or not a scenario of this kind explains the story of the Witham Bible, this reading of the Morgan Leaf has wider ramifications. The Morgan Leaf was created in two stages. The drawing on both recto and verso was the work of the Apocrypha Master, who also began to paint the scenes on both sides, but the painting was completed by the Morgan Master. The story of David and Absalom was just as relevant to Henry II after the first revolt of the Young King in 1173–74 as it was ten years later. The imagery makes little sense in any contemporary context prior to 1173, when the Young King was still the apple of Henry's eye. This suggests a possible date for the Apocrypha Master's work on the Winchester Bible in the mid 1170s. It also offers a plausible approach to the interpretation of the other two full-page drawings by the Apocrypha Master in volume two of the bible (Figures 11.4 and 11.5). The books of Judith and Maccabees are not the most obvious candidates for full-page illuminations, as Oakeshott recognised. He explained them on the grounds that the full-page illuminations were not part of the original scheme for the bible, but were only conceived when the first scribe was well on through the second volume.[45] Whether or not this is correct, it still does not explain why Judith (f. 331v) and Maccabees (f. 350v) were singled out for special treatment, rather than any of the New Testament which follows on immediately after Maccabees. Judith is one of the least well-known books of the bible, and it is mostly illuminated with no more than an initial, generally showing Judith killing Holofernes. Interest seems to have focussed on Judith as a type for the church. Narrative cycles are unusual, and no other 12th-century bible has such an extensive one. As with the Morgan Leaf, iconographical parallels can be found for the individual scenes in the Judith and the Maccabees pages, but the full cycles are unusual in the context of 12th-century bible illuminations.[46] Both concern the defence of Jerusalem in the face of infidel aggressors and focus on the roles of heroic individuals. Judith's assassination of Nebuchadnezzar's general, Holofernes, enabled the Israelites to defeat the invaders in battle before they reached Jerusalem, whereas the Maccabees page depicts the divine revenge on King Antiochus for setting up idols in the Temple at Jerusalem through the intervention of Judas Maccabeus, who laid down his life for the cause. Both stories find resonances in the Crusading spirit of the times. As part of his penance for the death of Becket, Henry II agreed in 1172 to pay for one hundred knights under the command of the Templars to assist in the defence of the Holy Land. Henry's own participation in the Crusades was also under discussion in these years and he continued to allocate annual sums for the purpose (while cannily refusing to let them be spent). He himself was supposed to set off on Crusade to the Holy Land within a year, though he repeatedly found reasons to postpone his departure.[47] As a set, the Morgan Leaf and the full-page illuminations to Judith and Maccabees with their bloody scenes of conflict and battle contrast markedly with the complex theological miniatures in the Bury Bible and the Lambeth Bible. A key to their significance, it may be suggested, is to be found in the political and military events of the mid-1170s.

This topic would merit further investigation. Meanwhile, it brings us back to the question of the origin of the Winchester Bible and the identity and role of its patron or patrons. As we have already seen, there are no firm grounds for connecting the original commission with Henry of Blois, and the dating of the first phase of work is debatable. If the narratives of the Morgan Leaf and the Judith and Maccabees pages were composed with a view to contemporary events, it means that the work of the Apocrypha Master should be dated to the mid-1170s. This is slightly later than the date usually assigned to him, but only by a few years. The date of the start of work would then depend on our assessment of the relationship between the Apocrypha Master and the Master of the Leaping Figures, and between the two of them and the first scribe. This

Figure 11.4

Winchester Bible, f. 331v. Frontispiece to the Book of Judith. Unfinished drawing by the Apocrypha Master. (John Crook)

FIGURE 11.5
Winchester Bible, f. v. Frontispiece to 1 Maccabees. Unfinished drawing by the Apocrypha Master. (John Crook)

is explored further in Appendix 1. It is usually assumed that the Winchester Bible was a purely ecclesiastical initiative. The possibility of Henry II's involvement in its making seems never to have been explored, but it deserves consideration. As noted above, the bible project cannot have been unknown to members of the royal administration in Winchester. Did Henry II not merely know about it, but contribute to it, financially or in some other way, perhaps through his international contacts? Winchester was not just his English capital; it had a particular personal significance for him. It was at Winchester in November 1153 that the settlement was agreed which brought an end to the civil war and paved the way for Henry to ascend to the throne on the death of King Stephen a year later. The agreement was negotiated with the help of the two leading churchmen of the day, Archbishop Theobald of Canterbury and Henry of Blois, and it was Theobald who, Samuel-like, anointed and crowned King Henry a year later.[48] In 1172, Henry the Young King was crowned a second time in Winchester Cathedral, and his young wife Margaret was anointed, consecrated and crowned queen of England. Had Henry II at any point felt inclined to make a thank-offering to the cathedral, the bible would have been an obvious focus for royal patronage. If he were involved, it would help explain his insistence on the Winchester Bible being sent to Witham and would make his intervention perhaps a little less high-handed, a little less like robbery. There are many avenues still to be explored.[49]

To conclude: the Winchester Bible continues to fascinate and tantalise with its combination of outstanding scribes and artists, its enigmatic origins and high-level connections, and the still elusive process of its creation. Much that has been taken for granted needs to be reassessed.[50] The Winchester Bible *was* the bible sent by Henry II to St Hugh at Witham. It was *not* a refectory bible, but more probably a sacrist's book designed to adorn the high altar. The date of its inception remains unclear. The involvement of Henry of Blois, so widely assumed, has still to be demonstrated, while the iconography of the full-page illuminations by the Apocrypha Master would be consistent with a date after his death in the mid-1170s. The abandonment of the project in 1185 (or a few months before or after) provides a precious fixed date in the history of 12th-century manuscripts. It has significant implications for our understanding of the careers of the illuminators (several of whom have been identified in other manuscripts). And it has wider ramifications. The late-12th-century wall-paintings in the Holy Sepulchre Chapel in Winchester Cathedral are close in style to the Morgan Master's illuminations, though opinion is divided as to whether the wall-paintings are actually to be attributed to him. A date of *c.* 1185 would seem appropriate.[51] Even more important are the celebrated wall-paintings from the chapter house at Sigena, which are remarkably close in style to the work of the Morgan Master in the Winchester Bible.[52] Oakeshott indeed concluded that the paintings at Sigena were probably created by the Morgan Master working with some of the other artists who had been employed at Winchester, including the Gothic Majesty Master. The royal nunnery of Sigena was founded in 1188 on the site of an earlier hospital. Placing the conclusion of work on the Winchester Bible in 1185, rather than the 1170s as some have suggested, brings the work of the Morgan Master and the Gothic Majesty Master very close in date to the Sigena paintings. Susanne Wittekind is currently exploring the circumstances of Sigena's foundation and the impact of its connections with the kingdom of Aragon on its buildings and decoration. In the present volume, Neil Stratford has demonstrated how the mission of the Patriarch of Jerusalem to England in 1185 (seeking assistance for the beleaguered kingdom of Jerusalem) occasioned direct personal links between the court of Henry II and Sigena. Although it is not known for certain whether the patriarchal mission visited Winchester or not, the links between them is symbolised by the appearance of Prior John of Winchester at the royal court at Dover on 16 April 1185 as the members of the mission waited to set sail with the king. The timing was exactly right. With the Winchester Bible project coming to a sudden close, the artists would have been on the look-out for new employment. It would seem that Henry II's intervention in the matter of the manuscript not merely resulted in the cessation of work on the Winchester Bible, it also had the effect of making available a team of outstanding artists to work on the wall-paintings at Sigena.

NOTES

[1] Principal bibliography: W. Oakeshott, *The Artists of the Winchester Bible* (London 1945); C.M. Kauffmann, *Romanesque Manuscripts 1066–1190* (A Survey of Manuscripts Illuminated in the British Isles, 3; London 1975), 108–11; W. Oakeshott, *The Two Winchester Bibles* (Oxford 1981) and review by T.A. Heslop, *Art History*, 5 (1982), 124–28; C. Donovan, *The Winchester Bible* (London 1993) which is the most accessible and best illustrated introduction to the bible. Other literature includes: T.S.R. Boase, *English Art 1100–1216* (Oxford 1953), 174–80; W. Oakeshott, *Sigena – Romanesque Paintings in Spain and the Winchester Bible Artists* (London, 1972), *passim*; L.M. Ayres, 'The work of the Morgan Master at Winchester and English painting of the early Gothic period', *Art Bulletin*, 76.2 (1974), 201–23; L.M. Ayres, 'The role of an Angevin style in English Romanesque painting', *Zeitschrift für Kunstgeschichte*, 37 (1974), 193–23; W. Cahn, *Romanesque Bible Illumination* (Fribourg 1982), *passim*; L. Ayres, 'Collaborative enterprise in Romanesque manuscript illumination and the artists of the Winchester Bible', in T.A. Heslop and V. Sekules, eds, *Medieval Art and Architecture at Winchester Cathedral* (BAACT VI, 1983), 20–27; D. Park, 'The wall paintings of the Holy Sepulchre Chapel', *ibid*, 38–62; *English Romanesque Art 1066–1200* (Exhibition Catalogue, London 1984), 120–22; C.R. Dodwell, *The Pictorial Arts of the West, 800–1200* (New Haven 1993), 363–73; C. Donovan, 'The Winchester Bible', in J. Crook, ed., *Winchester Cathedral – Nine Hundred Years, 1093–1993* (Chichester 1993), 80–96; H. Stirrup, 'A change of clothes on the Morgan Leaf: the Apocrypha Master's illustration of the transition of Saul', in M. Boulton, J. Hawkes and M. Herman, eds, *The Art, Literature and Material Culture of the Medieval World* (Dublin 2015), 232–48. For the most part, I confine subsequent references to the Winchester Bible to Oakeshott, whose work is both the most substantial and the most difficult to navigate. This study was carried out prior to the current conservation and rebinding of the bible. The bible was discussed by Christopher de Hamel in his Panizzi lectures at the British Library in 2014 and preliminary results from the research carried out during the conservation programme were presented at a seminar at the Bodleian Library on 27 June 2017, shortly before this paper went to press. I am

indebted to Harry Stirrup, Christopher de Hamel and Claire Donovan for discussing the bible with me, and to John McNeill for his patience.

2   N. Ker, *English Manuscripts in the Century After the Norman Conquest* (Oxford 1960), 35, 48, 51–52.

3   Cahn, *Romanesque Bible Illumination* (as n. 1), 234; C. de Hamel, *The Book – A History of the Bible* (London 2001), 81–83; R. Gameson, 'Book culture in northern Europe in the tenth and eleventh centuries', in E. Petersen, ed., *Living Words and Luminous Pictures – Medieval Book Culture in Denmark, Vol I – Essays, Vol II – Catalogue* (Copenhagen 1999), I 29.

4   Ker, *English Manuscripts* (as n. 2), 52; Oakeshott, *Sigena* (as n. 1), 142; Oakeshott, *Two Winchester Bibles* (as n. 1), 15–17 and *passim*; Donovan, *Winchester Bible* (as n. 1), 15–24 who attributes the quire signatures to the second scribe.

5   Compare Oakeshott, *Artists* (as n. 1), 4–16; Oakeshott, *Sigena* (as n. 1), *passim* and 142; Oakeshott, *Two Winchester Bibles* (as n. 1), *passim* and 113–15.

6   E. Bishop, 'Gifts of Henry of Blois, Abbat [sic] of Glastonbury, to Winchester Cathedral', *Downside Review*, 1884, reprinted in E. Bishop, *Liturgica Historica* (Oxford 1918), 392–401; G. Zarnecki, 'Henry of Blois as a patron of sculpture', in S. Macready and F.H. Thompson, eds, *Art and Patronage in the English Romanesque* (London 1986), 159–72; N. Stratford, 'The 'Henry of Blois plaques' in the British Museum', in Heslop and Sekules, *Medieval Art and Architecture at Winchester*, 28–37; N. Stratford, *Catalogue of Medieval Enamels in the British Museum, Volume II, Northern Romanesque Enamels* (London 1993), 53–58; Y. Kusaba, 'Henry of Blois, Winchester, and the 12th-century renaissance', in Crook, *Winchester Cathedral* (as n. 1), 69–79; Donovan, *Winchester Bible* (as n. 1), 13–15; N. Riall, *Henry of Blois, Bishop of Winchester: A Patron of the Twelfth-Century Renaissance* (Winchester 1994); J.F. King, 'The Tournai marble baptismal font of Lincoln Cathedral', *Journal of the British Archaeological Association*, 155 (2002), 1–21 and references there cited; J. West, 'A taste for the antique? Henry of Blois and the arts', *Anglo-Norman Studies*, 30 (2007), 213–30.

7   Oakeshott, *Two Winchester Bibles* (as n. 1), 8 and n.3. However, on p. 114 he writes much more cautiously that 'no documentary evidence connects Henry of Blois with the Bible, . . . unless we reckon that his endowment of 1171 'ad libros conscribendos' can be interpreted as being for illumination as well as writing'. Henry's involvement is taken as fact in (*inter alia*) the *Oxford Dictionary of National Biography*.

8   O. Lehmann-Brockhaus, *Lateinische Schriftquellen zur Kunst in England, Wales und Schottland vom Jahre 901 bis zum Jahre 1307*, 5 vols (Munich 1955–60), no. 4769.

9   G.V. Scammell, *Hugh du Puiset, Bishop of Durham* (Cambridge 1956).

10   The charters are printed in M.J. Franklin, ed., *English Episcopal Acta VIII, Winchester 1070–1204* (Oxford 1993), nos 17, 20, 126 and 132. The extract printed by Lehmann-Brockhaus, *loc.cit.*, is derived from a copy of the 1171 charter in the register of Bishop John of Pontoise (1282–1304).

11   The date of the Genesis Master's work is discussed below.

12   Donovan, *Winchester Bible* (as n. 1), 13, 34 and caption to fig. 11. C. Donovan, 'The Winchester Bible', in T. Ayers, ed. *The History of British Art, 600–1600* (London 2008), 68–69 states categorically that the bible 'was made between about 1160 and 1175 as one of the major projects of Henry of Blois'.

13   Petersen, *Living Words* (as n. 3), I, *Essays*, 12, and II, *Catalogue*, no. 8.

14   Franklin, *English Episcopal Acta VIII* (as n. 10), for Henry's career.

15   M. Biddle, ed., *Winchester in the Early Middle Ages: An Edition and Discussion of the Winton Domesday* (Winchester Studies, 1, Oxford 1976), 323–28.

16   Kauffmann, *Romanesque Manuscripts* (as n. 1), 121–22; D. Marner, 'The bible of Hugh of le Puiset (Durham Dean and Chapter Library, MS A. II. 1)', in D. Rollason, M. Harvey and M. Prestwich, eds, *Anglo-Norman Durham 1093–1193* (Woodbridge 1994), 471–84; R. Gameson *et al.*, *Manuscript Treasures of Durham Cathedral* (London 2010), 78–85.

17   Kauffmann, *Romanesque Manuscripts* (as n. 1), 88–90; T.A. Heslop, 'The production and artistry of the Bury Bible', in *Bury St Edmunds – Medieval Art, Architecture, Archaeology and Economy*, ed., A. Gransden, *British Archaeological Assocation Transactions*, XX (Leeds 1998), 172–85; R.M. Thomson, *The Bury Bible* (Woodbridge 2001); C.M. Kauffmann, *Biblical Imagery in Medieval England 700–1550* (London 2003), 89–104.

18   On the roles of Benedictine cantors and sacrists and their books, see D. Knowles, *The Monastic Order in England, 940–1216*, 2nd edn (Cambridge 1963), 428; M. Gullick, 'The hand of Symeon of Durham: further observations on the Durham martyrology scribe', in D. Rollason, ed., *Symeon of Durham, Historian of Durham and the North* (Stamford 1998), 14–31 at 20–21; C. Norton, 'Liber specialis et preciosus: a late twelfth-century illuminated Life of St Cuthbert' in P. Binski and W. Noel, eds, *New Offerings, Ancient Treasures: Studies in Medieval Art for George Henderson* (Stroud 2001), 210–34 at 224–25 and note 48.

19   The names of the officials in question are not well recorded. A Prior Geoffrey is mentioned in the 1140s, a Prior William died in 1165, and he was succeeded by Prior Robert, who held office till 1173 (D. Knowles, C.N.L. Brooke and V.C.M London, *The Heads of Religious Houses – England and Wales, 940–1216* (Cambridge 1972), 80). Henry of Blois' charter of 1142x1143 gives the name of the cantor then as Herbert, see reference in note 10.

20   All the details deriving from the 1148 survey are to be found in Biddle, *Winchester in the Early Middle Ages* (as n. 15).

21   This possibility was tentatively raised by Ayres, 'Collaborative enterprise' (as n. 1), 25, and compare Oakeshott, *Two Winchester Bibles* (as n. 1), 114.

22   D.L. Douie and H. Farmer, eds, *Magna Vita Sancti Hugonis – The Life of St Hugh of Lincoln*, 2 vols (London 1961–62 reprinted with corrections 1985), I, 85–88. The Latin is in places awkward, perhaps reflecting the awkwardness of the situation. I am indebted to Dr James Binns for discussing the translation of the Latin with me.

23   *Ibid.*, Introduction, for details concerning Adam, Hugh, Robert and Ralph. On the foundation of Witham and the early Carthusians, see M. Thompson, *The Carthusian Order in England* (London 1930); D. Knowles, *The Monastic Order in England, 940–1216*, 2nd edn (Cambridge 1963), 375–91; and D.H. Farmer, *Saint Hugh of Lincoln* (London 1985), 14–22.

24   R.W. Eyton, *Court, Household and Itinerary of King Henry II* (London 1878), 263; and summary itinerary in L.F. Salzmann, *Henry II* (London 1914), 249–50; Knowles *et al.*, *Heads of Religious Houses* (as n. 19), 80. Juxtaposing Henry's itinerary, Book II of the *Magna Vita* and the Pipe Rolls produces a coherent chronology for Henry's dealings with St Hugh, as follows:

Winter 1179–80. Hugh arrives in England, discusses the site and buildings before Henry leaves England in mid-April 1180, in time for a payment of £63 to appear in the Pipe Rolls for Michaelmas 1179 – Michaelmas 1180.

Mid-April 1180–26 July 1181. Henry II abroad. Payment of just £32 in the Pipe Roll for 1180–81, leading to a crisis in the works at Witham.

26 July 1181–4 March 1182. Henry, back in England, has second conversation with St Hugh. Funding increased to £126 in the Pipe Roll for 1181–82.

4 March 1182–10 June 1184. Henry abroad again. Funding of £40 in the Pipe Roll for 1182–83 and £110 for 1183–84.

10 June 1184–16 April 1185. Henry back in England. Third conversation with Hugh about books. Funding of £110 in the Pipe Roll for 1183–84, dropping to £12 for 1184–85 as building work comes to completion.

16 April 1185–27 April 1186. Henry abroad again.

27 April 1186–17 February 1187. Henry back in England, Hugh elected bishop of Lincoln in May 1186.

When at court, Hugh avoided getting sucked into administrative business (*Vita*, Bk II, Ch. VII), so his appearances there cannot be traced in charter witness lists or other such documents.

25   Kauffmann, *Romanesque Manuscripts* (as n. 1), 107–08; Oakeshott, *Two Winchester Bibles* (as n. 1), 33–43, 99–112; R.M. Thomson, *Manuscripts From St Albans Abbey 1066–1235*, revised edn, 2 vols (Woodbridge 1985), I, 33–36, 125.

26   Ker, *English Manuscripts* (as n. 2), 51–52; Oakeshott, *Two Winchester Bibles* (as n. 1), 30–32.

27   Ayres, 'The work of the Morgan Master' as n. 1), 211 n.33.

[28] It is incorrect to say that Hugh was offered 'an even bigger bible from Winchester, which was described as shortly to be finished' (Donovan, *Winchester Bible*, 15–17). The replacement bible was to be *made* (not finished) with the Carthusians in mind, and it was not to be 'bigger' but 'far better' (*longe meliorem*). Oakeshott and the editors of the *Vita* also mistranslated the adjective, as 'far finer'. The significance of the adjective is discussed below.

[29] For instance, de Hamel, *The Book* (as n. 3), 81.

[30] Cambridge University Library, MS Ee. 2.23, see P. Binski and S. Panayotova, *The Cambridge Illuminations – Ten Centuries of Book Production in the Medieval West* (London 2005), no. 29 and compare no. 31, a Parisian bible of *c*. 1260 from the Carthusian house of Vauvert in Paris founded by St Louis. For later examples of Carthusian bibles, see de Hamel, *The Book – A History of the Bible* (as n. 3), 183–85 and 196, and J.M. Luxford, 'Precept and practice: the decoration of English Carthusian books', in J.M. Luxford, ed., *Studies in Carthusian Monasticism in the Late Middle Ages* (Turnhout 2008), 225–68 at 233. On early Carthusian usage and readings in the refectory, see Thompson, *Carthusian Order* (as n. 23), 35–37, 104, 116–17. None of the three surviving English Carthusian refectories (including the one at Hinton) had a built-in pulpitum. G. Coppack and M. Aston, *Christ's Poor Men: The Carthusians in England* (Stroud 2002), 104–06.

[31] Adam of Eynsham chose his words with great care. In the conversation with the Winchester monk, Hugh is recorded as saying, not that he had been unaware that the bible came from the cathedral; merely, that he had not previously known *how* the king had managed to get hold of it.

[32] Oakeshott, *Artists* (as n. 1), 3 commented that much of the bible has been accented for reading aloud, and this notion has passed into the literature. On the other hand, Ker, whose opinion on textual matters carries greater authority, said that many of the alterations and corrections to the text 'are made in such a way that parts of the Winchester Bible can only be read with difficulty, and can hardly have been read aloud at all'. Ker, *English Manuscripts* (as n. 2), 5.

[33] Ayres, 'The work of the Morgan Master' (as n. 1), 209, attributed the unfinished Psalm 109 initials to the Morgan Master. The attribution is of little significance to the present analysis.

[34] Oakeshott's explanation is lame by comparison: volume two of the Winchester Bible was abandoned 'partly perhaps because (it seems) the fashion for these large bibles passed, partly because the scale of this one proved altogether too extravagant'. Oakeshott, *Two Winchester Bibles* (as n. 1), 35

[35] Ker, *English Manuscripts* (as n. 2), 51–52; Oakeshott, *Winchester Bible* (as n. 1), 32, shows that a *third* manuscript of the bible must have been used during the process of revising the Winchester Bible and the Auct Bible; and there were doubtless many other biblical manuscripts available for comparison. So the removal of the Witham Bible from circulation need not have stopped work on other manuscripts. A detailed comparison of the texts of the two bibles is much to be desired.

[36] The discussion of the text in Oakeshott, *Artists* (as n. 1), 2–3 contains some significant errors. It is not correct to say that Hugh 'was anxious to obtain copies of the Bible for his monastery'. Rather, Adam of Eynsham talks of the lack of books of spiritual edification, 'religious works', including books for the *lectio divina*, not just biblical manuscripts. It was the king's decision to send him a bible. Oakeshott also remarks that 'the Bible was later recognized by a Winchester monk, and returned, by the good offices of St Hugh to Winchester', implying that it was only by chance that the Winchester monk identified the bible at Witham. This is at variance with the text. Other commentators have also summarised Adam of Eynsham in potentially or actually misleading ways.

[37] For a scathing assessment of the Carthusians of Witham by a Winchester Cathedral monk, see J.T. Appleby, *The Chronicle of Richard of Devizes of the Time of King Richard the First* (London 1963), xiv, xvi, 1–3 and 26.

[38] *Magna Vita*, Bk II, Chs VI-VII.

[39] For a discussion of the Morgan Leaf's relationship to the rest of Winchester Bible, see Appendix One.

[40] Kauffmann, *Romanesque Manuscripts* (as n. 1), 111–12; Cahn, *Romanesque Bible Illumination* (as n. 1), 184–89; S. Wittekind, *Kommentar mit Bildern zur Ausstattung mittelalterlicher Psalmenkommentare und Verwendung der Davidgeschichte in Texten und Bildern am Beispiel des Psalmenkommentars des Petrus Lombardus (Bamberg, Staatsbibliothek, Msc. Bibl. 59)* (Frankfurt am Main 1994). I am indebted to Professor Wittekind for a copy of her book and for discussing the Morgan Leaf with me. C. Hourihane, ed., *King David in the Index of Christian Art* (Princeton 2002). For the Bury Bible, see also Kauffmann, *Biblical Imagery* (as n. 17), 94–97.

[41] On the Young King's rebellions, W.L. Warren, *Henry II* (London 1973), 108–36 and 580–93, and see now M. Strickland, *Henry the Young King 1155–1183* (New Haven 2016).

[42] See Strickland, *Henry the Young King* (as n. 41), 5, 206, 210–11, 303–04 and references there cited. Authors who compared the Young King to Absalom included Walter Map, Roger of Howden, Richard FitzNigel, and Richard archbishop of Canterbury in a letter to the Young King himself. Henry II's reference to Old Testament precedents was recorded by Peter of Blois.

[43] *Magna Vita*, Bk V, Ch XI. On Hugh's architectural projects as prior of Witham and bishop of Lincoln, see T.A. Heslop, 'Art, nature and St Hugh's Choir at Lincoln', in J. Mitchell and M. Moran, eds, *England and the Continent in the Middle Ages: Studies in Memory of Andrew Martindale* (Harlaxton Medieval Studies VIII) (Stamford 2000), 60–74. The Judgement Portal which gives access to the site of St Hugh's shrine in the Angel Choir of Lincoln Cathedral could usefully be considered in the light of this passage.

[44] Gerald of Wales in J.S. Brewer, J.F. Dimock and G.F. Warner, eds, *Giraldus Cambrensis, Opera*, 8 vols (Rolls Series 1861–91), VIII, 295–96; Warren, *Henry II* (as n. 41), 601; and see H.M. Colvin, ed., *The History of the King's Works, II, The Middle Ages* (London 1963), 857 for £3 10s spent on painting the king's chamber in 1181–82.

[45] See the discussion in Appendix 1.

[46] Cahn, *Romanesque Bible Illumination* (as n. 1), 199–204. On Judith imagery, see D. M Shepard, *Introducing the Lambeth Bible: A Study of Texts and Imagery* (Turnhout 2007), 219–222. On Maccabees iconography, see P. Binski, *The Painted Chamber at Westminster* (London 1986), 82–96.

[47] Warren, *Henry II* (as n. 41), 530–31, 604–08; H.E. Mayer, 'Henry II of England and the Holy Land', *English Historical Review*, 185 (1982), 721–39.

[48] Warren, *Henry II* (as n. 41), 50–53.

[49] For Henry II's involvement in monumental painting schemes abroad, see N. Stratford, 'The wall-paintings of the Petit-Quevilly', in *Medieval Art, Architecture and Archaeology at Rouen*, ed., J. Stratford, *British Archaeological Assocation Transactions*, XII (Leeds 1993), 51–59; R. Stalley, 'Design and function: the construction and decoration of Cormac's Chapel at Cashel', in D. Bracken and D. Ó Riain-Raedel, eds, *Ireland and Europe in the Twelfth Century – Reform and Renewal* (Dublin 2006), 162–75 at 173–75.

[50] In some respects my conclusions were anticipated in the 1970s by Larry Ayres (see references in note 1), though his work has tended to be overshadowed by that of Oakeshott.

[51] Oakeshott, *Sigena* (as n. 1), 135; Ayres, 'The work of the Morgan Master' (as n. 1), 213; W. Oakeshott, 'The paintings of the Holy Sepulchre Chapel', *Winchester Cathedral Record*, 50 (1981), 10–14; Park, 'The wall-paintings of the Holy Sepulchre Chapel' (as n. 1), dating them to *c*. 1175–85.

[52] O. Pächt, 'A cycle of English frescoes in Spain', *Burlington Magazine*, 103 (1961), 166–75; Oakeshott, *Sigena* (as n. 1); Ayres, 'The work of the Morgan Master' (as n. 1); Park, 'The wall-paintings of the Holy Sepulchre Chapel' (as n. 1).

APPENDIX 1: NOTES ON THE ARTISTS OF THE BIBLE

The relationships between the different artists in the Winchester Bible are complex and difficult to grasp. Tabulating the distribution of their work across the bible makes it easier to discern certain patterns. The accompanying Table is based on the work of Walter Oakeshott, who had a longer and closer acquaintance with the bible than any other scholar, supplemented by the listings by Kauffmann and Donovan.[53] It lists the illuminated initials in the order in which they appear in the bible, including some which have been cut out from volume one, and spaces where initials were planned but never executed. Oakeshott was able to attribute the underdrawings of almost all the painted historiated initials, but he was not always able to identify the designers of the painted decorative initials. The surviving full-page illuminations are also listed, including the Morgan Leaf; but full-page illuminations whose existence has been inferred but not proven are excluded. The contributions of the different artists are shown as follows:

D = Design drawing
P = Painting
DP = Drawing and painting by the same artist
* = Painting left unfinished
MLF = Master of the Leaping Figures
ApM = Apocrypha Master
GM = Genesis Master
MM = Morgan Master
AmM = Amalekite Master
GothM MGoM = Master of the Gothic Majesty

The sections allocated to the various artists are indicated by boxes, bold for the first phase of work, double line for the second. The original division into two volumes is indicated, the foliation is continuous throughout.

The first two artists to work on the bible were the Master of the Leaping Figures and the Apocrypha Master. Both of them left unfinished initials which were completed by four later artists. The relative chronology of the earlier and later artists is therefore not in dispute. The Master of the Leaping Figures worked across almost the entire manuscript and contributed to more of the initials than anyone else. In most cases, however, he never progressed beyond the stage of the underdrawings, some of which are themselves unfinished (Figure 11.1). A few of them were gilded but not painted. He only painted six of the surviving initials (colour plate IV), one of them being the double initial to Psalm 51. He was responsible for most of the unfinished decoration of volume two, namely the drawings for a series of initials at the start of the volume, from Psalm 1 (f. 218) to II Chronicles (f. 303), and another major sequence from II Maccabees (f. 363) through almost to the end of the New Testament (Philemon on f. 459). His contribution to volume one is, in its present state, less significant and more sporadic, consisting only of eight or nine initials between Exodus (f. 21v) and Micah (f. 205). However, he has probably suffered disproportionately from the mutilation of this volume.

The Apocrypha Master appears for the first time with the Morgan Leaf and the initial to I Kings (f. 88). He then has four initials in a row from Daniel (f. 193) to Joel (f. 200v) (colour plate VI top). Another set of initials runs from Zephaniah to Zechariah, all on folios 209 and 210. Lastly, he appears in volume two between f. 331v (the full-page Judith miniature) and f. 350v (the full-page Maccabees miniature). The Apocrypha Master painted only three of his own initials (ff 198, 200v and 342), but all of his other drawings for initials were painted over by the later artists. Of the four full-page illuminations which he designed, he started to paint only the Morgan Leaf. This was completed by the Morgan Master,[54] but the Judith and Maccabees pages remain unpainted and demonstrate the quality of the Apocrypha Master's drawing.

The Master of the Leaping Figures and the Apocrypha Master left very similar patterns of work in the bible. Both left most of their drawings unpainted, and neither artist painted any of the other's drawings.[55] Both worked on discrete sets of initials which do not overlap. In volume one each group consists of between four and six initials in a row, whereas in volume two the great majority are the work of the Master of the Leaping Figures, with just one, important contribution by the Apocrypha Master in the Old Testament Apocrypha. Some of the initials which were left blank in this first phase of work also fall into groups, on ff 1–5 and ff 169–90. These various groupings bear no obvious relationship to the text of the bible, but they do relate to the physical structure of the manuscript. The bifolios are assembled for the most part in standard quires of eight, and there are a few single leaves. The divisions between the groups reflect the quire structure. The first three blank initials are all on the first quire. Thereafter, for most of volume one, the successive groups cover a number of quires, reflecting the length of the texts. Then, towards the end of the volume, where the texts are shorter, the two artists alternate on successive quires. The initials for Daniel to Joel by the Apocrypha Master on ff 193–200v all belong to a single quire. The Master of the Leaping Figures drew the initials on the next (rather mutilated) quire (ff 201–08); and the Apocrypha Master reappears with a sequence of initials on the following quire, which completes volume one. In volume two, the Master of the Leaping Figures drew the initials from Psalms to II Chronicles. Then, after a gap of sixty folios, he drew the very last initial in the Old Testament Apocrypha, II Maccabees, on f. 363, followed by all of the New Testament initials.

On the assumption that the lost initials in volume one followed the same pattern, their designs can be attributed with reasonable confidence to one or the other of the two early artists, as suggested in the Table. The Isaiah initial by the Master of the Gothic Majesty (f. 131) (colour plate V), which appears on the replacement bifolium written by the second scribe, presumably replaced an original initial designed by the Master of the Leaping Figures.

Within the discrete groups worked on by the two early artists, there are a few initials which they never started. The ones in volume one were filled in by the

TABLE 11.1

QUIRE NUMBER	FOLIO NUMBER	ILLUMINATION	COMMENT	MLF	ApM	GM	MM	AmM	GoMM
VOLUME ONE									
i	f. 1	Letter to Paulinus				D P			
i	f. 3	Letter to Damasus				D P			
i	f. 5	Genesis				D P			
iii	f. 21v	Exodus		D P					
v	f. 34v	Leviticus				D P			
vi	f. 44	Numbers				D P			
viii	f. 57	Deuteronomy	Cut out			?		?	
ix	f. 69	Joshua		D				P	
x	f. 77v	Judges	Cut out		?		?	?	
xi	f. 85v	Ruth	Decorative				D P		
	Morgan Leaf recto		Single leaf		D P*		P		
	Morgan Leaf verso		Single leaf		D P*		P		
xi	f. 88	I Kings				D	P		
xiii	f. 99v	II Kings		D				P	
xiv	f. 109	III Kings		D				P	
xv	f. 120v	IV Kings		D P					
xvii	f. 131	Isaiah	Replaced bifolium						D P
xix	f. 148	Jeremiah		D P					
xxi	f. 167	Lamentations of Jeremiah	Cut out	?			?		
xxii	f. 169	Prayer of Jeremiah	Secondary				D P		
xxii	f. 169	Baruch					D P		
xxii	f. 170v	Preface to Ezekiel					D P		
xxii	f. 172	Ezekiel					D P		
xxiv	f. 190	Daniel					D P		
xxv	f. 193	Daniel Ch. 5	Secondary		D		P		
xxv	f. 197v	Preface to Minor Prophets	Decorative		D		P		
xxv	f. 198	Hosea			D P				
xxv	f. 200	Preface to Joel	Cut out						
xxv	f. 200v	Joel			D P				
xxvi	f. 201v	Amos		D			P		
xxvi	f. 203v	Obadiah		D		P			
xxvi	f. 204	Preface to Jonah	Decorative			D P			
xxvi	f. 204v	Jonah	Cut out						
xxvi	f. 205	Micah		?D		?D P			

QUIRE NUMBER	FOLIO NUMBER	ILLUMINATION	COMMENT	MLF	ApM	GM	MM	AmM	GoMM
xxvi	f. 206v	Nahum	Cut out						
xxvi	f. 207v	Habbakuk	Cut out						
xxvi	f. 208	Prayer of Habbakuk	Secondary				D P		
xxvii	f. 209	Zephaniah			D	P			
xxvii	f. 209v	Preface to Haggai & Zechariah	Decorative		D	P			
xxvii	f. 210	Preface to Haggai	Decorative		D	P			
xxvii	f. 210	Haggai			D	P			
xxvii	f. 210v	Preface to Zechariah	Decorative		D	P			
xxvii	f. 210v	Zechariah			?D	?D P			
xxvii	f. 213v	Malachi				D P			
VOLUME TWO									
i	f. 218	Psalm 1	2 initials	D		P			
ii	f. 232	Psalm 51	2 initials	D P					
iv	f. 246	Psalm 101	2 initials	D			P *		
v	f. 250	Psalm 109	Secondary 2 initials						D
vi	f. 260	Proverbs		D					P *
vii	f. 268	Ecclesiastes		D					
vii	f. 270v	Song of Songs		D P					
vii	f. 272v	Wisdom		D P					
viii	f. 278v	Ecclesiasticus		D					
x	f. 293	I Chronicles	Blank						
xi	f. 303	II Chronicles		D					
xiii	f. 316	Preface to Job	Decorative						
xiii	f. 316v	Job	Blank						
xiv	f. 326	Preface to Tobias	Decorative						
xiv	f. 326v	Tobias	Blank – *ad placitum*						
xiv	f. 329v	Preface to Judith	Decorative						
xv	f. 331v	Judith miniature	Full page on single leaf			D			
xv	f. 332	Judith	Blank						
xv	f. 337	Esther	Blank						
xvi	f. 342	Ezra				D P			
xvii	f. 350v	Maccabees miniature	Integral to quire			D			
xvii	f. 351	I Maccabees	Blank – *ad placitum*						
xviii	f. 363	II Maccabees		D					
xx	f. 375	Prologue to 4 Gospels		D					

(*Continued*)

TABLE 11.1 Continued

QUIRE NUMBER	FOLIO NUMBER	ILLUMINATION	COMMENT	MLF	ApM	GM	MM	AmM	GoMM
xx	f. 376v	Matthew	Decorative	D					
xxi	f. 387v	Mark		D					
xxii	f. 395	Luke		D					
xxiv	f. 407	John		D					
xxv	f. 417v	Acts	Blank						
xxvii	f. 429	Preface to Catholic Eps.		D					
xxvii	f. 430v	Peter		D					
xxvii	f. 434	John	Decorative	D					
xxvii	f. 434v	Jude	Decorative	D					
xxvii	f. 435	Preface to Pauline Eps.	Decorative	D					
xxviii	f. 436v	Romans		D					
xxx	f. 452v	Philippians	Decorative	D					
xxx	f. 453v	Colossians	Decorative	D					
xxx	f. 456	Thessalonians	Decorative	D					
xxx	f. 456v	Timothy	Decorative	D					
xxx	f. 458v	Titus		D					
xxx	f. 459	Philemon	Decorative	D					
xxxi	f. 460v	Hebrews	Blank						
xxxi	f. 463v	Apocalypse	Blank						

later artists, whereas all but one in volume two remain blank to this day. At first sight these initials seem to be scattered randomly across the manuscript, but on closer inspection a rationale does emerge. Most of them are what might be described as secondary initials – that is to say, they are either purely decorative, non-historiated initials; or they relate to subordinate divisions within the text; or both. The initial I to Ruth (f. 85v) is purely decorative (and when eventually designed by the Morgan Master was extended downwards well below the accompanying text in order to make it more impressive). The initial on f. 204, which was left blank by the Master of the Leaping Figures and subsequently created by the Genesis Master, is likewise decorative rather than historiated. It also marks the *preface* to Jonah, rather than the start of the actual biblical text, and it is noticeable that the initials to the other prefaces to the minor prophets towards the end of volume one are all decorative (f. 197v, f. 209v, f. 210 and f. 210v).[56] These were all designed (but not painted) by the Apocrypha Master. One other initial which was left out by the Master of the Leaping Figures is the double initial to Psalm 109 (f. 250). This is the theologically important Trinitarian initial referring to the opening words of Psalm 109 (*Dixit dominus* . . .), which was designed (but left unpainted) by the Master of the Gothic Majesty (colour plate VII bottom). The system of marking these four psalms with elaborate initials has a number of precedents and parallels. However, in terms of the divisions of the text of the book of Psalms, the initial to Psalm 109 can be considered a secondary one compared to those which commence the three sets of fifty psalms (Psalms 1, 51 and 101). A similar case is the prayer of Habbakuk of f. 208, at the end of a quire worked on by the Master of the Leaping Figures. This is a secondary initial marking a section of text *within* the book of Habbakuk, as also are the decorative initial to Daniel chapter 5 on f. 193 by the Apocrypha Master, and the initial to the prayer of Jeremiah marking the start of chapter five of the Lamentations (f. 169) (Figure 11.2). It is also noticeable that the final, largely unilluminated initials to the end of the Old Testament and the Apocrypha between ff 316 and 351 include blank initials to the prefaces to Job, Tobias and Judith, and to the books of Tobias and I Maccabees, both of which are marked *ad placitum* ('as you please'). These initials all seem to have been considered of lesser importance even though this is the section of the manuscript which includes the two famous full-page drawings by the Apocrypha Master on ff 331v and 350v.

Thus, taking into account what we can deduce about the missing initials and the secondary initials, we can say that the Master of the Leaping Figures and the Apocrypha Master both began all the major historiated initials within the sections which they worked on, with only a few exceptions. In volume one these are the initials to Leviticus and Numbers on ff 34v and 44, and perhaps Micah on f. 205, all in sections worked on by the Master of the Leaping Figures. The Malachi initial on f. 213v is at the very end of volume one, where the text was for some reason left unfinished by the first scribe. He stopped writing halfway through a word at the bottom of column one, and this probably explains why the Apocrypha Master left the initial blank. The second scribe added in the missing section of text as far as f. 214, and the initial was created by the Genesis Master in this second phase. In volume two there are a number of blank initials between Job (f. 316v) and I Maccabees (f. 351), with only the Ezra initial (f. 342) drawn and painted by the Apocrypha Master. His two unfinished full-page drawings to Judith and Maccabees are also in this section, and it may be that this was where the Apocrypha Master abandoned work on the bible. Otherwise, in volume two, the Master of the Leaping Figures drew all of the major initials except those to I Chronicles, Acts, Hebrews and the Apocalypse.

So, between them the Apocrypha Master and the Master of the Leaping Figures designed most of the initials in the bible. In volume one up to the Joel initial on f. 200v, the initials were divided between them in alternating groups of similar size, whereas the last two groups of initials at the end of the volume, which correspond to single quires, have more. The blank initials between ff 167 and 172 also form a group which for some reason does not seem to have been allocated to either artist. At any rate, it does not interrupt the pattern of alternation between the two. In volume two, the alternation continues, but in a different rhythm. The Master of the Leaping Figures designed a long set of initials between Psalm 1 and II Chronicles, followed by another sequence from II Maccabees onwards. The Apocalypse Master did just one initial (Ezra) and drew the designs for the two full-page illuminations to Judith and Maccabees. However, if all of the blank initials between Job and I Maccabees had been allocated to him; and if we count the full-page illuminations as the equivalent of perhaps six initials, then the division of labour between the two artists was much more balanced, and over the manuscript as a whole works out at about half each.

Within their allocated sections, both artists worked in similar fashion. Both prioritised the main initials over the secondary ones, and left some initials blank; both prioritised the design drawings over the painting; both painted just a handful of their initials, distributed through the manuscript in no obvious pattern. All of this suggests that the unbound quires of each volume were allocated to the two artists so as to give them approximately equal shares; that they both addressed their task in similar fashion; and that this *modus operandi* provided much greater flexibility than would have been possible with a linear progression through the illuminations of each volume.

A corollary of this is that the process of illumination would not have started in earnest until the text of volume one was complete, or nearly so – perhaps indeed not till the first scribe had finished the whole bible. This implies a gap of at least a year or two between the start of work on the text and the illuminations, perhaps longer. This helps make sense of some other features in the manuscript. Much of the puzzlement that has been felt by some commentators on the bible stems from certain assumptions about the process of its creation – assumptions which are questionable. If it is assumed that the illuminations 'ought' to have been created in order from Genesis through to the end, the pattern of work of the two artists is inexplicable. If it is believed that the entire cycle of illuminations was conceived in detail at the outset, and that the first artist(s) worked in close collaboration with the first scribe, then certain features are hard to explain. The initials, for instance, do not always correspond in outline to the spaces left for them by the scribe. Some overlap the text slightly, some fail to fill the spaces (Figure 11.1 and colour plate IV). But similar discrepancies can be found in other illuminated manuscripts of the period, even of the most lavish kind, and are not surprising when illuminators were working on pages of text written in advance. Inconsistencies in the bible in the display lettering which accompanies the initials can also be paralleled elsewhere. Such features need not be considered serious anomalies, or evidence of significant deviations from a pre-existing plan. Rather, they are indicative of a normal, on-going process of production involving scribes, illuminators and rubricators, whose work was not always precisely co-ordinated.[57]

More problematic are the anomalies connected to the full-page illuminations, which have been cited as evidence of a significant change in the original plan. The Morgan Leaf is a single folio which was designed to stand between f. 87v and f. 88 at the start of 1 Kings (colour plates IX and X). The Judith miniature is drawn on the verso of another single folio (f. 331v) at the start of a quire (Figure 11.4). Its recto is blank. Physically speaking, these two folios can be described as additions to the quire structure of the manuscript. On the other hand, the full-page Maccabees drawing on f. 350v is on the verso of a folio (whose recto is blank) which forms part of the normal quire structure (Figure 11.5). It therefore must have been intended when the first scribe reached the text of Maccabees. There are also four whole folios missing from volume two. At the start of the New Testament three folios have been cut out (numbered in the foliation as ff 372–74), and one has been lost at the very beginning of the very first quire of the volume (before f. 218). The former would almost certainly have been for the canon tables, the latter perhaps for a preface to the Psalms, and/or a full-page illumination of King David playing the harp. From the quire structure, it may be assumed that these were allocated to the Master of the Leaping Figures. There is also a folio missing at the start of the Book of Job, whose verso may have contained narrative scenes, and a blank page before the Book of Tobias (f. 325). So some full-page illuminations were planned as an integral part of volume two, at least. But that does not necessarily mean that the Morgan Leaf and the Judith folio were not envisaged when the text was being written. Full-page illuminations are mostly found in the twelfth century in luxury psalters, where they tend to be grouped together as distinct units before the start of the text of the psalms. Manuscripts with full-page illuminations distributed through the text are rarer, but there are examples where the full-page illuminations are variously part of the normal quire structure or on separate leaves, without any suggestion that the latter are additions or after thoughts. There may have been good practical reasons for using single leaves in some cases. A special quality of vellum may have been desirable, for instance, or it may simply have been easier to make elaborate illuminations on a separate sheet. There are other cases where the inclusion of a single illuminated leaf has resulted in a section of text appearing twice, rather as with the Morgan Leaf.[58]

By the same token, full-page illuminations may have been part of the design for volume one of the manuscript. The first quire begins with the Letter to Paulinus on f. 1. The three initials in this quire, including the Genesis initial on f. 5, are entirely the work of the later Genesis Master, having been left blank during the first phase of illumination. The initial F to Frater Ambrosius on f. 1 is relatively modest compared to the equivalent letters in both the Bury Bible and the Lambeth Bible.[59] The page which faces the start of the text of Genesis, f. 4v, is blank, and could have been intended for a full-page frontispiece. An even grander opening display could have been provided by full-page illuminations on a separate folio or folios at the start. If they ever existed, they would have been very tempting targets for any collector, and easily detached from the manuscript. Were any such full-page illuminations planned, they and the opening initials in the first quire would have made up a group of illuminations comparable in scale to the subsequent groups allocated to the first two artists. The pattern of work suggests that the start of the manuscript would have been allocated to the Apocrypha Master. Or it may be that, like many authors down the centuries, they decided to leave the start of the book till the end.

It has been disputed whether the Morgan Leaf was designed for the Winchester Bible, or even if it was, whether it was ever actually included.[60] However, Claire Donovan has pointed out that the differential discolouration in the current opening at the start of I Kings shows clearly that there was once another leaf here, and that the manuscript must have been repeatedly opened over the centuries to exhibit the verso of the Morgan Leaf and the I Kings initial.[61] Since this would have been the finest opening in the entire bible, it is exactly what one would expect.

When the first scribe reached this point in the text, he finished the preface to I Kings a quarter of the way down the second column of f. 87v (colour plate VIII). He then began the capitula to I Kings, which continued on to the first column of f. 88. After a short space, the main text begins at the top of the second column with the splendid historiated initial (colour plate XI). When writing such a lengthy manuscript it was impossible to control in advance exactly where the divisions between different sections of text would fall. F. 88 is the final folio in the quire. When planning the quire it may have been hoped that the end of the *capitula* would fall on the verso of f. 88. This would have made it possible to have a separate folio for the Morgan Leaf, followed by the start of the text of I Kings at the beginning of the next quire. Something of the kind was achieved with the Judith miniature. The preface to the Book of Judith comes at the end of a quire, and the text of Judith itself begins on the first recto of the next quire. Between the two is the single folio with a blank recto and the full-page Judith drawing on the verso, facing the start of the text of the book (Figure 11.4). At the start of I Kings, the *capitula* fall in an awkward position, spanning the middle of the opening. This made it impossible to incorporate the full-page illuminations without an anomaly of some kind. One option was simply to insert a fully-illuminated leaf in the middle of the opening, separating the two halves of the *capitula*. This would have had the effect of disrupting the reading of the *capitula* and perhaps as a consequence distracting the eye from the full-page illuminations. Instead, it was decided to write out the second column of the *capitula* a second time on the recto of the Morgan Leaf (colour plate IX). This meant that the reader would come to the end of the *capitula* before the start of the illuminations. This produced a more logical relationship between text and image, albeit at the cost of having the second half of the *capitula* repeated in the next opening when the page was turned.

The *capitula* on the recto of the Morgan leaf were written by the first scribe, so the leaf was begun during the first phase of work, irrespective of whether it was part of the original scheme or not. It is also interesting to note the position of the Morgan Leaf within the first group of illuminations allocated to the Apocrypha Master. If the Morgan Leaf had not been part of the original allocation, this group would have contained a maximum of just three initials – much fewer than any of the other sets of initials allocated to the two artists in volume one. This suggests that the Morgan Leaf would have been intended from the start, and that the slight anomalies in its relationship to the adjoining folios, like those of the other full-page drawings by the Apocrypha Master, are no more than quirks of execution of the kind that are often found in illuminated manuscripts.

To sum up this analysis of the illuminations by the Master of the Leaping Figures and the Apocrypha Master. The two men worked together on the manuscript. They were allocated similar amounts of work which was divided up into discrete sections. With the manuscript unbound, they were each able to work on several different quires at the same time, and although they never contributed to the execution of each other's illuminations, they followed a similar set of priorities. Both of them abandoned their work with the majority of their illuminations designed, at least in part, but with only a minority painted. This carefully co-ordinated, systematic approach indicates a considerable degree of control over the process. The broad conception of the scale and illumination of the manuscript must have been agreed at the outset with the first scribe, but the final decision of the relationship of the text, the illuminations and the rubrication was part of an on-going process which inevitably threw up some minor inconsistencies or anomalies along the way.

The Master of the Leaping Figures has been credited with being the original 'designer' in charge of the scheme of illuminations, but there does not seem to be any clear evidence to prioritise him over the Apocrypha Master, either chronologically or in terms of responsibility.[62] It is important not to overlook the input of the patrons, or their representatives, in the whole process. As well as ensuring the funding, they must have determined the overall conception of the manuscript, and probably also organised and supervised the processes of production. They were very likely instrumental in the choice of subject matter, particularly as regards the full-page illuminations, which could have been intended from the outset. If the design of the Morgan Leaf by the Apocrypha Master is to be dated after the Young King's rebellion in 1173, then the first phase of illumination probably dates to c. 1175, with the start of work on the text by the first scribe probably sometime in the first half of the 1170s. The reason for the abandonment of the first phase of work has yet to be determined.

Turning now to the four later artists, not a great deal needs to be added to what has been said above. Between them, they completed all of the illuminations in volume one, and volume two only as far as Proverbs (f. 260). The last two hundred folios of the manuscript were never completed. The contributions of the different artists can be seen in the Table. The Amalekite Master (Figure 11.3) and the Master of the Gothic Majesty (colour plate V) did only three surviving initials each. Everything else was the work of the Genesis Master and the Morgan Master. Like the Master of the Leaping Figures and the Apocrypha Master before them, they each took sets of consecutive initials, either painting over the design drawings of the earlier artists, or filling in the blanks by painting initials of their own design. The distribution of tasks is different in this phase. The Genesis Master created five initials at the start of volume one which had been left blank in the first phase of work (colour plate VI bottom). He also completed the final run of initials in volume one from Obadiah (f. 203v) to Malachi (f. 213v), except for the initial to the prayer of Habbakuk (f. 208) which is by the Morgan Master. The latter completed the entire set of illuminations in the middle of volume one, from Ruth (f. 85v) through to Amos (f. 201v), including painting both sides of the Morgan Leaf (Figure 11.2, colour plates IX and X). This means that each artist worked on separate quires, except for the penultimate quire in the volume (ff 201–08), which they both contributed to. It is uncertain to what extent each of them worked on the lost initials, since most of them fall either in this shared quire, or around the boundary between the two artists' allocations between ff 57 and 77v. But the lost initials would not significantly alter the pattern, which gave both artists about the same number of new initials to create and existing initials to paint. Once again, the distribution pattern strongly suggests that they were working together on the project.

The hand of the Amalekite Master has been identified in a number of initials in the Auct Bible. He has also been credited with painting the Joshua initial on f. 69 of the Winchester Bible and the initials to II Kings and III Kings on ff 99v and 109. It may be that he was also involved in the missing initials to Deuteronomy and Judges on ff 57 and 77v, but as far as the surviving initials are concerned, he did not design any at all. It is possible that his work represents an initial, abortive attempt to complete the unfinished work of the Master of the Leaping Figures and the Apocrypha Master. Or he may have been a junior partner to the Genesis Master and the Morgan Master who only worked on the project for a short time.[63]

Between them, these three artists completed all the illumination of volume one, with just one exception. The Master of the Gothic Majesty was responsible for the Isaiah initial on f. 131, which belongs to the replacement bifolium written by the second scribe. His style is generally agreed to be the latest of all the artists of the Winchester Bible, and it may be that he was drafted in at a late stage.

At the start of volume two, the pattern changes. The Genesis Master painted the double initial to Psalm 1 and the Morgan Master began to paint the double initial to Psalm 101 (colour plate VII top). The Master of the Gothic Majesty designed and gilded (but did not paint) the initial to Psalm 109 (colour plate VII bottom), and began painting the initial to Proverbs.[64] This illustrates the way in which an illuminator might be working on different initials at the same time. As we have seen above, the second scribe stopped emending the text at around the same point in volume two, and nothing further was done. The abandonment of the project can be dated to Henry II's intervention between the summer of 1184 and the summer of 1186, probably in 1185. There is no sign of any overlap between the first and second phases of work. The resumption of the project can therefore be dated to the first half of the 1180s, after a hiatus of perhaps only a few years.

APPENDIX 2: THE LATIN TEXT OF THE MAGNA VITA

From *Magna Vita Sancti Hugonis: The Life of St Hugh of Lincoln*, ed. D. L. Douie and H. Farmer (London, 1961–62), Vol. I, 84–88, Book II, Chapter XIII

CAPITULUM XIII

Quod sacris codicibus sollicite adquirendis plurimam impendit operam; et de bibliotheca Wintoniensium monachorum, quam regi datam et Withamensibus collatam, Hugo pristinis restituit possessoribus; et de prerogatiua dilectionis inter utrumque collegium.

Libet succincte quiddam ex gestis uiri spiritu pleni gemine dilectionis, Dei uidelicet ac proximi, referre, quod eiusdem que in illo uehementer enituit, sincerissime caritatis insigne documentum fuit. Igitur pene iam pro consuetudine illius ordinis integro fratrum numero edificiis quoque regularibus decenter consummatis, edificandis indesinenter in sancto proposito sibi commissarum ouium animabus boni huius pastoris inuigilabat sollertia. In cuius negotii non mediocre adiutorium, sacris codicibus conficiendis, comparandis, et quibus posset modis adquirendis, haut segnem operam impendebat. Hiis enim pro deliciis et pro diuitiis tempore tranquillo, hiis bellico sub procinctu pro telis uel armis, hiis in fame pro alimonia et in languore pro medela, religiosis quibusque, maxime uero solitariam gerentibus vitam, utendum esse memorabat.

Hinc contigit ut cum rege familiarius quodam tempore agens, de penuria librorum intersereret mentionem. A quo admonitus ut conscribendis insisteret per conductitios scriptores libris, membranas sibi deesse respondit. Tum ille: 'Et quantum,' ait, 'pecunie tibi uis conferri ad hunc supplendum defectum?' 'Una,' inquit, 'marca argenti diu sufficiet.' Rex ad hec subridens 'O', ait, 'quam immoderate grauas nos.' Iussitque incontinenti decem marcas fratri qui cum eo erat numerari. Promisit etiam unam bibliothecam, utriusque testamenti corpus integre continentem, se transmissurum ei. Rediit prior domum. Rex promissi sui non immemor inquirit sollicite bibliothecam optime confectam, quam ei conferre potuisset. Suggeritur demum studiosius querenti monachos sancti Swithuni egregiam recenti et decenti opere confecisse bibliothecam, in qua ad mensam edentium fratrum legi debuisset. Quo ille comperto opido gauisus est, accersitoque quamtocius priore illius ecclesie, sub multe recompensationis pollicitatione donari sibi munus optatum petiit, citiusque impetrauit. Itaque prior Withamie cum fratribus suis bibliothecam regio munere susceptam et inspectam non mediocriter et ipsi letati sunt, in eo potissimum gauisi quod stili elegantiam, totiusque operis uenustatem, operosior emendatio sublimius commendaret.

Contigit post hec quemdam ex monachis ecclesie Wintoniensis edificationis gratia uenisse Withamiam. Quem prior more suo summa cum affabilitate optato reficiens sancte discretionis sue colloquio, didicit repente ab eo cum quanta supplicatione dominus rex bibliothecam ipsam dignatus fuerit a priore suo postulare. 'Et nos quidem in eo', ait, 'etiam gratulamur impensius quod uestre illam contulit sanctitati. Que si uobis per omnia placet, bene res processit; sin alias, et si a uestra consuetudine dissidet aliqua sui parte, nos ista pro libitu uestro longe meliorem citius conficiemus, pro uestra in omnibus dispositione ordinandam. Hanc enim nostro usui nostreque consuetudini, nec sine magni sudoris impensa, fecimus consonare.' Ad hec prior admirans, nescierat enim prius quonam ordine rex optinuisset illam, fratri continuo ita affatus est: 'Itane dominus rex ecclesiam uestram fraudauit adeo necessario labore uestro? Crede michi, frater amantissime, restituetur uobis incontinenti bibliotheca uestra. Set et uestrorum fratrum deuote per uos supplicamus uniuersitati quatinus nostre dignentur humilitati indulgere, quod occasione nostri, nobis tamen id ignorantibus, defectum sustinuerunt codicis sui.' Hiis monachus auditis uehementer expauit, orans gemebundis uocibus ne talia cogitaret uel loqueretur, nullatenus expedire affirmans ecclesie sue, ut sibi utiliter conciliata tali exhennio regis gratia quauis occasione desciuisset. Hinc prior exultans, 'Estne,' inquit, 'hoc uerum quod de eius fauore solito plus presumitis, nec uobis triste est tali hunc munere negotiis uestris propitium esse effectum?' Cum ille fratribus suis omnibus ex hoc gaudium prouenisse assereret, Hugo subiunxit: 'Ut hoc,' inquit, 'gaudium perpetuetur in longum, cunctos necesse est lateat facta uobis restitutio pretiosi reuera laboris uestri. Si uero bibliothecam hanc recipere clanculo minime adquiescitis, ego illam ei restituo qui huc ipsam destinauit. Si uero modo eam reportaueritis, hoc illi per nos nullatenus innotescet.' Quid multa? Recipiunt monachi codicem suum quasi recenti dono acquisitum, multum de codice, set multo plus de transmittentis dulcedine et caritatis ipsius plenitudine exhilarati.

Quo facto, ut premissum est, euidentius innotuit, quanto gemine caritatis ardore mens uiri beati flagrauerit, qui, gratia sui commodi, uiris noluit religiosis opus ad honorem Dei elaboratum deperire, ne uel in modico eidem derogaretur diuino honori uel honorem exhibentium detraheretur utilitati. Proximos ergo et beneficio iuuit et exemplo, quatinus et per lectionem proficerent codicis, et uirtutem emularentur impense sibi fraterne dilectionis, ex utroque uero in amorem crescerent sui conditoris. In hunc sane finem omnis eius actio, sermo et cogitatio dirigi consueuit ut prestaret proximo, et tam ipse quam proximus ex eo placeret Deo. Set neque fraudari nouerat intentio eius pia et recta a spe sua. Conualuit siquidem ex illo presertim tempore inter utriusque loci accolas, Wintonienses uidelicet cenobitas et Withamenses heremitas, eximie dilectionis prerogatiua, prestante Dei gratia in euum duratura.

NOTES

[53] See references in Note 1. Oakeshott's conclusions as to the contributions made by different artists to the drawing and painting of the illuminations are usefully summarised in Table II in *Two Winchester Bibles* (as n. 1), 144, which, however, omits the initials which have been cut out.

[54] The fullest analysis of the painting of the Morgan Leaf is Stirrup, 'A change of clothes' (as n. 1), 239–48.

[55] Except that Stirrup, 'A change of clothes' (as n. 1), 240–41 has recently identified some highlights on the Apocrypha Master's paint on the recto of the Morgan Leaf which he attributes to the Master of the Leaping Figures.

[56] In the Winchester Bible, the books of the Old and New Testament generally start either with a list of *capitula* or with a preface, only occasionally with both. In some cases the preface covers a group of texts, such as the preface to the four Gospels. The prefaces usually have illuminated initials, the *capitula* do not, so the distribution of these prefatory initials is somewhat irregular. The prefaces and *capitula* are tabulated in Oakeshott, *Two Winchester Bibles* (as n. 1), 137–43.

[57] Compare for instance the discussion of the Bury Bible in Heslop, 'The production . . . of the Bury Bible' (as n. 17).

[58] See for instance the Durham manuscript of 1188 analysed in C. Norton, 'History, wisdom and illumination' in Rollason, *Symeon of Durham* (as n. 18), 61–105; and Ayres, 'The work of the Morgan master' (as n. 1), 203–07.

[59] See Heslop, 'The production . . . of the Bury Bible' (as n. 17) and Shepard, *Introducing the Lambeth Bible* (as n. 46) for the start of the two books and the anomalies which they present.

[60] Oakeshott, *Sigena* (as n. 1), 82–90; Oakeshott, *Two Winchester Bibles* (as n. 1), 58–63; and Ayres, 'The work of the Morgan Master' (as n. 1), 201–03 whose conclusions are similar to mine. See also now Stirrup, 'A change of clothes' (as n. 1) on the Morgan Leaf.

[61] Donovan, *Winchester Bible* (as n. 1), 33.

[62] *Inter alia*, Oakeshott, *Two Winchester Bibles* (as n. 1), 43.

[63] Stirrup, 'A change of clothes' (as n. 1), 242–44 for a re-assessment of the Amalekite Master's work. He has also discussed the Amalekite Master's innovative techniques of gilding in the Auct Bible in a lecture at the 13th York Manuscripts Conference in July 2014.

[64] See above, note 33.

PATRONS, INSTITUTIONS AND PUBLIC IN THE MAKING OF CATALAN ROMANESQUE ART DURING THE COMITAL PERIOD (1000–1137)

Manuel Castiñeiras

> Until the early fifteenth century, "author" meant "father", from the Latin word for "master", *auctor*. *Auctor*-ship implied authority, something that, in most of the world, has been divine right of kings and religious leaders since Gilgamesh ruled Uruk from a thousand years earlier
> Kevin Ashton, *How to Fly a Horse: The Secret History of Creation, Invention and Discovery and Discovery* (New York, 2015).

From the beginning of 20th century onwards both local and foreign scholars have pointed to the precocity of Catalan art and architecture around the first decades of the 11th century. If First Romanesque Architecture managed to recover Roman constructional techniques, such as *opus latericium* (Sant Martí del Canigó) and *caementicium* (Sant Miquel de Cuixà) (Figure 12.1),[1] in this same series of monuments (Girona and Urgell Cathedrals) we can see the carving of lavish marble altar tables decorated in their upper part with a border featuring arched lobes that evoke those of Early Christian Art in Aquitaine and the Narbonnais.[2] Nevertheless, the most striking phenomenon in this field is the ephemeral and intriguing appearance of the earliest sculpted façades of Romanesque Europe in Roussillon (St-Genis-des-Fontaines, Saint-André-de-Sorède, Arles-sur-Tech) and Empordà (Sant Pere de Rodes). Although scholars have so far been unable to find a reasonable explanation for this extraordinary development, it makes most sense to think that we are dealing with a transposition of formats, in which the long-standing Carolingian tradition of metal altar-frontals was literally exteriorised, and brought out from the interior of the church, to decorate the lintels of its entrance.[3]

In this respect, the emergence of these incipient façades might be related to the new function of the spaces adjacent to them: the *sagreres* or sacred spaces.[4] As a result of the violent feudal struggles in which the nobility tried to suppress the rights of the peasantry and seize their crops, the Church protected areas of up to 30 paces – named *sagreres* or *celleres* – around every church to avoid the voracity of the magnates.[5] Roussillon and the diocese of Elne was one of the centres of the Peace of God movement in the 1020s, which was precisely the decade which saw the emergence of these 'apotropaic' façades. The Synod of Toulouges, presided over in 1027 by the abbot-bishop Oliba, marked the peak of this process of the sacralisation of the space surrounding the church: 'neque aliquis auderet ecclesiam vel domos (clericum) in circuitu positas a XXX passibus violare aut assallire' ('No one should dare to violate or assault churches or houses of the clergy which are situated within a range of 30 steps').[6] The new apocalyptic carvings (Fontaines, Sorède) (Figure 12.2) and crosses (Arles) decorating the 'face' of these temples seem to have been thought to stress the protective role of the Church in the parish communities and the double function of the churchyard as cemetery and storage.

Oliba in his role as ecclesiastical reformer and promoter of the arts was undoubtedly one of the main protagonists in the development of this peculiar First Romanesque Art. Differences aside, the role he played is very similar to that of some of his contemporaries, such as St Dunstan in England, Gauzlin at Fleury and St Bernward at Hildesheim. Belonging to the comital family of Cerdanya, he took over some of the great ecclesiastical offices of 11th-century Catalunya, becoming abbot of the Benedictine monasteries of Ripoll and Cuixà (1008) and bishop of Vic (1017).[7] From its foundation Ripoll was the mausoleum for the counts of Barcelona, Cerdanya and Besalú, and from the second half of the 10th century became an international centre for the study of the *quadrivium*, having connexions with the most important abbeys in the post-Carolingian world. One of the main tasks of Oliba and his namesake, Oliva, the master of the *quadrivium*, was the improvement of the famous library of the abbey, increasing the number of books from 65 in 977 to 246 in 1047.[8]

Hence one can imagine frantic activity in the *scriptorium*, as well as a well-documented exchange of manuscripts, objects and relics with places such as Fleury in France, Lodi in Lombardy or Montecassino in southern

FIGURE 12.1

Sant Miquel de Cuixà, vault of the crypt (The Crib), 1035: opus caementicum (Manuel Castiñeiras)

FIGURE 12.2

Saint-Genis-des-Fontaines, western façade, lintel, 1019–20 (John McNeill)

Italy, where, according to the *Chronica Monasterii Casinesis*, Oliba's father, Oliba Cabreta, count of Cerdanya, retired in 988 and died in 990.[9] Understandably many scholars have speculated about the artistic consequences of the two journeys made by Abbot Oliba to Rome in 1011 and 1116–17 to obtain Papal immunity for the monastery of Ripoll, as well as confirmations of its lands.[10]

A long list of peculiar features or choices in Catalan art during the period of his active patronage has been attributed to this direct contact with the other side of the Western Mediterranean: was the *Pessebre* at Saint Miquel de Cuixà (1035) (Figure 12.1) a citation of the Crib at Santa Maria Maggiore? Were the round plan of the church of Santa Maria de Vic (1038), or the five-aisled plan of Ripoll (consecrated in 1032), respectively a medieval copy of Santa Maria ad Martyres (Pantheon) and St Peters in Rome?[11] Were the silver-altar-frontal and canopy of the monastic church at Ripoll, no longer extant, an evocation of the lavish furnishings of the major Roman basilicas such as Saint Peter's, The Lateran or Santa Maria Maggiore?[12] Why do the giant Ripoll Bibles remind us of the ancient traditions of Christian iconography, such as Roman depictions of Genesis (San Paolo fuori le Mura, San Giovanni a Porta Latina) or papyrus-style illustrations of the New Testament?[13] Were these bibles the result of a collection of images that had been gathered by Oliba's entourage specifically in order to provide iconographic patterns for the paintings of the basilica of Ripoll as was the case in the famous passage of the Life of Saint-Pancras of Taormina (8th century)?[14] Was the original aspect of Ripoll, as many scholars from the 19th century onwards have suggested, a true *basilica picta* following the model of the major Roman churches?[15]

ANGELS ON EARTH: OLIBA AND HIS ENTOURAGE

There are many open questions, but equally many clues that point to the agency[16] of Oliba, along with his inner circle of advisers, in taking the lead in the whole artistic process. When his beloved brother, Count Bernat Tallaferro of Besalú, tragically died in 1020 he bequeathed all his gold and silver vessels to Ripoll, where he had decided to be buried ('Vascula sua aurea et argentea quod ad ipso die habebat, donare faciant ad coenobium Sancta Maria Riopollenti, et cum corpus suum ibidem presentetur') ('The golden and silver vessels that at that time belong to him should be given to the monastery of Santa Maria at Ripoll, and brought there along with his corpse').[17] Shortly afterwards (1024–25), Oliba wrote a letter to the king of Navarre, Sancho III el Mayor, then the most powerful ruler in the Iberian Peninsula, asking for money for the work on the new basilica that he had begun some years before, and finally consecrated in 1032. In exchange for his generosity Oliba promised Sancho divine assistance against his enemies, the Muslims, as well as an eternal reward on the Day of the Last Judgement:

Precamur etiam, domine, aliquid impertiri famulis tuis **ad agendum ceptum opus Dei genetris Marie ecclesie** *quo illius ope fultus impenetrabilis consistere valeas adversus inimici iacula, et ab omni securus culpa vultum sui Filii placatum in die tremendi examinis conspicere.*[18] (We also pray, Lord, something to be bestowed upon your servants **to contribute to the starting work of the church of Mary, Mother of God**, which means to gain yourself an impervious support to stand against the enemy spears, and to be surely forgiven of any guilt beholding the face of her Son on the tremendous Day of Judgement).

(translation: author)

As with many Romanesque patrons, Oliba considered himself to be a true author, in the Latin sense of the word. According to Isidore of Seville the *auctor* is he who carries out a work or he who provides the resources to produce it.[19] Hence Oliba did not hesitate to display his name so that everyone could see it, both at the entrance to the basilica and on the silver altar-frontal:

Virginis hanc aulam sacravit Oliva beatam.
Hec domus est sancta **quam fecit domnus Oliva.**
+ + Coelitus accensus divini numins igne.[20]

+ Hoc altare sacrum Domini venerabile lignum
continet atque sui fragmen the mole sepulcri,
quod fide cum diva presul sacravit Oliva[21]

(At the entrance:)

Oliba consecrated this holy temple of the Virgin
This is the holy house **that Oliba made**
Inspired from Heaven by the divine will

(On the main altar:)

This venerable altar contains the Holy Rood of the Lord
as well as a fragment of the stone of his Sepulchre.
The bishop Oliba consecrated it with divine faith.

(translation: author)

Following a Neo-Platonist approach to art, Oliba presented himself as a true intellectual author who, having access to the divine will, was able to bring about the work of art. This is an ancient *topos* of Benedictine literature which describes its abbots as agents of the divine driving-force, and could even characterize them as angels, such as in the cases of Odo of Cluny (927–42) or Begon III of Conques (1087–1107). In this peculiar vision of the Father Abbot Oliba ('Abba pater'),[22] as *vir perfectus* (perfect man), celestial body and charismatic master, Ripoll became a type of showcase for the ideals of 11th-century monastic and cathedral schools, as discussed by Stephen Jaeger in his book *The Envy of Angels*.[23] Indeed, the abbot-bishop is described as recognisable as just such an angel by his face in a letter addressed to Oliba from Fleury in 1023 by Joan of Montserrat, a former monk of Ripoll: 'Angelus in facie semper dinosceris esse; pares cum luce, angelus in facie' ('Angel (you) will always be recognised by your face; with light, you are like an angel in your face').[24] It is not by chance that in his letter – sermon on the dedication of the new church of Cuixà in 1035, Garsias, a monk belonging to Oliba's entourage, describes

Garí (Warinus), the abbot responsible for finishing the first construction of the church in 974, as 'angelus vel caelestis homo' in order to praise his skills as *vir perfectus et charismaticus*:

> Eius in loco nempe rapitur, ut decuit, angelus vel caelestis homo Warinus identidem extruens basilica, parietes succinto opere in magnificencia fabricae cum admiratione mirabilis in sublime crexit, fastigia vero culminis proceritate simul trabium et ornamentorum claritudine illa venustissime operuit.[25]

In this same text, the author also mentioned a close collaborator of Abbot Oliba in the artistic enterprise of the restoration of the church of Sant Miquel de Cuixà in 1035: his namesake Oliba or Oliva,

> Itaque iuvit eum in omnibus quidam bonae famae monachus iter sequens magistri, ut ille Oliba, quique erat summae patientiae ac mansuetudinis vir, et sub eo vigilantissime in varias actiones tandem domum custodiebat.[26] (However, in all these things he was helped by a monk of good reputation, who followed in the steps of the master and was called Oliba (Oliva) like him. He was a man of great patience and gentleness, and under his watchful supervision in various activities he restored at length the house).

This monk should be identified with the master of *quadrivium* in the Ripoll abbey who stood out for being the author of a *Treatise on Music* (*Breviarium de musica* and *Versus monochordi*) (after 1036) (Barcelona, Arxiu de la Corona d'Aragó, Ms. Ripoll 42) and compiled a profusely illustrated compilation of *computus* and astronomy dated to 1055 (Città del Vaticano, Biblioteca Apostolica Vaticana, Ms. Reg. Lat. 123).[27] According to the sermon, the monk Oliva helped his master, Abbot Oliba, in all these things – 'iuvit eum in omnibus'–, but especially, as we can deduce from the aforementioned text, in the symbolism of one of the most innovative buildings of Cuixà: the famous circular and double-stored chapel located at the west end of the atrium. This had a lower crypt devoted to the Crib with side-chapels to the Archangels Gabriel and Raphael, and an upper level dedicated to the Trinity (Figure 12.3).[28] Indeed, it is not by chance that the passage with the mention of monk Oliva's accurate supervision directly follows the famous *ekphrasis* of this unique structure. Furthermore, it is no coincidence that the Trinitarian symbolism is also explicit in other works composed and signed by monk Oliva, *Breviarium de musica* and *Versus monochordi* (Barcelona, Arxiu de la Corona d'Aragó, ms. 42).[29] So, it is worth noting that the *prosopropeia* or commemorative signature of the manuscript containing these texts (f. 6r) – in which is mentioned the names of abbot Oliba as devisor of the work and those of the scribe (Arnaldus) and illustrator (Gualterus) – not only is accompanied on both sides by the word *Trinitas* (left) and the initials of the Holy Trinity in Greek (right) – P(ater), Vi(os), P(neuma) – but also preceded by a diagram depicting the tripartite division of music – *mundana, intrumentalis, humana*.[30]

In my opinion, this close collaboration between Oliba and his master of *quadrivium* can explain some

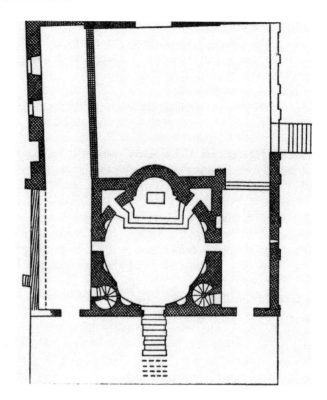

FIGURE 12.3

Saint-Michel de Cuxa, west-end of the atrium, ground plan of the church of the Trinity (M. Durliat, Roussillon roman, La Pierre-qui-vire)

peculiar numerical features of the architecture promoted by the abbot-bishop. Like Bernward at Saint Michael in Hildesheim,[31] Oliba's interest in the *quadrivium* (arithmetic, geometry, music and astronomy) seems to have extended to applying the principles of Boethius to this new architecture. For instance, the measures of the plan of the Ripoll basilica – 40 by 60 m – are based the sesquialtera proportion (2:3) (Figure 12.4), a well-known Boethian proportion related to the golden ratio that is explained in the *Treatise on Music* and accompanied by a schematic drawing (f. 10r).[32] Furthermore, the series of arches and columns of the new hypostyle halls of the crypts in Saint-Martin du Canigou (1009), the cathedral of Vic (1038) and Sant Vicenç de Cardona (1040) (Figure 12.5) seem to evoke numerical rhythms of even numbers such as that depicted in the 11th-century copy of Boethius's *De Arithmetica* made in the monastery (Barcelona, Arxiu de la Corona d'Aragó, Ms. Ripoll 168, f. 69r) (Figure 12.6).[33] Compelling evidence of this interest in making explicit Boethian arithmetic in the structure of the buildings is the depiction of the Temple of Solomon in the Ripoll Bible (Città del Vaticano, Biblioteca Apostolica Vaticana, Ms. Lat. 5729, f. 95v) (Figure 12.7). As the archetype of divine measures and proportions, the illuminator drew it as a large hypostyle hall in which rounded arches intersect like those in the *differentie pares* in the above-mentioned drawing.

It is worth noting that Oliba was not only concerned with presenting himself as the wise builder of those

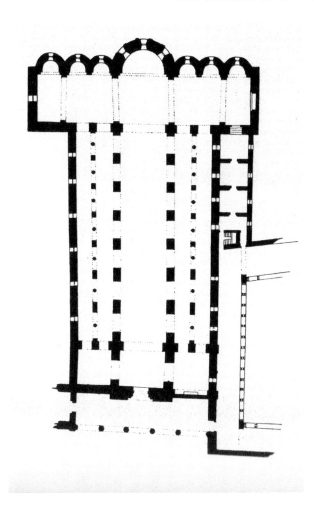

FIGURE 12.4

Ripoll: Santa Maria, ground plan (after Whitehill, Spanish Romanesque Architecture of the Eleventh Century)

FIGURE 12.5

Cardona: Sant Vicenç: crypt, 1040 (Manuel Castiñeiras)

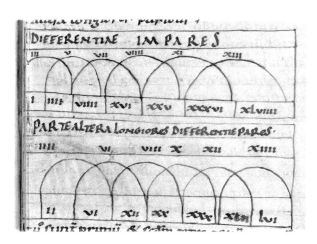

FIGURE 12.6

Barcelona, Arxiu de la Corona d'Aragó, MS Ripoll 168, f. 69r. Boethius, De Arithmetica, drawing with differentiae impares (upper) et pares (lower), eleventh century (© Barcelona, Arxiu de la Corona d'Aragó)

monuments directly related to him, such as Ripoll ('Praesul Oliva sacram struxit hic funditus aulam'), Cuixà or Vic – true indexes of Oliba's agency-, but also in being actively involved in a large number of buildings. Probably his participation in the first consecrations of Saint-Martin du Canigou (1009), Sant Pere de Rodes (1022), Girona Cathedral (1038) or Sant Vicenç de Cardona (1040) (Figure 12.5) can be related, particularly the latter three, to his role as bishop of Vic. The diocese claimed from the second half of the 10th century to be the successor of the metropolitan see of Tarragona in expectation of the eagerly-awaited re-conquest of that city.

It is very likely that his patronage provided a prestigious model for the laity. Among his major works were the now-destroyed lavish furnishings of the high altar of the monastery church of Santa Maria de Ripoll in 1032, especially a golden altar frontal decorated with precious stones and sixteen enamels, whose sides were covered by two smaller panels in silver: 'In primis, in altare sancte Dei genitricis Marie tabulam coopertam auro cum lapidibus et esmaltis XVI; tabulas cooperta argento II.'[34] It is not by chance that a few years later, in 1038, the Countess Ermessenda (c. 975–1058), sister of the Girona prelate, Pere Roger (1010–50) – both members of the comital family of Carcassone – and widow of Ramón Borrell II, Count of Barcelona, donated an enormous quantity of gold (300 *uncias*) for the construction of a golden frontal, during the consecration ceremony of Girona cathedral in presence of Oliba: 'ad honorem Dei et matris ecclesie trecentas auri contulit uncias ad auream construendam tabulam'.[35]

From the description made by J. Villanueva at the beginning of the 19th century, we know that this golden panel centered on a great mandorla enclosing the Virgin

FIGURE 12.7

Rome, Biblioteca Apostolica Vaticana, MS Lat. 5729, f. 95v (Ripoll Bible): Temple of Solomon (1027–32) (© Biblioteca Apostolica Vaticana) see also colour plate XII

FIGURE 12.8

Girona: Reconstruction drawing of the golden altar frontal of Girona Cathedral (Drawing: Ginés Baltrons)

Mary, surrounded by the four Evangelists in enamel and *tituli*, as well as thirty-two compartments in *cloisonné* enamel depicting the life of Christ (Figure 12.8).[36] This raises a number of questions: were the enamels of the golden frontal of Ripoll decorated with these same subjects? Were the models for these scenes taken from the New Testament cycle in the Ripoll Bible? At the foot of the central mandorla of the Virgin there were the names of the female patrons: 'Ermensindis' and 'Gisla cometissa fieri jussit' ('Countess Gisla ordered to make (this work)'). While the first was simply carved on a seal in chalcedony, the second surrounded an enamel with a seated portrait of the Countess Guisla de Lluçà (d. 1079). She was the second wife of Berenguer Ramon I (d. 1035), the son of Ermessenda and the count of Barcelona. After the death of the count, Guisla married Udalard II, viscount of Barcelona in 1037. Guisla probably offered the golden altar frontal to Girona cathedral with her former mother-in-law, between 1038, the date when the high altar was consecrated, and 1041, the year her step-son Ramon Berenguer I (1023–76), who was heir to the county and who was protected by Ermessenda, came of age.[37]

THE CHURCH AS A BRIDE: ARISTOCRATIC LINAGE AND FEMALE PATRONAGE'S AESTHETICS

The ubiquitous and varied role of women in the patronage of 11th-century Catalan art is also worth underlining and characterising. Ermessenda (972–1058), mentioned above, was very involved in financing the construction of Girona cathedral. First, together with her husband, in 1015 she paid the large amount of 100 golden *uncias* to buy the church of Sant Daniel at Girona from her brother, Pere Roger, bishop of Girona, who had started the new cathedral around 1010 and needed, according to this record, money to renew the covering of the cathedral church. A few years later, in 1018, Ermessenda founded a Benedictine nunnery at Sant Daniel with an important gift for the salvation of the soul of her husband, who had recently died in 1017.[38] Finally, in 1038, she gave the enormous amount of 300 golden *uncias* for the altar-frontal of the Cathedral and decided to be buried in the Galilee of this new building.[39] This new financial capacity resulted from the Catalan sack of Cordoba in 1010, after the collapse of the Caliphate, and the consequent expeditions of her husband to the valleys of the Ebro and Segre in 1015–16. So, as regent of the county of Barcelona and recipient of tributes from the Taifa Kingdom of Zaragoza, she had a seal in chalcedony showing a double signature in Latin and Arabic – which was precisely that set in the golden frontal of the cathedral of Girona[40] – and she used to enjoy playing chess with lavish Fatimid crystal chess pieces which she assigned in her will to the church of Saint-Gilles at Nîmes.

Aristocratic women played an important role in the making of the new feudal society as guarantors of the stability of a lineage as well as in alliances between members of the warrior class. The Church was extremely interested in protecting women. Furthermore, aristocratic women controlled the dowry they received from their fathers, and were given a special letter of marital donation or agreement (*scriptura donationis causa sponsalitii*), in which the husband gave to his wife a third of his heritage.[41] It seems that they freely used this dowry in the promotion or patronage of works of art as we have just seen in the cases of Ermessenda or Guisla of Llucà.[42] In the same years, another countess, Guisla of Cerdanya made an important gift of lands and textiles to Saint-Martin du Canigou, then under construction.[43] Finally, at the end of the century, it is very likely that the Norman princess Mahaut or Matilde (1060–1112), following female models such as Ermessenda and Guisla in Girona, or even her mother Sikelgaita at Montecassino, protected the Benedictine nunnery of Sant Daniel in order to make a special gift to Girona Cathedral of the Creation Tapestry made around 1097 (Figure 12.9).[44] This huge embroidery might have commemorated the coming of age of her son, Ramon Berenguer III, and celebrated the alliance between the reformed Gregorian Church and the new count of Barcelona and eventually was used as an Easter cloth – probably a ceremonial carpet – for the liturgy of the cathedral.[45]

This extraordinary item opens a new topic: the production of textiles by women in nunneries for the furnishing of altars, and the remarkable presence of the names of women on those fabrics as authors, as on the Stole of Saint Narcissus (MARIA ME FECIT) (c. 1038) (Figure 12.10) in the church of Sant Feliu in Girona or on the Saint Odo Banner (c. 1133–34) at the Cathedral of Urgell (ELISAVA ME FECIT).[46] On the one hand, this might be related to the legendary model of the Virgin Mary embroidering the Purple and the Scarlet of the Veil of the Temple of Jerusalem as is told in the Protoevangelion of St James (11:1).[47] Moreover, the sacred and biblical status of liturgical vestments as part of the new Ark of Covenant (altar) and Temple of Jerusalem (church) was especially highlighted in the liturgical texts in use during this period in Catalonia.[48] This is evident from the Narbonais-Catalan *Ordo* used in the Catalan dioceses as suffragans of the archbishopric of Narbonne until 1120–25. In the rite of consecration of the *Sacramentary, Ritual and Pontifical of Roda d'Isàvena* (Arxiu Capitular de Lleida, Ms. Re-0036, around 1000–18), the cloths covering the altar are compared to the embroideries made by Virgin Mary to adorn the *sancta sanctorum* of the Temple of Jerusalem: '(lintemina) que maria texuit et fecit in usum ministerii tabernaculis federis' ('cloths that Mary weaved and made to be used at the service of the covenant of Tabernacle').[49]

On the other hand, the charters made on the occasion of the consecration of a church, known in Catalonia as *dotalies*, were made following formulae used for marriage agreements, in which the patron gave a dowry to the church thus metaphorically marrying Christ.[50] In this connection, one might understand the preference of women such as Ermessenda, Guisla of Lluçà, Guisla of Cerdanya or Matilde for metalwork and textiles in their generous donations to the churches. Their precious gifts can be seen as a gender metaphor that expresses their identification with the role of Church as a bride.

Figure 12.9

Girona Cathedral Treasury: Creation Tapestry (c. 1097) (© Capítol Catedral de Girona) see also colour plate XIII

Figure 12.10

Girona: Sant Feliu; Stole of Saint Narcissus, c. 1038 (Manuel Castiñeiras)

UNDER THE SEAL OF THE GREGORIAN REFORM: PRINCELY PROGRAMMES AND DOGMATIC CHOICES AROUND 1100

At this point, it is worth noting that until the end of the comital period in 1137 – year of the union with the Crown of Aragon – Catalonia was not a centre but a periphery. Being outside the orbit of the major royal powers, and therefore without a courtly art, the *Marca Hispanica* remained distant from the artistic centres of Carolingian and Post-Carolingian art. Besides, it was without a true metropolitan see sited in its territory until the conquest of Tarragona from the Muslims in 1116–17 and the subsequent reestablishment of the ancient archdiocese in 1118. Hence, as has been seen, from the very outset the local Church, together with the lay magnates, promoted artistic patronage in an attempt to shore up their ecclesiastical and political status, based on their alliance with the Papacy. It is true that the Bishop-Abbot Oliba and his comital entourage had been able to lead in the first half of the 11th century what M. Zimmermann has defined as the Catalan *mini-renaissance classique*,[51] which is distinguished by very specific and peculiar features in architecture, manuscript illumination and written culture. However, in the third quarter of the century this inner phenomenon waned and a new external movement seems to have replaced it: that of the Gregorian Reform, in which the Roman Church took over the leadership of the Christian society and tried to promote dogmatic programmes based on the primacy of *Sacerdotium* over *Regnum*. Well-known examples such as that of Odo, bishop of La Seu d'Urgell (1095–1122) and his relatives, the Counts of Pallars, or that of Ramon, bishop of Roda de Isàvena (1104–1126), all eloquently demonstrate the transformation of the monumental arts during the late 11th and early 12th centuries, as well as the role of extensive painted figurative cycles as a privileged medium to display new content.

It is highly likely that the impressive Creation Tapestry that is kept in the Treasury of Girona cathedral was an attempt to combine the old and new trends of Catalan art. On the one hand, its rich repertoire of images, which mostly derived from biblical and astronomical manuscripts, witnesses the survival, at the end of the century, of the prestige of the monastic culture that had flourished at Ripoll some decades before.[52] Furthermore, the offering of an embroidery to enrich the liturgical furniture of the high altar connects with the long tradition of Catalan countesses to adorn the church as a bride. Notwithstanding this, the Creation Tapestry announces a new era of Catalan art, in which monumental pictorial programmes are used to express the leading role of the Church in society and the compromise of the comital houses to it.

To this extent, it is worth mentioning that in 1097, the Papal Legate, Bernard de Sedirac, archbishop of Toledo, presided over a Council in Girona to promote the pact between the new Count of Barcelona, Ramon Berenguer III (1097–1131), and the Count of Pallars, Artaud II (1081–1126), to conquer Tortosa and Tarragona.[53] It presupposed a new dynamic in the relationships between Rome and the Catalan counties in which the making of the Creation Tapestry – a true princely programme – can be seen as a political manifesto. In this respect, I have elsewhere tried to underline the implications of the exceptional depictions of Hercules (Figure 12.11), Samson (Figure 12.12) and Constantine in the embroidery and their possible relationship with the iconography of the Throne of St Peter (*Cathedra Petri*) and the political theories of the Gregorian Reform that were developed in this council.[54] Similarly, the bishop's throne in Girona (Figure 12.13) might belong to the same initiative and should be understood as a direct reference to the episcopal thrones of Norman southern Italy in Salerno, Canosa and Bari.[55] Moreover, the inclusion of a semi-nude Hercules bearing a lion skin close to a tree in the iconographic programme of the Creation Tapestry should be understood as an explicit reference to the Garden of the Hesperides. The alleged location of this eleventh Labour of the Greek hero in Hispania nourished the imagination of geographers and historians during the whole of the Middle Ages. They identified Hesperia with the Iberian Peninsula and Hercules became the mythical founder of many cities in these lands such as Barcelona or Urgell.[56] It is not a coincidence that in those years the Norman chronicle *Gesta Roberti Wiscardi* written by Willian of Apulia referred to Ramon Berenguer II, father of Ramon Berenguer III, as from the Hesperides ('partibus Esperiae'),[57] when he travelled to Southern Italy in 1078 in order to request a blessing for his marriage to the Italo-Norman princess, Matilde, who would eventually be the patron of the Creation Tapestry. As result, the exceptional presence of Hercules in the Tapestry highlights the leading role of the

FIGURE 12.11

Girona Cathedral Treasury: Creation Tapestry (c. 1097): Upper border, right side: Hercules ([Manuel Castiñeiras] © Capítol Catedral de Girona)

FIGURE 12.12

Girona Cathedral Treasury: Creation Tapestry (c. 1097): upper border, left side: Samson ([Manuel Castiñeiras] © Capítol Catedral de Girona)

FIGURE 12.13

Girona Cathedral: Episcopal throne (c. 1097) (Manuel Castiñeiras)

Count of Barcelona in the Christian Reconquista under the protection of the Church. Ultimately, the inclusion of Hercules was not only a reference to his mythical origins but also an example of *virtu*s and strength for any Christian ruler whose biblical prototype was Samson.[58]

It is not by chance that at the very same moment, in the other branch of the Catalan alliance in 1097, the County of Pallars-Sobirà, one can notice the emergence of a new art based on similar compromises between lay rulers and the Church, whose artistic language is deeply rooted in Roman and southern Italian sources. I am here referring to the mural paintings of San Pere del Burgal (1097–1106), currently kept in the Museu Nacional d'Art de Catlunya (MNAC 113138), that have been related to the activity of the so-called Master of Pedret workshop (Figure 12.14).[59] As many scholars have pointed out, the depiction of three lay figures occupied the lower part of the area of the central apse, with that of the Countess Lucy of Pallars (also known as Lucia de la Marca, † 1090) bearing a candle on the right side ((LUC)IA CONMITESA) (Figure 12.15), while other members of her family are represented in the left outer wall of the apse entrance (Figure 12.16). J. Ainaud was the first scholar to identify the standing female figure on the right as a depiction of Countess Lucy in the 1960s. As this was only the lay portrait belonging to the set visible at the time, Ainaud proposed that the paintings should be dated between 1081 and 1090, a period in which Lucy was involved in the county government after the death of his husband, Artaud I.[60] However, during the restoration carried out in the year

Figure 12.14

Mural paintings from the central apse of Sant Pere del Burgal (c. 1097–1106): middle and lower register (Barcelona MNAC, 113138 © Museu Nacional d'Art de Catalunya. Foto: Calveras/Mérida/Sagristà)

Figure 12.15

Mural paintings from the central apse of Sant Pere del Burgal (c. 1097–1106): funerary portrait of Lucy, countess of Pallars, bearing a candle.(Barcelona MNAC, 113138 © Museu Nacional d'Art de Catalunya. Foto: Calveras/Mérida/Sagristà) see also colour plate XIV

1998, a new layer of paintings depicting a religious man and a lay woman came to light on the left side of the outer wall of the entrance to the apse.[61]

It is obvious that these new findings raised new questions on the identity of the portraits, as well as on the date of the setting. First, it made sense that the isolated figure of Lucy had the privilege of being in the most sacred space of the apse, at the foot of the apostles, because it acted not as a portrayal of a woman alive but as a funerary portrait.[62] Second, her candle reminds us of the iconography of the Wise Virgins at Pedret (Figure 12.17) and, consequently, that she has already reached the delights of Paradise (Mat. 25:13).

In front of the altar, facing the aisles, there are the depictions of her son, Odo, the bishop of La Seu d'Urgell (1095–1122), and probably her daughter-in-law, Eslonça, the new countess of Pallars.[63] Both of them had showed a special devotion to the memory of the dead: Eslonça and her husband Artaud II gave a rent to the comital monastery of Santa Maria del Gerri to light a candle for their ancestors in 1099, while in 1106 Saint Odo favoured in the same monastery a lay confraternity for the remembrance of the patrons and the comital family. To this extent, it is worth noting that although Sant Pere del Burgal had been given at the beginning of the 9th century to the abbey of La Grassa, the monastery of Santa Maria of Gerri claimed its property.[64] So, it is highly likely that the iconographic programme of the paintings of El Burgal, with a depiction of the comital

FIGURE 12.16

Mural paintings from the outer wall (left side) of the entrance to the central apse of Sant Pere del Burgal, (c. 1097–1106): depictions of Eslonça, wife of count Artaud II of Pallars (?), and Odo, bishop of Urgell (?); Sant Pere del Burgal (Photo Laia Pérez)

family, was probably made between 1097 and 1106 as a means of highlighting the monastery's fidelity to the members of the house of Pallars-Sobirà and their ecclesiastical policy in order to keep their protection against the pretentions of El Gerri.

If the depiction of the comital family occupied the lower register of the paintings, the Church is displayed in the central register of the apse. It shows the Church of the Gregorian Reform, especially evoked by the depiction of a *synthronon* where some of the Apostles, the Virgin and Saint John the Baptist are seated. All the subjects are designed to stress their relationship to the principles of the Gregorian Reform as regards the primacy of the Pope or the defence of the dogma of the real presence of Christ in the Eucharist, against the ideas of Berenger of Tours.[65] So, the Byzantine iconography of the Deesis, where Mary and John the Baptist acted as mediators before God, became a means for emphasizing the Eucharist through the attributes held by Mary-Ecclesia (the chalice containing the blood of Christ) and Saint John the Baptist (the clipeus with the Lamb of God). Likewise, the depiction of the Apostles is a pretext for highlighting the central role of the visible heads of the Roman Church, Saint Peter (bearing the keys) and Saint Paul.[66]

EPILOGUE

From that time onward, the Catalan sees seem to adopt a policy to update their institutions in many fields, abandoning the old-fashioned Catalan-Narbonnais liturgy for the Roman liturgy, reforming their collegiate chapters and transforming or redecorating their buildings. Both Saint Odo at Urgell (1095–1122)[67] and Saint Ramon at Roda d'Isàvena (1104–26),[68] two contemporary prelates and rivals, are very good examples of this process.

FIGURE 12.17

Mural paintings from the south apse of Sant Quirze de Pedret, left side: Wise Virgins (c. 1097–1117) (Barcelona MNAC, 15973 © Museu Nacional d'Art de Catalunya. Foto: Calveras/Mérida/Sagristà)

Another fascinating topic related to the decade of the 1120s is the development of panel painting techniques under the wing of great ecclesiastic centres such as Ripoll, Vic or Urgell, whose institutions, being the repository of the necessary technical knowledge and a long-standing tradition of illumination, oversaw the work and training of the painters. These workshops, probably located in the actual cathedral or monastery buildings and formed by ecclesiastical painters (*clerici*), supplied the parishes of the diocese or of the territory of the abbey with liturgical furnishings (altar frontals, beams and canopies) that

ensured liturgically enriched worship and helped spread the dogma. They were clearly relatively cheap objects when compared with the magnificence of the great metalwork altars of the great production centres, but they were sufficiently eye-catching to contribute to the aesthetic of the Christian mystery of the Incarnation.[69]

Although the territorial expansion of the county of Barcelona and its incorporation into the Crown of Aragon in the middle of the 12th century marked a new era and dimension for Catalan art, many outstanding examples of the figurative arts at the period should be seen as a revival of earlier trends, or more specifically an extension of these earlier traditions into new media. This is the case, for instance, of the 'triumphal' Portal at Ripoll (1134–50), which epitomised all the traditions of the old monastic school of Ripoll (illumination, panel painting and the classical heritage) into the new language of monumental sculpture.[70]

ACKNOWLEDGEMENTS

I am indebted to John McNeill and Richard Plant for their help and patient editorial work. This contribution is the fruit of research developed for the projects carried out at the Universitat Autònoma de Barcelona: *Artistas, Patronos y Público. Cataluña y el Mediterráneo (siglos XI-XV)-MAGISTRI CATALONIAE* (MICINN-HAR 2 0 1 1–2 3 0 15) and *Movilidad y transferencia artística en el Mediterráneo medieval, 1187–1388: artisas, objetos y modelos.-MAGISTRI MEDITERRANEI* (MICINN- HAR2015–63883-P).

NOTES

[1] J.-A. Adell i Gisbert, 'L'aparició dels *Magistri Comacini* a Catalunya. Aspectes tecnològics i d'organització', in *Els "comacini" i l'arquitectura romànica a Catalunya*, ed. P. Freixas and J. Camps (Barcelona 2010), 51–59.

[2] P. Ponsich, 'Les tables d'autel à lobes de la province ecclésiastique de Narbonne (X–XIè siècles) et l'avènement de la sculpture monumentale en Roussillon', *Les Cahiers de Saint-Michel de Cuxa*, XIII (1982), 7–45

[3] P. Klein, 'Les Portails de Saint-Genis-des-Fontaines et de Saint-André-de-Sorède, *Les Cahiers de Saint-Michel de Cuxa,* 20 (1989), 121–59. See also: M. Durliat, *Roussillon roman* (Saint-Léger-Vauban 1958), 114–23; M. Durliat, 'L'apparition du grand portail roman historié dans le Midi de la France et le Nord de l'Espagne', *Les Cahiers de Saint-Michel de Cuxa*, 8 (1977), 7–24, at 9; O. Poisson, 'Le linteau dans la façade: note sur les portails de Saint-Genis-des-Fontaines et de Saint-André (Roussillon)", *Les Cahiers de Saint-Michel de Cuxa*, 45 (2014), 197–209 (with a state of the question).

[4] A. Trivellone, 'Le développement du décor monumental et la conquête de l'extérieur des églises: *sagreres* et façades catalanes au cours de la première moitié du XIè siècle, *Les Cahiers de Fanjeaux*, 46 (2011), 175–207.

[5] The holy ground of the *sagrera* or *cellera* usually encompassed a cemetery and a group of cellars in which parishioners kept their crops, A. Catafau, 'Paroisse et *cellera* dans le diocese d'Elne Xè–XIIè siècles', *Les Cahiers de Saint-Michel de Cuxa*, 20 (1999), 91–100. See also, A. Catafau, *Les celleres et la naissance du village en Rousssillon (Xè–XVè siècles)* (Perpignan 1998).

[6] E. Junyent, *Diplomatari i escrits literaris de l'abat Oliba*, ed. A. Mundó (Barcelona, 1995), doc. n. 92, p. 145.

[7] E. Junyent, *Esbós biogràfic del comte, abat i bisbe Oliba*, ed. R. Ordeig (Barcelona 2008), 11–14.

[8] M. Castiñeiras, 'Ripoll et Gérone, deux exemples privilégiés du dialogue entre l'art roman et la culture classique', *Les Cahiers de Sain-Michel de Cuxa*, 39 (2008), 161–80, at 161–70. For a general study of the library of Ripoll abbey during the office of Oliba, see R. Beer, *Los manuscrits del monestir de Santa Maria de Ripoll* (Barcelona 1909) (Butlletí de l'Acadèmia de Bones Lletres); M.E. Ibarburu, 'L'escriptori de Santa Maria di Ripoll i els seus manuscrits', in *Catalunya Romànica. X. El Ripollès* (Barcelona 1987), 276–82; M. Zimmermann, *Écrire et lire en Catalogne (IXè–XIIè siècle)*, II, Paris, 2003, 674 ff.

[9] *Chronica Monasterii Casinesis*, II, 19, in *Patrologia Latina*, 173, ed. J-P. Migne (Paris 1895), cols. 605–06.

[10] R, de Abadal, *L'abat Oliba, bisbe de Vic, i la seva època* (Barcelona 1948), 81–95.

[11] X. Barral, 'Culture visuelle et réflexion architecturale au début du XIè siècle: les voyages de l'abbé-évêque Oliba (2è partie)', *Cahiers de Saint-Michel de Cuxa*, 41 (2010), 211–26. See also my comments on this topic in: 'La cuestión lombarda en el primer románico catalán', in *Il Medieoevo delle Cattedrali. Chiesa e Imperio: la lotta delle immagini (secoli XI e XII)*, ed. A.C. Quintavalle (Università di Parma- Milano 2006), 345–55, at 352–53.

[12] For this liturgical furniture and their intepretation, see my contribution: 'El altar románico y su mobiliario litúrgico: frontales, vigas y baldaquinos', in *Mobiliario y ajuar litúrgico en las Iglesias románicas*, ed. P.L. Huerta (Aguilar de Campoo 2011), 9–76, at 45–47.

[13] M. Castiñeiras, 'From Chaos to Cosmos: the Creation Iconography in the Catalan Romanesque Bibles', *Arte medievale*, Nuova Serie, 1 (2002), 35–50 ; M. Castiñeiras, 'Le Nouveau Testament de la Bible de Ripoll et les anciennes traditions de l'iconographie chrétienne: du *scriptorium* de l'abbé Oliba à la peinture romane sur bois', *Les Cahiers de Saint-Michel de Cuxa*, 40 (2009), 145–64.

[14] For the text of the Life of St Pancras, see: C. Mango, *The Art of the Byzantine Empire, 312–1453* (Englewood Cliffs, N.J., 1972), 137 ff. For the Catalan Bibles of Ripoll and Rodes as a collection or catalogue of images, see: M. Castiñeiras and I. Lorés, 'Las Biblias de Rodes i Ripoll: una encrucijada del arte románico en Catalunya', in M. Guardia, C. Mancho (eds) *Les fonts de la pintura romànica*, Ars Picta. Temes, 1 (Barcelona 2008), 219–60.

[15] M. Castiñeiras, 'De l'obra vista al revestiment de l'arquitectura: l'església pintada a la Catalunya romànica', in *Els "comacini"* (as n. 1), 133–49, at 134–39; M. Castiñeiras, 'The Portal at Ripoll Revisited: An Honorary Arch for the Ancestors', in *Romanesque and the Past,* ed. J. McNeill, R. Plant (Leeds 2013), 121–42, at 124–27.

[16] I prefer to use here the term 'agency' instead of 'patronage' following Alfred Gell's book: *Art and Agency. An Anthropological Theory* (Oxford and New York 2010). Gell's art theory places the emphasis on 'agency' – action or intervention producing a particular effect- to understand the status of art objects. As a result art is seen as 'a system of action, intended to change the world rather to encode symbolic propositions about it' (p. 6), and hence it must be conceptualised in social terms. Indexes (material entities), prototypes (objects or persons that indexes represent or stand for), artists (intermediate causes or authors of the index) and recipients (those who are affected by indexes) are the elements that conform to the different parts of what he calls the art nexus, in which agency is always mediated by indexes. The formula *Recipient as Agent/ Index as Patient* is the elementary relation of patronage, in which the patron regards himself as the author (p. 33). In my opinion, this is clearly the formula that defines Oliba's artistic agency.

[17] Junyent, *Diplomatari* (as n. 6), doc. 65, p. 101.

[18] Junyent, *Diplomatari* (as n. 6), doc. 19, p. 333.

[19] 'Auctor ab augendo dictus' (*Auctor* – promotor- derives from *augere* : to develop or carry out), Isidore of Seville, *Etymologies*, X, 2, ed. J. Oroz Reta, M-A., Marcos Casquero (Madrid 1993), vol. I, 802–03. For the peculiar concept *of auctor* and *auctoritas* as someone or something that is worthy to be imitated, see: A.J. Minnis, *Medieval Theory of Authorship* (Aldershot 1984), 9–12; E. Palazzo, 'Le portrait d'auteur dans les manuscrits du Moyen Âge', in M.Bobin (ed.) *Portraits d'écrivains. La representation de l'auteur dans les manuscrits et les imprimés du Moyen Âge et de la première Renaissance* (Poitiers 2002), 21–34, at 21. See also Gell, *Art and Agency* (as n.16) for a formula of patronage as authorship.

[20] Barcelona, Arxiu de la Corona d'Aragó, Ms. 46, f. 21r. Cf. Junyent, *Diplomatari* (as n. 6), doc. 5, 308–09.

[21] This text was copied by Jaume Pujol, priest of Olot, between 1543–47, in a manuscript that belongs to Mr. Mascaró from Vilafranca del Penedès, J. Ainaud, 'Una inscripció inèdita en vers de l'escola de Ripoll', *Estudis Romànics* 8 (1961), 21–23; Junyent, *Diplomatari* (as n. 6), doc. 4, 308.

[22] The loving expression 'Abba Pater' to address Oliba was used in a letter dated to 1023 by the monk of Fleury, Joan, who earlier had been brought up in Ripoll abbey together with Oliba and later became abbot of Santa Cecília de Montserrat before entering Fleury, Junyent, *Diplomatari* (as n. 6), doc. 13, 324.

[23] C.S. Jaeger, *The Envy of Angels. Cathedral Schools and Social Ideas in Medieval Europe, 950–1200* (Philadelphia 1994), 21–25, 76–81. According to Saint Augustine's *De civitate dei* (XI, 29), angels as part of the divine Light can participate in the Wisdom of God and know better than anyone the art of Creation, *Angelic Spirituality. Medieval Perspectives on the Ways of Angels,* ed. S. Chase, E.H. Cousins (New York 2002), 89–90

[24] Junyent, *Diplomatari* (as n. 6), doc. 13, 324–25.

[25] Junyent, *Diplomatari* (as n. 6), doc. 28, 369–86, at 372. The letter-sermon of Garsias of Cuixà was written in 1043–44 and addressed to abbot Oliba as a reminder of the sermon that the latter had given in 1035 on the occasion of the restoration of the church:, see M. Zimmermann, 'Sur la terre comme au ciel: la paix chrétienne. Oliba (1008–46), pacificateur et guide des âmes', *Les Cahiers de Saint-Michel de Cuxa,* 40 (2009), 7–38, at 35–36; R. Ordeig i Mata, 'La documentació del monestir de Cuixà referent a Oliba i als anys del seu abadiat', *Les Cahiers de Saint-Michel de Cuxa* 40 (2009), 39–51, at 46–50. A French translation of the sermon is available: D. Codina, P. Bourgain, M. Besseyre, 'Lettre-sermon du moine Garsias de Cuxa à l'abbé Oliba', *Les Cahiers de Saint-Michel de Cuxa*, 40 (2009), 65–76.

[26] Junyent, *Diplomatari* (as n. 6), 379. See also: J. Puig i Cadafalch et alii, *L'arquitectura romànica a Catalunya*, vol. II (Barcelona 1911), 70, n.2; H. Anglès, *La música a Catalunya fins al segle XII* (Barcelona 1935), 66; M. Castiñeiras, 'Diagramas y esquemas cosmográficos en dos misceláneas de cómputo y astronomía de la abadía de Santa Maria de Ripoll (ss. XI–XII)', *Compostellanum*, 43 (1998), 593–646, at 602.

[27] Castiñeiras, 'Diagramas' (as n. 26), 594–620. Cf. A. García Avilés, *El tiempo y los astros. Arte, ciencia y religión en la alta Edad Media* (Universidad de Murcia 2001), 143–129.

[28] For the liturgical and iconographical interpretation of this building, see: A. Orriols, 'Les imatges preliminars dels evangelis de Cuixà (Perpinyà, Bibl. Mun. ms. 1)', *Locus Amoenus* 2 (1996), 31–46; M. Gros, 'Le culte des trois Archanges et de la Trinité à l'abbaye de Saint-Michel de Cuxa', *Études Roussillonnaises* 21 (2005), 93–98; D. Codina, 'La chapelle de la Trinité de Saint-Michel de Cuxa. Conception théologique et symbolique d'une architecture singulière', *Les Cahiers de Saint-Michel de Cuxa* 36 (2005), 81–88; E. Palazzo, 'Liturgie et symbolisme de l'espace rituel au temps d'Oliba', *Les Cahiers de Saint-Michel de Cuxa* 60 (2009), 77–89, at 79–82.

[29] K-W. Gümpel, "El Breviarium de Musica i els Versus monochordi del monjo Oliba de Ripoll", *Miscel·lània Litúrgica Catalana* 12 (2004), 23–57.

[30] Junyent, *Diplomatari* (as n. 6), doc. 7, 310; F. Rico, *Figuras con paisaje* (Barcelona 1994), 142–43.

[31] C. Heitz, 'Vitruve et l'architecture du haut Moyen Age', in *La cultura antica nell'Occidente latino dal VII all'XI secolo* (XXII Settimana di Studio del Centro di Studio sull'Alto Medioevo, 14–24 aprile 1974), II (Spoleto 1975), 725–752, at 749–50.

[32] Rico, *Figuras* (as n. 30), 139–41. See also: E. Tarracó, 'Le Portail de Ripoll: Symbologie, Style et Mathématique', *Les Cahiers de Saint-Michel de Cuxa,* 8 (1977), 69–92, at 85.

[33] M. Castiñeiras, 'Pensar con imágenes: los clásicos ilustrados en las bibliotecas de Ripoll y Vic en el siglo XI. Pervivencia y vivencia de la cultura visual antigua', in *Patrimonio artística de Galicia y otros estudios. Homenaje al Prof. Dr. Serafín Moralejo Álvarez*, vol. III, ed. A. Franco Mata (Santiago de Compostela 2004), 47–56, at 54–56, figs. 12–13; Castiñeiras, 'Ripoll et Gérone (as n. 8), 167–168, figs. 11–12.

[34] Junyent, *Diplomatari* (as n. 6), 396. Cf. Castiñeiras, 'El altar románico' (as n. 12), p. 45.

[35] R. Ordeig I Mata, *Les dotalies de les esglésies de Catalunya (segles IX–XII). II. Introducció. Documents 121–276 (segle XI). Primera part* (Vic 1996), doc. n. 160, p. 84

[36] J. Villanueva, *Viage literario*, vol XII (Madrid 1850), appendix XCIII, p. 180–82; F.A. Merino, J. de la Canal, *España Sagrada*, vol. XLV (Madrid, 1832), 8–9; J. Gudiol i Cunill, *Els Primitius. II. La pintura sobre fusta* (Barcelona, 1929), 26–29; J. Folch i Torres, *La pintura romànica sobre fusta* (Barcelona, 1956), 124.

[37] M. Castiñeiras, 'The Making of the Catalan Romanesque Altar Frontal (1119–50): Issues of Technical Training, Authorship and Patronage', in *Image and Altar, 800–1300, Papers for an International Conference in Copenhagen, 24 October-27 October 2007,* ed. Poul Grinder-Hansen (PNM, Publications from the National Museum Studies in Archeology and History, XX) (Copenhagen 2014), 97–120, at 99–100

[38] M. Marquès, *Col·lecció diplomàtica de Sant Daniel de Girona (924–1300),* doc. n. 5 (1015 June 8) and n. 6 (1018 March 16) (Barcelona 1997), 61–62, 63–66.

[39] M. Sureda, 'Architecture autour d'Oliba: le massif occidental de la cathédrale de Gérone', *Les Cahiers de Saint-Michel de Cuxa* XL, 2009, 221–36, at 224. See also: F. Español, 'Massifs occidentaux dans l'architecture romane catalane', *Les Cahiers de Saint-Michel de Cuxa* 28 (1996), 55–77, at 73.

[40] F. Español, J. Yarza, *El romànic català,* (Manresa 2007), 41. See also: J. Marqués Casanovas, 'El frontal de oro de la Seo de Gerona', *Anales del Instituto de Estudios Gerundenses* XIII (1959), 213–31; M. Sureda, *La catedral de Girona* (Madrid 2005), p. 84.

[41] M. Aurell, *Les noces del comte. Matrimoni i poder a Catalunya (785–1213),* (Barcelona 1998), 102–04, 111–17.

[42] Aurell, *Les noces del comte* (as n. 41), 226–27.

[43] F. Font, *Histoire de l'abbaye royale de Saint-Martin du Canigou (diocèse de Perpignan)* (Perpignan 1903), 33–35, 60–61

[44] M. Castiñeiras, 'Il Tappeto del Gigante: programma, cerimonia e committenza nell'Arazzo della Creazione di Girona', in *Medioevo: Natura e Figura. La raffigurazione dell'uomo e della natura nell'arte medievale,* ed. A.C. Quintavalle *(Actas del XIV Convegno Internazionale di Studi, Parma, 20–25 settembre 2011)* (Milan 2015), 359–78, at 373–74.

[45] Ramon Berenguer III turned 15 on 11 November 1097, and the council took place only some weeks later in Girona Cathedral, on 13 December, J.D. Mansi, *Sacrorum Conciliorum nova et amplissima,* vol. XIX (Venetiis 1774), cols 953–54: 'Anno Domine MXCVII Id. Decembris sub Bernardo archiepiscopus toletano apostolicae sedis legato celebratum est Gerundae concilium ad conrroborando ecclesiae libertatis dignitatem'); S. Sobrequés, *Els grans comtes de Barcelona* (Barcelona, 1969), 148–49; A. Benet., 'La tutoría de Ramon Berenguer III. La participació de Bernat Guillem de Queralt', *Quaderns d'Estudis Medievals* I, 7 (1982), 401–05, at 404. Cf. M. Castiñeiras, *The Creation Tapestry* (Girona 2011), 79–94; M. Castiñeiras, 'Le Tapis de la Création de Gérone: une oeuvre liée à la réforme gregorienne en Catalogne?', in *Art et réforme grégorienne en France et dans la Péninsule Ibérique,* ed. Barbara Franze (Paris 2015), 147–75, at 154–58.

[46] Castiñeiras, *The Creation Tapestry* (as n. 45), p. 36–40.

[47] For the topic of women, especially nuns, making cloths as imitation to Virgin Mary, there is an extensive literature: J. Hamburger, *Nuns as Artists. The Visual Culture of a Medieval Convent* (Berkeley 1997); E. Coatsworth, 'Cloth-making and the Virgin Mary in Anglo-Saxon literature and art', in *Medieval Art: Recent Perspectives. A Memorial Tribute to C. R. Dodwell*, G.R. Owen-Cracker, T. Graham (Manchester-New York 1998), 8–25; R. Parker, *The Subversive Stitch. Embroidery and the Making of the Feminine* (London 2010), 119–24; J. Ní Ghrádaigh, 'Mere Embroiderers? Women and Art in Early Medieval Ireland', in *Reassessing the Roles of Women as 'Makers' of Medieval Art and Architecture*, ed. T. Martin (Turnhout 2012), 93–125; S. Seeberg, 'Women as Makers of Church Decoration: illustrated textiles at the monasteries of Altenberg/Lahn, Rupertsberg, and Heiningen (13th-14th c.)', in *Reassessing the Roles of Women.* 356–91. See also. E. Fernández González, 'El artesano medieval y la iconografía en los siglos del románico: la actividad textil', *Medievalismo* 6 (1996), 63–119, at 76–82; J.L. Hernando Garrido, 'Por no perder el uso lleva la rueca y el huso: del gineceo de Skiros a las ruecas tradicionales', in *In Durii Regione Romanitas. Homenaje a Javier Cortes Álvarez de Miranda* (Palencia-Santander 2012), 115–20.

[48] M. Gros, 'Epíleg', in R. Ordeig Mata, *Les dotalies de les esglésies de Catalunya (segles IX–XII). IV. Estudi*, (Vic 2004), 268–78, at 272.

[49] J.R. Barriga Planas, *El Sacramentari, Ritual i Pontifical de Roda*, LIX, 48 (Barcelona, 1975), 2 vol., 505.

[50] Aurell, *Les dotalies* (as n. 41), p. 292.

[51] M. Zimmermann, 'La Catalogne de Gerbert', in *Gerbert l'Européen* (Actes du Colloque d'Aurillac, 4–7 juin 1996), ed. N. Charbonnet, J-E., Iung (Aurillac, 1997), 70–101, at 86. See also: I. Lorés i Otzet, 'L'église de Sant Pere de Rodes. Un exemple de «Renaissance» de l'architecture du XIè siècle en Catalogne', *Les Cahiers de Saint-Michel de Cuxa*, 32 (2001), 21–39.

⁵² Castiñeiras, *The Creation Tapestry* (as n. 45), 53–68.

⁵³ J. Roig I Jalpí, *Resumen de las grandezas y antigüedades de la ciudad de Gerona y cosas memorables*, (Barcelona 1678) 244.

⁵⁴ M. Castiñeiras, 'Hércules, Sansón y Constantino: el *Tapiz* de la Creación de Girona como *Speculum Principis*', in *L'officina dello sguardo. Scritti in onore di Maria Andaloro. I. Il luoghi dell'arte*, ed. G. Bordi, I. Carlettini, M.L. Fobelli, M.R. Menna, P. Pogliani (Rome 2014), 161–66.

⁵⁵ Castiñeiras, *The Creation Tapestry* (as n. 45), 92–94; Castiñeiras, 'Il Tappeto del Gigante' (as n. 44), p. 376.

⁵⁶ A. Rucquoi, 'L'héros avant le saint: Hercule en Espagne', in *Ab urbe condita. . .: fonder et refonder la ville: récits et représentations (second Moyen Âge – premier XVIe siècle)*, ed. V. Lamazou-Duplan, (Pau 2011), 55–75, at 55–59. See also R. Rodríguez Porto, 'The Pillars of Hercules: The Estoria de Espanna (Escorial Y. I.2) as Universal Chronicle', in *Universal Chronicles in the High Middle Ages*, ed. M. Campopiano, H. Bainton (York 2017), 223–53, and my recent contribution: 'Hercules in the Garden of the Hesperides. A Geographical Myth in the Creation Tapestry', in *Transformatio et Continuatio. Forms of Change and Constancy of Antiquity in the Iberian Peninsula 500–1500*, ed. H. Bredekamp, S. Trinks (Berlin and New York, 2017, 113–36).

⁵⁷ Cited in M. Aurell, 'Du nouveau sur les comtesses catalanes (IXe–XIIe siècles)', *Annales du Midi* 109, 219–20 (1997), 357–79, at 363

⁵⁸ For this role of Hercules and Samson as examples for the Christian ruler, see: C. Frugoni, 'L'ideologia del potere imperiale nella Cattedra di San Pietro', *Bulletino dell'Institutto Storico Italiano per il Medio Evo e Archivio Muratoriano* 86 (1976–77), 67–180, at 138–40.

⁵⁹ For a further discussion of the Master of Pedret's workshop and the peculiarities of the paintings of the church of Sant Pere de Burgal, see my previous contributions: 'Il "Maestro di Pedret" e la pittura lombarda: mito o realtà', *Arte Lombarda*, 156/2 (2009), 48–66; 'Le origini della bottega del cosiddetto Maestro di Pedret: una questione di metodo', in *Medievo: le officine*, ed. A.C. Quintavalle (XII Convegno Internazionale di Studi, Università degli Studi di Parma-AISAME, 22–27 settembre 2009) (Parma- Milano 2010) 276–90.

⁶⁰ J. Ainaud, *Pintura románica catalana* (Barcelona 1962), 26–28; J. Ainaud, *Art Romànic. Guia*, (Barcelona 1973), 79–83.

⁶¹ J-A. Adell, M. Guitart, 'La reproducció de les pintures murals de l'església del monestir de sant Pere del Burgal (la Guingeta d'Àneu, Pallars Sobirà', in *Burgal, Pedret, Taüll. Imitació o interpretació de la pintura mural romànica catalana* (I Taula Rodona dels Amics de l'Art Romànic) (Barcelona 2000), 53–61, at 59, fig. 4.

⁶² M. Guardia, C. Mancho, 'Pedret, Boí, o dels orígens de la pintura mural romànica catalana', in *Les fonts de la pintura romànica*, ed M. Guardia, C. Mancho, (Col·lecció Ars Picta, Temes, 1) (Universitat de Barcelona 2008) 117–159, at 129. See also: J. Camps e I. Lorés, 'Le patronage dans l'art roman catalan', *Les Cahiers de Saint-Michel de Cuxa*, 36 (2005), 209–23, at 220.

⁶³ Castiñeiras, 'Il Maestro di Pedret' (as n. 59), 63–65; M. Castiñeiras, 'Del Medioevo a la Modernidad. Conferencias sobre Románico Hispánico (2). Pintar hace mil años: recursos técnicos y programas iconográficos de los artistas del Románico catalán', *Junshin Journal of Studies in Humanities* 19 (2013), 241–58, at 248–49, fig. 23. Montserrat Pagès prefers to identify the figures as a depiction of Odo before his nomination as bishop and one of his sisters, 'Noblesse et patronage: El Burgal et Mur. Peinture murale en Catalogne aux XIè et XIIè siècles', Cahiers de Saint-Michel de Cuxa", 36 (2005), 185–94, at 189; M. Pagès, *La pintura mural romànica de les Valls d'Àneu* (Barcelona 2008), 91–92. See my comments on this latter hypothesis in; 'Il Maestro di Pedret' (as n. 59), 63–65; 'Del Medievo a la Modernidad' (as n. 63), 248–49.

⁶⁴ I. Puig i Ferreté, *El monestir de Santa Maria del Gerri (segles XI–XV)* (Barcelona 1991), vol. I, 479–80.

⁶⁵ For this controversy, see: H.E. Cowdrey, *The Abbot Desiderius. Montecassino, the Papacy and the Normans in Eleventh and Early Twelfth Centuries* (New York 1986), 90–95.

⁶⁶ Castiñeiras, 'Il Maestro de Pedret' (as n. 59), 66.

⁶⁷ E. Albert i Corp, *Saint Ot, bisbe d'Urgell, i la seva época* (Barcelona 1987), 36–62; A. Wunderwald, *Die Katalanische Wandmalerei in der Kiözese Urgell* (Stuttgart 2010).

⁶⁸ J. Goering, 'Bishops, Law and Reform in Aragon, 1076–1126 and the *Liber Tarraconensis*', *Zeitschrift der Savigny-Stiftung für Rechtsgeschichte: Kanonische Abeitlung* 95, (2009), 1–28; M. Castiñeiras, 'Los *ordines* de Roda: del Sacramentario-Pontifical a la *Collectio Tarraconensis*. Creación artística y *performance* litúrgica', in *Arquitectura y liturgia. El contexto artístico de las consuetas catedralicias en la Corona de Aragón*, ed. E. Carrero (Palma de Mallorca 2014), 209–24; I. Lorés, 'La réforme grégorienne et les église du diocèse de Roda dans la Ribagorce', in *Art et réforme grégorienne en France et dans la Péninsule Ibérique*, ed. Barbara Franze (Paris 2015), 91–107.

⁶⁹ M. Castiñeiras, 'The Making of the Catalan Romanesque Altar Frontal' (as n. 37), 101–15; M. Castiñeiras 'Il·luminant l'altar: artistes i tallers de pintura sobre taula a Catalunya (1119–1150)', in *Pintar fa mil anys. El colors i l'ofici del pintor romànic*, ed. Manuel Castiñeiras, Judit Verdaguer (Universitat Autònoma de Barcelona-Bellaterra 2014), 17–54, at 46–51.

⁷⁰ M. Castiñeiras, 'The Portal at Ripoll' (as n. 15) (with wider literature on the topic).

THE ARTISTIC PATRONAGE OF ABBOT GREGORIUS AT CUIXÀ: MODELS AND TRIBUTES[1]

Anna Orriols

Sant Miquel de Cuixà was one of the outstanding Catalan monasteries, particularly between the 10th and the 12th centuries. Founded in the 9th century and closely associated with the counts of Cerdanya, it enjoyed successive moments of splendour before starting to fade in the late 12th century.[2] As a result of the French Revolution, the monastery was secularised, after which its archives and many of its treasures were dispersed, some of them finding their way onto the international art market.

Fortunately, the monastic church survived. This was constructed in the second half of the 10th century and was consecrated during the abbacy of Guarinus in 975.[3] Although the church was built by conservative local labour, it is large and incorporates an innovative east end with multiple altars, which historiography has related to that of Cluny II. The well-known charter mentioning the consecration of this building is an interesting text, the work of Miro (Bishop of Girona 971–84 and Count of Besalú 965–84), who was also the author of the charter of the consecration of Santa Maria de Ripoll in 977. Written in a grandiose if refined style, it set a standard for later texts of a similar nature.[4] Material testimony of the consecration is the high altar stone, a large piece of reused Roman marble, which today stands on modern supports.[5]

For Cuixà, the second half of the 10th century was a period of intense contact with Italy that involved journeys to and from Rome, Venice and Monte Cassino on the part of the circle formed by Abbot Guarinus, Count Oliba Cabreta and the aforementioned Count-Bishop Miro.[6] Illustrious guests from Venice also visited the monastery, particularly the fugitive Doge Pietro Orseolo (†988), who ended his days as a hermit at Cuixà, where he was buried and would come to be venerated as a saint.[7]

OLIBA

From 1008, the Abbot of Cuixà was Oliba, a member of the family of counts of Cerdanya-Besalú, who simultaneously and until his death (1046) was abbot of the monastery of Ripoll. In 1018, he also became Bishop of Vic.

Oliba was one of the most notable figures of the first half of the 11th century.[8] It was during his mandate that the monastery at Ripoll became a rich and active cultural centre. Throughout a long career, Oliba promoted a number of major architectural projects, essentially at the places he governed, either as bishop (Vic Cathedral) or as abbot (abbeys of Ripoll and Cuixà).[9] All were major undertakings, evidently indebted to the prestigious models that Oliba had seen on his travels to Rome.[10] In addition, the documentary sources tell us that he was also responsible for a number of discrete artistic projects involving liturgical furnishings (the altar canopies in Ripoll and Cuixà)[11] and perhaps a series of paintings in the monastic church of Ripoll.[12] It should also be noted that it was during Oliba's abbacy that the most important illustrated bibles to have survived from Ripoll were produced.[13]

Oliba was the addressee of the valuable and well-known text written by the monk Garsies of Cuixà between 1043 and 1046 which, among other things, describes the architectural patronage of Guarinus and Oliba in considerable detail.[14] It is an anniversary sermon and, despite the nature of the text (a kind of *ekphrasis* that imitates the pompous style of the 975 act of consecration), it has been proved to be highly reliable.[15] The measurements given for the altar stone, for example, are as they are in reality. In his text Garsies also mentions the monastery's origins, and reports on its extraordinarily large collection of relics.

Oliba's activity in Cuixà was respectful of what already existed. It has been said, and it is interesting to note this now, that Oliba deliberately conserved the previous building because of its association with Guarinus.[16] Whatever view we take of that claim, Oliba surrounded the main apse with an aisle that opened onto three apse chapels to the east, he monumentalised the ends of the transepts with two enormous towers and he constructed a building on two levels a few metres to the west of the west façade. This consisted of a centralised sanctuary dedicated to the Trinity above a circular crypt dedicated to the Mother of God, the latter another work by Oliba influenced from Rome.[17] The crypt was probably inspired

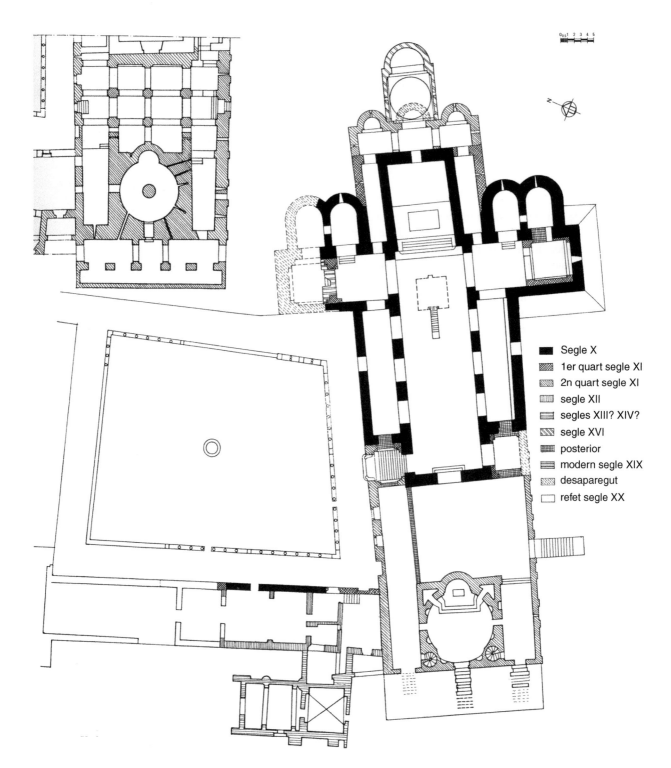

FIGURE 13.1
Sant Miquel de Cuixà: Plan of the abbey (R. Mallol)

by that at Santa Maria Maggiore, and which also invoked Christ's birthplace. It is no coincidence that the Cuixà crypt was known from the outset as the *crib* (*praesepium*; *pessebre* in Catalan; Figures 13.1 and 13.13).[18]

In the main church, Oliba erected a canopy above the altar that had been retained from the church of Guarinus. We can be sure of this thanks to Garsies' text, and I will specifically refer to it later. Although Garsies made no reference to any other liturgical furnishings, it is hard to believe that there were no altar frontals of precious metal, as we know existed in other abbeys of a similar status. The inventories that provide us with so much information about Ripoll have not been conserved in the case of Cuixà, and the documentary references are scarce and imprecise.[19]

Oliba died in 1046 and was buried at Cuixà (*sepultus est in Cocxano monasterio Sancti Michaelis*),[20] which by that date had become a wealthy monastery associated with a series of *uomini illustri*: the Abbots Guarinus and Oliba; the Counts of Cerdanya, who founded the monastery and included Oliba Cabreta, who is said to have ended his days as a monk at Monte Cassino; and the aforesaid Venetian Doge and saint, Pietro Orseolo.

GREGORIUS

A century later, Abbot Gregorius (c. 1120–46) promoted a new artistic era at Cuixà. The works which were undertaken, in all likelihood, during his abbacy can be understood in a context that was almost as splendid and ambitious as that of Oliba's period in office. The historiographical reputation of the great 11th-century abbot–bishop have rather overshadowed Gregorius, and reduced him to a background figure.

Fate has been unkind to Gregorius, depriving us of information about his person: we do not know when or where he was born, or anything about his family. And his name, unusual in Catalan onomastics of the era, makes this even more intriguing. We have a rich collection of charters that can be associated with Oliba, while for Gregorius – at least for now – we have to be content with scant and fleeting references in documents for which he is never the subject. Sometimes Gregorius doesn't even make it into general historical or artistic studies of 12th-century Catalonia, while the name Oliba is omnipresent, meaning his figure has become almost mythologised.[21] Of the latter we conserve news and proof of his magnificent task of artistic promotion (ranging from important buildings to extraordinary illustrated manuscripts), while works possibly commissioned by Gregorius remain undocumented. To add to the difficulty, what little information there is on Gregorius is neither clear nor uncontested, as the documentary sources are only known in later copies.

Thus it is not easy to reconstruct a life of Gregorius or assess the role he played. But let us review what we do know about him, and what works can be attributed to his abbacy at Cuixà. What we can say, with all due caution, is that the start of his abbacy may be placed around 1120, and that he apparently died on 25 March 1146.[22] At some time after he became Abbot of Cuixà he was appointed Archbishop of Tarragona. Certain historians assert that this happened in 1137, basically because this was the year when the previous Archbishop of Tarragona, Bishop Oleguer of Barcelona and future saint, died. However, Gregorius did not receive the pallium until 1144, as we know from a bull of Pope Lucius II granted at the Lateran Palace only days after acceding to the pontificate.[23] At this date, the Archbishopric of Tarragona was in a far from stable state. The consolidation of the conquest of Tarragona from the Muslims had been difficult, as was the restoration of the metropolitan see. It is thought that neither the first archbishop of the restored see, Sunifred, Bishop of Vic, nor the second, Oleguer, Bishop of Barcelona – both of whom retained their respective episcopal offices – even took up residence in Tarragona. The same may have happened to Gregorius, and it may not have been until the accession of his successor, Bernat Tort (1146–63), that things changed. Tarragona's *archiepiscopologia* have almost nothing to say about Gregorius.[24] At the time, then, the office of Archbishop of Tarragona must have been honorific rather than effective, and Gregorius probably maintained his close links with Cuixà.[25] The *Cronicon Rivipullense II* recorded his death, referring to him as *archiepiscopus Terragon(ensis) et abbas Cuxanensis*. We do not know where he was buried, and although this cannot yet be demonstrated, it is reasonable to assume that it was at the abbey of Cuixà and not at Tarragona.[26] His abbacy must therefore have lasted for twenty years, long enough to be able to engage in what was to become a notable artistic activity at the monastery. This is known indirectly from a chronology of the abbots of Cuixà written in the 14th century, where it is specified that Gregorius 'fecit claustra marmorea et postea fuit archiepiscopus Tarraconensis' ('made the cloister in marble and afterwards became archbishop of Tarragona'), a reference that is usually put forward to attribute the construction of the cloister to his abbacy.[27]

Approximately half the cloister is still in Cuixà (Figure 13.2), while the rest is mainly in the United States (New York, The Cloisters).[28] It is a praiseworthy project, not just because of its size but also its pioneering nature. It is considered the first sculpted cloister in Catalonia, and probably marks the beginning of what historically are known as the Roussillon workshops. The distinctive designs employed at Cuixà spread to other parts of Languedoc and Catalonia, becoming progressively diluted. The cloister at Cuixà is built of a characteristic pink marble from the nearby quarries at Vilafranca de Conflent, giving it its attractive colouring.

It is all the more remarkable when we note that it may have been during Gregorius' abbacy that a magnificent marble tribune decorated with carved reliefs may also have been built. Though this was dismantled at the end of the 16th century, and only fragments survive, we can get an idea of its overall appearance by examining the tribune at the neighbouring Augustinian priory of Santa Maria de Serrabona, although that at Cuixà was probably bigger.

Figure 13.2

Sant Miquel de Cuixà: Cloister (Jordi Camps)

Figure 13.3

Serrabona: west façade of tribune (Juan Antonio Olañeta)

As Eduardo Carrero has argued, the Serrabona tribune is still in its original position, and has always stood halfway along the nave, not at the western end as has usually been supposed. The Cuixà tribune will have occupied a similar location, near the presbytery.[29] Both structures give a notable role to sculpture, and share a common ornamental and iconographic repertoire, which eschews narrative imagery as was generally the case in buildings associated with the Roussillon workshops. Both are also made from the same pink marble as was used in the cloister at Cuixà. In terms of its material, ornamental profusion and type, there is no question that the tribune of Cuixà was as original as it was spectacular, as on a lesser scale is that of Serrabona (Figure 13.3). What survives, as with the cloister, is now divided between Cuixà and the United States.[30] Some of its elements ended up being used to frame two doors: the main door into the monastery and that of the abbot's house (Figure 13.4) as can be seen in 19th-century engravings.[31] During the 1950s restoration, these were transferred to the door between the church and the cloister, their current location (Figure 13.5).

Although we have practically no documentation on Gregorius, we do have a portrait. This is a marble relief representing an ecclesiastic with a mitre and crozier and wearing a pallium (Figure 13.6). He is holding a book on which we can read ABBAS and in the arch that frames him is the inscription GREGORIVS [A]RCHIEPIS[COPUS] (the second word in mirror writing). In a clear example of the dispersal of Cuixà's property, the plaque was found in 1986 at the Salon des Antiquaires in Toulouse, and was returned to the abbey. Its provenance was subsequently confirmed, as it was described when still at the monastery.[32] It has been speculated that the relief may have been originally sited in the cloister, since documents attribute its construction to Gregorius, and there are examples where the abbot responsible for a cloister is commemorated within the cloister. However, Ponsich suggested that it will have come from the tribune, a suggestion that has recently been confirmed by Anna Thirion, who proposed that Gregorius will have been set on its western façade, facing the nave and accompanied by symbols of the evangelists, all looking towards the *Agnus Dei* framed within a medallion.[33] This appealing location would allow Gregorius to 'sign' his work and perpetually offer it to Christ.

Although most authorities have dated the tribune to the 1140s, it has recently been argued that it was created in the 1150s or 1160s, after the abbacy of Gregorius, rendering his portrait commemorative.[34] However, no account has been taken of the manuscripts produced at Cuixà during the abbacy of Gregorius, abbotship, though these may offer important insights into the dating of the tribunes.

Proof that the Cuixà scriptorium was active during the abbacy of Gregorius is a *Commentary on the Psalms* (Perpignan, Bibliothèque Municipale, MS 3) whose colophon (f 176) tells us that it was commissioned by him: *Abbas Gregorius, prudens, discretus, honestus, me scribi iussit* (Figure 13.7).[35] The deliberately eye-catching style of this colophon (colourful, with large letters and a more intricate layout) uses a script that is comparable to that of the tribune inscriptions referring to the evangelists Matthew and Luke and on the representation of Gregorius. The colophon and the carvings even share some palaeographic details, such as the uncial *h* set amongst capital letters. This is not the only case where epigraphic inscriptions and highlighted texts from a manuscript have been related. Another well-known example is Moissac, where the similarity in both form and content of the commemorative inscription on the western face of the central pillar

FIGURE 13.4

Remains of the Cuixà tribune used as frame of the abbot's house door (from Taylor, Nodier and De Cailleux, Voyages pittoresques et romantiques dans l'ancienne France, II, Languedoc, Paris 1835)

FIGURE 13.5

Sant Miquel de Cuixà: Remains of the Cuixà tribune today used as frame for the entrance to the church from the cloister (Juan Antonio Olañeta)

FIGURE 13.6

Sant Miquel de Cuixà: Marble relief of Abbot Gregorius

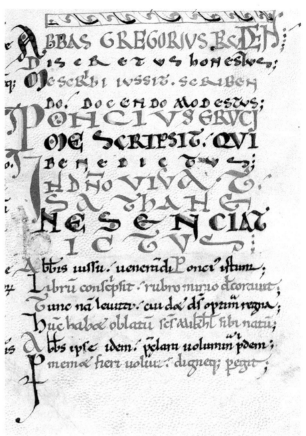

FIGURE 13.7

Commentary on the Psalms (Perpignan, Médiathèque municipale, MS 3, fol. 172) © Médiathèque de Perpignan

in the western gallery to the colophon of a manuscript has been pointed out.[36]

At Cuixà there are other significant links between sculpture and manuscript illumination. It is interesting to note that several ornamental motifs used in both tribunes are also found in manuscripts which must have been illuminated at the monastery. One is a late-12th-century liturgical Gospel Book (Perpignan, Bibliothèque Municipale, MS 2), whose link to Saint Michael of Cuixà is confirmed by its calendar of saints' days, (fols. 185–204v), which includes the feasts of Saints Flamidien and Nazarius, both of them represented by relics kept at the monastery.[37] But the manuscript which is most notable in respect of the ornamental repertoire it shares with the tribunes is an illustrated Gospel Book (Perpignan, Bibliothèque Municipale, MS 1).[38] This must belong to the time of Gregorius, as it seems to be contemporary to the aforementioned *Commentary on the Psalms*, undoubtedly commissioned by this abbot.

The Abbey within the book: commemorative images in the *Cuixà Gospels*

The Gospel book opens with a *Maiestas Domini* (fol. 2) (Figure 13.8), which, like many of the manuscript's illustrations, is uncoloured. Conversely, it is the only illumination that includes abundant foliate decoration. Close similarities can be recognised between this ornamental repertoire and what can be seen in both tribunes (both Serrabona and Cuixà). Thus the motif that resembles a cornucopia from which stems burst forth, on the spandrels of the image of the manuscript, is clearly present in several variations at both tribunes (Figures 13.8 and 13.9). The same occurs with the border formed by a series of quatrefoils, and, which we find again, transformed into a floral motif by the addition of a central button, with the same sequential repetition on the tribune at Serrabona and on the remains of the one at Cuixà. Finally, a palmette set within a semicircle between the feet Christ in the Christ in Majesty reappears under the hooves of some quadrupeds on the tribune at Serrabona (Figures 13.8 and 13.10).[39]

There is more to say about the relationship between this manuscript and the abbey. It includes, among its first folios, a series of images that, as I argued some time ago, cannot be understood as anything other than representations of the abbey's main places of worship, associated with the figures of the Abbots Guarinus and Oliba.[40] Moreover, apart from the illustrations which could be considered conventional for Gospel Books (like the

FIGURE 13.8

Cuixà Gospel Book (Perpignan, Médiathèque municipale, MS 1, fol. 2) (© Médiathèque de Perpignan)

FIGURE 13.9

Sant Miquel de Cuixà, Remains of the Cuixà tribune (Jordi Camps)

FIGURE 13.10

Serrabona: tribune pillar (Juan Antonio Olañeta)

Maiestas, canon tables and some Gospel episodes) there are three (fols 2v, 3 and 14v) that are as original as they are exclusive to this manuscript. They are full page and are to be found at the beginning of the book, which is indicative of their importance. The first (fol. 2v) is an early example of a *Gnadenstuhl Trinity*, or Throne of Grace (Figure 13.11). This must be related to the Church dedicated to the Trinity erected by Oliba to the west of the monastic church and praised by Garsies, of which vestiges remain. Underneath this is the crypt dedicated to the Mother of God, as invoked in another miniature in the manuscript (fol. 14v; Figures 13.12 and 13.13). In this case, the unidentified subjects surrounding the Virgin and Child could be martyrs buried in a circle around her feet, as was described by Garsies.[41] It is tempting to relate them to specific individuals, above all the two depicted without a halo: one a bishop or arch-bishop and the other wearing a crown. Any suggestion is necessarily speculative, but it is tempting to suggest these might have been intended to represent Gregorius and Ramon Berenguer IV.

The third of the images (fol. 3; Figure 13.14) shows a concentric circle, with the *Agnus Dei* at the centre, surrounded by the busts of sixteen haloed figures. Four other busts are set on the cardinals of the outermost circle, with the symbols of the evangelists, enclosed in medallions, at the corners. This folio must refer to the high altar of the monastic church, and most probably alludes to its now missing canopy. According to Garsies, it was Oliba who erected this canopy, just as Moses had built the mercy seat (*propitiatorium*). It featured sculpted images of the symbols of the four evangelists on the exterior (at the angles one supposes) and an image of the *Agnus Dei* in an elevated position, where it could be contemplated by the evangelists and apostles of the interior.

The canopy over the high altar

Garsies devotes a long description to the canopy.[42] This may have something to do with an aspect of his life which has been neglected in the scholarly literature: his participation in the design of the ciborium, which Garsies himself explains in the first part of the sermon, where he

FIGURE 13.11

Cuixà Gospel Book (Perpignan, Médiathèque municipale, MS 1, fol. 2v) (© Médiathèque de Perpignan)

FIGURE 13.12

Cuixà Gospel Book (Perpignan, Médiathèque municipale, MS 1, fol. 14v) (© Médiathèque de Perpignan)

FIGURE 13.13

Sant Miquel de Cuixà: crypt dedicated to the Virgin (Josep Renalias)

FIGURE 13.14

Cuixà Gospel Book (Perpignan, Médiathèque municipale, MS 1, fol. 3) (© Médiathèque de Perpignan)

states that he was responsible for the paintings and the figures of the evangelists (*Propitiatorii quoque coloribus et evangelistarum figuris si asignavi*). In his *ekphrasis*, he constantly alternates description with symbolic interpretation. This and the complex style of the text – 'confused and over-elaborate' in the words of Junyent – make it almost impossible to precisely visualise the structure. First, Garsies refers to the supports, four red marble columns topped by white capitals with diverse foliage and flowers. Then he expands on the symbolic reading of the colour red as the blood of the martyrs, and the purity of white, and has recourse to the stereotype of likening the bases to the doctors of the church:

> *Bases, inquam, iuxta unius hominis incessum quatuora calce procul altaris posuit, totidemque columnas e marmore rubicundi coloris e singularibus saxis in pedibus septem voluntaria fortitudine erexit [. . .] et in columnis martyrum gloriam praemonstrans, qui corporis pasioni rubicundi, spiritus puritate candidi [. . .] . . . doctorumque caterva qui constantia fortitudinis vel zelo rectitudinis in basibus sustentant plebemiunctam summo capiti in unitate fidei. Super capita etiam columnarum, ut candorem eclesiasticae castitatis imprimeret, ac spiritualium gratiarum flores proficientibus meritis, vanos timores tolleret, ex albo marmore capitella statuit, foliato corpore et flores diversarum modum.*

He goes on to describe the roof:

> *Desuper autem, ut ordo habebat, de lignis sectis in utraque parte propitiatorii contra se invicem positam columnas habentes tres semi cubitos ambientes arcus infra iuncturas vel secto et serrato ligno virtutes sanctorum innexuit, quae mutuo sibi quasi ad fenestras versa vice alter in altero proficuos fructus in arboream sustollerent firmitatem. Inter iuncturas autem arcus in arcemque ascensus fenestras in omni genere specierum sive operum multitudine diligentissima pictura variatas substraxit.*

It seems clear that this was a structure of some complexity, made of wood, with columns and arches, suggesting, perhaps, a two-stage roof with an intermediate tier of little columns. This caused Puig i Cadafalch to offer a reconstruction based on Roman *ciboria* of the Romanesque era, like those of San Clemente in Rome, San Nicola in Bari or at the basilica at Castel Sant'Elia.[43]

Finally, Garsies refers to the carved and painted motifs, possibly his own work as we have seen, on the ceiling:

> *Inter iuncturas autem arcus in arcemque ascensus fenestras in omni genere specierum sive operum multitudine diligentissima pictura variatas substraxit. Sculpsit quoque in giro per quadrum, ita ut facie a faciem se viderent, dolatili ligno imagines quatuor evangelistarum, subiitque eos infra status formae superioris et reclinationem arcus inferioris, sic ut aspectus eorum in quatuor mundi partes evangelii grata concordaret, altiori vero gradu Agnum eorum aspicerent. Interiori namque ambitu, non ad pompam et claritudinem vulgi opulentissimus praesul, sedin laudem duocdcim apostolorum bonique illorum magistri virtutem pretiosi ligni ordines XIII adfixit, ut apostoli inter semitas iustorum abintus filium hominis in spiritu gloriae suae illustrarent, ac sancta animalia exterius, Agnum Dei per cuncta tempora in una dominatione stantem proferrant, et intus vel fortis aeterni regis tribunal et solium mysterii revelationibus familiariter adornarent, atque pia munera offerentes in Christo unum corpus efficerent. Omnem enim materiam intrinsecus et extrinsecus in proceram celsitudinem fecit surgere, et manibus artificium faciem angulosque sic exornavit ut nusquam iunctura paginis apparet.*

If we accept that the folio from the Cuixà Gospels recreates the canopy over the main altar, it would appear to have had a domed or polygonal interior, embellished with an *Agnus Dei* surrounded by different figures, probably apostles and martyrs. A similar arrangement is found in the canopy at San Pietro al Monte in Civate (from around 1100) where the Lamb is worshipped by martyrs, on the basis of Chapter 7 of the Apocalypse, with the four winds on the pendentives and – as at Cuixà – the symbols of the evangelists carved on the exterior (Figures 13.15 and 13.16).[44]

Apart from Civate, we know of another canopy which had paintings inside its ceiling. This stood above the main altar in the cathedral of Compostela, and was erected by Archbishop Gelmírez, after his return from a trip to Rome. It has not been preserved but, as at Cuixà, we have a fairly detailed description, in this case in the *Codex Calixtinus*. As Serafin Morelejo pointed out, both descriptions reveal that the canopies had many features in common: namely the Lamb, the Evangelists, the *virtutes sanctorum* and the apostles, which in Compostela were sitting in a circle (*sedent per circuitum*).[45] Furthermore, the canopy of Gelmírez was painted on the interior (*deintus vero est depictus, deforis autem sculptus et depictus*), as is the case at Civate and as I think also happened at Cuixà.

We do not know when the Cuixà canopy disappeared: it may have been during the course of the reforms carried out at the end of the 16th century, when the church of the Trinity was demolished and the tribune dismantled.[46] Attempts have been made to associate with it four fine Corinthian capitals preserved at The Cloisters Museum in New York and originating from Cuixà.[47] They are made of white marble (not pink) and their size does not match the dimensions of either the cloister or the tribune. This, coupled with the fact that the decoration matches the description of Garsies (*ex albo marmore capitella statuit, foliato corpore et flores diversarum modum*), makes them ideal candidates to be from the canopy. However, several authors hold that the capitals at the Cloisters are much later, of around 1150, placing them a century after from the canopy.[48] On the other hand, a base of pink marble still preserved at Cuixà may have formed part of the piece.[49]

FIGURE 13.15

Civate: San Pietro al Monte; ciborium vault (Juan Antonio Olañeta)

FIGURE 13.16

Civate: San Pietro al Monte; ciborium seen from exterior (Juan Antonio Olañeta)

Marmore rubicundi colores. Fountains, red marble and Rome

As we have already seen, Garsies specifies that the canopy was supported on red marble columns crowned with white capitals decorated with leaves and flowers. The colours symbolised, respectively, the blood of the martyrs and spiritual purity. Various ancient Christian authors (such as Prudentius) had previously associated particular colours with martyrs, and with material elements of the sanctuaries that protected their bodies.[50] It is significant that when canopies are represented in the Ripoll bibles, the columns are reddish (*Rodes Bible*, vol. II, fols. 129v and 130v – colour plate XV, top), as are those of the canopy over the altar under which the souls of the martyrs are housed (*Rev.* 6, 9) in the painting in the apse at Sant Quirze de Pedret (Solsona, Museu Diocesà i Comarcal – colour plate XV, bottom).[51]

At Cuixà, access to pink marble from the nearby quarries in Vilafranca de Conflent, which ranged in colour from pale pink to red, was a happy circumstance that afforded the monastery access to stone with a chromatic range pregnant with symbolic potential. There is an intriguing possibility that these marble colours were deliberately exploited on Oliba's ciborium, not only to represent the martyrs' blood as alluded to by Garsies when he described their columns, but also to emulate the canopies with porphyry columns that Oliba would have seen on his travels to Rome, as Immaculada Lorès has proposed.[52] This brings us back to Gregorius, and the period when Vilafranca marble was used in the cloister and the tribune, and points to other possible works commissioned by this abbot.

A fountain currently on display in the Philadelphia Museum of Art and another now in a private property at Èze en Provence (Alpes-Maritimes), are both made of the same pink marble, and are believed to correspond to Gregorius' abbacy.[53] The presence of two fountains in a plan of the monastery drawn up in 1779 (one in the cloister and the other in a small cloister or garden between the abbot's house and the infirmary) could account for the existence of two. The Philadelphia fountain (Figure 13.17) consists of a circular font supported on six strong colonettes with foliated capitals. The font is embellished with a blind arcade, 'seemingly mirroring the arcade of the cloister in the midst of which the fountain stood', as Walter Cahn pointed out.[54] Today it stands in a modern catch basin in imitation of the one represented in a 19th-century engraving of Cuixà.[55]

The two 'fountains' thought to have come from Cuixà conform to a type of cloister laver that was widespread in the Romanesque era.[56] What we know about 12th-century cloister lavers, extant or otherwise, indicates that they were important elements of the cloister garth, and had a value over and above their practical function. In keeping with this, they received particularly careful treatment and were usually made of quality materials. The Moissac font, which has not survived, is mentioned in the chronicle of Abbot Aymeric of Peyrac (1377–1406): 'lapidem

FIGURE 13.17

Fountain from Cuixà (Philadelphia Museum of Art, 1930–79–1) (© Philadelphia Museum of Art)

fontis magni claustri predicti fecit aspotari'. It specifies that it was made of marble (*lapis fontis marmoreus*) and was attributed to Abbot Ansquitil (1086–1115), the builder of the cloister.[57] At Conques a magnificent cloister laver made of dark green serpentine survives, a special and valued stone obtained from the quarry at Firmy, some 20 kms from the monastery. Serpentine had also been used to carve elements of the funerary monument of Abbot Bégon (1087–1107), including the plaques that record his epitaph, and describe him as the promoter of the cloister – *Hoc peragens claustrum, quod versus tendit ad austrum*.[58] Finally, of particular interest is another font, also made of serpentine from the same source as the Conques example, and today located in the Place Saint-Géraud in Aurillac (Cantal), in front of the Romanesque hospital. It comes from the former monastery of Saint-Géraud, an important Cluniac house, and is one of the two lavers that we know were there: one in the cloister and the other in front of the abbot's *domus*.[59] The *Breve chronicon Auriliacensis abbatiae*, written around 1120, specifies: 'Petrus de Roca [. . .] claustra quae prius ligna fuerant, lapidea extruxit, marmorea altaria aedificavit. Cum diversa montanorum loca peragrasset, invenit lapidem marmoreum longe ab Auriliaco, de quo geminas conchas fabricavit, unam in claustro, alteram ante domum Abbatialem'.[60] The existence of two fonts at Aurillac parallels Cuixà and supports the proposition that at the Catalan abbey too, one of lavers stood in front of the abbot's residence.[61] Both the Moissac and the Conques lavers, as well as those at Aurillac, were commissioned by the very abbots who had built the respective monastic cloisters and are made of quality materials. All also seem to date from the first quarter of the 12th century. By virtue of typology, material and circumstance the laver in the cloister at Cuixà fits perfectly into these contexts.

In addition to the Cuixà laver, the Philadelphia Museum conserves a seat in which the pink marble is at the red end of its chromatic range (Figure 13.18). Although it is not certain that it came from Cuixà, and it has even been claimed that the cross on the back of the throne is a forgery, the seat would seem to be 12th century.[62] Could this also be related to Gregorius? He had outdone his already illustrious predecessors in the abbacy by obtaining the rank of archbishop, as proclaimed by the awkward inscription on the relief with his portrait. Achieving the role of *archiepiscopus* made him an ideal candidate to order a seat (a *cathedra*), which he could not use at the purely official see at Tarragona, but was possible at his abbey. Moreover, the intense colour is reminiscent of porphyry. For some time, the Church had appropriated the symbolic prestige of this material (and its substitutes). Especially in Italy (and even more so in Rome), where it was still being used in the guise of spolia columns furnishings and liturgical objects, the latter including ecclesiastical seats. It was precisely in the 1130s that the *sedes porphyreticae* were installed in the Lateran. These were twin Roman seats that would be used for papal coronations and which, despite their name, were not made of porphyry, but of *rosso antico*.[63]

Since the beginning of the 12th century and as a result of the Gregorian reform, Rome had been conducting an intense renewal of its churches, which frequently

FIGURE 13.18

Seat in reddish marble (Philadelphia Museum of Art, 1929–109–1) (© Philadelphia Museum of Art)

involved the embellishment of the presbytery with a new pavement and new liturgical furnishings. A prime example, which became a model in Rome and its region, is San Clemente, which at the time of Cardinal Anastasius (c. 1100–c. 1125) had been equipped with a new pavement and a canopy, plus a *schola cantorum* and a marble chair, both reusing previous material of special significance.[64]

In Cuixà it seems likely that Gregorius undertook an extensive refurnishing of the church which involved a choral tribune, a chair and quite possibly a mosaic pavement. Xavier Barral has already suggested that a few fragments of mosaic discovered in the 1960s may have come from the monastic presbytery and date to the time when the tribune was constructed.[65] The presbytery of the church of the monastery of Ripoll also housed a mosaic, probably dating from the 12th century, of which some remnants and a drawing have been preserved.[66] The fragments from Cuixà and Ripoll show several technical and material similarities that allow them to be considered as contemporaneous.

Our lack of knowledge about the life and movements of Gregorius make it hazardous to speculate about his exposure to art and architecture elsewhere, but he must have visited Rome at least once, as he received the pallium from Pope Lucius II in 1144. This is late in his abbacy (Gregorius died two years later) but it does not preclude an earlier journey to Rome. At the start of the 12th century, Archbishop Gelmírez of Compostela launched an important programme of renovation of the presbytery of the Cathedral of Saint James that included, among other features, the canopy referred to previously.[67]

Still conserved today in the cloister at Cuixà, flanking the door that leads to the church, are two pink marble pillars on one of whose faces are represented, respectively, the Apostles Peter and Paul. There are undoubtedly related by material and production with the sculptures of the tribune, which is where they originate (Figure 13.5).[68] Like the statues of Peter and Paul on the door at Ripoll or the former west portal at Sant Pere de Rodes, they invoke and vindicate the link with Rome.

Memory and tribute at Cuixà

Memory is important in all monasteries and the record of the consecration of 975 and the anniversary sermon of Garsies took the form of chronicles which were highly commemorative in nature. And although bibliographic activity at Cuixà has been overshadowed by that of Ripoll, it was clearly outstanding. It should be noted that Catalan historical writing can be first discerned at Cuixà in the late 10th century, to be transferred from there to Ripoll in Oliba's times. Also, in the final third of the 11th century, a *Vita* of Pietro Orseolo was composed on the basis of earlier texts that must also have been written at the abbey.[69] Moreover, as can be deduced from numerous indications, the history of the founder of the dynasty of the Counts of Barcelona, Wilfred the Hairy, was written at Cuixà before being included in the first version of the *Gesta Comitum Barcinonensium*.[70] It has been argued that Abbot Gregorius was the author, or inspirer, of this literary-historical work extolling the legendary dynastic origins of the then powerful House of Barcelona. It was presumably thanks to these links that Count Ramon Berenguer IV appointed him Archbishop of Tarragona.[71]

The mid-12th-century saw the compilation of the *Cartulari major* which, as happened with many cartularies, included several false documents, among them the opening two charters, which claimed that the founder and first abbot of Cuixà, Protasius, had accompanied Charlemagne to Rome for the imperial coronation.[72] In any event, the author of the falsification had a reasonable knowledge of history and was in good company in giving the monastery a legendary Carolingian origin, a practice then endemic throughout France and the Catalan counties.[73] Thus, from the late-10th-century until the 12th century, the writing of history had a prominent place at Cuixà.

Just as Guarinus may have preserved the memory of the original monastic oratory of Saint Michael in his ambitious apse, Oliba respected its shape with his intervention. The altar consecrated in 975 was sheltered by a canopy in Oliba's day, around 1040. To its west, a century later, Gregorius built the choral tribune and perhaps also added a seat of honour. In the tribune, the image of Gregorius would have stood beside that of the angel of Matthew, a possible visual metaphor which has been related to the terms in which Garsies' sermon described his predecessor Guarinus: 'angelus vel cœlestis homo', while the tribune itself establishes a dialogue with Oliba's canopy.[74]

Thus, the works that Gregorius commissioned equated him with his illustrious predecessors (Abbot Guarinus and Bishop-Abbot Oliba) while, in turn, he rendered tribute to their works. Moreover, Gregorius undertook a renovation that was materially and ideologically inspired by Rome. No text comparable to that of Garsies has been conserved from Gregorius' period, unfortunately. But the aforementioned Gospel Book, which was probably illustrated under his auspices, to a certain extent does serve this function. What Garsies evokes with words, the Cuixà Gospels records in images.

The artistic chapter which the virtually unknown Gregorius seems to have inspired at Cuixà, with its still poorly defined parameters, looks as rich as it is interesting. And its inspiring referents – Cuixà's monastic past and the present of the Rome of Gregorian reform – make it even more attractive. Gregorius died in 1146, exactly one hundred years after Oliba. This centenary, which we assume was beyond the abbot and archbishop's ability to control, constitutes an incomparable climax to his abbacy.

NOTES

[1] This paper is the result of research carried out for the project *Artistas, Patronos y Público.Cataluña y el Mediterráneo (siglos XI–XV)-MAGISTRI CATALONIAE* (MICINN-HAR 2011–23015). English translation by Joyce McFarlane.

² On the history of the monastery, see R. d'Abadal i de Vinyals, 'Com neix i creix un gran monestir pirinenc abans de l'any mil: Eixalada-Cuixà', *Analecta Monserratensia*, VIII (1954–1955), 125–337. This was later incorporated (although without the documentary annex) in *Dels visigots als catalans*, vol. I, *La Hispània visigòtica i la Catalunya carolíngia*, 3rd edn (Barcelona 1986), 377–484. Essential are the various studies by Pierre Ponsich, all of them quoted in the collective chapter P. Ponsich, O. Poisson and G. Mallet, 'Sant Miquel de Cuixà', in *La Cerdanya. El Conflent*, Catalunya Romànica, VII (Barcelona 1995), 357–395.

³ Many scholars cite 974 as the year of the church's consecration, though some suggest that this should be 975: P. Ponsich and R. Ordeig, *Els comtats de Rosselló, Conflent, Vallespir i Fenollet*, Catalunya carolíngia, VI (Barcelona 2006), part I, 20–21.

⁴ A detailed analysis of the text of the consecration can be found in J.M. Salrach, 'El comte-bisbe Miró Bonfill i l'acta de consagració de Cuixà de l'any 974' *Acta Historica et Archaeologica Medievalia*, 10 (1989), 107–124.

⁵ P. Ponsich, 'La table de l'autel majeur de Saint-Michel de Cuxa', *Les Cahiers de Saint-Michel de Cuxa*, VI (1975), 41–65.

⁶ Abadal, 'Com neix' (as n. 1), 465–478.

⁷ G. Ortalli, 'Quando il doge diventa santo. Fede e politica nell'esperienza di Pietro I Orseolo', *Studi veneziani*, 1 (2001), 15–48; C. Caby, 'Faire du monde un ermitage: Pierre Orseolo, doge et ermite', in *Guerriers et moines – Conversion et sainteté aristocratiques dans l'Occident médiéval (IXe–XIIe siècle)*, ed. M. Lauwers, (Antibes 2002) 349–368. D. Codina i Giol, 'Sources littéraires de la *Vita* ou *Gesta* de saint Pierre Orseolo', *Les Cahiers de Saint-Michel de Cuxa*, XLIII (2012), 199–204.

⁸ A. Albareda, *L'abat Oliba, fundador de Montserrat (971?–1046). Assaig biogràfic* (Montserrat 1931; new edition with prologue by A. Massot i Muntaner, Montserrat 1972); R. d'Abadal i de Vinyals, *L'abat Oliba, bisbe de Vic, i la seva època*, (Barcelona 1948), re-edited as 'L'abat Oliba i la seva època' in *Dels visigots als catalans*, vol. II, 3d ed (Barcelona 1986), 141–277; E. Junyent i Subirà, *Diplomatari i escrits literaris de l'abat i bibe Oliba*, posthumous ed, A.M. Mundó, (Barcelona 1992); and the various essays in *Le monde d'Oliba. Arts et culture en Catalogne et en Occident (1008–1046)*, published as *Les Cahiers de Saint-Michel de Cuxa*, XL (2009).

⁹ I.G. Bango Torviso, 'La part oriental dels temples de l'abat-bisbe Oliba', *Quaderns d'Estudis Medievals*, 23–24 (1988), 51–66; G. Boto, 'Monasterios catalanes en el siglo XI. Los espacios eclesiásticos de Oliba', in J. López Quiroga, A.M. Martinez Tejera, J. Morin de Pablos, eds, *Monasteria et Territoria. Elites, edilicia y territorio en el Mediterráneo medieval (siglos V–XI)*, (Oxford 2007), 281–320; I. Lorés and C. Mancho, 'Hec domus est sancta quam fecit domnus Oliva: Santa Maria de Ripoll', *Les Cahiers de Saint-Michel de Cuxa*, XL (2009), 205–219; X. Barral i Altet, 'Culture visuelle et réflexion architecturale au début du XIe siècle: Les voyages de l'abbé-évêque Oliba, I. Les premiers voyages, avant l'itinéraire vers Rome', *Les Cahiers de Saint-Michel de Cuxa*, XL (2009), 177–186.

¹⁰ X. Barral i Altet, 'Du Panthéon de Rome a Sainte-Marie la Rotonde de Vic: la transmission d'un modèle d'architecture mariale au début du XIe siècle et la politique 'romaine' de l'abbé-évêque Oliba', *Les Cahiers de Saint-Michel de Cuxa*, XXXVII (2006), 63–75; X. Barral i Altet, 'Culture visuelle et réflexion architecturale au début du XIe siècle: Les voyages de l'abbé-éveque Oliba, II. Les voyages à Rome et leurs conséquences', *Les Cahiers de Saint-Michel de Cuxa*, XLI (2010), 211–226.

¹¹ The Cuixà canopy is discussed later. The other canopy erected by Oliba at Ripoll must have combined a range of materials (wood covered with silver and perhaps stone bases) and was traditionally held to have been replaced inthe fifteenth century. However, it has been demonstrated that it was in fact pillaged in 1141 and renewed a few years later: F.X. Altés i Aguiló, 'La institució de la festa de Santa Maria en dissabte i la renovació de l'altar major del monestir de Ripoll a mitjan segle XII', *Studia Monastica*, XLIV (2002), 57–96. Four sturdy, carved stone bases have been preserved (two in the monastery and two in store at MNAC since 2011), thought to be the remains of the renewed 12th-century canopy, to which it is suggested other sculpture fragments preserved at Ripoll should be attributed: X. Barral i Altet, 'La sculpture à Ripoll au XIIe siècle', *Bull. Mon.*, 131 (1973), 311–359 [Le ciborium, at 316–331]; see also a recent state of the question discussion in B. Cayuela, 'Elements del baldaquí de Santa Maria de Ripoll', *El romànic i la Mediterrània. Catalunya, Toulouse i Pisa (1120–1180)*, ed. M. Castiñeiras, J. Camps, (Barcelona 2008), 244–247.

¹² M. Castiñeiras, 'De l'obra vista al revestiment de l'arquitectura: l'església pintada a la Catalunya romànica', *Els comacini i l'arquitectura romànica a Catalunya. Simposi Internacional* (Girona-Barcelona, 2005), Barcelona 2010, 133–149.

¹³ The so-called Ripoll Bible (Vat. Lat. 5729) and the Rodes Bible (París, BNF, MS lat. 6) and the dispersed remains of a third bible entitled the Fluvià Bible by its finder. See A.M. Mundó, *Les Bíblies de Ripoll. Estudi dels mss. Vaticà. Lat. 5729 i ParísBNF, Lat. 6*, (Vatican City 2002); M. Castiñeiras and I. Lorés Otzet, 'Las Biblias de Rodes y Ripoll: una encrucijada del arte románico en Catalunya', *Les Fonts de la Pintura Romànica*, ed, C. Mancho, M. Guardia, (Barcelona 2008), 219–260.

¹⁴ The text was first published in the 17th century by P. de Marca, *Marca hispanica sive limes hispanicus*, (Paris 1688), Ap. CCXXII col. 1072–82 and, again, in Junyent, *Diplomatari* (as n. 8), 369–386. It has been studied by E. Junyent, 'Le sermon du moine Garsias à l'occasion de la fête commemorative de la dédicace de l'église du monastère de Cuixa', *Tramontane, revue du Roussillon*, 35 année, núm. 340 (1951), 417–421. P. Ponsich, "Le sermon du moine Garsias", *Études Roussillonnaises*, 2 (1952), 28–39, and A.M. Mundó, 'Recherches sur le traité du moine Garsias à l'abbé-évêque Oliba sur Cuxa', *Les Cahiers de Saint-Michel de Cuxa*, I (1970), 63–74. It has also been translated into Spanish (A. Trías, 'Epístola-sermón del monje Garsías de Cuixà', *Anuario de Filología* 11–12 (1985–1986), p. 19–48) and into French (D. Codina, P. Bourgain et M. Besseyre, 'Lettre sermon du moine Garsias de Cuxa à l'abbé Oliba', *Les Cahiers de Saint-Michel de Cuxa*, XL (2009), 65–76.

¹⁵ Significant observations have been made on the nature of this text by R. Ordeig i Mata, 'La documentació del monestir de Cuixà referent a Oliba i als anys del seu abadiat', *Les Cahiers de Saint-Michel de Cuxa*, XL (2009), 39–51 [esp. 46–50].

¹⁶ Ponsich, 'Sant Miquel' (as n. 2), 367. The 10th-century building, with its layout including a rectangular apse, may recreate the original church dedicated to Saint Michael. See G. Mallet, *Églises romanes oubliées du Roussillon* (Montpellier 2003), 194; it has even been suggested that this apse was in fact the original chapel of Saint Michael (G. Gaillard,'Hypothèses sur le chevet de l'église de Saint-Michel-de-Cuxa', *Bulletin Hispanique*, XXXVI-3 (1934), 257–288, later included in his collected essays *Études d'art roman* (Paris 1972).

¹⁷ 'fecit caenaculum maximi et mirandi operis, qui divideret oraculum a priore, et ibi beatae et individuae Trinitaris clarum altare coram multis testibus piis manibus dedicavit' Junyent, *Diplomatari* (as n. 8), 379.

¹⁸ 'pulchro et arcuato opere beatae Mariae et archangelorum Dei in crypta quae ad praesepium dicitur extruxit ecclesiam' (ibid). J.Hubert, 'L'église de Saint-Michel-de-Cuxa et l'occidentation des églises au Moyen Age', *Journal of the Society of Architectural Historians*, XXI (1962), 163–170; B. Uhde-Stahl, 'La chapelle circulaire de Saint-Michel de Cuxà', *Cahiers de Civilisation Médiévale*, XX (1977), 339–351; C. Heitz, '"Beata Maria Rotunda". À propos de la rotonde occidentale de Saint-Michel de Cuixà', *Études Roussillonnaises offertes à Pierre Ponsich*, (Perpignan 1987), 273–277

¹⁹ Only two documents are known that allude to gold or silver work. For a recent review of the state of the question see J. Duran-Porta, *L'orfebreria romànica a Catalunya (950–1250)*, (unpublished Ph.D. thesis, Universitat Autònoma de Barcelona 2015), I, 303–305 and II, 221, 224–225.

²⁰ As is stated in a martyrology in Vic (Arxiu Capitular, Martirologi I, f. 126v); see Junyent, *Diplomatari* (as n. 8), 429; and Ordeig, 'La documentació' (as n. 15), 43.

²¹ For confirmation, see the studies mentioned in n. 8. See also M.-C. Zimmermann, 'La construction du mythe d'Oliba au XIXe siècle: *Canigó*, de Jacint Verdaguer (1886)', *Les Cahiers de Saint-Michel de Cuxa*, XL (2009), 341–353.

²² Without providing enough detail of the source, Font put forward 1121 as the start of his abbacy, indicating that the previous abbot had died in 1117 and concluding that there must have been a vacant period

between the two. F. Font, *Histoire de l'abbaye royale de Saint-Michel de Cuxa*, (Perpignan 1881), facsimile edition Rennes-le-Château 1989, 176. The date of death had already been given by J. Villanueva, *Viage literario á las iglesia de España*, XIX, Madrid 1851, p. 141–143, based on a necrology of Tarragona Cathedral. This dates from the 14th century and specifies (f 11v): 'Eodem die [March 25] anno MCXXXVI obiit Gregorius tertius Tarraconensis archiepiscopus' (S. Ramon and X. Ricomà, 'El necrologi de la Seu de Tarragona', *Miscel·lània Històrica Catalana, Homenatge al Pare Jaume Finestres, historiador de Poblet (1769)*, Abadia de Poblet, 1970 (Scriptorium Populeti, 3), 355 [343–398]. However, Villanueva himself had previously published a chronicle of the Monastery of Ripoll, the *Cronicon Rivupullense* II (*Viage literario á las iglesia de España*, vol. V, Madrid 1806, 247) which placed the date of Gregorius' death as two years earlier: '1144. Obiit Lucius papa et Gregorius archiepiscopus Terragon(ensis) et abbas Cuxanensis; et Berengarius Raymundi, comes Provinciae, occisus est'. In any event, the date of the Pope's death is wrong (he died in 1145) and that of Gregorius also seems to be mistaken.

[23] F. Fita, 'Doce bulas inéditas de Lucio II, Alejandro III, Lucio III, Celestino III, Inocencio IV y Alejandro IV históricas de Tarragona', *Boletín de la Real Academia de la Historia*, 29 (1896), 94–117.

[24] In the oldest of all, that of Lluís Pons d'Icart (1518/20–78), the author says that he has found no other document apart from a pair of bulls (one of which has already been mentioned in a previous note); J. Sánchez Real, *El archiepiscopologio de Luis Pons d'Icart* (Tarragona, 1954), 64. In that of the second half of the 17th century, Gregorius is the archbishop who has the briefest mention, which specifically underlines the lack of knowledge about his family and origins: J. Blanch, *Arxiepiscopologi de la Santa Església metropolitana i primada de Tarragona*, transcription and prologue by J. Icart (Tarragona, 1985, 2nd ed.), I, 85.

[25] In 1141 he founded a village in the grounds of the monastery (Font, *Histoire de l'abbaye*, (as n. 22), 180–181), which would be the new location of the village of Codalet.

[26] Annie de Pous, 'Les marbres inscrits de Saint-Michel de Cuxa", *Études roussillonnaises*, II, (1952), 117–125, considered that Gregorius must have been buried in Tarragona Cathedral, improbable at a time that the archbishopric and its see were little more than an aspiration.

[27] The Roussillon scholar A. Puiggarí copied this reference in the nineteenth century, though it was then mislaid amongst his papers, which were published some time later. A. Cazes, 'En parcourant les cartulaires', *Massana. Revue d'histoire, d'archéologie et d'héraldique du Roussillon*, IV (1972) 366–370; M. Durliat, 'La date du cloître de Saint-Michel de Cuxa', *Bull. Mon.*, 130 (1972), 364.

[28] Among various different studies dedicated to the eventful history of the cloister, see M. Durliat, 'La fin du cloître de Saint-Michel de Cuxa', *Les Cahiers de Saint-Michel de Cuxa*, II (1971), 1–16, and G. Mallet, 'Dispersion et restauration du cloître de Saint-Michel de Cuxa (XIXe–XXe siècles)', *Les Cahiers de Saint-Michel de Cuxa*, XXXIII (2002), 145–158, with extensive bibliography.

[29] E. Carrero, 'Centro y periferia en la ordenación de espacios litúrgicos: las estructuras corales', *Hortus Artium Medievalium*, 14 (2009), 159–179 (esp. 170–174), where there is a detailed critical review of the historiography on what the author argues were choral tribunes. Until very recently, scholars have argued that originally these tribunes would have been set at the west end of their respective churches, the one exception being Marcel Durliat. In the most recent publication on the subject, however, Carrero's interpretation is favoured. O. Poisson et al., *Les tribunes de Cuxa et de Serrabona deux clôtures de choeur exceptionnelles de l'époque romane*, (Montpellier 2014).

[30] A methodical analysis of all the remains – almost 200 – has allowed a hypothetical reconstruction. See A. Thirion, 'Proposition de reconstitution de l'ancienne tribune de Saint-Michel de Cuxa: De la sculpture à la structure, nouvelle approche', *Les Cahiers de Saint-Michel de Cuxa*, XLII (2011) 177–182. See also Poisson et al., *Les tribunes* (as n. 29).

[31] J. Taylor, Ch. Nodier, A. de Cailleux, *Voyages pittoresques et romantiques dans l'ancienne France*, II-1, *Languedoc*, (Paris 1835), pl. 161 and 163bis.

[32] Pous, 'Les marbres inscrits' (as n. 26), 119–122; D. Cazes and M. Durliat, 'Découverte de l'effigie de l'abbé Grégoire créateur du cloître de Saint-Michel de Cuxa', *Bull. Mon.*, 145 (1987), 593–608.

[33] P. Ponsich, 'Le problème des tribunes de Cuxa et de Serrabone', *Les Cahiers de Saint-Michel de Cuxa*, XVI (1985), 9–24 and XVIII (1987), 265–287 (esp. 271); A. Thirion, 'La plaque de l'abbé Grégoire et l'ancienne 'tribune' de Cuxa. Evaluer l'incertitude dans la maquette patrimoniale', *Les Cahiers de Saint-Michel de Cuxa*, XLV (2014), 175–187

[34] O. Poisson et al., *Les tribunes* (as n. 29), 34.

[35] The whole text of the colophon is transcribed in C. Samaran and R. Marichal, *Catalogue des manuscrits en écriture latine portant des indications de date, de lieu ou de copiste*, tome VI, *Bourgogne centre, sud-est et sud-ouest de la France* (Paris 1968), 345, and *Colophons de manuscrits occidentaux des origines au XVIe siècle*, V (Fribourg 1979), 169.

[36] C. Fraïsse, 'Le cloître de Moissac a-t-il un programme?', *Cahiers de civilisation médiévale*, 50 (2007), 245–270 (esp. 248–251).

[37] J. Lemarié, 'Le Sanctoral de Saint-Michel de Cuxa d'après le manuscrit Perpignan B.M. 2', *Liturgica* (Scripta et Documenta, 17), 3 (1966), 85–100.

[38] For a brief profile of the manuscript with earlier bibliography, see A. Orriols, 'Evangeliari de Cuixà', *El romànic i la Mediterrània* (as n. 11), cat. number 117, 436–437.

[39] I deal with these relationships in greater detail and in the context of other interchanges between the miniature and other arts in Romanesque Catalonia in: 'La miniatura en diàleg amb l'entorn: intercanvis artístics als scriptoria romànics catalans', *Entre la letra y el pincel: el artista medieval. Leyenda, identidad y estatus*, ed., M. Castiñeiras (Almería 2017), 165–183.

[40] A. Orriols, 'Les imatges preliminars dels Evangelis de Cuixà (Perpinyà, Bibl. Mun. Ms. 1)', *Locus Amœnus* 2 (1996), 31–46.

[41] 'Pulchro et arcuato opere beatae Mariae et atchangelorum Dei in crypta quae ad praesepium dicitur extruxit ecclesiam [. . .] Ad pedes etiam seu in sinu matris causa famulatus circumsepsit, et hinc inde martyres sepelivit'; Junyent, *Diplomatari* (as n. 8), 379.

[42] Junyent, *Diplomatari*, (as n. 8), 378–379.

[43] J. Puig i Cadafalch, *L'arquitectura romànica a Catalunya*, vol. II, *Del segle IX al XI*, (Barcelona 1911; facsimile ed. 1983), 406 (fig. 353), 408–409. Other reconstruction sketches have been produced: see that by C. Catanèse in Mallet, *Églises romanes oubliées* (as n. 16), 82; and an imaginative one, with arborescent forms not found on any known canopies, in Codina, Bourgain et Besseyre, 'Lettre sermon' (as n. 14), 73.

[44] V. Gatti, 'Il Ciborio della basilica benedittina di S. Pietro al Monte di Civate. Valore mistagogico dell'arte', in *Amen Vestrum. Miscellanea di studi liturgico-pastorali in onore di P. Pelagio Visentin*, a cura di A. Catella, (Padova 1994), 377–387; V. Gatti, 'Particolare iconografia degli Evangelisti nel contesto liturgico della medioevale basilica benedettina di S. Pietro al Monte sopra Civate', in C. Hediger, ed., *Tout le temps du veneour est sans oyseouseté'. Mélanges offerts à Yves Christe pour son 65ème anniversaire* (Turnhout 2005), 349–364.

[45] S. Moralejo, 'Ars sacra' et sculpture romane monumentale: le trésor et le chantier de Compostelle, *Les Cahiers de Saint-Michel de Cuxa*, XI (1980), 189–238 ['Le ciborium', 210–221 and fig. 5]. More recent studies propose a fresh reconstruction of the Compostela canopy and insist on the influence that the journeys to Rome would have had on their promoter in the layout of the Compostela presbytery (see below n. 67).

[46] As suggested by P. Ponsich, 'Le problème du ciborium d'Oliba', *Les Cahiers de Saint-Michel de Cuxa*, 24 (1993), 21–27.

[47] Numbers 25.120585–25.120588. Purchased from George Grey Barnard; J.L. Schrader, 'George Grey Barnard: The Cloisters and The Abbaye', *The Metropolitan Museum of Art Bulletin*, 37, (1979), 18.

[48] D.L. Simon, 'Romanesque Sculpture in North American Collections. XXIV. The Metropolitan Museum of Art. Part IV: Pyrenees', *Gesta*, XXV, (1986), 245–276 [esp. 267–270, figs 57–60]; P. Ponsich, initially considered the possibility that the capitals in the United States had belonged to the canopy. 'Saint-Michel de Cuxa du IXe au XIIe siècle. Aperçu historique', *Les Cahiers de Saint-Michel de Cuxa*, I (1970), 19–26 at 22, but he later ruled out their having been from the era of Oliba: Ponsich, 'Le problème du ciborium' (as n. 46), 24–27. The only

possibility that these capitals may have belonged to the canopy, according to Ponsich, would be if they had replaced the originals one century later.

[49] I. Lorés, 'La sculpture de Saint-Michel de Cuxa à l'époque de l'abbé Oliba', *Les Cahiers de Saint-Michel de Cuxa*, XXXVIII (2007), 183–191 [esp. 187–188]. Lorés revisits a previous proposal and contributes fresh arguments in favour of this base being part of the canopy.

[50] It should also be recalled that the altar stone of Santa Maria de Ripoll seems to have been a reddish colour. This has led to the proposal that it may be made from marble of this colour from the quarry near Cuixà. See J. Ainaud de Lasarte, 'Una inscripció inèdita en vers de l'escola de Ripoll', *Estudis Romànics*, 8 (1961), 21–23). The symbolic value of this colour for an altar would be clear, and it is tempting to think that Oliba, abbot of both monasteries, was responsible for this choice, though unfortunately the piece has not been preserved and nothing more can be said on the matter. The stone may belong to a consecration before Oliba's abbacy.

[51] If the canopy of Cuixà was deliberately evoked at Pedret, this would be another argument in favour of the influence of Oliba's heritage on the paintings of the so-called circle of Pedret, recently put forward by M. Castiñeiras, 'Il maestro di Pedret e la pittura lombarda: mito o realtà?', *Arte Lombarda*, 156 (2009), 48–66.

[52] Lorés, 'La sculpture' (as n. 49),190.

[53] W. Cahn, 'Romanesque Sculpture in American collections, XI. The Philadelphia Museum of Art', *Gesta* 13 (1974), 48–49. E. Diskant, 'Les fontaines du monastère de Saint-Michel de Cuxa', *Les Cahiers de Saint-Michel de Cuxa*, XXIII (1992), 135–141. The latter article is fundamental for clarifying some confusions about either source and dissipating doubts about possible falsifications.

[54] As n., 48.

[55] Diskant, 'Les fontaines' (as n. 51), 136.

[56] X. Barral i Altet, 'Fontaines et vasques romanes provenant de cloîtres méridionaux: problèmes de typologie et d'atttribution', *Les Cahiers de Saint-Michel de Cuxa*, VII (1976), 123–125 and figures; idem, 'Une vasque de cloître provenant probablement de Grandmont, au Musée de Cluny à París', *L'ordre de Grandmont. Art et Histoire* (Montpellier 1992), 209–213.

[57] R. de la Haye, 'La fontaine du cloître de Moissac', *Bulletin de la Société Archéologique de Tarn- et-Garonne* 110 (1985), 115–122.

[58] J.-C. Fau, 'Le bassin roman de serpentine du cloître de Conques', *Actes du Congrès d'Études de Rodez* (juin 1974), (Rodez 1975), 319–332; idem, 'Le cloître roman de Saint-Foy de Conques en Rouergue', *Archéologia*, 116 (1978), 36–47.

[59] Ibid., N. Charbonnel, 'La ville de Gerbert, Aurillac: Les origines', in N. Charbonnel and J.-É. Jung (eds), *Gerbert l'Européen. Actes du colloque d'Aurillac, 4–7 juin 1996*, (Aurillac 1997), 53–78 (esp. 66, 72–73).

[60] *Breve chronicon Auriliacensis abbatiae*, in J. Mabillon, *Vetera Analecta* (Paris 1723), 349–350.

[61] The old monastic buildings are currently being excavated and we must await the results. As regards the abbey church, during the abbacy of Pierre de Cisières (1079–1107), it had acquired an appearance very similar to that of Cuixà after Oliba's intervention (Charbonnel, 'La ville de Gerbert' (as n. 59), 66 and 70, with bibliography). Pierre de Laroque or de Roquenatou (Petrus de Roca) was abbot from 1107–c. 1119.

[62] In any event, some caution is in order. A red marble wall fountain in The Cloisters Museum, New York (num. 35.51a-d), acquired as a 12th-century work from Roussillon is now considered to be a forgery made at the end of 19th or the beginning of 20th century (see www.metmuseum.org/collection/the-collection-online/search/471180). On the seat, the ornamental motif formed by a succession of circles, which at first sight might seem inauthentic, is also found at the upper edge of the font, whose authenticity is beyond doubt. This is unusual and therefore links the pieces and allows us to see them as contemporary and sharing a possible common context.

[63] J. Déer, *The Dynastic Porphyry Tombs of the Norman Period in Sicily*, (Cambridge, Massachusetts 1959), 142–146; A. Paravicini Bagliani, *Le Chiavi e la Tiara. Immagini e simboli del papato medievale*, (Roma 1998), 64–66; idem, *The Pope's Body*, (Chicago – London 2000), 39–49.

[64] P.C. Clausen, 'Marmo e splendore. Architetura, arredi liturgici, spoliae', in M. Andaloro and S. Romano, eds., *Arte e iconografia a Roma dal tardoantico alla fine del medioevo* (Milan 2002), 151–174.

[65] X. Barral i Altet, *Els mosaics medievals de Ripoll i de Cuixà*, (Poblet 1971), 31–33, fig. 15, and, ídem, *Els mosaics de paviment medievals a Catalunya*, (Barcelona 1979), 95–100.

[66] X. Barral, *Els mosaics de paviment*, (as n. 65), 55–94. Considered a 12th-century creation, the Ripoll example has been dated at around 1151, when it is known that the new canopy was being constructed See Altés, 'La institució de la festa' (as n. 11), 61–69 [esp. 66]

[67] M. Castiñeiras, 'Roma e il programma riformatore di Gelmírez nella cattedrale di Santiago', in A.C. Quintavalle, ed., *Medievo: immagini e ideologie. V Convegno Internazionale di Studi*, (Parma-Milan, 2005), 211–26; and specifically on the canopy, M. Castiñeiras and V. Nodar, 'Para una reconstrucción del altar mayor de Gelmírez: cien años depués de López Ferreiro', *Compostellanum. Estudios Jacobeos*, LV (2010), 575–640 [esp. 599–607].

[68] M. Durliat, 'Les reliefs de St-Pierre et St-Paul à Saint-Michel de Cuxà', *Les Cahiers de Saint-Michel de Cuxà*, I (1970), 27–32. In his proposal for the reconstruction of the tribune, Pierre Ponsich also includes these, locating them in a western door of the structure: P. Ponsich, 'Le problème des tribunes' (as n. 33), II, 269–270); Thirion, 'Proposition de reconstitution' (as n. 30), 179.

[69] D. Codina i Giol, 'Sources littéraires de la *Vita* ou *Gesta* de saint Pierre Orseolo', *Les Cahiers de Saint-Michel de Cuxà*, XLIII (2012), 199–204.

[70] M. Coll i Alentorn, 'La historiografia a Catalunya en el període primitiu', *Estudis romànics*, III (1951–1952), 155–156; P. Ponsich, 'Le rôle de Saint-Michel de Cuxà dans la formation de la historiographie catalane et l'historicité de la légende de Wifred le Vélu', *Études Roussillonnaises*, IV, (1954–1955), 156–159.

[71] M. Coll, *Guifré el Pelós en la historiografia i en la llegenda* (Barcelona 1990), 20.

[72] The forgeries were detected by Abadal 'Com neix i creix' (as n. 2), 414–420.

[73] N. Jaspert, 'Carlomagno y Santiago, en la memoria histórica catalana', *El camí de Sant Jaume i Catalunya, Actes del Congrés Internacional celebrat a Barcelona, Cervera i Lleida, els dies 16, 17 i 18 d'octubre de 2003*, (Barcelona 2007), 91–104. For a general consideration of the phenomenon across southern France see A. Remensnyder, *Remembering Kings Past: Monastic Foundation Legends in Medieval Southern France* (Ithaca and London 1995).

[74] Thirion, 'La plaque' (as n. 33), 183–185. This is a further argument in favour of the idea of the tribute to bygone abbots at Cuixà, which I put forward in earlier studies. See notes 38 and 40.

A LIMOUSIN CIBORIUM IN MEDIEVAL CATALONIA

Joan Duran-Porta

A Limousin ciborium made of gilt copper with champlevé enamel decoration is preserved in the Museu Nacional d'Art de Catalunya in Barcelona (MNAC).[1] This outstanding eucharistic vessel was acquired by the Museum in 1918 after it was discovered in an unknown parish church in the Catalan region of la Cerdanya, in the Pyrenees, where it was still being used as a chrismatory. The discoverer, Joaquim Folch i Torres, published a monographic study shortly after in which he pointed out similarities with the famous Maître Alpais ciborium preserved in the Louvre, but suggested that the piece came from the Rhineland area.[2] However, his arguments attributing it to German origin do not offer any compelling evidence, and all later historiography has related the ciborium to Limousin workmanship. This is particularly based on contributions made by Marie-Madeleine Gauthier,[3] who studied the work closely in 1959 when she was invited to Barcelona to examine the Limousin enamels in the MNAC collection. Gauthier linked the ciborium to a group of Limousin works decorated with similar figures with wide expressive faces, which she called the *aux grands yeux* group. She also established the generally accepted chronology of the ciborium, claiming it was made between 1195 and 1200.

Although, as far as I am concerned, the ciborium was made slightly later (*vide infra*), this practically coincides with the earliest documented references found in Catalonia concerning the *oeuvre de Limoges*, such as those found in an inventory at the monastery of Sant Joan de les Abadesses (1217), the testament of canon Joan Colom (1229) and the purchase of a crosier in Rome by Pere d'Amenys, abbot of Sant Cugat del Vallès (1238).[4] Consequently the ciborium in Barcelona belongs to the earliest stage when Limousin products were first imported into medieval Catalonia, and this coincides with the beginning of the wide dissemination of Limoges enamels throughout Europe, brought on by the definitive development of international trade and also by Rome's explicit approval and recognition of the liturgical and decorative value of these products following the fourth Lateran Council in 1215.[5]

DESCRIPTION AND STYLISTIC ANALYSIS

The ciborium is a globe-shaped work in the form of a closed vessel with a striking gold effect. It is made up of a hemispherical bowl and cover that fit together to form a central body measuring some 140 mm in diameter (Figure 14.1). The knop or crowning feature has been lost as has the foot or lower support, which was not very tall and probably had a truncated conical shape. The whole of the outer surface of the ciborium is drawn together by a reticular strip of wide lines which gives rise to a series of rhomboidal compartments where the enamelled decoration is located. The latter combines detailed vegetal features (folded stems and stalks which end in tri-lobed fleurons) and human figures. This decoration was created by applying the enamel, whilst the whole of the background of the work remains completely in reserve. As noted, this procedure was common at the origin of champlevé enamelled works of southern Europe, but it was not so usual around 1200 when the workshops of Limoges were engaged in turning out objects with reserved figures on enamelled backgrounds.

The figures portrayed in the ciborium occupy two rows on the cover and one on the bowl of the vessel. There are eighteen half-length figures in all, none of which bear any special features and they can only be told apart by their postures and gestures, which are quite detailed and lively. Twelve of them are holding conversations in pairs and all (except one) hold a book in their hands, so they are most likely to be the apostles (Figure 14.2). The other six (those in the upper part) have been identified as being prophets or saints, yet they might also be angels portrayed without wings. Flanking these figures are three inscriptions, two of which have been identified (an alphabet and an angelic salutation) while the third is formed by a series of apparently unrelated letters and is still to be deciphered.[6] Completing the figurative decoration are two small engraved medallions in the inner part: a *Dextera Domini* on the cover and a beautiful angelical figure on the base (Figure 14.3).

From a typological viewpoint, this kind of short globe-shaped ciborium is quite characteristic of European metalwork from between the late 12th century and the early 13th century.[7] Two other similar examples of Limousin ciboria still survive: the famous Maître Alpais ciborium mentioned previously, dated *c.* 1200,[8] and a fragmentary replica of this in the British Museum collection, surely made slightly after (*c.* 1210–25).[9]

FIGURE 14.1

Barcelona: MNAC. Limousin Ciborium – general view (© Museu Nacional d'Art de Catalunya. Foto: Calveras/ Mérida/Sagristà) see colour plate XVI

FIGURE 14.2

Barcelona: MNAC. Limousin Ciborium – detail of apostle (© Museu Nacional d'Art de Catalunya. Photo: Calveras/Mérida/Sagristà)

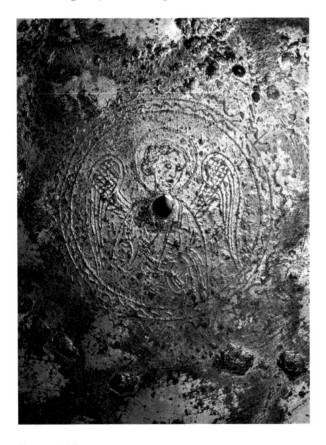

FIGURE 14.3

Barcelona: MNAC. Limousin Ciborium – inner medallion with angel figure (© Museu Nacional d'Art de Catalunya. Photo: Calveras/Mérida/Sagristà)

The Maître Alpais ciborium is probably the most outstanding Limoges work, at least in terms of historiography (Figure 14.4). It has a quite similar shape to the one displayed in Barcelona and still completely preserves the upper knop and conical foot. The main body is a little larger (168 mm in diameter) and is also drawn together with a pattern of rhomboidal cells which serve as a backdrop for the decorative figures and vegetation. Here also, as with most Limousin works from this period, the background is completely enamelled in blue and the decoration is always in reserve. The larger dimensions of this vessel enable more cells to be included in the pattern thus allowing the multiplication of figures portrayed, which also happen to be apostles (to which four more saints are added),[10] together with a series of thirty-two angels, this time with wings. The British Museum's ciborium is a simplified imitation of the Maître Alpais ciborium, yet lacks the quality and decorative ambition of the latter and features an iconography composed solely of angelical figures.

In contrast, the Barcelona ciborium is no mere humble imitation of the aspect and decorative formulas of the Alpais ciborium, despite the fact that whoever made it had clearly considered it when designing his piece. This obviously compels us to consider that it was made at a later date. Differences between the pieces are the presence of an abundance of glass cabochons, and an absence of inscriptions on the Alpais ciborium.[11] However we do find on the Alpais ciborium the same two medallions engraved on the inner face with the images of the *Dextera Domini* and the angel (next to which is the exceptional signature: 'Magister G. Alpais me fecit lemovicarum'). However, it seems clear that the maker of the Barcelona ciborium also drew on other sources and knowledge to create the work. It is along this path which I believe we should continue to investigate its ties to Catalonia. Thus, it is worth bearing in mind the two main differences between the ciboria: 1) the use of enamelled decoration

FIGURE 14.4

Paris: Louvre. Master Alpais ciborium (Louvre, © RMN/ Jean-Gilles Berizzi)

with elongated index fingers. A large upper arcade forms the backdrop of the scenes, in which the chromatic energy of the golden background clearly stands out, absorbing the space yet heightening the visual and material force of the whole work. Some of these stylistic features (though lacking the energy and the narrative quality of the panels) are repeated in a series of Limousin works which, in one way or another, derive from the Grandmontine altarpiece. Some of these were perhaps made by the same workshop, while the others were made by different workshops that were influenced by them. The obvious stylistic proximity of these works has, to a certain extent, enabled us to compile a *maniera* or Grandmontine style in the Limousin production of the time, in which particularly a series of altar crosses are to be found, dating from between 1185 and 1200. Significantly, when their origin is known, most of these works started out in the Grandmont priories.[14]

The style of the Barcelona ciborium may not be directly linked to this whole group, but it does share an important number of features, and at times the similar drawing of some of its figures is quite undeniable. For instance, it could be compared to the plaques found on a cross from Mathon Priory, part of the Metropolitan Museum's collection in New York, particularly as regards the angel of the Tetramorph (Figure 14.5). Even the vegetal

versus enamelled background; and 2) the style of the drawing, particularly on human figures.

As regards the first issue, we have already seen that in Limousin production from around 1200 enamelled backgrounds were widely used. The figures were generally reserved and often combined (such as on the Alpais ciborium) with appliqué features, particularly heads. However, some Limousin workshops rejected this evolution and kept on with the traditional procedures of enamelled figures on a reserved metal background, typical of early champlevé enamels. The nucleus of this second production style probably lies in the workshop or workshops which were working for Grandmont Abbey in the late 12th century. This monastery was the motherhouse of a reforming order founded in the middle of the same century which spread far and wide across most of Europe (particularly in western France) under the protection of the Plantagenet family.[12] The main altar in the abbey–church of Grandmont was splendidly decorated with enamelled work. The main feature of this installation was an altarpiece which was probably made around 1190, and of which still remain two outstanding panels, now part of the collection in the Musée de Cluny in Paris.[13]

These panels display large-sized figures, which are well proportioned with slender outlines and golden lines among the enamelled parts simulating the cloisonné technique, serene open-eyed faces outlined in gold and unusual hands

FIGURE 14.5

New York: Metropolitan Museum of Art. Plaque from a cross (Gift of J. Pierpont Morgan, 1917)

decoration on the ciborium is linked to this Grandmontine style. For example, the tri-lobed fleurons point directly to those on other works, such as the cross plaque found in 1869 in Cherves (Louvre), which could have come from a Grandmontine priory at Gandory.[15] In fact, all the pieces from the *aux grands yeux* group, among which Gauthier included the Barcelona ciborium, are in some way also linked to the Grandmontine works, despite the fact that the workmanship tends to be much less refined. Only the eyes that characterise this series, which are large, bulging and marked with dots of white enamel, are a specific feature of this group (the Grandmontine series of eyes tend to be reserved).[16]

There is still another series of Limousin enamels, which date from a little later, which continued to use the formula of the golden backgrounds and enamelled figures for decades later (until sometime between 1230s and 1240s). This later production bears some vague allusions to the expressive formulas and resources used by the workshops linked to Grandmont yet these usually feature a much more sketchy and expeditious style with images containing coarser and more expressionist features. They also bear some unique and exclusive ornamental features, such as the star-like or pseudo-floral motifs engraved throughout the golden reserved surface.[17] The most representative of the works from this series are two twin quatrefoil reliquaries devoted to St. Francis of Assisi, preserved at the Louvre and the Musée de Cluny. Curiously, the reliquary held at the Louvre is said to come from the island of Majorca (yet this lacks any documentary evidence), where it had been taken (from Catalonia?) following the conquest of King James I in 1229, perhaps coinciding with the dedication of the first Franciscan chapel on the island.[18]

The Barcelona ciborium bears hardly any features of this later series of reserved background Limousin works, except the use of the *guilloché* in the gilded surfaces (with a very elementary linear pattern) or the sharp definition of the inner lines of the figures. Moreover, were one to argue a similar later date for the ciborium (no earlier than 1225), it would be hard to understand the structural and iconographical resemblances with the Maître Alpais ciborium, nor the use of some stylistic features which clearly point to production prior to 1200, such as the fine use of chromatic combinations or the definition of human anatomy by means of firm vertical lines. On the other hand, the elegant, strictly harmonious vegetal motifs on the Catalan piece have little in common with the rigidity and schematisation of the vegetal motifs in later productions.

Having outlined and argued my case, I believe that a stylistic analysis of the Barcelona ciborium enables us to date it within a timeframe of between 1200 and 1215. That is to say, later than the Alpais ciborium (*c.* 1200), and also later than (but not much) the closest works on the Grandmont altarpiece, yet still not linked with the later series of works headed by the Franciscan reliquaries. The connection with Grandmont Abbey can still be upheld. By using information regarding this Abbey and the Order of Grandmont, I will attempt to explain the possible gestation of this work and the Catalan background of its patronage.

A WAY TO BARCELONA: THE BACKGROUND OF THE PATRONAGE

Despite the fact that the Order of Grandmont never established any priories in Catalonia, there were several important centres belonging to the order in the far reaching domains controlled by the Catalan kings in the Languedoc and Provence.[19] Moreover, the Grandmontine *bonis hominis* were directly in touch with the monarchs, who explicitly protected and provided them with several remarkable donations, and quite likely visited some of their houses. Indeed, the good relations between the kings and the order reflected to a large extent the attitude of Catalan allies, the powerful Plantagenets, who had protected the Order of Grandmont practically from the time of its foundation.

Documentary sources reveal the intensive nature of these contacts, which were established in the late 12th century. A significant document is the testament made by King Alfonso the Chaste, granted in 1194. The king bequeathed to the Order of Grandmont the sum of 500 *solidi* annually from rents paid in the town of Millau, and also 200 *morabatins* (maravedís) for the purchase of incense in exchange for prayers for his soul, as if the king were one of the brothers in the order.[20] This legacy was rather generous, and it was not the first donation to Grandmont made by the king. In fact, one year earlier Alfonso had granted the river Vézoubies with several mills to the Grandmontine priory of Comberoumal, located in the county of Rodez, over which Alfonso held feudal jurisdiction. The donation was confirmed later by his successor, Peter the Catholic, in 1194 and again in 1196.[21]

King Peter strengthened the relations with the southern Grandmont priories, partly due to his father's inheritance and partly to his marriage to Marie of Montpellier. His father-in-law, William VIII of Montpellier, was already the patron of the priory of Notre Dame of Montaubérau, situated a few kilometres from the city, and Peter the Catholic also put the monastery under his personal protection as mentioned in a document dating from 1206 in which he also placed under his direct patronage the aforementioned Comberoumal priory.[22] Needless to say, the monarch must have visited both monasteries himself: Montaubérau on his visits to Montpellier and Comberoumal, for example, on a trip to Millau which was documented in 1204.[23]

Naturally, the contacts between the Catalan monarchs and the Order of Grandmont lack any documented artistic implications and there is no evidence of Catalan kings or nobles ever visiting the Order motherhouse, nor any mention of interest in Limoges works. However, it must be recalled that the Grandmontines decorated most of their priories with *ornamenta* from Limoges workshops, and they must surely have done the same in their southernmost priories, situated in land then controlled by

Catalans, who surely knew and appreciated the Limousin enamelled work.

It is worth noting that Catalan intellectual circles were obviously aware of the Order of Grandmont, due to its proposal to renew western monasticism by way of austerity and asceticism (as practised by the Cistercians or Premonstratensians, who actually established centres in Catalonia). Even the order's internal problems, marked by a fierce struggle between monks and lay brothers,[24] were well known in Catalonia, as evidenced by the existence in the abbey of Ripoll of two copies of the famous poem *In Gedeonis area*, which describes the highpoint of the Grandmontine conflict.[25]

Having reached this point, I would like to outline my hypothesis: I believe it is reasonable to consider that the Barcelona ciborium is not only an object that was imported into Catalonia in the Middle Ages, but it is also an object that was specifically made under the patronage of a Catalan who was quite likely related to royal circles. I dare not assert that it was commissioned by a monarch (although the affordable prices of Limoges enamels would fit in quite well with the economic penuries habitually suffered by Catalan kings), yet this possibility should not be ruled out. To support my theory I have based my hypothesis on the stylistic relationship of the ciborium compared to the Limoges production linked to Grandmont, and on the close relationships between the Order of Grandmont and the kings of the House of Barcelona who emphatically supported this order.

Indeed, another Catalan work also points to the figurative culture of Grandmontine-style Limoges enamels. This is not a metalwork object but an illuminated manuscript: the renowned *Liber Feudorum Ceritaniae*, copied and illustrated in the early 13th century.[26] The miniatures in this royal cartulary are hard to understand without the enamelled works being used as visual models, an idea that was proposed some years back and must now be considered again.[27] Comparing these miniature works with the panels from the Grandmont altarpiece provides us with some interesting resemblances, such as the architectural setting, the flat golden background or its chromatic austerity subordinated to the brightness of the gold. Some features of the miniature paintings also even point to the style of the human figures in the Barcelona ciborium, such as the use of white dots (mainly in the eyes), the portrayal of large, oval faces or the expressive style of the hands, with long fingers outlined in black. The miniaturist of the *Liber Feudorum Ceritaniae* must therefore have known the Limoges works of the time, and links with the enamelled figures in the Barcelona ciborium are certainly suggestive, bearing in mind that the ciborium was discovered in la Cerdanya (and was perhaps even made for this area), i.e. one of the counties to which the cartulary is devoted.

Despite the indirect nature of the information, it is reasonable to consider the possibility that the Barcelona ciborium was directly commissioned by a member of the court of the Catalan kings (most likely in the entourage of Peter the Catholic), who could equally have been one of the lay councillors of the royal family or a high ranking ecclesiastical dignitary. Among the councillors of King Peter there were two eminent members of the clergy who are of special interest in this respect: Pere de Tavertet and his nephew Guillem, the bishop of Vic. The former had served in the accounts office with Ramon de Caldes (the head of the royal finances, and the compiler of *Liber Feudorum Maior*)[28] and later managed the Crown's finances, while Bishop Guillem de Tavertet was another important member of the King's circle, and a regular companion of Peter the Catholic in his travels. He was also ambassador to Rome several times, being on very good terms with Pope Innocent III, and he attended the fourth Lateran Council in 1215.[29]

In sum, the royal ties to the Grandmont priories might have enabled knowledge and love of Limoges champlevé enamelled works (favoured by their affordability), and would have incentivised the later acquisition of objects. In fact, this kind of process is well known in other lands. For example, a visit to Grandmont by the legate Lothario dei Conti di Segni, future Pope Innocent III, led to his interest in Limoges work and for Rome to commission several of Limousin works, particularly the decoration of the Vatican's *confessio* and also the reliquary casket in the shape of a basilica donated to the church of Saints Sergius and Bacchus.[30] Similarly, Cardinal Guala Bicchieri, founder of the abbey of Sant'Andrea in Vercelli (Piedmont), provided it with a large number of Limousin works following his visit to Limoges in 1209 also as a pontifical legate.[31] Shortly after, in 1242, Stephen of Lexington, then Abbot of Savigny, ordered five enamelled reliquaries following a visit to Grandmont Abbey and seeing its impressive decorated altar.[32]

As a result of a similar incentive, the Barcelona ciborium was commissioned from a Limousin enameller who followed the traditional procedures (enamelled figures on a reserved background) which were uncommon in the *oeuvre de Limoges* around 1200 but still used in the 'Grandmontine style' production. However, in order to conceive both the structure and the iconographic programme of the ciborium, the artist used the Maître Alpais ciborium as a prototype (and so must have been familiar with it). The internal engraved medallions are proof of this, as is the curious presence of one lone apostle without a book among the twelve figures portrayed, which also copies the presence of a lone saint without a book on the work in the Louvre. Access to the Alpais ciborium can be easily explained. It seems to have been part of the treasure at Montmajor Abbey, located in Provence (in the town of Arles, quite close to Montpellier),[33] and was thus within reach of the Catalan royal family's circle, who held fiefdoms (directly or indirectly) over the whole of Provence from the early 12th century.[34]

Therefore, combining the stylistic qualities of the 'Grandmontine style' and the format and decorative programme of an outstanding, Limousin work such as the Alpais ciborium, whoever made the Barcelona ciborium created a peculiar object, a veritable *unicum* among the Limoges work from that period. This work bears some quite unusual features, such as the tantalising presence and still unknown meaning of the engraved inscriptions, which we believe were either ordered by the unknown patron or made by the person who conceived its symbolic programme.

Bearing in mind the political background, it seems reasonable to argue that the ciborium was commissioned earlier than 1213. In that year, the Catalan and Occitan allies were defeated by northern French crusaders in the battle of Muret, after which Catalan influence north of the Pyrenees quickly fell into decline. Of course there were imported Limousin works in Catalonia by then, yet the outstanding quality and exclusive design of the ciborium at the Museu Nacional d'Art de Catalunya make this a particularly singular case. Moreover, this is perhaps one of the only commissions of Limousin enamelled pieces ever made for Catalan patrons, who generally acquired works such as these through other strictly commercial means or contacts and exchanges among religious institutions.

NOTES

[1] This study is part of the research project carried out by the Universitat Autònoma de Barcelona *Magistri Cataloniae – Artistas, patronos y público. Cataluña y el Mediterráneo (siglos XI–XV)* (MICINN HAR2011-23015).

[2] J. Folch i Torres, 'Copó esmaltat del Rin (segle XIII)', *Anuari de l'Institut d'Estudis Catalans* (1915–1920), 774–780. From 1920 to 1926, and later from 1930 to 1939, Folch i Torres was the director of the Museum in Barcelona.

[3] M.-M Gauthier, *Catalogue international de l'oeuvre de Limoges. 1. L'époque romane* (París 1987), 224–225.

[4] F. Español, 'Los esmaltes de Limoges en España', in B. Drake Boehm and J. Yarza (eds), *De Limoges a Silos* (Madrid 2001), 103

[5] M.-M. Gauthier, 'La clôture émaillée de la confession de Saint Pierre au Vatican, lors du Concile de Latran IV, 1215', *Synthronon, Art et Archéologie de la fin de l'Antiquité et du Moyen Age* (París 1968), 245.

[6] The alphabet (:A BC DE FG HI KL M) and particularly the angelic salutation (:AVE MARIA GRASIA PLENA DOMIN[US TECUM]) shows some Eucharistic flavour. I find it difficult to believe that the third inscription (D RC IA ML AO NI NL OI BL CD OI GL) is only decorative, but I am not able to suggest even a simple hypothesis about its meaning.

[7] P. Skubiszewski, 'Romańskie cyboria w kształcie czary z nakrywą: Problem genezy', *Rocznik Historii Sztuki*, 5 (1965), 7–46.

[8] É. Antonie, 'Ciboire de maître Alpais', *Corpus des émaux méridionaux, tome II: L'apogée 1190–1215* (Paris 2011), 144–149.

[9] B. McLeod, 'A ciborium in the British Museum', in S. La Niece, S. Röhrs and B. McLeod (eds), *The Heritage of 'Maître Alpais'* (London 2010), 1–5.

[10] Identified with saint Paul, the two non-apostolic evangelists Mark and Luke, and saint Trophime of Arles: É. Antoine, 'L'iconographie du Ciboire de Maître Alpais', in La Niece, Röhrs and McLeod (eds) *Heritage* (as n. 9), 21–26.

[11] There is only a meaningless pseudo-Kufic inscription on the Maître Alpais ciborium (and also on the British Museum ciborium): V. Porter, 'The Arabic Inscriptions on the Maître Alpais and British Museum Ciboria', in La Niece, Röhrs and McLeod (eds) *Heritage* (as n. 9), 17–20.

[12] J. Dubois, 'Grandmontains et chartreux, ordes nouveaux du XIIe siècle', in G. Durand and J. Nougaret (eds), *L'ordre de Grandmont. Art et Histoire* (Montpellier 1992), 3–21.

[13] On the enamelled works in Grandmont: G. François-Souchal, 'Les émaux de Grandmont au XIIe siècle', *Bull. mon*, 120 (1962), 339–357; 121 (1963), 41–64, 123–150, 219–235, 307–329; 122 (1964), 7–35, 129–159.

[14] G. Souchal, 'Autour des plaques de Grandmont: une famille d'émaux limousins champlevés de la fin du XIIe siècle', *Bull. mon*, 125, 1 (1967), 21–71.

[15] On both comparisions, see: Souchal, Autour (as n. 14) 47–48 and 59–60.

[16] Indeed, the *groupe aux grands yeux* is quite problematic, and deserves to be reconsidered. Perhaps the most similar work of the group to the Barcelona ciborium is the so-called Rusper Chalice: Gauthier, *Catalogue* (as n. 3), 223–224.

[17] F. Stohlman, 'The star group of champlevé enamels and its connections', *The Art Bulletin*, 32, 4 (1950), 327–330. Again, the uniformity of this group should be questioned, as pointed by: E. Taburet-Delahaye, 'Reliquiary of Saint Francis of Assisi', *Enamels of Limoges 1100–1350* (New York 1995), 306–309

[18] Taburet-Delahaye, Reliquiary (as n. 17), 306–309. Elisabet Antoine-König has convincingly proposed a later dating for both San Francis reliquaries, up to the third quarter of the 13th century: E. Antoine-König, 'New dating of the Limoges Reliquaries of the Stigmatization of St Francis', in J. Robinson, L. de Beer and A. Harnden (eds), *Matter of Faith: An Interdisciplinary Study of Relics and Relic Veneration in the Medieval Period*, London, 2014, 84–91. As the author points out, the re-dating of the reliquaries opens the possibility of a reassessment of the date of many other enamels that have been dated by taking them as point of reference.

[19] M. Aurell, 'Autour d'un débat historiographique: l'expansion catalane dans les pays de langue d'oc au Moyen Âge', *Montpellier, la couronne d'Aragon et les pays de langue d'oc (1204–1349)* (Montpellier 1987), 9–41

[20] J. Alturo, *L'Arxiu antic de Santa Anna de Barcelona del 942 al 1200* (Barcelona 1985), III, 150–151.

[21] G. Durand, 'Les Prieurés Grandmontains du Roergue: Comberoumal et Le Sauvage', *L'ordre de Grandmont. Art et Histoire* (Montpellier 1992), 154.

[22] Some years after, King James I renewed the royal patronage of these priories: J. Nougaret, 'Le prieuré grandmontain N.-D de Montaubérou, à Montpellier (Hérault)', *Durand and Nougaret (eds), L'ordre de* Grandmont (as n.12), 198

[23] J. Miret i Sans, 'Itinerario del rey Pedro I de Cataluña, II en Aragón (1196–1213)', *Boletín de la Real Academia de Buenas Letras de Barcelona*, IV (1905–1906), 274–276.

[24] J. Becquet, 'La Première crise de l'Ordre de Grandmont', *Bulletin de la Societé Archéologique et Historique du Limousin*, LXXXVII-3 (1959), 283–325.

[25] H. Anglès, *La música a Catalunya fins al segle XIII* (Barcelona 1935), 256.

[26] M.E. Ibarburu, 'Liber Feudorum Ceritanie', *Catalunya Romànica, vol. XX* (Barcelona 1992), 202–204. It was a partial copy (limited to charts related to counties of Cerdanya and Roussillon) of the *Liber Feudorum Maior*, the main Catalan royal cartulary at the times, compiled by the eminent jurist Ramon de Caldes under the reign of Alphonse the Chaste.

[27] M.E. Ibarburu, 'Los cartularios reales del Archivo de la Corona de Aragón', *Lambard* VI (1992–1993), 209. It should be noted that the influence of Limoges enamels (although not specifically in the Grandmontain style) is not uncommon in Catalan illuminated manuscripts: A. Orriols, 'La il·lustració de manuscrits a Catalunya al segle XII', *El romànic i la Mediterrània, Catalunya, Toulouse i Pisa, 1120–1180* (Barcelona 2008), 211.

[28] T. Bisson, 'Ramon de Caldes (c. 1135–1199): Dean of Barcelona and King's Minister', in Thomas N. Bisson (ed.), *Medieval France and Her Pyreneean Neighbours: Studies in Early Institutional History* (London 1989), 187–198.

[29] Bisson, *Fiscal Accounts of Catalonia Under the Early Count-Kings (1151–1213)* (Berkeley-London 1984) I, 148–149. Bishop Guillem de Tavertet is mentioned on several documentary sources travelling to Languedoc with King Peter in 1206–1207 and in 1212–1213: M.

Alvira Cabrer, *Pedro el Católico, Rey de Aragón y Conde de Barcelona (1196–1213). Documentos, testimonios y memoria histórica* (Zaragoza 2010), V, 187–198.

[30] B.D. Boehm, 'Opus lemovicensi: The Taste for and the Diffusion of Limousin enamels', *Enamels of Limoges, 1100–1300* (New York 1995), 44.

[31] S. Castronovo, 'Limoges et l'Italie: le cas du Piémont au XIIIe siecle', *L'Oeuvre de Limoges. Art et histoire au temps des Plantagenêts* (Paris 1998), 343–350.

[32] G. François, 'Une commande cistercienne d'émaux en 1242 pour l'abbaye normande de Savigny', *Bolletino d'Arte*, suppl. n. 95 (1996), 59–70.

[33] This information is provided by the former owner of the ciborium, painter Pierre Revoil (1776–1842): Antoine, 'L'iconographie' (as n. 10), 25.

[34] M. Aurell, 'L'expansion catalane en Provence au XIIe siècle', *La formació i l'expansió del feudalisme català* (Girona 1985), 175–197.

THE JACA IVORIES: TOWARDS A REVALUATION OF ELEVENTH-CENTURY FEMALE ARTISTIC PATRONAGE IN THE KINGDOM OF ARAGON

Verónica C. Abenza Soria

Over the last decade, knowledge of female artistic patronage during the Middle Ages has expanded significantly.[1] The Kingdom of Aragon, however, has been studied far less than other Romanesque *milieux* in the Iberian Peninsula.[2] For 11th-century Aragonese queens only limited documentary material survives, and the attention given to their artistic undertakings generally has been neglected in favour of that of their husbands, whose patronage is better documented.[3] One of the less-studied cases of Aragonese female patronage concerns the so-called Jaca ivories, which were commissioned by Queen Felicia of Roucy around 1100 (Figures 15.1 and 15.2). There is little scholarly consensus on many issues of broad importance regarding their manufacture, including the identity of their patron, their date, their function and the identification of the hands that were responsible for them. In this essay I will argue that the ivories created for the Jaca panels (Metropolitan Museum of Art, Accession no: 17.190.134; 17.190.33) may have been conceived as mementos. Alternatively, and just as intriguingly, the panels may have been made to resemble reliquaries in the manner of contemporary examples.

The two Jaca panels consist of wood supports, one displaying Byzantine and the other Romanesque ivory carvings, each surrounded by a precious metalwork frame. Their opulent decoration suggests they were conceived as a kind of liturgical *ornamentum*. In my opinion, on the basis of technical and stylistic arguments, the setting of the plaques may be attributed to the goldsmiths' workshop that, under Abbot Bégon III of Conques (r. 1087–1107), fashioned reliquaries out of diverse fragments of pseudo-filigree around 1100. The Byzantine ivory, which depicts the Crucifixion, originally formed the centre of a three-panelled icon dating from the late 10th century.[4] M. Cortés suggested a general stylistic affiliation with the elongated forms typical of 10th-century Byzantine carving, which are to be found in ivories such as The Borradaile Triptych (The British Museum, M&ME 1923 12–15,1) and the triptych from the Département des Monnaies, Médailles et Antiques of the Bibliothèque Nationale de France (Bibliothèque Nationale de France, Inv. 55 no. 301). However, far from displaying the common features of ivory icons connected to imperial workshops in Constantinople, this ivory seems to belong to an alternate type, more linked instead to intimate and private devotion. From my point of view, morphologically the ethereal and less naturalistic forms of the proposed models appear to be at odds with the simplicity of the folds, the swollen faces, the fleshy lips and the sensuous appearance of the figures in the Jaca ivory, which bear a greater resemblance to two Constantinopolitan ivory plaques depicting the Crucifixion and the Mission of the Apostles from the Museé du Louvre (second half of the 10th century) (Museé du Louvre, Département des Objets d'Art, MRR 354, 422).[5] It is most likely that the Romanesque ivory figures were carved purposely following the aesthetic trends of the artistic environment in which the Byzantine ivory was received: the nunnery of Santa María in Santa Cruz de la Serós (Jaca, Aragon).[6]

These Romanesque ivory figures are framed by repoussé silver epigraphs: IH(e)C(us) || NA | ZAR || EN(u)S [Iēsus Nazarēnus or 'Jesus the Nazarene'] (on top), FELI || CIA | REG || INA [Felicia Regina 'Queen Felicia'] (in the lower section), the latter providing the identity of the patron (Figure 15.3). Felicia (1063–1100?) was the daughter of the Count of Roucy (Picardy) and the second wife of King Sancho Ramírez, who ruled Aragon between 1063 and 1094.[7] His reign was defined by his determination to maintain the territorial integrity of the nascent kingdom of Aragon and he made several attempts to expand its boundaries. Sancho's association with the Holy See through the adoption of the Roman liturgy in 1071 and the acknowledgement of his status as a papal vassal eighteen years later fulfilled some of these high aspirations.[8] The king also encouraged French warriors to join Iberian Christian forces for the conquest of nearby Muslim-held lands, especially in the so-called siege of the city of Barbastro in 1063–64, which was sanctioned by Pope Alexander II. His marriage with Felicia assured the lasting nature of political and familial bonds, especially with Felicia's father Hildouin IV of Ramerupt, who had mediated in the relationship between the French King Philippe I and the Papacy,[9]

Figure 15.1

New York: Metropolitan Museum of Art: Jaca panel (Accession N. 17.190.134) © *The Metropolitan Museum of Art see also colour plate XVII*

FIGURE 15.2

New York: Metropolitan Museum of Art: Jaca panel (Accession N. 17.190.33) © The Metropolitan Museum of Art see also colour plate XVIII

but also with her brother Ebles of Roucy. Ebles in 1073 led the campaign to liberate the Aragonese city of Graus, which was endorsed by the same Pope Alexander,[10] and in 1084 defended Pope Gregory VII, alongside the Norman Robert Guiscard, during his military confrontation with Emperor Henry IV.[11] In this respect it is worth noting that the new queen and her siblings descended, on their mother's side, from the Carolingian kings of the Franks, the early Capetian kings, and the first Saxon king Henry I; they were therefore also distant relatives of Otto I, the great emperor of the Holy Roman Empire.[12] Likewise, by the mid 11th century, Hildouin IV of Ramerupt and Alice Adèle of Roucy, Felicia's parents, increased their power over northern France through the strategic marriages of their children. On the one hand, the marriage of their daughter Beatrice with Geoffrey II, count of Perche, afforded them important political profit and inheritances.[13] On the other, the wedding between Ebles, their heir, and Sybille of Hauteville, the daughter of the Norman ruler Robert Guiscard, secured the strong alliance between Rome and the House of Roucy.[14] Therefore, Felicia's family legacy made her a perfect choice of wife for King Sancho, and she helped his governmental ambitions flourish.

The intriguing complexity of the plaques' arrangement should be understood in light of the queen's familial and cultural heritage. The circumstances of the reception of

FIGURE 15.3

New York: Metropolitan Museum of Art: Jaca panel (Accession N. 17.190.33) © *The Metropolitan Museum of Art*

the Byzantine ivory possibly can be traced to the constant traffic of portable goods and gifts that played out through commercial and diplomatic networks.[15] Indeed, the practice of dismantling Byzantine ivory triptychs for their inclusion on liturgical objects is well attested beginning in the Carolingian and Ottonian periods. The circulation of these precious gifts to northern European lay and ecclesiastical rulers remained a custom well into the 11th and 12th centuries, as illustrated by the covers of the so-called Small Bernward Gospel (Dom-Museum Hildesheim, DS 13) and the Precious Gospels of Bernward of Hildesheim (Dom-Museum Hildesheim, DS 18). Moreover, the close relationship between the Roucy family and the Norman Sicilian dukedom may have been a potential path for the panel's acquisition and its later transmission to the queen. Thus, it is highly likely that the reception of the Byzantine ivory triggered Felicia's desire to commission the carving of the Romanesque ivories in order to create a more complex type of liturgical furnishing with them. It is plausible to argue that Felicia, sensitive to the artistic tastes of her own kingdom, was keen to ask an artist from Jaca familiar with the carving methods of Santa Cruz de la Serós to create these ivories.

These small figures featuring a Crucifixion, however, became part of a more significant creative process. In fact, one of the most striking peculiarities of the Romanesque figures lies in their *ad similitudinem* reformulation of the Byzantine panel. The composition provides an increased emphasis on the core motif turning the crucified Christ into the focus of attention (Figure 15.3). This is due to the framing supplied by the supporting figures attached to the repoussé silver ground and located on both sides of the cross, which divides the field into four panels. Even if the figures seem to have been created as appliqués, given that their size is consistent with the spaces delimited by the cross, and that Christ's nimbus forms part of the repoussé ground, it becomes apparent that the figures were precisely conceived for such a composition. Nonetheless, the Christ figure's body sways, breaking the unbending symmetry of the programme. This refinement may be attributed to the Romanesque artist's wish to render the figures with a strong expressiveness. Accordingly, pathos is achieved by facial expressions and gestures that show emotional attitudes and dramatic poses. At the same time, these gestures and grimaces contrast with the harmonious intentions of the carefully balanced composition. Even more revealing, perhaps, is the artist's tendency to distort the proportions of some body parts, especially heads and hands, as some sort of reinterpretation of the Byzantine ivory, where bodily schemata were accurately designed following the Byzantine canon of proportions.

Many scholars have found close parallels between the Romanesque crucifixion from Jaca and that of the Cross of Ferdinand and Sancha from the treasury of San Isidoro in León (Museo Arqueológico Nacional, 52.340), as well as the Carrizo Christ (Museo de León, 13) and the so-called Calvary of Corullón (Museo de León, 8, 10, 273).[16] I, however, am not convinced by such comparisons. Rather, I would suggest that the overall style of the carvings shows significant discontinuity with León's ivory carving tradition. It should be noted that the artist's tendency to naturalism and his particular treatment of volume create similar effects to those of other three-dimensional media, especially architectural sculpture. In his search for both intensely expressive figures and a balance of dramatic rhythms within a larger symmetry, the Jaca artist breaks with the schematic reduction of natural forms typical of León's monumental crucifixes. On the contrary, as already noted by Charles T. Little, the figures reveal 'an integrity associated with large-scale sculpture'.[17] This point leads to another interesting suggestion, that the ivories served, in poses and gestures, as models for a capital that originally came from the missing cloister of the same convent of Santa María in Santa Cruz de la Serós (Figures 15.4 and 15.5). This capital features scenes of the Flight into Egypt and the Massacre of the Innocents and has been attributed to the hand of the master who worked the front face of the Doña Sancha sarcophagus

FIGURE 15.4

Santa Cruz de la Serós: Capital depicting the Flight into Egypt and the Massacre of the Innocents from the lost cloister of the convent of Santa María (Verónica Abenza Soria)

FIGURE 15.5

Santa Cruz de la Serós: Capital depicting the Flight into Egypt and the Massacre of the Innocents from the lost cloister of the convent of Santa María (Verónica Abenza Soria)

(Benedictine monastery of Santa Cruz, Jaca). As a matter of fact, the ivories display a series of standard workshop style characteristics also visible in the works of the 'Doña Sancha master'.[18] These features include bell-shaped sleeves and wide, doubled triangular collars, almond eyes and flattened noses. The figures wear loose-fitting clothing that hide the body, and drapery which falls in parallel, trimmed folds with serrated edges. This suggests the ivory carver ostensibly was not only trained within the same environment, but also that he most probably worked within the same chronological framework as the sculptor (*c.* 1096/1097).

In this regard the artist was not unaware of other, coeval ivory productions,[19] namely the ivory panels that decorated the Reliquary of San Felices from the monastery of San Millán de la Cogolla (*c.* 1100) (La Rioja, Spain) (Figure 15.6). This is particularly well evidenced by his technique of tracing the most elementary forms of body parts and clothing with sketchy lines, without dwelling on details. As S. Moralejo pointed out, this formal language derived from the visual experiences of the Saint-Sever Beatus (Paris, Bibliothèque Nationale de France, MS. Latin 8878) and is also to be found in both series of ivory figures and panels from Jaca and San Millán. In my opinion, the ivories created for the Jaca panel provided the perfect testing ground to try out these aesthetic possibilities, which were to be later developed in sculpture in the mature Romanesque style from Toulouse to Compostela.[20] This set of ivories form the plastic expression of a renewed vocabulary built upon linear stylisation, and they might have played a major role in the assimilation and dissemination of this new language, especially by the late 11th and early 12th centuries, when later manifestations of Bernardus Guilduinus' sculpture in Jaca introduced effects associated with minor arts.

The transfer of models, the use of formulas that were fairly typical in pictorial arts and especially in miniatures (e.g. the cloud-like undulations of the upper ivory figures), and the widespread affinity with other artistic techniques together reveal an undeniable degree of complexity in the creative process of the Jaca ivories' carving. This interwoven dialogue between the arts was crowned with the addition of the bejeweled frames. Their decoration in silver-gilt pseudo-filigree and cabochons bears a

FIGURE 15.6

San Millán de la Cogolla (La Rioja): ivory panel from the Reliquary of San Felices (Verónica Abenza Soria)

FIGURE 15.7

Conques: Treasury of the Abbey of Saint-Foi – 'A' of Charlemagne (Térence de Monredon)

FIGURE 15.8

Conques: Treasury of the Abbey of Saint-Foi; pentagonal reliquary (Térence de Monredon)

close resemblance to a number of objects associated with the French abbey of Saint-Foy of Conques, including some fragments in the 'A' of Charlemagne, the so-called Pentagonal reliquary, the portable altar of Abbot Bégon III and the reliquary of Pope Paschal II, all in the abbey's treasury, which suggests that the frames were produced in the same artistic orbit (Figures 15.7, 15.8, 15.9 and 15.10).[21] Around 1100, the well-known Abbot Bégon III set up a new atelier of goldsmiths in order to carry out several commissions, including many reliquaries of the True Cross. Its productions are characterised by the use of silver instead of gold, as well as by the reuse of highly valued materials. They display a distinctive pseudo-filigree technique that creates complex visual patterns through specific vegetal and geometrical motifs, inviting comparison to the two diverse foliate patterns in the Jaca plaques. These and certain other features, such as the arrangement of the cabochons, their reinforcement by twisted threads, the use of slightly grainy tubular threading, and the highlighting of the edges of the frames with two larger, twisted threads, all link the silver-gilt frames from Jaca closely to the Conques workshop.[22] Even the fascinating presence in one of the frames of a cloisonné enamel, which appears to be one of the earliest surviving examples of this technique in Aragon, may be better understood in comparison with the cloisonné enamels of the 'A' of Charlemagne, specifically in terms of its colour scheme and its floral motifs' alveolar design.[23] Perhaps this may be explained by the close political and monastic links between the French abbey and the Kingdom of Aragon that argue for the creation of such reliquaries for affiliated communities by goldsmiths based in Conques, or perhaps travelling goldsmiths in monastic employ.

After Sancho Ramírez' death in 1094, the early reign of his son Pedro was still focussed on the conquest of the Muslim-held lands, especially the emblematic city of Barbastro located on the border of Muslim domains. In 1063, when King Sancho had briefly won Barbastro back from the Moors, he granted it to the Bishop of Roda. It was not by chance that between 1097 and 1100, and especially during the military campaign for the Conquest of Barbastro, King Pedro strengthened the kingdom's affiliation with the great abbey of Sainte-Foy de Conques, which was led at that time by Abbot Bégon III.[24] The exchange of monastic personnel is well documented since Pierre d'Andouque, formerly a monk at Conques, was bishop of Pamplona from 1083 to 1115. In addition, his contemporary Poncio, another former monk of Conques, was appointed Bishop of Roda in 1097 and two years later he hastened to request that Pope Urban II confirm the translation of the see from Roda to Barbastro.[25] It is highly significant that some months prior, in this same year, King Pedro had promised to donate to the abbey of Conques the first mosque of the city of Barbastro, even before its conquest.[26] At that time, the links between the abbey of Conques and the papacy appear to have been very close, as evidenced in Pope Paschal II's donation of relics of the *lignum crucis* to the abbey in 1100. This donation was probably made by April 1100 when a papal brief issued by the same Pope Paschal II and addressed to Bishop Poncio acknowledged the translation of the see from Roda to Barbastro. In fact, we know that some months later, on 26 June 1100, Bishop Poncio visited the abbey of Conques in order not only to consecrate the portable altar of Abbot Bégon III, but also to place there the relics of the True Cross[27] (Figure 15.9). It was within this context that Bishop Poncio might have communicated Felicia's commission and entrusted it to the workshop active in Conques at that time. This key example may not have been the last artistic exchange between the Kingdom of Aragon and the Conques ateliers. In this regard, the so-called reliquary-casket of Saint Valerius from Roda de Isábena (Huesca, Aragon) should be taken into consideration, since enamels have been attributed to Abbot Boniface of Conques' workshop (r. 1107–a. 1121).[28]

Despite the general assumption that the panels functioned as book covers for a missing gospel book,[29] not only is there no material or documentary evidence for the existence of such a manuscript, but also the wood support from the plaque with the Romanesque figures seems to suggest it was remounted at a later date.[30] At the same time, the two plaques do not have any visible means of attachment to a book and they lack the characteristic micro-tunnels of Romanesque bindings.[31] On the contrary, since there has been no formal consideration of the silver-gilt frames in connection with Bégon III's monastic goldsmiths' atelier, no one has taken into

Figure 15.9

Conques: Treasury of the Abbey of Saint-Foi; portable altar of Abbot Bégon III (Térence de Monredon)

Figure 15.10

Conques: Treasury of the Abbey of Saint-Foi Reliquary of Pope Paschal II (Térence de Monredon)

Figure 15.11

Nájera: Monastery of Santa María la Real; sarcophagus of Blanche of Navarre (Verónica Abenza Soria)

consideration the other works from Conques that functioned as reliquaries, although the possibility that the plaques functioned as book covers, or as another sort of votive object, cannot be entirely ruled out given the later remounting of the wood support.

The artistic response to the arrival of eastern fragments of the True Cross in the Christian kingdoms of the Iberian Peninsula and elsewhere in the Latin West during the 11th century was generally manifested in the creation of reliquaries that betray a close adherence to Western artistic traditions, such as caskets and crucifixes. As a result, it is rarely considered that among the surviving reliquaries of this early date, one may have been created with the intention of emulating a Byzantine model. Around 1160, one observes a Western interest in copying Byzantine reliquary forms, as shown by the renowned Stavelot Triptych (The Morgan Library and Museum, AZ001).[32] Yet, in this context it is worth remembering a notice from the *Vita Bernwardi Episcopi Hildesheimensis* of the German chronicler Thangmar, which records that having received a particle of the True Cross from Emperor Otto III, Bishop Bernward of Hildesheim created a 'container (*thecam*) richly decorated with gold and stones *in qua vivificum lignum includeret*'. Even if Holger Klein reads cautiously the uncommon term 'theca' as an indication that the reliquary 'was in some way based on a Byzantine exemplar' and suggests a cruciform reliquary, I am inclined to think that it could also refer to something similar to a box or a casket emulating, perhaps, the model of a Byzantine *staurotheke*.[33] Given the apparent remounting of the Jaca plaques, the identification of a specific Byzantine model proves difficult, even if its shape recalls other 11th-century Byzantine examples, such as the Reliquary of the True Cross from the Treasury of San Marco (Santuario, 75) or the Staurotheke of Svanéti in the monastery of St. Kvirike and St. Ivlita (Svanéti, Georgia). In the latter respect, we ought not to forget that both silver gilt plaques could be also arranged in the shape of a box, similar to the aforementioned reliquary of Pope Paschal II from Conques (Figure 15.10) or the reliquary-box with the Crucifixion from the treasury of Maastricht Cathedral of the first half of the 11th century (Musée du Louvre, Département des Objets d'art, MR 349).

In such a scenario, the dismantled Byzantine ivory panel and the Romanesque figures could have been rearranged at Conques in a manner inspired by the appearance of a Byzantine staurotheke, not with the aim of adapting the object to Eastern ceremonial practices, but to use the distinctive devotional function of this format in order to serve a sacred purpose within Western liturgical practices, especially those connected to Good Friday, when the solemn ceremony of the *Adoratio Crucis* was performed, and especial prayers were offered on behalf of the deceased.[34] It would justify the mysterious repetition in the Crucifixion theme. In fact, a closer look at the Romanesque ivories reveals something more akin to a lay mourning scene. Not only the absence of haloes, but also the sorrowful facial expressions and gestures of the figures in the upper zone, who touch their cheeks, and the Virgin on the left who grasps her belly,

almost as if her pain was objectified, refer other later examples of mourning scenes, as in the Sarcophagus of Donna Blanca in Nájera (Figure 15.11). In this regard it should be mentioned that the convent of Santa María of Santa Cruz de la Serós, the recipient of Felicia's donation, would become a centre exceptionally protected by the queen and her husband, as well as by king Sancho's grandmother, Donna Sancha de Aibar, and his sisters, Teresa, Urraca and Sancha, who had already died by the time of the donation and who had chosen to be buried there.[35] Consequently, the reliquary might have served a double function, as a devotional and commemorative object that was offered in fulfilment of the queen's desire to praise the dead and keep alive the memory of her closest relatives, especially within the celebration of the Good Friday veneration of the cross.

ACKNOWLEDGEMENTS

I would like to thank Manuel Castiñeiras and Charles T. Little for their scientific guidance. I am indebted to John McNeill and Richard Plant for their help in the final edition of this text. I am also grateful to Julia Perratore for reading the draft and making helpful comments. I gratefully acknowledge use of the services and facilities of The Metropolitan Museum of Art. This research was supported by a MICINN FPI research grant and the results are fruit of the research developed for my PhD Thesis: *Promoció artística femenina a l'Aragó i Catalunya (segles XI-XIII)* within the project Artistas, Patronos y Público. Cataluña y el Mediterráneo (Siglos XI-XV)-MAGISTRI CATALONIAE (MICINN-HAR2011–23015).

NOTES

[1] An extensive bibliography on medieval female patronage is provided in T. Martin, 'The Art of a Reigning Queen as Dynastic Propaganda in Twelfth-Century Spain', *Speculum*, 80 (2005), 1134–1171; more recent studies on the subject are to be found in the two volumes of T. Martin ed., *Reassessing the Roles of Women as 'Makers' of Medieval Art and Architecture*, 2 vols (Leiden 2012).

[2] Many scholars have especially turned their attention to the artistic patronage of the royal women of León-Castile during the 11th and early 12th centuries: S.H. Caldwell, 'Urraca of Zamora and San Isidoro in León: Fulfilment of a Legacy', *Woman's Art Journal*, 7 (1986), 19–25; J. Williams, 'León and the Beginnings of the Spanish Romanesque', in *The Art of Medieval Spain. A. D. 500–1200*, ed. The Metropolitan Museum of Art (New York 1993), 167–183; R. Walker, 'Sancha, Urraca and Elvira: The Virtues and Vices of Spanish Royal Women "Dedicated to God"', *Reading Medieval Studies* (University of Reading, Graduate Centre for Medieval Studies), 24 (1998), 113–138; S.H. Caldwell, *Queen Sancha's 'Persuasion': A Regenerated León Symbolized in San Isidoro's Pantheon and Its Treasures* (Binghamton 2000); T. Martin, 'The Art of a Reigning Queen' (as n. 1), 1134–1171; T. Martin, 'De 'gran prudencia, graciosa habla y elocuencia' a 'mujer de poco juicio y ruin opinión': recuperando la historia perdida de la reina Urraca (1109–1126)', *Compostellanum*, 50 (2005), 551–578; T. Martin, *Queen as King: Politics and Architectural Propaganda in Twelfth-Century Spain* (Leiden 2006); T. Martin, 'Mujeres, hermanas e hijas: el mecenazgo femenino en la familia de Alfonso VI', *Anales de Historia del Arte*, Volumen Extraordinario 2: Alfonso VI y el arte de su época (2011), 147–179.

[3] In recent years there been little progress in focussing attention on female patronage in the kingdoms of Aragon and Navarre, with the

exceptions of T. Martin, 'Sacred in Secular: Sculpture at the Romanesque Palaces of Estella and Huesca', in *Spanish Medieval Art: Recent Studies*, ed. Colum Hourihane (Tempe 2007), 89–117 and J. Mann, 'Piety in Action: Royal Women and the Advent of Romanesque Architecture in Christian Spain', in J. Mann, *Romanesque Architecture and its Sculptural Decoration in Christian Spain, 1000–1120* (Toronto 2009), 75–101.

[4] See C.T. Little, 'Two Book Covers from Santa Cruz de la Serós', in *The Art of Medieval Spain. A. D. 500–1200*, ed. The Metropolitan Museum of Art (New York 1993), 268–269.

[5] See M. Cortés, 'Acerca de la llegada a España de algunas obras bizantinas. Dos marfiles del siglo XI', in *Actas del XI Congreso Español del Comité Español de Historia del Arte: El Mediterráneo y el arte español*, ed. Comité Español de Historia del Arte (Valencia 1996), 14–18. For the ivories from the Département des Objets d'Art see: D. Gaborit-Chopin, 'Deux plaques: Crucifixion et Mission des apôtres', J. Durand et al., *Byzance. L'art byzantine dans les collections publiques françaises*, Paris, 1992, 245–246.

[6] The apparent lack of documentary evidence has led to an inevitable misinterpretation of the recipient, although the earliest modern reference to the plaques identified them as property of the female monastic community of La Serós: Ramón de Huesca, *Teatro histórico de las Iglesias del Reyno de Aragón*, ed. Ministerio de Cultura, Gobierno de España (Rolls Series, III, Leyre, Jaca y San Juan de la Peña, 1797), 338. Accordingly, D. Juana Castejón, who acted as secretary and accountant of the community at the moment when the plaques were sold on 28 November 1898, recorded the sale note in the community records, quoted in V. Abenza Soria, 'El Díptic de Jaca i la reina Felicia de Roucy' (unpublished M.A. thesis, Universitat Autònoma de Barcelona, 2013, http://ddd.uab.cat/). Authors have generally based the original provenance of the plaques from Jaca Cathedral's treasury on the information given by the catalogue of the *Exposición Histórico-Europea* (Madrid 1892), where it is stated that the Bishopric of Jaca acted as the lending institution: see *Catálogo abreviado y provisional de los objetos enviados por su Santidad, Cabildos Catedrales y varias Iglesias de España: comprende las salas V, VI, VII, VIII, IX y X de la Exposición Histórico-Europea*, ed. R. Velasco, (Madrid 1892), Sala IX, n. 24–25.

[7] The earliest documentary records of Felicia's ancestry and marriage are provided by the chronicle *Miracula Sancte Marie Laudunensis* of Hériman of Tournai (1095–1147), abbot of Saint Martin of Tournai: M. Bouquet, *Recueil des historiens des Gaules et de la France* (Paris 1833–1869), XII, 'Ex Hermanni Laudunen Monachi. De Miraculis B. Mariae Laudunensis Libris Tribus', 12, 267.

[8] See P.F. Kehr, 'Cómo y cuando se hizo Aragón feudatario de la Santa Sede. Estudio diplomatico', *Estudios de Edad Media de la Corona de Aragón*, I (1945), 302–303 and 319; D. Buesa, *Sancho Ramírez, Rey de Aragoneses y Pamploneses (1064–1094)* (Zaragoza 1996), 91–150.

[9] Hildouin IV of Ramerupt was sent with Elinand, bishop of Laon (1052–95) to Rome at an unknown date to serve as an ambassador: Bouquet, *Recueil* (as n. 7), 12, 268.

[10] P.F. Kehr, "El Papado y los reinos de Navarra y Aragón hasta mediados del siglo XII", *Estudios de Edad Media de la Corona de Aragón*, Vol. II (1946), 101–102, note 59; Á. Canellas, "Las Cruzadas de Aragón en el siglo XI", *Argensola: Revista de Ciencias Sociales del Instituto de Estudios Altoaragoneses*, 7 (1951), 224.

[11] See P.F. Kehr, *El papat I el principat de Catalunya fins a l'unió amb Aragó* (Barcelona 1931), 41; Canellas, 'Las Cruzadas de Aragón' (as n. 10), B. Guenée, 'Les généalogies entre l'histoire et la politique: lla fierté d'être capétien, en France, au Moyen Âge', *Annales. Économies, Sociétés, Civilisations*, 33, n. 3 (1978), 454; Buesa, *Sancho Ramírez* (as n. 8), 56, M. Aurell, *Les noces del Comte. Matrimoni i poder a Catalunya (785–1213)* (Barcelona 1998), 47.

[12] See K. Thompson, *Power and Border Lordship in medieval France: the County of the Perche, 1000–1226* (Woodbridge 2002), 48. cf. H. Moranvillé, 'Origine de la maison de Ramerupt-Roucy', *Bibliothèque de l'École des chartres*, 86 (1925), 168–184; G. Bernard, 'Les généalogies entre l'histoire et la politique: la fierté d'être Capétien, en France, au Moyen Âge', *Annales. Économies, Sociétés, Civilisations*, 3 (1978), 453–454.

[13] On the relationship between the House of Roucy and the Counts of the Perche, see Thompson, 'Power and Border Lordship' (as n. 12).

[14] It is most likely that this commitment to develop and maintain good relationships with the Holy See dates back to an uncertain moment when Hildouin IV was sent as ambassador to Rome accompanied by Elinand, bishop of Laon (1052–95), on behalf of King Philippe I of France: Bouquet, *Recueil* (as n. 7), 268.

[15] On the pathways for the arrival of these kind of portable objects from Eastern lands to Western recipients see E.R. Hoffman, 'Pathways of Portability: Islamic and Christian Interchange from the Tenth to the Twelfth Century', *Art History*, 24 (2001), 17–50. For a comprehensive study of gifts and luxury objects created for diplomatic exchange, see C.J. Hilsdale, *Byzantine Art and Diplomacy in an Age of Decline* (Cambridge 2014); K.N. Ciggaar, *Western Travellers to Constantinople. The West and Byzantium, 962–1204: Cultural and Political Relations* (Leiden-New York-Köln 1996), 295–323.

[16] See M. Gómez Moreno, *El arte románico español* (Madrid 1934), 26; A.K. Porter, *Romanesque Sculpture of the Pilgrimage Roads* (Boston 1923), I, 41.

[17] See Little, 'Two Book Covers' (as n. 4), 269.

[18] On the style of the master or the workshop that worked the front face of the Doña Sancha sarcophagus see: A.K. Porter, 'The tomb of Doña Sancha and the Romanesque Art of Aragon', *The Burlington Magazine for Connoisseurs*, 45/259 (1924), 165–179; D. Ocón, 'Los maestros de San Pedro el Viejo de Huesca: un ensayo de aproximación a los procesos de creación artística en la escultura románica', in *III Coloquio de Arte aragonés: El arte aragonés y sus relaciones con el hispánico e internacional*, ed. Diputación provincial de Huesca (Huesca 1985), 87–100; D. Simon, 'Le sarcophage de Doña Sancha à Jaca', *Les Cahiers de Saint-Michel de Cuxa*, 10 (1979), 107–124; D. Simon, 'El Sarcófago. Un monumento para la dinastía', in *La condesa doña Sancha y los orígenes de Aragón*, ed. D. Buesa and D. Simon (Zaragoza 1995), 57–95; M. Ll. Quetgles, 'Una nova lectura iconogràfica del sarcòfag de Doña Sancha', *Porticvm. Revista d'Estudis Medievals*, 2 (2011), 16–24; M. Ll. Quetgles, 'Les deux sculpteurs du Sarcophage de doña Sancha', *Les Cahiers de Saint-Michel de Cuxa*, 42 (2011), 209–214.

[19] N. Sentenach found stylistic continuity between the Jaca figures and the mid-11th-century workshop that was responsible for the creation of the ivories of the Reliquary of Saint Aemilian (Monastery of San Millán de la Cogolla, La Rioja, Spain): N. Sentenach, 'Bosquejo histórico sobre la orfebrería española', *Revista de Archivos, Bibliotecas y Museos*, Año XII (July–August 1908), 8.

[20] For the ivory carvings of the Ark of San Felices see: S. Moralejo, 'Placa de marfil del Arca de San Felices, con detalle de las bodas de Caná', *Boletín del Museo Arqueológico Nacional*, 7 (1989), 97–99. S. Moralejo argued for the Reliquary of San Felices as a link between the illuminations of the Saint-Sever Beatus and the mature style of Romanesque sculpture from Jaca and Toulouse: S. Moralejo, 'Placa de marfil del Arca de San Felices', *Boletín del Museo Arqueológico Nacional*, 7 (1989), 97–99.

[21] For a detailed study of these reliquaries, see D. Gaborit-Chopin and E. Taburet-Delahaye ed., *Le Trésor de Conques*. Exh. Cat. (Paris 2001), 38–43 and 50–61.

[22] For a full assessment of the technique of the goldsmiths who were responsible for these fragments of pseudo-filigree, see E. Garland, 'L'Art des orfèvres à Conques', *Mémoires de la Société Archéologique du Midi de la France*, 60 (2000), 83–114, esp. 88–91.

[23] For a comprehensive study on the 'A' of Charlemagne, see W. Cahn, 'Observations on the A of Charlemagne in the Treasure of the Abbey of Conques', *Gesta*, 45, 2 (2006), 95–107.

[24] M. Castiñeiras, '*Didacus Gelmirus*, Patron of the Arts. Compostela's Long Journey from the Periphery to the Centre of Romanesque art', in *Compostela and Europe: the Story of Diego Gelmírez*, ed. M. Castiñeiras (Milano 2010), 55–83.

[25] P.F. Kehr, 'El Papado y los reinos de Navarra y Aragón hasta mediados del siglo XII', *Estudios de Edad Media de la Corona de Aragón*, 2 (1946), 118–132.

[26] A. Ubieto, *Colección diplomática de Pedro I de Aragón y Navarra* (Zaragoza 1951), 302.

[27] *Le Trésor de Conques* (as n. 21), 56; E. Flórez et al., *España sagrada: theatro geographico-historico de la Iglesia de España. Tratado LXXXIV. De las Santas Iglesias de Lérida, Roda y Barbastro en su estado antiguo*, ed. Biblioteca de la Universidad de Alicante (Rolls Series, XLVI, 1836), 148–149.

[28] M. Ch. Ross, 'Un relicario esmaltado en Roda de Isábena', *Revista Zurita*, II (1933), 473–479; M. Iglesias, *Arte religioso del Alto Aragón Oriental. Arquitectura románica. Siglos X–XI, XII y XIII* (Barcelona 1985–1988), I/2, 2179. In fact, such exchanges of relics and sacred gifts would not be unfamiliar Felicia's close relatives as attested in Hériman of Tournai's dedicatory letter to *The Miracles of St. Mary of Laon*, where he mentions that Bishop Bartholomew of Laon (Felicia's nephew) once was in Spain to visit his cousin King Alphonse I (Felicia's son), who promised that when the bishop visited him again he would give him a relic of Hildefonsus of Toledo as well as the body of St. Vincent. See G. Niemeyer, 'Die Miracula S. Mariae Laudunensis des Abtes Hermann von Tournai. Verfasser und Entstehungszeit', *Deutsches Archiv für Erforschung des Mittelalters*, 27 (1971), 155–156.

[29] This prevailing idea is to be found in: E. De Leguina, 'Encuadernaciones romano-bizantinas', *Boletín de la Sociedad Española de Excursiones*, II (1895), 247; Sentenach, 'Bosquejo histórico' (as n. 19), 9; E. De Leguina, *Esmaltes españoles: los frontales de Orense, San Miguel in Excelsis, Silos y Burgos*, (Madrid 1909), 67; Porter, *Romanesque Sculpture* (as n. 16), vol. I, 41, Ill. 519; A. Goldschmidt, *Die Elfenbeinskulpturen aus der romanischen Zeit* (Berlin 1926), 32–33, n. 108, 110; J. Breck, *The Pierpont Morgan Wing: a handbook*, (New York 1929), 51–52; S. Huici and V. Juaristi, *El Santuario de San Miguel de Excelsis (Navarra)* (Madrid 1929), 58; Gómez Moreno, *El arte románico* (as n. 16), 26; H. Thomas, *Early Spanish Bookbindings, XI–XIV Centuries* (London 1939), 5–6; W.W.S. Cook and J. Gudiol Ricart, 'Pintura e imaginería románicas', *Ars Hispaniae*, 1st (Madrid 1950), VI, 293; *Spanish medieval art. Loan exhibition in honor of Dr. Walter W. S. Cook, arranged by the Alumni Association, Institute of Fine Arts, in cooperation with the Metropolitan Museum of Art. The Cloisters, New York, December 15, 1954 – January 30, 1955*, ed. New York University. Institute of Fine Arts. Alumni Association, (New York 1954), n. 22; J. Pijoan, 'El arte románico. Siglos XI y XII', *Historia general del arte. Summa Artis*, (Madrid 1961–1962), IX, 102; F. Steenbock, *Der Kirchliche Prachteinband im Fruhen Mittelater (Jahresgabe for 1965 of the Detsches Verin fur Kunstwissenschaft)*, (Berlin 1965), 160–161, n. 68; J. Bousquet, 'Les ivoires espagnols du milieu du XI siècle: leur position historique et artistique', *Les Cahiers de Saint-Michel de Cuxa*, 10 (1979), 40; M. Estella, *La escultura del marfil en España Románica y Gótica*, (Madrid 1984), 59–60; M.E. Frazer, 'Medieval Church Treasuries', *The Metropolitan Museum of Art Bulletin*, 43/3 (1985–1986), 13, 18–19; A. Naval, 'Evangeliario de Jaca', *Diario del Altoaragón. Cuadernos Altoaragoneses*, IV (16 June 1991), 5; S. Zapke, 'Manuscritos litúrgicos de la Diócesis Jaca-Huesca fuera de Aragón', *Signos. Arte y cultura en el Alto Aragón Medieval* (Jaca-Huesca 1993), 133–135; Cortés, 'Acerca de la llegada a España' (as n. 5), 14; I. Bango, 'Cubierta de evangeliario de la reina Felicia', in *La Edad de un Reyno. Las Encrucijadas de la Corona y la Diócesis de Pamplona*, ed. I. Bango, (Madrid 2006), 292; M. Dubansky, *Treasure hunt for book lovers: a self-guided tour of the Metropolitan Museum of Art*, (New York 2007), 4; M. Cortés, *Bizancio. El Triunfo de las imágenes sagradas* (Madrid 2010), 40–42.

[30] Little, 'Two book covers' (as n. 4), 269.

[31] J.A. Szirmai, *The Archaeology of Medieval Bookbinding* (Aldershot 1999), 140–172.

[32] For a comprehensive study of the Stavelot Triptych and its conscious adaptation of Byzantine reliquary forms see: H.A. Klein, 'Eastern Objects and Western Desires: Relics and Reliquaries between Byzantium and the West', *Dumbarton Oak Papers*, 58 (2004), 283–314.

[33] Ibid., 294, cf., Thangmar, *Vita Bernwardi Episcopi Hildesheimensis*, ed. G.H. Pertz, MGH, SS 4 (Hildesheim 1841), 762.

[34] According to Catalan and Aragonese conventions for the celebration of diverse ceremonies on Good Friday, at the moment of the veneration of the cross, exceptional prayers were said not only on behalf of the deceased, but also to ensure the health and safety of the king and his family, as documented in the 12th-century Sacramentary of Sant Cugat del Vallès (Barcelona, Arxiu de la Corona d'Aragó, MS Sant Cugat 47) cf. J. Bellavista, 'La Setmana Santa en el Sacramentari de Sant cugat del Vallès (MS Sant Cugat 47)', *Revista Catalana de Teologia*, XI/1 (1986), 108–109.

[35] The personal piety of the queen with respect to the convent of Santa Cruz de la Serós is reflected in a significant contribution in favour of the community made by Sancho and Felicia in 1093, consisting of the annual delivery of a generous 400-*solidos* pension, intended for the nuns' clothing and other essentials. In return, Sancho asks the servants of God to pray for his soul and his wife's: A. Ubieto, *Cartulario de Santa Cruz de la Serós* (Valencia 1966), 16–23 and 33–42.

THE AEMILIAN CASKET RELIQUARY: A PRODUCT OF INSTITUTIONAL PATRONAGE

Melanie Hanan

In the 13th century, a monk named Fernandus from the Riojan monastery of San Millán de la Cogolla, Spain, detailed how, in the 11th century, the monastery completed a new casket – or box-shaped – reliquary for the remains of its patron saint, Aemilian. According to Fernandus, on 26 September 1067, the Aemilian casket was carried in procession and placed on the newly consecrated high altar of the church in the monastery then being built at Yuso, about 20 kilometres from Nájera.[1] Given his devout and miraculous ways, the Visigothic hermit Aemilian (473–574) had attracted a following that led to the foundation of the original monastery in the cramped confines at nearby mountainous Suso in the 6th century. The new Yuso monastery – down the mountain from Suso – would provide not only ample space for the liturgical needs of a growing body of monks who had most likely recently switched over from the Visigothic to the Benedictine Office, but also for pilgrims coming to worship at the location of the saint's remains. Analysis of the appearance of the 1067 Aemilian casket reliquary reveals how its design and iconography were deliberately devised to serve the monastery's diverse devotional needs, as well as how this design constitutes a standard type of decorative programme for casket reliquaries that found widespread popularity in monasteries throughout Europe in the 12th and 13th centuries.[2]

The Aemilian reliquary must have been a spectacular sight when the monastery first displayed it. Originally 1,030 mm long, 580 mm tall, and 330 mm wide, it consisted of a wooden armature decorated with thirty-eight carved elephant-ivory plaques, gold and precious stones. Unfortunately, in 1809 Napoleonic soldiers stripped the armature of its gold and jewels, and the ivory plaques were dispersed. Many of the ivories today decorate a reconstructed version of the reliquary at San Millán that does not accurately reflect its original appearance. Other ivories can be found in museum collections around the world or have been lost. Recently, scholars have reconstructed the original appearance of the reliquary based on the shape of the original armature – the Arca Antigua – still located today at San Millán, as well as a description of the reliquary that the Spanish historian Prudencio de Sandoval made when he visited the monastery in 1601.[3]

The Arca Antigua originally featured ivory plaques in two registers on each of its long sides as well as groups of additional ivory plaques on the pinions (Figure 16.1). The different location of these plaques reflected two different cycles: hagiographic and commemorative. Both cycles served to promote the saint and his monastery. The hagiographic plaques were located on the long sides and featured didactic scenes from the life and miracles of Aemilian. These scenes closely followed the events in the only written biographical source of Aemilian's life – the *Vita s. Aemiliani* written by Braulio (*c.* 584–651), bishop of Saragossa, probably in 636.[4] The commemorative cycle was located on the two pinions, and it focussed on iconic images of Christ and the death of Aemilian. Inscriptions found above or below both the hagiographic and commemorative plaques closely match Braulio's text.[5]

Analysis of the imagery on the pinions provides the first clues as to how the Aemilian casket reliquary was used to facilitate worship. On one pinion, the extant Christ in Majesty plaque (Figures 16.2 and 16.3) served as the focal point, originally surrounded by now missing plaques of the tetramorph and images of archangels Michael and Gabriel in gold; it was topped with an ivory image of the *Agnus Dei*, or Lamb of God. To the sides of Christ, ivory plaques (now missing) depicted King Sancho IV (1054–76) and Queen Placentia – patrons of the monastery at the time – as well as San Millán's Abbot Blas and scribe Munius.[6] Accompanying inscriptions indicated that these contemporary figures represented those responsible for the creation of the casket paying homage to Christ at the moment of the Last Judgment.[7] The primary plaque of the other pinion, now split into two pieces, featured Aemilian's death (Figures 16.4 and 16.5).[8] According to Sandoval, a triangular ivory plaque above it (now missing) contained the image of an angel and Benedict dressed as a monk with wings presenting the soul of Aemilian to God in Majesty.[9] Smaller plaques depicting monastic figures from every station within the monastery[10] – including another San Millán abbot named Pedro – and other noble patrons and artisans responsible for the production of the reliquary surrounded the scene of Aemilian's death.[11] Above them in gold stood Gabriel and Michael. The general appearance of patrons

© British Archaeological Association 2018

FIGURE 16.1

San Millán de la Cogolla: Treasury. Arca Antigua of 1067 (Aemilian Reliquary). © Archivo Oronoz

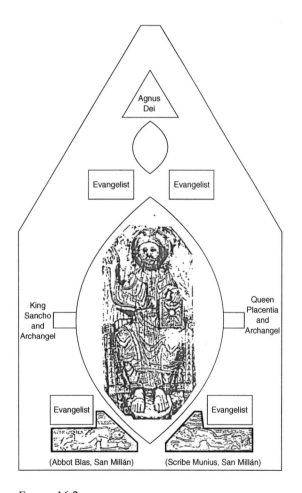

FIGURE 16.2

Reconstruction of front pinion by Julie Harris (prepared by Kevin Ames, titles by author). Aemilian Reliquary from San Millán de la Cogolla

FIGURE 16.3

Dumbarton Oaks, Washington, DC. Christ in Majesty from Aemilian Reliquary. © *Dumbarton Oaks, Byzantine Collection, Washington, DC*

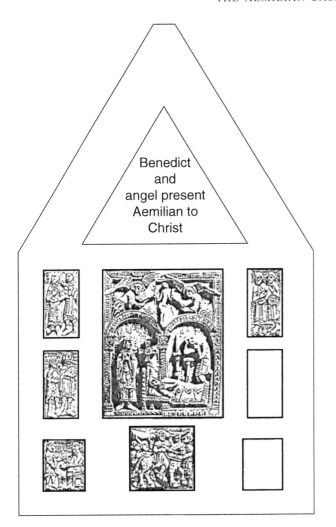

FIGURE 16.5

Florence: Museo Nazionale del Bargello and Boston: Museum of Fine Arts. Death of Aemilian from the Aemilian Reliquary

FIGURE 16.4

Reconstruction of back pinion by Julie Harris (prepared by Kevin Ames, titles by author). Aemilian Reliquary from San Millán de la Cogolla

and members of the monastery honouring Aemilian in his death in the presence of the archangels mirrors the arrangement of figures on the Christ in Majesty pinion.

The size, form and decorative scheme of the Aemilian reliquary appear to represent a change in the general design of such objects used in monasteries at the end of the 11th century. For example, before the Aemilian reliquary, casket reliquaries with iconic Christological imagery were not only considerably smaller than the Aemilian reliquary but also typically came in the shape of what Joseph Braun refers to as *Truhen*,[12] or caskets with a pyramidal or jewel-cut roof. Examples of this earlier type include the 1059 Pelagius-John the Baptist reliquary from San Isidoro in León, Spain: measuring 305 mm by 480 mm by 262 mm, it features ivory plaques of the *Agnus Dei* with a cross and of each of the four Evangelist symbols on its *Truhen* lid (Figure 16.6). In contrast, the pointed roof of the Aemilian reliquary resembles a house; this form is what Braun refers to as *Schreinchen*, or a shrine-shaped casket.[13] Therefore, earlier casket reliquaries were often small and *Truhen*-shaped with iconic Christological imagery located on their roofs in contrast with the large, shrine-shaped Aemilian casket reliquary with Christological imagery featured on one of its pinions.

It appears that the overall design of the Aemilian reliquary emerged because the small *Truhen*-shaped reliquaries became impractical. Evidence from Yuso indicates that the Aemilian reliquary was large in size because it was used as a major focal point on the high altar. Fernandus describes the high altar at Yuso as being separated from the rest of the church by a gate or screen, which would have made it imperative to have a large reliquary so that the congregation could see it from a distance. Increasing its size and moving the Christological imagery to one of its pinions guaranteed that worshippers could read this decoration. As Kurt Weitzmann points out, the Aemilian reliquary's ivory Christ in Majesty is carved in an extremely high relief that was uncommon in Spain at this time and was usually reserved for carvings of Christ on the cross made for the altar.[14] Therefore, the deep carving of the Christ in Majesty plaque on the Aemilian reliquary indicates that it was meant to be a focal point easily visible from a distance, analogous to how crucifixions would have been seen in churches at the time. Commensurate with the use of such imagery, Spanish sacramentaries and missals of this period usually started the canon of

197

FIGURE 16.6

León: Treasury of the Real Colegiata de San Isidoro. Reliquary of Pelagius and John the Baptist (1059). © Museo San Isidoro de León. Fernando Ruiz Tomé

the Mass with two illustrated pages of Christ in Majesty and the Crucifixion, alluding to the glory of Christ and his mission as redeemer;[15] as such, the monks could have focussed on the Christ in Majesty image on the Aemilian reliquary as they began Mass.[16] Given the reference to 'Christi triumphalis victoriae' in the opening *Missa* of the *Officium in diem Sancti Emiliani*,[17] the monks also could have done the same at the beginning of the celebration of Aemilian's Office.

The imagery on the pinions of the Aemilian reliquary also served another function. With its depiction of the monastery's patrons, monastic members and artisans surrounding the Christ in Majesty and Aemilian death plaques and accompanied by gold images of Gabriel and Michael, these pinions also would have aided the monks and other worshippers as they addressed prayers of intercession to their patron saint and the archangels.

The didactic hagiographic scenes from the life of Aemilian on the reliquary also played a role in facilitating worship at San Millán (Figure 16.7). Many of the plaques depicting scenes from Aemilian's life on the long sides were divided into two scenes, which could be read either from top to bottom or from bottom to top, apparently following no particular type of order, either chronologically or by subject matter. In attempting to explain the logic behind the organisation of the ivory plaques, scholars typically argue that the plaques' arrangement was random and that order in the modern sense of the word was not of concern at the time the Aemilian reliquary was created.[18] However, while the original positioning of the hagiographic scenes seems illogical to the modern viewer, evidence suggests that it served to echo and complement the celebration of the saint's Office.

The confusing ordering of hagiographical events relates both to how multiple scenes appear within individual plaques as well as to how the plaques themselves were arranged on the reliquary. Usually the top and bottom sections within a plaque are continuations of one scene or successive scenes chronologically, comprising what is referred to as a hinge composition where the action in one area continues into the next, and the saint acts as the 'hinge', or instigator, of the action.[19] One extant plaque featuring such a composition illustrates when thieves steal Aemilian's horse in the top section and then return it in the bottom one after God causes them to lose their sight for their actions (Figure 16.8). However, in other instances, scenes within the same plaque are grouped together because they carry a similar subject matter, but they are not related chronologically. For example, in the top section of one plaque, Aemilian cured a noble woman named Columba, daughter of the curial Maximus, who was possessed by the devil and experienced 'instability of her limbs': the plaque's bottom section showed Aemilian healing a different lame woman. The two scenes in this plaque – now missing but known through Sandoval's description – are based on Braulio's account of the Columba story in chapter 16 and the healing of a lame woman in chapter 10. It appears the designer of the reliquary grouped these scenes together as they both represent a similar type of miraculous healing – the curing of limbs.

In addition to placing two scenes along a common theme together within a plaque, the designer of the Aemilian reliquary appears purposefully to have situated

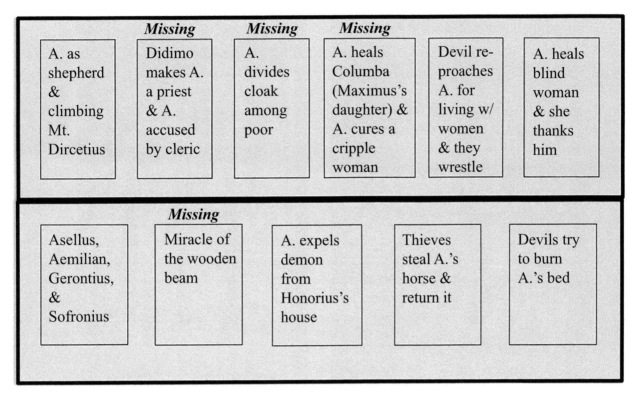

First Long Side

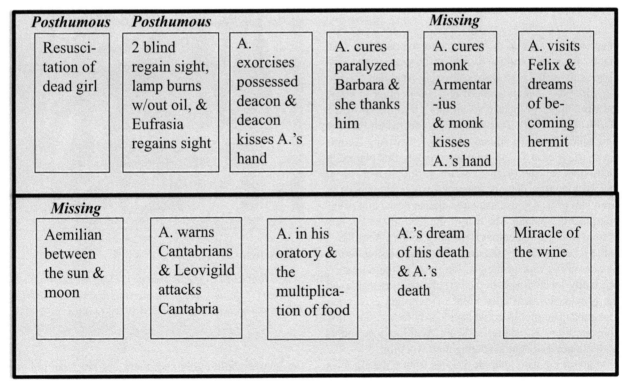

Second Long Side

FIGURE 16.7

Schematic of hagiographic scenes on the long sides of the Aemilian reliquary from San Millán de la Cogolla (Melanie Hanan)

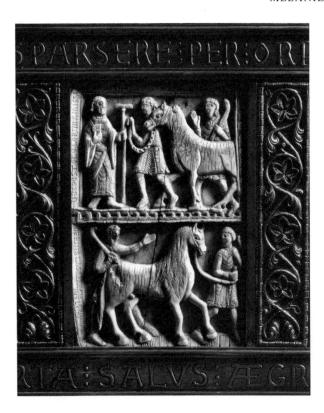

Figure 16.8

San Millán de la Cogolla: Treasury. Thieves steal and return Aemilian's horse, from the Aemilian reliquary. © Archivo Oronoz

plaques with similar themes near to one another. One plaque features Aemilian wrestling the devil in the wilderness as well as the devil chastising Aemilian for living with nuns, events grouped together in order to allow the worshipper to focus on Aemilian's triumphs over the devil (Figure 16.9). This plaque was located on the first long side while two additional scenes involving Aemilian's struggles with the devil were below this plaque in the bottom register (Figure 16.7). The middle ivory from this bottom row depicts Aemilian exorcising the devil from Honorius's house in a rare singular scene that occupies an entire plaque. The ivory from the right end of this bottom row shows demons attempting to burn Aemilian's bed as he sleeps. In addition, the now missing fourth plaque on the roof of the first long side of the reliquary, originally located next to the wrestling scene, displayed the previously mentioned event of Aemilian exorcising Columba. The monks could have easily focussed on this concentration of plaques showing Aemilian's struggles with the devil or demons during their worship.

Many of the hagiographic plaques feature the miracles that Aemilian worked, and interestingly all of the healing miracles appear in plaques that were located on the upper registers of the reliquary's roof. Furthermore, several plaques featuring curative acts are paired with a scene in which the healed person thanks Aemilian. It appears that these events were located in the upper registers in order to facilitate the public's access to them; at the upper levels

Figure 16.9

San Millán de la Cogolla: Treasury. Devil scolds Aemilian for living with nuns and Aemilian wrestles with the devil, from the Aemilian reliquary. © Archivo Oronoz

the viewer could easily spot them. As has been pointed out, the monastery attracted pilgrims through the promotion of Aemilian's miraculous acts of healing; through the modelling of thanks shown in these reliquary plaques, it hoped to encourage its pilgrims to make donations to the monastery.[20]

Many other types of groupings on the reliquary exist, and associating them with different liturgical contexts at San Millán further indicates how monks and pilgrims may have used them. As Julie Harris points out, scenes portraying Aemilian's posthumous miracles are arranged on the second long side of the reliquary (Figure 16.7).[21] In addition, a series of scenes show Aemilian holding a tau-shaped walking stick, the crosier of a bishop and a symbol of ecclesiastical power, and are grouped together on both sides of the reliquary. This stick was famous as Braulio specifically cites it as the tool Aemilian used to heal the lame woman in chapter 10. Despite the fact that the plaque representing this scene – originally located on the reliquary's first long side – is now missing, one can assume that it at least depicted Aemilian with his walking stick given that the passage upon which it was based is the sole mention of this object in all of Braulio's *Vita*. Next to the plaque featuring this event was the one depicting the devil confronting Aemilian about living with women, in which Aemilian is again depicted with his staff. Furthermore, the plaque featuring the horse theft, which was located below both of these scenes in the bottom register, also includes the staff (Figure 16.8). The concentration of these depictions in two top register scenes and one bottom register scene is repeated on the second long side as well.[22] The staff also appears in the back pinion's plaque of Aemilian's death (Figure 16.5).[23]

Liturgically, Aemilian's staff was significant, suggesting that it was depicted on the Aemilian reliquary because it was a cult object. In the *Officium in Diem Sancti Aemiliani* (London, British Museum, MS Add. 30.845), the *Inlatio* – the equivalent to the preface of the Mozarabic liturgy – celebrates the ability of the saint's walking stick to bring good health and to resolve divisions or open up avenues: 'Tu nunc per Emiliani tui baculum gressum quem orbi valitudo ligaverat, ut viam expedite carperet resolvisti'.[24] This reference, occurring in the build-up to the Communion, serves to celebrate the miraculous acts and instruments of Aemilian during the saint's Office.

In addition to mentioning Aemilian's miracle with his walking stick, the *Inlatio* in the Office for the saint's feast refers to three other miraculous acts, all of which were also represented on the reliquary: Aemilian caused a pint of wine to serve a multitude,[25] he grew a wooden beam cut too short for the construction of the granary (now missing)[26] and he enabled food to appear for his guests when none existed.[27] As discussed, the *Inlatio* of the Office mentions the miracle scene of the healing of the lame woman, the ivory for which was located on the upper register of the reliquary's first long side (Figure 16.7). After this reference, the Office describes the miracle of the wine, which was located at the end of the bottom register on the second long side of the reliquary. It then cites the third miracle – the growth of the wooden beam; the ivory for this scene was originally located on the bottom register of the first long side. Finally, the Office refers to the miracle of the food, which the reliquary displayed on the bottom register of the second long side. This alternation among the miraculous scenes located on either of the reliquary's long sides indicates that the designer of this object intended the worshippers – primarily the monks during the celebration of Aemilian's Office – to be present on both sides of the reliquary. Regardless of the side on which one stood, one still had the ability to focus on two of the four miracle scenes cited in this prayer leading up to the Communion.

This evidence indicates not only that thematic groupings lie behind the ordering of scenes on the reliquary, but it also points to the fact that the monks did not refer to these scenes in a chronological manner. They used them to meditate on Aemilian's deeds, especially during the celebration of the saint's Office. Their ability to do so appears to have been facilitated by their extensive familiarity with Braulio's *Vita*.[28]

With this information, one can reconstruct the order in which the monks viewed the different sides and scenes on the reliquary during the Office of Aemilian. The monks first started with the Christ in Majesty plaque of the main pinion – for example, during the opening *Missa* for the Office of Aemilian, as already cited. Then they progressed to one of the two long sides where they meditated on groupings of thematically related plaques while the Office made references to them at various points during the service. After worshipping before one of the two long sides, the monks could finish with the death of Aemilian plaque on the back pinion. In this scenario, a worshipper did not necessarily 'miss out' by having access only to one of the two long sides since similar themes or aspects of Aemilian's life were represented on each long side.

Finally, the mirroring of elements between the different parts of the reliquary also applies to the use of inscriptions. Sandoval describes the following one, 'de letras de oro esmaltado de negro y marfil', going all the way around the reliquary:

> *Per Moysem legem Domini mandata tenentem,/Actibus his sanctum cognoscimus Aemilianum,/Non iacet infirmus, pro quo petit Aemilianus./Ex Moysi fertur populus quo iure rogatur,/Aegri stant sani virtutibus Aemiliani/ Tristes accedunt, sed laeti quique recedunt.*[29]

The Moses passage was in two sentences, and, since Sandoval's description indicates that this inscription went around the reliquary, the first sentence was probably on one long side while the second one was on the other. Both Moses sentences seem to echo each other in sentiment and construction. Sandoval also transcribes two additional inscriptions, one on each side: 'Hiberum [sic] lumen proceres sparsere per orbem,/Facentis monstratur qualis fuit Aemilianus,/Certa salus aegris, spes et tutella misellis'[30] and 'Sanctorum conventus discipulorum/Vernant his signis virtutes Aemiliani/Aegris certa salus, quando vult Aemilianus'.[31] Perhaps each side featured a Moses inscription below the five bottom register scenes, as well as the other inscriptions about Aemilian's healing powers beneath the top register scenes.

An analysis of the inscriptions further helps in determining the Aemilian reliquary's liturgical use. The linking of Aemilian to Moses in the inscriptions recalls once again the *Inlatio* in the *Officium in Diem Sancti Aemiliani* (BM, MS Add. 30.845), which also compares the saint to

Moses.[32] Perhaps Aemilian was in part compared to Moses because both men were shepherds before becoming religious men. As Harris points out, the linking of Aemilian to Moses is echoed in the ivory plaque of the saint's climb up Mount Dircetius, which 'is based on a composition used to illustrate Moses receiving the Law'.[33] Also, perhaps the creators of the reliquary meant to link Aemilian to Moses through his staff. As Durand describes, 'Moses carried his staff; with us, the king follows the procession, sceptre in hand, and the bishop, supported by his crozier'.[34] Most importantly, all four sentences of the inscriptions emphasise how Aemilian cures the sick and would have echoed the miraculous healing scenes in the ivory plaques nearby.

As discussed, the Aemilian reliquary is the earliest extant example of a monastic casket reliquary with a decorative programme organised to have iconic commemorative imagery on its pinions and didactic hagiographic imagery on its long sides. However, by the 12th century, this organisational scheme became commonplace across Europe, as exemplified by the Hadelin casket reliquary (mid-11th to mid-12th century) from Saint Martin in Visé, Belgium, and the Heribert casket reliquary (c. 1160–70) from Saint Heribert in Cologne-Deutz, Germany (Figure 16.10). Evidence indicates that such casket reliquaries were often positioned on or near the high altar with the pinion facing out towards the nave, allowing processing clergy to focus on iconic imagery at the start of their liturgical practices.[35] Clergy familiar with the details of a saint's life could easily contemplate the detailed hagiographic imagery of the long sides while occupying the choir of the church. Clearly such a design supported the specific liturgical needs of monastic communities. This arrangement also would have allowed the laity to concentrate on an iconic image during their worship, much as they would come to use altarpieces in later periods.

In conclusion, the Aemilian casket reliquary – through its iconic commemorative imagery and didactic hagiographical scenes – represents the first extant example of a type of shrine-shaped reliquary that became a standard liturgical aid at medieval monasteries across Europe. The development of such a format appears to reflect the increasing number of worshippers at the time – monastic

Figure 16.10

Cologne-Deutz, Saint Heribert: Heribert casket reliquary (c. 1160–70).
© Archivo Oronoz

and otherwise – wanting access to casket reliquary imagery. The overall design of the Aemilian reliquary meant diverse audiences with varying amounts of knowledge about the saint and the liturgy could access the object for worship in different ways. With many aspects mirrored on different sides of the reliquary – from the Moses inscriptions and intercessory images to scenes of Aemilian's early life and of miracles with laity, religious figures and noblemen – worshippers could draw upon comparable features during their devotions regardless of which parts of the reliquary they could see.

NOTES

[1] See Fernandus's *De translatione Sancti Emiliani Presbiteri* in B. Dutton and G. de Berceo, *La 'Vida de San Millán de la Cogolla' de Gonzalo de Berceo: Estudio y edición crítica* (London, 1984), 34–35.

[2] This article is based on the author's dissertation, which is currently being revised into a monograph. M. Hanan, 'Romanesque Casket Reliquaries: Forms, Meanings, and Development' (unpublished Ph.D. thesis, New York University, 2013).

[3] P. de Sandoval, *Primera parte de las fundaciones de los monesterios [sic] del glorioso Padre San Benito* (Madrid, 1601); J.A. Harris, 'The Arca of San Millán de la Cogolla and its Ivories,' (unpublished Ph.D. thesis, University of Pittsburgh, 1989); and I. Bango Torviso, *Emiliano, un santo de la España visigoda, y el arca románica de sus reliquias* (San Millán de la Cogolla, 2007).

[4] Braulio, *Sancti Braulionis Caesaraugustani episcopi Vita S. Emiliani*, ed. Luís Vázquez de Parga (Madrid, 1943). Of the *Vita*'s thirty-one chapters, only four are not represented on the Aemilian reliquary (chap. 3, 13, 14 and 15).

[5] The inscriptions are not taken verbatim from Braulio but probably edited to enable them to fit the limited space in which they were placed. M. Ballesteros Gaibrois, *Los marfiles de San Millán de la Cogolla de Suso* (Valencia, 1944), 5 and 10.

[6] For images of the Blas and Munius ivory plaques as well as others not provided here, see I. Bango Torviso ed., *Sancho el Mayor y sus herederos: El linaje que europeizó los reinos hispanos*, 1 (Pamplona, 2006), 308–351.

[7] According to Sandoval, accompanying inscriptions for these figures stated 'Blasius Abbas huius operis effector', and 'Munio scriba politor supplex'. In addition, the gold border of the pinion contained an inscription in black enamel indicating Christ's role at the Last Judgment: 'Per secla futurus, / Scilicet in carne praesens ut iudicet orbem, / Unde Deum cernenti credulus atque; fidelis, / Et coram hic Domino Reges sistentur'. Sandoval, *Primera parte* (as n. 3), 27r.

[8] Half of this plaque resides today in the Museum of Fine Arts, Boston, while the other resides at the Museo Nazionale del Bargello, Florence.

[9] This pinion was accompanied with the inscription, 'Ubi Angeli Dei gaudentes ad coelum conscendunt, animam B. Aemiliani portantes'. Sandoval, *Primera parte* (as n. 3), 25v. The unusual scene of Benedict as an angel accepting the soul of Aemilian into heaven perhaps served to emphasise how, at the time the reliquary was made in the 11th century, the monastery functioned under the rule of Benedict as opposed to the Visigothic customs under which Aemilian would have acted and the monastery operated until Sancho el Mayor reformed it at the beginning of the 11th century. As Benedict died in 543, approximately thirty years before Aemilian, they were contemporaries.

[10] Bango Torviso describes this as an institutional representation of the monastery, indicating the responsibilities of its various members; Bango Torviso, *Emiliano* (as n. 3), 58.

[11] The Aemilian reliquary is unusual in this representation of the multitude of patrons, monks and artisans responsible for its creation. Many scholars have addressed this aspect of the reliquary's uniqueness, which unfortunately cannot be discussed in great detail here. For additional information and analysis of these patronage portraits and others, see Harris, 'The Arca of San Millán' (as n.3), 114–117. While the depiction of these figures may suggest that they participated in some sort of procession celebrating the reliquary's creation, no documentary information exists to indicate such an event occurred at San Millán during the period of the reliquary's production.

[12] J. Braun, *Die Reliquiare des christlichen Kultes und ihre Entwicklung* (Freiburg im Breisgau, 1940), 186–196.

[13] Ibid., 163–185.

[14] K. Weitzmann, *Catalogue of the Byzantine and Early Mediaeval Antiquities in the Dumbarton Oaks Collection, Ivories and Steatites*, 3 (Washington, DC, 1972), 86.

[15] S. Silva y Verástegui, *La miniatura en el monasterio de San Millán de la Cogolla: Una contribución al estudio de los códices miniados en los siglos XI al XIII* (Logroño, 1999), 57.

[16] For example, at the preface to the Mass in a missal created at San Millán in 1090 (Madrid, Biblioteca de la Academia de la Historia, cod. 18) and shortly after the creation of the Aemilian reliquary, an illumination depicts angels elevating the *Agnus Dei* in a mandorla, recalling the presence of the ivory plaque of the Lamb depicted over the Christ in Majesty in the apex of the main pinion of the Aemilian reliquary as Sandoval describes. Ibid., and Sandoval, *Primera parte* (as n. 3), 27r.

[17] M. Férotin, *Le liber mozarabicus sacramentorum et les manuscrits mozárabes* (Rome, 1995), col. 603, 482.

[18] Bango Torviso, *Emiliano* (as n. 3), 71–72; and Harris, 'The Arca of San Millán (as n.3), 176.

[19] O. Pächt, *The Rise of Pictorial Narrative in Twelfth-Century England* (Oxford, 1962), 14.

[20] Harris, 'The Arca of San Millán (as n. 3), 208; and Bango Torviso, *Emiliano* (as n. 3), 79–80.

[21] Harris, 'The Arca of San Millán (as n. 3), 176. This grouping is the only one Harris points out.

[22] Aemilian is depicted with his walking stick in two adjacent ivories depicting Aemilian's cure of a possessed deacon and his healing of Barbara. Below these plaques, Aemilian holds his staff in scenes of the saint's warning to the Cantabrians and of his miraculous provision of food for his guests when none existed.

[23] The walking stick also possibly appeared in other scenes that are either now missing or damaged.

[24] Férotin, *liber mozarabicus* (as n. 17), col. 606, 483. The Latin used here for Aemilian's walking stick – *baculum* – is the same word that Braulio uses in the *Vita* (chap. 10, 22). While no evidence exists today that a cult of Aemilian's walking stick existed at San Millán, inventory documents dating to 1047 from the monastery of Santa Maria of Ripoll, Spain, suggest that such a cult existed there related to the abbot Oliba, who died one year before: 'Baculos II, qui fuerunt de domno pontifice, unum cum cristillo et auro': E. Junyent, Oliba, and A.M. Mundó, *Diplomatari i escrits literaris de l'abat i bisbe Oliba* (Barcelona, 1992), 41–43, cited in M. Castiñeiras González, 'Le Nouveau Testament de la Bible de Ripoll et les Traditions Anciennes de l'Iconographie Chrétienne: Du scriptorium de l'abbé Oliba à la peinture romane sur bois,' *Les Cahiers de Saint-Michel de Cuxa*, 40 (2009), 1–19 at 4, n. 18. In addition, the treasury from the monastery of San Salvador in Celanova, Spain, still retains a 12th-century ivory *báculo* of Saint Rosendo that served as a cult item: M. Ángel González García, 'El culto a san Rosendo y la creación del 'tesoro de Celanova' en la edad media', in *Rudesindus: El legado del santo: Iglesia del Monasterio de San Salvador de Celanova, 1 de octubre – 2 de diciembre, 2007*, ed. F. Singul (Santiago de Compostela, 2007), 156–173 at 169. I thank Manuel Antonio Castiñeiras González for bringing these examples to my attention, and I hope to explore them in greater detail in relation to the Aemilian evidence in future research.

[25] 'Tu nunc per Emilianum licore vini paucissimo virorum multitudinem refecisti' (Férotin, col. 606, 483).

[26] Ibid.; 'Tu nunc per Emilianum succisum lignum protelans excrescere volvisti'.

[27] Ibid; 'Tu nunc Emiliano sumtus mittis ad prandium'.

[28] In discussing the 12th-century Heribert casket and its hagiographic scenes, Barbara Drake Boehm points out that its inscriptions, which were based on Heribert's legend, 'reinforced the visual narrative for members of the community for which they were made, but, within that community, the scenes would surely still have been comprehensible without them': B. Drake Boehm, '"A Brilliant Resurrection,"

Enamel Shrines for Relics in Limoges and Cologne, 1100–1230,' in *Treasures of Heaven: Saints, Relics, and Devotion in Medieval Europe*, ed. M. Bagnoli, H. Klein, C.G. Mann, and J. Robinson (New Haven / London, 2010), 149–161 at 155. Similarly, given the San Millán monks' familiarity with Braulio's *Vita*, it seems likely that they did not need ivory plaque inscriptions to understand the scenes on the reliquary.

[29] Sandoval, *Primera parte* (as n. 3), 27r – v. 'Keeping the Lord's commandments, through the Laws of Moses. Through these deeds we know Aemilian. They who call on Aemilian shall not lie sick. The people are led forth by Moses to whom that law is presented. The sick are healed by Aemilian's virtues. They approach in sadness but come away joyful'; quoted in Harris, 'The Arca of San Millán' (as n.3), 107–108.

[30] 'The nobles have spread the light of Spain throughout the world. Showing, by this, what kind of man was Aemilian. The sick are certain to be healed, he is hope and protector of the wretched'; quoted in Harris, 'The Arca of San Millán' (as n.3), 108.

[31] 'The assemblies of the holy disciples are renewed by Aemilian's virtues. The sick are certain to be healed whenever Aemilian wishes'; ibid., 108–109.

[32] 'Tu dudum per virgam Moysi rubri equoris profunda desiccans, ut viam inter fluctos aperires populo gradienti, spumosos sali gurgites et crebra fluctuatione vagabiles in cumulum religasti: tu nunc per Emiliani tui baculum gressum quem orbi valitudo ligaverat, ut viam expedite carperet resoluisti'; Férotin *liber mozarabicus* (as n. 17), col. 606, 483.

[33] Harris, 'The Arca of San Millán' (as n. 3), 110.

[34] G. Durand and Hugh, *The Rationale Divinorum Officiorum: The Foundational Symbolism of the Early Church, Its Structure, Decoration, Sacraments, and Vestments*, books 1, 3 and 4 (Louisville, KY, 2007), 274.

[35] Hanan, 'Romanesque Casket Reliquaries' (as n. 2), 177–188.

PATRONAGE AT THE CATHEDRAL OF TARRAGONA: CULT AND RESIDENTIAL SPACE[1]

Esther Lozano-López & Marta Serrano-Coll

THE MATERIALITY: WORDS AND IMAGES TO EVOKE MEMORY

On the wall of the cloister, near to the entrance connecting it to the church, there are three inscriptions that serve as our starting point (Figure 17.1). The oldest and largest, in the centre, is a Roman plaque whose meaning suggests it was intended to preserve the memory of the dead and to protect their property.

Leaving to one side the importance of relocating a marble plaque in the cloister,[2] what interests us here is the inscription's emphasis on remembering the dead.[3] Publius Rufius Flavius erected a monument, according to the epigraph, to the perpetual memory and honour of his wife Antonia Clementina. The clergy of Tarragona in the 12th century shared with the ancient Romans a desire to honour the memory of their dead companions because, for both parties, obscurity meant oblivion. On either side of the plaque to Clementina are two inscriptions from a stone necrology which would have been seen on a daily basis by the members of the religious community. On the west side, carved lettering invokes the memory of 'Raimundus de Karotitulo [. . .] presbiter et canonicus ac sacrista', who died in 1185[4] and, on the east side, another inscription commemorates the death in 1193 of 'Raimundus bone memorie [. . .] prepositus', who held the most important office in the chapter and whose existence is recorded from 1164 onwards.[5] Thus two clerics who died at the end of the 12th century flank a Roman inscription in a manner that illustrates the Tarragonan dignitaries' preoccupations regarding the Church's property. There is a reference to the *liberti* donation which was intended to turn them into heirs and carers of their tomb in perpetuity and meant in turn that they were required to pass this obligation onto their freemen and their descendants to ensure that the tomb should never fall into unwarranted hands.[6] Moreover, the structure of the Roman text follows a regulated testamentary format that expressly disallows any kind of interference[7] and is thus in keeping with the Order of Saint Rufus, well known for its emphasis on the study of law and for its clerical jurists, such as Oleguer (1118–37), who had trained at the Abbey of Saint Ruf before becoming archbishop of Tarragona.[8] These experts would have had an important role in promoting the preservation of Church property following the restoration of the metropolitan see after Tarragona was conquered by the Christians in 1129. In this regard, the episcopal documentation tells of a hard struggle over a period of decades to prevent the Church's property from falling into alien hands.[9]

The medieval inscriptions are thus inextricably linked to the engraved Roman stone, which must have been put in place when the wall was initially built given that its height follows that of the coursing of the rest of the stonework and that the size of the joints and the dressing of the stone are in keeping with the rest of the ashlar masonry.

The two people recorded on the walls of the cloister are probably the first Augustinian Canons Regular to live according to the rule of Saint Ruf.[10] Of particular note is 'Raimundus bone memorie [. . .] prepositus',[11] who we can identify as the *pavorde* (provost) Raimundus de Bages and whose death coincides with the epigraph.[12] His importance lies in the fact that he held the dignity of *post pontificalem* and thus governed the diocese *in sede vacante* and administered the community's property.[13] From among his properties, in 1169 the Archbishop Hug de Cervelló (1164–71) gave him lordship over La Selva del Camp, a position which was also held by his successors.[14] His importance is also attested in the documentation: in 1172 Alexander III sent a letter to him and to the chapter to confirm the religious community.[15] His role as a patron cannot be ascertained, but given his importance, his financial and administrative power and the information contained in the subsequent documentary records, it may be reckoned that he took an active part in the works, especially the chapter house, which had been in process since at least 1154.[16] There is also a document from several decades later, in 1214, which states that another provost, Raimundus de Sancto Laurentio, raised the vaults of the cloister at his own expense.[17]

Of Raimundus de Karotitulo[18] we know very little except that he was a presbyter, canon and sacristan, the latter position being instituted as a dignitary after his death during the ministry of Archbishop Berenguer de Vilademuls (1174–94). Of particular note is that his inscription is set at the same level as that of the provost,

© British Archaeological Association 2018

FIGURE 17.1

Tarragona Cathedral: epigraphs on the south wall of the cloister close to the entrance to the church. The central one is 1st-century Roman and flanked by the medieval ones of Raimundus and Raimundus de Karotitulo © Lozano and Serrano

the highest dignitary in the religious community. This equality of positioning may indicate that the commemoration of the dead extended to include all those who lived under the rule of the order. It is also significant that his successor, Poncius de Barberano, should have featured in a clause in Cervelló's will of 1171 regarding money for the *opus ecclesiae* and *officinas canonicae*,[19] which suggests that, despite not holding the rank of dignitary, these men were nevertheless important.[20]

It should be pointed out that these two Romanesque epigraphs are the only ones on the cloister's walls that commemorate the dead: the remaining stone-inscribed necrologies, which allude to some of the chapter's founders,[21] are located on the south face of the wall of the axial hall in the Flavian area and in the apse.[22]

The cloister has other commemorative features, but these are iconographic and in honour of the living. On the opposite gallery there are some imposts decorated with castles and chess-rooks that have traditionally been interpreted as emblems of the Archbishops Ramón de Castellterçol (1194–98) and Ramón de Rocabertí (1198–1215), above all because of when they are thought to have been sculpted. (Figure 17.2)

The highly distinctive appearance of these imposts, located on the northeast pillar and the third cluster of columns in the north gallery, causes them to stand out from the surrounding decoration. On a smooth background, and without alternating within the same piece, there is a linear and repetitive deployment of castles and chess-rooks that contrasts with the iconographic variety in the mouldings. It is also worth noting that they occur in two different places, which leads us to agree with those who interpret them as heraldic emblems, although not those of archbishops because there is no record of the episcopate using these before the 14th century. Wherever identifying elements were used for the archbishops, these were images or emblems of pastoral vocation, such as croziers, mitres or hands poised in blessing.[23] A clear example of this can be found in the seals used by the archbishops, which were the exclusive identifying property of the holder and which did not include any heraldic images until the 14th century,[24] as was the case throughout Europe.[25] This explains the mitred corbel in the northeast of the cloister which in this instance can be identified with Rocabertí, although only after he had been made archbishop, as we will subsequently see. Also significant is how these emblems were deliberately located together and related to one another; what at first sight seems to be a hastily assembled series of pieces is in fact the result of a particular way of working. Consequently, we have

FIGURE 17.2

Tarragona Cathedral: detail of the northeast pier of the cloister with imposts featuring the canting arms of the chamberlain Berengarius de Castelleto and the Archdeacon Raimundus de Rochabertino, ante quem 1999 © Lozano and Serrano

to assume the two men were contemporaries, which further rules out the possibility that these emblems refer to archbishops.

A review of the documentary records turns up only two candidates: Berengarius de Castellet[26] and Raimundus de Rochabertino, who later became archbishop of Tarragona. Both were among the first to use emblems to ensure recognition of their contribution to the cloister works. The castles and chess-rooks serve as an aid to identification and memory and are typical devices used as canting arms, of which Catalan heraldry has boasted so many examples since its beginnings.[27]

Castellet was descended from the first *castlà* of Reus[28] and is commemorated with a marble memorial stone, which, although no longer in its original setting, stands out as the first of this type to be found in the cathedral. He was a member of the community from at least 1173 before rising to the position of chamberlain in 1193, the second highest dignity *post pontificalem*, which meant that he was able to draw upon considerable resources in the execution of his duties. For example, in 1171 his predecessor, Iohannes Sancto Baudilio,[29] was made *seigneur* of Reus and his active patronage led him to be made *construatur et edificetur* of the church of Escornalbou under the supervision of the archbishop from 1162–70.[30] According to Morera, Castellet became provost in *sede vacante* after Raimundus de Bages died in June 1193.[31] His activities during the short time he occupied this dignity are important[32] because he decreed, among other rulings, that the novitiate period of canons was to be one year and that they had to be appointed unanimously.[33] This provision must be linked to concerns arising from the 3rd Lateran Council 1179, which Archbishop Vilademuls attended and which required every cathedral church to appoint a master to teach the clerics and the poor students of the church.[34] This provision was followed by other documents such as the constitution published in 1194 by Iohannes Sancto Baudilio, which stated that the members were to reside in the cloister permanently and throughout the whole year.[35] It should be no surprise that a chamberlain should participate actively in promoting the claustral works given that, again according to Morera, a parchment from 1214 states that this dignitary had paid the expenses of the cloister galleries since work began.[36]

His importance is also demonstrated by the fact that he was one of the signatories of Vilademuls' Constitutio Magna, dated 1 August 1193, where he appears as 'Berengarii camerarii'[37] alongside Rocabertino, Terraconensis archidiaconus. This document is significant because it refers to the new regular status of the dignitary of archdeacon. Among other things, it established that he should be made a canon regular and live in the church, for which reason he was bestowed with significant properties. The importance of this dignitary is also shown in the order of the signatures; Rocabertí appears after the archbishop and the papal delegate and just before the provost. As a descendent of one of the most important families in Catalonia and related to the Castellet through his mother, Rocabertí had a brilliant career: he was archdeacon from 1193 until he was crowned archbishop in 1198, a position that he held until his death in 1215.

We believe that both men acted as patrons of the cloister's galleries and consequently ensured that their emblems were sculpted on the imposts. In this regard, it should not be forgotten that some canons were intimately connected with the upper echelons of power and had consequently amassed considerable fortunes. We have yet to find documentary evidence that confirms the direct intervention of Rocabertí as archdeacon, but the presence of his coat of arms, which he used prior to 1199, suggests his patronage. The use of these identifying elements by members of chapter should come as no surprise given that, as Pastoureau states, 'en cette habitude, les simples curés et religieux semblent même avoir précedé les prélats'.[38] The morphology of the signs indicates an early date: first, of the two types of simultaneously sculpted chess-rooks, one is more decorated that the other, which suggests that this figure had yet to become a standardised heraldic symbol at the time they were made; second, the battlements of the castle towers are not covered with triangles, a feature which sets Catalan heraldry apart from that of the other Iberian kingdoms and those to the north of the Pyrenees and which can also be seen in the coat of arms at the back of the cathedral;[39] third, the type of construction directly recalls the altar frontal of Santa Tecla (Figure 17.3), which suggests it was carried out by the same workshop at roughly the same time, that is, the sculpture in the cloister (apart from the corbels, which are later) would have been completed during the 1190s.

THE SOURCE TEXTS: KEY DOCUMENTS IN RECORDING PATRONAGE

As in other cities of Roman origin, once the archdiocese of Tarragona had been restored, the new Christian acropolis was rebuilt by reusing the old monuments available to it,[40] which in Tarragona were from the Flavian period and located in the upper part of the city.[41] Oleguer, the first protagonist in the 12th century, played only a small role as a patron, his activities being mainly concerned with administering the recently conquered territory (Figure 17.4).[42] His successors created a network of parishes to satisfy the religious needs of the faithful in the city of Tarragona and the surrounding area;[43] however, the first man to show a real interest in creating the most important symbol of archiepiscopal power in the northern third of the Iberian Peninsula was Bernat Tort.

Bernat Tort (1146–63)

Tort's obsession with increasing the power of the church makes him a key figure in understanding how the cathedral was designed to emanate this power, particularly in opposition to the Bordet,[44] the joint lords of the city, and against Toledo, whose primacy Tort refused to recognise.[45] His efforts were facilitated by his connections with the counts of Barcelona.[46] Of particular note is the document from 1148 in which Robert Bordet swore loyalty to the archbishop as his lord and which features the

FIGURE 17.3

Tarragona Cathedral: Altar frontal of Santa Tecla, late 12th century © Lozano and Serrano

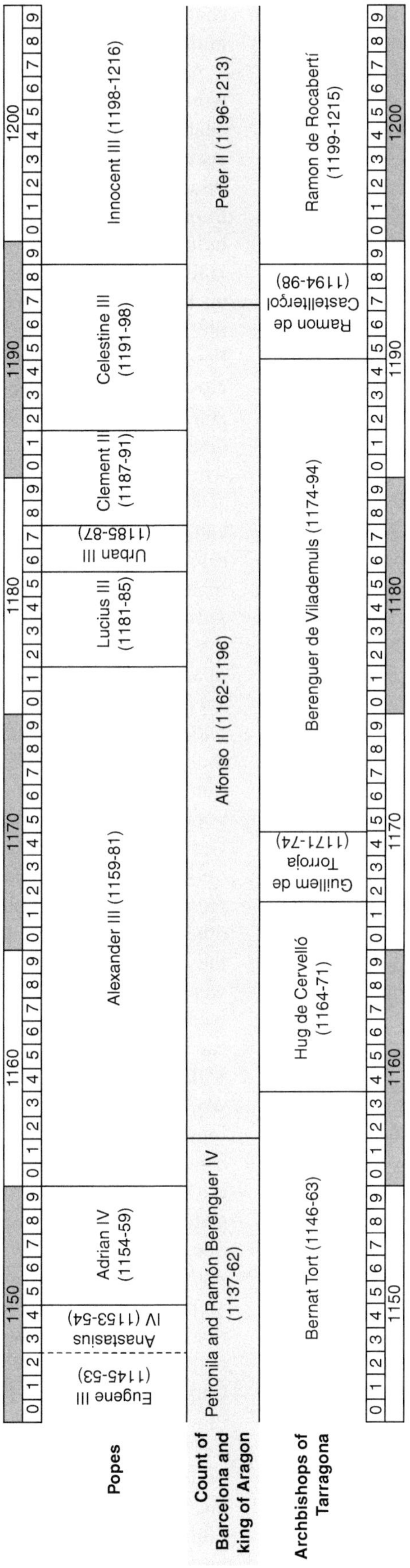

FIGURE 17.4

Popes, kings and counts of Aragon and archbishops of Tarragona from 1150 to 1200 © *Lozano and Serrano*

signature of 'Durandi canonicus sancti Ruphi',[47] thus indicating, in addition to Tort, the presence of other members of this community in Tarragona prior to 1154.[48]

The document that shows the archbishop's role as a patron is the problematic *Ordinatio te vita regulari in ecclesia Tarraconensi* from 1154.[49] It sets out the accommodation and equipment to be made available to the religious community for the daily execution of their duties,[50] for which it was to have storerooms, a refectory, a dormitory, a kitchen, a chapter house and a chapel, the location and characteristics of which are subject to varying interpretations in the records. This archbishop was responsible for delimiting the perimeter of the cloister by building the whole west side during his pontificate. On its northern end, where the wall of the claustral gallery features a blocked oculus, was the refectory[51] and on its southern end were the first dormitory and the chapterhouse. New studies will shed further light on this matter.[52]

In the 16th century Pons d'Icart mentioned Tort's role in the construction of the Archbishop's Castle, which 'he had made and built [. . .] up to the bartizans [. . .] and at the foot of the said castle he had a chapel built and dedicated to St. Mary'.[53] This is perhaps a misreading of the previous document which mentions the terms 'fortitudinem [. . .] quam ibi ediffico'.[54] Blanch, who incorrectly stated that Bernat Tort continued the building work on the church with the same opulence as his predecessor Oleguer,[55] points out that he had also built a church 'close to the walls of Tarragona [. . .] and named it St. Magdalena de Bell-Lloc',[56] which he donated to the monks of Sant Pere de Besalú.

Hug de Cervelló (1164–71)

Tort's successor, Hug de Cervelló, was of illustrious lineage and also extremely close the highest echelons of secular power.[57] This allowed him both to participate in political matters and to undertake a long journey that would take him to Aix-en-Provence, Silvacane, Montpellier and Arles,[58] places with similar repertoires to those used in the cloister and east end at Tarragona and which explain the connections with Provence. It is possible that at the end of 1167 he brought back with him a sculptor who worked on the monumental entrance to the cloister from the church, which we believe, on the basis of the latest research, was completed before 1171.[59]

Forceful in character, Hug de Cervelló's vigorous and wilful defence of the Church's interests was such that some held him responsible for the murder of Guillermo, the son of Robert Bordet, which in turn led to his own violent death. Testimony to this conflict can be found in, among other documents,[60] the letter sent by the king to Guillermo, in which the monarch urged the latter to abandon hostilities with the archbishop and also defined the city as 'capud tocius regni mei [. . .] Unde qui eam destruit capud meum destruit'.[61] His words indicate the level of his concern regarding affairs in Tarragona and his support for the prelate. In our opinion, the cathedral works motivated Cervello's obsession with money and led him to create the dignities of *pavorde* (provost) and chamberlain, the richest and most preeminent positions in the church.[62]

Although some authors, led by Morera,[63] believe that work had yet to begin by the time of Hug de Cervelló's death, it is nevertheless clear that he was responsible for accumulating the money needed to carry out the grandiloquent building work that the documents show was in progress thereafter. Although it cannot be said that he built the church, its design and the preparation of the land and the materials needed to build it all depended on his patronage. This is confirmed by, among others, the bequest made to the works in 1167 in the will of Pere de Queralt, brother-in law to the archbishop and closely linked to the comital house, which donated *mille [solitos] ad Ecclesiam Sancte Tecle faciendam*.[64] Other documents also refer to smaller donations made to the works.[65]

The best evidence of Hug de Cervelló's patronage can be found in his will,[66] which dates from 1171 and refers to a series of donations made to various buildings, including the *hospitali, quod ipso in Terracona incipierat* to which he bequeathed 300 *sueldos*, hospital for the poor (not the canons, as previously believed) which operated under the orders of the canon *Poncius de Barberano*.[67] He also gave 100 *morabetinos* to the *opus populetensis ecclesiae* and the remainder of his money to the *operi ecclesiae* in Tarragona.[68] These works are mentioned again when, in addition to the donation of other goods such as Saracen captives,[69] mules and small rings, Cervelló bequeaths the amount of 1,000 *morabetinos ad opus ecclesiae incipiendum et ad officinas canonicae faciendas* with half going to the *opere ecclesiae* and the other half to the *officinas canonicae*. A close reading of the document shows that the 1,000 *morabetinos* which were originally thought to be part of a donation to the works by the archbishop were actually donated by the sacristan. In reality, according to the text transcribed by Villanueva, this money was donated to the construction work by *Poncio de Barberano* before embarking on a journey to Rome. We do not believe that this money came from church taxes because the archbishop makes no mention of the money being church property and states solely that it was provided by Poncio or, as the document puts it, *quos tradiderat Poncio de Barberano*. Along with other bequests, this is the amount that the archbishop would leave in his will with the stipulation that half should be given to the church and the other half to the chapterhouse, thus complying with the instructions given to him by Poncio when the canon had given him the money before going to Rome.[70] The term *incipiendum* in relation to the church shows that work on this building had yet to begin, whereas *faciendas* in reference to the chapterhouse makes it clear that work on that building had long been underway. In his role as patron he also acted outside the confines of the cathedral complex; for example, according to Morera, the Romanesque façade of the monastery at San Miguel de Escornalbou once had an inscription (now vanished) that said 'Cervello archiep° Tarr. ereta fuit haec ecclesia'.[71]

Guillem de Torroja (1171–74)

Guillem de Torroja was bishop of Barcelona from 1144, brother of the Grand Master of the Knights Templar, Arnau,[72] and of the bishop of Zaragoza, Pedro. He was elected archbishop of Tarragona in 1172[73] after the murder of Cervelló, the electing suffragan bishops being urged by the Pope to choose a *personam idoneam, honestam et litteratam*.[74] Torroja was legate *ad latere* of Alexander III and had experience both of military campaigns (during which he mixed with the very highest levels of society)[75] and of the contentious issues arising from the city of Tarragona. Not only did he intervene in the trial between Cervelló and Robert Bordet in 1151,[76] he also coincided with his predecessor in Provence during his trip of 1167, the latter having awarded Torroja a series of prerogatives several years earlier.[77]

Under his pontificate, the issue of shared jurisdiction continued to cause problems to the point that he made an enemy of the king, to whom he had previously acted as tutor and with whom he was able to resolve some of the differences between them in 1171.[78] As Marí stated, his authority was undermined not only by the monarch but also by the feudal lords, who refused to pledge their loyalty to him and evaded paying the tithes and taxes that they owed to the church.[79] Nevertheless, as bishop of Barcelona Torroja had already demonstrated his willingness to expand and reorganise the church's property[80] and was thus able to appear as the strongman who *liberi ab homni iugo et oppressione laycalis personae*,[81] as is corroborated by the papal ratification of 1172 regarding the oath of loyalty that the men of the city of Tarragona and the surrounding area were required to swear to him[82] and by the agreement of 1173 known as *ad perennem*, which established the jurisdictions of the archbishop and the king.[83]

The documentary record contains little information regarding his patronage, although we suspect that he actively participated in the works. Only one diploma dated 1171 refers to this matter, with the phrase *ad opus canonice claustralis*.[84] This lack of documentary evidence must surely be the result of him occupying the post of archbishop for a mere three years because it contrasts markedly with his energetic patronage as bishop of Barcelona, where he was instrumental in the construction of the Hospital d'en Marcús and the Hospital de Santa Margarita (later renamed San Lázaro) and completed and consecrated various churches such as those of Sant Martí in Cerdanyola and Sant Vicenç de Sarrià.[85]

Berenguer de Vilademuls (1174–94)

The lengthy pontificate of Berenguer de Vilademuls, member of one of the most influential lineages in the area,[86] is notable for the good relations that he maintained with the monarchy and the continuation of his predecessors' policies aimed at strengthening the church. Particularly illustrative of this is the document dated 1182,[87] which put an end to the custom of giving church lands in fief to laymen who, the records clearly show, had accumulated considerable economic power. He also seems to have been instrumental in convening the Council of Tarragona in 1180, where he proposed that documents should be dated by the year of the Incarnation, an act which, leaving to one side the political and religious interests highlighted by Mundó, was of indisputable historical importance.[88]

The economic power of the church under his prelature is clearly evidenced by his loan in 1191 of 7000 *sueldos* to the king for his military campaigns in Roussillon and Cerdanya.[89] While it is true that a decade before he had reduced the number of canons to eighteen,[90] a decision determined by the war against the Muslims[91] and by the cost of the construction work, which was by now at its height,[92] we should also recall that in 1193, when the previous limit on the number of canons had expired after being in place for twelve years, he promulgated the *Constitutio Magna in favorem canonicae ipsius ecclesiae*.[93] Amongst other provisions, the *Constitutio* established a procedure whereby the possessions of converts, canons and intestate persons were distributed in such a way as to bring enormous benefits to the chapter.

The first documentary record from his reign that concerns us is the bull issued by Lucius III in 1184 which confirms the money assigned to the works and mentions the possessions of the *operarius*, whose post had by now been formally created and who was responsible for managing the funds destined for the construction of the cathedral.[94] We do not know if this post was held in 1184 by Geraldus de Aldeya, but he is mentioned in this capacity in two documents from the following year.[95] One of his many possessions was the parish of Figuerola, assigned to the building work in 1184 and which is mentioned again as *quae ad opus ecclesiae pertinet* in a bull dating from 1194.[96] Among his sources of income were the sale of benefices belonging to the *mensa episcopal* and the stipends that the chapter received during periods of *sede vacante*.[97]

We agree with Morera's hypothesis that Vilademuls advanced the works[98] to the point that the central apse was completed by 1184, as is confirmed by the epigraph on its axis[99] (Figure 17.5). This may explain the creation in 1192 of the post of minor sacristan, whose duty it was to look after the large amounts of money needed to clean the cathedral and take care of the ornaments, lights and incense[100] and for which he received important revenues such as that of Santa María del Milagro. We may say, therefore, that Vilademuls brought to fruition a project that had originated with Cervelló and erected it with hardly any modifications to the original plan.[101]

During his pontificate, Vilademuls also oversaw the sculptures in the cloister and on the altar frontal of Santa Tecla.[102] In our opinion, 1193–98 is a key period because

FIGURE 17.5

Tarragona Cathedral: inscription on the axis of the central apse belonging to Bonectus de Barberano. 1184 © Lozano and Serrano

it brought together Castellet as chamberlain and Rocabertí as archdeacon, dignitaries who, as has been mentioned, collaborated in building a cloister that displayed their respective canting arms on certain imposts on the north side. The political and religious context also helps us to understand the iconography of the capitals. Those that referred to external conflicts relating to the conquest and governance of the city and its territory would echo numerous fight scenes and certain themes taken from the Old Testament.[103] The defence of orthodoxy,[104] of utmost importance in a frontier territory such as Tarragona, was expressed on the northeast corner of the columns whose complex iconography alluding to baptism seems to be related to the use of the canonical space just in front of it as a baptistery.[105] We know that the archbishop, who would have had a central role in this ceremony, insisted on this sacrament after attending the Lateran Council of 1179 at which heresies were condemned and the perpetrators exhorted to convert to the true faith.[106] This episcopal element in a canonical space and the reference to conversion, in this case that of the Jews, may also be seen in the exceptional group of columns dedicated to Saint Nicholas, whose position is linked to the adjoining cathedral school, as a recently published study[107] points out, and which was one of Vilademuls' main interests.[108]

All of this leads us to believe that Vilademuls was responsible for the claustral sculptures and constructed a good part of the cathedral that we now see, and that both he and the building are thus of vital importance in late Spanish Romanesque art.

Ramón de Castellterçol (1194–98)

During the period after the murder of Vilademuls,[109] a series of financial abuses took place against the church which, according to the *Índex Vell*, led to a papal bull aimed at restoring the see's finances.[110] This interference by laymen, which had already occurred at other vacant sees, was complicated by relations between the new archbishop, Ramón de Castellterçol (previously bishop of Vic) and the monarchy.[111]

No document exists that allows us to determine the manner in which Ramón de Castellterçol exercised his patronage, although the will of Alfonso II from 1194 (of which the archbishop was executor),[112] shows a donation of 300 *solidos* in perpetuity until the completion of the church, *ad operam ipsius ecclesie donet sit hedificata*, which suggests that the building work was expected to conclude soon.

FIGURE 17.6

Tarragona Cathedral: cloister vaults, general view © *Rafael López-Monné*

Ramón de Rocabertí (1199–1215)

We are able to say rather more about Ramón de Rocabertí, who came from one of the most influential families of the time,[113] and was a member of the Tarragonan clergy from at least 1193 when he is recorded as archdeacon and when his coat of arms link him to the claustral works. Furthermore, he had a good relationship with the monarchy, which would in turn have a positive effect on the cathedral works and would foster mutual understanding in matters concerning the jurisdiction of Tarragona.[114] Nevertheless, his prelature was not free of strife due to the continuing conflict between the archbishop and his subjects; in 1214 there was a legal dispute between the prelate and the citizens as the latter demanded more places of worship.[115]

Proof of the church of Tarragona's financial strength are the successive loans of 11,500 and 10,000 *sueldos* made to Peter II who, *in maxima necesitate*, requested them from the archbishop, the latter receiving in return the king's protection and confirmation of his privileges.[116] In 1211 he again showed off his economic power by buying various territories, making it clear that the money was his own.[117] It is significant that Rocabertí should give the rights acquired in these territories to the chapter and the provost, who played a fundamental role in the cathedral works. According to Hernández and Torres, on 8 of January 1214 the Provost Raimundus de Sancto Laurentio, with the intervention of Rocabertí, *levantó á sus expensas las bóvedas del claustro aprovechando lo que estaba construido* (paid for the raising of the cloister's vaults)[118] (Figure 17.6). Although they do not cite their source, we believe that it is the same document as that cited by Morera; that is, an agreement bearing the same date and between the chamberlain Raymundus Guillelmi[119] and the aforementioned Ramón de Sant Llorenç.[120] According to Morera, the chamberlain had been charged with completing the cloister galleries; however, on finding himself without sufficient money to do so, he signed an agreement with the provost to obtain the funds needed to finish the work.[121] In our opinion it is beyond doubt that the galleries' marble structures had been completed by 1214 because, when discussing this now lost document, the aforementioned authors mention the vaults and the quarries from which the stone was taken to erect them. We believe that it was this provost who, in 1209, signed a document to the king as *Ego Raimundus de Sancto Laurentio, Terrachone ecclesie operarius*.[122]

We also know that in 1207 Peter II took the church of Tarragona under his protection and extended the royal safeguard to its building works and revenues.[123] Such favourable treatment was increased yet further in 1212 when, in gratitude for the men and money provided by the archbishop and his church, King Peter gave some properties and revenues *ad perpetuum* for the cathedral works,[124] a donation which Blanch believes was intended to ensure that the church building work that was underway should reach its conclusion.[125] Without doubt these munificent donations were motivated by the king's excellent relations with the archbishop and the provost.[126]

However, the nature of Rocabertí's patronage is best indicated by the will that he dictated when, judging by the phrase *gravi infirmitati detentus*,[127] he felt his death was drawing near. In addition to donating the work of various monasteries (Poblet, Escornalbou and Santes Creus), he provides a thousand *solidos* for the *operi claustri Terraconae*, and gives tithes for the *operi ecclesiae Terracona* which continued under his prelature.[128] As far as we can tell, Rocabertí financed the vaulting that we can see to this day, although the structural changes that it has suffered mean that it no longer retains its original covering. This would explain why his mitred bust was carved on the corbel in the north wall just on the opposite side, on the northeast corner of the columns where his archdeacon's insignia were sculpted. Further evidence of Rocabertí's patronage is his interest in the tomb that was being sculpted for him when he dictated his will and which prompted a donation of *CCC solidos ad tumulo meo marmoreo faciendo*, along with other quantities destined *ad opus sepulturae meae*. This again demonstrates the desire to be remembered after his death that we ascertained earlier on through our analysis of the epigraphic and heraldic evidence in the cloister.

CONCLUSIONS

Although the archbishops of Tarragona have traditionally been credited as being the principal patrons of the cathedral complex, our study shows that high-ranking dignitaries within the chapter, such as provosts, chamberlains and archdeacons, also played an important role. We have seen epigraphic evidence alluding to these figures and indicating the religious community's desire to commemorate the dead, and we have also seen the use of heraldic insignia aimed at perpetuating the memory of important individuals from the Castellet and Rocabertí families, both of which held considerable power within the chapter. This latter point also provides us with a *terminus ante quem* for the claustral sculpture of between 1193 and 1198.

A lack of evidence regarding some of the archbishops prevents us from stating to what extent each was involved in the cathedral works; nevertheless, four in particular stand out. First of all we have archbishop Tort, who conceived the cathedral space as a manifestation of power and was responsible for delimiting the cloister by erecting its west hall. His successor, Cervelló, put in place the entrance that provides access to the church from the cloister, prepared the site and raised the funds needed to execute the building project, which was enthusiastically continued by Vilademuls, who carefully administered the Church's estates and was thus in a position to complete the perimeter of the complex, including the apse, as is corroborated by the epigraphs placed on its walls in 1184.

Figure 17.7

Tarragona Cathedral: panoramic view © Creative Commons: Photo Michael Schumacher

The inscriptions dating from 1185 and the heraldic insignia on the imposts also show that the cloister was completed during his prelature, and before the vaults were raised in 1214 by Rocabertí, the provost *Raimundus de Sancto Laurentio* and *Raymundus Guillelmi*.

Despite the biases in the documentation available today, a rereading of a large part of it has shown us that neither common individuals nor monarchs played significant roles as patrons. Instead it is through the important role played by the ecclesiastical dignitaries of Tarragona (of varying ranks) that we can explain and understand this impressive monument to power (Figure 17.7).

NOTES

[1] This study forms part of the Projects funded by the Spanish Ministry of Economy and Competitiveness entitled *Sedes Memoriae. Espacios, usos y discursos de la memoria en las catedrales medievales de la Tarraconense. I: Memoria institucional, legados personales* [HAR2015-63870-R] and *Landscape and Identitarian Heritage of Europe: Cathedral Cities as Living Memories* [RecerCaixa 2015].

[2] Various Roman pieces were used throughout the cathedral walls and can generally be clearly seen in passageways and close to doors. Many are listed in *Pla d'Ordenació Urbanística Municipal de Tarragona*, 4ª revisió del Pla General d'Ordenació Urbana (Tarragona 2007).

[3] ANTONIAE CLEMENTINAE. VX. RVFIVS FLAVS / M. F. ET S. VIVINO. MEMORIAM PERPETVAM / HORTOS. COHERENTES. SIVE SVBVRBANVM TRADITIT / LIB. LIBERTABVSQ. EX. FAMILIA. VX. MARVLLO. ANTROCLO / HELENAE. TERTVLLINAE EXEPITQ. NE QVIS. EOS / VENDERET. SET. PER GENVS IPSORVM. POSESSIO DECVRRERE / VEL PER ATNATOS VEL MANVMISSOS: M.C.D. Gregorio, 'Antonia Clementina, propietaria de tierras en la *Colonia Iulia Urbs Triumphalis Tarraco*', *Lvcentvm*, 28 (2009), 150. Also G. Alfödy, *Die römischen Inschriften von Tarraco (rit 368)*, (Berlin 1975), plate XCV 2.

[4] Although there is no consensus, we interpret IIII IDUS FEBRUARII as 10 February 1185.

[5] S. Ramon, 'Canonges de la catedral de Tarragona', *Butlletí Arqueològic*, 21–22 (1999–2000), 241–595.

[6] Gregorio, 'Antonia' (as n. 3), 150.

[7] Gregorio, 'Antonia' (as n. 3),, 154.

[8] Oleguer was the right-hand man of Ramón Berenguer III. Details in: Th. Gergen, 'Els advocats i els mediadors al sud de França i Catalunya del segle XI al segle XV', *Revista de Dret Històric Català*, 11 (2011/2012), 33–53.

[9] See, for example, the following documents: the ordination of 1150 in which Ramón Berenguer IV vowed not to take the possessions of dead bishops: S. Ramon and X. Ricomà (eds.), *Índex Vell. Índex dels documents de l'arxiu de l'Aquebisbe 1679*, 1ª part, (Tarragona 1997), doc. 1, 7; the bull *ad notitiam* from 1151 which specified that on the death of an archbishop his possessions must remain in the chapter until the appointment of the new archbishop: J. Villanueva, *Viage literario a las iglesias de España. Viage á Barcelona y Tarragona*, (Madrid 1851), vol. XIX, appendix. 22, 275–279; the count's promise not to take the possessions of clerics, issued 6 August 1160: J. Blanch, *Arxiepiscopologi de la Santa Església Metropolitana i Primada de Tarragona* (Tarragona 1985), 71; and the *Constitutio Magna* of 1193, which stipulates the parts of an estate that are to go to the chapter and the archbishop after a death: Villanueva, *Viage* (as n. 9), appendix. 10, 226–230.

[10] 'Los mismos sin duda que introdujo del convento de S. Rufo en el Delfinado [. . .] en Noviembre del año 1153 el arzobispo D. Bernardo Tort [. . .]: el apellido estrangero del de la primera lápida confirma esta conjetura [. . .] que demuestran estos enterramientos en su colocación que ya entonces preexistia el Claustro actual' ('Without doubt the same as those who were brought from the Convent of San Rufus in the Dauphiné in November 1153 by Archbishop Bernardo Tort [. . .] the foreign name on the first stone confirms this conjecture [. . .] which these tombs demonstrate through their original location before the current cloister'): B. Hernández and J.M. Torres, *El Indicador arqueológico de Tarragona. Manual descriptivo de las antigüedades que se conservan en dicha ciudad y sus cercanías con designación de los puntos donde se encuentran y ruta que debe seguirse para recorrerlos con facilidad* (Tarragona 1867), 59.

[11] ANNO. M.C.XC.III / X. KA. IVLII. OBIIT / RAIMVNDVS / BONE. MEMORIE. HVIVS / ECLESIE. PREPOSITVS.

[12] According to the necrology: S. Ramon and X. Ricomà, 'El Necrologi de la Seu de Tarragona', in *Miscel·lània Històrica Catalana (Homenatge al Finestes)* (Poblet 1970), 343–398.

[13] On the cathedral dignitaries, see: E. Gort, *La cambreria de la seu de Tarragona. Segles XII i XIII* (Reus, 1990).

[14] For example, he received the castle of Albiol from the Archdeacon Iohannes Martorello (1158–64).

[15] Villanueva, *Viage* (as n. 9), appendix. 6, 218.

[16] *Ordinatio te vita regulari in ecclesia Tarraconensi* de 1154: Villanueva, *Viage* (as n. 9), appendix 4, 214–216; M. Marí, *Exposició cronologicohistòrica dels noms i dels fets dels arquebisbes de Tarragona*, llibre II, (Tarragona 1999), appendix 9, 118–120; E. Morera, *Tarragona Cristiana: Historia del Arzobispado de Tarragona y del territorio de su provincia (Cataluña la nueva)* (Tarragona 1897), vol. I, 696; J. Serra, *Santa Tecla la Vieja. La primitiva catedral de Tarragona* (Tarragona 1960), 52; *Índex Vell* (as n. 9), doc. 535, 141. For a recent study on the building process, see: G. Boto, '*Inter primas Hispaniarum urbes, Tarraconensis sedis insignissima*: Morphogenesis and Spatial Organization of Tarragona Cathedral (1150–1225)', in G. Boto and J. Kroesen (eds.), *Romanesque Cathedrals in Mediterranean Europe: Architecture Ritual and Urban Context* (Turnhout 2016), 85–105.

[17] Hernández and Torres, *Indicador* (as n. 10), 55.

[18] A. M.C.LXXX V IIII / IDVS. FEBRVARII / OBIIT. RAIMVNDVS / DE KAROTITVLO / PRESBITER. ET CANO / NICVS. AC. SACRISTA

[19] Villanueva, *Viage* (as n. 9), appendix. 18, 265–267. We will return to this document later.

[20] The fact that the inscription of *Poncius* is the only one out of all of those dating from the 12th century to have a *signum* would seem to corroborate this hypothesis. On the singular nature of this individual, see: M. Serrano and E. Lozano, 'La Catedral de Tarragona en el siglo XII: espacios de memoria y audiencias', in G. Boto and C. García de Castro (eds.), *Materia y acción en las catedrales medievales (siglos XI–XIII): construir, decorar, celebrar*, (Oxford, 2017), 277–303

[21] Among the eleven signatories from the chapter who feature on the document from 1173 confirming Guillermo de Torroja's donation of the municipality of Codony to Santes Creus in 1160 (Cod. De S. C., fol. 79v), there are nine individuals whose epigraphs have survived to the present day: *Raymundus de Tarracone prepositus Ecclesie* [Ramón de Bages, provost], *Pontius canonicus Tarracone* [Pons de Barberá], *Raymundi sacriste et presbyteri* [Ramón de Karo, sacristan]; *Vincentius presb.* [Vicente, presbyter], *Raymundus* [Raimundus de Término], *Bernardi presb* [Bernardo de Barberá], *Guillelmi presb.* [Guillermo de Modeliano, presbyter], *Berengarii canonici presb.* [Berenguer de Castellet] and *Petrus de Tarracona 'hoc scripsi'* [Pedro de Tarragona]. Some of these also signed a donation by Guillem de Torroja to Poblet in 1174 as *Raymundus Tarraconensis ecclesie prepositus, R. Tarracon. Ecclesie canonici, Pontii presb. et canonici* and *Petri Tarracone notarii*: Morera, *Tarragona Cristiana* (as n. 16), 697–698; and appendix. 24 bis.

[22] This hall functioned as a Flavian *aedes* that presided over the sacred area of the provincial forum, a space that was enriched by a sculptural and epigraphic programme in honour of the *genii* and the *flamines* from the *conventus iuridici* of the *Provincia Hispania Citerior*: R. Mar; J. Ruiz de Arbulo and D. Vivó, 'Los genios de los *conventus iuridici* y el lugar de reuniones del *concilium provinciae Hispaniae citerioris*. ¿Una «curia» de uso provincial en Tarraco?', in B. Soler et alii (eds.), *Anejos de Archivo Español de Arqueología. Las sedes de los ordines decurionum en Hispania. Análisis arquitectónico y modelo tipológico* (Mérida 2013), 25–41. We have suggested a discursive temporal analogy based on the epigraphs in this Roman space, which was brought back into use after the Christian restoration: Serrano and Lozano, 'Espacios de memoria' (as n. 20).

²³ V. de Cárdenas, *Vademecum heráldico: aplicación de la ciencia del blasón, con especial referencia a la heráldica eclesiástica* (Madrid 1961).

²⁴ F. de Sagarra, 'Antics segells dels arquebisbes de Tarragona', *Analecta Sacra Tarraconensia*, 5 (1929), 191–206.

²⁵ M. Pastoureau, *Traité d'Héraldique* (Paris 1979), 49, although according to him the date is slightly earlier: *rarement avant la seconde moitié du XIIIe siècle*.

²⁶ E. Liaño has also suggested Castellet, albeit in relation to Archbishop Rocabertí in 'La catedral de Tarragona', in *L'Art Gòtic a Catalunya, Arquitectura I. Catedrals, monestirs i altres edificis rellevants* (Barcelona 2002), 69 and 'Catedral de Santa Tecla (arquitectura)', in *Enciclopedia del románico en Cataluña, Tarragona* (Aguilar de Campoo 2015), 469. However, several years before he also put forward other possibilities such as Castellterçol, Castelló, Castellvell, Castellví: E. Liaño, 'Elementos ornamentales de orígen islámico en el claustro de la catedral de Tarragona', *Universitas Tarraconensis*, 9 (1987), 144.

²⁷ A. Even, 'L'héraldique catalane au Moyen Age', *Hidalguía*, 22 (1957), 472–473 according to M. de Riquer, *Heràldica catalana des de l'any 1150 al 1550* (Barcelona 1982), vol. I, 343.

²⁸ For more on this individual, see: Gort, *Cambreria* (as n. 13), 65–71; Ramon, 'Canonges' (as n. 5), 242 and 344.

²⁹ E. Morera, *Memoria o descripción histórico-artística de la Sta. Iglesia Catedral de Tarragona, desde su fundación hasta nuestros días* (Tarragona 1904), 115.

³⁰ The discrepancies in dating are analysed in A.I. Sánchez, *Alfonso II de Aragón, Conde de Barcelona y Marqués de Provenza. Documentos (1162–1196)* (Zaragoza 1995), doc. 87, 141–144, esp. n. 1. Some confusion surrounds this first chamberlain; Gort wonders whether he might be the founder and first prior of the monastery in Escornalbou. A 'third' contemporary with the same name could have been the sacristan: Gort, *Cambreria* (as n. 13), 58–63.

³¹ Morera, *Memoria* (as n. 29), 110.

³² Villanueva, *Viage* (as n. 9), appendix. 10, 226–230; Morera, *Tarragona Cristiana* (as n. 16), 607.

³³ Morera, *Memoria* (as n. 29), 110.

³⁴ 'Féu també una bona ordinatió per als canonges que anassen a les scoles, segons apar en lo dit Lib. Blanch de la Prepositura, en cartes XIII'. It was also ordered that the canons should go to schools, according to the said Lib. Blanch of the Prepositure: J. Sánchez Real, *El archiepiscopologio de Lluis Pons de Icart* (Tarragona 1954), 86.

³⁵ Morera, *Tarragona Cristiana* (as n. 16), Tarragona, 1981 [1897], doc. 45.

³⁶ Hernández and Torres, *Indicador* (as n. 10), 55.

³⁷ Ramon, 'Canonges' (as n. 5), 242.

³⁸ Pastoureau, *Traité* (as n. 25), 49.

³⁹ De Riquer, *Heràldica* (as n. 21), 277, 349.

⁴⁰ The example of Nîmes is significant, as are those of Narbonne and Saint Nazaire de Béziers. These cities also shared with Tarragona a high number of men-at-arms, which was also reflected in the urban landscape: M. Aurell, 'La chevalerie urbane en Occitaine (fin Xe-début XIIIe siècle)', in *Actes des congrès de la Société des historiens médiévistes de l'enseignement supérieur public*, 27(1996), 75–78.

⁴¹ For an exhaustive study of the city's Roman planimetry and the mark it has left on the modern urban landscape, see: J.M. Macias, *et alii* (dirs.), *Planimetria de Tarraco. Atles d'Arqueologia Urbana de Catalunya* (Tarragona, 2007).

⁴² Regarding the conquest of the city and its particular governmental structure, see: L. McCrank, 'Restoration and Reconquest in Medieval Catalonia: The Church and Principality of Tarragona 971–1177', 2 vols, PhD, University of Virginia, 1974; 'Norman crusaders in the Catalan reconquest: Robert Burdet and the principality of Tarragona, 1129–1155', *Journal of Medieval History*, 1/1 (1985), 67–82; or *The Tarragona Crusade Reconquest Strategy and Restoration Ideology*: www.academia.edu/4034719/The_Tarragona_Crusade_Reconquest_Strategy_and_Restoration_Ideology (consulted on 11/11/2014). Regarding the presence of the Christian community before the arrival of Norman troops in 1129, see: J.M. Macias, J. Menchón and A. Muñoz, 'De topografia urbana cristiana de Tarragona, a propòsit de dos documents medievals', *Annals de l'Institut d'Estudis Gironins*, 37 (1996–1997), 946–947.

⁴³ J. Menchón, J.M. Macias and A. Muñoz, 'Aproximació al procés transformador de la ciutat de Tarraco. Del Baix Imperi a l'Edat Mitjana', *Pyrenae*, 25 (1994), 225–243.

⁴⁴ On the Bordet's diminishing power, see: Marí, *Exposició* (as n. 16), appendix 37, 149–150; Villanueva, *Viage* (as n. 9), appendix 22, 275–279, appendix. 23, 280–283 and appendix 24, 283–285. Other documentary evidence shows that in 1151 they lost control of the church of San Fructuoso to the cathedral: Villanueva, *Viage* (as n. 9), appendix 23, 280–283.

⁴⁵ The conflict was serious: in 1154 Anastasius IV ordered the archbishop to accept the primacy of Juan of Toledo and to obey him, threatening to withdraw Tort's right to wear the pallium if he refused. Morera, *Tarragona Cristiana* (as n. 16), 577. The bull appears in F. Fita, 'Bulas inéditas de Anastasio IV. Nuevas luces sobre el Concilio nacional de Valladolid (1155) y otros datos inéditos', *Boletín de la Real Academia de la Historia*, 14 (1889), 530 and following. Several years later, in 1163, Alexander III ordered Juan of Toledo to cease any attempt to interfere in the governance of Tarragona during the *sede vacante* that arose on Tort's death. *Índex Vell* (as n. 9), doc. 172, 48; Morera, *Tarragona Cristiana* (as n. 16), 587. The problem continued without solution and in 1211 Innocent III told the archbishops of Toledo and Tarragona to stop squabbling amongst themselves and to concentrate on the expulsion of the Muslims: J.M. Martí, 'Tarragona Seu Metropolitana i Primada. Dels primers documents papals fins la restauració definitiva de Tarragona com a Seu Metropolitana i Primada', in J.M. Gavaldà, A. Muñoz and A. Puig (eds.), *Pau, Fructuós i el cristianisme primitiu a Tarragona (segles I-VIII). Actes del congrès de Tarragona (19–21 de juny de 2008)* (Tarragona 2010), 434.

⁴⁶ Tort participated in the conquest of Lleida in 1149, signed the sacramental will of Ramón Berenguer IV and, at the request of Queen Petronila, went to England to inform Henry II of the count's death, where Tort himself also died in 1163.

⁴⁷ Villanueva, *Viage* (as n. 9), appendix 8, 221–224.

⁴⁸ Villanueva, *Viage* (as n. 9), appendix 4, 214–216. For other canons from San Rufus with important positions in the archdiocese, see Gaufred de Aviñón: *Marca Hispánica sive limes hispanicus, hoc est, geographica & historica descriptio Cataloniae, Ruscinonis, & circumjacentium populorum* (Paris 1688), col. 500 and G. Aymerich, *Nomina et acta episcoporum Barcinonensium* (Barcelona 1769), 330, according to Marí, *Exposició* (as n. 16), 35, n. 101. He was ordained Bishop of Tortosa by Bernat Tort *in ecclesiae Sanctae Theclae* in 1151: Morera, *Tarragona Cristiana* (as n. 16), 568. See also: U. Vones-Liebenstein, *Saint-Ruf und Spanien. Studien zur Verbreitung der Regularkanoniker von Saint-Ruf in Avignon auf der Iberischen Halbinsel (11. und 12. Jahrhundert)* (Turnhout 1996).

⁴⁹ Villanueva, *Viage* (as n. 9), appendix. 4, 214–216.

⁵⁰ 'Confero [. . .] atque dono ipsam fortitudinem seu monitionem, quam ibi ediffico, ad manendum et habitandum in perpetum [. . .] et ut ibidem habeant suas officinas inferius et superius, subtus cellaria sua et orrea, supra vero reffectorio, et dormitorio cocinam et capitulum, sicut distinctum est. Dono item praefattis canonicis ipsam cappellam inferius et superios quae contigua est ipsi fortitudini'. loc.cit.

⁵¹ Tort was responsible for the old refectory, which would have been constructed in 1147, according to Hernández and Torres, *Indicador* (as n. 10), 62.

⁵² Boto, '*Inter primas*' (as n. 16).

⁵³ Sánchez, *Archiepiscopologio* (as n. 34), 68–69. Blanch repeats that it was Tort who ordered the archbishop's castle to be built as a fortress: Blanch, *Arxiepiscopiologi* (as n. 9), 86. Marí also believes that Tort's principal preoccupation was the 'patriarch's tower' as the castle was also known: Marí, *Exposició* (as n. 16), 35.

⁵⁴ Villanueva, *Viage* (as n. 9), appendix 4, 214–216 (see note 50).

⁵⁵ Blanch, *Arxiepiscopiologi* (as n. 9), 86.

⁵⁶ Blanch, *Arxiepiscopiologi* (as n. 9), 92.

⁵⁷ He accompanied Ramón Berenguer IV to Turin and, when the count died, was one of the executors of his will.

⁵⁸ The records state that this journey took place between September 1166 and September 1167: Sánchez, *Alfonso II* (as n. 30).

⁵⁹ The general consensus of opinion has always been that the entrance was moved here from elsewhere; however, we agree instead with

⁵⁹ Boto, 'Inter primas' (as n. 16), who argues that it was always intended for the place that it occupies.

⁶⁰ Such as the trial between the archbishop and Guillermo Bordet in 1168: Marí, *Exposició* (as n. 16), appendix 38, 150–151.

⁶¹ Sánchez, *Alfonso II* (as n. 30), doc. 59, 100.

⁶² Morera, *Tarragona Cristiana* (as n. 16), 588–589; Blanch, *Arxiepiscopologi* (as n. 9), chap. 17.

⁶³ E. Morera, *Tarragona antigua y moderna. Descripción histórico-arqueológica de todos sus monumentos y edificios públicos civiles, eclesiásticos y militares, y guía para su facil visita, examen é inspección* (Tarragona 1894), 67.

⁶⁴ E. Toda (ed.), *Cartulari de Poblet. Edició del manuscrit de Tarragona*, Barcelona, 1938, doc. 234, 141. McCrank dates this testament to 1166: McCrank, 'Restoration' (as n. 42), vol. II, 573. The will indicates that the completion of the cathedral was imminent.

⁶⁵ As little as 1 or 2 *sueldos* or even 6 dineros. See: Morera, *Tarragona Cristiana* (as n. 16), 699, or the donation made by Bernardo Vinater in 1171 *Offero domino Deo et Ecclesie Beate Tecle sedis Tarracone in vita et in morte corpus meum, et dono eidem ecclesie ac libens trado eiusdemque degentibus ac Deo servientibus*: Serra, *Santa Tecla* (as n. 16), 101.

⁶⁶ We take this opportunity to correct a mistake made in a recent publication where E. Lozano attributed words from the will of Cervelló to Tort: G. Boto and E. Lozano, 'Les lieux des images historiées aux galeries du cloître de la cathédrale de Tarragone. Une approche de la périodicité de l'espace et de la topographie du temps', *Cahiers de civilisation médiévale*, 56 (2013), 340, n. 9. Unfortunately, due to a minor error with the data, the note is partially incorrect.

⁶⁷ *Canonicus Terrachone ecclesie et gubernator hospitalis pauperum eiusdem ecclesie*, according to the transcription by M. Fuentes, 'El primer Hospital de Tarragona', *Diari de Tarragona*, 18/09/2014. The document shows that the hospital was funded by its own incomes and properties: '500è aniversari Fundació Hospital Sta. Tecla', *NotíciesT-GN*, diciembre 2014, VI.

⁶⁸ Villanueva, *Viage* (as n. 9), appendix 18, 265–267.

⁶⁹ As slaves, *servus* and *captivo*s: J.L. Cortés, 'Esclavos en medios eclesiásticos entre los siglos XII–XIV: apuntes para el estudio de la esclavitud en la Edad Media', *Espacio, Tiempo y Forma*, serie III, tomo 5 (1992), 423–440.

⁷⁰ Serrano and Lozano, 'Espacios de memoria' (as n. 20).

⁷¹ Alfonso II donated the church to Iohannes Sancto Baudilio in order that he build the temple under the bishop's supervision: Morera, *Tarragona Cristiana*, (as n. 16), 591. Document in Sánchez, *Alfonso II* (as n. 30), doc. 87, 141–142.

⁷² Regarding the role of Arnau de Torroja in resolving the jurisdictional conflicts surrounding the city and area of Tarragona, see: J.M. Sans, 'Arnau de Torroja: un català mestre major de l'orde del temple (1118/1120?–1184)', *Reial Acadèmia de Bones Lletres de Barcelona* (Barcelona 2006), 85–87.

⁷³ Blanch, *Arxiepiscopologi* (as n. 9), 101.

⁷⁴ Blanch, *Arxiepiscopologi* (as n. 9), 105.

⁷⁵ He accompanied Ramón Berenguer IV, with whom he maintained an excellent relationship, on the conquests of Tortosa and Lleida and the campaign in Almería. He was tutor to Alfonso II (Sans, 'Arnau de Torroja' (as n. 72), 86) and the principal executor of Petronila's will of 1152 (J. Mateu and M.D. Mateu, *Colectánea paleográfica de la Corona de Aragón: texto y transcripciones* (Barcelona 1991), lám. 53, 544–546).

⁷⁶ Villanueva, *Viage* (as n. 9), appendix 23, 280–283.

⁷⁷ He was stripped of these in 1164 by Alexander III: Villanueva, *Viage* (as n. 9), appendix 26, 286–287.

⁷⁸ 14 October 1171: Sánchez, *Alfonso II* (as n. 30), doc. 112, 175–177.

⁷⁹ Marí, *Exposició* (as n. 16), 42.

⁸⁰ Sans, 'Arnau de Torroja' (as n. 72), 24.

⁸¹ Villanueva, *Viage* (as n. 9), appendix 34, 294–297.

⁸² Villanueva, *Viage* (as n. 9), appendix 31, 292.

⁸³ Villanueva, *Viage* (as n. 9), appendix 34, 294–297. This was preceded by the bull issued by Alexander III in 1171 regarding those who withheld tithes from the church: F. Fita, 'Doce bulas inéditas de Lucio II, Alejandro III, Lucio III, Celestino III, Inocencio IV y Alejandro IV, históricas de Tarragona', *Boletín de la Real Academia de la Historia*, 29 (1896), 101. In 1172 the same pope confirmed the archbishop's prerogatives and gave him the power to excommunicate anyone who disobeyed him: Villanueva, *Viage* (as n. 9), appendix 31, 292. In 1174 Alfonso II confirmed the church's properties: Marí, *Exposició* (as n. 16), appendix 14, 125–126, although the document is dated a year earlier.

⁸⁴ Morera, *Tarragona Cristiana* (as n. 16), appendix 27 and Sánchez, *Alfonso II* (as n. 30), doc. 113, 177–179.

⁸⁵ Sans, 'Arnau de Torroja' (as n. 72), 24–25.

⁸⁶ S. Sobrequés, *Els Barons de Catalunya* (Barcelona 1989), 38–41.

⁸⁷ Marí, *Exposició* (as n. 16), 45.

⁸⁸ A.M. Mundó, 'El concili de Tarragona de 1180: dels anys dels reis francs als de l'encarnació', *Analecta Sacra Tarraconensia*, 67/1 (1994), 23–43. Perhaps related to this is the large number of representations alluding to the Incarnation, such as the Nativity (twice), the Epiphany (three times) and the *Visitatio Sepulchrii* (three times), which are concentrated on the claustral capitals, the east end and the north entrance of the west façade.

⁸⁹ The monarch promised to return the money: Morera, *Tarragona Cristiana* (as n. 16), 524.

⁹⁰ Morera, *Tarragona antigua* (as n. 63), 67.

⁹¹ By 1188 this situation led Clement III to issue the *Discretio vestra*, which stated that any laymen who had to go to Rome to seek the Pope's pardon for a grave offence would be absolved if he went to defend the city of Tarragona: Morera, *Tarragona Cristiana* (as n. 16), 604.

⁹² We agree with Pons d'Icart who stated that stipends came from the defence against the Muslims and the building work: 'en fer officinas y obras de la sglésia necessariament la dita Església feia gastos y despeses grans [in carrying out the duties and works of the church, the said church necessarily made large expenditures]': Sánchez, *Archiepiscopologio* (as n. 34), 86.

⁹³ Villanueva, *Viage* (as n. 9), appendix 10, 226–230.

⁹⁴ Morera, *Tarragona Cristiana* (as n. 16), 603–604, 699. The creation of the post would have been prior to the bull: Ramon, 'Canonges' (as n. 5), 340.

⁹⁵ An *operarius* is mentioned at the cathedral in1181: McCrank, 'Restoration' (as n. 42), vol. 2, 586. Furthermore, two documents from 1185 mention a certain Geraldus de Aldeya who was an *obrer* at the see and who later died in 1186, according to the following text: 'et anno MCLXXXVI obiit Geraldus de Aldeya canonicus et operarius huius ecclesie': Ramon and Ricomà, 'Necrologi' (as n. 12), 376. The first document is dated August and appears in *Índex Vell* (as n. 9), doc. 718, 197, and the second, dated December, is in *Catalunya romànica*, XXI, Barcelona, 1995, 123. The records mention other *operarii*: Guillem from 1190 to 1193, Ramón Guillem from 1198 to 1203 and Joan de Tortosa from 1206 to 1213: S. Capdevila, *La Seu de Tarragona. Notes sobre la construcció, el Tresor, els artistes, els capitulars* (Barcelona 1935), 131; Ramon, 'Canonges' (as n. 5); Gort, *Cambreria* (as n. 13), 1990, 96. Moreover, the necrology records the death of *A. de Palomarius canonicus et operarius* in 1221: Ramon and Ricomà, 'Necrologi' (as n. 12), 374.

⁹⁶ Marí, *Exposició* (as n. 16), appendix 15, 127.

⁹⁷ Marí, *Thesaurus Sanctae Metropolitanae Ecclesiae Tarraconensis*, fol. 231 (Arxiu Arxiepiscopal de Tarragona), according to McCrank, 'Restoration' (as n. 42), vol. 2, 573.

⁹⁸ Morera, *Tarragona antigua* (as n. 63), 67.

⁹⁹ S. Ramón, 'Epitafis inèdits de l'absis de la seu de Tarragona i un diable desaparegut', *Semana Santa*, 1976, n/p. Exhaustive study in Serrano and Lozano, 'Espacios de memoria' (as n. 20).

¹⁰⁰ Morera, *Tarragona Cristiana* (as n. 16), 605, appendix 44.

¹⁰¹ Boto, 'Inter primas' (as n. 16).

¹⁰² The similarities between the capitals and the frontal indicate that they were executed at around the same time: F. Español, 'El mestre del frontal de Santa Tecla i l'escultura romànica tardana a la Catalunya Nova', *Quaderns d'Estudis Medievals*, 23–24 (1988), 81–103. Nevertheless, our hypothesis moves the date back to the 1190s. A document from 1220 alludes to a lamp that was to be burnt daily *en lo altar de Sta. Tecla* [on the altar of Santa Tecla]: Blanch, *Arxiepiscopologi* (as n. 9), 133. It was there that obedience was sworn to the archbishop, *super altare sancta Theclae*, in a ceremony of vassalage first documented under

Aspàrrec de la Barca (1215–33), although it may already have occurred during the time of Guillem de Torroja: Morera, *Tarragona Cristiana* (as n. 16), 596–597. See also D. Cazes, 'L'art dans les pays de Toulouse, Comminges et Foix au temps de la bataille de Muret', J. Le Pottier, J. Poumarède, C. Marquez, R. Souriac (eds.), *Le temps de la bataille de Muret. 12 septembre 1213* (Montréjeau 2014), 443–458.

[103] E. Lozano and M. Serrano, *Los capiteles historiados del claustro de la catedral de Tarragona* (Tarragona 2010).

[104] The loss of the chapter library prevents us from corroborating which books were owned by the chapter on this subject. However, the presence of the *Liber antiheresis* (1150–1250) [Biblioteca Pública de Tarragona, Ms. 28(2)] from Santes Creus suggests there was something similar at Tarragona because there is evidence of links between the two libraries; Ramón de Rocabertí, in his will, gave this monastery a *salterium meum*: Villanueva, *Viage* (as n. 9), appendix. 19, 267–274.

[105] Boto and Lozano, 'Lieux' (as n. 66), 337–364.

[106] Blanch, *Arxiepiscopologi* (as n. 9), 45. This preoccupation would increase during the following pontificate when the archbishop advised the king to banish the Waldensians (op. cit., 125), which led to their expulsion by royal edict in 1194; document in Sánchez, *Alfonso II* (as n. 30), doc. 621, 797–798. In 1198 Innocent III made it compulsory to help the papal legates of Provence in their fight against the heretics: M. Alvira, *Pedro el Católico, Rey de Aragón y Conde de Barcelona (1196–1213). Documentos, Testimonios y Memoria Histórica* (Zaragoza 2010), I, doc. 147, 293–295. This issue is also highlighted in the stone inscriptions at Tarragona: Serrano and Lozano, 'Espacios de memoria' (as n. 20).

[107] M. Serrano, 'San Nicolás plural: el ciclo del santo obispo en el claustro catedralicio de Tarragona. Saint Nicholas the multifaceted: the sculptural cycle of the holy bishop in the cathedral cloister of Tarragona', *Codex Aquilarensis*, 30 (2015), 225–257.

[108] See the bull issued by Lucius III in 1184 which mentions the school and the *scriptorium* (Morera, *Tarragona Cristiana* (as n. 16), 603–604), or the document recording the ordination of the archbishop in 1192 which mentions the student clerics: Blanch, *Arxiepiscopologi* (as n. 9), 112. This preoccupation also continued after Vilademuls' death; in 1194 *Iohannes de Sancto Baudilio* decreed that novitiates should spend a year living permanently in the cloister: Morera, *Tarragona Cristiana* (as n. 16), appendix 45. In 1197, his successor, Ramón de Castellterçol, instituted the position of *succentoria primera* (a form of choirmaster) in relation to the *scolares canonicos*: *Índex Vell* (as n. 9), doc. 537, 142.

[109] The pope accused ecclesiastics of participating in the murder, and, in a bull dated 16 June 1194, directed at the canons and chapter of Tarragona, states that those who 'dieron favor, ayuda y consejo al dicho Guillermo Ramón de Montcada, para hacer aquella muerte, sean privados de los beneficios, oficios y dignidades, toda apelación postpuesta y los echen por siempre de sus iglesias [gave approval, help and advice to Guillermo Ramón de Montcada in carrying out that murder must be deprived of their benefices, offices and dignities and forever banished from their churches]': Blanch, *Arxiepiscopologi* (as n. 9), 118–119.

[110] *Índex Vell* (as n. 9), doc. 438, 116.

[111] For example the lawsuit that he launched against Alfonso II and the king's favourite Jiménez de Artusella after the former donated the port and municipality of Salou to the latter, or his initially poor relationship with Queen Sancha, which must have improved by 1194 because he is recorded as an executor of the king's will: Sánchez, *Alfonso II* (as n. 30), doc. 628, 808–820. By 1198 the tensions had been permanently resolved: Alvira, *Pedro* (as n. 106), doc. 139, 282–284.

[112] The executors were the archbishop of Tarragona, Gombaldo of Lleida, Ricardo of Huesca, the Grand Master of the Knights Templar and the abbot Pedro of Poblet, where the king was buried after his death: Sánchez, *Alfonso II* (as n. 30), doc. 628, 808–820.

[113] Sobrequés, *Barons* (as n. 86), 38–41.

[114] In 1205, the pope, in an attempt to prevent discord between the king and the archbishop, requested that possessions which were *pro indiviso* should be divided between the two parties: Alvira, *Pedro* (as n. 106), vol. 2, doc. 549, 657. These agreements were consolidated in 1209: op. cit., vol. 3, doc. 943, 1007–1008. In 1206 Peter II reminded Guillem Bordet of the oath of obedience that he had sworn to the archbishop: op. cit., vol. 1, doc. 637, 733–734. Marí extends this to all the soldiers and inhabitants of Tarragona and its territories, who were obliged to swear an oath of obedience and loyalty to the archbishop and his church: Marí, *Exposició* (as n. 16), 50. A bull dated 1207 confirmed the declaration of Peter II stipulating the need for royal consent before electing a new bishop: Blanch, *Arxiepiscopologi* (as n. 9), 129. A new example of these relations is the bull issued by Innocent III which allows the kings of Aragon to be crowned in Zaragoza by the archbishop of Tarragona: Alvira, *Pedro* (as n. 106), vol. 2, doc. 550, 657–658.

[115] *Índex Vell* (as n. 9), doc. 177, 49.

[116] Alvira, *Pedro* (as n. 106), vol. 2, doc. 767, 843–844 and doc. 856, 931–932.

[117] The money came from the benefices of the cathedrals of Girona, Barcelona, Pamplona and Elna: Morera, *Tarragona Cristiana* (as n. 16), 542–543.

[118] Hernández and Torres, *Indicador* (as n. 10), 55.

[119] During the period under study two individuals named Ramón Guillem are recorded in the chapter. One was a simple canon from at least 1192 until he became *operarius* in 1198, after which he was made archdeacon in 1203, a post he held until 1214. The other was a simple canon from at least 1187 to 1205 and then chamberlain from 1208 to 1236, when he became prior: Ramon, 'Canonges' (as n. 5), 252, 259, 340, 344, 346, 351, and Gort, *Cambreria* (as n. 13), 91–108.

[120] op. cit., 73–89.

[121] 'a la primera dignidad [camarero] le habían sido encomendados los gastos del pórtico claustral, de manera que aquellos se satisfacían de las rentas de la Camarería desde que comenzó la obra [. . .] mas como a la fecha citada alegara el camarero que no poseía rentas suficientes para terminarlo, firmó una concordia con el Pavorde. [the first dignity [chamberlain] was charged with providing the funding for the cloister portico, and from the start of the work this was paid out of the revenue of the *Camarería* [. . .] however, because on the date mentioned the chamberlain alleged that he did not have sufficient funds to complete it, he signed an agreement with the provost]'. Among the other donations mentioned are the usufruct of the parcel of land known as d'en Dalmau in the municipality of Codony, an annual pension of 200 *sueldos* from the revenue of the provostry, the provision of sustenance for the workers in the refectory while the work was carried out, and access rights to the quarries in order to source the stone; see Morera, *Tarragona antigua* (as n. 63), 110 and Gort, *Cambreria* (as n. 13), 88, who refers to Capdevila, *Seu* (as n. 95), 76.

[122] This is the document in which the grand master of the Order of Calatrava in Alcañíz, Martín Martínez, hands some land over to the king: Alvira, *Pedro* (as n. 106), vol. 2, doc. 889, 969–970.

[123] Blanch, *Arxiepiscopologi* (as n. 9), 129. This document does not appear in the full work: Alvira, *Pedro* (as n. 106).

[124] Morera, *Tarragona Cristiana* (as n. 16), 546, 699. During the *Cortes* of 21 April, Peter II brought the church works under his protection: Marí, *Exposició* (as n. 16), 52.

[125] Blanch, *Arxiepiscopologi* (as n. 9), 129.

[126] The record shows, for example, that all three took part in the Battle of Muret: tabla 7.9 'Orden de combate del ejército del rey de Aragón en la Batalla de Muret (1213)', in Alvira, *Pedro* (as n. 106), vol. 5, 2529.

[127] Villanueva, *Viage* (as n. 9), appendix 19, 267–274.

[128] In addition to the document from 1209 signed by Raimundus de Sancto Laurentio, *Terrachone ecclesie operarius*, we also have the confirmation of Aspàrrec de la Barca, from 1214, signed by, among others, *Arnaldus Tarraconens ecclae operarius*: Villanueva, *Viage* (as n. 9), appendix 9, 224–226.

AN ANGLO-NORMAN AT TERRASSA? AUGUSTINIAN CANONS AND THOMAS BECKET AT THE END OF THE TWELFTH CENTURY

Carles Sánchez Márquez

INTRODUCTION

The wall paintings which adorn the chapel of the south transept of Santa Maria at Terrassa are among the most notable works of art to bear witness to the early dissemination of an iconography of Saint Thomas Becket. They were discovered in 1917 as the result of restoration work in the Romanesque church, which itself was been consecrated on 1 January 1112 (Figure 18.1). The pictorial cycle immediately caught the attention of scholars. In addition to the pioneering studies of J. Soler i Palet, who first published the paintings in a series of four articles in the newspaper *La Vanguardia*, scholars such as Josep Gudiol i Cunill quickly picked up on the extraordinary discovery.[1]

In 1927 a private collector, Lluís Plandiura, financed the restoration of the paintings, which were detached and remounted in the apse by Arturo Cividini (Figure 18.2). Several years later, the American researcher and friend of Plandiura, Chandler Post, included the paintings of the martyrdom of Saint Thomas Becket in his survey of painting in Spain, lamenting the damage that the restoration had caused to the central area.[2] Recently, numerous studies have been done on the paintings, among which those of Milagros Guardia stand out for their contributions to the field of iconography.[3]

In spite of this attention, a number of questions concerning the selection of episodes and the commissioning of the paintings remain unresolved. Art historians have traditionally thought of Terrassa as the passive recipient of a cult that was already well established, and the creation of the paintings has been assumed to follow on from the acquisition of relics and/or of a work of art, such as an enamelled Limoges casket, which could have provided the iconographical model. However, this fails to address why Terrassa should have become associated with Becket at all, or address the route whereby the paintings came to faithfully illustrate events that took place in Canterbury Cathedral.

THE PAINTINGS: AN EXCEPTIONAL CYCLE OF BECKET'S PASSION

Terrassa certainly presents us with an extraordinary depiction of Becket's martyrdom, one that is notable not only for its precocious date, a matter that will be explored later, but also for its fidelity to the events that took place in Canterbury Cathedral.[4] The paintings are arranged in three registers, consisting of a theophanic image of Christ accompanied by two other figures in the semi-dome (colour plate XIX top), a hagiographical cycle dedicated to Thomas Becket (central register) and a band of fictive curtains (lower register).

Considering the iconography, the most interesting scenes are those in the central register, where we can see Thomas Becket, archbishop of Canterbury, murdered by men loyal to King Henry II of England on 29 December 1170.[5] The scenes at Terrassa are arranged as a frieze, in which three episodes of the martyrdom are represented (colour plate XIX bottom). Beginning from the left we see the initial meeting between Thomas, accompanied by Edward Grim, and three knights, who adopt a threatening or hostile attitude. One of the knights points a finger at the archbishop, while another readies himself to draw his sword. Becket wears the usual clothing of an archbishop: a white pallium decorated with black crosses, a red robe, chasuble and a mitre with lappets. He holds a crosier in his right hand, whose spiral top is decorated with the head of an animal in imitation of metalwork. The scene depicts three of the four knights (Reginald FitzUrse, William de Tracy, Hugh de Morville and Richard le Breton) who will execute the archbishop. All three are wearing a gambeson or short robe that gives us a glimpse of their underpants, fastened to the shorts with a cord according to the custom of the 12th century, and low boots of elongated profile, adorned with welts or leather strips. This is rare in representations of the martyrdom. The knights are usually shown with military clothing and are equipped with shields as well as swords, as in Cotton Claudius B II which

Figure 18.1

Santa Maria de Terrassa, wall paintings: murder of St. Thomas Becket (c. 1180–90; Photo Carles Sánchez)

FIGURE 18.2

Santa Maria de Terrassa, restoration work of the wall paintings by Arturo Cividini, 1927 © Arxiu Fotogràfic de Barcelona (Photo: F. Serra)

is considered the earliest surviving example (*c.* 1180) of a cycle dedicated to Thomas Becket (Figure 18.3).[6]

The second scene, in the centre, depicts the murder of the archbishop. The first of the assaulters raises his sword and removes the crown of Thomas's head, seen immediately beneath the airborne mitre, from which lappets and blood fall, here suggested by parallel lines. The English prelate tilts his head and raises his hand, while a second aggressor holds the saint by his chasuble and aims a blow to his neck. In an attempt to protect Becket, Grim embraces the archbishop and is wounded in his left arm. The scene shows certain similarities with the monumental cycle preserved in the presbytery of the church of Saints Giovanni e Paolo at Spoleto (Figure 18.4), where Grim is wounded and also embraces the archbishop. Nevertheless, there are variations, such as the depiction of an altar at Spoleto, a relatively common element in the iconography of Becket. We should also remember that although Becket was not in the act of celebrating the Eucharist, in most images of the murder he is represented in front of the altar, preparing to celebrate Mass. An altar also appears in the frescoes at Santa Maria di Reggimento – now preserved in the Museum of Casamari (Lazio) – where the murder is accompanied by the effigy of Becket with Saint Benedict and Saint Leonard.

The intention at Terrassa was clearly to represent Becket's martyrdom in detail, as well as to individualise the characters, by staying close to the story as it was told in the *Vitae*. The knight who holds Becket by his robe, the sword inwardly curved across the picture surface, together with other meticulously painted details – like the droplets of blood – suggest that an attempt is being made to depict events as they had occurred at Canterbury cathedral. In this respect, it is worth underlining how important Becket's blood was for the diffusion of the cult. Pilgrims who visited Canterbury took away with them small *ampullae* made of lead or tin, containing the so-called holy water of Saint Thomas – a mixture of water and traces of blood that had a beneficial effect on the sick. These *ampullae* might also carry scenes of Becket's murder, often accompanied by *tituli* referring to his miraculous abilities.[7]

The middle register of the cycle at Terrassa culminates with the deposition of the martyr's body in the tomb and the ascent of his soul, sustained by two angels. The shrouded body is placed in the tomb by two men (Figure 18.5). The one on the right is the same as appears in the earlier scenes, and therefore presumably represents Edward Grim. The character on the left is traditionally identified as John of Salisbury, one of the principal diffusers of the cult.[8] John of Salisbury played a major role

FIGURE 18.3

© *British Library Board, Cotton Claudius, B.II, f. 341*

FIGURE 18.4

Santi Giovanni e Paolo, Spoleto (Italy), wall paintings: murder of Thomas Becket (© Arcdiocesi di Spoleto-Norcia)

FIGURE 18.5

Santa Maria de Terrassa, wall paintings: burial of Thomas Becket (Carles Sánchez)

FIGURE 18.6

© *British Library Board, Harley 5102, f. 17*

in Becket's rapid canonisation, and vehemently defended the veracity of the miracles produced in Canterbury after his death.[9] It is a perfectly reasonable identification.

In this context it is worth remembering that John of Salisbury maintained that Becket was buried in a marble tomb (*sarcophago marmoreo*) in the crypt of the cathedral.[10] The tomb, henceforth, was a regular feature in the iconography of Becket, and appears in Cotton Claudius B 11 (*c.* 1180) as well as MS Harley 5102 of the end of the 12th century (Figure 18.6).[11] From the late 12th century onwards Becket's martyrdom and tomb also appear on Limoges enamel caskets where, just as at Terrassa, the soul of the deceased is carried in a *clipeus* by two angels. In some cases, such as the reliquary casket of the Victoria and Albert Museum of London (Figure 18.7), we find a complex ensemble of scenes presided over by a character with papal attributes who blesses the body of the martyr with the assistance of a cleric holding prayer books.

The upper part of the apse is dominated by an image of Christ in Majesty, enthroned within a *mandorla* decorated with four-petal flowers and blue and red circles (colour plate XIX top). Christ blesses and impresses a book on the heads of two characters, following a common scheme for the representation of ordination ceremonies. In this, I believe that Thomas Becket (on Christ's right) and Edward Grim (on the left) are represented. The range of colours of Becket's clothes is remarkable, fully corresponding with the robe of Christ, and establishing a clear connection in dignity. The fact that Grim was an eyewitness of Becket's martyrdom, and his prominence in the scenes of the middle register, would justify his presence next to the *Maiestas Domini*.[12] To better understand the scene, however, certain details should be pointed out. The representation of a maniple, an ornament of consecrated ministers, in the hands of both characters, reminds us that sacrifice and pain offered to God will be recompensed in celestial life. Moreover, seven candlesticks are depicted beneath Christ, an iconography usually associated with the Apocalypse, and whose appearance is strange in this context.[13] The inclusion of the candlesticks and stars surrounding the *Maiestas* is not fortuitous, however. It should be seen as an allusion to the Last Judgement and the Apocalypse, where Becket and Grim will receive eternal salvation as their reward. In the same way that Christ returned to the Father after his crucifixion, Becket's martyrdom ensures him a place beside God. We must not forget that the text corresponding to the opening of the fifth seal refers to the souls of the martyrs which, like Becket, 'had been slain for the word of God, and for the testimony which they held' (Revelation 6^{9-11}). In any case, the appearance of Christ in the apse is unique in the iconography of Becket, and otherwise unparalleled in surviving ensembles of paintings, miniatures and enamels that depict Becket's martyrdom.

Inscriptions

The three registers of the paintings are separated by two wide strips, which originally bore two inscriptions that are partially lost. A third inscription embellished the curtains of the lower register. The outlines of some letters can still be seen, giving the date of Becket's death – 29 December: 'THOMAS (. . .) IIII ·K(alendas)· IANVARII'. A second

FIGURE 18.7

© *Victoria and Albert Museum, London: reliquary casket with scenes from the life of St Thomas Becket (c. 1180–90)*

inscription, unpublished and currently illegible, was written on the red strip framing the apse.[14]

The third inscription is located just below the scene of the martyrdom: '[TH]OMA BO[NORUM] (damaged area) [NV]S S(an)C(t)A PLVS VALET ARTE SUA'. Finally, in the folds that form the curtains, a third epigraph is partially preserved: 'PRO XR(ist)O . . . . . SPOLIARI NON DUBITAVIT VIVIT QVM (damaged area) [THO]MAS QUE(m) SEMP(er) AMAVIT'. The *tituli* appearing at Terrassa could have their origins in the rich liturgical manuscripts documented in the Augustinian houses attached to Saint-Ruf d'Avignon. As we shall see, these contained numerous references to Thomas Becket. We have been able to identify certain similarities between the respective inscriptions and prayers for the office of the Feast of Saint Thomas Becket, which often directly relate Christ with the archbishop of Canterbury ('Christe Jesu, per Thome vulnera/ Que nos ligant/ relaxa scelera'), as occurs on the lower register of the paintings.[15] It was Tancred Borenius who first suggested that the inscriptions could be related to the offices of Saint Thomas, citing as a parallel the second antiphon for Matins of the Feast of the translation of St Thomas of Canterbury, established in 1220.[16] Analysis of the *tituli* reveals several points of connection between the rhyming verses of the office of Thomas Becket and the Terrassa paintings. In my opinion, the conceivers of the cycle knew this rich liturgical *corpus* and used it as a textual source for the paintings. As for its interpretation, on the one hand the epigraphs evoke the miraculous abilities of the archbishop (ARTE SUA), while on the other they connect his *Vita* and *Passio* with those of Christ. This latter parallel was frequently developed in texts of the *Vitae* by authors such as John of Salisbury, who compared Becket's Passion with the sacrifice of Christ in epistle 303.[17] Hence, the inclusion of scenes of the Passion of Christ in some Limoges enamel caskets. (Figure 18.8).

Finally, the extrados of the arch is ornamented with a series of concentric intertwined circles, integrating white eight-petal flowers. This decoration is interrupted by two angels with censers, holding a canvas in which there is a figure in a *mandorla* (Figure 18.9). The scene resembles the depiction of the ascent of Becket's soul in the lower register, and is almost certainly intended as Becket, thus duplicating the scene. The reason for the repetition is probably that the iconographic model for Becket's martyrdom was a Limoges enamel casket, where Becket's martyrdom was usually accompanied by the ascent of his soul (Figure 18.10).

THE ROLE OF THE CONGREGATION OF SAINT-RUF IN THE DIFFUSION OF THE CULT OF THOMAS BECKET

The rapid canonisation of Becket, just three years after his death, hastened the dissemination of his cult throughout the Latin West, being especially relevant in England, France and Italy.[18] From 1176 the consecration of churches, chapels and altars dedicated to Saint Thomas is documented, while references to his feast proliferated in liturgical manuscripts. The cult of Becket was adopted early in the Iberian Peninsula, particularly in the Kingdoms of Castile and León.[19] Remarkable imagery of Becket is also preserved, such as the relief from San Miguel de Almazán (Figure 18.11), the pictorial cycle of San Nicolás de Soria (*c.* 1300) or the effigy of Becket preserved in the church of Santo Tomás Cantuariensis at Salamanca.[20] Promotion of the cult in Castile and its consequent impact on the arts have traditionally been connected to Eleanor of England (1162–1214), daughter of Henry II, who married Alfonso VIII of Castile in the same year as Becket was martyred. Indeed, in 1179 the queen supported the endowment of a chapel dedicated to the archbishop of Canterbury that had been founded two years earlier at the Cathedral of Toledo.

The worship of Becket was also quickly adopted in the Kingdom of Aragon. In 1186 Bernat de Berga, bishop of Barcelona, consecrated an altar in Barcelona Cathedral, located above the galilee, and shortly afterwards, in 1190, a chapel dedicated to Thomas Becket is documented at Prat de Dalt (Caldes de Montbui). By *c.* 1180 the Feast of Saint Thomas of Canterbury appears in the *Llibre de les Refeccions* of the Monastery of Ripoll, while the *Liber Consuetudinum Vicensis Ecclesie* of canon Andreu Salmúnia should not be dated much later, and also contains the Feast of the English prelate.[21]

When it comes to the appearance of Becket at Terrassa, as will be developed later, the primary agents were members of the congregation of St-Ruf. This is also the reason why the cycle is positioned in so privileged a position, close to the main altar and on the route taken by the canons from the cloister into the church. Houses of canons regularly attached to the Augustinian abbey of Saint-Ruf at Avignon played a leading role in the spread of the cult of Becket in southern France and Spain. And the essential link between the congregation of St-Ruf, Catalonia and England was the sometime abbot of St-Ruf, and subsequent Pope Adrian IV, Nicholas Breakspear (died 1159).[22] Breakspear was fundamental to the expansion of the congregation of St-Ruf, and directly participated in the foundation of Augustinian houses in Catalonia. His close relationship with the count of Barcelona also encouraged contacts between Catalonia, Saint-Ruf at Avignon and England – contacts that clearly flourished from the middle of the 12th century onwards. St-Ruf was a conduit whereby liturgical texts and compilations of miracles concerned with Becket travelled from Canterbury to the Mediterranean, and on via its network of Augustinian monasteries.

Thus, Hispanic houses of canons regular were at the forefront of the adoption of the cult of Becket during the years that followed his martyrdom. A landmark in the expansion of the congregation of Saint-Ruf in the Iberian Peninsula was the foundation of Santa Cruz de Coimbra, in Portugal. Coimbra was the most influential Augustinian house in the Kingdom and one of the most notable cultural centres of the Iberian Peninsula.[23] During

FIGURE 18.8

Plaque from a Chasse for Relics of Saint Thomas Becket, 1220–25. Master G. Alpais (French) and workshop. (© The Cleveland Museum of Art).

FIGURE 18.9

Santa Maria de Terrassa, wall paintings: detail of the extrados of the arch. Ascent of Becket's Soul (Carles Sánchez)

FIGURE 18.10

Casket for relics of Saint Thomas Becket. (© Complesso museale e arqueologico della cattedrale di Lucca).

FIGURE 18.11

San Miguel de Almazán (Soria), altar frontal (Juan Antonio Olañeta)

the second half of the 12th century it became the most important monastic *scriptorium* in Portugal – along with Alcobaça – and its library was enriched with numerous codices that had been copied for it at the Abbey of Saint-Ruf.[24] One of these manuscripts, now in the library at Porto, contains a compilation of texts of special interest related to the archbishop of Canterbury.[25] It is a manuscript of the first third of the 13th century, comprising various books for the Divine Office and the Mass, along with the *Passio sancti Thome Cantuariensis archiepiscopi et martyris* by the anonymous author IV, and a compilation of *Miracula sancti Thome Cantuariensis* by Benedict of Peterborough, in two different codicological units.[26]

Coimbra exerted a notable influence on subordinated priories like San Vicente de Fora (Lisboa), where a late-12th-century sacramentary was made containing prayers for the Mass of Saint Thomas Becket.[27] Coimbra also maintained contact with Augustinian houses in the neighbouring Kingdom of León, specifically with Saint Isidore at León, where two manuscripts that refer to the archbishop of Canterbury are documented: a martyrology in which information related to Becket was added in the late-12th-century, and a text for liturgical use composed in 1187.[28] Besides these codices, a relic of Becket was preserved in León, documented in the *Translatio et miracula* of Saint Isidore.[29] Moreover, in February 1156 Pope Adrian IV had asked King Alfonso VII to yield a place to the canons of Saint-Ruf in the Diocese of Toledo for an Augustinian house.[30] The monarch gave the church of San Vicente de la Sierra to St-Ruf, located in a rural area near Toledo, where an important monastic scriptorium flourished in the second half of the 12th century, from which an Augustinian customary survives which also contains prayers dedicated to Becket.[31]

It is within this context that the choice of iconographic programme for the chapel might be better understood. In my opinion, the 'documental' character of the paintings of Terrassa and the faithful representation of events as described in the early accounts of Becket's martyrdom cannot be explained without direct knowledge of these texts, which at this period were copied and distributed through the congregation of Saint-Ruf. Although no codex of a similar nature to the Coimbra manuscript is preserved from Terrassa, it is probable that the agents involved in creating the paintings knew these liturgical manuscripts and that they were used as a source for the wall paintings.

CANON HARVEY

The driving force behind the paintings of Thomas Becket at Terrassa was, in all likelihood, a canon with

FIGURE 18.12

© *Arxiu Històric Comarcal de Terrassa. Manuscript containing the signature of canon Harvey. ACVOC-AHT. Fons de Sant Pere de Terrassa. Pergamí I-137 (3 August 1160)*

Anglo-Norman origins called Harvey, a very common name in England during the 11th and 12th centuries – as with Hervey le Breton (bishop of Ely, 1109–31) or Hervey of Keith (first marshal of Scotland, who died around 1196–99).[32] A priest and canon of Saint-Ruf, Harvey played an important role in the community of Santa Maria at Terrassa, and is the most prolific named scribe to transcribe and sign documents there during the second half of the 12th century. He wrote a total of seventeen surviving documents in two different periods: the first between 1158 and 1175 and the second between 1184 and 1186. The last document in which he is recorded as a canon (*Signum Arvei, presbiteri, canonici Sancti Rufi*) is dated 7 June 1207.[33] In addition to his name, his identification as a canon with an Anglo-Norman background depends on the character of his handwriting. This conforms with the rapid and more informal script used in many Anglo-Norman royal, episcopal and baronial charters of the third quarter of the 12th century, both in its letter forms and in the treatment of certain diagnostic forms, which reinforces our hypothesis as to his origins (Figure 18.12).[34] As is often the case at this period, his signature presents small variations: *harvey, ervey, arvey*. Most likely, Harvey came to the community of Terrassa through Saint-Ruf at Avignon which, as we have seen, maintained strong ties with the Anglo-Norman world through Pope Adrian IV. Even though Saint-Ruf had no daughter houses in England, many English Augustinian priories, such as Merton, where Becket himself had been educated, came into contact with the congregation and became familiar with their customs thanks to the role of Adrian IV.[35] Regarding the circulation of canons, we should note that in 1148 Nicholas Breakspear had ordered the transfer of monks from Saint-Ruf to Catalonia, to join the restored see of Tortosa under Gaufred of Avignon, a former canon at Saint-Ruf. Later, another canon of the congregation, Durand, became abbot of the Priory of Saint-Ruf at Lleida.

If we accept his Anglo-Norman origins, Harvey and the congregation of Saint-Ruf were the decisive agents for the introduction of Becket's cult to Terrassa. Of course, there is no way of knowing the precise role played by the canon and scribe in the process whereby the cult was received, nor can we prove with absolute certainty that Harvey directly participated in the commission of the paintings. However, given his origins, Harvey is the most likely candidate to have endowed an altar in the south transept chapel, and organised its consecration in honour of the archbishop of Canterbury, just as Pere de Ripollet had endowed the altar of Thomas Becket in the Cathedral of Barcelona in 1186.[36] It is very likely that the new painted cycle was made for the chapel of Terrassa in order to emphasise the *Passio* of Becket.

Thus, the role played by Harvey within the Augustinian house of Terrassa was potentially crucial. Furthermore, the fact that the canon-scribe is documented at Terrassa in two distinct periods may be relevant. Between 1179 and 1187, that is for most of the time that Harvey was absent, the priest Guerau de Santfeliu closed documents and was the most active scribe at Terrassa. However, between 1185 and 1187, that is during the time that Harvey had returned, Guerau wrote just three documents. Harvey seems to have left Terrassa for a short period (1175–84), and the reasons for his absence in the community are unknown, but his return in 1184 corresponds with our suggested date for the execution of the paintings. Although no documents have so far come to light that would enable us to trace Harvey's career while he was away from Terrassa, it does seem likely that Harvey was behind the chapel and its embellishment with a pictorial cycle of 'documental' character.

ARCHAEOLOGY AND DEDICATION

Traditionally it is thought that the south transept wall of Santa Maria at Terrassa was opened out in the later 12th century, sometime after the construction of the church, and that the apse was specifically built for the paintings. However, both the archaeological and the documentary evidence suggest the chapel formed part of the church that was consecrated in 1112, and that it was simply reconsecrated and painted in the late 12th century. From an archaeological perspective, the south transept wall is uniform: the arches used over the window, to form the small closet near the southwest angle, and over the chapel apse, are similar, and use an identical constructional technique (Figure 18.13). The mortar that is used is the same, as is the plaster used at the base of the south wall and chapel apse.

To that archaeological evidence, we should add the documentary record. The chapel could originally have housed the altar of Saint Adrian, documented from 1117 and consecrated by Oleguer, former prior of Sant Adrià del Besòs and abbot of Saint-Ruf at Avignon: 'Ego Berengarius Raimundi, bono spiritu ductus, dono et laudo atque evacuo domino Deo et ecclesie Sancte Marie Egarensi et altari Sancti Adriani, quod infra prescriptam basilicam est'.[37] Another document from 1153 tells us that the altar of Saint Adrian was 'in eadem ecclesia constructi', which indicates there was an altar and by extension a chapel dedicated to the saint at Terrassa. Saint Adrian was an important cult in the houses attached to the congregation of Saint-Ruf, used in the dedication of churches (Sant Adrià del Besòs) and chapels (Terrassa). It was also the papal title chosen by Nicholas Breakspear. Thus, the

FIGURE 18.13

Santa Maria de Terrassa, view of the south transept: chapel of St Thomas Becket (Carles Sánchez)

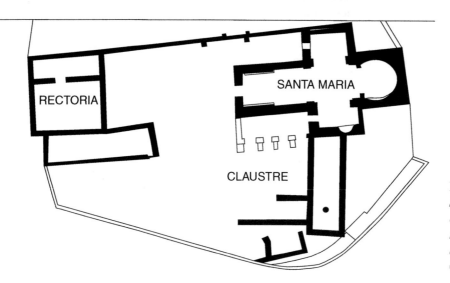

FIGURE 18.14 *Priory of Santa Maria de Terrassa, church, cloister and monastic dependencies according to A. Moro and G. Garcia Linares*

canons of Sant Adrià del Besòs, who had been moved and re-established in Terrassa, could have brought the dedication with them, and were given a space for the veneration of the saint at Terrassa from the outset.[38] The location of the chapel in the southern arm of the transept is not accidental: it was a prominent position, close to the altar of Saint Mary, above the floor level of the nave and positioned between the church, the cloister and the monastic dependencies (Figure 18.14). Around the middle of the 16th century the dedication of the chapel changed again, this time to Saint Lucy, and it was decorated with a Renaissance altarpiece in oils by A. Sabater in 1546. In consequence, we should assume that the installation of the 16th-century altarpiece precipitated the closing of the apse, as a result of which the wall paintings came to be hidden behind whitewashed walls until their rediscovery in 1917. A photograph made shortly after their rediscovery shows how the fixings for the 16th-century altarpiece had damaged the wall paintings (Figure 18.15).

Building chapels dedicated to the archbishop of Canterbury in Spanish churches was widespread in the last quarter of the 12th century. Thus, various altars dedicated to Thomas Becket are known, such as the aforementioned altar in Barcelona cathedral, located above the galilee. In addition, there were chapels in the cathedrals of Sigüenza, where Becket's chapel was consecrated by Bishop Joscelmo before his death in 1178, Toledo (1177), Zaragoza (*c*. 1200) and Burgos, the last endowed by Archdeacon Matthew in or shortly before 1202. The case of Toledo Cathedral is perhaps the most significant of all. The Augustinian reform became effective at Toledo around the middle of the 12th century. Then, in July 1177, Count Nuño Pérez de Lara with his wife, Teresa, endowed an altar dedicated to Saint Thomas Becket in the cathedral.[39] Two years later, Alfonso VIII and Eleanor Plantagenet brought the chapel under their protection. The altar was to be attended by a priest who served God and Becket and who prayed for their souls. This was similar to what

FIGURE 18.15

Santa Maria de Terrassa, wall paintings. Photograph made shortly after its discovery in 1917. © *Museu de Terrassa (Carles Sánchez)*

happened in Barcelona, where Pere de Ripollet, canon and sacristan, endowed the altar of Thomas Becket.

Narrowing down the position of Becket Chapels is more difficult. The chapel dedicated to Thomas Becket in the church of San Nicolás at Soria was located in the south transept, near to the presbytery, a privileged place close to the main altar, as at Terrassa. The chapel at Soria was also decorated with a cycle of mural paintings dedicated to Thomas Becket, though these are dated to around 1300. Everything suggests this was also the case at Sigüenza Cathedral, whose canons had lived *sub regula Augustini beati atque Ieronimi* from 1144. Some time later, the chapel was rededicated to San Juan and Santa Catalina. According to Gregoria Cavero the chapel was used as an episcopal mausoleum, becoming, in the 14th century, a pantheon of illustrious families.[40]

THE PAINTER: THE MASTER OF ESPINELVES

Historically, the wall paintings of Santa Maria at Terrassa have been attributed to the Master of Espinelves, a painter associated with Vic, and named after the altar frontal from Espinelves (*c.* 1187) now in the Episcopal Museum of Vic (Figure 18.16).[41] This altarpiece was probably made towards the end of the 12th century to complete the church which had been restored and re-consecrated in 1186.

As the result of collaboration between the *Magistri Cataloniae* project (UAB), the Episcopal Museum of Vic (MEV), the Centre de Conservació i Restauració de Catalunya (CRBMC) and the Autonomous University of Barcelona (CETEC-PATRIMONI), the wall paintings of Terrassa and the altar frontal of Espinelves have been analysed using infrared spectrography. This has demonstrated that the wall paintings at Terrassa share techniques with Catalan altar frontals, specifically the use of tinfoil (*Petula Stagni*) in the candlesticks and possibly also in some of the haloes (colour plate XXI, bottom).[42] There are also many stylistic similarities between Espinelves and Terrassa. The treatment of the hair is particularly symptomatic, conceived as large blocks of colour divided by curvilinear incisions, as we can observe in the Christ of Terrassa and the Christ Child on the altar frontal at Vic. The treatment of the garments is also remarkably close, where the Master of Espinelves shows great virtuosity and originality. We have already noted how short robes, showing a glimpse of underpants, feature at Terrassa. These appear similarly in the altar frontal. Certain other decorative details have gone unnoticed, however. In particular, the four-petal flower motif is used hierarchically in both works. This motif appears only in the robes of Christ and Becket in the paintings of Terrassa, and in the clothes of the Virgin, Christ, the prophets and two of the Magi on the altar frontal from Espinelves. The articulation of the bodies of the figures is also very distinctive. At Terrassa, John of Salisbury bends his head slightly and stretches his arms following the same model that was used for the figure of King Melchior in the frontal of Espinelves (Figure 18.17). The faces are similarly related, and are characterised by the presence of very marked contour lines, suggesting the artist had prior knowledge of working with drawings and miniatures.

The Master of Espinelves was most likely a painter trained in the workshop at Vic Cathedral. Given the relationship between Terrassa and Vic, both of which were houses of canons regular associated with the distinguished house of Saint-Ruf at Avignon, it is possible the painter would have been recommended by Vic as an artist suited to paint the chapel of Thomas Becket at Terrassa. Recent research by Manuel Castiñeiras on the training of painters in the 12th century suggests that they undertook a graduated and highly structured artistic apprenticeship that took in all forms of painting – manuscript illumination, panel painting and wall painting – probably under the protection of a large ecclesiastical institution, such as a monastery (Ripoll) or cathedral (Seu d'Urgell or Vic).[43] It is not possible to say if the Master of Espinelves was a cleric or a layman, but it is clear that his work was influenced by a clear sense of the 'religious'. Indeed, the numerous epigraphs – *tituli et explanationes* – which accompany the paintings from Terrassa and Espinelves, suggest the painter had enjoyed an education comparable to that

FIGURE 18.16

Vic, Museu Episcopal de Vic, MEV 7, altar frontal of Espinelves (photo: Museu Episcopal de Vic, photographers: Gabriel Salvans and Joan Mª Díaz)

FIGURE 18.17

King Melchior (Espinelves) and John of Salisbury (Terrassa)

of *clerici* or *conversi*, and had been instructed within a monastic or cathedral school. Not only are the inscriptions painted with skill in a well-developed hand, the painter seems to share a familiarity with monastic culture, suggesting he may have been resident within a religious community. If so, he would have been in reasonably good company. There are a number of documented instances of the artist *conversus* in the second half of the 12th century, as in the case of the painter Walter de Colchester, who entered the Abbey of Saint Albans as a monk; the *magister operis frater* Bernardus, the first architect whose name is recorded working on the Cathedral of Tarragona; or the

Master Pere de Coma, who was responsible for the construction of the cathedral at Lleida.[44]

CHRONOLOGY AND CONCLUSION

As far as the dating of these paintings is concerned, two events are relevant. First, in 1187 a new nave and apse were built for the church of Sant Vicenç d'Espinelves. The altar frontal will have been made and placed in the new church at around this date. Second, the canon Harvey, after a period elsewhere (1175–84), returned to Terrassa, where he can be detected signing documents once more between 1185 and 1187. It is likely, therefore, that the paintings were made in the half-decade between 1185 and 1190.

In conclusion, it seems clear that just as the proliferation of churches, chapels and altars dedicated to the archbishop of Canterbury underlines the extent to which the cult of Becket spread rapidly, the rich *corpus* of manuscripts concerned with his life and the liturgies developed for his feasts, underlines the role played by the Augustinians in the diffusion of the cult, especially those that belonged to the congregation of Saint-Ruf at Avignon. Becket appears in numerous codices made for Saint-Ruf's dependencies (San Vicente de la Sierra, Coimbra) and in wall paintings at associated houses such as Terrassa. We also should not forget that Becket was educated in the Augustinian Priory of Merton (Surrey), and even at the moment of his martyrdom, texts of the *Vitae* maintain he was wearing the vestment of a regular canon.[45] It is likely that Augustinian communities took an active role in promoting Becket because they saw him as one of their own – thus the *Vita*, *Passio* and *Miracula* were copied in various daughter houses of Saint-Ruf-to which an extensive liturgical *corpus* was soon added that played a significant role in the spread of the veneration of the archbishop of Canterbury.

ACKNOWLEDGEMENTS

The research undertaken on the paintings of Terrassa and developed in this article formed part of a Research Project *Movilidad y transferencia artística en el Mediterráneo medieval (1187–1388): artistas, objetos y modelos- MAGISTRI MEDITERRANEI*. HAR2015–63883-P. I am indebted to Manuel Castiñeiras for his help and suggestions during the preparation of this text. I would also like to express my most sincere thanks to Domènec Ferran and Antonio Moro (Museum of Terrassa), to John McNeill and to the staff of the Historical and Local Archive, for the facilities they provided and their help in enabling me to consult the documentation concerning the church of Santa Maria at Terrassa.

NOTES

[1] Published in *La Vanguardia* in the editions of 1 and 14 November, and 13 and 28 December 1917. The Catalan historian, Josep Soler i Palet, was the first to study the paintings: J. Soler i Palet, 'Descubrimiento de pinturas murales románicas en Santa Maria de Terrassa', *Museum: revista mensual de arte español antiguo y moderno y de la vida artística contemporánea*, 5/8 (1916–1917), 295–299; Idem, 'De les pintures murals romàniques i especialment de les recentment descobertes a Santa Maria de Terrassa', *Butlletí del Centre Excursionista*, 277 (1918), 24–36. See also J. Gudiol i Cunill, *La pintura migeval catalana. Els Primitius, II. La pintura mural* (Barcelona 1927), 411–427; J. Puig i Cadafalch, *Annuari de l'Institut d'Estudis Catalans: 1915–1920*, (Barcelona 1923), 772–773; C.L. Kuhn, *Romanesque mural painting*, (Cambridge 1930), 41–43; T. Borenius, *Thomas Becket in Art* (London 1932), 48–51.

[2] C. Post, *A History of Spanish Painting, I* (Cambridge 1930), 149–151.

[3] A. Borfo, 'Pintures de Santa Maria de Terrassa', in *Catalunya Romànica, XVIII, Vallès Occidental-Vallès Oriental* (Barcelona 1991), 259–261; A. Borfo, 'Les pintures murals sobre el martiri de Sant Tomàs Becket. La difusió d'un culte, la mort dins de la catedral o un conflicte social', *Terme*, 7 (1992), 12–18; M. Guardia, 'Sant Tomàs Becket i el programa iconogràfic de les pintures murals de Santa Maria de Terrassa', *Locus Amoenus*, 4 (1998–1999), 37–58; M. Guardia, 'Il precoce approdo dell'iconografia di Thomas Becket nella penisola iberica. Il martirio di Becket o il racconto di una morte annunciata', in *I santi venuti dal mare: Atti del V Convegno Internazionale di Studio, Bari-Brindisi, 2005*, ed., M.S. Calò Mariani (Bari 2009), 35–56; M. Guardia, 'La mort de Thomas Becket d'après l'Espagne', *Les Cahiers de Saint-Michel de Cuxa*, 42 (2011), 165–176; G. Cavero et al., *Tomás Becket y la Península Ibérica (1170–1230)*, (León 2013), 82–94. See also my recent contribution on this topic: 'Becket o el martiri del millor home del rei. Les pintures de Santa Maria de Terrassa, la congregació de Sant Ruf i l'anomenat Mestre d'Espinelves', in *Pintar fa mil anys. Els colors i l'ofici del pintor romànic*, ed., M. Castiñeiras and J. Verdaguer (Bellaterra 2014), 87–106.

[4] Even if the cult of Thomas Becket spread quickly in England, few pictorial cycles that depict the martyrdom are preserved. In 1538 Henry VIII ordered the destruction of all images of the archbishop, which probably caused the destruction of important narrative cycles. Notwithstanding this, wall paintings showing the martyrdom of Becket are preserved in the church of Saint Peter near Preston Park (Brighton), Saint Peter ad Vincula, South Newington (Oxfordshire), Saint Mary at Stow (Lincolnshire), Saint John of Winchester, Brookland (Kent), Saint James, Ashmansworth (Hampshire) and North Stoke (Oxfordshire). All of these are late, and none of the surviving examples predates the 13th century.

[5] For a general account of Becket's life and passion, see F. Barlow, *Thomas Becket* (London 1986); R. Foreville, 'Mort et survie de saint Thomas Becket', *Cahiers de civilisation medieval*, 14 (1971), 21–38. See also the more recent account by A. Duggan, *Thomas Becket* (London 2004) and idem, *Thomas Becket: friends, networks, texts, and worship*, Variorum Collected Studies Series 877 (Aldershot 2007).

[6] See London, British Library, MS Cotton, Claudius B 11, fol. 341. This manuscript contains the letters of Becket collected by the prior of Canterbury Alan of Tewkesbury, preceded by the *Vita* and the letters of John of Salisbury. The essential collection of documents is owed to A. Duggan, *Thomas Becket. A Textual History of his Letters* (Oxford 1980), 100–123.

[7] The extensive collection of miracles was gathered by William of Canterbury and Benedict of Peterborough. The latter was the first custodian of Becket's tomb and his interviews with pilgrims form the basis for the book of miracles. His *Passion of Thomas*, written between 1173–74, details the martyrdom and its consequences. See *Materials for the History of Thomas Becket archbishop of Canterbury (canonized by Pope Alexander III, A.D. 1173)*, ed., J.C. Robertson and J.B. Shepard, Rolls Series, LXVII, vols 1–7 (London 1875–1885).

[8] A. Borfo, 'Les pintures murals' (as n. 3), 14.

[9] See W.J. Millor, H.E. Butler and C.N.L. Brooke, ed., *The Letters of John of Salisbury* (Oxford 1979 and 1986), *passim*.

[10] 'Convenirent, ante altare Sancti Johannis Baptistae et Sancti Augustini Anglorum apostoli in sarcophago marmoreo sepelierunt', *Materials for the History of Thomas Becket* (as n. 7), 2, 321–322.

[11] London, British Library, MS Harley 5102, f. 17.

[12] Milagros Guardia identified the two figures in the upper of the paintings as Thomas Becket and Saint Stephen. Guardia, 'Sant Tomàs Becket' (as n. 3), 54.

[13] 'I turned to see the voice that spoke with me. Having turned, I saw seven golden lampstands. And among the lampstands was one like a son of man, clothed with a robe reaching down to his feet, and with a golden sash around his chest', (Revelation, 1^{12-13}).

[14] Josep Gudiol noted the presence of this inscription, whose existence we have been able to confirm thanks to the photographs made after its discovery. See J. Gudiol i Cunill, 'Pintura mural romànica a Terrassa', *Pàgina Artística de La Veu de Catalunya*, 406 (29 October 1917).

[15] Among numerous surviving manuscripts a liturgical text from Santa Cruz at Coimbra (a house of regular canons attached to Saint-Ruf) should be mentioned (Biblioteca Pública Municipal do Porto, MS Santa Cruz 40). This contains an opening prayer dedicated to the archbishop of Canterbury: 'Deus, pro cuius ecclesia Thomas gloriosus martir et pontifex gladiis impiorum occubuit, praesta, quaesumus, ut omnes, qui eius implorant auxilium, petitionis sue salutare consequantur effectum'. See R.B. Slocum, *Liturgies in Honour of Thomas Becket* (Toronto 2004), 192.

[16] 'Thomas coram Domino/ Vixit in timore/ Ideo cum Domino/regnat cum decore'. T. Borenius, *Thomas Becket in Art* (London 1932), 49.

[17] *The Letters of John of Salisbury* (as n. 9), 725–738.

[18] On this topic see R. Foreville ed., *Thomas Becket. Actes du colloque International de Sédières, 19–24 août 1973* (Paris 1975). Idem, *Thomas Becket dans la tradition historique et hagiographique* (London 1981).

[19] A document of 1180 relates of the celebration of the Feast of Saint Thomas of Canterbury in the Cathedral of Salamanca; in 1181 a church dedicated to Saint Thomas Becket is documented at Zamora and, shortly after, there is a chapel dedicated to the English prelate in Toro (Palencia). See Cavero et al., *Tomás Becket y la Península Ibérica* (as n. 3), 49–66. Toledo, Burgos and Sigüenza also adopted the cult of Thomas Becket. At Burgos, a chapel dedicated to the English martyr is documented in 1202; at Sigüenza, Bishop Joscelmo (1168–78) consecrated a chapel to the archbishop of Canterbury.

[20] J.M. Rodríguez Montañés, 'Iglesia de San Nicolás', in *Enciclopedia del Románico en Castilla León. Soria. III*, (Aguilar de Campoo 2002), 125–138.

[21] M.S. Gros i Pujol, 'El llibre de refeccions del monestir de Santa Maria de Ripoll', *Studia Monastica*, 46/2 (2004), 365–378. Idem, 'El *Liber consuetudinum Vicensis ecclesie* del Canonge Andreu Salmunia, Vic, Museu Episcopal, MS. 134 (LXXXIV)', *Miscel·lània litúrgica Catalana*, 7 (1996), 175–294.

[22] D.J. Smith, 'The Abbot-Crusader: Nicholas Breakspear in Catalonia', in *Adrian IV: The English Pope (1154–1159), Studies and texts*, ed., B. Bolton and A. Duggan (Aldershot 2002), 29–40; L. Villegas-Aristizábal, 'Anglo-Norman Involvement in the Conquest and Settlement of Tortosa, 1148–1180', *Crusades*, 8 (2009), 63–129; J. Pickworth, *Catalunya and the English Pope*, (Barcelona 2011), 75–80. See also C. Dereine, 'Saint-Ruf et ses coutumes aux XIe et XIIe siècles', *Revue Bénédictine*, 59 (1949), 161–182; D. Misonné, 'La législation canonial de Saint-Rufus d'Avignon à ses origines. Règle de saint Augustin et coutumier', *Annales de Midi*, 64 (1963), 471–489; Y. Lebrigand, 'Origines et première diffusion de l'Ordre de Saint-Ruf', in *Le monde des chanoines. XIe–XIVe siècles*, ed., M-H. Vicaire, Cahiers de Fanjeaux 24, (Toulouse 1989), 167–179.

[23] A. Figuereido Frías, 'O Mosteiro de Santa Cruz de Coimbra, perspectivaçao histórica', in *Catálogo dos Códices da Livraria de Mão do Mosteiro de Santa Cruz de Coimbra na Biblioteca Pública Municipal do Porto*, ed. A.A. Nascimento and J.F. Meirinhos (Oporto 1997) 71–78; S.A. Gomes, 'In Limine Conscriptionis: documentos, Chancelaria e Cultura no Mosteiro de Santa Cruz de Coimbra nos Séculos XII e XIV', *Lusitania Sacra*, 13–14 (2001–2002), 477–490.

[24] Ana Suárez has argued that it is likely that during the 12th century members of the community of Santa Cruz travelled to Saint-Ruf in order to copy books for the library of Coimbra. A. Suárez González, 'Tomás Becket: el reflejo escrito de su figura y de su culto', in *Tomás Becket y la Península Ibérica (1170–1230)*, (as n. 3), 123–201, at 185–201. A. Duggan, 'Aspects of Anglo-Portuguese Relations in the 12th Century. Manuscripts, Relics, Decretals and the Worship of St. Thomas Becket at Lorvao, Alcobaça and Tomar', *Portuguese Studies*, 14 (1998), 1–19; A. Duggan, 'The Santa Cruz Transcription of Benedict of Peterborough's Liber miraculorum beati Thome: Porto, BPM, cod. Santa Cruz 60', *Mediaevalia. Textos e estudos*, 20 (2001), 27–55.

[25] Biblioteca Pública Municipal do Porto, MS Santa Cruz 60.

[26] Five codices should be added to this example; two Psalters (Biblioteca Pública Municipal do Porto, MS Santa Cruz 26 and MS Santa Cruz 27, the latter dated 1179), a Missal (Biblioteca Pública Municipal do Porto, MS Santa Cruz 40) and two liturgical calendars (Biblioteca Pública Municipal do Porto, MS Santa Cruz 62 and MS Santa Cruz 74), both of them late 12th century. See A. Suárez González, 'Tomás Becket: el reflejo escrito' (as n. 28).

[27] Lisboa, Biblioteca Nacional, MS. IL. 218. See I. Vilares Cepêda, 'Dois manuscritos litúrgicos medievais do Mosteiro de S. Vicente de Fora de Lisboa (Lisboa, Biblioteca Nacional, MS IL. 218 e IL. 143)', *Didaskalia*, 15 (1985), 161–228.

[28] A. Suárez González, *Patrimonio cultural de San Isidoro de León. B. Serie Bibliográfica. Vol. II, Los Códices III.1, III.2, III.3, IV y V (Biblia, Liber Capituli, Misal)*, (León 1997), 330; idem, 'Dos calendarios litúrgicos leoneses de la segunda mitad del siglo XII', *Memoria Ecclesiae*, 25 (2004), 161–164.

[29] Besides the example of León, relics of Saint Thomas were kept at Santo Domingo de Silos and in the Cathedrals of Burgos and Oviedo. Furthermore, 19th-century chroniclers maintain that a relic of the cope of Becket was kept at the monastery of Sant Pere de Rodes (Girona).

[30] 'Pro ecclesia tamen Sancti Rufi, cuius uterus nos portavit et ubera lactaverunt'. The original text of the epistle can be found in J. Francisco Rivera, 'Cabildos regulares en la provincia eclesiástica de Toledo', in *La vita comune del clero nei secoli XI e XII. Atti della Settimana di Studio: Mendola, setembre 1959*, Miscellania del Centro di studi medievalli 3 (Milano 1962), 220–240.

[31] Madrid, Biblioteca Nacional, MSS 10100. See J. Janini, *Manuscritos litúrgicos de la Biblioteca Nacional*, (Madrid 1969), 132–133.

[32] The name Harvey, with its variations (Hervey, Hervie, Harvie, Herveus), has an etymological root of Breton origins (*Aeruiu*) and was introduced in England after the Norman Conquest. The study of English prosopography shows that it is a very common name in the 12th century. See S.E. Brydges, *Collin's Peerage of England; Genealogical, Biographical and Historical*, IV (London 1812), 139–161. See also C. Sánchez, 'Becket o el martiri del millor home del rei' (as n. 4), 98–99. All texts signed by canon Harvey can be found in P. Puig, V. Ruiz and J. Soler, *Diplomatari de Sant Pere i Santa Maria d'Ègara. Terrassa, 958–1207*, (Barcelona 2001).

[33] Arxiu Històric de Terrassa-Arxiu Comarcal del Vallès Occidental (AHCT). Perg. I-179. P. Puig, V. Ruiz and J. Soler, *Diplomatari* (as n. 32), 484, doc. 211.

[34] I would like to thank Dr. Teresa Webber (Trinity College, Cambridge) for her invaluable help in the paleographic study of the manuscripts from the Priory of Santa Maria at Terrassa.

[35] In a letter written by John of Salisbury to Pope Adrian IV (epistle 50), with whom he maintained a sincere friendship, he asks for his favour by the Augustinian house of Merton: 'May it profit the brethren of Merton that, while you were in the Church of Saint-Ruf their good odour reached even unto you, as your highness used to tell me, your servant, when we talked together'. See *Letters of John of Salisbury* (as n. 9), 3–14.

[36] This was consecrated by Bernat, bishop of Barcelona, on the feast of St Thomas of Canterbury, with the consent of Pope Clement II (1187–91) who confirmed its erection in 1188. J. Mas i Domènech, *Notes històriques del bisbat de Barcelona*, XII, (Barcelona 1915), 40, number 2174.

[37] P. Puig, V. Ruiz and J. Soler, *Diplomatari* (as n. 32), 354.

[38] The Augustinian community at Terrassa was given the use of Santa Maria at Terrassa in 1113. Originally, it had been founded at Sant Adrià del Besòs, and seems to have brought a devotion to St Adrian with it. See U. Vones-Liebenstein, *Saint-Ruf und Spanien. Studien zur Verbreitung der Regularkanoniker von Saint-Ruf in Avignon auf der Iberischen Halbinsel (11. und 12. Jahrhundert)*, Bibliotheca Victorina 6 (Paris 1996), vol. I 180–184, 194–224, 265–269 and II 583–660. See

also J. Ventalló i Vintró, *El priorato de Tarrasa. Notas históricas* (Terrassa 1894); F. Torres Amat, 'Egara (Terasa) y su monasterio de San Rufo', *Boletín de la Real Academia de la Historia*, 33 (1898), 5–30.

[39] 'Ego comes Nuno et uxor me comitissa dompna Tharesia, sane corpore et mente, damus et concedimus iure hereditario in perpetuum Deo et altari sancti martiris Thome, quod expermissione domni Cerebruni Toletani archiepiscopi et Hyspaniarum primatis et canonicorum ecclesie Toletane construi fecimus in ipsa ecclesia Toletana. F.J. Fernández, *Los cartularios de Toledo. Catálogo documental* (Madrid 1985), 173–174, doc. 180.

[40] G. Cavero et al., *Tomás Becket* (as n. 3), 69.

[41] On the basis of remarks by C. Kuhn, *Romanesque mural painting* (as n. 1), 41–43, who underlined the formal relationship between the paintings of Terrassa and the altar frontal, W. Cook and J. Gudiol established an identity for the two pieces, ascribing them to the Master of Espinelves. See W. Cook and J. Gudiol i Ricart, *Pintura e Imaginerias Románicas,* Ars Hispaniae, VI (Madrid 1950), 91–92. The first descriptions of the altar frontal can be found in J. Puiggarí, *Álbum de la sección arqueológica de la Exposición Universal de Barcelona* (Barcelona 1888), 22. Among other contributions see A. D'Espona and J. Serra, *Catálogo del Museo Artístico Episcopal de Vich* (Vic 1893), 71–72; C. Post, *A History of Spanish Painting,* I (Cambridge 1930), 243–247; J. Gudiol i Cunill, *La pintura migeval Catalana. Els Primitius, II. La pintura sobre fusta* (Igualada 1929), 116–124; J.M. Folch i Torres, *La pintura Romànica sobre fusta,* Monumenta Cataloniae, IX (Barcelona 1956), 166–167; M. Castiñeiras, 'Catalan Romanesque Painting Revisited (with Technical Report by A. Morer and J. Badia)', in *Spanish medieval Art, Recent Studies,* ed. Colum Hourihane (Tempe 2007),119–153.

[42] In undertaking this we have relied on the collaboration of the chemist Majo Alcayde (CETEC-PATRIMONI), and Judit Verdaguer (curator of the Museu Episcopal de Vic), both researchers of *Magistri Cataloniae* project. See J. Verdaguer and M. Alcayde, 'Descobrint o interpretant la matèria. La policromia de la pintura sobre taula romànica catalana segons els exemples de Puigbò, Ribes, Espinelves i Lluçà', in *Pintar fa mil anys. Els colors i l'ofici del pintor romànic,* ed. M. Castiñeiras and Judit Verdaguer (Bellaterra 2014), 125–142, at 135.

[43] M. Castiñeiras, 'Artiste-*clericus* ou artiste-laïque? Apprentissage et *curriculum vitae* du peintre en Catalogne et en Toscane', *Les Cahiers de Saint-Michel de Cuxa,* 42 (2012), 15–30; M. Castiñeiras, 'Clergue o laic? Algunes reflexions sobre l'estatus de l'artista i la qüestió de l'autoria a l'Europa romànica', *Medievalia,* 15 (2012), 83–87.

[44] C. Sánchez, 'Reconstruïu el temple: organització i rols professionals en els tallers catedralicis catalans', *Síntesi: Quaderns dels Seminaris de Besalú,* III (2016), 33–51. Idem, 'Organización y perfiles profesionales en los talleres catedralicios de la Corona de Aragón', in *Entre la letra y el pincel. El artista medieval: leyenda, identidad y estatus,* ed. M. Castiñeiras (Almería 2017), 221–238.

[45] 'Prius tamen, ut moris est, corpus mundissimum martyris lavandum expoliantes, sub habitu canonici regularis eum in habitu et ordine monachorum tam secreto diu reperiunt existitisse, ut etiam hoc suos lateret familiares'. *Materials for the History of Thomas Becket* (as n. 7), 2, 442.

AGENCY AND THE RE-INVENTION OF SLAB RELIEF SCULPTURE AT SAN ISIDORO DE LEÓN c. 1100

Rose Walker

Dissecting the twists and turns of artistic production in the Middle Ages is a challenging task. The multiple elements involved in the development of Romanesque art in Spain at a time of great invention and experimentation only serve to exacerbate this problem.[1] In an attempt to pinpoint some aspects of 'process', this paper will focus on one medium, relief sculpture; on one period, the early 12th century and on two specific areas of enquiry. First the possibility of an 'umbrella' level of direction emanating from the papacy, and second the agency of artists who may have intersected with multiple 'patrons'. The former relates to the mechanics of the implementation of reform. The latter considers the ways that artists may have dealt with such direction, which left room for interpretation by local recipients and for creative artistic responses to archetypes.

ART DIRIGÉ?

The idea that papal legates might have exercised artistic agency in the Iberian Peninsula from c. 1060 to c. 1100 formed the subject of an earlier paper, where I provided a narrative view of that process based on an accumulation of circumstantial evidence.[2] It shows papal legates were present on significant occasions and played a key role in networks. As a prelude to the main subject here, I wish to deploy a historical and social context: a friendship circle, or *réseau*, associated primarily with Pope Gregory VII (1073–85), although it had roots in earlier papacies and continued long after the death of Gregory VII.[3] This social network was formed by a closely managed group, whose members worked across institutional and political boundaries to form reciprocal relationships. Unlike the linear routes of 'pilgrimage road' art theory, this model of papal agency mirrors the circulation of artistic ideas, emphasises collaboration and nuances issues of precedence. The network grew over the last quarter of the 11th century, when it also supported the introduction of the Roman liturgy into the peninsula. It promoted a new generation of reformed churchmen and recruited like-minded supporters, so that by 1100 the web of connections had thickened and deepened. At the heart of papal artistic policy, as it was disseminated in Spain through this circle, was the use of Roman sarcophagi, both Pagan and Christian, as appropriate sources of artistic inspiration.[4] Serafín Moralejo has shown that sarcophagi were central to the development of Romanesque sculpture on capitals and corbels in Spain, and demonstrated how figurative poses, particularly those of the Roman sarcophagus at Husillos, were adapted to architectural forms (Figure 19.1).[5] I maintain that their role was even more important, and that they were identified as a suitable stimulus for diverse mental processes, technical, compositional and conceptual.[6] The policy enabled papal legates to retain a degree of control over local projects and to guide the available artistic expertise without imposing oppressive restrictions. Such a differentiated and subtle approach fits with that adopted for liturgical change, which also looked to antiquity for its rationale.[7] Sarcophagi not only directed artists towards archetypes from the period before the Muslim invasion, but avoided idolatrous associations with temples and freestanding sculpture. Within those limits, however, any type of sarcophagus seems to have been admissible as a source of inspiration, and the permitted responses to the subject were remarkably varied.

During the second half of the 11th century the popes identified men who could champion reform. In the 1060s Hugh Candidus from Remiremont, the legate of Pope Alexander II, began to establish relationships within the peninsula. His arrival was probably prompted by a conjunction of the temporary conquest of Barbastro (Aragón) in 1064, and by the death of Fernando I in 1065 and consequent instability in León and Castile. Both events were characterised by potential access to immense wealth. Hugh's legateship continued until 1068 and was renewed in 1071, during which time he built networks across Catalonia and Aragón, introducing the Roman liturgy to at least one site in Aragón. This early phase of ecclesiastical reform does not seem to have given rise to a particular visual expression or formulated a 'visual manifesto'.[8] Cardinal-Bishop Gerald of Ostia, the great Cluniac canon lawyer, continued the work begun by Hugh and was appointed legate to Spain in 1073. In that year he excommunicated a rival claimant to the see of Burgos-Oca and confirmed Bishop Jimeno (d. 1082), who was to remain

© British Archaeological Association 2018

FIGURE 19.1

Madrid, Museo arqueológico nacional; Husillos sarcophagus (John Batten Photography)

FIGURE 19.2

Toulouse, Musée Saint Raymond; Sarcophagus from St-Orens, Auch (John Batten Photography)

an important supporter of reform. Gerald may also have helped arrange Alfonso VI's gift of San Isidro de Dueñas to Cluny in 1073, a transfer that was confirmed by Jimeno.[9] This was the first of many gifts to Cluny that were part of a complex reciprocal relationship involving intercession for Alfonso VI's family at Cluny.[10] It foreshadowed the king's conspicuous generosity towards the abbey, culminating in the large quantity of gold that helped to build Cluny III. That gift may be the best-known example of such an exchange, but it was far from the only transaction that linked sites and individuals within the friendship circle. We should envisage a frequent exchange of precious metals and luxury goods in return for spiritual rewards and international status. Another example of gifts and friendship saw Bishop Peter of Pamplona welcomed into the Cluniac fold between 1094 and 1104, after he had brought largesse from the conquests of Pedro I.[11] Guidance on matters liturgical and artistic may have been amongst the less tangible benefits that came into the peninsula in return for the spoils of negotiated peace and war. The artistic expertise that can be seen on both sides of the Pyrenees may have travelled along the same routes of *amicitia*, perhaps in the form of craftsmen tied to members of the network.[12]

The first discernably visual phase of the Gregorian Reform can be detected during the papacy of Gregory VII, when the implementation of papal policy was carefully managed. The two dominant figures during this first phase were Amat, bishop of Oloron and, from 1089, archbishop of Bordeaux (d. 1101), and Richard, abbot of Saint-Victor of Marseille and, from 1106, archbishop of Narbonne (*c*. 1121). Amat began his career as a reformer in Aquitaine, where he was appointed legate by Gregory VII in 1074.[13] He may have been a Cluniac and was possibly a protégé of Gerald of Ostia.[14] Amat's sphere of activity in the peninsula encompassed Aragón and Navarre, and, in accordance with Pope Gregory's preferred management method, Amat shared this territory, his partner being Abbot Frotard of Saint-Pons-de-Thomières, who had a more permanent responsibility for the regions.[15] Both were probably involved in liturgical reform, as Juan P. Rubio Sadia has traced elements in the liturgical manuscripts of Aragón from Narbonne, the diocesan see for Saint-Pons-de-Thomières; from Auch, the diocese to which Oloron belonged, and from Bordeaux.[16]

In 1083 Frotard introduced two influential ecclesiastical protégés into Navarre, Peter of Rodez, a monk of Conques, who was preferred as bishop of Pamplona, and Raymond, who became abbot of Leire.[17] Frotard worked closely with King Sancho Ramírez, and together Amat and Frotard may have helped to negotiate the marriage in 1086 of Pedro, the son of Sancho Ramírez, to Agnes of Aquitaine. Women were also an important aspect of exchange across social networks. Both Amat and Frotard had access to Roman sarcophagi, especially those of Late Antique date. The feature singled out for use in Aragón and Navarre was the chrismon, which was common on ancient sarcophagi across Aquitaine, Catalonia, Toulouse and could even be found near Saint-Pons in Rodez. Adapted as a 'speaking chrismon' with added letters, the motif was carved over church doorways on both sides of the Pyrenees, where it probably signified a seal of papal protection.[18] Although Saint-Pons was in an area associated with marble carving, Frotard does not seem to have been in a position to introduce marble sculpture into Aragón or Navarre.

Amat's counterpart was Richard of Saint-Victor of Marseille, a member of the comital family of Millau, a county whose territory lay east of Conques and Rodez. A more senior figure, Richard, was made a cardinal-priest in 1078, and in the following year he succeeded his brother as abbot of Saint-Victor in Marseille and was made a legate by Gregory VII. The pope assigned him a major role in the implementation of the Roman liturgy in León and Castile, and Richard forged a good relationship with its king, Alfonso VI, one which seems to have lasted until the king's death in 1109. Richard and Amat were thus working as papal representatives at some remove from their own institutional areas of interest and in Spanish regions that were not immediately contiguous to them. Such careful checks and balances were typical of papal policy from the time of Gregory VII. This approach may have been particularly important in Richard's case, as not only did he have a considerable family network across the Rouergue and Provence but much of Catalonia had been reformed from Saint-Victor de Marseille, and the monastery had acquired a significant number of possessions there, including Ripoll. Under Richard's legateship the Roman liturgy was finally established in León and its introduction was confirmed at the Council of Burgos in 1080. Gregory VII also used Richard in 1083 to curb Cluniac ambitions at Saint-Sernin in Toulouse, where he employed rather blunt methods to reinstall the canons.[19] Alfonso VI relied on him at the 1088 Council of Husillos in an attempt to settle matters in Santiago de Compostela and in Osma. Richard may have subsequently helped to negotiate the marriage of Alfonso VI's illegitimate daughter, Elvira, to Raymond IV of Toulouse some time before 1094.[20] Although in some ways a controversial figure, Richard was briefly reappointed legate in 1101 by Paschal II, and his authority was further recognised when he was made archbishop of the sizeable archdiocese of Narbonne in 1106.

Collaboration between Amat and Frotard was mirrored by that between Cardinal Richard and Bernard of La Sauvetat. Bernard became abbot of Sahagún in 1080 and from 1086 was Archbishop of Toledo. Andrea Rucquoi has described Bernard as Richard's 'man', but their relationship was largely determined by the dynamics of papal management.[21] Bernard was a Cluniac, educated at Saint-Orens in Auch and at Cluny. He was sent to León with the personal support of Abbot Hugh of Cluny, and in background he had more in common with Amat of Oloron than with Richard of Saint-Victor. The partnership between Richard and Bernard was thus a highly successful example of the papal approach that set aside potential institutional rivalries in the expectation of greater goals. It was the hallmark of the friendship circle. Like Frotard, Bernard recruited immigrant churchmen from his home region. Several arrived initially to serve as canons in Toledo, but later went on to senior positions: Bishop Peter of Segovia, Peter of Palencia, and Bernard of Sigüenza were all from Agen, while Bernard's successor at Toledo in 1125 was Raymond who, like Bernard, came from La Sauvetat.[22]

Richard and Bernard were equally complementary in their artistic *milieux*. The region around Marseille retained a rich collection of classical art, including sarcophagi, notably at Aix-en-Provence and Arles, both cities where Richard's relations had considerable influence. Bernard, on the other hand, had access through his network to liturgical manuscripts from Auch, Agen, and Limoges, and his first monastery of Saint-Orens held a Late Antique sarcophagus, almost identical to one at Oloron (Figure 19.2). John Williams has shown a clear iconographic link between the sarcophagus at Saint-Orens and a capital depicting the Sacrifice of Abraham in the Pantheon at San Isidoro.[23] As some aspects of the sculptural style found in the Pantheon may also derive from the same source, specifically the heavy facial and corporeal features and cap-like hair found on several capitals, Bernard may have advised Alfonso VI's sister, Urraca, on the sculptural decoration. This style co-existed with the more classical approach that Serafín Moralejo has shown to be linked to the Orestes sarcophagus from Husillos (Figure 19.1), and thus to the Council of Husillos of 1088. Significantly it was Richard of Saint-Victor who presided over that Council, and he travelled with the archbishop of Aix-en-Provence. Aside from the presence of one of the finest sarcophagi in the peninsula, the venue had little to recommend it over Burgos, León or Palencia, so it may have been chosen for its artistic interest. The way that the capital with nude figures and serpents at nearby Frómista, only 25 km from Husillos, integrates responses to both types of sarcophagus could suggest that Richard and Bernard were also travelling with sculptors. The monastery of Husillos was in the territory of Alfonso VI's childhood friend, Pedro Ansúrez, the Count of Saldaña, who, like Alfonso VI's sister Urraca, may have had a particular interest in new works of art and architecture.[24] Certainly many of the subsequent developments in the carving of capitals took place in churches located in his territory. Another innovation, personally connected to him, came from the monastery of Sahagún, and it is this sculpture that introduces the subject of this essay, the fashion for slab relief sculpture *c.* 1100.

In 1093 Pedro Ansúrez's son, Alfonso, died and was buried at Sahagún in a tomb of white-grey marble, of which only the lid survives. As Alfonso was young, the tomb was probably posthumous. Alfonso VI's queen, Constance, niece of Abbot Hugh of Cluny, died in the same year, so it is possible that the sculptor was asked to carve more than one tomb.[25] Iconographically Alfonso Ansúrez's sarcophagus lid looks to the early-11th-century Empire and to Cluniac liturgical intercession.[26] In its gabled form it recalls Late Antique sarcophagi, but the decision to use marble and the use of a drill link it to classical sarcophagi and the renewal of techniques associated with them. As Moralejo noted, the faces of the flying angels, with fat cheeks and bulging eyes, recall other sculpted faces found near Palencia.[27] However, marble carving was also practised at this date in the regions associated with Richard of Saint-Victor and Frotard of Saint-Pons-de-Thomières. Judging by patterns of survival, the most probable source for a sculptor with the technique necessary to carve marble would be Saint-Sernin at Toulouse, a possibility which meetings of the friendship circle in 1095 and 1096 would support. Against this, the portrait-like image of the deceased on the Sahagún tomb, and the ample use of script, suggest another possible source.[28] Both features are found on a relief slab from Saint-Victor at Marseille, one that depicts their renowned mid-11th-century reformer Abbot Isarn. Often dated earlier, this piece is probably a retrospective *memoria* of c. 1100, celebrating the reforming ancestry of the abbots of Marseille.[29] The relief from Saint-Victor and the Sahagún tomb lid also share an innovative approach to the relationship between the body and the slab, even if the results diverge. Whilst Alfonso Ansúrez appears to float towards the Hand of God that receives him into heaven, the equally individualised Abbot Isarn is flattened beneath the script that contains him.

The multiple references found on the tomb lid of Alfonso Ansúrez and on capitals in the Spanish kingdoms reflect connections between members of the friendship circle, which were becoming more complex around this time. The increased frequency of their meetings was matched by a change in the rhythm of artistic interaction. Richard of Saint-Victor attended the Council of Piacenza in March 1095, where most distinguished clerics of period, including Abbot Hugh of Cluny, gathered under Pope Urban II (1088–99) to set out a renewed reform agenda. The attendance list and canons have been pieced together from a variety of sources, confirming the presence of Archbishop Amat of Bordeaux and Abbot Frotard of Saint-Pons, along with Archbishop Peter of Aix-en-Provence. Bernard Reilly has argued that some Spanish representatives were also in attendance but others think that Richard presented their petition.[30] Archbishop Bernard of Toledo was present, however, at the larger Council of Clermont in November 1095, accompanied by the Cluniac Dalmatius, bishop of Iria-Santiago de Compostela, who successfully requested the translation of his see to Santiago and its direct dependence on Rome.[31] By now designated a permanent 'native' legate like Frotard, Bernard was with Urban II again the following year for the consecration of the high altar at Saint-Sernin in Toulouse.[32] Other recorded attendees included Archbishop Amat of Bordeaux, Bishop Walter of Albi, Bishop Peter of Pamplona and Count Raymond of Toulouse, Alfonso VI's son-in-law.[33] Richard of Saint-Victor seems to have been absent, but Urban II confirmed Saint-Sernin's independence, so vigorously established by Richard, at the Council of Nîmes shortly afterwards. The number of attendees with Spanish connections at the consecration may indicate communal, and reciprocal, support for the collegiate church.[34] The Spanish clerics may have even been amongst the *confratres* mentioned on the altar's inscription.[35] Such bonds of *amicitia* would certainly help to explain the artistic dialogue between Toulouse and the Spanish kingdoms from the late eleventh century onwards.

The long papacy of Paschal II (1099–1118) opened in a spirit of optimism, after Pedro I of Aragón's conquest of Huesca in 1096, and the success of the First Crusade in 1099.[36] An ancient church in Huesca, renamed San Pedro el Viejo, was quickly ceded to Frotard's abbey.[37] Amat of Bordeaux, as papal legate, working again with Frotard of Saint-Pons, consecrated the mosque as a new cathedral.[38] The focus of the circle appeared to be shifting eastwards in the wake of military success, following the acquisition of new wealth and perhaps expertise, which continued with Pedro I's reconquest of Barbastro in October 1100. Even so Paschal II reappointed Richard of Saint-Victor as papal legate to León and Castile in that same year. Paschal may have retained a particular interest in the region, as in 1090 he was sent as Urban II's papal legate to preside over a Council at León. His brief was to bring order to the vacant see of Iria-Santiago, to restore the archbishopric of Tarragona (in name at least), and, perhaps, to help Hugh of Cluny collect the arrears of his annual donation from Alfonso VI.[39] In December 1100 Richard was to attend a Council at Palencia, a short distance south of Husillos, where he would work again with Alfonso VI and Archbishop Bernard of Toledo.[40] On this occasion, he travelled with Ghibbelin, archbishop of Arles. Part of the business of the Council was to restore Braga to metropolitan rank, and its new archbishop Gerald of Moissac was in attendance. The Council of Palencia probably also ratified the election of Diego Gelmírez as bishop of Santiago de Compostela, as he confirmed one of its charters as bishop-elect. Gelmírez was now clearly a full member of the circle. His *amicitia* with Peter of Pamplona may date from their joint attendance at the Council, and possibly gave new impetus to artistic exchange between Santiago, Conques and Toulouse. Richard of Saint-Victor's return to Palencia may also have been behind a renewed attempt to use Roman sarcophagi as sources of artistic inspiration and extend slab relief sculpture to the exterior of churches in the peninsula. Bernard of Toledo's visit to Saint-Sernin in Toulouse in 1096 might alone be sufficient to account for this, but given Richard and Bernard's probable artistic collaboration over a decade earlier Richard's return to Spain seems a more timely catalyst.

RELIEF SCULPTURE ON THE PUERTA DEL CORDERO AT SAN ISIDORO DE LEÓN

Slab reliefs in stone and ivory were initially carved in Spain for interior spaces – tombs, liturgical furniture and shrines. The tomb of Alfonso Ansúrez at Sahagún constitutes the surviving example in stone, but others may have been lost. Morales, for example, writing in the 17th century described a tomb carved for the infanta Urraca (d. 1101) at San Isidoro as having a 'very fine white marble' chest, and being 'strangely rich'.[41] Within a short time relief carving came to adorn the exterior of buildings around doorways and to announce the church as *domus dei*, or as a reliquary in stone. The biblical model for such decoration was the Temple of Solomon (1 Kings 6; 2 Chronicles 2–5), which glittered with marble, precious metals and gems donated by King David (I Chronicles 29[2–5]). Exterior slab relief sculpture may be found in Spain around 1100 over the south doorways at San Isidoro in León; over the transept doorways at Santiago de Compostela, and at Jaca cathedral, where it is now mounted on the exterior of the southern apse, and over the portal of the fortified collegiate church at Loarre.[42] Some of this sculpture is carved on reused marble, a material that emphasises the earlier deployment of relief sculpture in interior funerary and liturgical spaces. Whether the repurposing of Roman marble slabs also carried imperial connotations at this period remains under discussion.[43]

The slab relief sculpture that decorates the exterior of the south nave portal of San Isidoro at León, known as the Portal of the Lamb (Puerta del Cordero), is the focus of the rest of this study. The reliefs appear in four different forms: a tympanum in two tiers; a row of zodiac symbols on separate slabs of grey-white marble; a set of slabs in a pinker-tinged marble-like stone depicting King David's musicians and a soldier holding a shield and a sword; and two larger slabs sculpted with single figures in higher relief, one labelled as St. Isidore and the other traditionally identified as St. Pelagius (Figure 19.3). The coherence and date of the ensemble have long been a source of controversy, as elements may have been moved since their manufacture.[44] I shall discuss the reliefs in five groups, as I will revert to Sauerländer's view of the 'tympanum' and argue that it is an amalgam of two types of sculpture originally conceived separately[45] (Figure 19.4). This opinion is strengthened by recent petrological analysis, which has shown that the lintel was carved in dolomitic limestone from the local Boñar quarry, whereas the upper reliefs – a *clipeus* containing the Lamb of God held by two victory angels, and two angels holding cross-staves – are of grey-white marble.[46]

A thick lime wash covers the slabs today and rather homogenises the tympanum, but differences between the slabs are clear in photographs taken by John Williams in the early 1970s.[47] Other slab reliefs have clearly been moved into tympana at a later date, for example at Notre-Dame de Luçon (Vendée) and at Santiago de Compostela.[48] Most significantly, however, this suggestion is confirmed by recent archaeological analysis by María de los Ángeles Utrero and José Murillo. Although John Williams argued that the reliefs were carved for their present position and purpose, more trimming is evident than he identified.[49] The lintel is clearly cut unevenly along the upper edge, but damage is also visible on the slabs that bear angels carrying cross-staves (Figure 19.5). The tops of both wings on the right-hand angel have been cut; the halo has been trimmed across the top, and possibly its toes as well. The left-hand angel has been clipped at the top of its right wing. Williams pointed to some foliate carving continued from one of the marble pieces onto the lintel slab, but it would have been a simple matter to add such a feature when the sculptures were re-assembled as a tympanum. Most problematically these angels are now mounted to look outwards at the roll mouldings.[50] Moreover the angel slabs at San Isidoro have no parallels on the capitals inside or outside the church. In style they are emphatically Toulousain, sharing hairstyle and features with the larger angels reset within the ambulatory at Saint-Sernin. Although the original disposition of the Saint-Sernin angels is uncertain – they may have been behind the altar table, or set into the walls of the sanctuary where they would recall other angelic members of the celestial liturgy as were later painted in Catalan apses, or have ornamented the shrine around the sarcophagus of St. Saturninus – they clearly originated inside the church.[51] Like those at Toulouse, the San Isidoro angels are highly classical.[52] Indeed the marble in which they were recut probably came from a Roman structure in León. Given these questions, it is worth considering other ways in which the San Isidoro angels might have been displayed. One possibility is that they formed part of an ensemble inside the church, perhaps around the shrine of St. Isidore, or even above the tomb of the Infanta Urraca. If so, the angels would have acted as psychopomps in the manner of the archangels on the tomb of Alfonso Ansúrez. Contemporary parallels for a funerary use are lacking, but given the experimental nature of early Romanesque sculpture and descriptions of other precious objects, such as a crucifix with a figure of Urraca kneeling at its base, this remains a possibility.[53] The removal of Urraca's body to the centre of the Pantheon, probably c. 1148 when Augustinian canons took over the double monastery, could explain Morales's reference to the marble tomb, especially if part of its sculptural decoration had been removed. Alternatively, the panels could have been mounted in a gable over an earlier nave portal. Both suggestions assume that the angels were carved for San Isidoro, though they could, of course, be spolia from another site.

Similar questions might be asked of the zodiac panels now mounted as a frieze below the baroque cornice of the Portal of the Lamb (Figures 19.6 and 19.7). Is this their original position? What role do they play in the iconography of the portal? Although the rectangular slabs vary in size, shape and depth of relief, they clearly form a set, both stylistically and iconographically. They are full of invention and, as Serafín Moralejo noted, the sculptor drew on the figure of Orestes from the Husillos sarcophagus to create the naked male figure of Aquarius. The snakes held by

FIGURE 19.3

León, San Isidoro; Portal of the Lamb (John Batten Photography)

FIGURE 19.4

León, San Isidoro; Portal of the Lamb, tympanum (John Batten Photography)

FIGURE 19.5

León, San Isidoro; Portal of the Lamb, tympanum detail (John Batten Photography)

FIGURE 19.6

León, San Isidoro; Portal of the Lamb, zodiac panels, left side (John Batten Photography)

FIGURE 19.7

León, San Isidoro; Portal of the Lamb, zodiac panels, right side (John Batten Photography)

the Furies on the same piece may have inspired the snake-like tails on the Capricorn and Leo panels.[54] The sculptor who employed the pose from the Husillos sarcophagus to carve the naked figure on the showpiece capital at Frómista may thus have worked on the zodiac panels at San Isidoro, and perhaps on the 'Sacrifice of Abraham' at Jaca cathedral. It remains possible, however, that the sculptors were not identical but working with the same visual stimulus.[55] It is possible that these panels always decorated the exterior of the portal, and some of the inscriptions on separate stones that once named each zodiac sign survive in a fragmentary state. Zodiac signs appear on the exterior of churches in other circumstances, and sculpted examples from the late-11th-century are found as metope friezes or metope-voussoirs in Aquitaine, notably at Saint-Pierre at Melle.[56] In such cases the zodiac signs are thought to represent earthly or liturgical time, and they often appear in association with the labours of the months.[57]

An original interior function for these zodiac panels, in association with a tomb or shrine, is another possibility, as the inscriptions, cut into a different stone, could have been added at a later date. Zodiac signs sometimes appear on Roman sarcophagi, where they are thought to symbolise eternal fame and bliss.[58] However, it is difficult to envisage the San Isidoro panels decorating a tomb, partly because of their size. Although the zodiac and angel panels are carved on slabs of the same white-grey marble, they are completely different in style and are unlikely to have been combined in a single work of art. Reliquaries provide another possible context for the zodiac reliefs. The St. Servatius reliquary from Quedlinburg (Saxony) preserves Carolingian ivory panels (*c.* 870) that depict the twelve zodiac signs above Christ and the apostles. Although this ivory box was not remodelled until *c.* 1200, it may have been the focus of attention in the early-11th-century as a gift from Emperor Henry II (d. 1024) to the abbey of Quedlinburg and its abbess Adelaide.[59] Another link between zodiac signs and a reliquary can be found in the description of the shrine of St. Giles (Egidius) from Saint-Gilles-du-Gard, in the *Pilgrim's Guide* from the Codex Calixtinus.[60] Saint-Gilles-du-Gard was a neighbour of Saint-Victor at Marseille. The *Guide* describes how all twelve zodiac signs formed the second register on the great gold shrine, organised from Aries to Pisces, and how they were interspersed with gold flowers in the form of a vine. Regardless of the accuracy or otherwise of the *Guide*, it shows that such panels were perfectly appropriate on a major shrine. One unusual feature at San Isidoro suggests an awareness of liturgical furniture. This is the carving of small round circles on each plaque. Moralejo argued forcefully that these represent scattered stars, similar to those found in astronomical manuscript illustrations.[61] If so, the sculptor or designer misunderstood their primary use in the manuscripts, where the most important stars are aligned with a defining part of each figure. If they were painted, perhaps in gold, these circles might equally imitate gilded nail-heads, of the kind that fix ivory or enamel plaques to reliquaries. Such attention to the physical construction of the panels would imply a methodical interest in making and artisanship. Ultimately, given the stylistic commonalities between the zodiac panels and the other reliefs on the Portal of the Lamb, they were probably all carved to decorate the exterior wall above the doorway. They may also have helped to denote the church as a holder of relics, and had other associations. Moralejo argued that the zodiac at San Isidoro was based on a sermon of the 4th-century bishop, Zeno of Verona, and that each panel had a moral dimension. He saw its appearance at San Isidoro as an assertion of Christian orthodoxy and as an anti-Islamic statement, and agreed with Williams's interpretation of the tympanum.[62] Astronomy and astrology were certainly controversial, and both Petrus Alfonsi from Aragón in the early-12th-century and, a decade later, Raymond of Marseille, a scholar from Richard of Saint-Victor's region, felt obliged to write in their defence.[63] Arabic treatises on astrology were also available in Toledo and, in accordance with Islamic thought, the zodiac might have been seen to confer talismanic protection on San Isidoro.

Below the zodiac panels a row of musicians is carved on six slabs cut from a different marble-like stone, with a pinker tone than that used for the angels in the tympanum or for the zodiac (Figures 19.6 and 19.7). Certain stylistic traits are shared between the zodiac panels and the musicians. The flowing hair and drapery of the female personification of Virgo is paralleled on some of the musicians; whereas the squashed features of another musician recall faces found on the Late Antique sarcophagus from Saint-Orens at Auch (Figure 19.2). The sculpted musicians appear to have always been intended for exterior use, and the panels probably never formed part of a tympanum but were always mounted above and to the side of the doorway. The current arrangement seems unbalanced, but this may be because some reliefs have been lost. This use of relief sculpture is paralleled by slabs of similar scale over the Porte des Comtes in Toulouse and on the Puerta de las Platerías at Santiago de Compostela, as well as by comparable developments in the Loire valley and Aquitaine.[64] The panels at Santiago that are closest to the San Isidoro reliefs are those that were once over the *Puerta Francigena*, the north transept portal where pilgrims first entered the cathedral.[65] Two scenes of Adam and Eve, God reproaching them and their Expulsion from the Garden of Eden, flank a slab depicting Christ in Majesty surrounded by the four evangelists. Although these sculptural vignettes, their frieze arrangement, and their repeated figures could be said to derive from the separate scenes found on early Christian sarcophagi, the subject found on so many sarcophagi, including that from Saint-Orens, Adam and Eve with the Tree of Knowledge, is oddly omitted or perhaps lost.[66] Around this date sculptors in Aragón also experimented with slab relief carving. Framed plaques, used as metopes between the corbels on the south apse of Jaca cathedral, depict emblematic animals and figures. Antonio García Omedes has identified other blocks, now almost entirely eroded and embedded in the later central apse, which once carried images of the signs of the zodiac. These plaques may have originated as metopes from the earlier central apse, as he suggests, or they could have formed a frieze above earlier doorways on the west or south sides of the cathedral. The south doorway at Jaca has been reconstructed with a tympanum, but it is possible that the portal originally had only slab relief decoration including the frieze. It is likewise not entirely unthinkable that, before the construction of the porch, the west doorway at Jaca may have had slab reliefs. It is clear that the artists at San Isidoro were not working in isolation and that their experiments were paralleled at other sites. As Therese Martin has noted, there are stylistic similarities between the Portal of the Lamb sculpture and certain reset capitals in the apses at San Isidoro, which in turn have resonances with the capitals at Frómista and Jaca that Moralejo connected to the Husillos sarcophagus.[67] These links suggest that the carvings were produced by craftsmen who worked across the friendship circle, and not for any single monarch, bishop or monastic order.

The sculpted figures at San Isidoro play a variety of instruments, while one wears a small crown indicating that these are King David's musicians accompanying the psalms. Two musicians playing rebecs emerge from small circles surrounded by rough roll mouldings. As this gives the impression that they are playing their instruments amongst clouds, the musicians may also evoke a celestial liturgy. The reference to King David fits with the significant role the Old Testament monarch played in the *memoria* of King Fernando I, linking him in turn to the Carolingian and Ottonian emperors.[68] This theme was particularly appropriate in a building whose prime purpose was liturgical intercession for the king.[69] The *Historia 'Silense'*, probably written at San Isidoro in the second decade of the 12th century, ends with a vivid description of the last hours of Fernando I: the king kneels before the altar of St. John the Baptist, and the relics of St. Isidore and St. Vincent, to recite the Davidic canticle *Benedictus es Domine Deus Israel* (I Chronicles 29^{10}).[70] The Book of Chronicles concentrates on the later part of David's life and his death, and in particular on his arrangements for the worship of God. The association between Fernando I and the canticle had been established many decades earlier.[71] This identification worked even during Fernando's lifetime, as the Davidic canticle was included in the *Liber Diurnus* (fol. 179v), the book of prayers given to Fernando I by Queen Sancha, where an initial portraying King David resonates with that used for Fernando I on the dedication page.[72] The correlation between King David and Fernando I was doubtless strengthened by chapter 29 verse 28 of I Chronicles that speaks of David dying 'in a good old age replete with days, riches and glory, and that his son Solomon reigned in his place', as this encapsulated the legacy claimed by Alfonso VI from his father.[73] Another of the slab figures may also belong with the narrative of David: the soldier that uncomfortably abuts the figure of St. Isidore (Figure 19.8). Stylistically this relates to the group of musicians, but is usually considered separately. The figure is often described as an executioner of St. Pelagius, on the assumption that the figure paired with St. Isidore depicts Pelagius. However, the size of the soldier matches neither the musicians nor the large saints, and the way he turns suggests that he belongs in a narrative scene. Had he been carved in the same marble as the zodiac signs, he might have represented a planet, but given the importance of King David at San Isidoro, it is possible that he represents Goliath and that a smaller more lightly armed David has been lost.

The figures of St. Isidore and the saint that flank the doorway are a pair, carved by the same sculptor, who used discreet lion thrones to support each with only minor variations in the drapery and poses[74] (Figures 19.8 and 19.9). St. Isidore has the accoutrements of a bishop-confessor with a crosier, episcopal cap and vestments, whilst the second figure has long wild hair, bare feet and carries a book in his veiled hand. The use of a veiled hand to hold a book indicates the figure was once a member of the clergy, in which case he is most likely to be the deacon St. Vincent, whose bishop charged him to preach, and not the boy martyr of Córdoba, St. Pelagius.[75] It is true that painted figures of St. Isidore and St. Pelagius appear at the small remote Palencian church of San Pelayo, as Manuel Castiñeiras has noted, but a pairing of St. Isidore and St. Vincent at León fits better with the account of Fernando I's death in the *Historia 'Silense'*.[76] St. Pelagius does not figure in Fernando I's choice of intercessors in that text, but the relics of St. Isidore and St. Vincent play an important role in his last days. Combined with the reliefs of King David's musicians, these large-scale saints suggest a mini-programme, closely tied to the memory of Fernando I and announcing the purpose of this royal monastery, which was liturgical intercession on his behalf. The Sacrifice of Abraham, carved in the lintel, continues this theme to the extent that verse 18 of the canticle '*Benedictus es Domine Deus Israhel*' addresses the 'Lord God of Abraham, Isaac, and Israel, our fathers', after expressing thanks to God for the abundance (*copia*) that enables the temple (*domus*) to be built in His name. Thus the Davidic canticle provides a textual framework for San Isidoro. Not only is Fernando I an antitype of King David, and Alfonso VI an antitype of Solomon, but the church of San Isidoro is also a re-embodiment of the temple of Solomon built with the riches gathered by David. The immense wealth of the temple is expressed in verse 2:

> Now have I prepared with all my might for the house of my God the gold for things to be made of gold, and the silver for things of silver, and the brass for things of brass, and wood for things of wood; onyx stones, and

FIGURE 19.8

León, San Isidoro; Portal of the Lamb, St Isidore and soldier (John Batten Photography)

FIGURE 19.9

León, San Isidoro, Portal of the Lamb, St. Vincent (?) (John Batten Photography) stones to be set, glistering stones, and of divers colours, and all manner of precious stones, and marble stones in abundance.

The emphasis on multi-coloured stones may even have suggested the three hues of stone found over the Portal of the Lamb, the yellow-brown limestone, the pinker stone and the white-grey marble. A specific reference in verse 4 to gilding the walls of the temple might have reinforced the decision to place the slabs across the walls, and the stipulation in verse 5, 'all manner of work (*opus*) to be made by the hands of artificers (*artificum*)', could have inspired the self-conscious artisanship displayed on the zodiac panels if the small circles depict gilt nail-heads. The decision to put zodiac signs over the doorway at San Isidoro may also allude to the last verse of I Chr. 29 that reflects on David: 'With all his reign and his might and the times that went over him (*temporum quae transierunt sub eo*), and over Israel, and over all the kingdoms of the countries.' The close dynastic identification with King David and King Solomon suggests strong local agency for the overall conception of the portal decoration, an impression that is reinforced by the long-standing importance of the canticle in the mythology of Fernando I. As Alfonso VI's daughter Urraca did not claim the *infantaticum*, including San Isidoro, until after the death of her husband, Raymond of Burgundy in 1107, it is probable that Alfonso VI himself would have taken on responsibility for the infanta's project in the meantime.[77] As he had been close to his sister Urraca, he may have wished to monumentalise her devotion to the memory of their father, as well as giving visual expression to his own legitimacy over the enlarged kingdom of León-Castile.

THE SACRIFICE OF ABRAHAM AT THE CENTRE OF A CREATIVE NEXUS

The sculpture on the lintel, the largest slab on the portal, was carved in the same local limestone as most of the church (Figures 19.4 and 19.5). The sculptor – or sculptors – worked in an idiom that relates to some of the zodiac panels, for example the centre-partings found on Hagar and the Angel are similar to that of the surviving twin in Gemini (Figure 19.7), but he does not seem to have worked at San Isidoro long-term. The subject of this large relief is the Sacrifice of Abraham, which would have been familiar from many sarcophagi including that from Saint-Orens. As Francisco Prado Vilar has shown, this slab is a response to the ways narrative is displayed on pagan sarcophagi, specifically that at Husillos (Figure 19.1).[78] In its size, rhythms and composition this relief reinvents the carving on the classical sarcophagus, whilst substituting a narrative of the Old Testament for the classical myth. The figure of Orestes is repeated cartoon-fashion on the Husillos sarcophagus: in the centre he carries out the murder of his mother Clytemnestra and her lover Aegisthus, to the right he is driven to remorse by the Furies and to the left tormented by them even in his sleep. On the San Isidoro lintel Isaac appears three times: on the right, his mother Sarah watches him depart on a horse; once dismounted Isaac removes his sandals to make himself a fitting sacrifice, and in the central scene Isaac is on the point of being sacrificed. Whilst the other slab reliefs at San Isidoro derive generically from sarcophagi, the lintel is in explicit dialogue with the Husillos sarcophagus. The sculptor found a way of reinventing the whole sarcophagus relief that went well beyond the use of techniques and isolated motifs found after the Council of Husillos in 1088. As on the Husillos sarcophagus, ritual death occupies the centre of the space, creating a physical and narrative core for the design, and both the reliefs have a dynamic symmetry that is carefully balanced around that central scene. Although there is almost no stylistic engagement with the Husillos figures, the faces of the figures on the San Isidoro lintel share a certain bland sweetness with some of those at Husillos. There may also be an awareness of the Saint-Orens sarcophagus, which also includes Abraham's wife Sarah in the scene, and an aedicule, although in that case it forms the tomb of Lazarus.[79]

The intellectual conception of the lintel is as subtle as the engagement of the sculptor with the physical form of the sarcophagus. Normally this image is emblematic and consists of only one abbreviated scene: Abraham about to plunge the knife into his son with an angel intervening and a ram waiting in the wings to replace Isaac. In contrast an exceptional extended version of the scene is found on the lintel. In the centre is the familiar core scene: Abraham about to sacrifice Isaac when an angel appears and offers a ram as a substitute. The additional scenes on each side precede the Sacrifice of Abraham chronologically and thus lead towards the centre. The figures of Hāgar and her son Ishmael are placed to Abraham's right, balanced on the left by those of Sarah and Isaac. Williams sees the figures of Sarah and Hāgar as a representation of the Pauline Letter to the Galatians (chapter 4[22-31]), where they stand for the Old and New Covenants, for the sons of the free descended from Isaac and those of the unfree descended from Ishmael. In the same text Hāgar is described as mount Sinai, whereas Sarah is Jerusalem. Consequently Williams, in common with most other interpreters of the tympanum, sees opposition, conflict and a negative view of Islam in this sculpture.[80] For him it is a representation of *reconquista*. He reinforces this interpretation by highlighting a detail in the carving of Hāgar, for him a figure of *luxuria* and an exemplar of the lascivious nature attributed to Muslim women in Christian thought, because her left hand slightly lifts her skirt.

However, Williams also notes another aspect of the design which suggests that this may not be straightforward triumphalism: Isaac is unusually approaching from Abraham's left, often considered the less favoured side, ceding the right side, the more favoured, to Hāgar and Ishmael.[81] More significantly Hāgar stands very close to the angel, a proximity that recalls her two conversations with angels in the Book of Genesis. Hāgar is not a negative figure in the Old Testament; she is a foreigner and a servant, but not an enemy. Moreover Hāgar's gesture is ambiguous: she lifts her skirt with only her left hand, not two as if dancing, and her left-hand side is closest to the angle. This suggests another possibility, a reference to a Midrashic tradition, which says that Abraham tied a garment to Hāgar to indicate her enslaved status. She had to drag this behind her as she walked amongst the mountains searching for water that she finally received from the angel Gabriel. This popular story intimates a change in Hāgar's status, which subverts St. Paul's juxtaposition of the enslaved and the free woman. If the sculptor had intended a simpler triumphalist reading of Galatians, a more obviously enslaved Hāgar could have been placed on the far left to contrast with Sarah on the far right. He could have included Mount Sinai, and placed Sarah outside the city of Jerusalem, not her simpler dwelling. He could have placed the angel on the other side of the ram. A more aggressive Ishmael could have been put closer to the centre as if threatening and in opposition to the submissive figure of Isaac. Instead Ishmael is placed on Hāgar's right and shown riding in the wilderness on the point of leaving the scene. His body twists as he raises his bow and arrow, which he points upwards and away from the other figures. This depiction of Ishmael, as an archer, refers specifically to another biblical verse: 'And God was with the lad; and he grew and dwelt in the wilderness, and became an archer' (Genesis 21[20]). This biblical portrayal of Ishmael is again not negative but runs parallel to that of Isaac, like the symmetry of the sculpture. In Genesis Ishmael attends the burial of Abraham and is the father of twelve sons that beget twelve tribes, as was Jacob. His descendants are as God-given as Isaac's, even though his mother is a bondwoman.[82] Meyer Schapiro notes another non-biblical element in the central scene: the angel is presenting the ram and not merely pointing to it. He found this iconography mostly in Spain or the Languedoc and was able to relate it to both Jewish and Islamic texts but not to Christian ones.[83] Taken together these details suggest a different interpretation of the lintel sculpture.

First, and most importantly, I want to suggest that the symmetry of the Abraham relief may indicate not opposition but unity under the rule of Abraham's people. It represents the idea of negotiated reconciliation, and not the dominance of reconquest. This connects to I Chronicles 29[30] to King David's rule in Israel and 'in all the kingdoms of the lands' (*in cunctis regnis terrarum*). The covenant between God and Abraham, made possible by Abraham's demonstration of faith, was a blessing for all the peoples of the earth and represented a bond with Abraham's other descendants, the Ishmaelites.[84] I do not intend this as some kind of idealised *convivencia*, but something closer to an inversion of the *dhimma* or pact, whereby other Peoples of the Book could be protected under Muslim rule provided they paid a tax and conformed to certain rules. Since the conquest of Toledo in 1085, Alfonso VI had ruled not only over León, Castile and Galicia, but also over much of the old taifa kingdom of Toledo. He now had responsibility for a mixed population, where Christians were at the top of the pyramid with a duty to protect the Jews and Muslims. As Prado Vilar has highlighted in this context, lacking a male heir with his aristocratic European queens, Alfonso VI promoted Sancho, his son by Zaida, his Sevillian concubine, as a member of the court, and by 1106 as his heir.[85] The relief sculpture from the Portal of the Lamb seems to fit into this historical and political situation, after the Council at Palencia in 1101 but before the death of Sancho in 1108, during the years when a Leonese-Castilian version of al-Andalus still seemed viable.

The details of the lintel carving may suggest its agency. It seems probable that the ultimate patron was the king, as his sister, the infanta Urraca who had been the *domina* of San Isidoro, died in 1101. But the complex nature of this work suggests the involvement of others. Given the lintel's dialogue with the Husillos sarcophagus, the sculpture may have been planned at the Council of Palencia in 1100, perhaps in front of the pagan sarcophagus. This return to the Husillos sarcophagus as a stimulus for creativity is a strong indicator of fresh guidance from Cardinal Richard of Saint-Victor. Pope Paschal II had given him renewed authority through his re-appointment as papal legate and an opportunity to revive his partnership with Archbishop Bernard of Toledo.[86] Richard's role in the friendship network could also have exposed him to theological debates around intellectual and artistic dependence on pagan culture, most notably those of St. Augustine.[87] Julie Harris has shown how St. Augustine's reading of the notion of 'spoiling the Egyptians' (Exodus 11[2] and 12[36]) in his *De doctrina christiana*, so popular with rhetoricians, could have been used to legitimise the repurposing of Muslim objects and buildings.[88] It would have been equally suitable as a justificatory framework for stylistic, technical and compositional borrowing from pagan sarcophagi. Augustine says that when 'the Christian severs himself in spirit' from pagans, he could take their treasures 'for the lawful service of preaching the Gospel', and that it is also right to receive 'their clothing' (*vestis*) or practices (*instituta*) which should be converted (*convertenda*) to Christian use. This describes the process underlying the creation of the lintel, when both motifs and compositional elements from the Husillos sarcophagus were converted for a Christian narrative.[89] The lack of any surviving manuscript of Augustine's *De doctrina christiana* in Visigothic script suggests that such scholarly thinking was not indigenous. Bernard of Toledo might have known the text, as there was a 10th-century copy at Cluny, but Richard of Saint-Victor is a more plausible candidate. Not only was he surrounded by pagan sculpture in Provence, so would have had greater motivation to engage with this question, but, judging from the earliest inventory to have survived from the library at Saint-Victor, he had access to the *De doctrina*.[90]

Although Archbishop Bernard had considerable experience of negotiating with the Mozarabic population of Toledo and Cardinal Richard had direct contact with the city between 1088 and 1099 when his abbey administered San Servando on behalf of the papacy, it is hard to attribute the demonstrable knowledge of Jewish and Islamic scholarship in the lintel carving to them. Another possibility is the involvement of Jewish advisors at

Alfonso VI's court.[91] A third possibility is the participation of educated men from Toledo, perhaps Mozarabs, perhaps Muslims, perhaps even converts to Christianity. Amongst these may have been the sculptors themselves. The prevailing assumption is that craftsmen were skilled but ill-educated artisans, although the sophistication of Caliphal ivory carvers suggests that this was not necessarily so. Such sculptors worked at the forefront of artistic exploration in form, style and composition and were responsible for much ingenious 'Romanesque' invention. Their formation is the subject of debate, but it is probable that some of these sculptors had been trained in the taifa kingdoms.[92] If they came from Toledo, for example, this raises questions about their status, confessional identity and language. They may have been free, manumitted or unfree, Muslims, converts or Christians. Their world was one of shifting identities, lively debate and translation.

It may be worth recalling one notable case of a convert in this decade: the Jewish scholar Moses who became Petrus Alfonsi. He was baptised on the feast day of SS Peter and Paul in 1106 in the cathedral (previously a mosque) at Huesca, in Aragón. The occasion was sufficiently important for the bishop to baptise him, and for the king, Alfonso I 'the battler', to stand as his godfather. Petrus was then able to travel as far as England, to have access to libraries and intellectual circles from Canterbury to Malvern, and possibly to serve as physician to King Henry I.[93] Although he had only moderate success as a teacher in France, his works have survived, from aphorisms and fables to astronomy, astrology and exegesis of both the Talmud and the Qu'ran. But it is his critique of Judaism – and incidentally of Islam – presented as a dialogue with himself, that received most attention in the Middle Ages.[94] This world in which the lintel sculpture was created was one where conversion to Christianity opened doors and gave entreé to royal and ecclesiastical networks. Both the lintel and the zodiac panels suggest the involvement of someone with the breadth of knowledge of a Petrus Alfonsi, a command of both Judaic and Islamic scholarship, and an engagement with debates between the three religions. It is this dimension that gives the lintel sculpture its exceptional complexity. The role of such an individual, as advisor to the king, as translator for the sculptors, must remain the subject of speculation.

CONCLUSION

The Portal of the Lamb as a whole reflects an environment in which experimentation was allowed to flourish. The sculpture seems to emerge from a deep and lengthy dialogue, and the sum of the innovations introduced on the Portal of the Lamb remains our best guide to its agency. The over-arching typological narrative has solid foundations in the imaginative landscape of León, which was forged in the last years of Fernando I or in the first decade of Alfonso VI's reign. Its re-invention on the portal suggests the close participation of the king, perhaps fulfilling a wish of his sister Urraca. The return to the Husillos sarcophagus as a stimulus for creativity implies that the old team, the king, Richard of Saint-Victor and Bernard of Toledo, had reunited. The execution of the scheme, however, represents a considerable creative leap in a number of ways. The use of slab relief sculpture on the exterior of a building was new not only to San Isidoro but also to the peninsula; only the small panels at Jaca may predate those from Portal of the Lamb. The clear precedent for this kind of sculpture, and for marble carving, is, of course, Saint-Sernin at Toulouse, but the sophistication of the programme at San Isidoro goes beyond the Porte des Comtes.[95] The intersection between archetypes, materials, style and form in León is remarkably inventive. One of the keys to this phenomenon may be the movement of artists. These sculptors do not form a Leonese 'workshop', and they do not seem to have worked at San Isidoro for any significant amount of time before or after the completion of the Portal. Amongst surviving buildings, their artistic dialogue is with other innovative centres, with Toulouse, Frómista, Jaca and later with Santiago de Compostela. These sites may be on the 'pilgrimage roads', but that does not provide a plausible rationale for the sculptors' arrival in León. This team, which may have worked together some ten years before, would have been carefully assembled for the project. The underlying stylistic connections between San Isidoro, Frómista, Toulouse and Jaca fit with the ecclesiastical network, the friendship circle in which Cardinal Richard of Saint-Victor played a major role. Other links can be found between León and Toulouse through the marriage of Raymond IV and Elvira, but only the network, bound together by gifts and counter-gifts, had the same breadth and depth as the artistic dialogue.[96] Ultimately the bonds between the sculptors and their multiple patrons produced a complex self-aware work of art that continues to provoke debate.

NOTES

[1] This article is based on a paper delivered at the BAA Romanesque conference in Barcelona in April 2014, and I should like to thank Manuel Castiñeiras and John McNeill warmly for giving me that opportunity. J. Caskey, 'Whodunnit? Patronage, the Canon, and the Problematics of Agency in Romanesque and Gothic Art', in C. Rudolph ed., *A Companion to Medieval Art: Romanesque and Gothic in Northern Europe* (Oxford 2006), 193–212.

[2] R. Walker, 'The influence of papal legates on the transformation of Spanish art in the second half of the eleventh century', B. Franzé, ed., *Art et réforme grégorienne en France et dans la péninsule ibérique* (Paris 2015), 77–90.

[3] I. Robinson, *The Papacy 1073–1198: Continuity and Innovation* (Cambridge 1990), 149–156; and ibid., 'Reform and the Church 1073–1122' in *The New Cambridge Medieval History*: pts. 1–2. c. 1024-c.1198 (Cambridge 2004), 326–328; see also K.R. Rennie, 'Collaboration and Council Criteria in the Age of Reform: Legatine Councils under Pope Gregory VII', *Annuarium Historiae Conciliorum*, 38 (2006), 95–115; ibid., 'Uproot and destroy, build and plant': legatine authority under Pope Gregory VII, *Journal of Medieval History*, 33 (2007), 166–180; ibid., 'Extending Gregory VII's 'Friendship Network': Social Contacts in Late Eleventh-Century France', *History*, 93/312 (2008), 475–496.

[4] Walker, 'papal legates', (as n. 2); for the equal role of pagan and Christian art, see H. Toubert, *Un art dirigé. Réforme grégorienne et iconographie* (Paris 1990), 99 n.2

⁵ S. Moralejo, 'La reutilización e influencia de los sarcófagos antiguos en la España medieval', in B. Andreae and S. Settis ed., *Colloquio sul reimpiego dei sarcophagi romani nel Medioevo* (Marburg 1984), 187–203, and in A. Franco Mata ed., *Patrimonio artístico de Galicia y otros estudios. Homenaje al Prof. Dr. Serafín Moralejo Álvarez*, I (Santiago de Compostela 2004), 279–299.

⁶ Works of art produced in the cause of reform could also be used in this way: S. Riccioni, *Il mosaico absidale di S. Clemente a Roma: 'Exemplum' della chiesa riformata* (Spoleto 2006), including the introduction by H. Kessler, xii.

⁷ E. Kitzinger, 'The Gregorian Reform and the Visual Arts: A Problem of Method', *Transactions of the Royal Historical Society*, 22 (1972), 87–102, esp. 101; R. Walker, *Views of Transition. Liturgy and Illumination in Medieval Spain* (London and University of Toronto 1998), 208–223.

⁸ D. Glass, 'Revisiting the 'Gregorian Reform', in C. Hourihane, ed., *Romanesque Art and Thought in the Twelfth Century* (Princeton, 2008), 200–218, esp. 204.

⁹ B.F. Reilly, *The Kingdom of León-Castilla under Alfonso VI, 1065–1109* (Princeton 1988), 78; C.M. Reglero de la Fuente, *El monasterio de San Isidro de Dueñas en la Edad Media: un priorato cluniacense hispano (911–1478), estudio y colección documental* (León 2005), 334–348 nos 24–28.

¹⁰ H.E.J. Cowdrey, *Two Studies in Cluniac History, 1049–1126* (Rome 1978), 159–160: 'domno Alfonso Hispaniarum rege, nostro fideli amico, qui tanta ac talia bona nobis fecit et adhuc indesinentur facit'.

¹¹ Cowdrey, *Two Studies* (as n. 10), 162–164: 'cum suis praeclaris muneribus uenit secumque etiam munera domni Petri regis detulit'.

¹² Cowdrey, *Two Studies* (as n. 10), 159–160: 'dedimus ei in ecclesia beatorum apostolorum Petri et Pauli noua, quam ipse de propriis facultatibus construxisse videtur, unum altare de praecipuis, quo scilicet diuina mysteria ibidem celebratur saluti eius ualeant suffragari'. '*Facultates*' could encompass skilled labour as well as funds.

¹³ H.E.J. Cowdrey, *Pope Gregory VII, 1073–1085* (Oxford 1998), 366–369.

¹⁴ B. Cursente, 'L'action des légats. Le cas Amat d'Oloron (vers 1073–1101)' in *La réforme 'grégorienne' dans le Midi (milieu XIe – début XIIIe siècle*, Cahiers de Fanjeaux 48 (Toulouse 2013), 181–207.

¹⁵ Cowdrey, *Pope Gregory VII* (as n. 13), 366, 374–375, 473.

¹⁶ J.P. Rubio Sadia, 'Narbona y la romanización litúrgica de las Iglesias de Aragón', *Miscellània Litúrgica Catalana*, 19 (2011), 267–321.

¹⁷ J. Goñi Gaztambide, *Historia de los obispos de Pamplona, I, Siglos IV–XIII* (Pamplona 1979), 280.

¹⁸ D. Ocón Alonso, 'El sello de Dios sobre la iglesia: tímpanos con Crismon en Navarra y Aragón', in R. Sánchez Ameijeiras and J.L. Senra, eds., *El Tímpano románico. Imágenes, estructuras y audiencias* (Santiago de Compostela 2003), 75–101.

¹⁹ H.E.J. Cowdrey, *The 'Epistolae Vagantes' of Pope Gregory VII* (Oxford 1972), 120–121, doc. 50. For a full account see E. Magnou, 'L'introduction de la réforme grégorienne à Toulouse', *Cahiers de l'association Marc Bloch de Toulouse: études d'histoire méridionale*, 3 (1958)

²⁰ The circumstances of this betrothal are obscure. Reilly, *Alfonso VI* (as n. 9), 92–93; Raymond seems to have been on good terms with Saint-Victor in Marseille from c. 1094

²¹ A. Rucquoi, 'Diego Gelmírez: Un archevêque de Compostelle 'pro-français'?', *Ad Limina*, 2 (2011), 164.

²² S. Barton, 'El Cid, Cluny and the Medieval *Reconquista*', *English Historical Review*, 126 (2011), 525–529; Rucquoi, 'Diego Gelmírez' (as n. 21), 164.

²³ J. Williams, 'A Source for the Capital of the Offering of Abraham in the Pantheon of the King in León', in C. De Benedictis, ed., *Scritti di Storia dell'arte in onore di Roberto Salvini* (Florence 1984), 25–28.

²⁴ B. Reilly, 'The rediscovery of Count Pedro Ansúrez', in S. Barton and P. Linehan, ed., *Cross, Crescent and Conversion, Studies on Medieval Spain and Christendom in Memory of Richard Fletcher* (Leiden and Boston 2008), 109–126, esp. 122; T. Martin, *Politics and Architectural Propaganda in Twelfth-Century Spain* (Leiden and Boston 2006), 92.

²⁵ Reilly, *Alfonso VI* (as n. 9), 240–241.

²⁶ S. Moralejo, 'The Tomb of Alfonso Ansúrez (d. 1093): Its Place and the Role of Sahagún in Beginnings of Spanish Romanesque Sculpture', in B. Reilly ed., *Santiago, Saint-Denis, and St Peter. The Reception of the Roman Liturgy in León-Castile in 1080* (New York 1985), 63–100; *The Art of Medieval Spain* (New York 1993), 234–235, cat. no. 107; D. Hassig, 'He Will Make Alive Your Mortal Bodies: Cluniac Spirituality and the Tomb of Alfonso Ansúrez', *Gesta*, 30 (1991), 140–153 esp. 142.

²⁷ Moralejo, 'The Tomb of Alfonso Ansúrez' (as n. 26), 75–77

²⁸ A. Miguélez Cavero, 'La *impaginatio* como punto de partida: la relación entre texto e imagen en la cubierta del sarcófago de Alfonso Pérez procedente de Sahagún', in M.E. Martín López and V. García Lobo ed. *Impaginatio en las inscripciones medievales* (León 2011), 72–97.

²⁹ M.F. Hearn, *Romanesque Sculpture. The Revival of Monumental Stone Sculpture in the Eleventh and Twelfth Centuries* (Oxford 1981), 64, Pl. 41.

³⁰ Reilly, *Alfonso VI* (as n. 9), 261; R. Somerville, *Pope Urban II's Council of Piacenza* (Oxford 2011), 9–11.

³¹ Reilly, *Alfonso VI* (as n. 9), 262.

³² Robinson, *The Papacy* (as n. 3), 124–125.

³³ P. Cabau, 'Les données historiques relatives à la reconstruction de Saint-Sernin de Toulouse (XIe–XIIe siècles): réévaluation critique', in *Mémoires de la Société archéologique du Midi de la France*, 58 (1998), 29–66; Q. and D. Cazes, *Saint-Sernin de Toulouse: De Saturnin au chef-d'oeuvre de l'art roman* (Toulouse 2008), 53. For the presence of Raymond of Toulouse at the dedication ceremony see J-P. Migne, *Patrologiae Cursus Completus Series Latina*, 151 (Paris 1881), col. 478–480: 'Candelas quoque cereas, quas filius noster Raimundus Tolosanus comes, in ecclesiae dedicatione nobis praesentibus abdicavit.' For the high altar see T. Lyman, 'Le table d'autel de Bernard Gilduin et son ambiance originelle', *Cahiers de Saint-Michel de Cuxa*, 13 (1982), 53–67; M. Durliat, 'La construction de Saint-Sernin de Toulouse, étude historique et archéologique', *Actes des congrès de la société des historiens médiévistes de l'enseignement superior public*, 3 (1972), 201–211 esp. 203; C. Devic and J. Vaissete, *Histoire générale de Languedoc*, vol. 5 (Toulouse 1875), col. 49–50.

³⁴ See notes 12 and 13 above.

³⁵ Durliat, 'La construction de Saint-Sernin de Toulouse' (as n. 33), 207–208; for confraternities see M. McLaughlin, *Consorting With Saints: Prayer for the Dead in Early Medieval France* (Ithaca and London 1994), 83–98.

³⁶ Reilly, *Alfonso VI* (as n. 9), 282–283

³⁷ A. Ubieto Arteta, *Colección diplomática de Pedro I*, 241–243, doc. 24, dated 17 December 1096: 'illam antiquam sancti Petri'; R. Crozet, 'L'art roman en Navarre et en Aragon. Conditions historiques.' *Cahiers de civilisation médiévale*, 17 (1962), 54.

³⁸ Ubieto, *Colección diplomática de Pedro I*, 251–253, doc. 30, dated 5 April 1097; J.A. Harris, 'Mosque to Church Conversions in the Spanish Reconquest', *Medieval Encounters*, 3 (1997), 166.

³⁹ Reilly, *Alfonso VI* (as n. 9), 216–219.

⁴⁰ *Ibid.*, 299–301.

⁴¹ R. Sánchez Ameijeiras, 'The Eventful Life of the Royal Tombs of San Isidoro in León', in T. Martin and J.A. Harris, eds., *Church, State, Vellum, and Stone. Essays on Medieval Spain in Honor of John Williams* (Leiden and Boston 2005), 166, 485; E. Flórez, *Viage de Ambrosio de Morales por orden del rey D. Phelipe II a los reynos de León, y Galicia, y Principiado de Asturias. Para reconocer Las Reliquias de los Santos, Sepulcros Reales, y Libros manuscritos de las Cathedrales, y Monasterios* (Madrid 1765), 44: 'su sepulcro estrañamente rico'.

⁴² The small church of San Esteban at Corullón (El Bierzo) should perhaps be added to this list, if the small relief of the martyrdom of St. Stephen now mounted on one of the houses in the village was once on the exterior of the church.

⁴³ D. Kinney, '*Spolia* as signifiers in twelfth-century Rome', *Hortus Artium Medievalium*, 17 (2011) 155–166; M. Greenhalgh, *Marble Past, Monumental Present. Building with Antiquities in the Medieval Mediterranean* (Leiden and Boston 2009), 2–6.

⁴⁴ J. Williams, '*Generationes Abrahae*: Reconquest Iconography in Leon', *Gesta*, 16 (1977), 3–14.

⁴⁵ W. Sauerländer, 'Über die Komposition des Weltgerichts-Tympanons in Autun', *Zeitschrift für Kunstgeschichte*, 29 (1966),

46. 261–294, esp. 264 and 286 n. 16, reprinted in idem., *Romanesque Art. Problems and Monuments*, vol. 1 (London 2004), VIII 223–267.

46. This took place as part of the work done under the Plan PAHIS 2004–2012 by the Patrimonio histórico de Castilla y León. Junta de Castilla y León, but remains unpublished. The conservation architects were Carlos Sexmilo and Ramón Cañas, who worked with researchers of the Architectural Photogrammetry Laboratory, E.T.S. Arquitectura, Universidad de Valladolid.

47. For Williams's photographs, see T. Martin, *Queen as King: Politics and Architectural Propaganda in Twelfth-Century Spain* (Leiden 2006), figs 50 and 51. My analysis has relied on such photographs as well as examination *in situ*. Although carried out independently, it coincides in general and in many particulars with the archaeological analysis by Utrero and Murillo: M.A. Utrero Agudo and J.I. Murillo Fragero, 'San Isidoro de León. Construcción y reconstrucción de una basílica románica', *Arqueología de la Arquitectura*, 11 (2014), 1–53, esp. 42–46, doi: http://dx.doi.org/10.3989/arq.arqt.2014.011; the doorway was reset within its present moulding in the middle of the 12th century.

48. Utrero and Murillo, 'San Isidoro' (as n. 47), 43; A. Tcherikover, *High Romanesque Sculpture in the Duchy of Aquitaine c.1090–1140* (Oxford 1997), 34 and plate 116.

49. Williams, '*Generationes Abrahae*' (as n. 44), 4–6; Utrero and Murillo, 'San Isidoro' (as n. 47), 42–44.

50. I owe thanks also to Laura Jacobus, at the International Medieval Congress in Leeds (2016), for pointing out that in the current arrangement Isaac seems to be aiming his arrow at the Lamb of God.

51. For a review of the discussion see Q. and D. Cazes, *Saint-Sernin* (as n. 33), 206–216.

52. M. Gómez Moreno, *El arte románico español de un libro* (Madrid 1934), 108: 'de un bizantinismo bien clásico'.

53. R. Walker, 'Sancha, Urraca and Elvira: the virtues and vices of Spanish royal women 'dedicated to God'', *Reading Medieval Studies*, 24 (1998), 119–120.

54. S. Moralejo, 'Sobre la formación del estilo escultórico de Frómista y Jaca', *Actas del XXIII Congreso internacional de la historia del arte (Granada 1973)*, I (Granada 1976), 427–434.

55. Martin, *Queen as King* (as n. 47), 92–93.

56. Tcherikover, *Sculpture in Aquitaine* (as n. 48), Pl. 66.

57. M. Panadero, *The Labors of the Months and the Signs of the Zodiac in Twelfth-century French Façades* (Michigan 1984). For an overview of this association, see M. Castiñeiras, *El calendario medieval hispano. Texto e imágenes (siglos XI–XIV)* (Salamanca 1996).

58. P. Zanker and B. Ewald, *Living with Myths. The Imagery of Roman Sarcophagi* (Oxford 2012), 166.

59. C. Hahn 'Relics and Reliquaries. The Construction of Imperial Memory and Meaning with Particular Attention to Treasuries at Conques, Aachen, and Quedlinburg', in R. Maxwell, ed., *Representing History 900–1300. Art, Music, History* (University Park Philadelphia 2010), 133–148 esp. 137–143: Henry II gave an almost identical ivory box to Bamberg.

60. A. Shaver-Crandell and P. Gerson, *The Pilgrim's Guide to Santiago de Compostela* (London 1995), 76–77; Castiñeiras, *El calendario* (as n. 57), 41–42.

61. S. Moralejo, 'Pour l'interpretation iconographique du Portail de l'Agneau à Saint Isidore de León: les signes du zodiaque', *Les Cahiers de Saint-Michel de Cuxa*, 8 (1977), 145–146.

62. Moralejo, 'les signes du zodiaque' (as n. 61), 137–173. For the anti-Islamic argument, see 170 and n. 141, 'une précoce réaction pour l'orthodoxie. Resuscitée la maladie, il fallait ressusciter l'antidote'.

63. J. Tolan, 'Reading God's will in the stars', *Revista española de filosfía medieval*, 7 (2000), 13–30.

64. Tcherikover, *Sculpture in Aquitaine* (as n. 48), passim.

65. Shaver-Crandell and Gerson, *The Pilgrim's Guide* (as n. 60), 88–91; the Pilgrim's Guide mentions sculptured 'months of the year and many other beautiful works' on the left of the north portal, but no signs of the zodiac. A lost panel portraying the Annunciation is usually located in a tympanum over the left-hand doorway, on the basis that the Pilgrim's Guide says that it is 'over the doorway which is on the left' and '*in cimborio*'. However, architectural vocabulary, like the forms themselves, was far from fixed at this period. Abbot Suger of Saint-Denis in Paris, for example, used *in arcu* when referring to a tympanum. The phrase *in cimborio* could equally mean 'on the drum', that is above the arch and not inside it.

66. M. Castiñeiras, '*Didacus Gelmirius*, Patron of the Arts. Compostela's Long Journey: from the Periphery to the Center of Romanesque Art, in idem., ed., *Compostela and Europe. The Story of Diego Gelmírez* (Santiago de Compostela 2010), 64–70; idem., 'La *Porta Francigena*: una encrucijada en el nacimiento del gran portal románico', in J. Martínez de Aguirre and M. Poza Yagüe, eds., *Anales de Historia del Arte: Alfonso VI y el arte de su época*, Volumen Extraordinario 2 (2011), 93–122; J. Williams, 'Framing Santiago', in C. Hourihane, ed., *Romanesque Art and Thought in the Twelfth Century: essays in honor of Walter Cahn* (Princeton 2008), 219–238 esp. 224–230.

67. Martin, *Queen as King* (as n. 47), 90–91; see also M.V. Herráez, M.C. Concepción and M. Valdés, 'La escultura de San Isidoro de León y su relación con otros talleres del Camino', *De Arte*, 12 (2103) 41–58.

68. F. Prado Vilar, '*Lacrimae rerum*: San Isidoro de León y la memoria del padre', *Goya*, 328 (2009), 195–221; I.H. Garipzanov, *The Symbolic Language of Authority in the Carolingian World (c. 751–877)* (Leiden 2008), 225–228.

69. R. Walker, 'The Wall Paintings in the Panteón de los Reyes at León: A Cycle of Intercession', *Art Bulletin*, 82 (2000), 200–225.

70. S. Barton and R. Fletcher, eds., *The World of El Cid: chronicles of the Spanish reconquest* (Manchester 2000), 63–64, para. 106; J. Pérez de Urbel and A. González-Zorrilla, *Historia Silense. Edición crítica e introducción* (Madrid 1959), 207

71. Charles Bishko points out that the same canticle was quoted in the charter that recorded Alfonso VI's first gift to Cluny in memory of his father in 1073. C.J. Bishko, 'The Liturgical Context of Fernando I's last days according to the so-called Historia Silense', *Hispania Sacra*, 17–18 (1964–1965), 47–59, reprinted in *Spanish and Portuguese Monastic History 600–1300* (London 1984), no. VII.

72. Prado, '*Lacrimae rerum*' (as n. 68), 206–208; J. Williams, 'Fernando I and Alfonso VI as Patrons of the Arts', in J. Martínez de Aguirre and M. Poza Yagüe, eds., *Anales de Historia del Arte: Alfonso VI y el arte de su época*, Volumen Extraordinario 2 (2011), 415–424.

73. I Chronicles 29–28: 'et mortuus est in senectute bona plenus dierum et divitis et gloria regnavitque Salomon filius eius pro eo'.

74. The figure of King David at Santiago de Compostela may have developed from these saints at San Isidoro.

75. E. Thunø, *The Apse Mosaic in Early Medieval Rome: Time, Network, and Repetition* (Cambridge 2015), 66.

76. M. Castiñeiras, 'El *labora*: los trabajos y los días en la iconografía románica', in *XVII Seminario sobre Historia del Monacato, Vida y Muerte en el monasterio románico* (Aguilar de Campoo 2004). 65–83, esp. 78–80; Barton and Fletcher, *The World of El Cid* (as n. 70), 63–64.

77. T. Martin, 'Hacia una clarificación del infantazgo en tiempos de Urraca y su hija la infanta Sancha (ca. 1107–1159)', *e-Spania* [Online], 5 June 2008, Online since 01 February 2008, connection on 1 June 2015. URL: http://e-spania.revues.org/12163; DOI 10.4000/e-spania.12163.

78. F. Prado Vilar, '*Saevum facinus*: estilo, genealogía y sacrificio en el arte románico español', *Goya*, 324 (2008), 173–199 esp. 188–190.

79. J. Williams, 'A source for the capital' (as n. 23), 25–28.

80. Williams, '*Generationes Abrahae*' (as n. 44), 3–14; T. Martin, *Queen as King* (as n. 47), 101–105 and idem., 'Un nuevo contexto para el tímpano de la portada del cordero en San Isidoro de León', in R. Sánchez Ameijeiras y J.L. Senra, eds., *El tímpano románico. Imágenes, estructuras y audiencias* (Santiago de Compostela 2003), 181–205; Prado, *Lacrimae rerum* (as n. 68), 209–215; I understand some of these interpretations are under revision.

81. Williams, *Generationes Abrahae* (as n. 44), 14, n. 47.

82. Genesis 2113: 'And also of the son of the bondwoman will I make a great nation, because he is thy seed.'; 'sed et filium ancillae faciam in gentem magnam quia semen tuum est'.

83. M. Schapiro, 'The Angel with the Ram in Abraham's Sacrifice: A Parallel in Western and Islamic Art', *Ars Islamica*, 10 (1943), 134–147 esp.135–139, reprinted with an appendix in ibid., *Late Antique, Early Christian & Medieval Art. Selected Papers* (London 1980), 288–318; Williams, *Generationes Abrahae* (as n. 44), 5 and 12, n. 11.

[84] R. North, 'Abraham', in B. Metzger and M. Coogan, eds., *The Oxford Companion to the Bible* (Oxford 1993), 4–5; S. Calvo Capilla, 'La Mezquita de Córdoba, San Isidoro de León y el debate doctrinal entre asociadores (cristianos) y agarenos (musulmanes), in M. Varela and G. Boto, eds., *Islam y Cristiandad. Civilizaciones en el mundo medieval*, (Girona 2014), 79–118, esp. 113; B. Anderson, 'Covenant', in B. Metzger and M. Coogan, eds., *The Oxford Companion to the Bible* (Oxford 1993), 138–139.

[85] Reilly, *Alfonso VI* (as n. 9), 328, 338; A. Christys, 'Picnic at Madinat al-Zahra', in S. Barton and P. Linehan, eds., *Cross, Crescent and Conversion. Studies on Medieval Spain and Christendom in Memory of Richard Fletcher* (Leiden 2008), 102–107.

[86] Kitzinger, 'The Gregorian Reform' (as n. 7), 101.

[87] M. Carruthers. *The Craft of Thought: Meditation, Rhetoric, and the Making of Images, 400–1200* (Cambridge 1998), 125–129.

[88] J. Harris, 'Muslim Ivories in Christian Hands: the Leire Casket in context', *Art History,* 18 (1995) 213–222, esp. 213–214, n. 7.

[89] M.M. Gorman, 'The diffusion of the manuscripts of Saint Augustine's 'De doctrina christiana' in the early Middle Ages', *Revue Benedictine,* 95 (1985), 18.

[90] D. Nebbiai-Dalla Guarda, *La bibliothèque de Saint-Victor de Marseille (XIe–XVe siècle)* (Paris 2005), 73, 82, 86, 145–155, 165–180, 197, 215.

[91] For example, Cidellus, mentioned in J. Fernández Valverde, ed., *Roderigo Ximenez De Rada, Historiae de rebus Hispanie sive historia gothica.* Corpus christianorum 72 (Turnholt 1987), VI. XXXIII.12.

[92] R. Walker, 'Sculptors in Medieval Spain after the Conquest of Toledo in 1085', in R. Bacile and J. McNeill, eds, *Romanesque and the Mediterranean* (Leeds 2015), 259–275.

[93] J. Tolan, 'Afterword', in eds. Carmen Cardelle de Hartmann & Philippe Roelli, *Petrus Alfonsi and his Dialogus. Background, Context, Reception,* 2014, 371–377.

[94] J. Tolan 'Petrus Alfonsi', in ed. Georgia Greenia, *Dictionary of Literary Biography* vol. 337: Castilian Writers 1200–1400 (Farmington Hills, Michigan 2008) 192–199; R. Szpiech, *Conversion and Narrative: Reading and Religious Authority in Medieval Polemic* (Philadelphia 2013) 76–82.

[95] The decision to carve a lintel provides another link to Saint-Sernin at Toulouse.

[96] Herráez, 'La escultura de San Isidoro de León', 49.

PATRON AND LITURGY: THE LITURGICAL SETTING OF THE CATHEDRAL CHURCH OF SAN MARTINO IN LUCCA AFTER 1070 AND THE GREGORIAN REFORM

Carlotta Taddei

THE PATRON: ANSELMO DA BAGGIO/ POPE ALEXANDER II

Anselmo da Baggio became bishop of Lucca in 1057 and remained bishop even after he was elected Pope, when he took the title Alexander II (1061–73). He was a leading member of the Gregorian Reform movement, and the most illustrious of the patrons of the church of San Martino in Lucca (Figure 20.1).[1] Little of the 11th-century architecture of San Martino survives, but the written sources provide plenty of evidence for Anselmo's patronage. Chronicles and inscriptions celebrate this period as the golden age of San Martino, and present Bishop Anselmo I as the man who renewed the building and chose for it a Romanising style – 'grande sed augusto'.[2] The realisation of this project was not without difficulties however, primarily as the result of persistent opposition from the canons of San Martino.

The purpose of this paper is to use the written sources to examine the late 11th-century reorganisation of Lucca Cathedral. These sources cast light on how a number of churches in Lucca co-operated in ensuring liturgical provision across the city. They also say something as to the nature of the relations between those churches. During the immediately 'pre-gregorian' period, the church of San Frediano at Lucca had become a centre for religious reform, with a large community of canons who lived communally and led a life of strict observance (Figure 20.2). Indeed, Alexander II brought canons from San Frediano to Rome in order to reform the Lateran, at the request of Peter Damian. Lucca's own cathedral canons seem to have been more resistant to reform, however. Most were drawn from influential families within Lucca, closely allied to the city's temporal authorities, wherein clerical marriage was commonplace and correspondingly harder to uproot. In this context Anselmo moved only very gradually to promote the *vita comune*, and discourage *simonia* and *concubinato*. But his election to the papacy took him

FIGURE 20.1

Lucca, San Martino: façade (Wikimedia Commons)

away from Lucca for long periods, and in 1073 Anselmo died in Rome.

Anselmo I's initial attempts to reform Lucca Cathedral created difficulties for his nephew, and the next-in-line to the bishopric, however, the homonymous Anselmo II

FIGURE 20.2

Lucca, San Frediano. Nave to east (A.C. Quintavalle)

(later sainted as Sant'Anselmo da Lucca). Anselmo II pursued a more radical policy, in line with Pope Gregory VII's more confrontational methods, so strengthening resistance within the opposition. In 1081 Anselmo II was pushed out of Lucca, dying in exile in 1086. Meanwhile the canons elected their own (schismatic) bishop, Pietro. Though the sources gloss over this and celebrate the reformist initiatives in Lucca as an unalloyed triumph, which from a 12th-century perspective, the perspective of success, they may have appeared to be, it would be more accurate to describe the last third of the 11th century in Lucca as a time of crisis.

Success eventually came with Rangerius, who was elected bishop of Lucca in 1097. It was Rangerius who wrote a poetic biography of Anselmo II entitled the *Vita metrica Sancti Anselmi Lucensis episcopi*,[3] which gives prominence to Anselmo II's predecessor, Anselmo I (Pope Alexander II), in recording the events of the late 11th century, as well as a polemical treatise on institutional conflict – *De anulo et baculo*. Rangerius is also considered by many scholars to be the author of a number of documents that describe the liturgical organisation of Lucca Cathedral during this period.[4] It is for this reason that Rangerius is considered to be Anselmo I's true successor, and the effective creator of his reputation as bishop and reform-minded architectural patron.

THE *CURTIS AECCLESIAE*

Documents inform us that, before Anselmo's intervention, the *curtis aecclesiae* consisted of several churches (Figure 20.3 and colour plate XX). These included the church of Santi Giovanni, Pantaleone e Reparata, which, with its baptismal font, has long been considered the first cathedral of Lucca (Figure 20.4). Excavations on the site have revealed a complex sequence of archaeological phases. The 4th-century *basilica episcopalis*, was followed by a second building in the 8th or 9th centuries, which in turn seems to have been extended westwards in a probably 10th-century third phase. It was in relation to this latter phase that archaeologists discovered the bases of two towers, composed in the manner of a *westwerk*.[5] These western towers faced the town, and could also, perhaps, have acted as a fortified entrance to the *curtis aecclesiae*. Both the church and its baptismal font were subsequently rebuilt in the 12th century. Meanwhile, the church of San Martino was described as the cathedral from 724 onwards, and extended to *porticalia*, a *schola* and a chapel, known as Santa Maria ad Praesepem, were recorded until 1021 on its north side.

Local tradition holds that the title 'Cathedral' moved from Santi Giovanni, Pantaleone e Reparata to San Martino, though no documents survive to corroborate the tradition. In addition, the *curtis aecclesiae* ran to a rectory (*canonica*) – known to have been on the north side of the cathedral from 941 – the church of San Pietro in Vincoli, – founded in 818 and recorded until 1055 – a hospital from the early 11th century, and a *domus episcoporum* – this last probably positioned between Santi Giovanni, Pantaleone e Reparata and San Martino. Finally, a church dedicated to San Salvatore stood behind the Cathedral and arguably first housed the Volto Santo, though this was demolished in 930.[6]

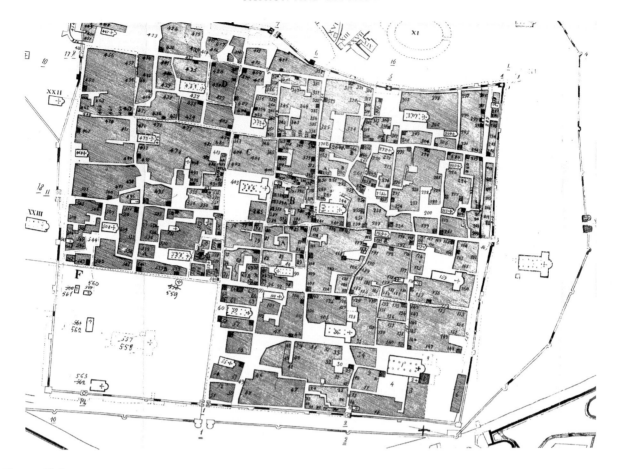

Figure 20.3

G. Matraia, Plan of Lucca c. 1200

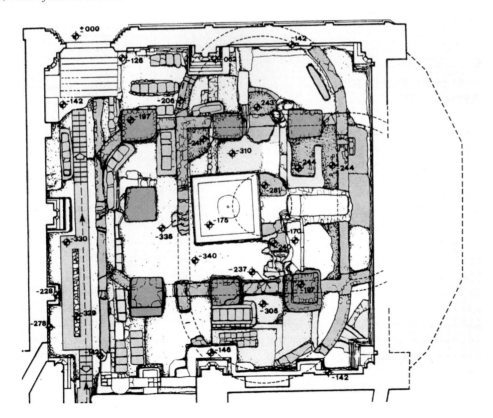

Figure 20.4

Lucca, archaeological plan of baptistery of San Giovanni attached to the church of Santi Pantaleone e Reparata

FIGURE 20.5

Lucca, Biblioteca Capitolare Feliniana, Passionario P+, f. 123 r

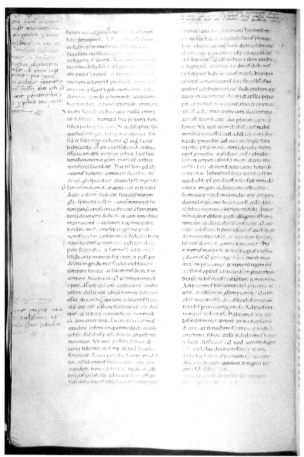

FIGURE 20.6

Lucca, Biblioteca Capitolare Feliniana, Passionario P+, f. 123 v

THE LITURGY BEFORE AND DURING ANSELMO'S EPISCOPATE

Four important sources, all now in the Biblioteca Capitolare Feliniana in Lucca, enable us to reconstruct Lucca's late-11th-century liturgy. The first is the *Sermo in dedicatione aecclesie*. This was copied into the 12th-century cathedral passionary, known as P+, and has been edited by Pietro Guidi.[7] The text was probably composed by Bishop Rangerius (1097–1112), and records the modifications that were made to the building and to the liturgy over the second half of the 11th century (Figures 20.5 and 20.6).[8] The second is the *Ordo officiorum* of the Cathedral of Lucca, written in the late-13th-century but witness to more ancient uses of the Cathedral as well as to the city at large.[9] This text, as was usual, is divided between *temporale* and *santorale*, and describes a liturgy in Lucca that for the most part follows the Roman liturgy as practised in secular churches.[10]

The third source is a simple list of twelve altars in the cathedral, together with their relics, which was casually transcribed alongside other notes, in MS 124 in the Biblioteca Capitolare Feliniana. The original list offers a rare insight into devotion within the cathedral at a critical moment, and can be dated to between 1065 and 1109. The list reads:

[I] Altare ante Vultum in honore XII Apostolorum, Cornelii et Cipriani atque Concordii, Gregorii martyris Spoletini.

[II] Ante crucem Veterem: Blasii, Valentini, Remigii et Xmilium Martyrum

[III] Supra porticum: Eadmundi

[IV] In angulo septentrionali: corpus Lucinae, Cristinae et Felicitatis.

[V] Iuxta: Agathae et Agnes

[VI] Deinde: Mariae et Teclae

[VII] Altare Maius: Martini, Hilarii et Prosperi.

[VIII] In confessione: corpus Reguli.

[IX] Dehinc: Michaeli et utriusque Iohannis.

[X] Iuxta Agnelli, Zenonis et Stephani pontificis

[XI] Prope: corpora sanctorum Iasonis et Mauri et Ilariae matris eorum

[XII] In capella: Apolenaris et Pancratii et Dionisii

Finally, the *Sermo in traslatione corporum sanctorum martirum Reguli, Iasonis et Mauri atquae Hilariae*, recorded in Biblioteca Capitolare Feliniana MS 47, describes the cathedral between 1109 and 1112.[11] This is also likely to have been written by Bishop Rangerius, and refers to the closure of the crypt and the translation of relics within the cathedral.[12]

Thus it can be seen that the renovation of the Cathedral under Anselmo I (Alexander II) was followed by a new dedication recorded in the *Sermo in dedicatione aecclesie*. This followed a standard text for the rededication in its first part, but goes on specifically to describe the situation in Lucca.[13] The dedication was performed in the presence of twenty-two bishops and a 'clericorum multitudinem infinitam', while the account explains that Anselmo enlarged the Cathedral, and centralised all solemn masses in the one church. Until then, it seems that solemn masses were split on a seasonal basis, and were celebrated in Santi Giovanni, Pantaleone e Reparata between Easter until November, and in San Martino from November to Easter (colour plate XX).[14]

The *Ordo officiorum* of Lucca Cathedral confirms this division and describes in detail the ancient liturgical system of Lucca as it applied to both the Cathedral and the rest of the city. As in Rome, Lucca enjoyed a *liturgia stationale*, which extended to seven churches over the week following Easter. This was organised as a penitential procession that visited a precise sequence of churches where a Mass would be celebrated each day. On Easter Sunday, the first *statio*, the solemn Mass was celebrated in Santi Giovanni, Pantaleone and Reparata. On Monday the Mass was celebrated in San Martino. The procession then left the *curtis aecclesiae* to visit San Donato on Tuesday, Santa Maria Forisportam on Wednesday, San Pietro on Thursday, San Frediano on Friday and, finally returned to the *curtis aecclesiae* on Saturday, where a Mass was celebrated in San Martino, closing the circle.[15] This procession went out from the holy precinct so that the *sacrum* radiated and unified the whole of Lucca. The *Ordo* is copied in a late-13th-century hand, but it reflects earlier practice, documented for San Frediano as early as 687 and known to have been in use for all six *ecclesiae sedales* until 1173. The Gregorian sources of this liturgy are clear and serve to underline a hierarchy among the churches.[16]

Thus, the seasonal *trasmigratio* between Santi Giovanni, Pantaleone e Reparata and San Martino was inserted into this Easter path. Indeed, the first *statio* of the Easter week in Santi Giovanni, Pantaleone e Reparata overlapped with the beginning of the liturgical season for that church. Since the texts indicate that the liturgy was split between two churches before Anselmo I became bishop, one for summer and one for winter, we might suppose that the city operated a system of twin cathedrals, for in addition to the seasonal division, we can detect a functional division. San Martino was the canons' cathedral while Santi Giovanni, Pantaleone e Reparata housed baptisms, and perhaps functioned as the bishop's cathedral (with the *domus episcoporum* nearby).

The debate about the nature and authority of twin cathedrals remains an open one, and it is not my purpose here to say anything about the form, function or symbology of this phenomenon.[17] I simply wish to consider the liturgical *praxis* for the Church of Lucca that the documents describe so well. The shared liturgical organisation tells us something about the relationship between the buildings, and offers a reason as to the silence of the sources concerning the supposed movement of the Cathedral church from San Giovanni, Pantaleone e Reparata to San Martino.

As was the case in Milan, so it was in Lucca. Both churches in the twin cathedral complex could operate contemporaneously and throughout the year. It was simply the solemn masses that were divided seasonally. In changing this, so that the major masses would be celebrated in San Martino all year round, Anselmo promoted a new liturgical system focussed on a single cathedral church. For this purpose he restored the Cathedral building, which thereafter became known as the *ecclesia matrix*.[18] Moreover, he introduced a *vita comune* for the canons, and in 1062, perhaps in mitigation or as an encouragement to accept reform, granted the canons the right to wear mitres in procession.

The plan of Anselmo's Cathedral remains arguable. Pietro Guidi, Clara Baracchini, Antonio Caleca and Romano Silva believe the cathedral had twin aisles, like Pisa, while Anna Rosa Masetti argued that it consisted of a nave flanked by single aisles, as at Sant'Alessandro in Lucca.[19] The list of altars (see above) tells us that there were twelve in total. The high altar was dedicated to San Martino, with an altar *ante Vultum* and another *ante Crucem Veterem*.[20] There was a crypt beneath the presbytery containing the relics of Saint Regulus (as in Carolingian times), while the church boasted a porch with an altar for Saint Edmund above. The *Sermo in traslatione corporis* (source 4) also records the relics of Giasone, Mauro and Ilaria, placed in Anselmo's time on the right side of the church, near the inner face of the façade, and adds that the relics of Lucina were on the left, while again confirming that the relics of St Regulus were in the crypt.

THE REASONS WHY ANSELMO REARRANGED THE CATHEDRAL

From the middle of the 9th century, clerics began to use written rituals to define the boundaries of the Church, both as an institution and as a community, a process which intensified over the second half of the 11th century. One aspect of this was the establishment of a correspondence between Christian society and the buildings in which it worshipped. Dominique Iogna Prat has shown how, and when, the *ecclesia* as a building became the mirror of the *Ecclesia* as an institution.[21] During the Gregorian Reform, church buildings increasingly came to be celebrated as if they were themselves the body of a saint. The church as a container came to represent, as a metonym, its contents, as the Gregorian elite strove to create cathedrals that encompassed the whole of Christian society.

Thus it was that in the years when Anselmo was Pope, and chose to remain bishop of Lucca, the town became the focal point of a struggle between the papal reform party and the local clergy, as Rangerius relates in his *Vita Metrica*. This same Rangerius also wrote the *Sermo in dedicatione aecclesiae*, in which he described the dedication of a church in the name of a saint as 'a baptism' of the building.[22] That is a striking simile to use. Michael Lauwers has pointed out that the consecration of a building is a means of advertising and ratifying the authority that built it. It either validates the initial establishment of authority, a transfer of authority, or it reflects a liturgical rearrangement, all of which affect those who staff or use the church in question.[23] For Lucca Cathedral we don't have a consecration sermon, but we do at least have the *Sermo in traslatione corporis*. What emerges from that is a story in which longstanding relations between social groups were reorganised, not without conflict, and cathedral worship was eventually centralised in a single building with a complex of altars and spaces.

From San Martino the *sacrum* radiated to the *curtis* and on into the town, which then, ideally, identified with Lucca's principal church – the one and only Cathedral. Of the area around the Cathedral, the *Sermo* states that Anselmo, 'sub anathemate quoque ex auctoritate divina et apostolica praecepit, ut nullus in circuitu et atrio et canonica ipsius ecclesiae irato animo vim alicui inferat, aut assaltum facere, aut personam capere pr(ae)sumat', revealing the bishop's determination to take charge of the *curtis* and protect it from violation.

Through the newly reformed church (*ecclesia*/building), the bishop/Pope wanted to project a new concept of the Church as a community, one which would act as a mirror of Christian society in a peaceful city. The building he chose as the new cathedral was the canons' church, a course of action that was fraught but, if successful, would bring them into body of a reformed Church. The project failed, at least in its 11th-century form, and a few years later, in 1077, Gregory VII excommunicated the still rebellious canons of the cathedral. Resolution only came with Bishop Rangerius, who finally won over the city's mercantile community, which had previously supported the schismatic Bishop Pietro.[24] Rangerius also suppressed the crypt at some point between 1097 and 1112, translating the relics of St Regulus out of the dark (crypt) and into the light (presbytery). For the crypt had been a '*locus vanitati* [. . .] *occasionem confabulationis*'.[25] What had been begun by Anselmo was concluded by Rangerius. The *curtis episcopale* became the *Curtis Ecclesia Sancti Martini*, where, in the early 12th century, civic worship of the *Volto Santo* emerged. So, concluding the *Sermo in dedicatione ecclesie*, Rangerius was able to state 'quid valet vobis eorum habere reliquias, quasi quoddam manna reconditum, quorum vitam spernitis, labores aborretis, coronam non curatis? [. . .] Ad pacem unanimitatem redeamus'.[26]

NOTES

[1] Anselmo was born in Milan of a noble family; where he took an active part in the Patarin movement. His appointment as bishop was approved by the Emperor, as Anselmo was then identified with a moderate wing within the Gregorian movement. C. Violante, 'I laici nel movimento patarino', in *I laici nella 'societas cristiana' dei secoli XI e XII*. Atti della III settimana internazionale di studio, Mendola 21–27 agosto 1965, (Milan 1968), 597–687. After he became bishop, Anselmo proved himself an energetic supporter of Ildebrando di Soana (subsequently Gregory VII) in endeavouring to suppress simony and enforce clerical celibacy. The papal election of 1061, which Hildebrand had arranged in conformity with the papal decree of 1059, was not however sanctioned by the imperial court of Germany. See also the essays collected in C. Violante (ed.), *Sant'Anselmo vescovo di Lucca (1073–1086) nel quadro delle trasformazioni sociali e della Riforma ecclesiastica* (Rome 1992).

[2] Our principal source is the biography of Anselmo II written by one of his successors, Bishop Rangerius (1097–1112), who celebrated Anselmo I's actions. According to Rangerius. 'Aspice nunc aedem primam, mirare columnas / ordine quasi gemino ducit utrumque latus. / Aspice structuram lapidum, quas arte decora. / Docta manus posuit sub Salomone novo. / Quae sub Alexandro Romam Lucamque regente / Grande sed angusto tempore fecit opus'. Rangerius also composed several liturgical texts that mention Anselmo's patronage, and within the Cathedral porch, an inscription reads:'HUJUS QUAE CELSA RADIANT FASTIGIA TEMPLI/SUNT SUB ALEXANDRO. PAPA CONSTRUCTA SECUNDO.' In addition to these sources, Anselmo's patronage is mentioned in several chronicles and histories, such as the Annales Tolomei. See. B. Schmeidler (ed.), *Tholomei Lucensis Annales*, MGH (Monumenta Germaniae Historica), Scriptores Rerum Germanicarum, New Series, VIII (Munchen 1984).

[3] The *Vita metrica Sancti Anselmi Lucensis episcopi* is published in MGH, Scriptores, XXX, 2, (Lipsia 1929), 1152–1307. See also R. Savigni, 'Rangerio, vescovo di Lucca, agiografo', *Dizionario Biografico degli Italiani* (forthcoming).

[4] According to Pietro Guidi, Rangerius is probably the author of the *Sermo in dedicatione ecclesiae*, and the *Sermo in traslatione corporum sanctorum martirum Reguli, Iasonis, et Mauri atque Ilarie* (see n. 7 and n. 11).

[5] G. Piancastelli Politi Nencini (ed.), *La chiesa dei Santi Giovanni e Reparata in Lucca, dagli scavi archeologici al restauro*, Lucca 1996. The *basilica episcoporum* was built after 391 with a baptistry and a cemetery; this church is referred to as Santa Reparata from 754, to which the dedications to San Giovanni (known from 881) and San Pantaleone (known from 984) were added.

[6] G. Concioni, 'San Martino di Lucca. La cattedrale medioevale', *Rivista di archeologia, storia, costume*, XXII, n. 1–4, (1994), 11–13.

[7] Lucca, Biblioteca Capitolare Feliniana, Passionario P+, f. 123 (r and v). See: P. Guidi, 'Per la storia della Cattedrale e del Volto Santo', *Bollettino Storico Lucchese*, IV (1932), 182–184.

[8] The relevant sections of the *Sermo in dedicatione aecclesie* read: 'Ubi cum Romanae sedis pontifice Alexandro, qui tunc et Lucensis specialiter erat episcopus, ad hanc solempnitatem XX duos episcopos et abbatum numerositatem non modicam convenire fecit. [. . .] Aecclesie vero huic talem attribuit dignitatem, ut ab hac die dominicis diebus missas solempnes habeat, quas in aecclesia beati Pantaleonis a Resurrectionis die usque ad kalendas novenbris caelebrari mos erat; sub anathemate quoque ex auctoritate divina et apostolica praecepit, ut nullus in circuitu et atrio et canonica ipsius ecclesiae irato animo vim alicui inferat, aut assaltum facere, aut personam capere pr(ae)sumat.

'Ut autem etiam de thesauris nichil minus esse potuisset, vel ad illa quae in tabernaculo per Moysen, vel quae in templo sunt reposita per Salomonem, Roma detulit memoratus pontifex et praelibate aecclesiae obtulit sanctorum corpora Iasoni et Mauri et eorum matris Hylariae et ea in dextro latere honorifice reposuit. In sinistro vero beatae Lucinae corpus, quod Iohannes episcopus predecessor suus item Roma detulerat, magna cum devotione collocavit. Sanctum quoque Regulum iam multo ante tempore divina largitione huic Lucensi aecclesiae datum, cum debita reverentia in cripta recondidit. Iutuemini igitur, obsecro, paulo diligentius honorem vestrum et divitias vestras conservate. Quid valet vobis eorum habere reliquias, quasi quoddam manna reconditum, quorum vitam spernitis, labores aborretis, coronam non curatis? [. . .] Quamobrem mutemus studia, discordias omittamus, fraudes, periuria corrigamus. Ad pacis unanimitatem redeamus'.

[9] Lucca, Biblioteca Capitolare Feliniana, MS 608.

[10] M. Giusti, *L'Ordo officiorum' della cattedrale di Lucca*, in *Miscellanea G. Mercati*, II (Vatican 1964), 552–566.

[11] Lucca, Biblioteca Capitolare Feliniana, MS 47, f. 1–6. The text is headed *Sermo in traslatione corporum sanctorum martirum Reguli, Iasonis et Mauri atquae Hilariae,* and has been edited by P. Guidi, 'Storia della Cattedrale' (as n. 7).

[12] The relevant sections read: 'Cum autem ad [A]lexandri tempora ventum esset et vir, summe industrie Romanam Cathedram a Domino suscepisset, placuit Lucanam ecclesiam non deserere et contritiones illius suo solatio refovere. Que cum olim divitiis et honoribus floruisset, per quorumdam occupationes potius quam regiminis pastoralis curas pervilegis ita foris pressa et consumpta erat, ut ipsa quoque sarta tecta maioris ecclesie pre vetustate vacillarent; unde et habito, quorum oportuit, consilio, quam cernitis fabricam, ab eo fundata est et sacrata brevi quidem tempore, sed non levi su[m]pto a[c] labore. [. . .] Lectio VII [. . .] Sed dum per negligentiam custodum et importunitatem pulsantium sacra illa intentio solveretur et locus ille iam non tam rarus fieret pietati, quam frequens et pervius vanitati, visum est his, quorum interrat, viam et occasionem confabulationi claudere et corpus sanctum [S. Reguli] de tenebris ad lucem revocare. [. . .] Lectio IX. Sed et beatorum Iasonis et Mauri et matris eorum Hylarie reliquias transferendi ea causa est, quia nec aliter altare, ubi est [corpus] beati Reguli levari poterat, nisi ex alio quoque latere aliud locaretur, nec erat aliud quod nobis ad transferendum sic abile videretur tum propter loci incommoditatem non ferendam. Erat enim ut est, locus ille nec ad quietem idoneus, nec ad evidentiam perspicus et decere visum est, ut quos necessitas tranferebat'.

[13] In the *Sermo in traslatione corporum sanctorum martirum Reguli, Iasonis et Mauri atquae Hilariae*, Rangerius wrote '[Alexandro] unde et habito, quorum oportuit, consilio, quam cernitis fabricam, ab eo fundata est et sacrata brevi quidem tempore, sed non levi su[m]pto a[c] labore'. See n. 11.

[14] 'ab hac die dominicis diebus missas solempnes habeat, quas in aecclesia beati Pantaleonis a Resurrectionis die usque ad kalendas novenbris caelebrari mos erat; sub anathemate quoque ex auctoritate divina et apostolica praecepit, ut nullus in circuitu et atrio et canonica ipsius ecclesiae irato animo vim alicui inferat, aut assaltum facere, aut personam capere pr(ae)sumat'. See also C. Taddei, *Lucca tra XI e XII secolo. Territorio, architetture, città* (Parma 2005), 15–20.

[15] Giusti, *Ordo officiorum* (as n. 10); C. Buchanan, 'Spiritual and Spatial Authority in Medieval Lucca; Illuminated Manuscripts, Stational Liturgy and the Gregorian Reform, *Art History*, 27 (2004), 723–744. C. Taddei, 'Sanctificare vias. Lo spazio sacro nella città e la liturgia stazionale a Lucca', *Codex Aquilarensis*, 32 (2017), 155–170.

[16] R. Savigni, *Episcopato e società cittadina a Lucca da Anselmo II a Roberto* (Lucca 1996), 284–288.

[17] See in particular R. Krautheimer, 'The twin cathedral at Pavia', in R. Solomon, ed., *Opicinus de Canistris* (London 1936), 325–337; A. Grabar, 'Cathédrales multiples et groupement d'églises en Russie', *Revue d'Etudes Slaves*, XX (1942), reprinted in A. Grabar, *L'Art de la fin de l'Antiquité et du Moyen Age*, II (Paris 1968), 919–938; J. Hubert, 'Les *cathédrales doubles* et l'histoire de la liturgie', in *Atti del I Congresso internazionale di Studi Longobardi*, (Spoleto 1951), 167–176; A. De Capitani D'Arzago, *La 'Chiesa Maggiore di Milano: S. Tecla*, (Milan 1952); R. Bauerreis, *Stefanskult und frühen Bischoffstadt*, (Munich 1963); C. Violante and C.D. Fonseca, 'Ubicazione e dedicazione delle cattedrali dalle origini al periodo romanico nelle città dell'Italia centro-settentrionale', in *Il romanico pistoiese nei suoi rapporti con l'arte romanica dell'Occidente*, Atti del I Convegno internazionale di studi medioevali di storia e d'arte. Pistoia-Montecatini Terme 1964, (Pistoia 1979), 303–346; P. Piva, *La cattedrale doppia* (Bologna 1990); A. Pracchi, *La Cattedrale antica di Milano* (Bari 1996); P. Piva, *Dalla cattedrale doppia allo 'spazio' liturgico canonicale: linee di un percorso*, in *Canonici delle cattedrali nel Medioevo* (Verona 2003), 69–93; A. Calzona, *Cremona, dalla cattedrale doppia paleocristiana a quella dei 'cives' del 1107*, in *Immagine e ideologia*, Studi in onore di Arturo Carlo Quintavalle (Milano 2007), 191–206. None of the proposals made by these scholars can be considered definitive. Moreover, although discussion of this subject was active in the 1960 s and 1970s, it has now subsided. In Lucca there is no obvious reason to presume a paring of churches, as is evident in dedications to St Mary and St Stephen, for example. Instead, we find a liturgical/seasonal division between an ancient basilica (Sant Giovanni, Pantaleone e Reparata) adjacent to a second and more recent building.

[18] Savigni, *Episcopato* (as n. 16), 284–288.

[19] Guidi, *Storia della Cattedrale* (as n. 7), 169–186; C. Baracchini-A. Caleca, *Il duomo di Lucca*, (Lucca 1973), 14; R. Silva, *La ricostruzione della cattedrale di Lucca (1060–1070): un esempio precoce di architettura della riforma gregoriana*, in *Sant'Anselmo* (as n. 1), 297–309. A.R. Calderoni Masetti, 'Anselmo da Baggio e la cattedrale di Lucca', *Annali della Scuola Normale Superiore di Pisa*, s. III, VII (1977), 91–116.

[20] This is a witness of the presence of two crosses, one more ancient (*crucem veterem*) and another that could be that known as the *Volto Santo* (*Vultum*).

[21] D. Iogna-Prat, *La maison dieu. Une histoire monumentale de l'Eglise au Moyen Age (800–1200)*, (Paris 2006).

[22] M. Lauwers, 'Consécration d'églises, réforme et ecclésiologie monastique' in *Mises en scènes et memoires de la consécration de l'église dans l'Occident médiéval*, ed., D. Mehu (Turnhout 2008), 145–194.

[23] Ibid., 146–147.

[24] An inscription of 1111 in the cathedral porch (whose authenticity is contested) reads

+ AD MEMORIA(M) HABENDA(M) ET IUSTITIA(M) RETINENDA(M) CURTIS / ECCLESIE BEATI MARTINI SCRIBIMUS IURAM(EN)TUM QUOD CAMBIATORES / ET SPECIARII OM(NE)S ISTIUS CURTIS TEMPORE RANGERII EP(ISCOP)I FECERUNT / UT OM(NE)S CU(M) FIDUCIA POSSINT CA(M)BIARE VENDERE ET EMERE / IURAVERUNT OM(NE)S CAMBIATORES ET SPECIARII QUOD AB ILLA ORA / IN ANTEA NEC FURTUM FACIENT NEC TRECCAMENTU(M) NEC FALSI / TATE(M) INFRA CURTE(M) SANCTI MARTINI NEC IN DOMIBUS ILLIS IN QUIBUS / HOMINES HOSPITANTUR HOC IURAM(EN)TUM FACIUNT QUI IBI AD / CAMBIUM AUT AD SPECIES STARE VOLUERINT / SUNT ETIA(M) INSUPER QUI SEMPER CURTEM ISTA(M) CUSTODIUNT ET QUOD / MALEFACTU(M) FUERIT EMENDARE FACIUNT AN(NO) D(OMI)NI MCXI / ADVENIENS QUISQUA(M) SCRIPTURA(M) PERLEGAT ISSTA(M) ET QUA CONFIDAT ET SIBI NIL TIMEAT

[25] See n. 11. A section of the *Sermo in traslatione corporum sanctorum martirum Reguli, Iasonis et Mauri atquae Hilariae,* reads 'sed dum per negligentiam custodum et importunitatem pulsantium sacra illa intentio solveretur et locus ille iam non tam rarus fieri pietati, quam frequens et pervius vanitati, visum et his, quorum interrat, viam et occasionem confabulationi claudere et corpus sanctum [sancti Reguli] de tenebris ad lucem revocare'.

[26] See n. 11

THE 'LITERATE' LAY DONOR: TEXTUALITY AND THE ROMANESQUE PATRON

Robert A. Maxwell

Patronage of artistic works could be likened to a performance, one played out by a cast of individuals, each of whom fulfils a particular role or roles. There are those that request the work or finance it, others that oversee its production, and still others that commit themselves to the work's fabrication, installation and perhaps even consecration. The roles vary in scope and detail according to the circumstances but also according to the individuals' aims and interests, and any one of a number of roles could, depending on the commission, earn the distinction of 'patron' (which is not always aligned with the modern usage). The personal dynamics among the actors also play a role, with relationships pivoting on economic, social, religious, personal or other factors, and sometimes generating friction or even patent conflict. All of these varied elements that make up the social performance of patronage undergo yet further inflection when the performance becomes representation; that is, when the negotiated relations undergo translation as pictorial subject.

Patronage images are not uncommon in medieval art. They often present a figure kneeling deferentially before the person or institution to whom a gift is made. Sometimes the institution is represented by spiritual proxy, namely a saint, the Virgin, or Christ himself. The kneeling figure also usually proffers a symbolic miniature of his or her gift, such as a model-sized representation of a church, chapel or monastery. The model helps to connect the presenter with the real-world gift.[1]

In spite of appearances, however, this motif's seeming straightforwardness can be misleading. The nature of the gift, the identity of the donor and the role of the recipient can all undergo subtle (or even not-so-subtle) transformation when cast as visual representation. The Crucifixion window in the east axial chapel at Poitiers Cathedral, for example, seems to follow customary form by showing Eleanor of Aquitaine and Henry II of England kneeling as they hold up their gift of a stained glass panel to the martyred Peter, Paul and crucified Christ above them (Figure 21.1). (The little white panel is a 19th-century restoration, but the object they originally held was nonetheless likely a representation of a window.) The image gives pause on several accounts.

First, no written evidence suggests that the royal couple financed the cathedral's construction, and nothing – other than this representation – ties them specifically to the choir glazing as the miniature gift would suggest. While one could take the image at face value and consider it evidence, it may just as well make an invented argument. Second, the image's layers of reference build a complex *mise-en-abyme*: its constructed visual rhetoric suggests the window gift is made not to Christ, Peter and Paul but to a window – a representation – of Christ, Peter and Paul, suggesting that the gifted window is the window in which the Plantagenet couple finds themselves represented. One outcome of this representation within a representation is to suggest that the gift includes, beyond any material patronage, the offer of themselves to the cathedral, in the sense of becoming its spiritual subjects. Much more could be said about this image, but suffice it to say that it projects complex ideas about the relationship of the royal couple to the church under construction, while it elucidates very little about what was given (funds, privileges, quarries, glazing, etc.) and to what ends (political, spiritual, salvational, etc.).[2]

A hemicycle capital at Notre-Dame-du-Port in Clermont-Ferrand (Auvergne-Rhône-Alpes) suggests a similar web of questions (Figure 21.2). On one of the capital's faces, a lay donor – identified by the inscription as Stephanus but otherwise unknown to us – bears a gift of a foliate capital.[3] As at Poitiers, the depicted capital stands for the object on which he himself is carved and stands synedochally for the whole church as both material and ecclesiastical body. The *mise-en-abyme* once again establishes a visual relationship that makes the figure the agent (broadly construed) and the gift itself. An inscription adds to the rhetorical play through its mischievously opaque use of 'fieri jussit', which could mean that Stephanus commissioned the work (as through a monetary gift), or perhaps authorised it (in a legal or protectorship sense), or perhaps oversaw the gift's transfer as representative of a family lineage or corporate body. On the surface of it, the text does not clarify the relationship shown in the image any more than the image helps untangle the text.

FIGURE 21.1

Poitiers Cathedral, choir. Eleanor of Aquitaine and King Henry II, with their four sons, offering a window (photo: Robert A. Maxwell)

FIGURE 21.2

Clermont, Notre-Dame-du-Port: Stephanus offering a capital (Robert A. Maxwell)

These images project complex ideas about patronage relations, even while hewing to a seemingly conventional iconography of presentation. Recent scholarship has usefully drawn attention to the ambiguities often found in the represented relationship of the recipient and patron (or the person whom we assume to be the patron).[4] Jill Caskey, for example, has shown in an excellent study that the denomination by inscription on a group of southern Italian bronze doors of a certain Panteleone as '*auctor*' – a term with juridical overtones – made him the legal overseer rather than actual donor.[5] The visual language too can reveal more tendentious and contingent implications, as in Elizabeth Pastan's study of the Bayeux Tapestry that calls for a re-consideration of what one can learn about patronage from image and text.[6] These art historical treatments echo important research by historians that emphasise the negotiated, shifting parameters of the patron-client relationship.[7] Many of those historical studies draw attention to new inflections of patronage performance in a crucial period beginning in the 10th and 11th centuries.

This paper builds on those studies and, in keeping with this volume's emphasis on process, suggests ways that imagery contributed to changing notions of patronage. Whereas laymen and laywomen had always made gifts to the Church, the 11th and 12th centuries saw a dramatic rise in images that represented these deeds. The Poitiers window is a good 12th-century example of the common royal type, but increasingly the diffusion of this iconography extended also in a significant way to non-royal figures, as at Clermont.[8] Non-royal laity usually adopted the traditional donor-with-church-model iconography, as in the mid-10th-century wall painting of the Sylvester Chapel at Goldbach (Lake Constance) showing a local lord and in the 12th-century image of Graf Eberhard von Nellenburg as founder of Schaffhausen monastery. The proliferation of lay subjects represents an expansion of iconography to embrace a social class that previously figured only exceptionally in donor representation.[9]

A second aspect of transformation concerns the written record. This period experienced unprecedented writing activity, particularly in the realm of record-keeping and historical accounting, and indeed an enormous number of texts produced in this period concern gift-giving that record patrons' actions, notably in charters, annals and chronicles. At Clermont, one could regard the inscription as a mere *titulus* that does little more than name the figure and ambivalently identify his role. But the inscription's presence may be suggestive in subtle ways of donorship's new textual environment.

This paper argues that allusions to textual culture combined with an emerging class of patron yielded a novel kind of donor imagery. The resulting iconography situated laymen and laywomen in a culture of textual, and specifically diplomatic, production. The emerging image of patronly performance reveals something about the ongoing process of defining what it meant to be a donor: as suggested here, donorship's pictorialisation increasingly textualised the patronly performance, just as the performance increasingly textualised the laity.

TEXTUALISING DONORSHIP

Images of lay donorship multiplied in the 11th and 12th centuries, but as noted previously, there was already a tradition of royal, and especially imperial, imagery throughout the Early Middle Ages. These often showed the sovereign proffering a work in miniature or with a book. The 10th century includes several exceptional examples of non-royal donors, and these images show either a miniature church model (as at Goldbach, cf. *supra*) or a book offering.[10] The latter scenes by extension implicate the layperson as a contributor to the literate preoccupations of the religious class in that the layperson provides a Gospel book, sacramentary or other codex needed for clerical or monastic use.

Those examples are sufficiently rare to merit our attention, yet what is distinctly novel in the Romanesque period is the appearance of images that depict the donor as an actor within the textual culture *specific* to donorship. By the start of the 11th century, some images of offering, sponsoring or commissioning a gift emphasise the donation as having an expressly notarial component; that is, a textual record is shown as part of the patronage performance. This textualisation of patronly action engages a different set of reference points in cultural practice than does the traditional model-in-miniature motif. This is the case whether the gift is a book or something else entirely.

When, for instance, Hugh the Poitevin set in writing the history of his abbey at Vézelay along with the abbey's legal documents, the resulting chronicle-cartulary (*c*. 1170) commemorated the abbey's 9th-century founders, Girart of Roussillon and his wife Berthe, with portrait images (Figure 21.3). The image shows Girart holding a vegetal sceptre and gesturing across his body as his wife touchingly places her hand on her husband's shoulder. These portraits inaugurate the cartulary proper, which begins with Girart's *testamentum*, the text that identifies him as the monastery's founder.[11] The image departs from the more familiar iconography of a kneeling presentation and, given the juxtaposition to the text, works instead to establish the couple as part of a textual tradition of gift recording.

FIGURE 21.3

Auxerre, BM 227, fol. 22r. (Chronicle-Cartulary of Vézelay): Girart of Roussillon, with spouse Bertha (photo: CNRS-IRHT)

The figures' juxtaposition to the neighbouring text even confers on them a kind of authorship, in so far as their donation is conveyed exclusively as a textual event and not as part of a conveyance scene. In fact, their own bodies become part of the donation's textualisation, as they occupy the first letter of the act ('Omnibus'). While the traditional visual language of donorship – showing a kneeling, offering donor – is discarded, the motif of the 'portrait' medallion aligns with other iconographic traditions, notably funerary and dynastic. Indeed, the presence of portraits to introduce a *testamentum* suggests those specific commemorative traditions, which are also in keeping with the general archival nature of a cartulary. Cartularies proliferated only at the end of the 10th century as a means of preserving an institution's acts, quickly becoming common notarial equipment of clerical, monastic and eventually lay archives. Although relatively few cartularies from the period contain images, the medium provided illuminators a ready occasion to depict donors as textual agents of their actions.

The Vézelay work demonstrates one way this was done, but frequently in cartularies the act of giving was represented with the aid of a depicted charter. For example, a combined cartulary-chronicle from San Vincenzo al Volturno (Molise) records gifts made by the local duke Gisulf that led to the monastery's foundation (Figure 21.4).[12] The privileges and lands he offers are absent from the scene – that is, they are not figured with a kneeling donor – yet they are nonetheless evoked through the image of the scroll, a motif that suggests an enacted transfer of a document (before an altar, no less) that would have been part of the donation's diplomatic ceremony.[13] In this case, the scroll also depicts some written text, the opening words of the invocation, thus underscoring its standing as the charter upon which the duke's gifts were recorded. The textual implication of the duke's patronage is thus in effect doubled, as it is shown first symbolically through the performance of the proffered scroll and second through the transcribed document that the image accompanies. In a sense, the kneeling offer of a scroll takes the place of the traditional gift-in-miniature motif. But it is not so simple as a motif's migration from one offered object to another; the importance of diplomatic praxis is fundamental to this new object, as is discussed further below.

The motif of transferring a charter became something of a visual trope for cartularies. In the *Libro de las Estampas*, a compilation of royal *testamenta* enumerating the respective donations to the cathedral of León, each of the seven royal portraits is shown wielding a charter with a dangling seal (Figure 21.5).[14] In the *Tumbo A* of Santiago de Compostela many of the depicted royal figures hold charters in images that precede their transcribed acts.[15] The *Cartulary of Mont-Saint-Michel* also includes several images of donors holding written scrolls.[16] Patrons holding scrolls were so common in later medieval art that it is easy to forget how strangely novel the motif was just a short time before.

In practical terms the scroll motif resolves a pictorial problem for the artist, namely how to represent the sundry gifts and privileges that may be contained in a single donation. In the *Libro de las Estampas* the portraits preface texts that recount the extent of the subject's largesse over a lifetime. A single depicted scroll can symbolically account for them all. Yet the prominent inclusion of a represented document is more than a convenience. In the León manuscript, Countess Sancha deliberately clutches a scroll with its conspicuously pendant seal, even while being brutally murdered by her nephew (Figure 21.6).[17] Sancha brandishes the scroll (inscribed 'ego sancia comitissa confirmo') as if its contents – confirming her pious largesse to the Church – would parry the blow. The painted scroll stands in for the various written records – the actual diplomatic production – that she has signed and sealed over a lifetime and that here collectively provide her defence and hope for salvation. In all of these images, the scroll motif acquires greater meaning because of what it suggests about the donor's historic relationship to diplomatic process and, more generally, the increasing importance of written texts in that process.

Charters had long recorded gifts and various other engagements for institutions and individuals, but the culture of written acts, including written forms of donorship, intensified in the 11th and 12th centuries to complement dependency on orality and memory. Michael Clanchy noted that while approximately 2,000 written acts survive for the entire Anglo-Saxon period, one could conjecture at least eight million from the 13th century alone in England.[18] Among surviving private acts in Italy, A. Bartoli Langeli tallies 500 for the 8th century and over 9,000 for the 11th and another 9,000 for the 12th.[19] To be sure, these estimates also reflect low survival rates for documents produced in the Early Middle Ages, but the later boom in record-keeping is undeniable.[20]

The phenomenon embraced not simply the literate, clerical ranks. Rosamond McKitterick, Alice Rio and others have demonstrated the importance of written production to the laity, including non-literates, at least as early as the late 9th century.[21] Non-literates understood that written documents bound them to duties and also guaranteed their rights. As Matthew Innes has argued, 'the ability to read, still less to write, a charter did not need to be widespread for the written word to play a central role in legal practice'.[22] Laymen eventually achieved a form of pragmatic literacy in the 11th and 12th centuries,[23] suggesting even, as Clanchy has claimed, that 'lay literacy grew out of [the new] bureaucracy' of written production.[24]

The performance of donorship in the 11th and 12th centuries thus played out within a culture that increasingly expected, and indeed imposed, a textual element. The diplomatic expectations of the textual elements were themselves increasingly systematised in terms of script, language, formulae and validation marks, not to mention the performed rites and ceremonies, yielding new legal 'standards' of *instrumentum publicum*. All these elements of diplomatic practice provided a new kind of stage for the performance of donorship, and, as already suggested, for the representation of that performance. The laity's role in the visual discourse of 'diplomatic' patronage

FIGURE 21.4

Rome, Biblioteca Apostolica Vaticana, Barb. Lat. 2724, fol. 47v. (Chronicon Vulturnense): Duke Gisulf presenting donation charter (photo: Biblioteca Apostolica Vaticana)

FIGURE 21.5

León, Archivo de la Catedral, Cód. 25, fol. 12v. (Libro de las Estampas): Ordoño III (photo: after Galván Freile, Testamentos de los Reyes de León [León 1997])

implicates more strategies than can be discussed here, but the following remarks isolate three specific ways that can be taken as representative: 1) instances in which laymen appear as agents of manuscript production; 2) projections of laymen as writers; and 3) laymen as readers. Proffering a scroll may have been the most common means to associate a patron with the diplomatic performance, but there were other ways to construct donorship as a 'literate' act.

As a final preliminary remark, it is worth noting that the historical figures discussed previously – Countess Sancha (d. 1045), Girart of Roussillon (d. 877?) and Duke Gisulf (d. 706) – all lived long before their visual representation as 'literate' donors. (Further examples are found in the works discussed later.) Though donations before the 10th or 11th century were never not always recorded, these figures were involved in the production of charters, including some that recorded gifts. Nonetheless, it is striking that the 12th-century manuscripts in which they appear bestow on these ancestral figures – in spite of their belonging to a time dominated by oral tradition – 12th-century expectations for specific signs of diplomatic culture. A pervasive discourse of writing in the 11th and 12th centuries bore so greatly on notions of what it meant to be a donor that the past could, in images, be re-written.

AS RECORD-KEEPER

One long-standing iconographic tradition concerning lay patronage involves the gift of a book, as noted above. In the 11th and 12th centuries, however, a book in a donor image could suggest something else. In a notarial context – in cartularies, for example – the book could

FIGURE 21.6

León, Archivo de la Catedral, Cód. 25, fol. 41v. (Libro de las Estampas): Condesa Sancha, murdered by her nephew (photo: after Galván Freile, Testamentos de los Reyes de León [León 1997])

suggest not so much a gift as the figure's role as legal authority in the diplomatic process.

The mid-12th-century cartulary of St-Pierre at Vierzon (Cher) includes a half-page illumination of the 9th-century lord of Vierzon, Ambrannus, kneeling in typical donor fashion (Figure 21.7).[25] He kneels before the local monastery's abbot to present a bound codex. His actual gift was not a manuscript, but rather, as the text following the image says, lands and several churches. The codex he presents could signify the symbolic importance of those gifts, made in three separate acts; that is, his gifts were so numerous and important that a single scroll, as seen in the previous examples, would not have done justice to his magnanimity. It is more likely, however, that the offered codex represents the entirety of this very manuscript, Vierzon's cartulary, making a statement on all the diversely transcribed acts and the entirety of the monastery's agreements since its 9th-century foundation.

This illumination, the largest in the manuscript and covering nearly one-third of the page, comes early in the codex and after a set of prestigious bulls and diplomas. While those preceding acts establish papal, episcopal and royal privileges, the act introduced by this illumination inaugurates texts of a more 'local' flavour. Ambrannus's lordship was decisive for the monastery and a source of justification for the monks when claiming their authority over neighbouring lands and a nearby monastery. This makes Ambrannus in this image not so much the patron, in the modern sense of the term, but rather a public authority exercising his legal oversight to the archival collection.[26] Some of the monastery's key possessions were in dispute when the cartulary was made, which may explain why the monastic artist chose to draw upon a long-ago lord to plead for the perpetual legitimacy of past agreements.

His legal commitment is confirmed by his two witnesses – a veiled woman (presumably his wife, mentioned in the acts) and a bearded man behind her – both of whom seem to look at and gesture towards the book. The notion of witness is important (the abbot has his own witnesses as well) as it evokes diplomatic ritual. Showing Ambrannus as 'giver' of the collected acts, thus endorsing the acts' authoritative transcription into codex, the image makes him the lay representative – the local public authority – in a scene of diplomatic ritual.

The transformation of the familiar kneeling donor motif into a figure that offers his oversight to an institutional archive embraces the new place cartularies and records occupied in 12th-century society. Vierzon after all, produced a cartulary (with nearly a dozen images), so it was not unaware of the importance of written records and their diverse archival forms. What is striking, however, is how the image makes Ambrannus, through his personal handling of the monastery's archive, a diplomatic representative. Ambrannus's offering of the complete codex posits him as diplomatic agent for the monastery's records, those of the deep past and also those to come.

A remarkable image from a secular cartulary conveys a similar message (Figure 21.8). The opening folio of the *Liber Feudorum Maior* (*LFM*) shows Alfonso (d. 1196), count of Barcelona and king of Aragón, conversing with Ramón de Caldes, dean of the cathedral and keeper of the count's archives. The two exchange a sheet of parchment, as more sheets lay in a heap behind them.[27] Their conversation concerns the careful selection of the documents that Alfonso will charge Ramón with transcribing, resulting in the codex in which the illumination appears.[28] To the right, a smaller figure, a scribe, busily works at a desk, presumably already recording the selected charters onto codex-ready parchment.

The *LFM*, originally in two volumes of nearly 900 folios, collected documents stretching from the 10th century to Alfonso's own time. The white scraps depict in legible lettering the names of historical persons entered in the cartulary's many acts, adding a touch of anecdotal authenticity to the *mise-en-abyme*. While the acts deal with a range of affairs, they generally serve to confirm – both in their subject but also in their geographic range – numerous gifts, particularly those that establish Alfonso's land rights in Catalonia and surrounding areas, reinforcing claims at a time when he sought to consolidate his territorial power.[29]

Figure 21.7

Paris, BNF lat. 9865, fol. 5v. (Cartulary of Vierzon): Ambrannus of Vierzon, offering a codex to the abbot (photo: BNF)

FIGURE 21.8

Barcelona, Arxiu de la Corona d'Aragó, Cancelleria reial, reg. 1, fol. 1r. (Liber Feudorum Maior): Alfonso and Ramón de Caldes discussing the cartulary's redaction (photo: Barcelona, ACA)

The surprising opening illumination provides a kind of behind-the-scenes look at the cartulary's creation. Ramon is undoubtedly the master of the archive (as his dedicatory preface following the image makes perfectly clear), but the image suggests Alfonso pored over each document himself and gave his approval. It asks us to believe that he drew upon his own discernment, perhaps upon his political but also diplomatic sensibilities, to determine the appropriateness of each document's inclusion in the new codex. Such studious review effectively reconfirms the commitments, for one imagines that any irrelevant or dubious document would not have passed muster. It is as if Alfonso's personal consultation of each charter offers a new signature by his own hand – *manu mea*, per the customary phrase – as once again courtly witnesses look on to observe the new 'diplomatic' performance. The image places Alfonso in the role of agent in the cartulary's production, a symbolic overseer of stored records and guarantor of their archival value, and as in the Vierzon example, it makes him the validating authority even of acts passed centuries before.

AS AUTHOR

Alfonso's depicted investment in the diplomatic archive may be exceptional, but other contemporary images insinuate lay donors' involvement in diplomatic production. In a general way, for instance, patrons shown transferring scrolls as representative of their gifts evince personal involvement in the diplomatic process. Sometimes the scroll's pictorial role receives special emphasis. The centrality accorded scrolls in the *Libro de las Estampas*, for example, suggests their role as more than mere visual props. The image of Ordoño III (d. 956) shows the king handling differently his kingly attribute (the sceptre) and his charter (Figure 21.5). The latter he grasps energetically with both hands, while the sceptre wielded in the crook of one hand seems to get in the way.[30] The inclusion of a sceptre is expected. Yet if the sceptre represents the investment of royal authority, one could imagine the scroll, in parallel fashion, as an attribute too, namely of diplomatic authority. Indeed, the image's acute emphasis on tactile engagement with the charter scroll, as elsewhere in the codex, seems to invest it with more than mere symbolic proxy for a visually absent gift. The pictorial emphasis suggests the charter's *material* significance, as if the energetic embrace of scrolls is the artist's way of showing the rulers' personal implication in his own diplomatic production.

Some examples remove the ambiguity. For a royal charter recording the gift of tithes from Pedro I (d. 1104) of Aragon to the bishop of Huesca, a line-drawn image shows Pedro presenting a charter (Figure 21.9).[31] More precisely, he extends a wax tablet (discussed later) to the bishop (Figure 21.10). The image thus records for posterity an imagined scene of diplomatic conveyance. The diplomatic quality is further generated by the image's placement: coming at the end of the text and just adjacent to Pedro's signing phrase, it assumes the role of a pictorial signature. Pedro's signature – 'hoc signum manu mea facio' – constitutes a personal enunciation that bestows on its accompanying *imago* the weight of pictorial *ego*. The image and signature work together as joint aspects of a deictic utterance, a self-declaration of personal implication, just as they are two forms of notarial validation.

Most importantly, the image specifically renders the king as scribe: while he extends a wax tablet in one hand, he clearly holds a stylus in the other. Not content merely to bestow a scroll or charter as seen previously, Pedro has taken it upon himself to write out his donation. The choice of a wax tablet in the scene is also significant. Tablets, apart from their utilitarian uses, participated in a particular visual discourse concerning practices of writing.[32] They appear in scenes that highlight the activities of scribes and authors; sometimes their presence highlights the ephemeral quality of wax writing vis-à-vis parchment writing, and sometimes their presence also underscores the orality of an event or performance.[33]

The charter's wax tablet offers such allusions. It alludes to the donation ceremony and the initial oral agreement, as it suggests a hastily noted initial textual rendering before being ultimately recorded for posterity onto parchment by a chancery scribe. The image of the wax tablet strives to recover lost immediacy, even authenticity, by imaging Pedro's personal authorship in an initial, fugitive

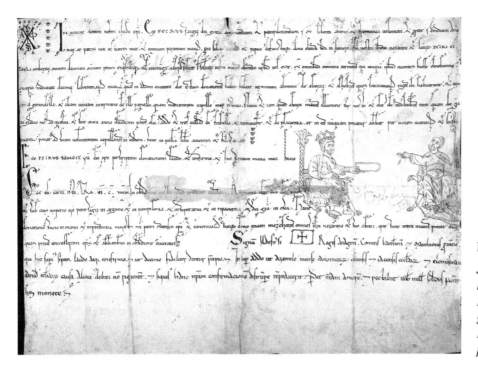

FIGURE 21.9

Jaca, Archivo de la Catedral, leg. 1, docs. reales, 10-E: Pedro I of Aragón offering a gift to Bishop Pedro (photo: Robert A. Maxwell, with permission)

FIGURE 21.10

Jaca, Archivo de la Catedral, leg. 1, docs. reales, 10-E Pedro I of Aragón offering a gift to Bishop Pedro, detail (photo: Robert A. Maxwell, with permission)

medium. It is a reminder of immediacy that a simple parchment record might otherwise allow one to forget.

Even more remarkable is that this particular parchment is itself a later confirmation, a 12th-century copy of the 1098 original. The original survives, and it is undecorated, so this imagined scribal donation scene is this copy's invention. That fact suggests that the episcopal chancery of the mid 12th century desired a visualisation of Pedro's commitments, perhaps as a means of re-authenticating the act in more than just a juridical sense: the performance of the donor writing carried great weight and was worth memorialising pictorially. With the signature of Pedro's successor, Alfonso, added to the confirmation copy, the new document constructs an implied scribal genealogy from one ruler to the next. It projects for Alfonso a heritage of 'literate' donorship that the episcopal chancery must have felt strengthened its archival copy.

A similarly retrospective *mise-en-scène* of writerly diplomatic is on display in the chronicle-cartulary of Saint-Martin-des-Champs (Figure 21.11).[34] Two illuminations on one folio present a two-part performance of Henry I's patronage towards the Paris abbey. The upper scene signals Henry's agency as founder of the new church. It shows him enthroned on a folding stool under a royal canopy; he gestures towards the church that he had provided for in his foundation charter of 1059–60 but had not yet seen built by the time of his death in August 1060.

In contrast to the top image, the bottom of the page features a scene of royal audience (Figure 21.12). A half-dozen tonsured clerics approach and petition the crowned, seated king. Henry addresses the group, brandishing a curling sheet of parchment with one hand as he wields a stylus in the other. The illumination reproduces legibly the words 'Libertas æcclesiæ Sancti Martini' that clearly identify the document's gist. The stylus is positioned just beneath the king's signature: 'Henrici regis signu[m]'. More precisely, the stylus indicates the mark of the cross, reinforcing the idea that Henry's own hand – *manu mea* – has made the cross, validating his signature that ratifies

FIGURE 21.11

London, British Library, Add. 11662, fol. 4r. (Cartulary of Saint-Martin-des-Champs): Henry I shown founding a monastery and in a diplomatic ceremony (photo: © The British Library Board)

FIGURE 21.12

London, British Library, Add. 11662, fol. 4r. (Cartulary of Saint-Martin-des-Champs). Henry I in a diplomatic ceremony (photo: © The British Library Board)

the charter's contents. The staged scene allows one to imagine Henry signing the document just before handing it over the waiting clerics. The clerics hold still additional parchment charters, no doubt to suggest that each of those, in turn, will receive confirmation by the king's own hand.

The scenes juxtapose two kinds of actions within a performance of patronage: Henry commands or supervises the foundation above, while he exercises his writerly, diplomatic role below. This juxtaposition offers a stark demonstration of patronage iconography's shifting concerns, from that privileging the donor with his church model (above), to a scene implicating the donor in a textual, and specifically diplomatic, performance (below). In the latter scene, furthermore, the gifts spelled out are intangibles (the 'libertates') difficult to pictorialise but which a written document could elaborate and guarantee. These two pendant images suggest that in the new diplomatic culture the gesture of foundation found its confirmation not solely in the erected church, but in its diplomatic trace.

When the church was completed in 1067, Henry's son, Philip, presided over the dedication.[35] The chronicle-cartulary, consisting of just three acts, was probably completed about that time.[36] The first document is one of Henry's, the foundation charter itself that is the subject of the illuminations. 'Libertas' on the brandished scroll, beyond its obvious message, may also refer to a passage in which Henry rhetorically makes an oath to the canons.[37] Philip issued the two other diplomas included in the cartulary, one of which in particular (no. 2) confirms the liberties granted by his father. As at Huesca, *picturing* of writing – played out as notarial performance – was part of the creative 're-validation' of earlier agreements by a successor. The retrospective casting of an earlier donor as a stylus-holding performer of diplomatic practice may have lent greater authenticity through an imagined 'literate' ancestry.

AS READER

Prior to the widespread increase in textual records, performance and orality – and the memory thereof – were essential to agreements and transactions. The written document, with its signatures and wax seals of authentication, translated performance and memory into a material trace for posterity. Cartularies were direct products of this interest in re-presenting one kind of material trace (sealed charter) as another (bound codex), with all of the archival advantages a cartulary offered.[38] Sometimes an interest in transforming the material document spread to monumental contexts, as donations and privileges were sometimes recorded on church façades and choirs, and even on city gates and bridges. These inscriptions often used the language, formulas and even validating signs of contemporary diplomatic. At Sant'Antimo in Tuscany, the steps leading to the altar include an inscription of a local layman's gifts for a re-foundation (Figure 21.13).[39] The

FIGURE 21.13

Sant'Antimo: donation inscription before and around the altar (photo: Robert A. Maxwell)

inscription continued onto a column flanking the altar, containing the eschatocol, witness and notary names, and date. Its location before and around the altar is pregnant with sacred meaning, and not least because, in keeping with common practice, the initial donation would have been made at a ceremony that included an oath upon the altar. At the Asturian church San Salvador de Fuentes, a 12th-century inscription on the jambs of an interior door transcribes the foundation gift made long before by a local layman in the 1020s, listing three 'signing' witnesses (Figures 21.14, 21.15).[40] Inscriptions such as these do not qualify as charters per se, as their standing in legal use is unclear at best, but like parchment charters they constituted a material trace of an earlier performance, and they clearly aimed to affect diplomatic style.[41] Some inscriptions even emulated the visual effect of a charter, as at Treviño (Burgos), where a rectangular relief recording the founding donation by a local layman imitates a charter form, including even a seal (Figure 21.16).[42]

As an object of public regard, these monumentalised acts entered the public discourse.[43] Their importance may have been more as *images* of text than as legible documents, as they must have been a challenge to read even for the most accomplished lector. Regardless of their legibility, however, the public rendering of the document promoted the named lay figures as actors in a textual discourse. It rendered patrons as performers in the social community of textual production.

These public images at the same time transform the spectator into a diplomatic 'participant'. They draw the viewer into a witnessing role, insofar as the inscribed image constitutes a recreation (of sorts) of an earlier diplomatic performance. Given that acts of donation were often not located finitely in the past but were revived when disputes arose – even to the point where any living witnesses to the original agreement might be summoned, or the original charter was produced for inspection – the monumental inscriptions present a renewed diplomatic staging. The public viewer becomes party to that restaging.

Donor images could emphasise readership in a similarly public way, drawing attention to the donor as the reading subject of his own donation's diplomatic ceremony. On a relief from Clérieu (Drôme) a layman dressed in a long mantle sits facing a clerical figure, recognisable as such by the tonsure, mantle and incised cross (Figure 21.17).[44] The cleric holds a book and demonstratively points at its open page, as if inviting his interlocutor, the layman, to

FIGURE 21.14

Fuentes, donation inscription on jambs of a lateral door (photo: Robert A. Maxwell)

FIGURE 21.15

Fuentes, donation inscription on door jambs, detail (photo: Robert A. Maxwell)

FIGURE 21.16

Treviño, foundation donation above entrance (photo: Pedro Novella)

FIGURE 21.17

Clérieu: donation relief (Ottawa, National Gallery of Canada, #116.959; after De Galier 1869)

see what is written. The relief's inscription, while difficult to interpret, qualifies a certain Hugh as 'magister', a title that (along with the incised cross) has led scholars to consider him a Templar. It names another individual 'Silvius', recently identified as Silvius II, lord of Clérieu.[45] The scene thus portrays the cleric holding up the text of the layman's gift for his inspection. The composition fixes Silvius in a visual discourse of written text. It presents him as a 'reader' in the sense that he is shown in the act of recognising the probative textual record.[46]

A somewhat different, yet still readerly portrayal commands a tympanum scene at the small church of Mervilliers (Eure-et-Loire) (Figure 21.18).[47] A local knight, dressed in chain mail and a helmet and identified in the inscription as Rembaud, kneels as if in an attitude of vassalage before St George, patron of *milites*, to offer him a gift in the form of a vase or pyx-reliquary.[48] Behind St George stands a priest, who acknowledges the gift by his blessing gesture. The priest stands before an altar bearing a Eucharistic chalice that is itself blessed by the hand of God emerging from the tympanum's frame.[49] Further to the right, crouching in the corner, a small tonsured scribe busily records the donation. His parchment scroll continues in a ribbon encircling the entire tympanum to provide the sculpture with a frame of text. The scribe's text appears not incised but in relief, just as ink sits raised in relief upon parchment. It reads: 'Herbert, just as William, granted, and the knight Rembaud his descendent transferred to me [his] present [terrestrial] treasures in order to gain those that have no end'.[50] Rembaud hopes that with his gift of an earthly possession, he will receive in return the eternal gifts of Heaven, juxtaposing an act of giving to an eschatological purpose. The reciprocity described in the inscription is a classic feature of medieval gift economy.

The inscription's nod to forebears Herbert and William makes the scene, like others discussed previously, a retrospective confirmation.[51] As in those other works, the scribe at Mervilliers writes this patronage performance as a new charter; he is recording not an original performance but a notarial confirmation of an original performance that is renewed in front of a contemporary signatory, Rembaud. Visually, too, the composition emphasises this new notarial process: the scribe's confirmation text literally circumscribes the event. Unfurling around the tympanum, the charter encompasses the full experience of the diplomatic act, embracing at once the terrestrial and celestial, the priestly and lay, the liturgical and feudal. This performance of patronage is rendered through a textual prism, just as it is also the written word that provides the stage for the actors to assume their roles. The scene makes Rembaud as much the reader of the text as he is its producer: without his generous gesture, this textual performance would not take place.[52]

The Clermont capital assembles several of these codes, making the donor a reading actor in a textualised performance. The layman Stephanus points to a book, but unlike at Clérieu it is an angel that holds the codex (Figure 21.19). With one hand the angel graces the inscribed lettering of Stephanus's name, while with the other he guides the layman's hand over the inscription. Stephanus's fingers point to the precise words spelling out his agency – 'fieri jussit' – although as noted previously, the phrase lacks precision to identify Stephanus's particular

FIGURE 21.18

Mervilliers, former tympanum, scene of donation (photo: Robert A. Maxwell)

FIGURE 21.19

Clermont: Notre-Dame-du-Port, hemicycle capital. Stephanus offering a capital, detail (photo: Robert A. Maxwell)

intervention. In the context of the present discussion, one could understand the book as a medium of diplomatic, as a cartulary or other notarial record – and indeed, the paired figures with text between them recall somewhat the motif of proffering a scroll, discussed previously (cf. Duke Gisulf). The book's role, however, is more likely symbolic. Prompted by the angel's presence, the open codex surely represents the Book of Life, although it is not out of the question that an ecclesiastical institution may have considered their archival records of gifts as having bearing on the latter. Stephanus's generosity would earn him mention in the *liber vitae* – which he seems to read – with the hope of receiving heaven's counter-gift, salvation.[53]

The scene emphasises the material, textual recording of patronage in other important respects, most notably in Stephanus's touching, indeed fingering, of the written record, a detail also noted in examples discussed previously. The tactile performance may have reminded viewers of the phrase '*manu mea*' and that here would be introduced by an angelic 'scribe'. The touching hand could also be construed a gesture of guided reading, as at Clérieu, as Stephanus personally confirms the donation's material trace as text. Of course, the materiality of the gift is registered on another level by the miniature leafy capital just above the book. Yet even while Stephanus's donation is rendered by the miniature capital he offers – employing the venerable donor-and-his-model motif – the scene's imagery recasts the donation – and the old motif – into a textual performance.

Though this is the only face that records the donation, the capital's flanking scenes of *Psychomachia*, where *Caritas* and *Largitas* trample vices, complement the donor motif's message of salvational economy (Figure 21.20). Like the battling Virtues, Stephanus too, participates in the triumph over a vice: Avarice spills out from the adjacent *Psychomachia* face and thus finds himself defeated not only by *Largitas* but also trampled by Stephanus. Stephanus's feet land upon Avarice's clasped hands that mimic a vassalage gesture, and indeed mimic Stephanus's own hand above that is received by the angel. The message is clear: vassalage to Avarice is broken, as Stephanus's victory was won through his material largesse to

FIGURE 21.20

Clermont: Notre-Dame-du-Port, hemicycle capital. Psychomachia (photo: Robert A. Maxwell)

Notre-Dame. That the angel's gesture towards Stephanus resembles the taking of hands in the vassalage rite, only further reminds one that gifts to the Church were above all commitments to saints and that the saints reciprocally offered their patronage, or protection. All of these elements conjure the complex oral, aural and increasingly diplomatic cast of donorship in the 12th century, and of the new visual vocabulary deployed to convey that intertwined complexity.

CONCLUSIONS

Brian Stock's fundamental study of literacy in the 12th century offered a new framework for reconsidering the traditional binary model of literacy/illiteracy.[54] Stock proposed instead a model that included shades of orality, literacy and textuality, wherein literacy was a middle ground. Stock's literacy described not so much a medium of communication, as a shifting, interpretive cultural space that derived its discursive existence from the opposing poles of oral and textual means of communication. Scenes of donation, with their inclusion of diplomatic practices, could be considered to occupy that middle space described by Stock. Representations of donor performance in these centuries drew on both oral traditions and textual novelties, the two bleeding into one another to produce ultimately an image that suggests a new relationship of the donor to past oral and present textual cultural conditions. These images furthermore project a form of 'literacy' based not on the layman's ability to read or write, but on his belonging to a culture that imposed new ideas about the place of writing in society. The rise in diplomatic practice and the importance of written documents redrew expectations for how patronage could be, or should be, visualised.

It would probably not be accurate to interpret these images as tacit celebrations of advances in 'literacy' by the laity or of their mastery of textual knowledge, even if both were indeed on the rise.[55] Instead, these images may present a more sober reality: the laity's subjection to a textual discourse that it scarcely controlled and only modestly mastered. Whereas donors had long benefited from the majestic, even auric, power of donation ceremonies, with their gestural rites, sworn oaths and witnesses, these images reinforced the rising diplomatic component of donations. The laity was obliged to keep step with the new textual discourse of donation, and those responsible for these images – ecclesiastical institutions for the most part – may have wanted to show patrons as subjects within that discourse. The fact that many of the examples are also retrospective scenes featuring ancestral figures only further suggests that these institutions understood the importance of showing patronage, even that of the past, as occupying a place in a textual diplomatic community and of the gifts themselves having a textual history. While rising diplomatic practice clearly impacted how lay patronage was performed, the transformation clearly also involved the pictorial assimilation of patrons into a discourse of diplomatic literacy, with all of the social changes and ideological impositions implied.

NOTES

[1] See E. Lipsmeyer, 'The Donor and his Church Model in Medieval Art: From Early Christian Times to the Late Romanesque Period', (unpublished Ph.D. thesis, Rutgers University, 1981, 2 vols.); B. Decron, 'Images de fondateurs, donateurs et personnages historiques gravitant autour d'un établissement réligieux, France XIIème siècle', (unpublished D.E.A., Université de Poitiers, 1985); and E.S. Klinkenberg, *Compressed Meanings: The Donor's Model in Medieval Art to around 1300: [The] Origin, Spread and Significance of an Architectural Image in the Realm of Tension between Tradition and Likeness* (Turnhout 2009).

[2] A partial inscription survives but is too enigmatic to clarify these questions; see V. Debiais, "Les inscriptions du vitrail de la Crucifix," in *La cathédrale Saint-Pierre de Poitiers: enquêtes croisées*, eds. Cl.-A. Schmitt, M.-Th. Camus, V. Debiais, B. Fillion-Braguet, C. Treffort (La Crech 2013), 70.

[3] See B. Boerner, 'L'image romane d'un donateur exemplaire', *Le plaisir de l'art du Moyen âge: commande, production et réception de l'oeuvre d'art, mélanges offerts à Xavier Barral I Altet*, ed. R. Alcoy, D. Allios and M.A. Bilotta (Paris 2012), 169–174; A. Heyman, *'That Old Pride of the Men of the Auvergne': Laity and Church in Auvergnat Romanesque Sculpture* (London 2005), 6–10, 146ff. The date of the hemicycle capitals is debated, with propositions ranging from the early decades of the 12th century to *c.* 1180s–90s (cf. J. Wirth, *La datation de la sculpture médiévale* (Geneva 2004), 73, 144–145). Heyman (146–148) prefers the 1120s–30s.

[4] Art historical interest, with its varying approaches, is effectively traced in J. Caskey, 'Whodunnit? Patronage, the Canon, and the Problematics of Agency in Romanesque and Gothic Art', in *A Companion to Medieval Art: Romanesque and Gothic in Northern Europe*, ed. C. Rudolph (Oxford 2006), 193–212, esp. 196–198. Anthropological studies – ranging from the work of Marcel Mauss to Alfred Gell – have had much to do with this critical awakening.

[5] J. Caskey, 'Medieval Patronage & its Potentialities', in *Patronage, Power and Agency in Medieval Art*, ed. C. Hourihane (Princeton 2013), 3–30.

[6] E. Pastan, 'Imagined Patronage: The Bayeux Embroidery & its Interpretive History', in *Patronage, Power and Agency in Medieval Art*, ed. C. Hourihane (Princeton 2013), 54–76. For a similarly critical art-historical view of how patronage has been investigated, see M.H. Caviness, 'Anchoress, Abbess and Queen: Donors and Patrons or Intercessors and Matrons?', in *The Cultural Patronage of Medieval Women*, ed. J.H. McCash (Athens, Ga. 1996), 105–154.

[7] Barbara Rosenwein, for example, demonstrated that a primary aim of gifts to Cluny prior to about 1050 was to create a perpetual bond between monastery and individual that fostered 're-gifting' (*'To Be the Neighbor of Saint Peter': The Social Meaning of Cluny's Property, 909–1049* (Ithaca, NY 1989)). Other important studies include G. Duby, 'Taking, Giving and Consecrating', in *The Early Growth of the European Economy*, trans. H.B. Clarke (Ithaca, NY 1974), 48–57; A. Angenendt, 'In honore Salvatoris. Vom Sinn und Unsinn der Patrozinienkunde [I & II]', *Revue d'Histoire écclésiastique* 97 (2002), 431–456 & 791–823; A.-J. Bijsterveld, 'The Medieval Gift as Agent of Social Bonding and Political Power: A Comparative Approach', in *Medieval Transformation: Texts, Power, and Gifts in Context*, eds. E. Cohen and M. de Jong (Leiden 2001), 123–156; B. Jussen, 'Religious Discourse of Gift in the Middle Ages: Semantic Evidences (Second to Twelfth Centuries)', in *Negotiating the Gift: Pre-Modern Figurations of Exchange*, eds. G. Algazi, V. Groebner, B. Jussen (Göttingen 2003), 173–192. A good brief historiographic overview: L.S. Benkmann, 'Schenken als historisches Phänomen: Gewandelte Sichtweisen zum mittelalterlichen Schenken im Gang der Forschung', in *Moderne Mediävistik: Stand und Perspektiven der Mittelalterforschung*, ed. H.W. Goetz (Darmstadt 1999), 206–212.

[8] Similar donor capitals are found at several nearby Auvergnat churches, including Volvic, Trizac and Saint-Nectaire. These are studied as a group in Heyman, *'That Old Pride'* (as n. 3), 1–73, 141–151.

[9] In Lipsmeyer, 'The Donor' (as n. 1) the primary concern is to trace an evolution in representations of the church-model type, and for these examples Lipsmeyer detects a shift away from the purely symbolic meaning that was prevalent in earlier periods towards greater historicising significance. See also Klinkenberg, *Compressed Meanings* (as n. 1), 59–70, 76ff, 117ff. There is at present no reckoning of the number of lay donor images produced in these centuries; the donor-model type is duly inventoried in the works by Lipsmeyer and Klinenberg, but no accounting is yet available for all other types, including the ones discussed in the present essay. Some additional material is found in C. Sauer, *Fundatio und Memoria: Stifter und Klostergründer im Bild, 1100 bis 1350* (Göttingen 1993).

[10] e.g. The Hague, Kgl. Bibliothek, MS 76-F-1, the *c.* 900 Egmond Gospels, whose donor images were added *c.* 975. They show (fols 214v–215r) Graf Dietrich von Friesland with his wife Hildegard placing this codex on the altar at Egmont. (Cf. J. Prochno, *Das Schreiber- und Dedikationsbild in der deutschen Buchmalerei, bis zum Ende des 11. Jahrhunderts [800–1100]* (Leipzig 1929), 63; also *Bernward von Hildesheim und das Zeitalter der Ottonen, Katalog der Ausstellung, Hildesheim, 1993* (Mainz 1993), 2: 262–263, cat. V-8.)

[11] Auxerre, Bibliothèque municiaple, MS 227, fol. 22. More precisely, Girart offered a *villa* for the new foundation of nuns, *c.* 859–60. See R.B.C. Huygens, ed., *Monumenta Vizeliacensia* (Turnhout 1976), xix, where he dates the manuscript to *c.* 1170 at the latest (post-1168). For the *testamentum* text, see Huygens, 243–248.

[12] Vatican, Biblioteca Apostolica Vaticana, Barb. Lat. 2724, fol. 47 (*c.* 1110s-20s). For the text: *Chronicon Vulturnense*, ed. V. Federici, 3 vols. (Rome, 1929–1933), I: doc. 9. Gisulf made a gift of lands and other privileges to three Beneventan brothers, Paldo, Taso and Tato, who in turn used the gift for the founding of the monastery. The document accompanying the image, the only record of the gift, is a forgery.

[13] There are a handful of such scenes in the manuscript, some involving kings. Depicting gift-giving in this manner levels the social playing field for royalty and nobility; for both, gift-giving is equated with textual exchange.

[14] León, Archivo de la Catedral, Cód. 25 (*c.* 1200), e.g. on fols 12v, 17v, 21v.

[15] Santiago de Compostela, Archivo de la Catedral, s.n., e.g. on fols 11r, 12r, 17r. The manuscript is dated *c.* 1129–34 for the first forty folios.

[16] Avranches, Bibliothèque municipale, MS 210 (*c.* 1154), e.g. on fol. 23.

[17] On the shadowy Countess Sancha, see M. Torre Sevilla Quiñones de León and F. Galván Freile, 'La condesa doña Sancha: una nueva aproximación a su figura', *Medievalismo: Boletín de la Sociedad Española de Estudios Medievales* 5 (1995), 9–30.

[18] M.T. Clanchy, *From Memory to Written Record*, 2nd ed. (Oxford 1993), 2–3, 28–29.

[19] A. Bartoli Langeli, 'Private Charters', in *Italy in the Early Middle Ages, 476–1000*, ed. C. La Rocca (Oxford 2002), 205–219, at 206–207.

[20] Arguments against overestimation, though with merit, are polemically overstated in P. Bertrand, 'A propos de la révolution de l'écrit (x–xiii siècle). Considérations inactuelles', *Médiévales* 56 (2009), 75–92.

[21] R. McKitterick, *The Carolingians and the Written Word* (Cambridge 1989), 77ff and 211–270; A. Rio, *Legal Practice and the Written Word in the Early Middle Ages: Frankish Formulae, c.500–1000* (Cambridge 2009), 13ff.; K. Bullimore, 'Folcwin of Rankwell: The World of a Carolingian Local Official', *Early Medieval Europe* 13 (2005), 43–77; J. Nelson, 'Literacy in Carolingian Government', in *The Uses of Literacy in Early Medieval Europe*, ed. R. McKitterick (Cambridge 1990), 258–296, esp. 266–267, 269–271. From a sample of some 2,000 charters from 10th-century Catalonia (however exceptional that territory's writing production may be) studied by Adam Kosto, some 45% concerned lay men and women exclusively ('Laymen, Clerics and Documentary Practices in the Early Middle Ages: The Evidence from Catalonia', *Speculum* 80, 1 (2005), 44–74).

[22] M. Innes, *State and Society in the Early Middle Ages: The Middle Rhine Valley, 400–1000* (Cambridge 2000), 111–118, at 118.

[23] P. Wormald, 'Charters, Law and the Settlement of Disputes in Anglo-Saxon England', in his *Legal Culture in the Early Medieval West* (London 1999), 289–311, e.g. 303: 'many later Anglo-Saxon laymen were as careful in their muniments as Aethelric had been in the early ninth century. Thus, precisely those most accustomed to pre-literate transactions were exploiting the implications of literacy'; M.B. Parkes, 'The Literacy of the Laity', in *The Mediaeval World*, eds. D. Daiches, A. Thorlby (London 1973), 555–577; also Clanchy, *From Memory* (as n. 18), 234ff, esp. 236–237. A recent collection highlights the advances in this domain: Warren Brown, et al., eds., *Documentary Culture and the Laity in the Early Middle Ages* (Cambridge 2013).

[24] Clancy, *From Memory* (as n. 18), 19, also 234–237.

[25] Paris, Bibliothèque nationale de France, MS lat. 9865, fol. 5v; for the text, see G. Devailly, ed., *Le cartulaire de Vierzon* (Paris 1963), 110–120. Three charters concern Ambrannus (nos 12, 13, 14): the first (844) was ratified by Charles the Bald and Archbishop Raoul of Bourges, offering among other things, the churches of Saint-Georges-sur-Moulon, Saint-Quentin-sur-Yèvre, Neuvy-sur-Barangeon and a chapel at Orçay; the second (844), also ratified by Charles the Bald and Archbishop Raoul, lists the lord's donation to Vierzon's affiliated abbey at Dèvres, including several churches and lands; the third (also 844), ratified by the same two dignitaries, lists additional offerings to the abbey of Dèvres, including Ambrannus's church St-Pierre at Vierzon. All three of these charters have raised suspicions by modern scholars (cf. Devailly, *Cartulaire*, 111). In the 12th century, Vierzon argued, against claims made by rival monastery Déols and the cathedral chapter at Bourges, its rights over Dèvres and all that latter's possessions; these three acts are crucial to those claims (Devailly, *Cartulaire*, 44–46). For more on Ambrannus and his role in the monastery's history, see R.A. Maxwell, "Le livre-objet entre oralité et 'literacy'. La *memoria* du medium dans le monde juridique," *Revue d'Auvergne*, spec. num. *Le livre à l'époque romane* (25ème Colloque International d'art roman à Issoire, 2015), in press.

[26] Cf. Caskey's argument in her 'Medieval Patronage' (as n. 5).

[27] Barcelona, Arxiu de la Corona d'Aragó, Cancelleria reial, Registres 1. The surviving folios were edited into a single-volume reconstruction (1 volume, 9 + 199f.) by F. Miquel Rossell; see his *Liber Feudorum Maior. Cartulario real que se conserva en el Archivo de la Corona de Aragón*, 2 vols. (Barcelona 1945).

[28] The text begins with a prologue in which Ramón offers praise to his patron and explains the archival project ('ut, his intrumentis ad memoriam revocatis . . . tum propter eternam magnarum rerum memoriam, ne inter vos et homines vestros, forte obliviionis occasione, aliqua questio vel discordia posset oriri'). See Miquel Rossell, *Liber Feudorum Maior* (as n. 27), 1: 1–2.

[29] See A.J. Kosto, 'The *Liber feudorum maior* of the Counts of Barcelona: The Cartulary as an Expression of Power', *Journal of Medieval History* 27 (2001), 1–22; T. Bisson, 'The Problem of Feudal Monarchy: Aragon, Catalonia, and France', *Speculum* 53, 3 (1978), 460–478, at 468–469; L.J. McCrank, 'Documenting Reconquest and Reform: The Growth of Archives in the Medieval Crown of Aragon', *American Archivist* 56 (1993), 256–318, esp. 280ff.

[30] Nonetheless, there can be no doubting the symbolic weight of the sceptre as a symbol of rule; here it even inserts itself in the written form of Ordoño's 'ego'.

[31] Jaca, Archivo de la Catedral, leg. 1, docs. reales, 10-E, a 12th-century copy of a 1098 original; see *Colección diplomática de Pedro I de Aragón y de Navarra*, ed. A. Ubieto Arteta (Zaragoza 1951), 276–279 (doc. 47). The image is discussed in J. Pijoán, *El arte románico*, 5th ed. (Madrid 1966), 105–106; and most recently in a short catalogue entry by L. Diego Barrado in *Sancho el Mayor y sus herederos: el linaje que europeizó los reinos hispanos. Baluarte, Pamplona, 26 de enero al 30 de abril de 2006*, ed. I.G. Bango Torviso (Pamplona 2006), 1: 189 (cat. 38). See further comments in R.A. Maxwell, 'Les chartes décorées à l'époque romane', *Bibliothèque de l'École des Chartes* 169 (2011), 11–39, at 22–28; and Susanne Wittekind, ' "Ego Petrus Sangiz rex donationem confirmo et hoc signum manu mea facio": Formen der Autorisierung in Illuminierten Urkundenabschriften des Hochmittelalters in Nordspanien', in *Buchschätze des Mittelalters: Forschungsrückblicke – Forschungsperspektiven*, ed. K. Gereon Beuckers, C. Jobst and S. Westphal (Regensburg 2011), 215–235, at 218–221. An early-13th-century copy – reproducing faithfully the scene of the 12th-century copy – also survives (Huesca, Archivo de la Catedral, 2–3–102).

[32] E. Lalou, 'Les tablettes de cire médiévales', *Bibliothèque de l'École des Chartes* 147 (1989), 123–140, who notes their importance in managing the affairs of abbeys and towns. On their role in images, see K. Graf, *Bildnisse schreibender Frauen im Mittelalter, 9. bis Anfang 13. Jahrhundert* (Basel 2002), 142–177, who studies their contributions to notions of writerly '*auctoritas*'.

[33] A telling juxtaposition of wax tablets as a hastily written scratch pad, on one hand, and the labour-intensive codex, on the other, is found in manuscripts of the visions of Hildegard of Bingen, e.g. Lucca, Biblioteca statale, MS 1942, fol. 1v, *Liber divinorum operum*. Orality is also often assumed with the inclusion of tablets, as in the Codex Manesse (Heidelberg, Universitätsbibliothek, Cpg. 848), where *Minnesänger* are shown with tablets that recall the ephemeral quality of music composition and performance. See Graf, *Bildnisse schreibender Frauen* (as n. 32); Maxwell 'Les chartes décorées' (as n. 31).

[34] London, British Library, Add. 11662, fol. 4r (*c.* 1067, before 1079), originally six folios, currently only five. It consists of a versified chronicle interspersed with three diplomas. The text and its images were copied in the mid 13th century (Paris, BNF, MS n.a.l. 1359); that version served J. Depoin for his edition in *Recueil de chartes et documents de Saint-Martin-des-Champs, monastère parisien* (Paris 1912), 1: 13–22, 27–31. On the images: M. Prou, 'Dessins du XIe siècle et peintures du XIIIe siècle', *Revue de l'art chrétien* 33, 4th ser., v.8 (1890), 122–128.

[35] Canons were installed *c.* 1059–60 at Henry's encouragement, but Philip I transferred the establishment to Cluny in 1079. For a historical summary, see most recently C. Denoël, 'La bibliothèque médiévale de Saint-Martin-des-Champs à Paris', *Scriptorium* 65, 1 (2011), 67–108, and pl. 26–36.

[36] At least before 1079 when Phillip transferred the collegiate church to the monks of Cluny.

[37] 'Et ut sine solicitudine, magis divinis quam seculi curis vacantes, valeant vivere, de facultatibus meis dotem faciens ecclesie, ob remedium patris mei matrisque meae animarum, atque pro mei, necnon conjugis et prolis salute et pace, haec illis largior possidenda perpetuo jure: Altare in primis ejiisdem basilice omni clarificatum libertate, et terras quas circa eandam ecclesiam prius habebam, et quas ibidem Ansoldus cum nepotibus suis Milone scilicet et Warino mihi dédit, concedente Hugone comite'. The word appears a few lines later as well, referring specifically to lands given immediately around the church, 'concedo, ea videlicet libertate ut nullus in eis aliquam redibitionem exigere presumat'. (Dupoin, *Recueil* [as n. 34], 1: 15–16.) More generally, the act emphasises Henry's role as Saint-Martin's 'restorer', reinforced with biblical analogies, including a preamble describing Henry's deeds for the Sponsus/Sponsa and a paraphrase of Ps. 25, 8 that gives Henry the voice of David: 'ego Henricus, Dei gratia rex Francorum, sedula cogitatione recolens qualiter "decorem domus Domini et locum habitationis ejus dilexi" '.

[38] The critical literature on cartularies as archive, source of *memoria*, monastic propaganda, among other issues, has developed significantly in recent decades. To name but one important work in this growing field: P. Geary, *Phantoms of Remembrance: Memory and Oblivion at the End of the First Millennium* (Princeton 1994).

³⁹ In 1118 Bernard, a local count, ceded to Ildebran, son of Rusticus, the possessions and rights that he held in all Italy; the latter in turn presented these gifts to Sant'Antimo. The agreement amounts to more than a simple *testamentum*, however, as it involves complex agreements with several individuals, including Emperor Henry V; see W. Kurze, 'Zur Geschichte der toskanischen Reichsabtei S. Antimo im Starciatal', in *Adel und Kirche: Gerd Tellenbach zum 65. Geburtstag dargebracht von Freunden und Schülern*, J. Fleckenstein, K. Schmid, eds. (Freiburg 1968), 295–306, who explains that the inscription amounts to a declaration of refoundation.

⁴⁰ See the text and discussion in F. Diego Santos, *Inscripciones medievales de Asturias* (Oviedo 1994), 214–219.

⁴¹ Insofar as the inscriptions provide a material trace of a diplomatic performance, they achieve what charters sought to achieve. They differ, however, in legal value: charters were summoned in cases of dispute, and thus had the weight of juridical probity. See the measured discussion on inscriptions' legal parameters in V. García Lobo and M.E. Martín López, 'Las inscripciones diplomáticas de época visigoda y altomedieval (siglos VI a XII)', *Mélanges de la Casa de Velázquez* 41 (2011), 87–108; and more generally R. Favreau, 'Fonctions des inscriptions au Moyen Âge', *Cahiers de civilisation médiéval* 32, no. 127 (1989), 203–222; idem, 'La notification d'actes publics ou privés par des inscriptions', in *Cinquante années d'études médiévales: à la confluence de nos disciplines. Actes du Colloque organisé à l'occasion du cinquantenaire du CESCM, Poitiers, 1er-4 septembre 2003*, C. Arrignon, et al., eds. (Turnhout 2006), 637–664.

⁴² It includes a 'seal' set in high relief, as a real wax seal would be in relief on parchment, thereby producing a striking visual analogy. Rather than the seal of the donor or church, the seal reproduces the monogram of Christ, the Chi-Rho, asserting that the church confirms the donation in the name of Christ. On Treviño, see M.J. Portilla Vitoria, and J.E. López de Sabando, eds., *Catálogo monumental, Diócesis de Vitoria. 2: Arciprestazgos de Treviño-Albaina y Campezo* (Vitoria 1968), 217–218. I am grateful to Juan Antonio Olañeta for bringing this example to my attention.

⁴³ Cf. Favreau, 'La notification d'actes publics' (as n 41). See also more generally A. Petrucci, *Public Lettering: Script, Power, and Culture*, trans. L. Lappin (Chicago 1993).

⁴⁴ Ottawa, National Gallery of Canada, 16.959, 520 x 130 mm. The toponym corresponds today to Clérieux in the Drôme.

⁴⁵ On the lower frame in two lines: SILVIVS FVNDAVIT VG/VS MAGISTER R(ECEPIT). In the pictorial space, between the two heads: GVIRALD STEFANE. See W. Cahn, 'A Romanesque Relief from Clérieu (Drôme)', in *Iconographica. Mélanges offerts à Piotr Skubiszewski*, eds. R. Favreau, M.-H. Debiès (Poitiers 1999), 23–27. Cahn proposed Silvius II and identified a set of donations that Silvius made to the Templar community Richerenches in Vaucluse. Cahn adds (27) that, 'Images of donors or scenes depicting transactions intended to enhance the trustworthiness of these legal instruments in the eye of beholders, and perhaps foster on them a degree of "liturgical" solemnity. This, no doubt, was also the intention of the Clérieu relief'.

⁴⁶ The other two inscribed names continue to cause scholars problems. One possibility, though purely conjectural, is that rather than Silvius and Hugh, the sculptor portrayed the other two named figures, Giraldus and Stephanus. The relief thus would represent an updated accounting, presided by Stephanus and Giraldus, of an earlier donation by Silvius – a kind of pictorial confirmation or commemoration of an earlier agreement, as seen in some examples discussed here where the image of a written text assumes historical, even historicising, status; see also Mervilliers, below.

⁴⁷ The parish church St Fiacre, in the diocese of Orléans, was secularised in *c.* 1810. Today the surviving church walls are part of a private farm. The relief and especially its inscription have inspired study, including: J. Quicherat, 'Une donation du XIIe siècle figurée en bas-relief', *Revue archéologique* 1 (1854), 171–173; G. Sainsot, 'Le tympan du portail de Mervillers', *Congrès archéologique* 67 (1900), 97–119; C. Maines, 'Good Works, Social Ties, and Hope for Salvation: Abbot Suger and St.-Denis', in *Abbot Suger and Saint-Denis: A Symposium*, ed. P.L. Gerson (New York 1986), 76–94, at 83–84; and most recently C. Voyer, 'Le geste efficace: le don du chevalier au saint sur le tympan de Mervilliers', in *Chevalerie & christianisme aux XIIe et XIIIe siècles*, eds. M. Aurell, C. Girbea (Rennes 2011), 101–121, emphasising liturgical context and the symbolic gestures of the social space. Dates attributed to the relief range from the 1110–20s to the last decades of the century. As several authors have pointed out, the scene bears certain similarities to the St Anne Portal in Paris, e.g. W. Cahn, 'The Tympanum of the Portal of Saint-Anne at Notre-Dame de Paris and the Iconography of the Division of the Powers in the Early Middle Ages', *Journal of the Warburg and Courtauld Institutes* 32 (1969), 55–72, at 61–62.

⁴⁸ The object may simply be a symbolic token, as tokens were offered in ceremonies of homage (cf. *infra*). The posture is suggestive of Rembaud's vassalage to St George and, more broadly, to the Church. On the liturgical resonance of gift-giving, see I. Rosé, 'Commutatio: le vocabulaire de l'échange chrétien au haut Moyen Age', in *Les élites et la richesse au haut Moyen Age*, eds. J.-P. Devroey, L. Feller, R. Le Jan (Turnhout 2011), 113–138.

⁴⁹ In diplomatic ritual, symbolic objects, including charters, were often set upon altars. See Clanchy, *From Memory* (as n. 18), 256–257; A. Angenendt, '"Cartam offerre super altare." Zur Liturgisierung von Rechtsvorgängen', *Frühmittelalterliche Studien* 36 (2002), 131–158; and for further literature, see R.A. Maxwell, 'Sealing Signs and the Art of Transcribing in the Vierzon Cartulary', *Art Bulletin* 81 (1999), 576–597, at 580 and esp. n. 24. Sainsot, 'Le tympan de Mervilliers' (as n. 47), 107–109, discusses a ritual tradition in this region that employed a gesture called 'per thecam', thus with a box or reliquary.

⁵⁰ HERBERTUS GUILERMUS SIMILITER / CUNC[ESSIT] / RENBAUDUS MILES / EIS [=EIUS] HERES / MICHI C[ON]TULIT / GAZA P[RAE]SENTES / UT HABERET / FINE CARENTES. This new transcription, by V. Debiais, is provided in Voyer, 'Le geste efficace' (as n. 47). The gains that have 'no end' may be a reference to Matthew 6, 19–20 and its 'treasury in heaven'.

⁵¹ Voyer, 'Le geste efficace' (as n. 47), 111: 'le tympan de Mervilliers offre une définition en image de la valeur efficace de l'acte diplomatique'.

⁵² The inclusion of an open book in Christ's hands (inscribed with the Alpha and Omega) extends the relief's theme of writing (by the scribe) to one of reading, inviting the viewer to contemplate Rembaud's donation presented for the viewer in the Book of Life

⁵³ Boerner points out the 'synchronization' of the two actions, which indicates that the one (the name in the *liber vitae*) is the direct result of the other (the gift): 'Un donateur exemplaire' (as n. 3), 171.

⁵⁴ B. Stock, *The Implications of Literacy; Written Language and Models of Interpretation in the Eleventh and Twelfth Centuries* (Princeton 1983).

⁵⁵ See nn. 21–24, *supra*.

REMARKS ON PATRON INSCRIPTIONS WITH RESTRICTED PRESENCE[1]

Wilfried E. Keil

On and in medieval churches there are a number of different types of inscription, among which are building inscriptions. These include patron- and foundation-inscriptions, inscriptions for the laying of the foundation stone, consecration inscriptions, which also include altar inscriptions, and inscriptions by the master of the workshop, and signatures.[2] There are also building- and foundation stone-inscriptions of limited visibility, in other words: inscriptions of *restricted presence*. They can be positioned up high on a church building, invisible to anyone passing by, like the AVE MARIA at Worms Cathedral (Figure 22.1), near the fifth level of the south-eastern tower (Figure 22.2), which was first documented in 2009 during our thorough examination of the building.[3] At the other extreme would be a foundation-stone inscription, like the one at Saint Michael in Hildesheim, discovered in 1908 during excavations (Figure 22.3).[4] The inscription reads: S(ANCTVS) · BENIAMIN/S(ANCTVS) · MATHEVS · A(POSTOLVS)/B(ERNWARDVS) + EP(ISCOPVS)/M(ILLESIMO) X (DECIMO).[5] It was not until the discovery of this particular foundation stone that the beginning of constructions at Saint Michael could be securely dated to the year 1010.

To explain the concept of *restricted presence* it is necessary to clarify the term *presence*. The production of presence is now, as it was in the Middle Ages, a central concept of Christian liturgy, especially during the holy sacrament where the real presence of God on earth is expressed and celebrated.[6] The term *production of presence* was established by literary scholar Hans Ulrich Gumbrecht. *Presence* is meant primarily in terms of space:[7] if something is *present* for us, it 'is in front of us, in reach of and tangible for our bodies'.[8] The production of presence can therefore be understood as an 'act of "bringing forth" an object in space'.[9] It 'implies that the (spatial) tangibility effect coming from the communication media is subjected, in space, to movements of greater or lesser proximity, and of greater or lesser intensity'.[10]

One can extend this definition of *presence* to the concept of an object's visibility. If it is only marginally visible, or not visible at all, we have a special case of *presence*; we have *restricted presence*. This term was first introduced by Assyriologist Markus Hilgert in the theoretical framework *Text-Anthropology* of the Heidelbergian Collaborative research centre 933 'Material Text Cultures'.[11] The restriction of presence can occur in terms of space, in terms of time, or in terms of person.

During the Middle Ages patrons sought to receive intercession for their donations. The purpose of donation was also to be part of the liturgical *memoria*.[12] The liturgical commemoration, the *memoria* for the living and the deceased, was written down in memorial books.[13] In the monastic community the living and deceased members, their relatives, their masters, friends and benefactors were united in the memorial acts of prayer and Eucharistic sacrifice. This association of the living and the dead in a spiritual community was made visible by the *libri memoriales* and necrologies.[14] The historical *memoria* is the realisation of the incidents and doings of a person, it stands for the knowledge and history of a person.[15] In the Middle Ages the personality of a person did not end with the death. The deceased were still legal subjects with legal capacity and actionability.[16] By mentioning the name, the presence of dead is reached and thus the *memoria* caused a mode of real presence of those physically absent. This applied not only to the dead, but also to individuals who were alive but physically not present.[17] Mentioning their name gave them a presence even after death and they could therefore, in a way, attend the ceremony.

In order to keep track of who was to be mentioned, the names were written down in the *liber memoralis* or the *liber vitae*.[18] The *libri memoriales* and necrologies were used in the Eucharistic liturgy and the Liturgy of the Hours of the monks.[19] Daily during Eucharist the names were recited from the *liber memorialis*, which lay on the altar.[20] In order not to forget the names of the entries sometimes they were inscribed together with the day of death on the wall of the apse or directly on the altar table in the early Middle Ages.[21] Around the 11th century the *libri memoriales* lost their importance, because there were simply too many names on the lists to be recited during the mass.[22] Thereafter they were recited only on specific days, for which purpose they used necrologies in the form of a calendar which also strengthened memory

© British Archaeological Association 2018

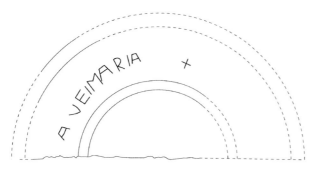

Figure 22.1

Worms Cathedral: south-eastern tower, fifth level, inscription AVE MARIA + (Aquilante De Filippo)

Figure 22.2

Worms Cathedral: south-eastern tower, view from south-west (Wilfried E. Keil)

of the individual.[23] These necrologies, where the deceased were recorded, were called sometimes furthermore *Liber memorialis* or *Liber vitae* throughout the Middle Ages.[24] To be part of the community as a layperson, it was necessary to act as a benefactor.[25] For the benefactors the concept of substitutional intercession was important: prayers by another person contributed to the salvation of the intended person.[26] For a donation, therefore, the patron received a counter-donation in the form of liturgical commemoration.[27] The entry in the *liber memorialis* recorded the commitment before God and the participants.[28]

Donations were made, therefore, to attain salvation. The entry into a memorial book and the reading of the name were connected with the idea of the heavenly book of life. Those who gained an entry in the memorial book hoped analogously for an entry in the heavenly book of life.[29]

To ensure the commemoration of specific donations, some patron inscriptions were carved in stone.[30] These inscriptions were usually placed in a visible place making them present for a possible viewer. Most of them mention the patron's name and his donation. There are also shorter versions, which mention little more than the name. An example of this is the patron inscription on the portal sculpture of a lion from the former south-portal of Worms Cathedral dating to around 1160,[31] which states in Romanesque majuscule: ADELR(ICVS) · ME · EM(IT). I was bought by Adelrich (Figure 22.4). The letters have a height of about 60 to 70 mm.[32] The lion is 600 mm high and was built into the western wall of the Anne-Chapel around 1300 (Figure 22.5), when a new gothic portal was built, together with other sculptures (Daniel in the lion's den, Habakkuk, two lions) from the former Romanesque portal.[33] The lion's inscription must have been clearly visible to church visitors in its original placement as part of the portal, identifying a patron of parts of the portal or its whole decoration. Portal inscriptions provide a special kind of presence, due to their placement near the entrance. The patron's name was seen by churchgoers as they entered, who then could commemorate him inside the church. In addition, portals were often used as important stations during processions. So, the patron's liturgical *memoria* was safely ensured.

Inside Worms Cathedral there is another patron inscription. This one, however, is much less visible. It is an inscription with *restricted presence*. It is part of the Juliana-relief, which is placed at the foot of a pilaster in the eastern sanctuary. The relief has three inscriptions in Romanesque majuscule: one which identifies the scene (IVLIANA), the artist's name (OTTO/ ME/FE/CIT) and the name of the patron (AD/EL/BR/AHT/MO/NE/TA/RI/VS) (Figures 22.6, 22.7).[34] In some cases the phrase

Figure 22.3

Hildesheim: St Michael, foundation stone (Wilfried E. Keil)

FIGURE 22.4

Worms Cathedral: Anne-Chapel (former Romanesque south portal), lion (photo of c. 1931) (E. Seebald, 'Das romanische Südportal', in Das Südportal des Wormser Doms, ed. W. Brönner, Denkmalpflege in Rheinland-Pfalz, Forschungsberichte, 5 (Worms 1999), 13, Figure 3 / Archiv of Worms Cathedral Doms zu Worms, W. Hege)

FIGURE 22.5

Worms Cathedral, Anne-Chapel (former Romanesque south portal), sculptures (photo of c. 1931) (E. Seebald, 'Das romanische Südportal', in Das Südportal des Wormser Doms, ed. W. Brönner, Denkmalpflege in Rheinland-Pfalz, Forschungsberichte, 5 (Worms 1999), 13, Figure 3 / Archiv of Worms Cathedral Doms zu Worms, W. Hege)

ME FECIT can be interpreted as a patron's inscription. This is primarily the case if the name has an addition, which refers to the donor. Such an interpretation, however, is also possible without such an addition. ME FECIT can be translated with the causative meaning 'he has had me made' as well as 'he has made me'.[35] In this case, however, the additional patron inscription clearly classifies the OTTO ME FECIT as the artist inscription. Since the relief is placed in the sanctuary, it was not accessible to the laity (Figure 22.8). The relief is also facing towards where the altar must have stood. For church visitors today the relief is still not visible. The inscriptions were therefore only noticeable for a specific circle of clerics. We have here a case of *restricted presence* in terms of person. The inscriptions were only visible to clerics who had access to the sanctuary.

The relief is 1250 mm high and shows Saint Juliana of Nikomedia standing on the shoulder of the devil in front of her, around whose neck she has slung a rope. To her left stands an angel on a pedestal, grabbing the devil's hair with its left hand and poking him with a lance. Parts of the relief on the right side have been damaged because of installations in a later period. According to the martyr's legend, the virgin Juliana refused marriage with the pagan prefect of Nikomedia on account of her faith. She was betrayed by her own father, and sentenced to torture and death. In her dungeon the devil, concealed behind an angel's appearance, tried to tempt Juliana into making a pagan sacrifice. Juliana recognised him, however, threw him to the ground and beat him with the chains she herself was held in. On the way to her own execution, she pulled the devil in the chains behind her and threw him down into a latrine. Juliana was executed in 305 in Nikomedia.[36] The helping angel in the picture could be interpreted as a depiction of the moral support of the Redeemer. Why the relief of Saint Juliana was placed in the eastern sanctuary of Worms Cathedral has not yet been plausibly explained: perhaps the reason is related to the patron of the relief.

The patron inscription ADELBRAHT MONETARIUS is written to the right side of the relief, with up to three letters per line. The letters have a height of 35 to 40 mm. Between the letters A and R of MONETARIUS is an H. It is cut deeper into the stone than the other letters or might have broken off. Rüdiger Fuchs of the Commissions of German Inscriptions assumes its origin to be around the same time as the rest of the relief.[37] However, it looks rather that the H was carved before the inscription, because the following letters of the inscription take consideration of the H: this is the only line where the letters of the inscription do not start at the same position. The meaning of this letter H has not been deciphered yet; it might be a technical mark, formed before the sculpture was made.

Adelbraht the moneyer is assumed to be a person found in several medieval documents. In one of them from around 1106 a *praepositus Adalbertus* is mentioned. In

281

1110 we find the name *Adelbraht praepositus* among the *majores clerici et laici* in the disclaimer of the properties of the provost of Saint Paul in Worms.[38] Both cases very likely refer to Adelbraht the moneyer. The relief demonstrates the ministeriales' activity in making donations to their new cathedral church right from the start of construction. The fast progress at the beginning of the building project might only have been possible through their support. The ministeriales of the city had the necessary economic capacity as well as influential political positions.[39]

After the dendrochronological re-dating of the eastern part of the Cathedral in the late 1970s and the early 1980s,[40] the relief was dated in the decade before 1132.[41] Rüdiger Fuchs compared the relief's inscriptions to others around that time and concluded that the ones of the Juliana relief are different. They seem simpler, or less progressive than the rest. He kept the *c.* 1130 dating due to the building's construction history, even though the formal aspects of the inscription made him contemplate a much earlier origin.[42] In 2009 Matthias Untermann undertook a new dating of some parts of the eastern sanctuary,[43] which is supported by stylistic assessment of the architectural constructional sculpture.[44] The new building of the cathedral is now seen as an initiative of Emperor Henry V, with construction beginning around the time his reign began in 1106. A consecration is also documented for 1110.[45] This revised dating fits well with an earlier dating of the inscription and the documents mentioning Adelbraht.

How strong an influence must Adelbraht have had if he was allowed to place his name at such an important place? More broadly, who was allowed to place his name there in general? It can't have been easy to get permission for such commemoration inside the sanctuary and more especially near the altar. It is not clear whether Adelbraht only donated the Juliana-relief or parts of the sanctuary as well. In any case, being allowed to place his name where he did shows his great influence. Maybe he was not the only patron, or he might have been the chief moneyer? It could be that his was not the only inscription on the walls of the sanctuary. During the baroque period the walls in the apse were smoothed and plastered for the placing of the high altar by Balthasar Neumann.[46]

FIGURE 22.6

Worms Cathedral: eastern-sanctuary, Juliana-relief (Wilfried E. Keil)

FIGURE 22.7

Worms Cathedral: eastern-sanctuary, Juliana-relief, inscription ADELBRAHT MONETARIVS (Wilfried E. Keil)

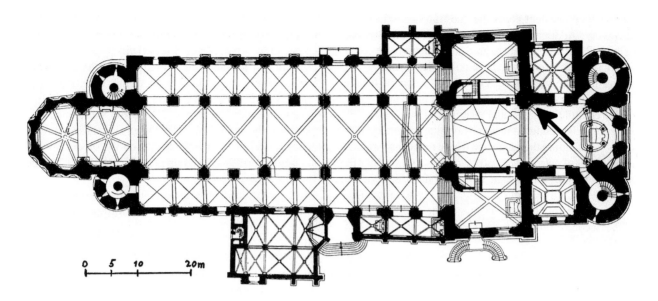

FIGURE 22.8

Worms Cathedral: plan with position of the Juliana-relief (modified from W. Hotz after R. Kautzsch)

The great influence moneyers had in Worms can be grasped if we take an event that took place somewhat later. Their community belonged to the economic and political elite of Worms and in 1165 they received, after their own request during a festive court-day, an imperial privilege from the Emperor Frederick I Barbarossa. It secured them their economic and political advantages, freed them of liabilities of common society and granted them their own jurisdiction, which in turn laid the ground for the city's jurisdiction fifteen years later.[47] Probably due to the moneyers' advance, Worms itself received similar privileges from Barbarossa in 1184, which also acknowledged and confirmed some privileges given by former emperors in 1074 and 1114.[48] Among the important privileges of the 1184 diploma were the granting of civil liberties and the lifting of the annual head-tax. Crucial parts of society were thereby given personal and economic freedom.[49] The privilege was made permanent in an inscription plaque above the north portal of Worms Cathedral, which was built between 1160 and 1165 (Figure 22.9).[50] It is not recorded from what material the plaque was made, but parts of its architectural frame in stone can still be seen today. The inscription itself only survived in its content, and in 1981 a bronze-image of the emperor along with the transcribed original wording of the inscription was put in its former place, after the design of sculptor Gustav Nonnenmacher.[51] The moneyers' privileges can be seen as the foundation for the advance in jurisdictional and other privileges for the city, which reached their peak in 1184.

The question remains: who might have been able to see the Adelbraht patron inscription? Who was supposed to

FIGURE 22.9

Worms Cathedral: north portal (Wilfried E. Keil)

read it? Its placement poses the question of its function. Why would Adelbraht put his name in a place of restricted visibility? Did he just want to mark his donation? He could have had other reasons than the purely legal function of having his name inscribed. During my research I have noticed a general tendency, especially in the eastern parts of church buildings, of name inscriptions with *restricted presence* to be found on the walls or other structural elements surrounding the sanctuary. These name inscriptions are not only of patrons but also of masons.[52] For example, on the south-eastern tower at Worms, at the fifth floor the name HERICKE (Figures 22.10, 22.11), written upside-down, can be found,[53] and in one of the window jambs of the second floor the name Georius (Figure 22.12).[54]

But this is not only a phenomenon in Worms. On the three apses from the end of the 12th century of the collegiate church in Neuchâtel, Switzerland[55] we have several inscriptions with the names of Guido (Figure 22.13) and WIEO (Figure 22.14) in altering forms, sometimes also written upside-down. The name GUIDO appears in two types with several subtypes. The WIEO sometimes also appears in the short form WI.[56] Other sanctuaries provide names as well, such as PONCIVS on the inner walls of Saint-Honorat-des-Alycamps in Arles, Provence, France (Figure 22.15).[57]

Not only patron inscriptions but also artist inscriptions could be made for commemoration and to ask for intercessions.[58] Name inscriptions, especially ones with *restricted presence*, can have another meaning.[59] This is to be found in the Old Testament, as well as the Revelations of the New Testament, where we are told that God has an account of all living souls. One can be crossed out of this 'Book of Life' by committing sins.[60] On judgment day this book will be opened and everyone will be judged according to his or her deeds and accomplishments.[61] Whoever's name is not found in the 'Book of Life' will go to hell.[62] In order to be able to connect the deed with a name, in this case

FIGURE 22.10

Worms Cathedral: south-eastern tower, fifth level, inscription HERICKE (Wilfried E. Keil)

FIGURE 22.11

Worms Cathedral: south-eastern tower, fifth level, inscription HERICKE (Aquilante De Filippo)

FIGURE 22.12

Worms Cathedral: south-eastern tower, second level, inscription Georius (Wilfried E. Keil)

284

FIGURE 22.13

Neuchâtel: Collegiate Church of St Mary. Apse inscription, Guido (Wilfried E. Keil)

FIGURE 22.14

Neuchâtel: Collegiate Church of St Mary. Apse inscription WIEO (Wilfried E. Keil)

FIGURE 22.15

Arles: Saint-Honorat-des-Alycamps. Main apse interior, inscription PONCIVS (Wilfried E. Keil)

the donation or the artwork, it was marked with the name of the artist or the patron. For the inscribing of the names there is thus also a possible eschatological reason.[63]

In the case of the inscription of Adelbraht Monetarius and the artist Otto, the proximity to the altar could be explained by their wish to be as close as possible to the celebration of the Eucharist. The hope of a secure place in the book of life could have been decisive for this. It can also be seen in the context of *memoria*. A priest would see their names during the service, think of the persons and thereby include them in his prayers. This should be seen in the context of liturgical *memoriae* for which sometimes special precautions were made and the names were written down in the church, for example on the wall of the apse or of the altar table.[64] Just the presence of a name at the place of the Eucharist produces a connection to this.[65] So it could be that the bare presence of a name was enough to 'attend' the ceremony without the name being mentioned during the service.[66]

With name inscriptions with extreme *restricted presence*, like the HERICKE inscription, such a concern is not conceivable. The 'Book of Life' interpretation seems more likely, especially when the inscription is close to the altar: the closer the name is to the altar, the less likely that it will be removed from the 'Book of Life'. If a position inside the sanctuary was not possible, then one tried to write it outside, as near to the altar as possible, such as on the walls of the sanctuary or the nearby structural elements.

This idea can also be connected to burial practices. In the ancient world it was forbidden to bury someone inside the city walls.[67] Christians kept this tradition and buried their martyrs and saints outside the city walls according to this rule. Chapels and churches were built above the tomb of a saint. The altar always stood close to the original grave.[68] From an early date the desire of *sepultura ad sanctos* evolved, the wish to be buried close to the martyrs and saints in order to have them as intercessors on judgment day.[69] When the saint's remains were transferred into city churches and placed beneath the altar,[70] the wish to be buried *intra muros* evolved.[71] At the synod of Vaison-la-Romaine in 442 a prohibition on burial inside churches was proclaimed for the first time.[72] In 563 at the synod of Braga a complete prohibition of burials inside churches was decided.[73] This was confirmed subsequently several times.[74] There were, nevertheless, repeated unofficial exceptions. These were first granted only to popes and bishops. After some time worthy clerics, rulers and church founders also found places of burial within the church.[75] At the synod of Mainz in 813 bishops, abbots, worthy priests and faithful laymen were given the same privilege.[76] Even within the church there was the wish to be buried as close as possible to a saint's relics or the altar.[77] The faithful who could not be buried in the church found burial in the cemetery around the church, still close to the honoured saint and the sacraments at the altar.[78] Taking this context into account, and by assuming name inscriptions like the one of Adelbraht Monetarius show an analogous desire, the wish to have one's name written near the altar and thereby to secure ones place in the 'Book of Life', can be considered as a very plausible explanation for patron inscriptions of *restricted presence*.

NOTES

[1] This article emerged from the Collaborative Research Centre 933 "Material Text Cultures. Materiality and Presence of Writing in Non-Typographic Societies" (Subproject A05 "Script and Characters on and in the Medieval Artwork") at the University of Heidelberg. The CRC 933 is financed by the German Research Foundation (DFG).

[2] For a definition of building inscription see E. Hohmann/H. Wentzel, 'Bauinschrift', *Reallexikon zur Deutschen Kunstgeschichte*, 2 (Stuttgart 1948), 34–53; R. Funken, 'Bauinschrift', *Lexikon des Mittelalters*, 1 (München, Zürich 1980), 1631. For a distinction concerning the content see also R. Funken, *Die Bauinschriften des Erzbistums Köln bis zum Auftreten der gotischen Majuskel*, 19. Veröffentlichung der Abteilung Architektur des Kunsthistorischen Instituts der Universität zu Köln (Köln 1981, also PhD. thesis Köln 1980), 2–3.

[3] For the inscription, see A. De Filippo and W.E. Keil, 'Zu den Versatzzeichen und Inschriften am Südostturm des Domes zu Worms', *Der Wormsgau*, 27 (2009), 205–215, at 211; W.E. Keil, 'Überlegungen zur restringierten Präsenz mittelalterlicher Bauinschriften', in *Verborgen, unsichtbar, unlesbar – zur Problematik restringierter Schriftpräsenz*, Materiale Textkulturen, 2, ed. T. Frese, W.E. Keil and K. Krüger (Berlin, Boston 2014), 117–142, at 120. The Bauforschung, in which the author was involved, was done by the Institut für Europäische Kunstgeschichte of the University of Heidelberg under the supervision of Prof. Dr. Matthias Untermann and under the local management of Aquilante De Filippo M.A.

[4] K. Mohrmann, 'Ein Grundstein aus der Zeit Bernwards', *Die Denkmalpflege*, 10 (1908), 64. A little later K. Mohrmann found a fragment of a second foundation stone, see K. Mohrmann, 'Grundsteine aus der Zeit Bernwards', *Die Denkmalpflege*, 10 (1908), 71.

[5] For the inscription see W. Berges, *Die älteren Hildesheimer Inschriften bis zum Tode Bischof Hezilos († 1079). Aus dem Nachlass herausgegeben und mit Nachträgen versehen von Hans Jürgen Rickenberg*, Abhandlungen der Akademie der Wissenschaften in Göttingen, Philologisch-Historische Klasse, Dritte Folge, 131, 50–54, No. 5; C. Wulf, *Die Inschriften der Stadt Hildesheim. Teil 2: Die Inschriften, Jahreszahlen und Initialen*, Die Deutschen Inschriften, 58 (Wiesbaden 2003), 185–187, No. 6. For the foundation stones in Hildesheim also see C. Wulf, 'Grundsteine von St. Michael', in *Bernward von Hildesheim und das Zeitalter der Ottonen*, 2, catalogue of the exhibition of the Dom- und Diözesanmuseums Hildesheim and the Roemer- und Pelizaeus-Museums Hildesheim, ed. M. Brandt and A. Eggebrecht (Hildesheim, Mainz 1993), 533–534, cat.no. VIII-10; M. Untermann, '"primus lapis in fundamentum deponitur". Kunsthistorische Überlegungen zur Funktion der Grundsteinlegung im Mittelalter', *Cistercienser. Brandenburgische Zeitschrift rund um das cisterciensische Erbe*, 6, issue 23 (2003), 5–18, at 14–15; C. Schulz-Mons, *Das Michaeliskloster in Hildesheim. Untersuchungen zur Gründung durch Bischof Bernward (993–1022)*, Quellen und Dokumentation zur Stadtgeschichte Hildesheims, 20, 2 vols (Hildesheim 2010), vol. 1, 194–221 and vol. 2, 96–104; E. Bünz, '"lapis angularis" – Die Grundsteinlegung 1010 als Schlüssel für den mittelalterlichen Kirchenbau von St. Michael in Hildesheim', in *1000 Jahre St. Michael in Hildesheim. Kirche-Kloster-Stifter*, ed. G. Lutz and A. Weyer (Petersberg 2012), 77–87; W.E. Keil, 'Abwesend und doch präsent? Zur restringierten Präsenz von Grundsteinen und ihren Inschriften', *Gründungen im archäologischen Befund. Mitteilungen der Deutschen Gesellschaft für Archäolgie des Mittelalters und der Neuzeit*, 27 (Paderborn 2014), 17–24, at 18–19.

[6] For the sacramental/theological category of the real presence see J. Betz, *Die Realpräsenz des Leibes und Blutes Jesu im Abendmahl nach dem Neuen Testament* (Freiburg 1961). For the actual and real presence of Christ during the holy mass see T. Frese, *Aktual- und Realpräsenz. Das eucharistische Christusbild von der Spätantike bis ins Mittelalter* (Berlin 2013, also Ph.D. Thesis, Frankfurt a. M. 2009), 110–112.

[7] H.U. Gumbrecht, *Production of Presence. What Meaning Cannot Convey* (Stanford 2004), xiii and 17.

[8] Gumbrecht, *Production* (as n. 7), 17.

[9] Gumbrecht, *Production* (as n. 7), xiii.

[10] Gumbrecht, *Production* (as n. 7), 17.

[11] For the definiton of *restricted presence* see M. Hilgert, '"Text-Anthropologie": Die Erforschung von Materialität und Präsenz des Geschriebenen als hermeneutische Strategie', in *Altorientalistik im 21. Jahrhundert. Selbstverständnis, Herausforderungen, Ziele. Mitteilungen der Deutschen Orientgesellschaft*, 142 (Berlin 2010), 87–126, at 99, note 20: 'Einen typologischen Sonderfall stellen diejenigen Arrangements von Objekten und Körpern dar, innerhalb derer ein oder mehrere Artefakte mit Sequenzen sprachlicher Zeichen so platziert sind, dass nur bestimmte oder gar keine Akteure dieses Geschriebene temporär oder permanent rezipieren können. Solche Arrangements weisen eine *restringierte Präsenz* des Geschriebenen auf'.

[12] C. Sauer, *Fundatio und Memoria. Stifter und Klostergründer im Bild 1100 bis 1350* (Göttingen 1993, also Ph.D. Thesis, Munich 1990), 19.

[13] O.G. Oexle, 'Memoria und Memorialüberlieferung', *Frühmittelalterliche Studien*, 10 (1976), 70–95, at 70.

[14] K. Schmid/J. Wollasch, 'Die Gemeinschaft der Lebenden und Verstorbenen in Zeugnissen des Mittelalters', *Frühmittelalterliche Studien*, 1 (1967), 365–405, at 365.

[15] Sauer, *Fundatio* (as n. 12), 19; Oexle, 'Memoria' (as n. 13), 79–82.

[16] Oexle, 'Memoria' (as n.13), 81; Sauer, *Fundatio* (as n. 12), 19–20.

[17] Oexle, 'Memoria' (as n. 13), 84. O.G. Oexle refers here also to R. Berger, 'Die Wendung "offerre pro" in der römischen Liturgie', *Literaturwissenschaftliche Quellen und Forschungen*, 41 (Münster 1964), 233: 'Der Name zwingt den Genannten herbei, das Aussprechen des Namens schafft die Gegenwart des Genannten'.

[18] Oexle, 'Memoria' (as n. 13), 71–73; Sauer, *Fundatio* (as n. 12), 20. See also Schmid/Wollasch, 'Gemeinschaft' (as n. 14), 366–389.

[19] Oexle, 'Memoria' (as n. 13), 70–71.

[20] Oexle, 'Memoria' (as n. 13), 71.

[21] Oexle, 'Memoria' (as n. 13), 85. For examples see Oexle, 'Memoria' (as n. 13), 74–75.

[22] Sauer, *Fundatio* (as n. 12), 20–21. See also Oexle, 'Memoria' (as 13), 77–79 and 85–86.

[23] Schmid/Wollasch, 'Gemeinschaft' (as n. 14), 367–368; Oexle, 'Memoria' (as n. 13), 74–79.

[24] Schmid/Wollasch, 'Gemeinschaft' (as n. 14), 365.

[25] Sauer, *Fundatio* (as n. 12), 21–22.

[26] A. Angenendt, 'Theologie und Liturgie der mittelalterlichen Toten-Memoria', in *Memoria. Der geschichtliche Zeugniswert des liturgischen Gedenkens im Mittelalter*, Münstersche Mittelalter-Schriften, 48, ed. K. Schmid and J. Wollasch (München 1984), 79–199, at 143–148 and 150–152.

[27] Oexle, 'Memoria' (as n. 13), 87–88.

[28] Angenendt, 'Theologie' (as n. 26), 181.

[29] Oexle, 'Memoria' (as n. 13), 90; Angenendt, 'Theologie' (as n. 26), 182; Sauer, *Fundatio* (as n. 12), 20. For some entries that show this analogous desire, see Angenendt, 'Theologie' (as n. 26), 182–183.

[30] R. Favreau proposed that Patron inscriptions have a double function, one is the memorial function and the other seeks intercession. See R. Favreau, 'Fonctions des inscriptions au moyen âge', *Cahiers de civilisation médiévale*, 32 (1989), 203–232, at 315.

[31] The dating is given by some wood from scaffold cross-bars of the north wall of the nave, which were dendrochronologically dated to the years between 1161 and 1163 see Hotz, *Der Dom zu Worms*, (Darmstadt 1981), 83–84; D. v. Winterfeld, *Der Dom zu Worms*, 3rd edn (Königstein im Taunus 1994), 11. W. Hotz dates the sculpture to around 1165, see W. Hotz, *Dom* (as this n.) 75, footnote 123. D. v. Winterfeld dates the sculpture to perhaps before 1160, see v. Winterfeld, *Dom* (as this n.), 16, 18; D. v. Winterfeld, *Die Kaiserdome Speyer, Mainz, Worms und ihr romanisches Umland*, (Würzburg 1993), 204.

[32] For the inscription see R. Fuchs, *Die Inschriften der Stadt Worms*, Die deutschen Inschriften, 29 (Wiesbaden 1991), 24, No. 22.

[33] E. Seebald, 'Das romanische Südportal', in *Das Südportal des Wormser Doms*, ed. W. Brönner, Denkmalpflege in Rheinland-Pfalz, Forschungsberichte, 5 (Worms 1999), 11–24, 11. The sculpture with Daniel in the lion's den has an inscription in Romanesque majuscule: DANIEL INLAC / + LEONVM, see Fuchs, '*Inschriften*' (as n. 32), 22–23, No. 21.

[34] For the inscription see Fuchs, *Inschriften* (as n. 32), 19–21, No. 18. Another monetarius-inscription is written on a capital of the southeastern apse of Saint-Hilaire-le-Grand in Poitiers from the late 11th century: VGO MONEDARIVS, see R. Favreau, *Corpus des inscriptions de la France médiévale, 1 Poitou-Charente, 1 Ville de Poitiers* (Poitiers 1974), 66–67, No. 62.

[35] For this problem see W.E. Keil, 'Von sichtbaren und verborgenen Signaturen an mittelalterlichen Kirchen', ed. I. Berti, K. Bolle, F. Opdenhoff and F. Stroth, *Writing Matters. Presenting and Perceiving Monumental Inscriptions in Antiquity and the Middle Ages*, Materiale Textkulturen, 14 (Berlin, Boston 2017), 309–351.

[36] For the legend, see Jacobus de Voragine, *Legenda Aurea. Goldene Legende*, ed., trans. and commented B.W. Häuptli, 2 vols, Fontes Christiani (Freiburg i. Br. 2014), vol. 1, 572–575; G. Kaster, 'Juliana von Nikomedien', in *Lexikon der christlichen Ikonographie, 7, Ikonographie der Heiligen. Innozenz bis Melchisedech*, ed. E. Kirschbaum and W. Braunfels (Freiburg i. Br. 1974), 228–231.

[37] Fuchs, *Inschriften* (as n. 32), 20.

[38] G. Bönnen, 'Dom und Stadt. Zu den Beziehungen zwischen der Stadtgemeinde und der Bischofskirche im mittelalterlichen Worms', *Der Wormsgau*, 17 (1998), 8–55, 15 with footnote 21. The name Adelbreth is also found among the witnesses in an enactment of the bishop for Saint Paul from April 1140. In the diploma for the moneyers of Worms from Emperor Frederick I Barbarossa from September 1165 can be found among the witnesses a person with the name Adelbert. See Bönnen, 'Dom und Stadt' (as this n.), 15, footnote 21. R. Fuchs believes that the inscription is the oldest name document for a moneyer of Worms, see Fuchs, *Inschriften* (as n. 32), 20. Under Bishop Burchard II (1115/20–49) coins are documented with the letter A, see Fuchs, *Inschriften* (as n. 32), 20. This can be seen as an additional record.

[39] See Bönnen, 'Dom und Stadt' (as n. 38), 15. Later, at the beginning of the 13th century, we have in other churches in Worms name inscriptions, which could also be interpreted as inscriptions of lay patrons. At Saint Martin we have on the tympanum of the south portal, which dates to around 1220, the following inscription in early Gothic majuscle: · HEI(N)RIC(VS) · DE OP(PEN)H(EIM) · ADVOCAT(VS), that is, of the reeve Heinrich von Oppenheim; see Fuchs, *Inschriften* (as n. 32), 38, No. 31. At Saint Paul we both outside and inside several name inscriptions in Gothic majuscle from the 13th century, which can be interpreted as patron inscriptions. Two of the inscriptions mention the names of men and five of them mention in each case a woman and a man. One of the male name inscriptions is for a cleric, but the others seem to be laypersons. For one couple we know from documents that they are lay patrons, and can assume this for two others from the same document. For the inscriptions see Fuchs, *Inschriften* (as n. 32), 40–41, No. 34; 41–42, No. 35; 47–48, No. 40; 49–50, No. 44; 50, No. 45; 50–51, No. 46; 51–52, No. 47.

[40] In the upper parts of the transept they found some wood in the putlog holes which was dendrochronologically dated to the years from 1132 to 1137, see E. Hollstein, 'Dendrochronologische Datierung von Bauhölzern des Wormser Doms', *Neues Jahrbuch für das Bistum Mainz* (1979), 45–46; E. Hollstein, 'Neue Bauholzdaten des Wormser Doms', *Neues Jahrbuch für das Bistum Mainz* (1981), 125–134; W. Hotz, *Dom* (as n. 31), 43.

[41] Fuchs, *Inschriften* (as n. 32), 19–20.

[42] R. Fuchs, 'Wormser Inschriften. Zur Schriftgeschichte und Quellenkunde', in *Deutsche Inschriften. Fachtagung für mittelalterliche und neuzeitliche Epigraphik. Lüneburg 1984. Vorträge und Berichte*, ed. K. Stackmann, Abhandlungen der Akademie der Wissenschaften in Göttingen. Philosophisch-Historische Klasse, 3. Folge, 151, (Göttingen 1986), 82–99, 85.

[43] M. Untermann, 'Der Ostbau des Wormser Doms. Neue Überlegungen und Befunde zu Bauabfolge und Datierung sowie zur Weihe von 1110', *Der Wormsgau*, 27 (2009), 189–203.

[44] M. Untermann and W.E. Keil, 'Der Ostbau des Wormser Doms. Neue Beobachtungen zu Bauabfolge, Bauentwurf und Datierung', *Insitu. Zeitschrift für Architekturgeschichte*, 2 (2010), 5–20, 16–19.

[45] Untermann, 'Ostbau' (as n. 43), 196–197; Untermann and Keil, 'Ostbau' (as n. 44), 20.

[46] Which dates to 1741; see E. Kranzbühler, 'Der Wormser Dom im 18. Jahrhundert', in *Studien aus Kunst und Geschichte. Friedrich Schneider zum siebzigsten Geburtstag gewidmet* (Freiburg i. Br. 1906), 295–312, 303.

[47] Bönnen, 'Dom und Stadt' (as n. 38), 16–17.

[48] Bönnen, 'Dom und Stadt' (as n. 38), 17–18. In 1074 Emperor Henry IV granted economic advantages through toll benefits and in 1114 Henry V introduced innovations in marriage and inheritance law, see Fuchs, *Inschriften* (as n. 32), 33; S. Happ, *Stadtwerdung am Mittelrhein. Die Führungsgruppen von Speyer, Worms und Koblenz bis zum Ende des 13. Jahrhunderts*, Rheinisches Archiv 144 (Köln, Weimar, Wien, 2002), 76–77.

[49] Bönnen, 'Dom und Stadt' (as n. 38), 18.

[50] The dating comes from wood from the scaffold cross-bars of the north wall of the nave, which were dendrochronologically dated in the years from 1161 to 1163; Hotz, *Dom* (as n. 31), 83–84; Winterfeld, *Dom* (as n. 31), 11.

[51] Fuchs, *Inschriften* (as n. 32), 32–33. The inscription was after the chronicle of Friedrich Zorn (1538–1610) in Romanesque majuscule. The first part of the privilege was written in two distiches and two leonine hexameter and the second part as a leonine hexameter: SIT TIBI WORMACIA LAVS HINC ET FRVCTVS HONORIS / QVOD PIA QVOD PRVDENS QVOD BENE FIDA MANES / A CENSV CAPITVM SIS LIBERA MVNERE NOSTRO / LIBERTATE FRVI DIGNA

FRVARIS EA / DIGNA BONA LAVDE SEMPER WORMACIA GAVDE / TE MIHI SACRAVIT CRVX TE MIHI MVCRO DICAVIT. – TE SIT TVTA BONO WORMACIA PETRE PATRONO. (Glory to you, Worms, henceforth may you enjoy honour as long as you stay pious, wise and loyal. May you be free of rulers by our grace; may you enjoy freedom in its worth, highly praised shall you be, Worms, always rejoice, mine consecrated by the cross, mine given by the sword. – With you as their good shepherd, Peter, Worms shall be safe.). For the inscription, see Fuchs, *Inschriften* (as n. 32), 32–43, No. 27; W. Müller, *Urkundeninschriften des deutschen Mittelalters*, Münchener Historische Studien, Abteilung Geschichtliche Hilfswissenschaften, 13 (Kallmünz 1975, also PhD thesis Munich 1972), 69–70, No. 11. The installation of an inscription of the privilege on the portal relates to the importance of church portals in the medieval period: some portals, for example, were used for the administration of justice. There are several reasons for placing an inscription at a portal: the durability of the material, in order to publicise the content, public preservation, the inscription as certification, legitimisation, protection of the content by placing it on a sacred building, meeting place of the municipality. For this summary see Bönnen, 'Dom und Stadt' (as n. 38), 20. For more details see Müller, *Urkundeninschriften*' (as this n.), 26–33. At Speyer cathedral the privilege of Emperor Henry V had already been placed at the portal in 1111. For the inscription see Müller, *Urkundeninschriften* (as this n.), 23–26, 43–48, No. 2. For the privilege see S. Weinfurter, 'Salisches Herrschaftsverständnis im Wandel. Heinrich V. und sein Privileg für die Bürger von Speyer', *Frühmittelalterliche Studien*, 36, (2002), 317–335.

[52] Where only a name is inscribed it could be a mason's inscription but also a patron's inscription. The old thesis of P.C. Claussen that names on their own were always artist's inscriptions can no longer be held. For this thesis see P.C. Claussen, 'Künstlerinschriften', in *Ornamenta Ecclesiae. Kunst und Künstler der Romanik in Köln*, exhibition catalogue, vol. 3, ed. A. Legner (Köln 1985), 263–276, at 265. C. Treffort argued that names on their own could be connected to masons, donors or pilgrims. See C. Treffort, 'Inscrire son nom dans l'espace liturgique à l'époque romane', *Les Cahiers de Saint-Michel de Cuxa*, 34 (2003), 147–160, at 148. A. Hartmann-Virnich argued that in these cases it could be the signature of a foreman, purchaser or a donor. See A. Hartmann-Virnich, 'Steinmetzzeichen im provençalischen Sakral- und Profanbau des 12. bis 14. Jahrhunderts. Forschungsaspekte und Forschungsperspektiven', *Naturstein als Baumaterial. Jahrbuch für Hausforschung*, 52 (Marburg, 2007), 103–138, at 116. For name-only inscriptions, which could be interpreted as patron inscriptions, see Keil, 'Überlegungen' (as n. 3), 132–135 and Keil, 'Signaturen' (as n. 35) , 337–341.

[53] The name inscription has a height of 110 mm and a width of 260 mm and is written in Romanesque majuscule. For the inscription see Fuchs, *Inschriften* (as n. 32), 21, No. 19. R. Fuchs thought that the inscription was lost. It was rediscovered during the building investigations in 2009, see De Filippo/Keil, 'Versatzzeichen und Inschriften' (as n. 3), 209–211; Keil, 'Überlegungen' (as n. 3), 130–135.

[54] The name inscription, which was first documented in 2009, has a height of 90 mm and a width of 250 mm and is written in Romanesque minuscule. For the inscription see De Filippo/Keil, 'Versatzzeichen und Inschriften' (as n. 3), 208–209.

[55] J. Courvoisier, *Les monuments d'art et d'histoire du Canton de Neuchâtel 1: La ville de Neuchâtel*, Les monuments d´art et d´histoire de la Suisse, 33 (Basel 1955), 77.

[56] J. Courvoisier only mentions the name GUIDO, see: Courvoisier, 'Neuchâtel' (as n. 55), 81. J. Christoph wants to recognise two variations with GVIDO and GUIGO. But this does not apply according to newer investigations. In the second variation he wants to recognise the uncial D as a G. For the name inscriptions see J. Christoph, *Corpus inscriptionum Medii Aevi Helvetiae 2: Die Inschriften der Kantone Freiburg, Genf, Jura, Neuenburg und Waadt*, Scrinium Friburgense, Sonderband 2 (Freiburg i. Üe. 1984), 136–137, No. 60. J. Christoph mention only thirty name inscriptions, see Christoph, *Inschriften*, 136. J. Zierer counts in her thesis sixty-one name inscriptions on the outside and four inside the building. She also counts some single letters, which she interprets as abbreviations of the name inscriptions: see J. Zierer, 'Steinmetzzeichen an der Collégiale de Notre-Dame in Neuchâtel. Eine Untersuchung der vorkommenden Steinmetzzeichen und Namensinschriften an den Apsieden der Collégiale de Notre-Dame in Neuchâtel (NE)' (unpublished thesis (Lizentiatsarbeit), University of Zürich 1994), 67–68, 72–74. The author had the opportunity to investigate the name inscriptions during the last restoration in the years 2012/2013 from a scaffold and found around fifty. Many thanks to Christian de Reynier (Archéologue du bâti, Office de la protection des Monumentes et des Sites, Neuchâtel) for the kind permission.

[57] For the inscription see Keil, 'Überlegungen' (as n. 3), 126–127. On the stones around the name inscriptions the mason's mark PO is carved. This is probably an abbreviation of the name inscription. For this see also A. Hartmann-Virnich, *Saint-Paul-Trois-Châteaux et Saint-Trophime d'Arles et l'église romane à trois nefs en Provence rhodanienne: architecture, construction, évolution*, 2 vols (Lille 2000, also Ph.D. Thesis, Aix-en-Provence 1992), 536–537; A. Hartmann-Virnich, 'Steinmetzzeichen' (as n. 52), 110–111.

[58] For patron inscriptions; Favreau, 'Fonctions' (as n. 30). Favreau also establishes that artist's inscriptions have a double function, one for personal glory, the other to seek intercession. See Favreau, 'Fonctions' (as n. 30), 217–218.

[59] For the following argument, see also Keil, 'Überlegungen' (as n. 3), 135–137.

[60] For example see Psalm 69, 29 and Revelation 3, 5.

[61] Revelation 20, 12–13.

[62] Revelation 20, 15, 'And whosoever was not found written in the book of life was cast into the lake of fire', but also mentioned several times previously in the Bible, for example Revelation 17, 8.

[63] Tobias Burg mentions the Book of Life and this related possible interpretation in only a single sentence in the last chapter of his book 'Fazit: Warum Signieren?': 'Zum anderen diente die Verewigung des Namens der Selbstvergewisserung, in das Buch des Lebens eingetragen zu werden und damit am Tag des Gerichts zur Schar der Erlösten zu gehören'. He sees this reason only in connection with scribes and illuminators of medieval manuscripts. For him, religious motives do not matter in other art forms. See T. Burg, *Die Signatur. Formen und Funktionen vom Mittelalter bis zum 17. Jahrhundert* (Berlin 2007, also PhD. thesis Dresden 2003), 542. Cécile Treffort argues that inscribed names are to build not only the terrestrial church, but also the spiritual and celestial church, the *Ecclesia*. The names which are inscribed in churches and cloisters are like a huge book of living stones which she connects to the book from which God reads the names of the righteous on Judgement Day, and which participate materially and spiritually in the building of the *Ecclesia*. See Treffort, 'Inscrire' (as n. 52), 159–160.

[64] Oexle, 'Memoria' (as n. 13), 74–75, 85; Treffort, 'Inscrire' (as n. 52), 154–155.

[65] Treffort, 'Inscrire' (as n. 52), 153–155.

[66] For this theory, see Treffort, 'Inscrire' (as n. 52), 158.

[67] B. Kötting, *Der frühchristliche Reliquienkult und die Bestattung im Kirchengebäude*, Arbeitsgemeinschaft für Forschung des Landes Nordrhein-Westfalen. Geisteswissenschaften, 123 (Köln, Opladen 1965), 10–11; B. Kötting, 'Die Tradition der Grabkirche', in *Memoria. Der gesellschaftliche Zeugniswert des liturgischen Gedenkens im Mittelalter*, Münsterische Mittelalter-Schriften, 48, ed. K. Schmid and J. Wollasch (München 1984), 69–78, at 69–70; H. Körner, *Grabmonumente des Mittelalters* (Darmstadt 1997), 7–8.

[68] Kötting, *Reliquienkult* (as n. 67), 13–15; Kötting, 'Grabkirche'(as n. 67), 70–72.

[69] Kötting, *Reliquienkult* (as n. 67), 24–28; Kötting, 'Grabkirche'(as n. 67), 74–76. See also F. Zoepfl, 'Bestattung (Bestattungswesen)', *Reallexikon zur Deutschen Kunstgeschichte*, 2 (Stuttgart 1948), 332–355, at 334; Körner *Grabmonumente* (as n. 67), 8.

[70] Kötting, 'Grabkirche'(as n. 67), 72–74. For more details on the translation of martyr's relics and the reasons for this, see Kötting, *Reliquienkult* (as n. 67), 15–24.

[71] Körner *Grabmonumente* (as n. 67), 9. The prohibition of the burial of non-saints inside the city walls was abolished by the Eastern Roman Emperor Leo I (457–474). See Zoepfl, 'Bestattung' (as n. 69), 335. Emperor Leo VI (886–912) abolished all restrictions on burial within Byzantine churches. See Kötting, *Reliquienkult* (as n. 67), 30.

[72] Kötting, *Reliquienkult* (as n. 67), 33; Kötting, 'Grabkirche'(as n. 67), 77. The prohibition, however, is not recorded in the Canons of the Synod, see Kötting, '*Reliquienkult*' (as n. 67), 33.

[73] Kötting, 'Reliquienkult' (as n. 67), 31–33; Kötting, 'Grabkirche' (as n. 67), 77; S. Scholz, 'Das Grab in der Kirche – Zu seinen theologischen und rechtlichen Hintergründen in der Spätantike und Frühmittelalter', Zeitschrift der Savigny-Stiftung für Rechtsgeschichte, 125 (1998), Kanonistische Abteilung, 84, 270–306, at 287.

[74] Kötting, Reliquienkult (as n. 67), 31–34; Kötting, 'Grabkirche'(as n. 67), 77–78.

[75] Zoepfl, 'Bestattung' (as n. 69), 335; Kötting, 'Grabkirche'(as n. 67), 76–78. For the burial of church founders in their foundation, see Sauer, Fundatio (as n. 13), 110–115. On the question how they get their coveted burial places, see Scholz, 'Grab' (as n. 73), 274–275.

[76] Kötting, Reliquienkult (as n. 67), 35; Kötting, 'Grabkirche' (as n. 67), 78; Sauer, Fundatio (as n. 13), 111–112; Scholz, 'Grab' (as n. 73), 299. For more details on the question of the burial rights, see Scholz, 'Grab' (as n. 73), 285–306.

[77] H. Wischermann, Grabmal, Grabdenkmal und Memoria im Mittelalter, Berichte und Forschungen zur Kunstgeschichte, 5 (Freiburg i. B. 1980), 5; Scholz, 'Grab' (as n. 73), 273–275.

[78] Körner Grabmonumente (as n. 67), 9.

THE TWELFTH-CENTURY PATRONS OF THE BRIDEKIRK FONT

Hugh Doherty

The font of the parish church of Bridekirk in Cumberland – one of the finest Romanesque church furnishings to survive in northern Britain – has not wanted for antiquary, artistic and scholarly attention. The existence of the font and the interest of its runic inscription was first noted by Reginald Bainbrigg (1544–1613), headmaster of Appleby School, an enthusiastic (as well as intrepid) obtainer of Roman antiquities.[1] Bainbrigg communicated details of the font to William Camden, whose publication of these engravings in the sixth and final edition of his *Britannia* in 1607 introduced the font to Jacobean England and set it on its course to wider fame.[2] Over the course of the next four centuries, the font has been the subject of numerous studies by some of the leading antiquaries, gentlemen experts and professional scholars of the British Isles.[3] It has been engraved, drawn and photographed by numerous artists and visitors, most elegantly by the accomplished draughtsman Charles Stothard in the summer of Waterloo.[4] It has also been a regular feature of any serious itinerary of the Lakes and Wall country since the so-called rediscovery of the region in the 18th century.[5] The font's pretensions as a monument worthy of national (and even international) standing were confidently declaimed when Colonel Frecheville Ballantine-Dykes (1800–67), the squire of Dovenby Hall, who owned the presentation to Bridekirk church and who took an active interest in the Roman antiquities of his neighbourhood, presented a cast of the font to the Museum of Manufactures (as the earliest incarnation of the Victoria & Albert Museum was known) in 1863.[6] Further fame followed a century later when, in 1953, the font graced the front of the dust wrapper of George Zarnecki's *Later Romanesque Sculpture* and then, in 1967, was chosen as the back cover of the dust jacket for Pevsner's *Buildings of England* volume on Cumberland.[7] Yet for all this attention and interest, the judgement offered by a visitor to the church in 1814 that the font is 'very ancient and very curious ... about which much has been written, but little that is satisfactory', continues to possess an element of truth: the font has been more often admired – and certainly more engraved and photographed – than studied in detail.[8]

There are two recent exceptions to this trend. The first is the study of the font made by C. S. Drake towards his catalogue of Romanesque fonts in Scandinavia and northern Europe, published in 2002.[9] The second is a detailed study of the inscription offered by M. Barnes and R. I. Page as part of their corpus of Scandinavian runic inscriptions from the British Isles, published in 2006.[10] Both works have certainly helped sharpen our understanding of different aspects and features of the font – yet there still remains much to say. Apart from early misinterpretations drawn from the runic inscription, and a rather later, misguided effort by one of the county's most learned scholars of pre-Conquest sculpture, there has been almost no consideration of the identity of the patron or patrons whose investment resulted in the construction of so lavish a furnishing. This paper, in seeking to address this theme, will use neglected evidence – evidence that has been in print for more than 300 years, but almost entirely ignored – in order to offer a new identification of these patrons and to explore the intersection of their devotional priorities and territorial interests. What follows is less, therefore, a study of the font's sculptural details, iconographic programme, and process of construction than an exploration of the world of lordship, power and devotion – the world of 12th-century secular hearts and minds – represented by the font.

THE BRIDEKIRK FONT

The Bridekirk font (Figure 23.1) is found in the present parish church, five miles north of Cockermouth, in the historic county of Cumberland. The original medieval church was almost entirely demolished in the course of the construction of the present church in 1868–70. The original church had clearly suffered major alterations in the late medieval and modern periods, but a description of it in 1835, the best description we possess prior to its demolition, observes that the church was 'an ancient edifice, principally in the Norman style'.[11] In place of this church, the two architects, John Cory and Charles Ferguson, built a more coherent structure in a neo-Romanesque style – precisely the sort of 'new imposing church' that its Victorian parishioners had always dreamed of possessing.[12] Cory and Ferguson – both, we should note, founding

FIGURE 23.1

The Bridekirk Font (Hugh Doherty)

members of the Cumberland and Westmorland Archaeological and Antiquarian Society and regular contributors to the society's *Transactions* on a range of learned subjects – were nevertheless sensitive to the church's Romanesque fabric and preserved some of this fabric in their new building.[13] The 12th-century chancel arch was thus reused as the north transept arch, a 12th-century door and tympanum as the south porch entrance, and a second 12th-century door as a doorway at the east end of the south transept. A number of gravestones and other fragments, including what may be a late 12th-century carved panel, were also preserved. So, too, of course, was the font, which now stands – or, rather, stands cemented – on a later plinth close to the western end of the present church, so close, indeed, that it is almost impossible to examine in detail (or even photograph) the western face of the font.[14]

Our understanding of the origins of the font has been complicated by the view – a minority view, it must be stated, but one given fresh life by the rather equivocal comments of Barnes and Page in their recent survey of Scandinavian runic inscriptions – that the font was originally discovered at the Roman settlement of Papcastle.[15] As was stated earlier, our earliest written reference to the font occurs in notes made by the antiquary, Reginald Bainbrigg, for his correspondent and friend, William Camden. According to Bainbrigg, the Bridekirk inscription 'was in a stone found at Papcastle and now made a font stone at Bridekirk'. Camden himself describes how the font, which he describes (in the words of his earliest translator) as 'a broad vessell of a greenish stone', presumably because of the green moss on the font, was discovered 'among many monuments of Antiquity'.[16] This detail is not found in Bainbrigg's report, so Camden is likely to have obtained this information from one of his local informants, possibly Oswald Dykes, possibly John Senhouse.[17] According to William Stukeley, who visited Papcastle on 22 August 1725, 'the famous font, now at Bridekirk, was taken up at this place, in the pasture south of the south-east angle of the city, by a lane called Moorwent'.[18] Again, the precision of his details suggests the existence of a robust local tradition, one very likely communicated to him by his friend, Mr Humphrey Senhouse, who hosted Stukeley at his residence in Ellenborough and who accompanied him on his visit to Papcastle.[19]

There are good reasons, however, to doubt the veracity of this tradition. We should begin by observing that, in his notes for Camden, Bainbrigg had first written that 'the inscription was found in Papcastle' before erasing the 'in' and replacing it with 'at'.[20] His correction would suggest that he himself was unsure as to the details of the font's discovery. The informants behind the statements made by Camden in 1607 and Stukeley in 1725 may have been local men with a usable store of information, but the discrepancy behind their reports – the font being discovered 'among many other ancient monuments' or in a precise corner of a local field – would imply that this information was not drawn from a fixed local tradition and, moreover, was subject to revision and improvement. The discovery of Roman sculpture and coins at Papcastle must have made the site an evocative, even convenient, location for the purported origins of many items of perceived antiquity. There is evidence that the vill had been a significant seigneurial centre in the early history of the lordship of Allerdale, and one of the early 12th-century lords, who we shall meet in due course, was credited with making his headquarters at Papcastle, perhaps within the surviving Roman remains. Yet the only known ecclesiastical building at Papcastle was a chapel dedicated to Saint Zita, which was in existence by the early 1470s. This chapel can have been raised no earlier than the 14th century and is unlikely to have possessed a baptismal font.[21] We must therefore conclude that the ascription to Papcastle, if at all accurate, must refer to no more than the re-use and recycling of Roman stone from Papcastle rather than the discovery of the entire font in the grounds of the former Roman settlement. The Bridekirk font, we must stress, began and ended its life as a baptismal font at Bridekirk church.

Before we proceed to a description of the font, it is first essential to discuss the visit to Bridekirk church made by William Dugdale in the spring of 1665. This visit, as will become clear, marked a significant event in the history of the font, and is an event of central importance to the thesis advanced by the present paper.[22] As Norroy King of Arms, Dugdale was responsible for all heraldic business in the counties north of the Trent; his visit to Cumberland and Westmorland in March and April 1665 was in fact the first heraldic visitation of these counties since 1615. In the course of his visitation – very likely on Saturday, 1 April – he and his young amanuensis and assistant, Gregory King, visited Bridekirk church and inspected the font. During their visit, King made drawings of the four sides of the font (Figure 23.2).[23] Though his drawings are the earliest depiction of the font, they have never, remarkably, been published. What makes them particularly

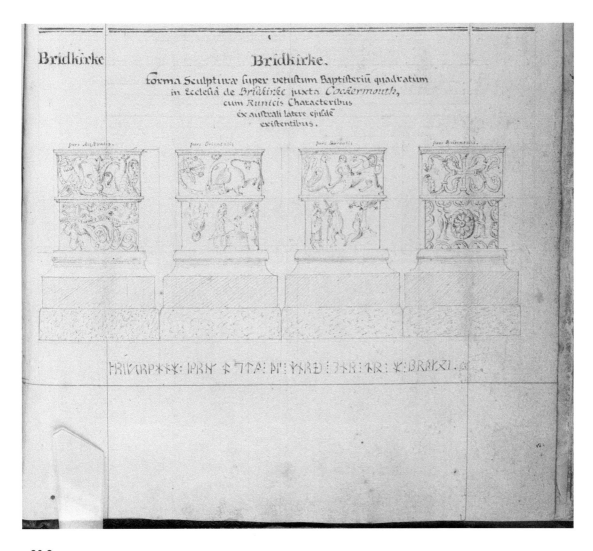

FIGURE 23.2

Drawing by Gregory King of the four faces of the Bridekirk Font (College of Arms MS C. 39, Monuments of Cumberland section, 13). Reproduced by permission of the Kings, Heralds and Pursuivants of Arms

valuable is the fact that he labelled each of the four sides with the directions of the compass. This has significant implications for our understanding of the font's orientation. Our only description of the location of the font in the original church is provided by the Cumbrian man of letters, George Smith, who, in a brief description published in 1749, stated that the font 'faces the porch door'.[24] Since this porch appears to have been the vestibule created by the collapsed west bell tower, the font was very likely situated towards the western end of the church.[25] Unless the font was moved in its late medieval or early modern existence, itself unlikely but not impossible, its position at the western end must represent its location in the 12th-century church. King's labelled drawings, when combined with Smith's useful detail, thus allow us to recreate what may have been the original orientation of the font in the medieval church, which was significantly different, it is clear, from the font's present orientation. This has implications for what follows: for when this paper refers to the north face of a font, it will be referring to the face labelled north by Gregory King.

As to the font itself, this consists of a rectangular tub, which is 600 mm high and has a depth of 220 mm. A plain roll-moulding decorates the top of the font, while a second roll-moulding divides each of the four sides into two tiers. Each side of the font is thus divided into two separate registers. All eight of these registers carry rich sculptural decoration.[26] On each of the four sides there is a combination of foliage, fruit, beasts and figural scenes. There is movement and drama in many of the scenes. Two basilisks devour a plant from either direction, their front paws almost touching; a dog bites eagerly into the stem of fruit-bearing vegetation; and a centaur fights in desperate combat with two beastly assailants. There is no coherent or integrated artistic programme, but rather a collection of visually arresting scenes. Perhaps the most significant of these scenes – the critical scene on any font – is found in the lower register of its east face (Figure 23.3). This depicts the baptism of Christ: a mighty John the Baptist holds a smaller Christ by the shoulders in the Jordan river; 'the Spirit of God' descends as a dove directly on to Christ's head, with all the tautness and will, it must

FIGURE 23.3

Bridekirk Font: Original east face (now north face) (Hugh Doherty)

be conceded, of a bird of prey; and a small sphere, presumably the sun, sits in the top left corner, perhaps as a representation of the tearing open of heaven on Christ's baptism. An equally gripping scene is found in the lower register of the south face. Running across the top of this register is a horizontal band, which carries an inscription. Beneath the band, on the left, is a kneeling mason, who raises a mallet in his right hand and gently edges his long chisel into the beading of the stems. We will return to both the inscription and the figure of the mason in due course. Now it is enough to observe the quality of the sculptural detail of these various scenes, from the pellets on the belt of the centaur through the texture of John the Baptist's camel-skin garment to the richness of the mason's hair and beard.

The complex interplay of ideas that informed both the design of the font and the responses of its viewers, especially its secular viewers, is clearest from the lower register of the north face of the font (Figures 23.4–23.5). This depicts a dramatic scene. On the far left is an elegant figure, brandishing a sword with one hand and pointing in the opposite direction with the other. Close to him a man raises his arm in exclamation while a female figure clutches the base of what may be a tree with mournful desperation. The possibility that this scene represents an episode from the life of St Brigit, possibly the episode in which she surrendered her father's sword to a leper, can probably be rejected, since the only apparent correlation between this episode and the scene on the font is the individual on the left bearing a sword.[27] The more standard view that the scene depicts episodes from the Fall seems on the whole a more compelling interpretation of its details. Identifying which episodes is less than straightforward, however. The view that the scene depicts either 'the Expulsion from the Garden of Eden' or 'both the Temptation and the Expulsion' fails to explain why Adam and Eve are fully clothed and why Eve appears to be clutching the base of a tree.[28] Examination of the font itself reveals, in addition, that there was once an object in Adam's left hand, which has since been obliterated. King's drawing of the font in 1665 reveals that the item was some sort of tool, possibly even the traditional spade. His posture may even indicate his foot resting on the edge of the spade's blade. The entire lower register is more likely, therefore, to represent a moment (or, perhaps, a combination of moments) following the Expulsion of Adam and Eve. These fortunes

FIGURE 23.4

Bridekirk Font: original north face (now west face) (James F. King)

FIGURE 23.5

Bridekirk Font: lower register of original north face (James F. King)

were not an unpopular subject for artistic and devotional expression in 12th-century England: wall paintings from the parish church of Hardham (in Sussex), for instance, appear to narrate the various labours and penitence of the couple following the Expulsion.[29] They feature, too, in the 12th-century drama, *The Play of Adam*, which was written in French for what may have been a predominantly (if not exclusively) élite Anglo-Norman audience.[30] Such dramatic entertainment, of which the *Play of Adam* is a valuable, but not unique, survival, appears to have exercised an important influence on contemporary – and especially secular – familiarity with events from the Biblical past and the lives of the saints.[31]

The parallels between the *Play of Adam* and this register on the font are striking. In the play, God stations an angel, 'dressed in white', at the gate of paradise and commands him to guard the way 'with this sword that shines so brightly': on the font, a magnificently garmented angel holds up his sword in threatening fashion.[32] The stage instructions in the *Play* likewise required Adam to turn back to 'look back to paradise' and to 'lift up his hands in its direction': on the font Adam does, indeed, look back to paradise and hold up his left hand in its direction.[33] More problematic, perhaps, is the depiction of Eve clutching the tree or shrub on the right side of the register. The play stage instructions narrate that Satan sowed thorns and thistles to strangle the crops planted by Adam and Eve and direct that both should 'fall prostrate' when they discovered his malice.[34] One of the wall paintings at Hardham certainly shows Adam clasping the branches of a tree or shrub. This has generally been interpreted as Adam engaged in the cultivation of the land, but could easily represent his efforts to uproot the thorns planted by Satan.[35] The register on the font may depict a similar scene, with Eve either cultivating the soil or, prostrate in grief, clutching the weeds planted by Satan. These details – however interpreted – underline the complex influences that not only determined the creative process represented by the carving, but also framed and informed the responses and reactions of its audience, including, perhaps, its patrons.

One of the most striking and most significant features of the font is its remarkable runic inscription (Figure 23.6). In fact, since Camden published the inscription in 1607, it was the first runic inscription ever published in the British Isles.[36] The inscription is inscribed in the horizontal band that runs along the top of the lower register on the south face of the font. It is composed of a combination of mixed runes and Roman bookhand characters and offers a rhyming couplet in early Middle English verse:

Rikard he me iwrocte |
And to dis merd ger . . . me brocte.

In their survey of runic inscriptions, Barnes and Page have offered the following translation of this verse:[37]

Rikard he made me |
And to this splendour . . . brought me.

As is often the case with runes, no translation is necessarily straightforward. It is possible, for instance, that the

FIGURE 23.6

Bridekirk Font: lower register of original south face (now east face) (Hugh Doherty)

Middle English word *mērthe*, meaning 'splendour', could be taken to mean Bridekirk itself – 'this splendid place'. More challenging is the reading of the word beginning 'ger . . . '. This word has generally been taken to be ME *gernr* and translated as an adverb or adjective. On this reading, the inscription could be translated as:[38]

> Rikard he made me |
> And to this splendour carefully [or eagerly] brought me.

Barnes and Page have raised the possibility, however, that this word represents a personal name. On this reading, the verse could be translated as:[39]

> Rikard he made me |
> and to this splendour NN brought me.

The personal name represented by the graphs NN, depending on how they are read, could represent either various forms of the Old Norse *Arnórr*, which might be rendered *Arner*, *Artur* or *Arnther* in Middle English, or a rare form of the Old English *Earnweard*. The inscription may therefore, in effect, carry a double signature containing the names of the two leading craftsmen or, just possibly, the names of the senior mason and the font's commissioner and patron. Such a reading must remain no more than a possibility.

The earliest efforts to identify a patron of the Bridekirk font focussed exclusively on the identity of this *Rikard*. For the first generation of commentators, *Rikard* (or *Ekard* as his name was transliterated) was the patron himself, 'a General, or other great officer in the Danish army', keen to erect a monument to his conversion to Christianity and to his baptism, even perhaps Erik Bloodaxe, the early 10th-century Norwegian warrior who was once, possibly even twice, king of the Northumbrians.[40] It was the antiquary, William Hamper (1776–1831), who, in 1821, proposed that *Rikard* was 'the ingenious sculptor' rather than the patron and that the inscription was nothing less than his signature.[41] Better readings and transliterations of the runic inscription have confirmed Hamper's proposition. The fact, moreover, that *Rikard*'s name in the horizontal band sits directly above the depiction of the mason at work only strengthens this identification. But what can we say about this *Rikard*? When publishing the second volume of his four-tome work, *The Old-Northern Runic Monuments of Scandinavia*, in 1868, George Stephens (1813–95) – the 'pioneering, erratic, and irascible' scholar of runes and runic inscriptions – believed very little: 'Richard', he reminded his readers, 'was a very common name'.[42] By 1884, however, Stephens had formulated a more exciting thesis: that this *Rikard* was the same Richard the engineer whose career in the bishopric of Durham can be reconstructed from a range of evidence, including a fascinating miracle narrative.[43] This evidence establishes that Richard was employed by Hugh du Puiset, bishop of Durham, to rebuild and renew the castle at Norham and that he was very likely responsible for the phase of major reconstruction dated to the 1160s.[44] Stephens's identification of *Rikard* the mason with Richard the engineer has been influential and is occasionally cited, not least, we may suspect, because the challenge of reconstructing the career of an individual craftsman – to compare with other 12th-century *virtuosi* – has always been an attractive one for historians.

We should nevertheless be cautious. What little we know about these careers of 12th-century masons and metalworkers – as the recent identification, for instance, of an Anglo-Norman mason working for Muirchertach Ua Brian, king of Munster and high-king, on his oratory of St Flannán in the 1090s has demonstrated – hints at complex and competitive networks of artisanal recruitment and employment in the early-12th-century British Isles.[45] Stephens was not incorrect in his statement that Richard was a common name in the 12th-century north. Attributing two very different works – the first requiring the abilities of a sculptor with some skill in the carving of runes, the second demanding the expertise of an engineer versed in the business of tower-construction and in the latest fashions of seigneurial comfort – may do an injustice to the range, depth and vitality of artistic talent in 12th-century northern Britain. Even if we reject the possibility that the runic inscription carries the signature of two masons, *Rikard* is unlikely to have carved the font on his own. The acquisition of the stone and its transport to Bridekirk would at least have required a number of trained hands. *Rikard* may also have worked on the rebuilding and decoration of the church, but we must presume that this, too, was the work of more than one craftsman. At Bridekirk, therefore, we may therefore be looking at a small team of masons and sculptors – of *Rikard & Co.*, as it were – rather than at one 'ingenious sculptor' working in precocious isolation. Stephen's original identification of this *Rikard* with Richard the engineer should not only be treated with caution, but should not be allowed to obscure the extent of *Rikard*'s collaboration with other masons and craftsmen.

The details of the inscription and the depiction of *Rikard* on the font nevertheless tell us something important about the font's patrons. There may have been other members of his team, and there may even be a second name included in the inscription, but it is *Rikard*'s name that was awarded such prominence in the inscription and which stands over the figure of the mason. The details of this figure – the long, braided hair (as long, indeed, as the hair of the angel in the Expulsion scene), the neat, trimmed beard, the decorated, belted and elegant garment (Figure 23.7) – bespeaks a clear pride in his professional calling and personal standing. This is the very ideal of a mason, and constitutes one of the finest depictions of a Romanesque craftsman in action.[46] *Rikard*'s professional zeal was certainly shared by some of his contemporaries. So proud was Snarri of York in his office of toll-collector that his ivory seal-matrix depicts him elegantly dressed and holding a money-bag into which coins fall easily – but inescapably.[47] In his miracle narrative concerning Richard the engineer, builder of Norham castle, Reginald of Durham declares that Richard is – he was evidently still alive – most famous 'among the inhabitants of the region for his skill (*ars*) and reputation (*nomen*)' and is

FIGURE 23.7

Bridekirk Font: figure of Rikard on lower register of original south face (Hugh Doherty)

called 'by his name Richard the engineer'. This is exactly how Richard was styled in deeds drafted in his name for the monks of Durham: he evidently took satisfaction in his standing as 'the engineer'.[48] The pride taken by both Snarri and Richard in their professional status was likely to have recommended them to their lords and fellow citizens in York and Durham. The patrons of the Bridekirk font may have recruited *Rikard* the mason for exactly the same reasons: as much for his reputation as for his skill. The fact that it was this face of the font, the face which may have been seen on entry through the church's southern door, may reveal the desire of the patrons to demonstrate *Rikard*'s contribution to the font's creation. The pride expressed by *Rikard* in the elegance of his figure and in the pre-eminence of his name in the inscription must surely reflect, in its own way, the pride of his patrons.

Let us turn, finally, to the more problematic issue of when the font was carved. Zarnecki advanced a date range of the 'third quarter of the 12th century', but as a characteristically oracular statement, without any meaningful explanation of his reasoning.[49] Dodwell discussed the font only within the context of the Dover Bible, which he dated to '1150–1160', but, once again, offered no discussion of his criteria.[50] Pevsner and his successor looked instead to 'the mid-twelfth-century'.[51] Such efforts should be treated with caution, dependent, as all such efforts are, on variable and subjective interpretations of style, expertise and technological change, and complicated by the difficulties of dating architectural and sculptural fashions at a local level.[52] Certainly, as Drake has observed, the closest parallel to the Bridekirk font, in its shape and design, is the font now preserved at Lenton (in Nottinghamshire) that Zarnecki himself, it should be noted, dated to 1140 × 1160.[53] The runic inscription offers only the most tentative help here. Barnes and Page observed that the use of the one of the runic graphs found in the inscription 'seems to begin after 1150', but were nevertheless only prepared to offer 'a twelfth-century dating' for the font.[54] Then there is the related issue of the date for the surviving sections of the 12th-century church. These sections have been almost entirely ignored by the extensive literature on the font, so there has been little consideration of their date, but Pevsner and his successor volume dated them to the mid 12th century.[55] Since there can be no certainty here, and since we are in danger of running around in ever more confusing circles, this paper will propose (in the light of the documents to be considered shortly) that the church was rebuilt and the font carved in the course of the 1140s, but that this was the climax of a process that began in the late 1120s or 1130s. Compelling evidence frames the historical context and leaves any later date unconvincing.

THE PATRONS OF ST BRIGIT'S CHURCH

Who, then, were the patrons of *Rikard* and his colleagues? Critical evidence here is supplied by four documents published by William Dugdale in 1673, in the third and final volume of the *Monasticon Anglicanum*, that learned enterprise initiated by the Yorkshire antiquary, Roger Dodsworth, in the 1630s and 1640s, but completed by Dugdale himself over the course of the two decades following the publication of the first volume in 1655.[56] In his source note for these four documents, Dugdale reveals that they had been in the possession of Richard Tolson 'in April 1665' – when Dugdale was conducting his heraldic visitation of the counties of Cumberland and Westmorland in his capacity as Norroy King of Arms. The precise circumstances in which this Richard Tolson shared his documents with Dugdale remains frustratingly unclear. Richard is known to have submitted his family descent and arms for Dugdale's verification at Cockermouth on Friday, 31 March, and this may have been the occasion for the presentation of his muniments. Since, however, he also held the manor of Bridekirk, it is possible that he produced them when Dugdale made his visit to Bridekirk church. The story is complicated by the fact that there is evidence that Richard Tolson presented these documents to Dugdale – perhaps for a second time – in London in the early summer of 1666. Their eventual fate remains unknown, but they have long since disappeared, and may even have been destroyed in the Great Fire of London. No copy of these documents survives in the many notebooks belonging to William Dugdale or Gregory King. We are therefore dependent for the texts of these documents on their printing of 1673. This should not obscure their importance. Since Henry VIII had granted the manor of Bridekirk to Henry Tolson, the great-grandfather of Richard Tolson, in July 1543, the four documents must have passed into the possession of the Tolson family directly from the church of Bridekirk.[57] What these four documents represent, in other words, is the archive of a 12th- and early-13th-century parish church.

For the purposes of the present paper, only two of the four documents directly concern us here. The first is a deed of Waltheof, son of Earl Gospatric, granting the vill of Appleton to the church of St Brigit (in Bridekirk) and confirming E. the priest and El. son of Erlaf the priest in their possession of the church. The second is a deed of Alan, son of this Waltheof, confirming his father's gift of Appleton, supplementing this gift with the tithe of the mill of Broughton, and confirming Athelwold, son of Erlaf the priest, in possession of the church. Both deeds, it should be stated immediately, are not without their complications: there is tentative evidence that they were reworked, very likely in the first decade of the 13th century, but they both possess enough legitimate forms and enough verifiable detail to suggest that they were reworked from authentic single-sheet originals. They offer the best evidence discovered so far for the identities of the patrons of the font at Bridekirk and for the material investment made by these laymen in their church. We should stress that these deeds do not constitute the 12th-century equivalent of that contract between the canons of Beverley and the apprentice of a London goldsmith for the construction of a new reliquary shrine in 1292 – the earliest surviving artisanal contract from northern England – with its specific injunctions on the details of the design, the terms of the payment and the obligations on the goldsmith.[58] But they nevertheless provide a clear and direct link between these laymen, their relations and followers, the priestly personnel of the church and the carving of the font.

Waltheof, son of Earl Gospatric, and his son Alan belonged to one of the élite families of northern England. Waltheof's paternal kin had ruled Northumbria from their seat at Bamburgh since the early 10th century. More recently, his father, Earl Gospatric, had ruled as earl of Northumbria in the late 1060s, and his (considerably older) brother, Dolfin, had exercised some form of control over the territory centred on Carlisle in the 1080s and early 1090s. Waltheof and Alan were themselves lords of Allerdale in the shire of Cumberland, in what is now north-west England. They exercised their leadership and authority over a small set of vills in the coastal lowlands, over a share of the western lake fells, and over a spread of churches, enjoying a handsome array of services, revenues and rights and commanding a body of active tenants and followers.[59] Waltheof had certainly been recognised as lord of Allerdale by the early 1120s, but may have been established there from still earlier. He appears to have died at some point early in the reign of King Stephen and probably by 1136.[60] His son and successor, Alan, succeeded in the 1130s, but died sometime before June 1152. Waltheof's deed for the church of St Brigit can very likely be dated 1126 × 1136, while Alan's deed was very likely drafted soon after his succession and can probably be dated 1136 × August 1139.[61] Both men enjoyed close ties to the premier rulers in northern Britain, the kings of Scots, and especially to King David, son of King Mael Coluim III. Waltheof himself can be seen attending upon David when he was *princeps* of Cumbria in the early 1120s, and he appears later to have entrusted custody of his son and possibly his lordship to David when king in the late 1130s.[62] Alan, in turn, was an active supporter of David's efforts to rule the northern shires of the English kingdom. Their ties to the king and his court has bearing on some of what follows.

The deeds of Waltheof and Alan for their church of St Brigit offer a rare and revealing insight into the nature of their devotional life. Retrieving the character and quality of that life – as for the 12th-century secular élite as a whole – from the surviving evidence is no easy task. Perhaps Waltheof (as the late-11th-century monks of Worcester believed of Leofric, earl of Mercia) was accustomed 'to drink very little' – but still 'be happy with drinking companions'; 'to pray in secret'; and to hear 'two masses each day'.[63] But perhaps he was more inclined to spend nightly vigils at the shrines of the saints (as Guibert of Nogent has his bête noire, John, count of Soissons, declare) 'because beautiful women spend the night here'.[64] Waltheof is certainly known to have fathered sons by many sexual partners.[65] There is much that we do not know. According to the early-17th-century historian John Denton, who very likely drew on material from the archive of Carlisle cathedral priory, Waltheof acquired a significant share of relics when on pilgrimage to Jerusalem and Constantinople.[66] Such a pilgrimage is not, in itself, unlikely, but our uncertainty about so significant a moment in Waltheof's spiritual formation underscores the gaps – or rather gulfs – in our knowledge.

What evidence there is reveals that both Waltheof and Alan were as sensitive and as responsive to the currents and fashions of religious reform and renewal as other lords in 12th-century northern Britain. Two examples will have to stand for many. The first concerns the priory of Hexham. In his history of his own community, Richard, prior of Hexham, credited Waltheof and his son Alan with giving four bovates of land and a house for fishing herring in their lordship of Allerdale.[67] The community at Hexham, possessing the relics of its episcopal triumvirate of Wulfric, Acca and Alchmund, had been refounded as an Augustinian community in the course of 1113, and the gifts made by Waltheof and his son reveal their commitment to its refoundation. The fact that they were served by a priest who bore the name of Acca – he witnessed Alan's deed for the church of St Brigit's – can only have reinforced the appeal of the refounded community of Hexham. The second example concerns Alan's foundation of a Cistercian abbey on the isle of Holm Cultram. We possess no deed drafted in Alan's name, partly because both Alan and his own son Waltheof appear to have died in unknown circumstances before they could complete their intended gift. But the deed of Henry, son of David, king of Scots, and earl of Northumberland, is explicit that Alan and his son had given the monks a share of their estate in Holm Cultram.[68] Alan and his son appear to have been as electrified by the reformed life lived by the brethren of Cîteaux – by 'the citizens of the saints', as Bernard of Clairvaux put it with characteristic vehemence to another secular lord – as other leading laymen in the Latin West of the 1140s.[69]

Significant collaborators and sources of counsel in the rebuilding of the church of St Brigit, so the deeds of Waltheof and Alan reveal, must have been the clerical personnel of the church. The deed of Waltheof explicitly confirmed the church and all its pertinences to E. the priest and to El. son of Erlaf the priest, while the deed of Alan fitz Waltheof confirmed the church to Athelwold the clerk, son of Erlaf the priest. This Athelwold the clerk, son of Erlaf the priest, is likely to have been the same individual as the El. son of Erlaf the priest referred to in Waltheof's deed; his name may have been some variation on Elwold (or even Aelwold). These deeds thus identify three different priests of St Brigit's church in Bridekirk: E. the priest, Erlaf the priest and Athelwold the clerk, son of Erlaf the priest. Since by the time Alan had his deed drafted for the church, Athelwold the clerk appears to have succeeded both his father and E. the priest as sole custodian of the church, we may be dealing here with a line of hereditary priests, similar, in effect, to the custodians of Hexham church. These custodians were clearly men of status and standing: Waltheof refers to Athelwold the clerk as his 'kinsman and foster brother' (*cognatus meus et alumpnus*). The lords of Allerdale were evidently bound to the priests of St Brigit's church and the priests of St Brigit's to the lords of Allerdale by a complex weft of ties. There was honour and prestige for both sets of men in the association.

These three men – E. the priest, Erlaf the priest, and Athelwold the clerk – may have been more than familiar with the expectation that priests should decorate and embellish their churches.[70] The hereditary priests of Hexham were celebrated by their descendant, Aelred of Rievaulx, in the 1150s 'for restoring, adorning, and preserving the churches of Christ', and the priests of Bridekirk were unlikely to have been any different.[71] When composing his treatise on recluses for his sister in the 1160s, however, Aelred took a rather more hostile line, but his criticism – a rejection, in effect, of the artistic munificence for which his family seems to have been famed – nevertheless offers one of the most revealing insights into the investments of parish priests in the furnishing and decoration of their churches: 'I would not wish you, on the grounds of devotion, to strive for that glory vested in painting or sculpture, in hangings decorated with birds or beasts or depictions of different flowers'.[72] A more sympathetic expression of the value of such efforts was made by Sigar, parish priest of Newbald (in the East Riding, Yorkshire), in his *Vita et uisio simiplicis Orm*, which he composed in 1126 or soon afterwards.[73] Sigar, it is clear, was no isolated and marginalised *curé*, but an active and widely regarded participant in a well-connected literary network.[74] His *Vita et uisio* is none the less one of the few texts written by a parish priest (rather than by their monastic detractors) to have survived from early-12th-century northern Britain, and takes us closer to the values and aspirations of E. the priest and his colleagues than perhaps any other work. Even if his text, which recounts the visionary experience of a young boy by the name of Orm, who lived in the parish of Howden, owes more to the literary pretensions of Sigar than to the recollections of Orm himself, Sigar is explicit that the details of the vision were both widely verified and excitedly discussed by the 'priests, monks, clerics, and the laity' of the neighbouring parishes.[75] His work is unlikely, therefore, to have strayed too far from the essential components of the narrative. The nature of the sights described by Orm – of the crucified Christ; of Michael the Archangel holding a book depicting the passage of time, its letters written in gold; of the open jaws of hell – surely underline, as has been observed, the impact of the visual experience of a parish church and of its furnishings on the imaginative landscapes and devotional practices of lay parishioners.[76] In many ways, therefore, Sigar offers his readers (primarily, if not exclusively, the monks of Durham) an eloquent – if not necessarily deliberate – validation of the devotional purpose and effective power of 'the paintings and carvings' so denounced by Aelred and others. The idealised parish world evoked by Sigar was likely to have been one endorsed and cherished by his professional colleagues in Bridekirk.

As priests of the church of St Brigit, both E. the priest and his colleagues would have had every reason to welcome the rebuilding and furnishing of their church. The font – as Gillebertus, bishop of Limerick, described it in his contemporary treatise – was one of the essential furnishings for every parish church.[77] The new emphasis on the sacramental efficacy of baptism, as articulated by Hugh of St Victor and others, may have been slow to reach northern Britain, though not as slow, perhaps, as we might imagine, but the liturgical and even cultic power that possession of a font gave to its custodians was unlikely to have been lost on the priests of St Brigit's.[78] They were even less likely to have been blind to the more temporal advantages offered by 'the sacred font'. The carving of a new stone font was a powerful reminder of St Brigit's status as a baptismal church and an equally effective statement of their own authority and standing. Fonts were also, moreover, valuable sources of profit. The prohibition on the taking of money for the baptism of children – as condemned, for example, at the legatine council of London in 1138, the *acta* of which were certainly still read at Hexham in the 1140s – was doubtless more honoured in the breach than the observance.[79] It is not impossible that the second name identified by Page and Barnes in the Bridekirk inscription, a name which may be a form of the Old English *Earnweard*, is in fact the same individual as E. the priest. Even if this reading is rejected, E. the priest and Athelwold the clerk surely have as much right to be called the patrons of the Bridekirk font as the lords of Allerdale.

They were certainly in an excellent position to recommend the rebuilding and renewal of their church. Only two deeds of Waltheof have survived, but only one – for the church of St Brigit – includes a witness list. It is therefore impossible to assess how often he was attended upon by the priests of Bridekirk, but given the ties of kinship and friendship between Waltheof and Erlaf the priest, their interaction was likely to have been not infrequent. The seven surviving deeds of Alan are, in this regard, good evidence. Athelwold the clerk witnesses three of them.[80] His attestation denotes that he enjoyed a prominent place in Alan's household and perhaps even a significant role in his private chapel. The fact, moreover, that he is entered as the last witness in two separate deeds lets us infer – for it was a convention – that he was the scribe responsible for the drafting of both documents. There is the possibility, therefore, that Athelwold the clerk served the lords of Allerdale as their scribe, household clerk and keeper of their treasure, including their small array of relics. The impact of such local and household clergy on the devotional ideals and practices of the northern secular élite should not be underestimated. If the lessons taught by E. the priest and his colleagues were as arresting and as compelling as those recounted by Sigar to his own parishioners – that the daughter of a local knight had achieved salvation through her vow of virginity (rather than through the alms invested by her father), that the denizens of the earthly paradise were dressed 'in rich vestments of many colours', and that even the apostles were equipped with swords, which they were all too ready to unsheath in judgement – they are likely to have found a ready audience among Waltheof, his family and his following.[81] Both men would thus have enjoyed multiple opportunities to encourage Waltheof and Alan to rebuild and renew the church of St Brigit and to remind them of the many advantages to be had – in the here and now as well as in the next world – in doing so. The Bridekirk font may, in effect, be the most lasting visible result of their encouragement.

WALTHEOF AND THE ENDOWMENT OF ST BRIGIT'S CHURCH

The deeds printed by William Dugdale in 1673 reveal that a significant stage in the renewal and rebuilding of the church was represented by Waltheof's gift of the vill of Appleton and his quittance from the obligation to render multure. His gift and exemption can be no more narrowly dated than 1122 × 1136. The beneficiary of his generosity was 'the church of St Brigit the virgin'; indeed his deed provides the earliest evidence for the church's dedication to this saint. While the church had a stone cross from the late 10th century or soon afterwards, the church itself was still very likely a wooden structure by the time Waltheof succeeded as lord of Allerdale.[82] What he and those who witnessed his deed knew about the origins and early fortunes of the church is now lost to us, but their store of information is unlikely to have been negligible. Among those who must have known more than most, who will have played a significant part in the formulation and communication of this foundation narrative and history, were E. the priest and his colleagues. The testimonies of other 12th-century Cumbrian priests would establish that what they related to Waltheof and his family and followers was both detailed and full of resonance for themselves and for their listeners.[83] They may have known, as is now widely believed, that the cult of St Brigit was brought to the north-west by Scandinavian settlers operating in the Irish Sea world, but they may not: they may have nurtured and developed an entirely different narrative of how their church came to be dedicated to this most powerful of female Irish saints. The Bridekirk font should thus be considered a silent memorial to the complex local narratives once vested in the church and its furnishings.

As lord of Allerdale, Waltheof was a lord of churches. The landscape of his territory was dominated by a spread of powerful churches dedicated to a range of saints, and many of these churches – including those of Aspatria, Brigham, Bromfield, Crosthwaite, Dearham, Isel and Torpenhow – belonged directly to him. They were his to retain or relinquish, even, indeed, to grant as a gift on the marriage of his own daughter.[84] The priests who served them will have recognised him as their primary protector and benefactor; the prayers offered in them will have been made for his salvation and for the salvation of his relations; the tithes and revenues that sustained them will have been counted as a significant component of his own wealth; and the obligation to maintain and furnish them will have been his responsibility.[85] Another one of these churches, so the deeds of both Waltheof and his son establish, was the church of St Brigit. Since he did not grant this church to one of the new religious communities in the north-west, since he retained it in his own hands, we must presume it was one of his favoured churches.[86] The precise nature of its status by the early 12th century has been complicated, however, by the recent suggestion that it was originally founded as a chapel subject to the wealthy parish church of Brigham.[87] On this interpretation, Waltheof would have made his gifts as a contribution to the chapel's refoundation as a baptismal church. But we might note that this suggestion about its early lower status was primarily based on the supposition that both churches shared the same dedication to St Brigit. Against this, there is clear evidence that the medieval dedication of Brigham was to St Michael and that it was very likely changed to St Brigit – perhaps on false etymological grounds – no later than the 18th century.[88] While there is record of litigation between the parish priest of Brigham and the lords of Cockermouth over the tithes of the chapel of Cockermouth castle, there is no such evidence for any dispute between the priest of Brigham and the custodians of Bridekirk, even when those custodians (from the early 13th century onwards) were the rather litigious Augustinians of Guisborough.[89] The fact that the church of St Brigit was served by what may have been a hereditary line of priests would strengthen the likelihood that it was a church of independent standing by the beginning of the 12th century. By the 1290s, the living of Bridekirk was valued at £60, one of the highest in the former lordship of Allerdale, rivalled only by the figure returned for the church of Brigham, which was valued at £80.[90] The gifts made by Waltheof and his son can only partially explain this high valuation, which was more likely to have been founded on a combination of other resources, including lands, tithes and fisheries.[91] In making his gift to the church of St Brigit, therefore, Waltheof was not converting a chapel into a baptismal church, but investing some of his wealth for the renewal of a *matrix ecclesia* of established status and standing.

Waltheof's deed for the church of St Brigit is explicit that he had made his gift for the salvation of himself, his wife, sons, kinsmen and friends. This in itself, of course, was no trivial request: the nature of their eternal destinies must have been an essential priority for many members of the laity. But Waltheof doubtless had other reasons to invest in his church of St Brigit. For Waltheof to have made his gift in the first place we must presume a sequence of events – a combination of actions and aspirations – that ended in the drafting and sealing of his deed. What this sequence of events might have been is revealed by two very different accounts of lay encounters with favoured churches and their saints. The first is found in the in the foundation history of the abbey of Saint Martin of Tournai by Herman, monk and abbot of the same community, in the early 1140s. Herman reports that when Fastrad, advocate of Tournai, would pass by the little church (*ecclesiola*) of St Martin – 'riding with his knights' – he would extend his hands and with tears declare: 'Oh Saint Martin! Why do you have no concern for this church of yours, desolate for so long? Now, I beseech you, show mercy and grant that it be restored!' So often did this occur, in fact, that his men, presumably those knights who rode in his company, pleaded with him to refound the church.[92] Perhaps Waltheof was similarly accustomed, when riding with his own knights, to make similar requests on seeing the church of St Brigit. Hermann's compelling description of the intervention made by Fastrad's knights reminds us that the part played by Waltheof's own followers – the Waltheof fitz Bueth, Roger fitz Aldan, and Uhtred fitz Gamel, for instance, whose names were entered in the witness-list of his deed – may have been no less influential in encouraging his own devotion to St Brigit and mobilising his investment in her church.

The second narrative is found in two *miracula* composed by Reginald of Durham. Reginald's collection of miracles worked by St Cuthbert, which he composed in the early 1160s and then supplemented with further *miracula* in the 1170s, offers one of the most detailed insights into the social and devotional fabric of 12th-century northern England; his collection will be an essential source for our further discussion.[93] Reginald relates that the people of Leighton in Cheshire were reluctant to visit their little church there because – even 'though a baptismal church' – it was 'built of unshapely wattle' and was thus 'held in low esteem and thought to be of no importance'.[94] Only when St Cuthbert appeared to a rich young man of the locality during a nocturnal vigil in the church and healed the deformity of his face – by forcibly pressing the young man's face on the altar – was the young man prompted, together with his wife and their son, to demolish the wooden church, rebuild it 'in coursed stone in a most seemly manner' (*lapideo tabulatu decentissime*) and enrich it 'with many gifts of land'.[95] These two *miracula* establish that members of the secular élite were not only credited with a decisive role in the renewal of their local churches, but were believed to enjoy a close relationship with the patron saints of these churches. In the same way that Cuthbert of Durham intervened in the sleeping hours of the laity, so we may wonder if St Brigit – 'in the stillness of the evening air, half-heard and half-created' – haunted the dreams of Waltheof, his wife, and their son.[96]

Every parish church, in Cumberland as in other corners of 12th-century Christendom, was, first and foremost, the possession of their patron saint. This possession found clearest expression in the multiplicity of customs associated with each church, especially – as Reginald of Durham's collection reveals – the diversity of celebrations that marked their feast days: the drinking and dining, the singing and dancing, even the slaughter of a donated bull.[97] Parish churches were also, significantly, the primary location for the saint's continuing miraculous interventions. Reginald of Durham reports that Plumbland church in the *prouincia* of Allerdale – less than five miles to the north-east of Bridekirk – had been the site of many miracles worked by the saint before proceeding to narrate one of the latest and more remarkable of these.[98] His statement may have served his rhetorical purpose, but must surely reflect the contemporary expectation that saints should, and often did, intervene within the space of their parish churches. St Cuthbert was in this regard no way exceptional. The small dossier of miracles compiled by a monk of St Bees in the first decades of the 13th century recounts miracles worked by St Bega since the refoundation of her church in Kirkby as a Benedictine priory in the 1120s.[99] The dossier provides a valuable insight into the sort of miracles that might been worked by other saints in other churches in 12th-century Cumbria – of the many miracles, for instance, credited by Reginald to Cuthbert at Plumbland. The dossier thus narrates her miraculous interventions to preserve her rights, to punish oath-breakers, and to protect the denizens of her vill from the depredations of the men of Galloway. When, therefore, a monk of Glasgow, completing his life of St Kentigern in 1147 × 1164, declared that the saint's miracles 'still appear in Cumbria (*in Cambria*)', there was more than rhetorical flourish to his claim.[100] The lordship of Allerdale, which possessed at least one church and possibly more dedicated to St Kentigern, would certainly have been one venue for the performance of such *miracula*.[101]

St Brigit the virgin may have been as dynamic a force in the lives of the lay patrons and priests of Bridekirk as St Cuthbert was at Plumbland and St Bega at Kirkby. Waltheof doubtless had many reasons to visit the church of St Brigit. His ties of kinship and fosterage to the priests of the church, as detailed in his deed, may have endowed him with an early and enduring attachment to the church. Given the proximity of Bridekirk to his headquarters at Papcastle, the church is likely to have been a regular stop in the moveable feast that was his itinerary. The church will have offered him and his family a convenient location for the celebration of some of the major feasts of the church and for the performance of their private devotions.[102] It may also have offered them, as other churches offered, a comfortable venue for them to take rest and refreshment with kinsmen, friends and followers – Cumbrian weather permitting.[103] But they must have come, too, in search of St Brigit. If her feast day on 1 February was celebrated there with the same solemnity and conviviality as that accorded to the saints of other parish churches, Waltheof and his family would have been immersed in the liturgical drama of her feast and versed in the miracles that formed part of her lesson.[104] They may also have been treated to lavish suppers by E. and Erlaf the priests.[105] Such occasions will have provided the priest with a welcome opportunity to press upon the lord the significance of the saint and the need for the further endowment of her church (even, perhaps, to complain of the heavy burden of Waltheof's mill at Broughton on the community). Perhaps like the rich young man of Leighton and his family, Waltheof and his wife were accustomed to spend nocturnal vigils in the church of St Brigit and to seek out her miraculous intervention. If, like the monks of St Bees, one of the priests at St Brigit had also compiled a small dossier of miracles in the first decades of the early 13th century, we might have as revealing an insight into the impact of St Brigit on the *prouincia* of Allerdale as we do for the intervention of St Bega in the lordship of Copeland. According one of the *miracula* in the St Bees dossier, Godard, the constable of Egremont castle in Copeland and a contemporary of Waltheof's, was taught the temerity of his arrogance when one of his men was punished by St Bega herself for pasturing his favourite horse on a field belonging to the new priory.[106] Godard was evidently known to Waltheof: not only do they both witness one of the earliest deeds for the monks of St Bees, but Waltheof also attests Godard's own deed of gift for the same community. Beyond the statement that it was drafted 'on the day of the dedication of the church', the deed reveals little about the events and experiences that prompted Godard to make his gift to the community.[107] His encounter with St Bega may not have occurred on the lines recounted by the compiler of the miracle collection, but his devotion to the saint was evidently significant enough to deserve remembrance in her community. Godard and Waltheof doubtless had much to discuss whenever they met, but that their conversation occasionally turned to the power of St Bega and St Brigit seems a not unreasonable possibility.

Interest in the life of St Brigit was not confined, however, to the talk of Waltheof and his circle. That this was a conversation enjoyed in many different corners of the North Sea world in the first half of the 12th century is clear from the presence of her statue, complete with *titulus*, in the golden altar carved in *c.* 1135 for the church in Lisbjerg in Denmark – an altar more or less contemporary with Waltheof's own deed of gift for her church in Bridekirk.[108] Her inclusion in an early-12th-century monastic calendar from Durham Cathedral priory and in a later one from St Bees's priory would hint at similar talk from Waltheof's own orbit.[109] But the clearest evidence for interest in the cult of St Brigit – from within circles very close to Waltheof and his son – is the *uita* of the saint composed by Lawrence of Durham, monk of the community of St Cuthbert. Lawrence dedicated his work to the future Aelred of Rievaulx, and in his letter of dedication declares that he was simply rewriting a life of St Brigit which had been given to him by Aelred's father Eilaf, the priest of Hexham. He describes this life as being *semibarbarus*, which might mean that it was written in an inferior style or possibly even in the vernacular.[110] What is striking is that when Lawrence composed his work and wrote his letter of dedication to Aelred, sometime in the late 1120s or early 1130s, Aelred was serving as seneschal (*dispensator*) at the court of David, king of Scots, and was thus still very much immersed – as Waltheof and his household would remain immersed – in the values, obligations and priorities of the secular world, so immersed, in fact, that he did not refrain from an unpleasant dispute with a knightly courtier (*militaris*) at the court of King David.[111] Lawrence's *uita* of St Brigit reveals, in other words, a close interest in the life of St Brigit by priestly, monastic and secular élites with whom Waltheof and his family entertained close and collaborative ties. There must have been multiple opportunities for Waltheof, when conversing with the brethren and benefactors of Hexham, and when sharing company and conviviality with Aelred and his courtier companions, including his knightly rival, to have been both informed and inspired by talk of the virtues and miracles of St Brigit.[112] The interest expressed by Eilaf and his son at Hexham, by Lawrence and his confrères at Durham, and by his readers at the court of King David in the *uita* of St Brigit may therefore have played no small part in encouraging and increasing the devotion of Waltheof, his family, and his followers.

The refoundation of the church of Kirkby (now St Bees) by Waltheof's contemporary, William Meschin, lord of Copeland, may have offered a further source of inspiration and encouragement. By the early 12th century, the church of Kirkby may have enjoyed the status and rights of a *matrix ecclesia*, may have been served by a hereditary priest and may already have become the focus for a local cult dedicated to a virgin by the name of Bega. The church of Kirkby was therefore in many respects similar to the church of St Brigit. At some point in the 1120s, William Meschin refounded the church of Kirkby as a Benedictine priory dependent on St Mary's, York, the wealthiest monastic community in northern Britain. The refoundation of the church, the first phase of which was signalled by the consecration of the church by Archbishop Thurstan of York, breathed fresh life into the fortunes of both the church and the cult. A finely carved early-12th-century lintel – distinguished enough to merit inclusion in the Romanesque exhibition at the Hayward Gallery in 1984 – provides some indication at William Meschin's investment in the church.[113] Waltheof was closely involved in this campaign of refoundation. He was present on the day of the church's formal consecration, and he himself gave the church of Stainburn, near Workington, to the new foundation.[114] The successful refoundation and enrichment of the church of Kirkby will have offered Waltheof and his family a model for what could be achieved through action and investment. Waltheof may not have not refounded the church of St Brigit as a Benedictine priory, but he did renew a church dedicated to a female saint of noted local power.

ALAN FITZ WALTHEOF AND THE CAMPAIGN OF REBUILDING

What Waltheof began, so his son and successor, Alan fitz Waltheof, continued. Alan not only confirmed his father's gifts, but supplemented them with a tithe of the mill of Broughton, presumably in Great Broughton, which remained within the parish of Bridekirk until 1863. Waltheof had granted the church exemption from multure, and it was presumably to his mill at Broughton that this due was owed. Alan's gift not only confirmed their exemption from multure, but – more valuably – endowed the church with a share of the mill's profits. By the time Alan's deed was drafted, which was probably in the late 1130s, Athelwold the clerk, son of Erlaf the priest, had succeeded as sole priest of the church. The collaboration of Athelwold and Alan was to result not only in the gift of the tithe of Broughton mill, but also in the realisation of an even more ambitious project: the rebuilding of the entire church in stone. A date of rebuilding in the 1140s would sit happily with the rather imprecise mid-12th-century dating offered for the surviving fabric of this church. Such rebuilding was no small undertaking, requiring the recruitment of suitably skilled craftsmen and representing a sizeable financial outlay. Craftsmen and builders, especially if they were as talented as *Rikard* the mason, were unlikely to have come cheap. Richard the engineer was rewarded by Hugh, bishop of Durham, with two modest estates in the bishopric of Durham and with citizenship of the city of Durham, but Bishop Hugh evidently hoped to retain Richard on a long-term basis, presumably for future building projects.[115] Richard was even admitted to the bishop's circle of household officials and men of business.[116] Alan and Athelwold were unlikely to have offered anything as generous for *Rikard* and his team, who presumably settled for payment in cash or kind.

How Alan and Athelwold divided the costs of such payment remains unknowable, but that gifts made by Alan and his father helped meet them – directly or otherwise – seems likely. By the 1140s, rents collected from the vill of Appleton and money saved through the exemption from multure – the gifts, of course, of Waltheof – would have complemented the existing resources of the priests of Bridekirk for perhaps more than a decade. By the 1140s, in other words, Athelwold may have had enough cash to spare to initiate the rebuilding campaign. It is not impossible, indeed, that this had been Waltheof's intention from the beginning: that these gifts should serve as a first step towards the rebuilding of the church, as a down payment, in effect, for the recruitment of masons as talented as *Rikard*. Alan may likewise have made his gift of the tithe of the mill of Broughton in order to sustain the financial position of the church during – or towards the end of – the rebuilding campaign. But Alan's investment was not confined to his gift of the tithe. As lord of Allerdale, he was very likely responsible for the supply of the distinctive local red sandstone employed for the construction of the church. Evidence from the 13th century reveals that most of this sandstone originated in quarries in Aspatria, which was less than seven miles north of Bridekirk, and that the lords of Allerdale controlled these quarries closely.[117] An alternative source of stone may have been the Roman remains at Papcastle: various Roman altars and building stones from Papcastle were later certainly used in the construction of Cockermouth castle in the 1230s and 1240s.[118] These remains would have belonged to Alan in his capacity as lord of Allerdale. The church of Bridekirk, in other words, can fairly be described as his, down to the very stonework.

The campaign initiated by Alan resulted in the construction of a single-aisle church. The surviving fragments of that church – the cushion capitals of the chancel arch, the figure of Christ in majesty on the tympanum over the south door – suggests that the finished church, though comparable in size to many other northern parish churches, was the product of some investment. It is possible, as Malcolm Thurlby has proposed, that the tympanum was painted.[119] There is no reason to suppose that the significance of their decision to rebuild the church – of the visual power and theological resonance of what William of Malmesbury memorably described as a 'new style of architecture' – was somehow lost on Alan and Athelwold.[120] Goscelin of Canterbury believed that no church could rival the structures built by 'the noble architect of the eternal palace' (*eternii palatii architectus*), but he was doubtless speaking for many when he conceded that churches should, ideally, be 'magnificent, radiant, spacious, full of light, and very beautiful'.[121] His sentiments were as likely to have been shared as much by the secular élite as by his monastic – and indeed female – readership. According to Reginald of Durham, it was the local rich man and his family who choose to rebuild their baptismal church of Leighton 'in dressed stone' so that it was not 'held in low esteem and thought to be of no importance'. In replacing the church of St Brigit with a new stone structure, Alan and his wife may have hoped to do something similar at Bridekirk. Lay patron and priest thus constructed a church where they could celebrate the feast of St Brigit in appropriate splendour and where they could bring family, friends and followers to share in its admiration – a church, in other words, of which they could be proud.

Alan may have had further reason to rebuild the church in stone. The location of his father's tomb remains unknown. Subsequent members of the family were buried within the precincts of reformed religious communities: Alan's nephew, Gospatric, earl of Dunbar, with the Benedictines of Durham, and his early-13th-century successor as lord of Allerdale, Alice de Rumilly, with the Cistericians of Fountains.[122] Alan buried his only son and heir, Waltheof, in the Arrouaisian priory in Carlisle, and he himself may have been buried in the same location.[123] But, in the late-11th and early-12th century, before the fashion for burial within reformed monastic communities became established for leading landholders in northern England, many great men appear to have been buried in their favoured parish churches. Waltheof's own father, for instance, had been buried at the door of Norham church.[124] Michael, bishop of Glasgow, was buried in Morland church (in Westmorland), another high-status church, in 1114: since he may have been a native of Cumbria, it is likely that there was some local, even filial, attachment represented in his choice of burial location.[125] The survival of a small number of late-12th-century grave slabs from Bridekirk establishes that priests and local knights were choosing to be buried in the church's cemetery (or just possibly in the church) in the two generations following Alan's own death.[126] Waltheof may have chosen the church of St Brigit as a suitable venue – a 'splendid place', as the inscription on the font proclaimed – for his own eternal commemoration. Alan was doing more than rebuilding the church: he may have been rebuilding the location of his father's tomb. This possibility adds resonance to his deed confirming his father's gift to the church of St Brigit. Where this deed fits in the sequence of the building campaign is difficult to fix with any certainty, but internal details suggest that it was drafted in the late 1130s and thus at the beginning of the campaign. When Alan, his widowed mother, Sigerith, and his followers assembled to witness the drafting of his deed, they may have done so inside the church soon to be rebuilt in stone and close to Waltheof's tomb.

THE CARVING OF THE FONT

With the church completed (or nearing completed), Alan fitz Waltheof and Athelwold the clerk would have now turned to the business of its adornment with furnishings and lighting. The bestowal and installation of such furnishings were rarely entered in any written record and have all too often fallen victim to the vagaries of devotional fashion, sectarian violence and cross-border warfare.[127] It is indicative that one of the few 12th-century references to the presence of crosses (and just possibly of a *Trumphkreuze*) in northern parish churches should be a description of their destruction and humiliation by Gallovidian raiding partings in the late 1130s.[128] The survival of a late-12th-century reliquary cross from St Helena's church in Kelloe (in County Durham), decorated with scenes celebrating the part of St Helena in the discovery of the true cross and still bearing the remains of the iron fittings for the burning of votive candles, is a striking reminder of what we have lost.[129] All that remains now at Bridekirk is, of course, the font; yet it was likely to have been joined by many other items. The rich array of sumptuous vestments, books, altar furnishings, reliquaries and relics given by the royal clerk and official, Thomas of Burgh, to his chantry in Brigham church in the 1320s – known only because carefully itemised in an indenture of 1348 – may offer some idea of the sort of gifts made by his 12th-century predecessors.[130] E. the priest and Athelwold the clerk are likely to have taken the initiative here, being more than happy – like their Somerset contemporary, Wulfric of Haselbury – to spend some of their income on 'reliquaries and books and vestments' (*phylacteria et libri et uestimenta*) so as to crown their parish church 'with glory'.[131] But Alan fitz Waltheof and his family are likely to have made their own such gifts to the church. Alan may have known that his grandfather, Earl Gospatric, had conveyed two embroidered altar cloths (*dorsalia*), presumably from his private chapel, to the two recluses who heard his death-bed confession; both cloths could still be seen in the church of Durham in the 1190s.[132] In a form of gift-giving that may have been more common than the surviving evidence indicates, David, king of Scots, would donate silver chalices to those parish churches in Craven (in Yorkshire) damaged by warfare in the early 1150s.[133] Alan himself, in what was clearly a terrible and devastating moment in his life, would convey possession of his family's cherished relic of the holy cross, together with the body of his only son and heir, to the Arrouaisian canons of Carlisle.[134] If Alan was willing to make the sort of investment recorded in his deed, he was surely inclined to have made other gifts to their church of St Brigit. The font at Bridekirk may therefore be a lasting reminder of the other, all too perishable, but nevertheless valuable furnishings given by the lay patrons and priests of Bridekirk to their church.

Behind countless Romanesque fonts there was a necessary negotiation between craftsmen, priests and patrons. The design and iconographic details of the Bridekirk font were likely to have been the result of such negotiation.

As the craftsmen entrusted with the creative process of carving the font, the contribution of *Rikard* and his team was likely to have been significant. Such craftsmen were in no way uneducated: they may have been more than familiar with relevant and recondite chapters of biblical history and more than sensitive to the scriptural and theological value of their artistic decisions. Theophilus Presbyter may have written his text for other monk-artisans active in the monastic community, but his dedication to the moral purpose of his craft and his delight in the virtues of artistic workmanship were unlikely to have been confined exclusively to his Benedictine readership.[135] Reginald of Durham's miracle narratives concerning Richard the engineer is here revealing. According to Reginald, Richard possessed a 'book on the life of St Cuthbert, which he kept suspended by a cord round his neck' and a small relic of the cloth (*pannus*) in which St Cuthbert's body had been wrapped, which he stored within the book. Richard was so enamoured of his relic and book that he was accustomed, 'when sitting with his companions', to regale them with their precious character.[136] On this evidence, it seems, 12th-century masons and builders did not require instruction in the lives and miracles of the saints; they carried their relics with them, boasted about their power to their friends and colleagues and were empowered by their protection – even when undertaking so secular a business as the construction of a seigneurial residence. That *Rikard* and his team may have possessed their own share of relics and texts, conversed with each other and with others about the power of their favoured saints and entertained a similar conviction about the moral purpose of their task should not be ruled out.

Athelwold the clerk is likely to have been a no less forceful contributor to the carving of the font. As the sacred custodian of the font, it was presumably Athelwold who must have conversed directly with *Rikard* and his team – perhaps in the early Middle English of the inscription – and who must have been most active (and perhaps most articulate) in determining some of the decoration of the font. It was presumably they, in collaboration with *Rikard* and his colleagues, who decided that the face of the font (on the orientation recorded by Gregory King in 1665) that looked towards the chancel – the liturgical heart of the church – should depict the baptism of Christ. Distinguishing between the respective contribution of mason and priest, of *Rikard* the mason and Athelwold the clerk, is far from straightforward, however. The parallels between decorative features on the Bridekirk font and on Roman monuments from the region – the patterns of the flowers, the beading on the stem, even, perhaps, the use of the inscription – invite particular comment.[137] Are these parallels the result of observations made by *Rikard* and his team when working *in situ*? Or are they the recommendations of Athelwold the clerk? Athelwold may not only have been familiar with the surrounding monuments, but he may have taken particular delight – as Aelred believed other northern priests delighted – in 'birds or animals or flowers of one sort and another'.[138] We may suspect that these decorative features were the consequence of conversation between both mason and priest.

A third voice of no less weight in this conversation may have been that of Alan fitz Waltheof. Alan had every reason to take an interest in the carving and completion of the font. It is possible, for instance, that he intended the font to be finished for the baptism of his only known son and heir, Waltheof. The date of Waltheof's birth is unknown, but must have occurred at some point in the 1140s. Be that as it may, it is worth recalling that it will have been Alan who, as lord of Allerdale, permitted *Rikard* and his team to take local stone from his quarries to carve the font. But his contribution was likely to have been more than simply the supply of resources: he may have expressed his own recommendations on the design of the font. The laity were unlikely to have been silent partners in such enterprises, relegated, as some recent works have relegated them, to the role of passive beneficiaries of a clerically controlled educational programme. Sigar, priest of Newbald, may have cast the young Orm as an 'idealized impression of child piety', but his presentation of the boy's knowledge and interpretative skills were presumably believable enough not to stretch the credulity of his learned readership and thereby discredit his text.[139] An ability to recognise and interpret the identity and accoutrements of Christ and his saints was surely one as useful in a parish church as it was in paradise. Theophilus Presbyter may have been correct to suppose that representations from the passion of Christ and the martyrdom of the saints could inspire the faithful to embrace 'the observance of a better life', but such responses can only have been effective if the laity were already familiar with these episodes.[140] A diet of private prayer, sermons, sacramental ritual and liturgical drama was likely to have ensured that many members of the secular élite possessed more than a passing knowledge of biblical, theological and sacramental detail. The household of Hugh, earl of Chester – a friend, no less, of Anselm of Bec – was unlikely to have been unusual in its passionate commitment both to the business of the hunt and in its devotion to some of the greatest soldier-martyrs.[141] The possibility that Alan and his household possessed both enough knowledge to formulate views on the decoration of the font for his new church and the confidence to express such views with eloquence and insight deserves to be taken seriously.

Examination of the north face of the font underlines the possibilities of his contribution. The upper register shows a centaur in mortal struggle with two beasts, while the lower register depicts an episode (or episodes) from the Expulsion narrative (Figure 23.4). As the current interest implies, Alan would not have been the only 12th-century laymen to express an interest in the features and meaning of beasts. The fact that the monks of his foundation of Holm Cultram possessed an unillustrated copy of Philippe de Thaon's poem, *Bestiaire*, by the final third of the 12th century underlines the existence of wider interest in the theological resonance of such beasts in this corner of Cumberland.[142] If Philippe's *Bestiaire*, composed in the 1120s, is any guide to the sort of conversations that might have occurred on this subject within the élite circles of Allerdale, lay as much as monastic and clerical, Alan may have been more than sensitive to the theological resonance of the dove, the dragon and the centaur – all beasts, of course, carved in the registers of the font. The depiction of the centaur – a beast divided, as Philippe de Thaon put it, between 'truth' (*verité*) and 'villany' (*vilainie*) – in violent and desperate combat with two dragon-like enemies must have spoken eloquently to lay conceptions of their duties and obligations in a sinful and compromised world.[143] Alan's interest in the centaur's struggle may have been more than matched by his interest in the narrative of the Expulsion in the lower register. As was seen earlier, there is tentative evidence that this depiction of the Expulsion was inspired by some sort of dramatic or literary tradition. Perhaps Athelwold the clerk was as accustomed to staging similar dramas for Alan and his household as his contemporary, Geoffrey, school-master of Dunstable, was for the laity of his own town.[144] Since, as Philippe de Thaon contended, beasts 'keep in memory the fact of the ancient crime' committed at the Fall, the depiction of the centaur's struggle can only have reinforced the drama of the post-Expulsion fortunes of Adam and Eve in the lower register.[145] These two registers were not separate, one designed for the laity, the other for the clerical élite; they formed a united and compelling whole. The laity were more than equipped to take a devotional interest in the theological status of Adam: Alan's cousin, Waltheof, even appears to have changed his name to Adam, possibly on taking clerical vows, in the 1120s or 1130s.[146] There is no reason to believe, then, that the general scheme and details of the north face of the font could not have been requested by Alan and his family in conversation with Athelwold the clerk and *Rikard* the mason.

The evidence reviewed in the course of this paper, most notably two deeds printed by William Dugdale in 1673, has revealed a complex process behind the carving of the Bridekirk font. An important moment in this process was marked by Waltheof's generous gifts to the church of St Brigit, which can be dated to the late 1120s or early 1130s. But far from representing the beginning of this process, these gifts were likely to have been the product of an existing relationship between Waltheof and the church – a relationship inspired, perhaps, as much by the magnetism of St Brigit as by the words and encouragement of E. the priest. His gifts provided a significant contribution to the church's endowment and may have supplied some of the wealth for its subsequent rebuilding in the 1140s. The process continued when Waltheof's gift was confirmed and enhanced by his son and successor, Alan, in the late 1130s. In the following decade, in close collaboration with Aethelwold the clerk, Alan undertook the rebuilding of the old wooden church in stone, complete with sculptural and painted decoration. The construction of the church was accompanied or soon followed by the provision of furnishings and other items. Among these furnishings was the font itself. There can be no fixed date for the completion of the font, but the chronology offered in this paper, which would do no violence to the date-range proposed by Pevsner and others, would point to a date in the second half of the 1140s. Its completion by *Rikard* and his team very likely marked the formal end of the campaign of renewal initiated by Waltheof and E. the priest and his colleagues. If *Rikard* the mason has occupied most previous considerations of the font, this is perhaps only just. But this paper has revealed the contribution of others – not only of the lay patrons and priests of the church, but also of their wives, knightly followers and neighbours. Out of their interaction came the rebuilding of the church and the carving of the font. The Bridekirk font, when examined in the context of other evidence, thus allows us to listen in on conversation and chatter about the Expulsion of Adam and Eve, the virtues and vices of centaurs and other beasts, the power of saints as vested in their parish churches, and, above all, the continuing appeal of St Brigit. The font, together with the surviving remains of the church raised by its patrons and priests, stand as lasting memorials to the breadth and vitality of this long-distant conversation.

ACKNOWLEDGEMENTS

I should like to thank Trevor Lloyd (of Whitehaven) for his gentlemanly hospitality and good humour on my many visits to the north; Claudia Contreras Rojas for her superb printing skills all the staff of the Cumbria Archives Service at Carlisle and Whitehaven for their energetic and informed assistance; Lynsey Darby, archivist at the College of Arms, for her generosity and guidance; Richard Sharpe and Nicholas Vincent for their forensic reading; Agata Gomołka for teaching me the difference between a hammer and a mallet; Jim King for letting me use his photographs of the present west front of the font (Figures 23.4–23.5); and Richard Plant, John McNeill and Manuel Castiñeiras for their monumental patience and unfailing encouragement.

NOTES

[1] For Bainbrigg's notes, see London, British Library, MS Cotton, Julius F. VI, fols. 300r – 44r, at fol. 305r; printed in F. Haverfield, 'Cotton Julius F. VI. Notes on Reginald Bainbrigg of Appleby, on William Camden, and on some Roman inscriptions', *Transactions of the Cumberland and Westmorland Archaeology and Antiquarian Society*, Second ser. 11 (1911), 343–378, at 351. Bainbrigg (unlike Camden) was even brave enough to venture into the Debatable Land – into Redesdale and North Tynedale – in order to visit the Roman forts of Risingham and High Rochester in the course of 1601 (on which, see L.W. Hepple, 'Sir Robert Cotton, Camden's *Britannia*, and the early history of Roman Wall studies', *Archaeologia Aeliana*, Fifth ser. 27 (1999), 1–19).

[2] W. Camden, *Britannia, sive florentissimorum regnorum Angliae, Scotiae, Hiberniae, et insularum adiacentium ex intima antiquitate chorographica descriptio, nunc postremo recognita* (London, 1607), 632–633, with drawing of inscription at 632.

[3] For a bibliography of published works on the font, see *Bibliographie der Runeninschriften nach Fundorten 1 Runeninschriften der Britischen Inseln*, ed. H. Marquardt (Göttingen, 1961), 29–31. The font was the subject of correspondence between the Danish scholar, Ole Worm (1588–1654), and Henry Spelman (1562–1641), in 1629–34: *Olai Wormii et ad eum doctorum virorum epistolae*, 2 vols (Copenhagen,

1751), i. 423–426, at 426 (no. 425); i. 426–432, at 431–432 (no. 426) i. 440–443, at 41 (no. 431 [recte 432]). Their correspondence, omitted by Marquardt, is one of the earliest discussions of the font's runic inscription, even though the font is no more specifically identified than as a monument 'sub Brigantibus Cumberlandae' or 'in comitatu Brigantino' – rather unhelpfully rendered as 'Brighton in Cumberland' or 'the Brighton region' (*Brighton-Egnen*) in the excellent modern Danish translation of these letters (*Breue fra og til Ole Worm*, ed. H.D. Schepelern, 3 vols (Copenhagen, 1965–1968), i. 169–171, at 171 (no. 271); i. 174–180, at 179 (no. 284); i. 329–331, at 330 (no. 536)).

⁴ For Stothard's drawing, see D. Lysons and S. Lysons, *Magna Brittania; Being a Concise Topographical Account of Several Counties of Great Britain* (London, 1816), iv. two plates between pp. cxcii–cxciii. For the date of his visit, see Stothard's letter to his father, dated 15 September 1815, printed in *Memoirs, including Original Journals, Letters, Papers, and Antiquarian Tracts, of the Late Charles Alfred Stothard, F.S.A.*, ed. Mrs Charles Stothard (London, 1823), 199–208. Stothard's original drawings survive as BL, MS Add. 9462, fol. 139v.

⁵ For the visits of Thomas Pennant in 1772, William Hutchinson in 1773, and John Skinner in 1801, see T. Pennant, *A Tour in Scotland and Voyage to the Hebrides; MDCCLXXII* (Chester, 1774 [First printing]), 43–44; W. Hutchinson, *An Excursion to the Lakes in Westmorland and Cumberland . . . in the Years 1773 and 1774* (London, 1776), 249–249, plate 11; K.S. Painter, 'John Skinner's observations of Hadrian's Wall in 1801', *British Museum Quarterly* 37 (1973), 18–70, esp. 63–68, plate XXXV (a).

⁶ For his gift of the cast, see V&A Repro. 1863–1826. For his publication on Roman antiquities, see his *A Survey of the Roman Road from Maryport to Papcastle* (London, 1868), partially summarised in his 'On the Roman road from Maryport to Papcastle', *Transactions of the Cumberland and Westmorland Antiquarian and Archaeological Society*, 1 (1874), 169–175.

⁷ G. Zarnecki, *Later Romanesque Sculpture 1140–1210* (London, 1953); N. Pevsner, *The Buildings of England. Cumberland and Westmorland* (Harmondsworth, 1967). It should be observed that Pevsner's driver and companion in Cumberland in 1965 was one of the other contributors to this volume: S. Harries, *Nikolaus Pevsner. The Life* (London, 2013), 656–657.

⁸ For this comment, made by Walter Fletcher, then chancellor of Carlisle diocese, see J. Platt, *The Diocese of Carlisle, 1814–1855. Chancellor Walter Fletcher's 'Diocesan Book' with Additional Material from Bishop Percy's Parish Notebooks*, Surtees Society 219 (2015), 139. It is possible, as Platt has proposed, that Fletcher 'seized upon' a statement by Hugh Todd in his unpublished history of the diocese of Carlisle, that the interpretation of the inscription had been 'arbitary and conjectural' (ibid 139 note 177). But since Todd applied this assessment only to the interpretation offered by the Danish scholar, Ole Worm, Fletcher's judgement may have been better informed and had wider application than his modern editor allows (Carlisle, Cumbria Archives Service [hereafter CAS], DA 1915/3, fol. 238r).

⁹ C.S. Drake, *The Romanesque Fonts of Northern Europe and Scandinavia* (Woodbridge, 2002), 10, 175, and plate 7.

¹⁰ M.P. Barnes and R.I. Page, *The Scandinavian Runic Inscriptions of Britain* (Uppsala, 2006), 278–288, plate 73.

¹¹ This description is found in the third edition of Samuel Lewis's *Topographical Dictionary of England*, 5 vols (London, 1835), i. 202, but not in the first two editions of 1831 and 1833, and was presumably supplied by one of his 'resident gentlemen' (ibid, unpaginated preface). For a slightly earlier description of the church as 'an ancient structure', see W. Parson & W. White, *History, Directory, and Gazetteer of the Counties of Cumberland and Westmorland* (Leeds, 1829), 304.

¹² For the quotation, see the account of the visit made to Bridekirk by the earliest members of the newly founded Cumberland and Westmorland Antiquary and Archaeological Society in June 1878 (Anon., 'Excursions', *Transactions of the Cumberland and Westmorland Antiquarian and Archaeological Society*, 1 4 (1879), 82). It is a revealing insight on 19th-century priorities that Col. Ballantine Dykes, who gave the cast of the Bridekirk font to the earliest incarnation of the V&A, should have been a leading force behind the building of the new church, and that the foundation stone should have been laid by his widow, as is clear from various (unpaginated) entries in Carlisle, CAS, PR 65/35, Churchwardens' Account Book for Bridekirk.

¹³ For their membership of, and contribution to, the society, see A.J.L. Winchester, 'The society's first 150 years', in *Revealing Cumbria's Past. 150 Years of the Cumberland and Westmorland Antiquarian and Archaeological Society*, ed. M. Winstanley et al (Kendal, 2016), 3–59, at 9, 13, and 16.

¹⁴ Access to the west face of the font is made difficult by the proximity of shelves on the western wall of the church, but Lucien Musset – or his photographer – solved the problem by propping a mirror against the wall and photographing the image (L. Musset, *Angleterre romane*, 2 vols (La-Pierre-qui-Vire 1983–1988), ii. 147–149, at 148).

¹⁵ In their analysis of the inscription, Barnes and Page appear rather more certain about the Papcastle origins of the font ('some confirmation of the Papcastle . . . provenance'), but in their introduction offer a rather more guarded judgement: *Scandinavian Runic Inscriptions* (as n. 10), 107–108, 279.

¹⁶ For these words, see P. Holland, *Britain: or A chorographical description of the most flourishing kingdomes, England, Scotland, and Ireland, and the ilonds adjoining, out of the depth of antiquitie* (London, 1610), 768.

¹⁷ For Oswald Dykes, who was rector of Wensley (in the North Riding, Yorkshire) when he accompanied Camden and Robert Cotton on their visit to the wall in 1599, see Hepple, 'Sir Robert Cotton, Camden's *Britannia*', (as n. 1), 7, and B.J.N. Edwards, 'Reginald Bainbrigg, Westmorland antiquary', *Transactions of the Cumberland and Westmorland Antiquarian and Archaeological Society*, Third ser. 3 (2003), 119–125, esp. 124–125 note 140. We might note that Oswald Dykes was a younger brother of Thomas Dykes of Ward Hall (in Plumbland), which was less than seven miles to the north of Papcastle, and had been rector of Distington church, just over ten miles to the south-west of Papcastle, since 1568 (Whitehaven, CAS, YDRC 10/8/10; Carlisle, CAS, Senhouse family of Netherhall, Maryport, DSen Box 4, unsorted deed dated December 1576). He would thus have been more than familiar with the Roman remains at Papcastle.

¹⁸ W. Stukeley, *Iter Boreale*, in W. Stukeley, *Itinerarium curiosum. Centuria II*, Second edn (London, 1776), 17–77, at 51. For the date of his visit, see Stukeley's original accounts of his itinerary in the north and the Wall country: Oxford, Bodleian Library, MS Top. Northumberland e. 2, p. 19; Bodl., MS Eng. misc. e. 384, p. 74.

¹⁹ For his residence with Senhouse, 'who inherits a true for love for these studies', and their visit to Papcastle, see Stukeley, *Iter Boreale* (as n. 18), 49–51.

²⁰ BL, MS Cotton Julius F. vi, fol. 305r. The deletion was not printed by Haverfield, 'Cotton Julius F. vi.' (as n. 1), 351.

²¹ For this chapel, see Whitehaven, CAS, Wyndam Family, Earls of Egremont and Cockermouth Castle, DLec 299 (D/Lec/1/1/2), unnumbered manorial roll for 13–14 Edward IV, mem. 9 dorse. Charles Boucher, misled, it seems, by an unpublished 19th-century misreading of this manor roll, declared that the chapel was dedicated to St Oysth: C.M.L. Boucher, *Prelates and People of the Lake Counties. A History of the Diocese of Carlisle 1133–1933* (Kendal, 1948), 160. For the later medieval cult of St Zita in England, see S. Sutcliffe, 'The cult of St Sitha in England: An introduction', *Nottingham Medieval Studies* 37 (1993), 83–89.

²² For the events of this visit, see my forthcoming study of William Dugdale's visitation of the north-west in 1665.

²³ For King's pen and ink drawings of the font, see College of Arms MS C. 39, p. 13 [in Monuments of Cumberland section]. For a second copy of these drawings, in the formal copy of the visitation notebook submitted by Dugdale to the College of Arms in May 1667, see College of Arms MS, Visitation of Lancaster, Westmorland, and Cumberland [Item 887], on fold-out page between fols. 244v and 245r.

²⁴ G. Smith, 'Description of an antique font', *Gentleman's Magazine* 19 (May 1749), 271. On the antiquary, George Smith, a Scot who made his home in Cumberland and who witnessed the Jacobite invasion of his adopted county, see S. Matthews, *The Gentleman who Surveyed Cumberland* (Carlisle, 2014).

²⁵ A plan and elevation for a new church tower at Bridekirk, made in the late-18th-century, appears to show no porch either to the north or

south of the church (Carlisle, CAS, PR65/37). For the entrance formed from the original tower, see the description of the original church in a newspaper clipping, dated 8 March 1870, from an unidentified local newspaper: Carlisle, CAR, DRC 56/1/1, collection of photographs and newspaper clippings made by Harvey Goodwin, bishop of Carlisle between 1869 and 1891.

[26] For a sober and detailed survey of the font's decoration, see Drake, *Romanesque Fonts* (as n. 9), 10; for a more dramatic description, complete with sketches and tracings by W.G. Collingwood, see W.S. Claverley, *Notes on the Early Sculptured Crosses, Shrines and Monuments in the Present Diocese of Carlisle*, ed. W.G. Collingwood (Kendal, 1899), 68–71.

[27] For this episode, see, for instance, *Vita Prima*, c. 16, ed. J. Colgan, *Triadis Thaumaturgae seu divorum Patricii, Columbae et Brigidae, trium veteris et maioris Scotiae, seu Hibernaie sanctorum insulae communium patronorum acta* (Louvain, 1647), 527–542, at 528, and Lawrence of Durham, *Vita S. Brigidae*, c. 31–34, ed. W.W. Heist, *Vitae sanctorum Hiberniae e codice Salmanticensi* (Brussels, 1965), 1–37, at 13–14. The notion that this scene has some connection to the cult of St Brigit is a lesson in the uncritical transformation of a tentative suggestion into an established fact. In 1988 Lucien Musset speculatively proposed some association with St Brigit: 'S'agit-il d'un martyre (que ne subit point, en tout cas, sainte Brigide, patronne du lieu)?' (Musset, *Angleterre romane*, ii. 346). In 1996 A.K. Wagner suggested a connection with the episode concerning the sword, even though, as she herself conceded, 'depictions of St Brigid with a sword are not forthcoming at present' (A.K. Wagner, 'An investigation of the twelfth-century baptismal font in the parish church in Bridekirk, Cumbria', University of Washington MA Thesis (1996), 39, citing only A. Dunbar, *A Dictionary of Saintly Women*, 2 vols (London, 1904–1905)). Wagner could also offer 'no explanation' for the figure clutching the base of the tree in the scene. In 2008 F. Altvater, in a rather harsh review of Drake's *Romanesque Fonts*, criticised the author's failure to reference 'the substantial literature that offers a counter-reading of the iconography as the locally venerated saint Brigid' (*The Medieval Review* online).

[28] For exponents of these views, see, respectively, Hyde, *Cumbria* (as n. 51). and Drake, *Romanesque Fonts* (as n. 9), 10.

[29] On the cycle at Hardham, see A.M. Baker, 'Adam and Eve and the Lord God: The Adam and Eve cycle of wall paintings in the church of Hardham', *Archaeological Journal* 155 (1998), 207–208.

[30] For the text of the play, see *The Play of Adam (Ordo representacionis Ade)*, ed. and trans. C.J. Odenkirchen (Brookline, MA, 1976); for its date and audience, see the still useful L.R. Muir, *Liturgy and Drama in the Anglo-Norman Adam* (Oxford, 1973), esp. 118–120. While examination of the play's responsories suggests an author familiar with the liturgical tradition practiced in monasteries in southern France, study of the dialect suggests it was performed for English or Anglo-Norman audiences: C.T. Downey, '*Ad imaginem suam*: regional chant variants and the origins of the *Jeu d'Adam*', *Comparative Drama* 36 (2003), 359–390.

[31] For the significance of such drama, see the observations in P. Dronke, *Nine Medieval Latin Plays* (Cambridge, 1994), esp. xvii – xix, and J.C. Caldewey, 'From Roman to Renaissance in drama and theatre', in *The Cambridge History of British Theatre* 1 Origins to 1660, ed. J. Milling and P. Thomson (Cambridge, 2008), 3–69, esp. 40–47.

[32] *The Play of Adam*, ed. Odenkirkchen, 100–101, esp. ll. 516–517.

[33] Ibid., 102–103.

[34] Ibid., 100–103.

[35] Baker, 'Adam and Eve' (as n. 29), 209.

[36] J.A.W. Bennett, 'The beginnings of Runic studies in England', *Saga-Book of the Viking Society* 13 (1946–1953), 269–283, at 269–270.

[37] Barnes and Page, *Scandinavian Runic Inscriptions of Britain* (as n. 10), 283.

[38] Ibid., 284.

[39] Ibid., 284.

[40] For *Rikard* as 'General', see W. Nicolson, 'Two letters from Mr. W. Nicolson, concerning two runic inscriptions at Beaucastle, and Bridekirk' *Philosophical Transactions* 15 (1685), 1287–1295, at 1294; for the font as a monument to his baptism, see C. Lyttelton, 'Description of an antient font at Bridekirk, in Cumberland', *Archaeologia* 2 (1778), 131–133, at 132; and for the identification with Erik Bloodaxe, see H. Howard, 'Observations on Bridekirk font and on the Runic column at Bewcastle in Cumberland, *Archaeologia* 14 (1803), 113–118, at 115–116.

[41] W. Hamper, 'The Runic inscription of the font at Bridekirk considered, and a new interpretation proposed', *Archaeologia* 19 (1821), 379–382, at 382.

[42] G. Stephens, *The Old-Northern Runic Monuments of Scandinavia and England*, 4 vols (London and Copenhagen, 1866–1901), ii. 489–491, at 491. For the quotation, see A. Wawn, 'George Stephens, Cheapinghaven, and Old North Antiquity', in *Studies in Medievalism* VII, ed. L.J. Workman and K. Verduin (Cambridge, 1996), 63–104, at 63.

[43] Stephens, *Old-Northern Runic Monuments* (as n. 42), iii. 221–222.

[44] For discussion of his work at Norham, specifically the construction of private chambers, a gallery, and a tower, see P. Dixon and P. Marshall, 'The great tower in the twelfth century: the case of Norham castle', *Archaeological Journal* 150 (1993), 410–432, at 416–426.

[45] R. Gem, 'St Flannán's oratory at Killaloe: a Romanesque building of c. 1100 and the patronage of king Muirchertach Ua Briain', in *Ireland and Europe in the Twelfth Century: Reform and Renewal*, ed. D. Bracken and D. Ó Riain-Raedel (Dublin, 2006), 74–105.

[46] Matched only, perhaps, by the remarkable depiction of a mason on the tympanum of the parish church of Larrelt bei Emden (in Lower Saxony): for which, see K. Gerstenberg, *Die Deutschen Baumeisterbildnisse des Mittelalters* (Berlin, 1966), 4–5, with plate on p. 7.

[47] G. Zarnecki, J. Holt and T. Holland (eds), *English Romanesque Art, 1066–1200*, exh. cat. (London 1984), 318, no. 373.

[48] For these deeds, which survive as authentic single-sheet originals, see his two original deeds printed in *Feodarium Prioratus Dunelmensis: A Survey of the Estates of the Prior and Convent of Durham Compiled in the Fifteenth Century*, ed. W. Greenwell, Surtees Society 58 (1872 for 1871), 140 note – 141.

[49] Zarnecki, *Later Romanesque Sculpture*, 59, nos 71–72.

[50] C.R. Dodwell, *The Pictorial Arts of the West 800–1200* (New Haven, CT, 1993), 353–354.

[51] Pevsner, *Cumberland and Westmorland* (as n. 7), 78; M. Hyde, *Cumbria: Cumberland, Westmorland, and Furness*, Pevsner Architectural Guides: Buildings of England (New Haven, CT, 2010), 183–185.

[52] For wise words of warning, see R. Gem, 'The English parish church in the 11th and 12th century: A great rebuilding?' in *Minsters and Parish Churches: The Local Church in Transition, 950–1200*, ed. J. Blair, Oxford University Committee for Archaeology Monograph 17 (Oxford, 1988), 21–30.

[53] G. Zarnecki, 'The Romanesque font at Lenton', in *Southwell and Nottinghamshire: Medieval Art, Architecture, and Industry*, ed. J.S. Alexander (Leeds, 1998), 136–142, at 140; Drake, *Romanesque Fonts* (as n. 9), 10–11.

[54] Barnes and Page, *Scandinavian Runic Inscriptions* (as n. 10), 285.

[55] Pevsner, *Cumberland and Westmorland* (as n. 7), 78. Such a date is likewise implied by M. Thurlby, 'Romanesque architecture and Romanesque sculpture in the diocese of Carlisle', in *Carlisle and Cumbria: Roman and Medieval Architecture, Art and Archaeology*, ed. M. McCarthy and D. Weston (Leeds, 2004), 269–290, at 273–274.

[56] For these four documents, see R. Dodsworth and W. Dugdale, *Monasticon Anglicanum*, 3 vols (London, 1655–1673), iii. 46, reprinted in *Monasticon Anglicanum*, ed. J. Caley, H. Ellis and B. Bandinel, 6 vols in 8 (London, 1817–1830), vi. 270–271. For a new edition of these four documents, see my forthcoming study (as n. 22).

[57] *Letters and Papers, Foreign and Domestic, of the Reign of Henry VIII*, ed. J. Gairdner and R.H. Brodie (London, 1901), xviii, pt 1, 543 (no. 981/106).

[58] The contract, dated 18 October 1292, is printed from the earliest London letter book in *Memorials of Beverley Minster: The Chapter Act Book of the Collegiate Church of St John of Beverley AD 1286–1347*, ed. A.F. Leach, 2 vols, Surtees Society 98, 108 (1898, 1903), ii. 299–301.

[59] For the earliest and most complete survey of the resources of the lordship of Allerdale, see National Archives, Cumberland, Feet of Fines, CP 25/1/35/2, no. 13; calendared in detail in J. Bain, *Calendar of*

Documents relating to Scotland, i. *AD 1108–1272* (Edinburgh, 1881), 202–204, no. 1106.

[60] For his enfeoffment by Henry I, see the statement of jurors summoned to give evidence in June 1212, printed from the original return, see *Liber feodorum. Book of Fees (1198–1293)*, ed. H.C. Maxwell Lyte, 3 vols. (London, 1920–1931), i. 197–200, at 198. A narrative composed in the 1270s held that Waltheof had been established in Allerdale by Ranulf Meschin, lord of the *potestas* of Carlisle, in the first two decades of the 12th century; for this narrative, see National Archives, Chancery, Chancery Miscellanea, Scotland, C47/22/9/3; printed in J. Wilson, *Register of the Priory of St Bees*, Surtees Society 126 (1915), 530–533, Illustrative Documents, no. vi, at 531. For his family's earlier claims to Allerdale, see the remarkable, if deeply problematic, evidence of 'Gospatric's writ': *Anglo-Saxon Charters* 16 *Charters of Northern Houses*, ed. D.A. Woodman (Oxford, 2012), 361–378, with text at 370–371. For critical discussion, see R. Sharpe, *Norman Rule in Cumbria 1092–1136*, Cumberland and Westmorland Antiquarian and Archaeological Society, Tract ser. 21 (2006), esp. 53–54.

[61] For the date-ranges of these deeds, see my forthcoming edition of the deeds (as n. 22).

[62] For Waltheof's connections to David, see the text of David's inquest into the possessions of the church of Glasgow in Cumbria (G.W.S. Barrow, *The Written Acts of David I, King of Scots, 1124–1153, and of his son Henry, Earl of Northumberland, 1139–1152* (Woodbridge, 1999), 60–61 (no. 15)). For David's custody of Alan, see the narrative printed in Wilson, *Register* (as n. 60), 530–533, Illustrative Documents, no. vi, at 531.

[63] For this memory of Leofric, see P.A. Stokes, 'The vision of Leofric: Manuscript, text and context', *Review of English Studies* 63 (2012), 529–550 (text at 548–550, quotations at 548 and 549).

[64] For the scandalous behaviour of Jean, count of Soissons, see Guibert of Nogent, *De uita sua*, III 16, ed. and trans. E – R. Labande, *Guibert de Nogent. Autobiographie* (Paris, 1981), 424–426.

[65] According to his deed for the church of St Brigit, Waltheof made his gift for the souls of his wife and of his sons, Gospatric and Alan (Dodsworth and Dugdale, *Monasticon* (as n. 56), iii. 46). Gospatric did not succeed his father, and was later remembered as illegitimate (Wilson, *Register* (as n. 60), 530–533, Illustrative Documents, no. vi, at 531).

[66] John Denton, *History of Cumberland*, 91. For Denton's possession of 'dyvers bookes and peces of books' belonging to the former priory, see J. Wilson, 'The first historian of Cumberland', *Scottish Historical Review* 8 (1910), 5–21, esp. 18–19.

[67] Richard of Hexham, *Historia Haugustaldensis ecclesie*, c. 13, ed. J. Raine, *The Priory of Hexham*, Surtees Society, 2 vols, 44, 46 (1864–1865), i. 1–60, at 58–60.

[68] Earl Henry's deed is printed from an antiquary copy of the lost original in Barrow, *Written Acts of David I*, 150–151, no. 197 (as n. 62).

[69] Bernard of Clairvaux, *Ep.* 109, in *Sancti Bernardi Opera*, ed. J. Leclercq, C.H. Talbot, & H.M. Rochais, 8 vols (Rome, 1957–1977), vii. 280–282, at 281.

[70] For useful discussion, even if one heavily dependent on evidence from the dioceses of Salisbury and London, see H.M. Thomas, *The Secular Clergy in England, 1066–1216* (Oxford, 2014), 307–317.

[71] Aelred of Rievaulx, *De sanctis ecclesiae Hagustaldensis*, c. 11, ed. J. Raine, *The Priory of Hexham*, 2 vols, Surtees Society 44–45 (1864–1865), i. 173–203, at 191.

[72] Aelred of Rievaulx, *De institutione inclusarum*, c. 24, ed. C.H. Talbot, *CCCM* 1 (1971), 637–682, at 657.

[73] For this work, see Sigar, *Vita et uisio simplicis Orm*, ed. H. Farmer, 'The vision of Orm', *Analecta Bollandia* 75 (1957), 72–82.

[74] Sigar dedicated to his work to Symeon, precentor, historian, and pamphleteer of Durham (ibid. 76). For his connections to Malachy, bishop of Armagh, see Bernard of Clairvaux's *Vita Malachie*, c. 35, in *Sancti Bernardi Opera*, ed. Leclercq, Talbot, and Rochais, iii. 297–378, at 341–342.

[75] Sigar, *Vita et uisio simplicis Orm* (as n. 73), 82.

[76] This, indeed, was the suggestion of the text's editor: ibid. 74.

[77] Gillebertus of Limerick, *De statu ecclesiae*, ed. and trans. J. Fleming, *Gille of Limerick (c. 1170–1145). Architect of a Medieval Church* (Dublin, 2001), 154–155. For discussion of the compilation and purpose of this text, and for the copy of the text made at Durham by the end of the 12th century, see M.T. Flanagan, *The Transformation of the Irish Church in the Twelfth Century* (Woodbridge, 2010), 54–91, 119–125.

[78] On the contribution of Hugh of St Victor and Peter Lombard to the contemporary understanding of the sacramental power of baptism, see P. Cramer, *Baptism and Change in the Early Middle Ages, c. 200 – c. 1150* (Cambridge, 1993), 258–261, together with the lucid commentary in P.S. Barnwell, *The Place of Baptism in Anglo-Saxon and Norman Churches*, Deer Hurst Lecture (2013), esp. 14–16.

[79] For the Hexham text of the council's *acta*, see Richard of Hexham, *De gestis regis Stephani et de bello standardii*, ed. Raine, *Priory of Hexham*, i. 101–103 at 101 (*Councils & Synods with Other Documents Relating to the English Church* I *A.D. 871–1204*, ed. D. Whitelock, M. Brett, and C.N.L. Brooke, 2 vols (Oxford, 1981), ii. 768–779, at 774).

[80] For these deeds, see Wilson, *Register* (as n. 60), 80–81, 316–317, nos. 49, 308, and C.R. Davey, 'Medieval grants to the priory of Carlisle', *Transactions of the Cumberland and Westmorland Antiquarian and Archaeological Society*, 2 71 (1971), 285–286 (§ b).

[81] For these details, see Sigar, *Vita et uisio simplicis Orm* (as n. 73), 79 (*c.* 3), 81 (*c.* 5), 81 (*c.* 81).

[82] For this cross-head, see *Corpus of Anglo-Saxon Stone Sculpture* II *Cumberland, Westmorland and Lancashire North-of-the-Sands*, ed. R.N. Bailey and R. Cramp (Oxford, 1988), 74. For the 13th-century statement that the chapel of Triermain remained a wooden one until the time of Bishop Athelwold (d. 1153), see the narrative printed in J.M. Todd, *Lanercost Cartulary*, Surtees Society 203 (1997), 384–385, no. 346. For the statement that Lytham church in Lancashire remained a wooden structure until at least the beginning of the 12th century, see Reginald of Durham, *Libellus de admirandis Beati Cuthberti*, ed J. Raine, Surtees Society 1 (1835), 282–283 (*c.* 33).

[83] For the statement of six named priests of the rural deanary, which can be no more narrowly dated than 1178 × 1195, see Wilson, *Register* (as n. 60), 114–115, no. 86.

[84] For the gift of the vill and church of Torpenhow to the husband of Waltheof's daughter, see the original deed calendared in K.J. Stringer, 'Acts of lordship: the records of the lords of Galloway to 1234', in *Freedom and Authority. Scotland c. 1050 – c. 1650. Historical essays presented to Grant G. Simpson*, ed. T. Brotherstone and D. Ditchburn (East Linton, 2000), 203–234, at 216, no. 10, and the deed printed in C.T. Clay, *Early Yorkshire Charters* 9 *The Stuteville Fee*, Yorkshire Archaeological Society (1952), 125, no. 54.

[85] For commentary on these issues, see M. Brett, *The English Church under Henry I* (Oxford, 1975), esp. 229–230, and S. Wood, *The Proprietary Church in the Medieval West* (Oxford, 2006), esp. 584–651.

[86] For his gift of Bromfield to the Benedictines of St Mary's, York, see the confirmation of his gift in the charter of King Henry I, forged in the 1150s, in Add. MS 38816, fols. 22v – 24r. For his gift of the church of Cross Canonby and the chapel of St Nicholas to the Arrouaisians of Carlisle, see the early 17th-century copy of his deed in Davey, 'Medieval grants' (as n. 80), 285 (§ *a*).

[87] As proposed by C. Phythian-Adams, *Lands of the Cumbrians. A Study in British Provincial Origins A.D. 400–1120* (Aldershot, 1996), 127, and followed by F. Edmonds, 'Saints' cults and Gaelic-Scandinavian influence around the Cumberland coast and north of the Solway Firth', in *Celtic-Norse Relationships in the Irish Sea in the Middle Ages 800–1200*, ed. J. Vidar Sigurdsson and T. Bolton (Leiden, 2014), 39–63, at 55–56.

[88] For the record of a baptism 'in the church of St Michael of Brigham' (*in ecclesia sancti Michaelis de Brigham*), see the inquisition *post mortem* dated October 1300: National Archives, Chancery, C135/49, no. 19, mem. 2; calendared in *Calendar of Inquisitions Post Mortem and other Analogous Documents Preserved in the Public Record Office*, viii. 45, no. 76. See, too, the stipulation, in an indenture between the lord of Cockermouth and the priest of Brigham, dated December 1330, that the former render an annual rent 'to God and the blessed Michael the archangel and the aforesaid church' (*deo et beato Michaeli archangelo et predicte ecclesie*): Whitehaven, CAS, Wyndam Family, Earls of Egremont and Cockermouth Castle, D/Lec 301 ('The Lucy Cartulary'), rot. 12 (no. 155).

[89] For the resolution of this litigation, see the indenture of December 1330 between Anthony de Lucy, lord of Cockermouth, and Thomas de Burgh, priest of Brigham, cited in n. 85 above.

[90] For these figures, see *Taxatio Ecclesiastica Angliae et Walliae Auctoritate Nicholai IV*, ed. T. Astle, S. Ayscough, and J. Caley (London, 1802), 308, 318–320. For the challenges posed by these diocesan returns, and for a discussion of the limitations of the Record Commission edition, see J.H. Denton, 'Towards a new edition of the *Taxatio Ecclesiastica Angliae et Walliae Auctoritate Nicholai IV CIRCA AD 1291*', *Bulletin of the John Rylands Library* 79 (1997), 67–79.

[91] A dossier of 12th-century documents relating to the *matrix ecclesia* of Camerton establishes that its wealth was founded on just such a combination of tithes, lands and fisheries: all the texts were calendared in F. Grainger and W.G. Collingwood (eds), *Register and Records of Holm Cultram* (Kendal 1929)23, nos. 53, 53a, and 53b, and a single *actum* from this dossier was printed in *Twelfth-Century English Archidiaconal and Vice-Archidiaconal Acta*, ed. B.R. Kemp, The Canterbury and York Society 92 (Woodbridge, 1991), 5–6, no. 7.

[92] Herman of Tournai, *De restauratione monasterii Sancti Martini Tornacensis*, c. 9, in MGH SS XIV (Hanover, 1883), 274–317, at 278.

[93] On Reginald's construction and the contemporary richness of his *Libellus*, see, for instance, V. Tudor, 'The cult of St Cuthbert in the twelfth century: The evidence of Reginald of Durham', in *St Cuthbert, His Cult and His Community*, ed. G. Bonner, D. Rollason, and C. Stancliffe (Woodbridge, 1989), 447–467, and H.T. Antonsson, S. Crumplin, and A. Conti, 'A Norwegian in Durham: An anatomy of a miracle in Reginald of Durham's *Libellus de admirandis beati Cuthberti*', in *West over Sea: Studies in Scandinavian Sea-Borne Expansion and Settlement before 1300: A Festschrift in Honour of Barbara E. Crawford*, ed. B.B. Smith, S. Taylor, and G. Williams (Leiden, 2007), 195–226.

[94] Reginald of Durham, *Libellus* (as n. 82), 138–141 (c. 68). For the identification of *Lixtune* as Leighton, see G.W.S. Barrow, 'Northern English society in the early middle ages', *Northern England*, 4 (1969), 1–28, at 4; repr. in G.W.S. Barrow, *Scotland and its Neighbours in the Middle Ages* (London, 1992), 127–153, at 129.

[95] Reginald of Durham, *Libellus* (as n. 82), 141–142 (c. 69).

[96] William Wordsworth, 'Yet once again', in *Lyrical Ballads, and Other Poems, 1797–1800*, ed. J. Butler and K. Green (Ithaca, NY, 1992), 274.

[97] For these customs, see Reginald of Durham, *Libellus* (as n. 82), 179 (c. 85) (gift of bull to Kirkcudbright church); 126–130 (c. 64) (celebratory meal at Shustoke church in Warwickshire) and 182–185 (c. 87) (singing and dancing at unidentified parish church in Lothian).

[98] Reginald of Durham, *Libellus* (as n. 82), 275–278 (c. 129).

[99] For this dossier, which was very likely compiled by the author the *uita* of St Bega, see Wilson, *Register* (as n. 60), 497–520, Illustrative Documents, no. I, at 509–520.

[100] For this claim, reported in a life of St Kentigern composed at the request of Herbert, bishop of Glasgow (1147–64), see *Vita Kentigerni*, ed. and trans. Forbes, *Lives of S. Ninian and S. Kentigern Compiled in the Twelfth Century*, 243–252, at 244.

[101] For the dedication of Great Crosthwaite to Kentigern, see see the will, dated 22 November 1361, printed in R.S. Ferguson, *Testamenta Karleolensia: The Series of Wills from the Prae-Reformation Registers of the Bishops of Carlisle 1353–1386* (Kendal, 1893), 36–37 (no. 36), and just possibly the reference in Jocelin of Furness, *Vita S. Kentigerni*, ed. and trans. A.P. Forbes, *The Lives of S. Ninian and S. Kentigern Compiled in the Twelfth Century* (Edinburgh, 1874), 200 (c. 23). Aspatria, Bromfield, and Dearham were also dedicated to the same saint, but the earliest evidence for these dedications (so far discovered) is entirely 17th century: T.H.B. Graham and W.G. Collingwood, 'Patrons saints of the diocese of Carlisle', *Transactions of the Cumberland and Westmorland Antiquarian and Archaeological Society*, Second ser. 25 (1925), 1–27.

[102] For the expectation on one Cumberland knight to attend the feast days of Christmas, Candlemas, Pentecost, Trinity Sunday and the Assumption at the *matrix ecclesia* of Wetheral, see the text of the 1160s settlement printed from an antiquary copy of the cartulary in J.E. Prescott, *Register of the Priory of Wetherhal*, Cumberland and Westmorland Antiquarian and Archaeological Society, Record Series 1 (1897), 98–101, no. 44. A similar settlement concerning Longnewton chapel in Roxburghshire, probably datable to 1140 × 1151, specifies that mass should be celebrated in the chapel at Christmas, Candlemas, the three days before Easter, Easter, Rogationtide and Whitsun (printed from the original in *Scottish Episcopal Acta 1 The Twelfth Century*, ed. N. Shead (Woodbridge, 2016), 167–168, no. 142).

[103] For the memory of the Worcestershire thegn who feasted and played dice under the great tree in the churchyard of his favourite parish church, see William of Malmesbury, *Vita Wulfstani*, II 17, ed. M. Winterbottom and R.M. Thomson, *William of Malmesbury. Saints' Lives*, Oxford Medieval Texts (Oxford, 2002), 94–95.

[104] For one such lesson, see A. Macquarrie, *Legends of Scottish Saints. Readings, Hymns and Prayers for the Commemoration of Scottish Saints in the Aberdeen Breviary* (Dublin, 2012), 48–53.

[105] According to Reginald of Durham, the parish priest of St Cuthbert's church, Shustoke in Warwickshire, was accustomed to throw small feasts for any secular member of the élite visiting on St Cuthbert's feast-day: Reginald of Durham, *Libellus*, 126–130 (c. 64). For the identification of the church, see Reginald's own marginal entry, ibid., 127, and the commentary in A Hamilton Thompson, 'The MS list of churches dedicated to St Cuthbert attributed to Prior Wessyngton', *Transactions of the Architectural and Archaeological Society of Durham and Northumberland*, 7 (1935), 159.

[106] For this *miraculum*, see Wilson, *Register* (as n. 60), 512–513, Illustrative Documents, no. I.

[107] For deed witnessed by both Godard and Waltheof, see Wilson, *Register* (as n. 60), 26–27, no. I; for Godard's deed, see ibid., 106–107, no. 76.

[108] For the Lisbjerg altar, and for the recent dendochronological dating, see P. Nørlund, *Jysk Metalkunst fra Valdemarstiden. Golden Altars from the Romanesque Period* (Copenhagen, 1926), 73–86, and K. Stemann-Petersen, S. Kaspersen, P. Grinder-Hansen, and N. Bonde, 'Guldets tale. Gamle og nye blik på middelalderens gyldne altre', *Nationalmuseets Arbejdsmarks 1907–2007* (Copenhagen, 2007), 131–146.

[109] For the calendar from Durham, see F. Wormald, *English Benedictine Kalendars after A.D. 1100*, 2 vols, Henry Bradshaw Society 77, 81 (1939, 1946), esp. i. 161–179, at 169, and for the calendar from St Bees, see Bodl. MS Lat. liturg. g. 1, fol. 11v.

[110] For the most accessible edition of the text, but which lacks the preface and the opening chapters, see Lawrence of Durham, *Vita S. Brigidae*, ed. Heist, 1–37. For this preface, see A. Hoste, 'A survey of the unedited work of Laurence of Durham with an edition of his letter to Aelred of Rievaulx', *Sacris eruditi* 11 (1960), 249–265, text at 263–265 and quotation at 263.

[111] For Aelred's time as *dispensator*, and for this dispute, serious enough to be remembered forty years later, see Walter Daniel's untitled life of the abbot, ed. and trans. F.M. Powicke, *Walter Daniel's Life of Ailred Abbot of Rievaulx*, Nelson Medieval Texts (London, 1950), 3–9.

[112] For one such occasion, at Dunfermline in 1128 × 1136, see Barrow, *Written Acts of David I*, 72, no. 36 (as n. 62).

[113] Zarnecki, Holt and Holland (eds), *English Romanesque Art, 1066–1200*, 166, no. 124 (as n. 47).

[114] Ibid., 28–30, no. 2.

[115] For his holdings in Wolviston and Newton Hall, see the entries in *Boldon Boke: A Survey of the Possessions of the See of Durham, Made by Order of Bishop Pudsey in the Year MCLXXXIII*, ed. W. Greenwell, Surtees Society 25 (1852), 2, and the two deeds printed in *Feodarium Prioratus Dunelmensis* (as n. 48), 140 note – 141 note.

[116] For one of Hugh's *acta* witnessed by Richard, see the authentic single-sheet original printed in *English Episcopal Acta 24 Durham, 1153–1195*, ed. M. Snape (Oxford, 2002), 31, no. 35.

[117] For gift of a quarry (*quarera*) in Aspatria by Alice de Rumilly, see BL, MS Harley 3911 (cartulary of Holm Cultram abbey, s. xiii/xiv), fol. 69r – v, briefly calendared in *Register and Records of Holm Cultram* (as n. 91), no. 54a. For the continuing use of these quarries into the 1290s, see the letter printed in *English Episcopal Acta 30 Carlisle 1133–1292*, ed. D.M. Smith (Oxford 2005), 156–157, no. 196.

[118] On these inscriptions, see, for instance, J.W. Curwen, 'Cockermouth castle', *Transactions of the Cumberland and Westmorland Antiquarian and Archaeological Society*, Second ser. 11 (1911), 129–158, at 151, and *RIB* 882, 883, 884.

[119] Thurlby, 'Romanesque architecture' (as n. 55), 273–274.

[120] William of Malmesbury, *Gesta regum Anglorum*, III 246, ed. and trans. R.A.B. Mynors, R.M. Thomson, and M. Winterbottom, OMT (Oxford, 1998), 460–461.

[121] Goscelin of Canterbury, *Liber confortatorius*, ed. C.H. Talbot, *Analecta Monastica* 3 *Studia Anselmiana* 37 (1955), 1–117, at 93.

[122] For the discovery of a burial slab inscribed COSPATRICIUS COMES at Durham Cathedral in 1821, and for discussion of the occupant's identity, see W. Greenwell, 'The house of Gospatric', in *History of Northumberland* VII, ed. J. Crawford Hodgson (Newcastle upon Tyne, 1904), 14–106, at 45, and E. Hamilton, *Mighty Subjects. The Dunbar Earls in Scotland c. 1072–1289* (Edinburgh, 2010), 31. For Alice's wish to be buried at Fountains, see the cartulary copies printed in *Early Yorkshire Charters*, vii. 78, no. 32, and calendared in W.T. Lancaster, *Abstracts of the Charters and other documents contained in the Chartulary of the Cistercian Abbey of Fountains*, 2 vols (Leeds, 1915), i. 52, no. 49.

[123] For the burial of Alan's son, Waltheof, in Carlisle priory, see Wilson, *Register* (as n. 60), 530–533, Illustrative Documents, no. vi, at 531.

[124] For Earl Gospatric's burial at the door of Norham church (*in ipso ecclesie exitu*), in what may have been a requested act of humiliation, see the addition made by Roger of Howden to the narrative history of the earls of Northumbria (Roger of Howden, *Chronica*, ed. W. Stubbs, 4 vols, Rolls Series 51 (1868–1871), i. 59).

[125] Hugh the Chanter, *Historia Eboracensis ecclesiae*, ed. C. Johnson, M. Brett, C.N.L. Brooke, and M. Winterbottom (Oxford, 1990), 52–53.

[126] For these grave slabs, see L.A.S. Butler, 'Some early northern grave covers – a reassessment', *Archaeologia Aeliana*, Fourth ser. 36 (1964), 207–220, at 215, and P. Ryder, *The Medieval Cross Slab Grave Covers in Cumbria* (Kendal 2005), 116–118.

[127] According to an inventory made in 1552, the church possessed two chalices, two silk copes, two bells, one surplice, two corporals and one candlestick (Exchequer, Inventories of Church Goods, Cumberland, E117/1/53, fol. 8v; printed, with commentary, in H. Whitehead, 'Church Goods in Cumberland in 1552', *Transactions of the Cumberland and Westmorland Antiquarian and Archaeological Society*, First ser. 8 (1886), 186–204, at 201).

[128] Richard of Hexham, *De gestis regis Stephani et de bello standardii*, ed. Raine, *Priory of Hexham*, i. 63–106, at 78. For discussion of the implications of this detail, drawn from Henry of Huntingdon's account of the same atrocities, see R. Marks, 'From Langford to South Cerney: The rood in Anglo-Norman England', *JBAA* 165 (2012), 172–210, at 196–197.

[129] For the St Helena cross, see *English Romanesque Art* (as n. 47), 208–209, no. 176, and the commentary, with excellent photographs, in B. Baert, '*In hoc vinces*. Iconography of the stone cross in the parish church of Kelloe (Durham, ca 1200)', in *Archaeological and Historical Aspects of West-European Societies: Album Amicorum André Van Dooselaer*, ed. M. Lodewijckx (Leuven, 1996), 341–362.

[130] For this indenture, which survives as a near contemporary copy, see I. Fletcher, 'Brigham church', *Transactions of the Cumberland and Westmorland Antiquarian and Archaeological Society*, First ser. 4 (1880), 149–177, at 164–165. For Thomas's career, and for the construction of his chantry chapel, see M. Markus, 'The south aisle and chantry in the parish church of St Bridget, Brigham', *Architectural History* 39 (1996), 19–35.

[131] John of Ford, *Vita S. Wulfrici*, ed. M. Bell, *Wulfric of Haselbury*, Somerset Record Society 47 (1932), 65 (*c*. 47).

[132] For Earl Gospatric's gifts, see the additions made by the royal clerk and chronicler, Roger of Howden, to the memorandum narrating the history of the earls of Northumbria (Roger of Howden, *Chronica* (as n. 124), i. 59).

[133] For these chalices, see John of Hexham, *Historia XXV annorum*, ed. T. Arnold, *Symeonis monachi opera omnia*, Rolls Series 75, 2 vols (1882–1885), ii. 284–332, at 326.

[134] For this event, see the narrative of the monks of Holm Cultram printed in Wilson, *Register* (as n. 60), 530–533, Illustrative Documents, no. vi, at 531.

[135] For the possibility that Theophilus Presbyter was *Rikard*'s contemporary, the monk and metalworker, Roger of Helmarshausen, see Theophilus Presbyter, *De diuersis artibus*, ed. and trans. C.R. Dodwell (London, 1961), xxxiii – xliv. For what is still a compelling study of his theological and polemical purpose, see J. van Engen, 'Theophilus presbyter and Rupert of Deutz: The manual arts and Benedictine theology in the early twelfth century', *Viator* 11 (1980), 147–163.

[136] Reginald of Durham tells this miracle twice, but only mentions Richard the engineer in one telling: Reginald of Durham, *Libellus* (as n. 82), 94–98 (*c*. 47), 111–112 (*c*. 54). In fact, *c*. 47, very likely represents a more polished reworking of the second version in *c*. 54, in which he supplies the name.

[137] For the potential parallels between the font and Roman altars from the region, as observed by John Higgitt 'in conversation', see Wagner, 'An investigation' (as n. 27), 30 note 34.

[138] Aelred of Rievaulx, *De institutione inclusarum*, *c*. 24 (as n. 72), 657.

[139] For this quotation, see C.S. Watkins, 'Sin, penannce and purgatory in the Anglo-Norman realm: The evidence of visions and ghost stories', *Past & Present* 175 (2002), 3–33, at 12.

[140] Theophilus, De *diuersis artibus* (as n. 135), 62–64.

[141] For this shared passion for hunting and sacred history, see Orderic Vitalis, *Historia ecclesiastica*, ed. M. Chibnall, *The Ecclesiastical History of Orderic Vitalis*, 6 vols (Oxford, 1969–1980), ii. 260–263, iii. 216–217. For his correspondence with Abbot Anselm, as remembered by Eadmer, see Eadmer, *Historia nouorum in Anglia*, ed. M. Rule, *Eadmeri Historia novorum in Anglia*, Rolls Series 81 (1884), 27–28.

[142] For their copy of Philippe de Thaon's *Bestiaire*, see BL MS Cotton Nero A. v, fols. 41r – 82v, from which the text was edited by E. Walberg, *Le Bestiaire de Philippe de Thaün* (Lund, 1900), text at 1–115. The manuscript may be unillustrated, but there is a pencil drawing of a lion on fol. 62v. For the date of the manuscript, see *Livres et écritures en français et en occitan au XIIe siècle: catalogue illustré*, ed. M. Careri, C. Ruby, and I. Short (Rome, 2011), 74–75, no. 33, with image of fol. 54r at p. 77.

[143] For his commentary, see Walberg (ed.), *Le Bestiaire* (as n. 142), 42 (ll. 1119–1122).

[144] Matthew Paris, *Vitae abbatum*, in H.T. Riley, *Gesta abbatum monasterii sancti Albani a Thome Walsingham, regnante Ricardo secundo, eiusdem ecclesiae precentore, compilata*, 3 vols, Rolls Ser. 28 (1867–1869), i. 73. For the same Geoffrey's connections to Alan's uncle and cousin, see n. 146.

[145] Walberg (ed.), *Le Bestiaire* (as n. 142), 54 (ll. 1465–1469).

[146] For Adam, *qui prius uocatus est Waldief*, see the *couencio* with Geoffrey, abbot of St Albans (printed from the authentic single-sheet original in W. Gibson, *The History of the Monastery founded at Tynemouth in the Diocese of Durham to the Honour of God under the Invocation of the Blessed Virgin Mary and S Oswin, King and Martyr*, 2 vols (London, 1846), ii. Appendix, p. xx – xxi, no. xxx). For Adam's connections to the church of St John the Baptist in Edlingham (in Northumberland), see the evidence collected and discussed in W. Greenwell, 'The house of Gospatric' (as n. 122), 38.

THE SCOPE OF COMPETENCE OF THE PAINTER AND THE PATRON IN MURAL PAINTING IN THE ROMANESQUE PERIOD

Anne Leturque

To represent what a mural work site might have looked like in the 12th century, we need to consider the physical constraints involved in the enterprise: feasibility, cost, materials, time, etc. These aspects were necessarily a subject of discussion or negotiation between the various protagonists, that is to say, at the very least, the patron and the craftsman who gathered a team around him to produce the desired decoration. Any agreement between the two parties would have been based on a binding contract, written or oral. It seems hard to imagine, even in the 12th century, that this commitment would simply rely on the good faith of the parties involved, either in regard to the money required for its realisation, or the ability to execute it. If we accept this as a precondition, the question of the draft drawing inevitably arises. But to produce such a draft, the painter would need to have acquired a certain amount of knowledge. This knowledge was assimilated in the course of his training and the exercise of his profession. He had knowledge of materials and techniques, of drawing and the practice of pictorial representation. The tools required to carry out his work and the preliminary tasks like setting up a scaffold, preparing the wall by coating it prior to painting it (unless these tasks had been already been carried out by stonemasons), the laying out of the pictorial composition by tracing or the use of preparatory drawings, the preparation of pigments and binders and choice of the application technique are all steps that were essential to realising the mural itself.[1]

In the *Liber diversarum artium* or *LDA* (Ms H277, inter-university medical library of Montpellier), the first skill to be acquired by the painter is the mastery of drawing.[2] Moreover, this ability is presented as the foundation of all painting and the first stage of artistic training. Aside from the *LDA*, the only other manuscript that refers to the importance of drawing skill in the artist's training is that of Cennino Cennini, in his *Libro dell'arte* written in 1437: 'The foundation of art and the beginning of all manual work is based on drawing and colour'.[3] In the other treatises, drawing is only mentioned in passing, as, for example, in the 12th century, by Alexandrer Neckam (1157–1217), who considered it part of the artist's apprenticeship without giving details of the process.[4] The *LDA* is therefore the only treatise on painting prior to that of Cennino Cennini to measure the importance of learning how to draw and master proportions, as well as the ability to fabricate and use drawing and painting implements.

LEARNING THE RUDIMENTS OF DRAWING

In the *LDA*, the apprentice is first taught how to draw on what might be called a rough copy, which was a wooden tablet bleached with soap and bone white, on which the shapes were drawn using a stylus (probably made out of wood, bone, copper or silver).[5] This practice is also described by Cennino Cennini, with the young apprentice painter starting by drawing on such tablets and continuing to do so for a year.[6] The English monk, Alexander Neckam also advises apprentice goldsmiths to use tablets to sketch their first drawings of jewels. It is easy to see the connection between these wooden tablets, bleached with soap and bone white, and the wax tablets known since Antiquity and widely used in the Middle Ages[7] (Figure 24.1). Another parallel can be drawn with the glaziers' templates or tables referred to already in the 12th century by the monk Theophilus.[8] He describes the drawing of a pane of stained glass on a wooden board coated with chalk, whose other side is left free to lead out the window. The board was used not only to mark out the main drawing, which was identical to the lead lines, but probably also the interior drawing and perhaps even the shading. The colours of the various parts were marked with letters. The collaboration between glaziers and painters tends to be well documented, even if it is complex. Documentation about making stained glass often appears to refer to the work of painters, including the making of cartoons.[9] These templates were evidently considered to be valuable work instruments, to the point of being subject to theft or bequest. In 1398, one of Jean de Berry's painters, Jacquemart de Hesdin, was accused by Jean de Olanda of having broken the lock on one of his trunks preserved in the palace of the Duke of Poitiers, in order to steal some of his colours and templates.[10]

FIGURE 24.1

Wax tablet © Yoan Martoglio

In the first stage of apprenticeship described in the *LDA*, the apprentice painters learned how to do things correctly: drawing a straight line, a true curve, a square, etc. They also had to learn to draw human figures, known as *ymagines*, flowers, foliage, vine tendrils, twisted strands, long, straight lines, square and rectangular thrones, various kinds of birds, animals, fish – in short, everything that can be seen and touched on the earth. We are not far from the concept of drawing developed by Cennini who also considered drawing from nature as the first step, even before studying the great masters.[11] In the fifth part of his treatise he summarises the entire cycle of apprenticeship for painters: drawing on a tablet for a year, learning how to prepare the materials and supports for six years, studying colours, making gold draperies, learning how to work on walls for another six years, while never abandoning drawing. Talent or a predisposition for painting did not exist as far as Cennini was concerned. The science was considered to be the result of long, hard work that was always accompanied by a master. So anyone who claimed to have learnt by themselves and without discipline was considered to be lying.

REPRODUCING MODELS

The author of the Montpellier text makes explicit reference to models that had already been drawn elsewhere, which one kept after having traced them out. His description of making a tracing is quite succinct. He says to take a sheet (of parchment) that has been finely abraded, and to prepare it with linseed oil and chicken fat. It must then be coated in a circular motion or in such a way that it dries without cracking. To make a model to use as an example, a sheet must be placed over it, and the work appears like the shadow of the original. The directives provided by the monk from Mount Athos Dionysius in the 1st chapter of *The Painter's Manual* entitled 'How to make copies' are much more detailed, like those provided by Cennino Cennini.[12] The latter devotes four chapters of his Treatise to the manufacture of transparent paper. It is hard to imagine that he would dwell on this subject had it not been in widespread use in the late 14th century and probably even before that, as indicated by the *LDA*. He describes how to trace onto parchment or transparent paper, to obtain a copy of a head, a figure or a half-figure according to what is produced by the hand of the great masters. He adds more information that is worthy of interest, describing how to make copies on tracing paper of panel paintings, frescoes and drawings on parchment.[13] These models on parchment or paper are easily transported from one site or workshop to another, and can be reused, reduced or enlarged elsewhere.

The widespread use of transparent paper has also been highlighted by sources from Westminster Abbey, informing us that the templates were models made of parchment or paper impregnated with wax. Indeed, since classical Antiquity, models have been used in the preparatory drawings for painting, especially with the mysterious 'catagraphs' whose invention was attributed by Pliny to Cimon of Cleonae.[14] It is also noteworthy that in Book II of the *LDA*, devoted to painting on wood, there is also a description of cutting a stencil out of a sheet of parchment. Archaeological investigations at Meaux Abbey (England) have brought one of these to light, probably dating back to the 14th century.[15]

MASTERING THE ART OF DRAWING

Learning to draw is accompanied in the *LDA*, by knowledge of the proportions of the human body, directly inspired by Vitruvius, i.e. that in the relationship between the size of the head and that of the body, the face represents one tenth of the body and the whole head, one eighth. It is clear that in the text of the *LDA*, as it has been handed down to us, these proportions have been modified, the face representing one eighth of the body. It is difficult to comment on how this change came about. After at least two successive copies, it may have been the result of a misinterpretation, but one could also envisage a deliberate reinterpretation according to the context in which the treatise was written. The Byzantine proportions described by the monk Dionysius of Fournar also differ from those described by Vitruvius: 'Learn, my student, that the body is nine heads high, that is to say nine measures from the forehead to the heels'.[16] The few experiments on some of the Catalonian ensembles of paintings show a great deal of irregularity in the relationship of ideal human proportions. However, these proportions are maintained throughout the work for all the figures of identical importance, generally corresponding to each of the registers of the paintings, which are often separated by a decorative frieze. As human bodies present a wide variety of shapes and proportions, we can assume that painters adapted these proportions to the subject of the work and the hierarchy of the figures.

Geometry also makes it possible to draw pictures that are proportional at much bigger scales than the human scale. Juliette Rollier-Hanselmann has begun work on this subject through the study of the monks' chapel in Berzé-la-Ville. She emphasises that the painter created an extremely dense composition, with over forty figures in a small space (L. 2.94 x W. 3.26 x H 6.62 m.), which demanded strict internal organisation and meticulous preparation of the semi-circular surface. String was used to draw the boundaries of the register as well as the mandorla of the Christ figure. For the latter, which is located on a virtually flat surface, the length of the nose corresponds to the space between the two pupils and the radius of the first circle. The same principle was applied for the heads of the apostles, producing great uniformity of composition. The use of a three-circle system is even more apparent on the female head (in the scene of the martyrdom of St. Blaise) where the preparatory drawing shows through the worn paint layer. The middle circle, previously hidden under the veil, is visible in the gaps in the painted layer, which verifies her hypothesis.[17] A study by Hjalmar Torp recalls the Byzantine principles that dictated how artists should paint sacred images. The use of models had several functions: to teach young artists the basic principles for building an image, to respect the proportions of the sacred archetypes and to give the work hidden structure, based on simple geometrical shapes.[18] The realisation of an apse decoration presented a number of difficulties for the medieval painter. Curved surfaces and the height of the figures produced deformations and optical effects that had to be rectified. This made the use of geometry and suitable tools even more indispensable.

Drawing a mandorla implies not only the use of a compass system, by means of a string turning around a nail for example, but also knowing how to construct an ovoid element. This basic form, called *vesica piscis* (fish bladder), had been well mastered since the time of the Carolingian manuscripts and appeared to be well known by Romanesque painters (Figure 24.2). The drawing of two flamingos by Villard de Honnecourt (13th century – Paris, BnF, ms fr. 19093, fol. 18v) demonstrates the practical and relatively simple use of this geometrical shape.[19] The mnemonic method of the flamingos goes back to the geometry of Euclid (*c*. 325–265 BC).[20] The principles used by this Greek scholar have survived through the centuries and could be found in the 6th-century Latin translations of Boethius and Cassiodorus.[21] In medieval decoration,

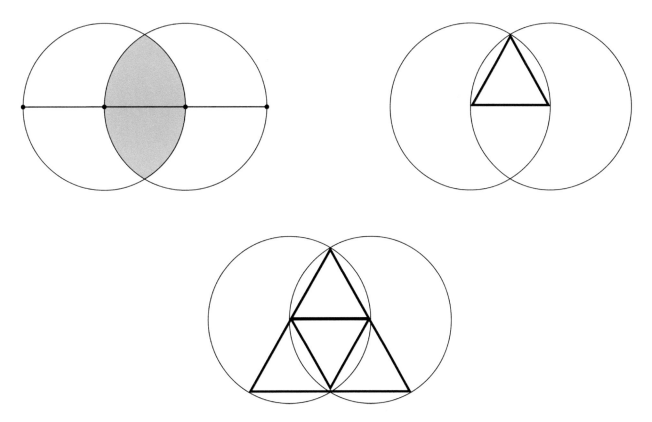

FIGURE 24.2

Motif called a vesica piscis (fish bladder) © Yoan Martoglio we must not overlook the importance of the use of decorative friezes to structure the composition and clearly separate the various subjects depicted.[22]

Technical knowledge is often hidden behind the enigmatic figures of horsemen, human faces or animal figures in the lodge-book of Villard de Honnecourt: they are all mnemonic figures, which the historian and architect Roland Bechmann has deciphered and interpreted. Villard de Honnecourt's sketches are there to remind those working on the site of geometrical constructions, when needed, in much the same way that figures of animals, objects and characters in the sky chart help to recall and recognise the arrangements of the stars in the constellations. This is what Villard underlines when he writes that they are useful for working with. In folio 38 of the lodge-book, the four nude figures serve to construct a square grid; in folio 36, the flamingos help to draw a right angle with a compass and the sheep to form a golden rectangle.[23] The system of building on the basis of a square grid to be able to transpose and enlarge the drawing is nothing new. An Egyptian papyrus from the 2nd century BC, conserved in Berlin, already depicts different patterns drawn on a grid.[24] Another demonstration of this can be seen in the church of San Vincenzo Galliano (11th century, Italy).[25] Later, among the many technical details that appear in *De Pictura* by Leon Battista Alberti (1436) there is one concerning the scaled enlargement of a draft drawing using a grid system.[26]

As the painter acquires his skills, from learning to draw on a tablet, to constituting his own stock of traced copies, painting on parchment and then on wooden panels, he gradually prepares the way for wall painting, and the ability to change scale. The transition from producing a 'small' drawing to laying out a 'very large' decoration therefore requires specific knowledge and tools.

LAYING OUT A WALL DECORATION

When we talk about drawing, particularly large-scale wall drawing, the question of tools is fundamental and warrants closer attention. The author of the *LDA* specifies that the objects used for wall drawing include an iron or steel tip (Figure 24.3), a paintbrush (documented in Book I of the *LDA*), a compass, a ruler (or rather, a rod), a string or a *condermenia fectam de carta*. The fabrication of a paintbrush is described and documented in the *LDA*, with a sketch illustrating the following text: 'Fabricate a paintbrush with a small tuft of hairs from the tail (of a squirrel?), bind them together, cut off the base of a feather and insert them into it to give them the shape'[27] (Figure 24.4). A brush might be made from the hairs of a squirrel's tail as described, or from pig bristles as seen in Cennino Cennini.[28] Several types of compasses were used at the time of Villard de Honnecourt. In his lodge-book we find a sector in which the quadrant, fixed to one of the legs, slides across the other leg, to block the compass in certain open positions and use the graduations engraved on the curved part to find the angles and proportions (Figure 24.5). Compasses with leg joints were made in variable sizes, usually on the site itself, with dividers, as a precision factor[29] (Figure 24.6). The ruler (or measuring rod, *virga*) was a simple measuring tool by definition. It was the standard used to measure lengths on the site, it met the need for economy of materials, ease of handling, it took up little space in the workshop and on the

FIGURE 24.4

Cennino Cennini: Liber Diversum Artium (Montpellier, Bibliothèque inter-universitaire de médecine, MS H277, fol. 92v. Paintbrush.) © Bibliothèque inter-universitaire de médecine – Montpellier

FIGURE 24.3

Medieval drawing tip © Yoan Martoglio

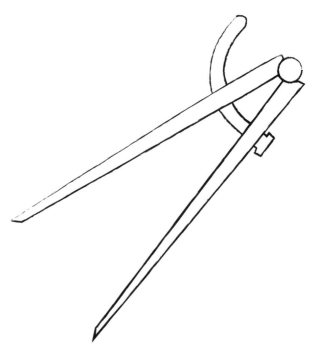

FIGURE 24.5

Sector © Yoan Martoglio

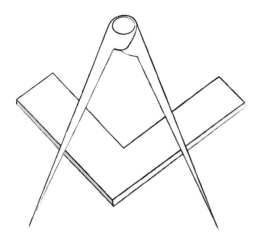

FIGURE 24.6

Compass with leg joints and set square © Yoan Martoglio

site, and was easy to use as it did not require the ability to read. It also made it possible to draw straight lines[30] (Figure 24.7). The string line was a simple, practical tool found on any site. When weighted, it served as a plumb line and defined the vertical. It was also used to draw radii converging to the centre, the joints of an arc from the centre, or circles of any size[31] (Figure 24.8). We do not know the precise meaning of the word *condermenia* referred to previously. If used in the sense of cartoon, it could apply to the craft of stonemasonry (in which case it would be called a *mole*) but also to glassmaking and painting, as has already been pointed out.

This is hardly surprising when we picture life on a site in the Middle Ages and the exchanges between people working in the different trades. As we saw in the discussion on proportions, craftsmen in the Middle Ages used measures that were directly related to the morphology of the human body. The problem with such units of measurement (cubit, line, pace, span, palm, foot, etc.) was that they varied according to the place and the person using them[32] (Figure 24.9).

There are several ways of making under-drawings or of marking out the surface to be painted according to the technique used. Works painted from the 12th century onwards in Catalan (or neighbouring) territories illustrate several types of under-drawings: *sinopia* (Figure 24.10), incisions in the lime plaster (Figure 24.11), drawn with a line (Figure 24.12), drawn in diluted ochre (Figure 24.13) but also, more rarely, in blue. Observation of some decorations shows that several techniques can be employed for the same work, depending on the desired drawing.

Clearly, one does not proceed in the same way for a fresco as for tempera. The latter does not involve the same constraints, especially in regard to time, as the surface is dry. One of the characteristics of fresco painting is that it is done in phases of a day, lasting about six hours (depending on climate conditions) that is to say the time during which the *intonaco* applied to the wall stays wet (*intonaco* being the name of the lime plaster on which the fresco is painted). Therefore, every morning, one had to start by defining the area to be painted in a day (*giornata*). Thus, on big sites, it was common to divide up the work, allowing several people to work simultaneously on different *giornate*. Every morning one had to know exactly which task to give to the men on the scaffolding. One also had to know exactly where to place the bowls of *intonaco* to coincide as closely as possible with the silhouettes of the subjects represented, the figures, decorative areas, etc., and to best conceal the junctions between the different *giornate*. The *Sinopia* is the wall sketch and the division of the spaces executed on the *arriccio* (lime plaster to which the *intonaco* is applied). The *Sinopia* was sometimes applied directly to the wall, even if the pigment used was not the red earth that gave its name to this kind of drawing. The proper function of *sinopia* was to serve as a guide for the later execution of the painting on the *intonaco*. Preparatory drawings and scale drawings are also visible on the *intonaco* or distemper intended to receive the painting.

DRAFT DRAWING

An initial draft drawing had to precede the composition and execution of a wall painting. This raises two key aspects in regard to the usefulness of this reduced model. The first is to consider that most of the transactions between the patron of a wall painting and the painter himself could not have been simple tacit agreements, whether we are talking about the 12th, 13th or 14th centuries. As noted by Philippe Lorentz, the proliferation of work contracts is linked to the growth of cities in the 12th and 13th centuries, the development of independent crafts and the emergence of what we call 'artists' today.[33] However we do not see contracts for works of art prior to the 13th century. The examples presented by Lorentz show that the assumption of a contract containing information on the programme of the work is based on an assumption.

FIGURE 24.7

Ruler © Yoan Martoglio

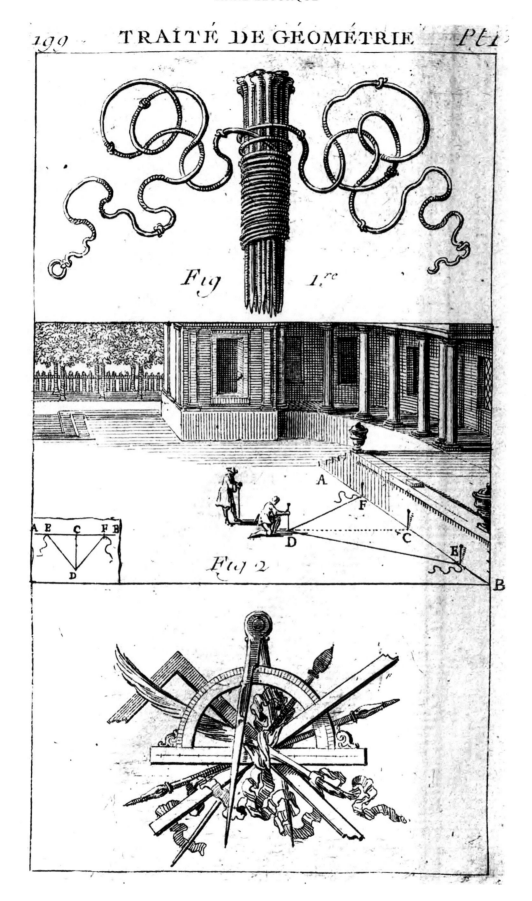

FIGURE 24.8

Image taken from the Traité théorique et pratique de géométrie, à l'usage des artistes by Sébastien le Clerc (1764)

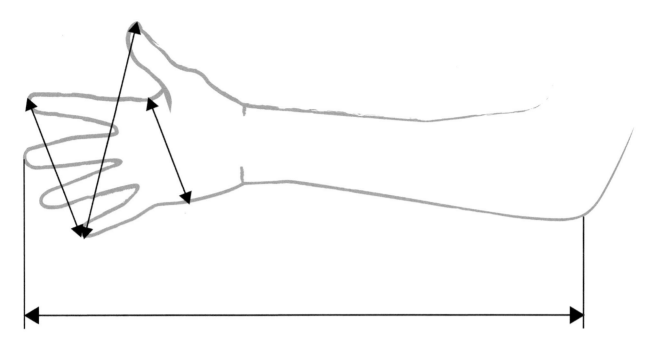

FIGURE 24.9

Medieval measuring units © Yoan Martoglio

FIGURE 24.10

Taüll: Sant Climent, Sinopia of face of Christ (Manuel Castiñeiras)

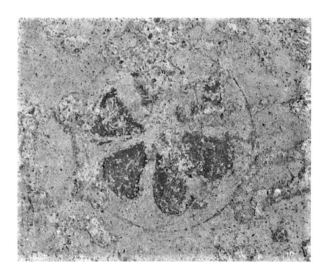

FIGURE 24.11

Arles-sur-Tech: Sainte-Marie. Incisions in the plaster in south-west tower (Anne Leturque)

Indeed it was considered pointless to go into details about questions of iconography in a legal act. It was more a case of determining the wages of the artist and the details of execution and payment. The formal aspects of the work, based on the agreement between the patron and the artist prior to executing the work, were included in a formal document, the 'devise' (the division or written draft) that is often mentioned, sometimes summarised and, very rarely, copied out verbatim in the notarial act.[34] When Philippe Lorentz examines the relative share of the artist and the patron in the genesis of a work, he admits how difficult this is to assess. However, in the rare cases where the 'devise' and the finished work have both been preserved, one can see that the patron is not necessarily the main actor.[35] Moreover, the draft model of the wall decoration is not merely to meet the patron's very legitimate desire for advance knowledge of the work to be paid for. Executing a wall painting implies preparation beforehand, with a scaled-down design of the scheme. This question is not dealt with in the *LDA* but the preparation

FIGURE 24.12

Arles-sur-Tech: Sainte-Marie. Drawings made with a string line in south-west tower (Anne Leturque)

FIGURE 24.13

Villelongue-dels-Monts: Notre-Dame-del-Vilar. Drawings in red ochre (Christian Bachelier)

of draft drawings intended for the site is confirmed by Cennino Cennini in his treatise when he says: 'If you want to make houses, make them in your drawing in the size you wish'.[36]

It would be difficult to improvise painted scenes populated by a large number of figures without first thinking out the precise details of the composition, or taking the time to make a sketch. The technical, i.e. material, execution of the painting could not be improvised and only the presence of a very detailed draft drawing would have addressed the issue of the extremely meticulous organisation of the work before starting on a cycle of wall paintings, if only in terms of provision or the coordination and division of tasks. Unfortunately, although these draft drawings probably existed, they have since disappeared, which is understandable in light of the fact that they had no intrinsic value for their contemporaries, and could be scraped off and reused until they were worn away.

A CASE-STUDY: SAINT-MARTIN DE FENOLLAR AND THE MAKING OF A MURAL PAINTING

The wall paintings of Saint-Martin-de-Fenollar (Pyrénées-Orientales, France) illustrate the point in question. In the 12th century, this building was part of the Diocese of Elne and the property of the Viscount of Castellnou. It appears to have been owned by the Abbey of St. Mary of Arles-sur-Tech from 844. It is located on the old Roman road that passed through the fortified post of Clausures, north of the Perthus Pass. Oral tradition identifies the Church of St. Martin-de-Fenollar as the 'Chapel of Mahut', associated with Mahaut, daughter of Raymond Berenger III, Count of Barcelona, who inherited the land where the church is located, in 1131.

The church consists of a nave (which was apparently vaulted in the 12th century) and a rectangular chancel. The painting ensemble of Saint-Martin-de-Fenollar remains the largest painted area and the best preserved of the wall paintings of Pyrénées-Orientales. The walls of the chancel are covered with frescoes and a few fragments remain on the walls of the nave.

On the vault of the chancel, at the centre of the composition, stands a Christ in Majesty. He is depicted accompanied by symbols of the evangelists, and carried by angels. They are designated by four verses from the *Carmen Paschale* by Coelius Sedulius, poet of the mid 4th century (Figure 24.14). On the eastern wall of the chancel, above the axial window, the Virgin Mary appears (Figure 24.15). This head-and-shoulders image of the crowned Mary is midway between the divine space, represented by Christ and the Tetramorph on the vault, and the history of the Incarnation painted beneath it, in which she is the main protagonist. At the springing of the vault, on both sides, against a background of horizontal stripes, are the Elders of the Apocalypse (Figure 24.16). They are arranged on an intermediate register converging both towards the Christ in Majesty and the Virgin in prayer. The elders flank the chancel, walking towards its centre. This is clearly to emphasise the fundamental role of the Virgin in this iconographic cycle. The second register presents a cycle of the Incarnation (Figure 24.17): from left to right the scenes depicted are the Annunciation, the Nativity, the Annunciation to the Shepherds and the Adoration of the Magi (Figure 24.18). The lowest register depicts pale yellow scalloped draperies. On the southern wall of the nave, in the first span, two quadrupeds with clawed feet confront one another on either side of a tree, against a background of drapery. This decoration was made slightly later than the wall paintings previously mentioned.[37]

The historiography of these paintings has proposed a chronology that runs through the first half of the 12th century, but the research of Pierre Ponsich on the Viscountess of Castellnou has really advanced the dating of these paintings. He dates them in the second quarter of the 12th century, arguing that Mahaut could not have taken possession of her property until after her marriage to Jasper II, Viscount of Castellnou, in around 1135. At the age of about forty, Mahaut probably played an important role in the restoration of the church of Arles-sur-Tech. This is recalled by the act of consecration of the abbey in 1157.[38]

Parallels have been drawn between the Fenollar paintings and those of the Church of Saint-Sauveur-de-Casesnoves (in the treatment of the faces and clothing). In addition, the inscription accompanying Matthew the Evangelist at Fenollar presents the same variant of the *Carmen Paschale* as at Casesnoves. Elements such as these would tend to assert the existence of a common culture between Fenollar and Casesnoves, with the same desire to highlight the figure of the Virgin Mary. Casesnoves belonged to the Abbey of Saint-Michel-de-Cuxa in the 12th century, where the cult of Mary was also highly developed. This finding brings us to the idea that the influence of the culture of the prestigious monastery on the painter of Fenollar should to be taken into account.[39] From this historiographical overview, we can deduce that common models circulated for some time, enriched with local cultures and that, in all likelihood, a simple vector was needed for this to spread: an illuminated book of religious inspiration could have fulfilled this function. The question of the sources from which the Fenollar painter could have drawn the elements of his wall painting is difficult to resolve. Nevertheless, the hypothesis that the Gospels of Saint-Michel-de-Cuxa could have been included in the sources is quite plausible.[40] Indeed, these Gospel verses include the *Carmen Paschale* which has already been referred to and which existed in several copies in the inventory of the Ripoll manuscripts.

Both the decorative profusion of the painter of Fenollar and the intensity of the associated colours used in this setting are extraordinary: the angels have bicoloured wings, the nativity scene is displayed on a checkered red and white background, the Christ Child is supported on capitals formed like giant palms; the modelling of the flesh is done with thick dabs of pure tones, curvilinear

FIGURE 24.14

Saint-Martin de Fenollar: Christ in Majesty and Tetramorphe © *Christian Bachelier*

red triangles denote the cheeks and corners of the nose, a red dot is placed between the eyes, there is hatching on the wrists, neck, palms and feet. A number of these features and certain ornamental recurrences can also be found in the paintings of the church of Saint-Nazaire of Hautes-Clauzes.

Technical investigations in the *Factura* research programme now allow us to relativise this perspective.[41] The murals of Saint-Martin-de-Fenollar and Santa Maria des Hautes-Clauzes were frescoed with dry highlights but were executed using very different techniques. Although the composition of the original plaster tends to be the same in both churches, the technique used in Fenollar is very simple. Except for the highlights, it only contains two layers of preparation and one paint layer. On the contrary, the paintings of Hautes-Clauzes have two preparatory layers, covered with three paint layers. Moreover, even if they reveal certain thematic similarities, their stylistic treatments are also very different.[42]

The palette of pigments used has a common base but there are also some notable differences. At Fenollar, the identified pigments are green earths, cinnabar, an ochre mixture for the orange colour, the white is based on lime,

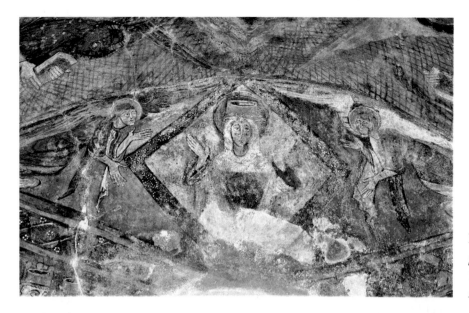

FIGURE 24.15

Saint-Martin de Fenollar: Virgin in prayer (Christian Bachelier)

FIGURE 24.16

Saint-Martin de Fenollar: Elders of the Apocalypse (Christian Bachelier)

FIGURE 24.17

Saint-Martin de Fenollar: Nativity (Christian Bachelier)

FIGURE 24.18 *Saint-Martin de Fenollar: The Magi. (Christian Bachelier)*

FIGURE 24.19

Saint-Martin de Fenollar: general view of the chancel (Christian Bachelier) see also colour plate XXI

the blues are lazurite and indigo, the grey is made with a yellow ochre mixed with carbon black and lime. However, in the Hautes-Clauzes, the pigments comprise a mixture of ochre and cinnabar for the red colouring, a red ochre and lazurite overlay, a mixture of lime and red ochre for the skin tones, a superposition in various places of red ochre, lime white and *minium* and green with a copper base.[43]

In regard to drawing and representation, the wall painting of Fenollar is an exemplary source of information. Markings for the lay out of the decoration were made with incisions (for the separation of registers), the protruding edge of the wall was also used in the composition, drawings were made using a string line for the hanging and the diluted ochre used for the under-drawings for some of the decoration is visible. The composition of this wall-painting cycle demonstrates the importance of the Virgin. The elders of the Apocalypse are arranged on an intermediate register converging both towards the Christ in Majesty and towards the Virgin in prayer. They are placed around the chancel, walking towards the centre of it. Their size decreases as they advance. The bands encircling the register are spaced further apart as they move away from the figures of Christ and the Virgin. The purpose underlying this form of representation is undoubtedly that of a commission calling for Christ and the Virgin to be strongly featured. The intercession of the Virgin thus becomes one of the essential elements of this iconography. While it is easy to imagine this as the desire of a literate patron, who was as product of his or her time, it would seem that the substance given to this desire, through this particular pictorial representation of the Elders and the visual effect it produces, comes under the role of the painter (Figure 24.19). By placing the scene of the Adoration of the Magi in a right-to-left direction, unlike the rest of the cycle of paintings, the painter was able to direct the viewer's gaze to the Virgin and Child, doubly represented in the centre of the chancel, on one hand by the throne in the register of the Adoration of the Magi, and on the other, by the glory at the edge of the theophanical space.[44] This dual representation and the central position it occupies reinforces the idea of the essential role of the Marian figure in the Fenollar cycle of paintings.

CONCLUSION

Painting in the context of a monumental site implies specific knowledge and skills that make the painter a privileged partner of the patron. His role in the medieval process of creating painted ensembles was probably more significant than we are prepared to admit today. The question of composition, and thus of drawing, is a fundamental aspect of the skills acquired by the painter during his training, and the testimony left by painted cycles such as that of Saint-Martin Fenollar or sources of artistic technology such as the *LDA*, are quite remarkable in this way. Each of the tools used by the painter in the process of learning (wax tablets), reproducing (copies, templates, grids) or laying out the decoration (tools for drawing, working out proportions, geometry, draft drawings) made him the custodian of a craft, and thus of specific knowledge that was essential in the design and execution of a pictorial programme.

NOTES

[1] According to the *Vita Gauzlini* written by André de Fleury (11th century) and published by Robert-Henri Bautier, we learn that the painter worked on a lightweight platform, probably accessed from the ground by means of a simple rope ladder with rungs. R.-H., Bautier, 'Le monastère et les églises de Fleury-sur-Loire', *Mémoires de la société nationale des antiquaires de France*, 4/74(1969), 116.

[2] The *LDA* dates to the 1470s but the original text goes back to the 14th century. The textual sources for the *LDA* derive from different European areas, where they were widely disseminated. They mainly date to the 12th and 13th centuries, thereby reflecting the painting techniques in practice at those times, regardless of the western medieval area referred to. It is not the codicological and philological aspects of the text published by Mark Clarke in 2011 that are discussed here, but an analysis of the contents. M. Clarke, *Mediaeval Painters' Materials and Techniques – the Montpellier* Liber Diversarum Arcium (London, 2011).

[3] Cennino Cennini (c. 1370–c. 1440) late Gothic Florentine painter, is the author of the *Libro dell'arte*, The Craftman's Handbook, a treatise on painting written around the turn of the 15th century, probably in Padua, V. Mottez, *Le livre de l'art ou traité de la peinture par Cennino Cennini* (Paris, 1982), 32.

[4] T. Wright, *A Volume of Vocabularies, Illustrating the Conditions and the Manners of our Forefathers, as Well as the History of the Forms of Elementary Education and of the Languages Spoken in the Island, From the Tenth Century to the Fifteenth* (London, 1857), 96–110.

[5] In chapter 26 of Book I of the *LDA*, we find the soap recipe said to have come from Judea, Gaul or Sparta. The recipe involves boiling filtered tallow with caustic lye and adding the ash of lupins, beans, lentils or peas. In chapter 15, we find how to produce good quality whites. These include one that is made from burnt bone or eggshells. Clark, *Medieval Painters* (as n. 2), 119 and 111–112.

[6] Mottez, *Livre de l'art* (as n. 3), 7–8.

[7] E. Lalou, 'Les tablettes de cire médiévales', *Bibliothèque de l'école des chartes*, 147/1 (1989), 123–140.

[8] Theophilus, *On Diverse Arts*, ed. and trans. John G. Hawthorne and Cyril Stanley Smith (New York, 1979), 61–62.

[9] V. Nieto Alcaide, 'Vidrieros y pintores: el problema de los cartones y la vidriera del siglo XV', in *Imagenes y promotores en el arte medieval* (Barcelona, 2001), 555–562. On this subject, see the description by Cennino Cennini, clearly reflecting the issue of the division of labour between painters and glassworkers in the making of stained glass windows. The painter is considered as the creator and the glass craftsman as the executor. However it is difficult to generalise about this viewpoint, which was probably more suited to the Italian Trecento.

[10] B. Zanardi, 'Projet dessiné et patrons dans le chantier de la peinture murale au Moyen Age', *Revue de l'Art*, 124 (1999), 47.

[11] Mottez, *Livre de l'art* (as n. 3), 17–19.

[12] M. Didron, *Manuel d'iconographie chrétienne grecque et latine* (Paris, 1865), 17.

[13] Mottez, *Livre de l'art* (as n. 3), 16.

[14] Zanardi, 'Projet dessiné' (as n. 10), 44.

[15] Clark, *Medieval Painters* (as n. 2), 141; R. Rosewell, *Medieval Wall Paintings in English and Welsh Churches* (Woodbridge, 2008), 130.

[16] Didron, *Manuel d'iconographie* (as n. 12), 52.

[17] J. Rollier-Hanselmann, 'Géométrie et modules de construction à l'époque romane: de Constantinople à Berzé-la-ville', in C. Père (ed.) *Arch-I-Tech* (Bordeaux, 2011), 99–108.

[18] H. Torp, *The Integrating System of Proportion in Byzantine Art*, Acta ad archaeologiam et artium historiam pertinentia, Institum romanum norvegiae, 4, (Rome, 1984).

[19] R. Bechmann, *Villard de Honnecourt. La pensée technique au XIIIe siècle et sa communication* (Paris, 1991), 305.

[20] M.T. Zenner, 'Villard de Honnecourt and Euclidean Geometry', *Nexus Network Journal*, 4 (2002), 65–78.

[21] V. Robert, *L'art du trait. Tracés à la corde des bâtisseurs romans* (Busloup, 2010), 24–29.

[22] M. Castiñeiras, A. Leturque, J. Rollier-Hanselmann, A. Mazuir, 'Histoire et perspective des peintures de Saint-Sauveur de Casesnoves (Ille-sur-Têt, Pyrénées-Orientales): la restitution 3D de l'église et de ses décors peints', in G. Mallet and A. Leturque (ed.) *Arts picturaux en territoires catalans (XIIe–XIVe siècle) – Approches matérielles, techniques et comparatives* (Montpellier, 2015), 171–198.

[23] The manuscript of Villard de Honnecourt is composed of leaves of parchment with drawings on both sides, bound in a book comprising a variable number of leaves. The format is that of a small book, measuring about 140 mm by 220 mm, bound and covered in brown leather. It is kept at the National Library of France. Between a third and half of the leaves of the manuscript, originally estimated at one hundred, have disappeared. Others have been modified or scraped. 33 folios remain, or 66 pages. Bechmann, *Villard de Honnecourt* (as n. 19), 71.

[24] R.W. Scheller, *Exemplum – Model-Book Drawings and the Practise of Artistic Transmission in the Middle Ages (ca. 900-ca. 1470)* (Amsterdam, 1995), 91.

[25] M. Rossi, 'Le committenze di Ariberto d'Intimiano e le botteghe di pittori e di miniatori a Milano nella prima metà del secolo XI', in M.Castineiras (ed.) *Entre La Letra y el Pincel: el Artista Medieval. Leyenda, identidad y estatus* (Barcelona, 2017), 249–262.

[26] Zanardi, 'Projet dessiné' (as n. 9), 44.

[27] Translated by Anne Leturque (Université Paul Valéry, Montpellier III, CEMM, EA 4580 – Universitat Autonoma de Barcelona).

[28] Mottez, *Livre de l'art* (as n. 3), 47.

[29] A. Séné, 'Un instrument de précision au service des artistes du moyen âge : l'équerre', *Cahiers de civilisation médiévale*, 13 (1970), 349–358.

[30] Robert, *L'art du trait* (as n. 21), 18–21.

[31] Ibid, 18–21.

[32] Robert, *L'art du trait* (as n. 21), 13.

[33] Lorentz,'Histoire de l'art du Moyen Âge occidental'*, Annuaire de l'École pratique des hautes études, Section des sciences historiques et philologiques*, 142 (2011), 178.

[34] Ibid, 180.

[35] Ibid, 181.

[36] Mottez, *Livre de l'art* (as n. 3), 66.

[37] A. Leturque, 'Étude des peintures de Saint-Martin de Fenollar : remarques préalables à l'étude technique en laboratoire', in G. Mallet and A Leturque (ed.) *Arts picturaux en territoires catalans (XIIe–XIVe siècle) – Approches matérielles, techniques et comparatives* (Montpellier, 2015), 63–85.

[38] P. Ponsich, 'Le maître de Saint-Martin de Fenollar', *Les cahiers de Saint-Michel de Cuxà*, 5 (1974), 117–129

[39] Castiñeiras, Leturque, Rollier-Hanselmann and Mazuir, 'Histoire et perspective' (as n. 22), 171–198.

[40] M. Durliat, *Arts anciens du Roussillon* (Perpignan, 1954), 15–28 ; M. Durliat, 'La peinture romane en Roussillon et en Cerdagne', *Cahiers de civilisation médiévale*, 4 (1961), 1–14 ; A. Leturque, 'Du trait à la couleur: les arts picturaux en Catalogne aux âges romans. La peinture monumentales et les parements d'autel des Pyrénées-Orientales' (unpublished MA thesis, Université Paul Valéry, Montpellier, 2010).

[41] http://factura-recherche.org/

[42] I. Bilbao, J.-M., Vallet, 'Les peintures murales romanes de Saint-Martin-de-Fenollar et des Cluses-Hautes : étude de la technique et éléments de conservation' in G. Mallet and A Leturque (ed.) *Arts picturaux en territoires catalans (XIIe–XIVe siècle) – Approches matérielles, techniques et comparatives* (Montpellier, 2015), 87–100.

[43] Ibid, 89.

[44] N. Piano, 'Locus Ecclesiae. Passion du Christ et renouveaux ecclésiastiques dans la peinture murale des Pyrénées Françaises. Les styles picturaux (XIIe s.)' (unpublished PhD thesis, University of Poitiers, 2010), 106–123.

THE DEATH OF THE PATRON: AGENCY, STYLE AND THE MAKING OF THE *LIBER FEUDORUM MAIOR* OF BARCELONA

Shannon L. Wearing

During the reign of Alfonso II, king of Aragon and count of Barcelona (reigned 1162–96), the palace chancery in Barcelona produced a massive two-volume cartulary that has come to be known as the *Liber Feudorum Maior* (Barcelona, Archivo de la Corona de Aragón, Real Cancillería, Registros, núm. 1). Alfonso commissioned this book to consolidate the documentary evidence of his authority in the kingdom of Aragon, the counties of Catalonia, and the recently acquired county of Provence. It was the end product of an immense archival project spearheaded by the dean of Barcelona Cathedral, Ramon de Caldes, who oversaw the collection, organisation and transcription of over 900 documents.[1] The resulting manuscript was virtually unprecedented: the *Liber Feudorum Maior* (hereafter *LFM*) is one of the earliest extant lay cartularies (most others having been produced by monastic and cathedral scriptoria to document ecclesiastical privileges and territorial holdings), and one of very few examples of its genre to be enhanced with illuminations.[2] The novelty of the *LFM* as a cartulary both secular and illuminated prompted its creators to develop innovative iconographic strategies for the illustration of its various charters, which document an array of socioeconomic arrangements, including treaties, agreements (*convenientiae*), oaths, judgements, donations, sales, wills and betrothals. Most of the cartulary's illustrative programme is dedicated to scenes of homage or vassalage, represented through the repeated depiction of figures kneeling and offering their clasped hands to a seated lord (Figure 25.1).[3] It also includes scenes of treaties, the bestowal of castles, a marriage, the exchange of gold coins for land and an enigmatic circular composition featuring an enthroned couple surrounded by a radially arranged group of gesticulating courtiers (Figure 25.2).[4]

PATRONAGE AND REPRESENTATION

The *LFM*'s best-known image, however, is its extraordinary frontispiece, which ostensibly re-enacts the patronage of the book itself (Figure 25.3 and cover). Beneath a characteristically Iberian polylobed arch, King Alfonso and Ramon de Caldes sit to either side of a pile of charters, selecting source material for their cartulary.[5] To the right, an amanuensis in secular garb works on a new sheet of parchment that will presumably be incorporated into the new codex. To the left, six courtiers attend the proceedings, though their collective gaze is fixed not directly on the action within the chancery, but slightly upward: they appear to be admiring the elaborate, turreted architectural frame that describes the urban environment in which Alfonso's palace is embedded. Thematically, the frontispiece can be compared to the medieval tradition of presentation scenes: illuminations that depicted codices – the very codices of which they were themselves a part – being presented to a secular patron or recipient, or to a saintly dedicatee.[6] Like presentation scenes in general, the *LFM* frontispiece self-reflexively constructs a mythologised origin story for itself, but with a very different set of implications regarding the role of the patron, who is shown not as the book's recipient but as an active agent in its production. This is a significant iconographic shift, for the illuminator might easily have opted to (or been instructed to) represent the archivist Ramon de Caldes deferentially presenting the work he had overseen to the king, who had commissioned it. Instead, the painting depicts the cartulary not as a gift intended to glorify a ruler, nor as a luxurious commodity purchased by a client, but as both an in-house project and a work in progress – one with which the patron was closely involved.

The frontispiece might thus be interpreted as the pictorial 'signature' of Alfonso as the cartulary's patron. However, unsolved mysteries surrounding the manuscript's chronology complicate such a reading. Much early scholarship on the *LFM* presumed that it had been completed before King Alfonso's death in 1196 at the age of thirty-nine – an assumption stemming largely from its prologue, which appears on the verso of the frontispiece.[7] This eloquent prologue, written by Ramon de Caldes himself, addresses King Alfonso as the cartulary's patron and recipient, implying that it was completed before his

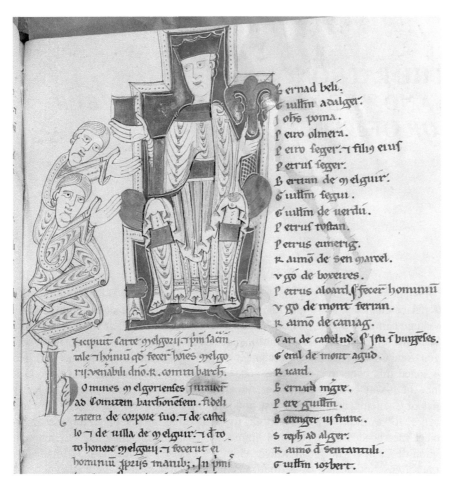

FIGURE 25.1

Liber Feudorum Maior, Barcelona, Archivo de la Corona de Aragón, Real Cancillería, Registros, núm. 1, fol. 85r, detail ('style A')

FIGURE 25.2

Liber Feudorum Maior, Barcelona, Archivo de la Corona de Aragón, Real Cancillería, Registros, núm. 1, fol. 93r ('style B')

FIGURE 25.3

Liber Feudorum Maior, Barcelona, Archivo de la Corona de Aragón, Real Cancillería, Registros, núm. 1, fol. 1r ('style B')

Figure 25.4

Las Huelgas Beatus, New York, Pierpont Morgan Library, MS M.429, fol. 12r (detail)

death. If the painting on the folio's recto eschews the formula of a presentation scene, the prologue on the verso has been interpreted as a kind of textual translation thereof. To be sure, there is no doubt that the work of transcription took place during Alfonso's reign; according to the palaeographic study of Anscari Mundó, the primary scribal campaign was complete by 1192, with various additions made in later years.[8] But several art historical studies have suggested that its illustrative programme should be dated decades after his death. These assessments cite as evidence the stylistic characteristics shared by the *LFM* and the Las Huelgas Beatus (also known as the Later Morgan Beatus – Figure 25.4).[9] This manuscript, made for the royal foundation of Santa María la Real de Las Huelgas, a community of Cistercian nuns just outside Burgos (Castile), includes a colophon stating that it was completed in September 1220. A rare and valuable clue for art historians attempting to date illumination through formal analysis, the 'magic number' 1220 has in turn been applied to objects perceived to be related to the Las Huelgas Beatus, including the *LFM*. The illuminations of the Barcelona cartulary have likewise been dated to the early 13th century by several scholars in recent decades.[10] If, following these style-based analyses, the *LFM* was illustrated as late as the 1220s, its pictures would significantly postdate King Alfonso's death. This has profound implications for our understanding of his cartulary's patronal history, as well as our interpretation of its frontispiece. Should this miniature be understood as a tribute to a dead king rather than the 'signature' of a living patron? If so, whom should we credit as being responsible for the cartulary's illumination?

Patronal analysis of the *LFM* is further complicated by the fact that it was illustrated in two radically different styles. One, which I call 'style A', is rooted in the Romanesque pictorial traditions of 12th-century Iberia, especially Catalan liturgical manuscripts (Figure 25.1).[11] Style A is characterised by an emphasis on draughtsmanship over colour – a two-dimensional linearity that renders figures in a hieratic, anti-illusionistic manner, with facial features and clothing stylised to have an elaborate ornamental rather than naturalistic effect. The other, which I call 'style B', is exemplified by the *LFM*'s frontispiece and circular composition (Figures 25.2–25.3). This set of illustrations, which was carried out by at least two artists, points towards the novel formal developments associated with the so-called Year 1200 and Gothic styles. Figures are comparatively elongated and their gestural interactions are more nuanced and diverse. Whereas surfaces in style A are articulated with schematic meanders and geometricised shapes, in style B drapery is defined through the application of bold pigment overlaid either with striations and swirls or textile patterns. The question remains, however, as to the amount of time that might have elapsed between these two campaigns. The *LFM* was certainly meant to be illustrated from its inception, for its scribes allotted spaces for images as they executed their work in the early 1190s. It is reasonable to assume that the style-A illustrations were carried out in these same years or immediately thereafter. We must then consider whether there was a significant break in production, with the artists responsible for style B working on the manuscript as late as the 1220s, as certain scholars have suggested.

My own investigations have led me to conclude that the tendency to assign the year 1220 to the *LFM* as either an approximation or a terminus ante quem should be re-evaluated. Despite their stylistic similarities, there is no evidence that the cartulary of Barcelona and the Beatus of Las Huelgas shared a hand. David Raizman, the foremost expert on the Las Huelgas Beatus, has concluded as much:

> 'Similarities are of a generalized rather than specific type, and appear superficial upon closer inspection, related only in their adaptation or transformation of Byzantinizing tendencies. . . . Differences in drawing, poses and heads, and especially in modeling, are too great to suppose an identity of authorship between these two manuscripts.'[12]

Moreover, we can point to other illuminated books dated to the late 12th century that are no less similar in style to the *LFM*. Two manuscripts now in the National Library of the Netherlands, dated by Walter Cahn to *c.* 1180 and the late 12th century respectively, exhibit resonances with *LFM* style B that remain unexplored: a psalter which can be connected either to Fécamp or Ham (The Hague, Koninklijke Bibliotheek, MS 76 F 13) and a psalter fragment connected to the Abbey of Saint-Bertin in Saint-Omer (Hague, Koninklijke Bibliotheek, MS 76 F 5) (Figures 25.5–25.6).[13] While these manuscripts may not share a hand with the *LFM*, the commonalities evident in their treatment of bodily proportions, facial features, drapery and architectural frames testify to a shared stylistic vernacular – one passed from masters to students/assistants and disseminated on both sides of the English Channel and into the Iberian peninsula by itinerant artists. The Fécamp Psalter would represent an early incarnation of this idiom, and the Las Huelgas Beatus a late example. As for *LFM* style B, I contend that the scenario of patronage at the court of Barcelona makes a dating of *c.* 1200 more likely than *c.* 1220.

With this chronological shift in mind, we should return to the curious coexistence of the *LFM*'s two pictorial styles. How might we 'diagnose' this stylistic juxtaposition? One possible explanation is that the death of the manuscript's patron resulted in an interruption in its illustration and a subsequent change in style; we might then speculate as to who would have stepped in to take up the project and hire the second group of artists.[14] Following this hypothetical

FIGURE 25.5

Psalter. The Hague, Koninklijke Bibliotheek, MS 76 F 13, fol. 5v.

FIGURE 25.6

Psalter fragment. The Hague, Koninklijke Bibliotheek, MS 76 F 5, fol. 3v.

scenario, there are three likely candidates for the role of 'substitute patron'. The first and perhaps most convincing is Ramon de Caldes (d. 1199), who as the head of Alfonso's chancery was responsible for the compilation and is lionised in the frontispiece. Assigning the role of 'patron' to Ramon, however, might not be entirely appropriate in the sense that he would not have provided funds himself, but may have distributed them as an intermediary between the crown and the artists. Whether before and/or after Alfonso's death, Ramon may also have directed the cartulary's iconographic programme, and even memorialised himself by requesting his presence in the chancery scene. In any case, it is difficult to imagine Ramon featuring so prominently in the frontispiece had it been painted twenty years after his death.[15] The monumental treatment afforded Alfonso's archivist in this painting only makes sense in the context of his direct involvement in the making of the cartulary. There is, however, a second possibility, which is that work on the cartulary was taken over by Alfonso's wife, Queen Sancha of Castile (d. 1208), who served as regent following the death of the king and was the primary patron of the Hospitaller monastery of Santa María de Sigena in Aragon, known for its Byzantinising chapterhouse frescoes. It may be Sancha herself who is depicted in the manuscript's other full-page illumination, the radial throne scene (Figure 25.2); if the queen regent did indeed take over the decoration of the cartulary, she might have instructed the painters to memorialise her and her dead husband with this apotheotic composition. A third possibility is that Alfonso's son and successor, King Pedro II el Católico (d. 1213), commissioned a second series of illuminations after he came of age.[16] The text of the *LFM* was, in fact, updated during his reign, with Pedro's scribes making use of the blank folios that had been strategically included to ensure that the manuscript could be kept up-to-date.

On the other hand, having wrested the *LFM* from its ties to the year 1220, we might consider an alternative scenario: that there was no 'patronal break' at all, nor any significant chronological separation between *LFM* styles A and B. To some extent, the tendency to temporally distance the cartulary's two styles is informed by art historical narratives that presume a linear, teleological model of stylistic progress – according to which 'Gothic' is regarded as the successor to, and an improvement on, 'Romanesque'. In the case of the *LFM*, the coexistence of two distinct illustrative modes has prompted art historians to reveal a conspicuous bias in favour of one over the other: specifically, the more naturalistic style B over the more abstract style A. This preference dates back to the survey of medieval Catalan painting written by Josep Gudiol i Cunill (1872–1931), who described the more Romanesque illustrations in the *LFM* as 'the most barbarous [style] imaginable' – the product of a 'very bad hand' that can't help but create 'deformed' figures.[17] Regarding the image illustrating the oath of fealty made by the men of Melgueil (today Mauguio) to the Count of Barcelona (fol. 85r; Figure 25.1), Gudiol writes: 'If ever the men of Melgueil saw the drawing in question, they would be none too pleased to find themselves represented in such an excessive manner'.[18] Gudiol's comments are extreme almost to the point of comedy, and I think we can rest assured that the medieval citizens of Melgueil are not rolling in their graves over their depiction in Alfonso's cartulary. Yet the derogatory attitude underlying his assessments has survived even today, with recent art historians describing the style A illustrations as 'archaising',

FIGURE 25.7

Liber Feudorum Maior, Barcelona, Archivo de la Corona de Aragón, Real Cancillería, Registros, núm. 1, fol. 109r (detail)

'mediocre' and 'inferior' to style B, which is lauded as 'superior' or of 'higher quality'.[19]

Such assessments amount to an erroneous conflation of style and quality, one that is at odds with the trajectory of art history in recent decades, as value judgements concerning artistic beauty and quality have been justifiably problematised. I propose that the *LFM*'s stylistic pluralism should instead be interpreted as a demonstration of medieval viewers' ability to appreciate a variety of representational strategies, even within a single work of art. The Barcelona cartulary is hardly unique among medieval works in incorporating multiple styles, whether carried out in quick succession or over the course of long stretches of time: the mid-12th-century Winchester Psalter and the Parma Ildefonsus of *c*. 1200 also combine Romanesque and Byzantinising illuminations, while the cloisters of Silos, San Juan de la Peña and Elne integrate different sculptural styles.[20] Given the persistence of Romanesque pictorial and architectural traditions on the Iberian peninsula, we might view *LFM* style A as an alternative contemporary style rather than an archaising or outmoded, let alone faulty, one.[21] One particular idiosyncrasy of the *LFM* supports this reading: remarkably, on two folios (23r and 109r) we find both styles combined within a single illustration (Figure 25.7). In each case, the artist responsible for style B painted multiple vassals over the single vassal drawn by his predecessor. The fact that only the left half of the illustration was painted over, and the enthroned lord left behind, suggests that medieval audiences were untroubled by certain styles being 'retardataire' or 'archaising' (to use terms frequently employed by art historians). Whether this repainting was done weeks or years after the execution of the original images, we cannot be certain. But in either case, we should view this cartulary's two styles not as different stages of a teleological formal development, but rather as equally legitimate, coexisting artistic expressions.

PATRONAGE, COLLABORATION AND ARTISTIC PRODUCTION

While the precise chronology of its decorative programme remains elusive, the *LFM*'s incorporation of the unreservedly Romanesque style A and the comparatively modern style B brings to the fore issues of patronal intent and the medieval reception of style. Questions concerning the cartulary's patronage also have methodological implications. Is it preferable to date artworks and buildings through formal analysis, or by focussing on cultural and socioeconomic factors such as patronage? Can a social history of art lead to more accurate conclusions than the 'old-fashioned' style-based methods of the discipline? Over the past several decades, art historians have sought to problematise the Romantic view of the artist as creator-genius; medievalists, facing a dearth of artists' signatures, have in many cases adopted the study of patronage as a means of analysing artworks as products (and perpetuators) of social and economic forces.[22] Problems arise, however, when the role of the patron is aggrandised, and he or she is upheld as the primary author-genius responsible for an artwork; one thinks of the debates over the role of Abbot Suger at Saint-Denis, for instance.[23] Dare we declare the death of the patron as the literary theorist Roland Barthes did for the author?[24]

In several recent studies, historians of art and architecture have sought to destabilise assumptions about patronage and agency. Jill Caskey has spoken of an expanded 'patronal field' in which works were commissioned by individuals acting within the context of a larger 'cultural fabric'.[25] Stephen Perkinson has identified patronage as more 'diffuse' than is often assumed, involving not only the commissioners who supplied funds for projects but 'conduit[s]' responsible for distributing those funds to labourers such as scribes and artists; such intermediaries might themselves exercise control over imagery to some degree.[26] And Aden Kumler has encouraged us to consider patrons not just as initiators but as 'effects' of artworks, following Foucault's model of the 'author-function', according to which an author is not so much an individual creator as a discursive entity giving rise to 'a series of *egos* or subject-positions'.[27] These and other studies have been helpful in critiquing and nuancing art historical narratives of patronage, but we should also avoid applying the term too broadly. There is, I believe, a value in maintaining a narrow economic definition of the patron as a provider of capital, while framing medieval artistic production in terms of a multiplicity of different types of makers: scribes, artists, designers, masons, architects and patrons alike.[28] This resists the modernist tendency to seek an overarching creator-genius responsible for a given artwork or building, while also noting the special power of the individual who possesses the material means to commission art and architecture. Patronage thus remains a useful line of inquiry because it helps us glimpse how rulers constructed their identities and their legacies in order to support their ideological aims. But as recent studies have emphasised, we must bear in mind that the making of medieval art involved complex interactions between donors, designers, artisans and audiences, with each party exercising a varying degree of control depending on the circumstances.

The collective nature of medieval artistic production is brilliantly illustrated by the frontispiece of Alfonso's cartulary, which highlights the extent to which royal patronage was an institutional activity rather than an individualised one (Figure 25.3). The network of gazes and gestures performed by the various figures clearly articulates the contribution of each: the king commands the production of the cartulary; the dean of the cathedral serves as archivist and designer; the amanuensis transcribes the documents and converts them into a codicological format; and the six courtiers testify to the legitimacy of the entire process and, by implication, represent the cartulary's future readers. Given its emphasis on patronage as process, this illumination might be compared to the well-known image in the Toledo *Bible Moralisée* depicting that book's patron(s) and producers (colour plate XXII).[29]

This full-page miniature – which dates to the late 1220s or 1230s and is therefore later than the *LFM* – is organised according to an 'upstairs/downstairs' architectonic scheme, with the royal figures responsible for the commission at the top and the manuscript's creators below. Each of the four figures is isolated within a discrete space defined by a trefoil arch: reading left to right and top to bottom, we find the book's patron, Blanche of Castile, Queen of France; its likely recipient, her son, King Louis IX; a secular cleric consulting a codex and issuing iconographic instruction; and finally a lay artist completing the mise-en-page of one of the folios.[30] As Aden Kumler has noted, the composition describes the creation of the manuscript as 'embedded within, and productive of, a profoundly relational social, intellectual, and aesthetic economy'.[31] The book is portrayed not as the product of a single artistic or patronal genius, but as a truly collaborative endeavour.[32]

This collaborative dimension is heightened in the *LFM* frontispiece, which dispenses with architectural divisions and presents the participants within the same ambit (Figure 25.3). By constructing an ostensibly realistic glimpse into Alfonso's chancery, the illuminator unites the book's various makers according to their common goal. The king's open right hand, like Blanche's left hand, demonstrates his agency as the book's patron, while the sceptre in his left underscores his royal prerogative to commission a project of this type. And much like the cleric in the Toledo Bible, the Augustinian canon Ramon consults a text and raises an index finger, indicating that he is actively articulating his plans for the codex. The parchment Ramon holds aloft, like those piled below (as well as that on the scribe's desk), bears legible Latin script, all of which correspond to texts copied within the *LFM* itself.[33] While most of these meta-documents are oaths and agreements, that in Ramon's right hand is identifiable as a judgement (*iudicium*). The fact that it is the *only* judgement in the painting invites us to interpret it as a canny allusion to the wisdom Ramon has exercised in the selection and arrangement of the cartulary's contents.[34]

While King Alfonso is indisputably the cartulary's patron, we might identify Ramon de Caldes with Beat Brenk's notion of the 'patron-*concepteur*' – the intellectual director or designer of a given project as opposed to the provider of funds.[35] That Ramon had the intellectual sophistication required for such a task is made clear by the erudition of his prologue, in which he creates playful patterns with word order and quotes the Justinianic *Corpus Juris Civilis*. Each side of the folio thus highlights Ramon as a spokesman for the cartulary: the recto depicts him speaking, while the verso records his words. Moreover, both recto and verso, image and text distribute credit for the book to both Alfonso and Ramon. The prologue specifies that the king was responsible for the cartulary insofar as he expressed a wish (*viva expressistis voce*) that Ramon compile the documents drawn up during his own reign and the reigns of his ancestors, to preserve the memory of past deeds and prevent future conflict.[36] Ramon then goes on to describe in detail his methods of compilation, barely able to contain his pride at having completed this massive project in such an organised and comprehensive fashion, but careful to insist – in feigned humility – that he elaborates thus 'not to boast, but to express the truth'.[37] For it is ultimately to the glory of the patron that he has dedicated his labour, to ensure *eternam magnarum rerum memoriam* – the 'eternal memory of great things'.

ACKNOWLEDGEMENTS

I would like to thank Manuel Castiñeiras, Abby Kornfeld, Therese Martin, and Kathryn Smith for their helpful comments on an earlier draft of this essay. I am also grateful to the staff of the Arxiu de la Corona d'Aragó, especially Albert Torra, for allowing me to view the *Liber Feudorum Maior* on two separate occasions over the course of my dissertation research.

NOTES

[1] While the book itself is a product of the 1190s, the documents were compiled over the course of the previous decade; see A.J. Kosto, 'The *Liber feudorum maior* of the Counts of Barcelona: The Cartulary as an Expression of Power', *Journal of Medieval History*, 27 (2001), 1–22 at 3–8. On the role of Ramon de Caldes in the administrative reform of the palace chancery, see T.N. Bisson, 'Ramon de Caldes (*c.* 1135–99): Dean of Barcelona and King's Minister', in *Medieval France and her Pyrenean Neighbours: Studies in Early Institutional History* (London 1989), 187–198. The modern edition of the text is F. Miquel Rosell, *Liber Feudorum maior: Cartulario real que se conserva en el Archivo de la Corona de Aragón*, 2 vols (Barcelona 1945).

[2] The most in-depth art historical analysis of the *LFM* is S.L. Wearing, 'Power and Style: The *Liber Feudorum Maior* and the Court of Alfonso II, King of Aragon and Count of Barcelona (r. 1162–96)' (unpublished Ph.D. thesis, Institute of Fine Arts, New York University, 2015).

[3] J. Le Goff, 'The Symbolic Ritual of Vassalage', in *Time, Work, and Culture in the Middle Ages*, trans. A. Goldhammer (Chicago 1980), 237–287.

[4] This folio (93r) was one of many removed around the turn of the 19th century during a period of archival mismanagement. It was rediscovered in 1944 along with twenty-six others, all of which had been recycled as book covers. J.E. Martínez Ferrando, *Hallazgo de miniaturas románicas en el Archivo de la Corona de Aragón* (Barcelona 1944). Because it is bereft of text and no longer in its original position, its subjects cannot be identified with certainty. Given their monumentality and reverential treatment, a likely identification of the pair is the patron of the manuscript itself, Alfonso, and his wife, Queen Sancha (d. 1208, daughter of King Alfonso VII of León-Castile and Queen Riquilda).

[5] The architectural vocabulary depicted here has its roots in Islamic Spain, and would undoubtedly have been familiar to Alfonso. His residence in Zaragoza was the Islamic palace known as the Aljafería, renowned for its stucco polylobed and interlacing arches. Within Barcelona, the cloister arcade at Sant Pau del Camp also uses polylobed arches, but, in what might be called a more 'Romanesque' take on the form, the individual lobes are round rather than horseshoe arches. The precise chronology of the cloister is unknown, but see the following essay which makes a convincing case for the last quarter of the 12th century (hence roughly contemporaneous with the *LFM*): J. Camps i Sòria, 'Catalonia, Provence and the Holy Land: Late 12th-Century Sculpture in Barcelona', in *Romanesque and the Mediterranean*, ed., R. Bacile and J. McNeill (Leeds 2015), 327–336. I would like to thank Jordi Camps for sharing this essay with me prior to its publication. See also Carles Sánchez Márquez, 'Monasterio de Sant Pau del Camp', in

Enciclopedia del Románico en Cataluña: Barcelona, vol. II (Aguilar de Campoo 2014), 1131–1140 (1136–1139 on the cloister specifically), and J. Camps i Soria and I. Lorés i Otzet, 'El claustre de Sant Pau del Camp en el context de l'escultura barcelonina del segle XIII', *Lambard* 6 (1991–1993), 87–111 and 469–472.

[6] As Anna Orriols has deftly observed, the *LFM* frontispiece is particularly reminiscent of the presentation scene in the Montecassino Lectionary (*c.* 1070), which shows Abbot Desiderius (later Pope Victor III) offering the codex to St Benedict (Vatican, BAV MS. Lat. 1202, fol. 2r). A. Orriols Alsina, 'Liber feudorum maior', in *El románico y el Mediterráneo: Cataluña, Toulouse y Pisa, 1120–1180*, ed., M. Castiñeiras and J. Camps (Barcelona 2008), 236.

[7] See, for example, Miquel Rosell, *Liber* (as n. 1), vol. 1, viii (with a transcription of the prologue at 1–2). A 16th-century register in the ACA that describes the *LFM* indicates that it originally appeared twice in the cartulary, introducing each of its two volumes. Only the prologue on what is now fol. 1v survives today. Barcelona, ACA, Memoriales 70, vol. 2, fols 318v–320r.

[8] See A.M. Mundó, 'El pacte de Cazola del 1179 i el *Liber Feudorum Maior*. Notes paleogràfiques i diplomàtiques', in *X Congreso de Historia de la Corona de Aragón: Jaime I y su época* (Zaragoza 1980), 119–129, as well as Kosto, 'The *Liber*' (as n. 1), 4–5 and 8–10, regarding the dating of the transcription.

[9] New York, Pierpont Morgan Library, M.429. The two manuscripts have been linked at least since the 1940s, when Jesús Domínguez Bordona pointed out their stylistic similarity to the director of the ACA; Martínez Ferrando, *Hallazgo* (as n. 4), 14–15. The *LFM* has also been stylistically linked to a group of undated objects: a painted beam with scenes of the Passion (Barcelona, Museu Nacional d'Art de Catalunya, MNAC 15833); a copy of St Ildefonsus' *De Virginitate Beatae Mariae* (Madrid, Fundación Lázaro Galdiano, Mss. R14424); and a Cistercian Bible (Dijon, Bibliothèque municipale de Dijon, B.M. 3).

[10] See for instance P. Bohigas, 'Les derniers temps de l'enluminure romane en Catalogne: la transition en gothique', *Les Cahiers de Saint Michel de Cuxa*, 5 (1974), 33–44 at 40–41; M.E. Ibarburu, 'Los cartularios reales del Archivo de la Corona de Aragón', *Lambard: Estudis d'art medieval* 6 (1994), 197–213 at 206; D. Raizman 'The Later Beatus (M.429) in the Morgan Library: Description, Function, Style, and Provenance', in *Beato del Monasterio de Las Huelgas: Ms M.429* (Valencia 2004), 209–236 at 228–229. While Bohigas and Ibarburu propose that the two codices do share a hand, Raizman argues against this.

[11] Style A is especially close to (but not of the same hand as) the illustrations found in two Augustinian manuscripts from the second half of the 12th century, the Tortosa Sacramentary (Tortosa, Arxiu Capitular, Ms. 41) and Girona Sacramentary (Paris, Bibliothèque nationale de France, Ms. Lat. 1102), and is also comparable to a sacramentary dating to *c.* 1200 from the Benedictine monastery of Sant Cugat del Vallès (Barcelona, Archivo de la Corona de Aragón, Sant Cugat 47).

[12] Raizman, 'The Later Beatus' (as n. 10), 228–229.

[13] W. Cahn, *Romanesque Manuscripts: The Twelfth Century* (London 1996), cat. 134 and 138. More specifically, the Fécamp Psalter should be compared to the style of the artist dubbed Artist B1 in my dissertation, while the psalter fragment resembles the style of Artist B2 (note especially the strong outlines of the facial features, garments, and hair on fol. 3v; Cahn, *Romanesque*, fig. 337). Wearing, 'Power and Style' (as n. 2), chap. 3.

[14] Of course, we could alternatively credit this to the death of the first artist (that responsible for the more 'Romanesque' style A). Either scenario is speculative.

[15] Bisson dates Ramon's death to '1199 or soon thereafter'; Bisson, 'Ramon de Caldes' (as n. 1), 187.

[16] Personal names of rulers present a complicated problem. The ruler here called Alfonso II is Alfonso II of Aragon and Alfons I of Catalonia. His son is known as Pedro II (because he is the second king of Aragon by that name) but as Pere I in Catalonia. For the sake of consistency, the Aragonese numbering system has been used.

[17] 'una faisó la més barbre que pugui imaginar-se'; 'miniatures de tan pèssima mà'; 'homes . . . que sortiren de la ploma del miniador deformats i antinaturalment arraulits'. J. Gudiol i Cunill, *Els primitius: Els llibres illuminats* (Barcelona 1955), 141–144.

[18] 'Els homes de Merqueuil, si mai vegeren el disseny que ens ocupa, deurien estar ben poc contents en veure's efigiats amb aquella forma tan extravagant'. Ibid., 144.

[19] See, among others, M.E. Ibarburu, *Catalunya Romànica*, vol. XX: *El Barcelonès, El Baix Llobregat, El Maresme* (Barcelona 1992), 196, and idem, 'Los cartularios reales' (as n. 10), 202. Most recently, the press release of 2014 announcing the discovery of two folios from the *LFM* described the two styles in terms of a discrepancy in quality: 'Su estilo es geométrico, sin sentido de volumen. . . . El segundo artista, de más calidad que el primero aunque también perteneciente a una tradición formal conservadora, presenta una mayor variedad cromática y de recursos decorativos'. Archivo de la Corona de Aragón, 'Dossier de prensa: Hallazgo de nuevas miniaturas del *Liber feudorum maior*', 9 June 2014, www.mcu.es/archivos/docs/MC/ACA/Dossier_Prensa_LFM.pdf.

[20] On the Winchester Psalter (London, British Library, MS Cotton Nero C IV), see F. Wormald, *The Winchester Psalter* (London 1973). Throughout his career, Meyer Schapiro was sensitive to heterogeneity in medieval art: 'If in all periods artists strive to create unified works, the strict ideal of consistency is essentially modern'; M. Schapiro, 'Style' [1953], in *Theory and Philosophy of Art: Style, Artist and Society* (New York 1994), 51–102 at 62. In his 1964 study of the Parma Ildefonsus (*The Parma Ildefonsus: A Romanesque Illuminated Manuscript from Cluny and Related Works*), Schapiro recognised its duality of styles without denigrating this multiplicity or explicitly favouring one over another. Likewise, he described the asymmetry and inconsistencies of the façade of Chartres Cathedral in positive terms, as evidence of 'architectural invention' and an 'empirical approach' (or 'empirical solutions'); M. Schapiro, *Romanesque Architectural Sculpture: The Charles Eliot Norton Lectures*, ed., L. Seidel (Chicago 2006), 71–74.

[21] Expressive abstraction and ornamental surfaces are the hallmarks of a number of Catalonian liturgical manuscripts dated *c.* 1200, such as a missal from Tortosa Cathedral (Tortosa, Arxiu Capitular, Ms. 56) and the aforementioned Sant Cugat sacramentary (as n. 11). On architecture, see E.P. McKiernan González, 'The Persistence of the Romanesque in the Kingdom of Aragón', in *Church, State, Vellum, and Stone: Essays on Medieval Spain in Honor of John Williams*, ed., T. Martin and J.A. Harris (Leiden 2005), 443–478.

[22] There has been a welcome flourishing of historiographical and methodological considerations of patronage in recent years. See especially J. Caskey, 'Whodunnit? Patronage, the Canon, and the Problematics of Agency in Romanesque and Gothic Art', in *A Companion to Medieval Art: Romanesque and Gothic in Northern Europe*, ed., C. Rudolph (Malden, MA 2006), 193–212; H. Flora, 'Patronage', *Studies in Iconography*, 33 (2012): 207–218; and the essays in *Patronage: Power and Agency in Medieval Art*, ed., C. Hourihane (Princeton 2013).

[23] 'At times, it would seem, art historical recuperation of intention in the name of the patron has inadvertently smuggled a persistent conception of *individual* authorial agency, authority, and presence into explanations of how . . . medieval works of art came to be'. A. Kumler, 'The Patron-Function', in Hourihane, ed., *Patronage* (as n. 21), 302–304. For a critique of the conceptualisation of Suger as mastermind, see P. Kidson, 'Panofsky, Suger, and St-Denis', *Journal of the Warburg and Courtauld Institutes* 50 (1987), 1–17.

[24] R. Barthes, 'The Death of the Author' [1968], in *Image – Music – Text*, trans. S. Heath (New York 1977), 142–148.

[25] Caskey, 'Whodunnit?' (as n. 22), 196.

[26] S. Perkinson, 'Portraits and Their Patrons: Reconsidering Agency in Late Medieval Art', in Hourihane, ed., *Patronage* (as n. 22), 274.

[27] A. Kumler, 'The Patron-Function' in Hourihane, ed., *Patronage* (as n. 21), 304–305 and passim.

[28] Therese Martin has encouraged the use of the word 'makers' given that medieval audiences did not consistently distinguish between artificers and patrons in the way we do today, as exemplified by the ambiguity of the verb *facere* in Latin texts and inscriptions. T. Martin, 'Exceptions and Assumptions: Women in Medieval Art History', in *Reassessing the Roles of Women as 'Makers' of Medieval Art and Architecture* (Leiden 2012), 1–33.

[29] New York, Pierpont Morgan Library, M.240, fol. 8r.

[30] I here generally follow Lowden's iconographic analysis as well as his convincing argument that Blanche commissioned the Bible as a wedding gift for Louis. J. Lowden, *The Making of the Bibles Moralisées* (University Park, PA 2000), vol. 1, 127–132. See also Lowden's comments on this manuscript in 'The Holkham Bible Picture Book and the *Bible Moralisée*', in *The Medieval Book: Glosses from Friends & Colleagues of Christopher de Hamel*, ed., J.H. Marrow, R.A. Linenthal, and W. Noel ('t Goy-Houten 2010), 75–83. Here he emphasises the constructed nature of what we might call 'production scenes' (as opposed to, yet also parallel with, 'presentation scenes'). Lowden suggests that the inclusion of ecclesiastic advisors/iconographers in these depictions – as in the Toledo and Holkham Bibles – may have been intended to make a claim for religious authority rather than reflect actual circumstances of production.

[31] Kumler, 'The Patron-Function' (as n. 27), 297. This painting is also cited as an example of the complex, relational nature of medieval artistic patronage and production in Caskey, 'Whodunnit?' (as n. 22), 199.

[32] For additional examples of patronage as 'network' or 'circuit', see Perkinson, 'Portraits and Their Patrons' (as n. 26), 273, and Kumler, 'The Patron-Function' (as n. 26), 310.

[33] This attention to detail and, we might say, medium specificity, is also found in the Toledo *Bible moralisée*, where the empty roundels on the artist's parchment reveal an acute self-awareness – an impulse to acknowledge the genre and format of the manuscript within the depiction of its production. In the case of the *LFM* frontispiece, the tiny meta-documents testify to an appreciation of the material shift from charter to codex, while implying a direct and correct transformation from original to copy. (Ramon's prologue on the verso likewise makes a case for the cartulary's accuracy: 'Licet grande sit opus et magne egens inquisitionis, non credo me errasse, vel in aliquo articulo aliqua pretermississe, vel ex parte mea etiam punctum unum addidisse'.) For a list of the inscriptions of the documents depicted on the frontispiece, see Mundó, 'El pacte' (as n. 8), 129.

[34] As Adam Kosto has noted, it is neither Alfonso nor Ramon, but this very document, that is the true centre of the composition. Kosto, 'The *Liber*' (as n. 1), 20. Its wording ('Hoc est iudicium a Barchinonensi curia legaliter et usualiter') corresponds with *LFM* doc. 511. On the judgement in question in the context of the frontispiece, see T.N. Bisson, *The Crisis of the Twelfth Century: Power, Lordship, and the Origins of European Government* (Princeton 2009), 373–374.

[35] B. Brenk, 'Committenza', in *Enciclopedia dell'arte medievale*, ed., A.M. Romanini and M. Righetti, vol. 5 (Rome 1994), 203–218. 'Non sufficientemente indagati restano ancora i meccanismi della collaborazione certamente esistente, di norma, fra il committente-*concepteur* e l'artista, determinante in ogni caso per la configurazione dell'opera. . . . Il committente-*concepteur* interveniva nella concezione dell'opera d'arte definendone la tematica e soprattutto il programma e talvolta anche lo stile' (203).

[36] It is nevertheless possible that Ramon, having already worked in the king's chancery for several years, was himself responsible for the conception as well as the design of the cartulary, and only chose to credit the king to further exalt and flatter him.

[37] *Nec ad iactantiam loquor, sed ad maioris veritatis evidentiam.*

INDEX

(Page references in **bold** refer to illustrations.)

Adam of Eynsham, 121–26
Adelbraht, moneyer, **282**, 283, 284–85, 286
Adelrich, 280
Adorno, Anselm, 86
Adrian IV pope, 224, 226, 227
Aeci, bp of Barcelona, 39, 41, 42
Ælfheah, St, 4
Aemilian, St, 195, 200
Æthelsige, abbot of St Augustine's, 6
Alban, St, 4–6, 10
Alberbury (Shropshire), 94, 106
Alberico, abbot of San Benedetto Po, 17
Aldo, bp of Piacenza, 19, 32
Alexander II, pope, 3, 6, 183, 235, 251, 252, 255
Alexander III, pope, 205, 211
Alfonso I the Battler, king of Aragon and Pamplona, 57, 247
Alfonso II, king of Aragon, 109, 178, 212, 265, **266**, 327, 330, 332, 334
Alfonso II, king of Castile-León, 66
Alfonso VI, king of Castile-León, 63, 65, 66, 69, 94, 236–38, 243, 244, 246, 247, 249n.71
Alfonso VII, king of Castile-León, 63, 69, 226
Alfonso VIII, king of Castile, 224, 228
'Amalekite Master', 117, **127**, 139
Amat, bp of Oloron, 236
Ambazac (Haute-Vienne), 96, **97**
Ambrannus, lord of Vierzon, **265**
Anavarza (Turkey), 87
Ani (Turkey) cathedral, 86, **87**, 90
Anketil, goldsmith, 10
Anselm, abbot of Bury St Edmunds, 120
Anselm, St, archbp of Canterbury, 3–8
Anselmo II, bp of Lucca, 251, 252
Ansúrez, Alfonso, 238, 239
'Apocrypha Master', 117, 119, 127, **128**, **129**, 130, 133, 136–39, **plates VI, IX–XI**
Arduino, bp of Piacenza, 19, 33
Arles (Bouches-du-Rhône) Saint-Honorat-des-Alyscamps, 284, **285**
Arles-sur-Tech (Pyrénées-Orientales) Sainte-Marie, 143, **319**, **320**, 321
Arnaldus, scribe, 146
Arnolfo da Velate, bp of Cremona, 18
Auch (Gers) Saint-Orens, **236**, 243
Auct Bible, 117, 123–25, 139
Aurillac (Cantal), 170
Avignon (Vaucluse) Saint-Ruf, 224, 226, 227, 229, 231

Bainbrigg, Reginald, 291, 292
Ballantine-Dykes, Frecheville, 291
Baños de Cerrato (Palencia), 73

Barcelona (Catalonia)
　cathedral, 41, 42, **44**, 45, 224, 227, 228, **plate II**
　claustra, 39, 42
　episcopal palace, 42
　Holy Sepulchre, 41, 44
　St Eulalia, 44
　Santa Maria, 41
　Sant Pau del Camp, 334n.5
Bari (Apulia) San Nicola, 168
Battle (Sussex) abbey, 8
Beatrice of Canossa, 17, **27**
Bec-Hellouin (Eure) abbey, 3, 4
Bede, 4, 5
Bégon III abbot of Conques, 145, 170, 183, 189, **190**
Berengarius de Castellet, **207**, 208, 212
Berenguer de Vilademuls, archbp of Tarragona, 205, 207, 211, 212, 214
Bernardo degli Uberti, bp of Parma, 15, 19
Bernard of Cluny, 4
Bernard of La Sauvetat, archbp of Toledo, 237, 238, 247
Bernard the Elder, stonemason, 68
Bernardus Gilduinus, 52, 187
Bernat de Berga, bp of Barcelona, 224
Bernat Tort, archbp of Tarragona, 161, 208, 210, 214
Bernward, St, 143, 146, 191
Beuil (Haute-Vienne) abbey, 103, 104
Blanche of Castile, queen of France, 334
Blanche of Navarre, **190**, 191
Blasco Gardéliz, bp of Pamplona, 56
Blitherus, master mason, 9
Bois-Rahier (Indre-et-Loire), 106
Bonectus de Barberano, **212**
Boniface, abbot of Conques, 189
Boniface of Canossa, 15, 17, 27
Bonizone, bp of Piacenza, 19
Bonlieu (Creuse) abbey, **103**, **104**
Bonsignore, bp of Reggio Emilia, 18, 21
Borradaile Triptych, 183
Borrell, bp of Vic, 41
Borrell II, count of Barcelona, 41
Boschaud (Dordogne) abbey, 103
Brandin, 95
Braulio, bp of Saragossa, 195, 198, 201
Bridekirk (Cumberland), 291–312, **292–96**, **298**
Buckland (Somerset), 110, 111
Burgos (Castile)
　cathedral, 228
　Santa María la Real de Las Huelgas, 330
Bury Bible, 120–21, 127, 138

337

INDEX

Caen (Calvados) St Etienne, 3, 5, 7–9
Cairo, Bab-al-Futuh, 88
Cambrai (Nord) Holy Sepulchre, 44
Camden, William, 291, 292, 296
Canossa (Emilia)
    castle, **17**, **18**
    Sant' Apollonio, 15, **17**, **18**, 27, 28n.8
Canterbury (Kent)
    Christ Church cathedral, 2, 5, 7–9
    St Augustine's abbey, 2–6, 9, 10
Cardona (Catalonia) Sant Vicenç, 77, 78, **79**, 146, **147**
Carpi (Emilia) Santa Maria in Castello, 23, **24**
Castel Sant' Elia (Lazio), 168
Celanova (Galicia) San Salvador, 203n.24
Centula, St-Riquier (Somme) abbey, 41
Chartres (Eure-et-Loir) cathedral, 95
Chassay-Grandmont (Vendée), 106
Cherves (Vienne), 96, 178
Civate (Lombardy) San Pietro al Monte, 168, **169**
Clairvaux (Aube), 95
Clement III, pope, 19, 94
Clement VII, pope, 42
Clérieu (Drôme), 269, **271**, 272, 273
Clermont-Ferrand (Auvergne) Notre-Dame-du-Port, 259, **260**, 272, **273**, **274**
Cluny (Saone-et-Loire) abbey, 15, 17, 48, 49, 77, 81n.10, 94, 159, 236, 246, 249n.71
Coimbra (Portugal) Santa Cruz, 224, 226, 231
Cologne (North Rhine-Westphalia) St Maria im Kapitol, 22
Comberoumal (Aveyron) abbey, 104, **105**, 178
Conques (Aveyron), 170, **188**, 189, **190**, 191
Conrad, prior of Christ Church Canterbury, 8
Constance (Baden-Württemburg) St Maurice, 44
Cordoba (Andalusia) Great Mosque, 89
Corullón (León) San Esteban, 248n.42
Craswall (Herefordshire) abbey, 94, 104
Cremona (Lombardy) cathedral, 15, 18, 19, **20**, 21–24, **25**, 32, **33**, 34

Dalmacio, bp of Iria Flavia, 63, 68, 238
Damasus, pope, 120
Damianus, abbot of Nonantola, 15
Diego I Peláez, bp of Iria Flavia, 63, 65, 66, 68, 69
Diego II Gelmírez, bp of Iria Flavia *see* Gelmírez, archbp of Santiago de Compostela
Dionigi, bp of Piacenza, 19
Dodone, bp of Modena, 18, 21
Donizo, 15, 17, 27
Dugdale, William, 293, 298, 299, 301, 307
Dunstan, St, 4, 143

Eadmer Anhaende, 8
Eadmer of Canterbury, chronicler, 3, 4, 6
Eberhard von Nellenburg, 261
Edward Grim, 219, 223
Eleanor of Aquitaine, 259, **260**
Eleanor Plantagenet, queen of Castile, 224, 228
Elne (Pyrénées-Orientales)
    St Eulalia, 40
    St Mary, 40
    St Peter, 40
    St Stephen, 40
Enrico, abbot of San Benedetto Po, 17
Ermengol, bp of Urgell, 39, 42, 45
Ermessenda, countess of Barcelona, 147, 149
Ernulf, prior of Christ Church Canterbury, 8
Escornalbou (Catalonia) San Miguel, 207, 210, 214
Eskdale-Grosmont (Yorkshire), 94
Eslonça, countess of Pallars, 153, **154**
Espinelves (Catalonia) Sant Vicenç, 231
Esteban, architect, 58

Estella (La Rioja), 94
Etienne de Liciac, prior of Grosmont, 94, 96
Etienne of Muret, St, 94
Eulalia, St, 41, 42

Fabrizio Ferrarini, Nicola, 17
Fagildo, abbot of Anteoltares, 65, 66
Felicia, queen of Aragon, 183, 185, 186, 189, 191
Fernando I, king of Castile-León, 235, 243–45, 247
Fernando II, king of Castile-León, 63, 69
Fernandus, monk of San Millán de la Cogolla, 195, 197
Fontevraud (Maine-et-Loire), 94
Frassinoro (Modena), 15, 17
Frederick I Barbarossa, emperor, 283
Froger de Sées, 96
Frómista (Castile), 237, 242, 243, 247
Frotard, abbot of Saint-Pons-de-Thomières, 236–38
Fulda (Hesse) St Michael, 42
Fulk Fitz Warin III, 94

Garcia, bp of Aragon, 52, 54, 56, 57
Gari, abbot of Cuixà, 146
Garnier de Nablous, 111, 112
Garsies, monk of Cuixà, 145, 159, 161, 165, 168, 169, 171
Gauzlin, abbot of Fleury, 143
Gelmírez, archbp of Santiago de Compostela, 63, 64, 68, 69, 168, 171
Geminianus, St, 18, 23, 27, 32, **33**
Geoffrey, abbot of St Albans, 10
Gerald, magistrum operis, 96
Gerald of Ostia, 235
Germanus, bp of Auxerre, 5
Gervase, chronicler, 4, 8, 94, 111
Giordano da Clivio, archbp of Milan, 19
Girart of Roussillon, **261**, 264
Girona (Catalonia)
    cathedral, 39, **40**, 41, 42, 45, 143, 147, **148**, 149, **150–52**
    domus canonice, 39
    Sant Daniel, 149
    Sant Feliu, 149, **150**
Gisulf, duke, 262, **263**, 264, 273
Goldbach (Lake Constance) Sylvester Chapel, 261
Goscelin of Saint-Bertin, 4, 5, 9
Grandmont (Haute-Vienne) abbey, 93–108, **94**, **98–100**, 177, 179
Gregorius, abbot of Cuixà, 161, 163, **164**, 165, 169–71
Gregory I, pope, 6
Gregory VII, pope, 18, 52, 54–57, 235–37, 252, 256
Gregory the Chain-Bearer, patriarch, 83
Guadamir, bp of Vic, 41
Guala Bicchieri, cardinal, 179
Gualterus, illustrator, 146
Gualtiero, bp of Cremona, 18
Guarinus, abbot of Cuixà, 159, 161, 164, 171
Guglielmo, abbot of San Benedetto Po, 17
Guillaume de Treignac, 96
Guillem, bp of Vic, 179
Guillem de Torroja, archbp of Tarragona, 211
Guillermo, bp of Pamplona, 57
Guisla, countess of Cerdanya, 149
Guisla de Lluçà, countess of Barcelona, 149
Gundesindo, abbot of Santiago de Compostela, 68
Gundulf, bp of Rochester, 6, 8

Haghpat (Armenia), 88
Hamper, William, 297
Hardham (Sussex), 296
Harvey, scribe, 226, **227**, 231
Hautes-Clauzes (Pyrénées-Orientales) Saint-Nazaire, 321, 323
Henry I, king of England, 6, 95, 247
Henry I, king of France, 267
Henry II, emperor, 242

INDEX

Henry II, king of England, 93–97, 103, 106, 110–12, 114, 121–27, 130, 140, 259, **260**
Henry III, king of England, 7, 94
Henry IV, emperor, 18
Henry V, emperor, 282
Henry of Blois, bp of Winchester, 119–21, 130
Henry the Young King of England, 93, 96
Hildesheim (Lower Saxony) St Michael, 22, 146, 279, **280**
Himerius of Cremona, St, 19
Honorius II, pope, 19
Honorius Augustodunensis, 5, 9
Hôpital-Saint-Blaise (Pyrénées Atlantiques), 89
Horomos (Turkey), 90
Huesca (Aragon) mosque, 50
Hug de Cervelló, archbp of Tarragona, 210, 211, 214
Hugh Candidus, 235
Hugh de Flori, abbot of St Augustine's abbey, 3
Hugh du Puiset, bp of Durham, 120, 297
Hugh le Brun de Lusignan, 98
Hugh of Avallon, St, 103, 121, 123–26, 130
Hugh of Cluny, St, 26, 237, 238
Husillos sarcophagus, 235, **236**, 237, 239, 242, 243, 245–47

Innocent III, pope, 179
Iohannes Sancto Baudilio, 207
Isarn, abbot of Saint-Victor, Marseille, 238
IVORIES
   Boston, Museum of Fine Arts.
      Death of Aemilian from the Aemilian Reliquary, 197
   Florence, Museo Nazionale de Bargello.
      Death of Aemilian from the Aemilian Reliquary, 197
   León, Treasury of the Real Colegiata de Sa Isidoro.
      Reliquary of Pelagius and John the Baptist, 197 **198**
   London, British Museum.
      M&ME 1923 12–15,1 *Borradaile Triptych*, 183
   New York, Metropolitan Museum of Art.
      Accession N, 17, 190. 134. *Jaca Panel*, 183, **184**, plate **XVII**
      Accession N 17, 190. 33. *Jaca Panel*, 183, **185**, **186**, plate **XVIII**
   Paris, Bibliothèque nationale de France.
      Inv 55 no. 301, 183
   Paris, Musèe du Louvre, Département des Objets d'Art.
      MRR, 354, 422, 183
   Quedlinburg abbey.
      St Servatius reliquary, 242
   San Millán de la Cogolla.
      Aemilian reliquary, **200**
   San Millán de la Cogolla.
      Reliquary of San Felices, 187, **188**
   Washington DC, Dumbarton Oaks.
      Christ in Majesty from Aemilian Reliquary, **196**

Jaca (Aragon)
   cathedral, 47, **50**, 51, **52–57**, 60, 239, 242, 247
   San Pedro, 52
   Santa Cruz de la Serós, 183, 186, **187**, 191
Jaca panels, 183, **184–86**, plates **XVII, XVIII**
Jean Gâtine, 96
Jerusalem
   Anastasis Rotunda, 90
   Holy Sepulchre, 44, 45, 84, 87–89, 91
   St Anne, 87, 88
   St Helen's chapel, 87, 88
   St Menas chapel, 83
   Saints James cathedral, 83–92, **84–86**, **88**
Jimeno, bp of Burgos-Oca, 235, 236
Joan Colom, 175
Joan of Montserrat, 145
John, bp of Pamplona, 47
John, king of England, 93–95, 126
John, prior of St Swithun's, Winchester, 111, 123, 130

John of Salisbury, 221, 222, 224, 229
John of Würzburg, 83

Khorakert (Armenia), 89, 90
Khoranashat (Armenia), 90
Khtskonk (Turkey) monastery, Surb Sargis **plate III**
King, Gregory, **293**, 294, 295, 306

La Chapelle-Taillefert (Creuse), 98
Lagrasse (Aude) abbey, 77, **78**
Lambeth Bible, 127, 138
Lanfranc, archbp of Canterbury, 2–9
Lanfranco, architect, 18, 21, 22, 27, 32
L'Artige (Haute-Vienne), **101**, **102**, 103, 104
Las Huelgas Beatus, **330**, 331
Le Breuil-Bellay (Maine-et-Loire), **105**, 106
Leire (Navarre) abbey, 47, **48–50**, 54
Le Liget (Indre-et-Loire), 99
León
   cathedral, 262
   San Isidoro, 52, 69, 197, **198**, 226, 239, **240–42**, 243, **244**, 245, 247
Le Mans (Sarthe) cathedral, 95
Le Pin (Vienne) abbey, 104
Lenton (Nottinghamshire), 298
Les Châtelliers (Vendée) abbey, 103
Levens (Alpes-Maritimes), 75
Liber diversarum artium, 313
Liber Feudorum Maior, 179, 265, **266**, 327–36, **328**, **329**, **332**
Limoges (Haute-Vienne)
   Saint-Augustin, 103
   Saint-Martial, 95, 96
Lisbon, San Vicente de Fora, 226
Lleida (Catalonia) cathedral, 42, 231
Loarre (Aragon), 239
London
   Clerkenwell Hospital, 111
   Temple Church, 111
   Tower of London, 8
Louis IX, king of France, 334
Lucca (Tuscany), **253**, **plate XX**
   cathedral, 251, 252, 255, 256
   San Donato, 255
   San Frediano, 251, **252**, 255
   San Martino, **251**, 252, 255, 256
   San Pietro in Vincoli, 252, 255
   San Salvatore, 252
   Sant' Alessandro, 255
   Santa Maria Forisportam, 255
   Santi Giovanni, Pantaleone e Reperata, 252, **253**, 255
Lucius II, pope, 161, 171
Luçon (Vendée) Notre-Dame, 239
Lucy, countess of Pallers, 152, **153**, **plate XIV**

Macarius, bp of Jerusalem, 83
Mahaut, dau of Raymond Berenger III, 320, 321
Mahaut, dau of Robert Guiscard *see* Matilde
Maïeul, abbot of Cluny, 77
Maitre Alpais ciborium, 175–79, **177**
Mantua (Lombardy), 15
MANUSCRIPTS
   Auxerre, Bibliothèque municipale
      MS, 227, **261**
   Barcelona, Arxiu de la Corona d'Aragó
      MS Ripoll 42. *Treatise on Music*, 146
      MS Ripoll 168. *De Arithmetica* (Boethius) 1456, 146, **147**
      Real Cancilleria, Registros, núm. 1. *Liber Feudorum Maior*, 179, 265, **266**, 327–36, **328**, **329**, **332**
   Durham, Dean and Chapter Library
      MS A II.1 *Puiset Bible*, 120
   Hildesheim, Dom-Museum

INDEX

DS13 Small Bernward Gospel, 186
DS18 Precious Gospels of Bernard of Hildesheim, 186
Jaca, Archivo de la Catedral
    leg.1, docs, Reales, 10-E, **267**
León, Archivio de la Catedral
    Cód, 25. Libro de las Estampas, **264**, 266
Lleida, Arxiu Capitular.
    MS. Re-0036. Sacramentary, Ritual and Pontifical of Roda d'Isàvena, 149
London, British Library
    Add MSS 30845. Officium in Diem Sancti Aemiliani, 201
    Add MSS 11662. Cartulary of St-Martin-des-Champs, 267, **268**
    Cotton Claudius B. 11, 222
    Cotton Nero C IV, *Winchester Psalter*, 114
    Harley 5102, 222
London, College of Arms
    MS C.39, **293**
Lucca, Biblioteca Capitolare Feliniana
    Passionario P+, **254**
    MS, 123–24, 254
    MS, 47, 254
Modena, Archivio capitolare
    MS II.11, **33**
Montpellier, Inter-university Library
    MS H277. Liber diversarum artium, 313
New York, Pierpont Morgan Library
    M.429. *Las Huelgas Beatus*, **330**, 331
    M.240. *Toledo Bible Moralisée*, 333, 334, **plate XXII**
    M 619. Leaf related to the Winchester Bible (*Morgan Leaf*), 137–39, **plates IX, X**
Oxford, Bodleian Library
    MS Auct. E inf 1–2. *Auct Bible*, 117, 123–25, 139
Paris, Bibliothèque nationale de France
    MS Lat 6. *Rodes Bible*, 169, **plate XV**
    MS Lat 8878. *Saint-Sever Beatus*, 187
    MS Lat 9865. Cartulary of Vierzon, **265**, 266
Perpignan, Bibliothèque municipale
    MS 1 Gospel Book, 164, **165–67**, 168, 171
    MS 2 Gospel Book, 164
    MS 3 Commentary on the Psalms, 163, **164**
Rome, Biblioteca Apostolica Vaticana
    Barb Lat 2724. Chronicon Vulturnense, **263**
    Lat. 123, 146
    Lat. 4922. Donizo, Vita Mathildis, **26**
    Ms Lat 5729. *Ripoll Bible*, 146, **148**, **plate XII**
The Hague, Koninklijke Bibliotheek
    MS 76 F 5, **331**
    MS 76 F 13, **331**
Winchester Cathedral Library
    Winchester Bible, 109, **110**, 112, 114, 117–41, **118**, **119**, 127–29, **plates IV–VII, XI**
Marignac (Charente-Maritime) Saint-Sulpice, 88
Marseille (Bouches-du-Rhône) Saint-Victor, 238, 242
'Master of Espinelves', 229
'Master of Pedret', 152
'Master of the Genesis Initial', 117, 120, 124, 125, 136–39
'Master of the Gothic Majesty', 117, 124, 125, 130, 133, 136, 139, **plates V, VII**
'Master of the Leaping Figures', 117, **118**, 119, 124, 125, **127**, 133, 136–39, **plates IV, VII**
Mateo, architect, 63, 69
Mathon (Switzerland) priory, 177
Matilda, empress, 94
Matilda of Canossa/Tuscany, 15, 17–19, 21, 26, 27, 31
Matilde, dau. of Robert Guiscard, 149, 151
Matthew Paris, 7, 9, 10
Melisende, queen of Jerusalem, 84, 90, 91
Melle (Deux-Sèvres) Saint-Pierre, 242
Mervilliers (Eure-et-Loire), **272**
METALWORK

Ambazac, Saint-Antoine.
    Ambazac shrine, 96, **97**
Barcelona, Museu Nacional d'Art de Catalunya. *Limousin ciborium*, 175–81, **176**, **plate XVI**
Cleveland Museum of Art.
    Becket reliquary plaque, **225**
Cologne-Deutz, St Heribert.
    Heribert casket reliquary, **202**
Conques, Treasury of the Abbey of Saint-Foi.
    'A' of Charlemagne, **188**, 189
    Pentagonal reliquary, **189**
    Portable altar of abbot Bégon III, 189, **190**
    Reliquary of Pope Paschal II, 189, **190**, 191
London, Victoria and Albert Museum.
    Becket reliquary casket, **223**
Lucca, Complesso Museale e Arqueologico della Cattedrale.
    Becket reliquary casket, **225**
New York, Metropolitan Museum.
    N17. 190, 33. *Jaca panel*, 183, **185**, **186**, **plate XVIII**
    N17. 190, 134. *Jaca panel*, 183, **184**, **plate XVII**
    Plaque from a cross, 177
New York, Morgan Library and Museum.
    AZ 001. *Stavelot Triptych*, 191
Paris, Louvre.
    Maitre Alpais ciborium, 175–79, **177**
St Alban's cathedral.
    St Alban's shrine, 10
Visé, Saint Martin
    Hadelin casket reliquary, 202
Mezonzo, bp of Iria Flavia, 64
Milan (Lombardy) Museo del Castello Sforzesco, 24, **25**
Miro, bp of Girona, 159
Miró Viven, 44
Modena (Emilia) cathedral, 15, 17–19, **20**, 21, **22–25**, 28n.5–6, 31, **32**, 36
Moissac (Tarn-et-Garonne), 163, 169, 170
Montaubérau (Hérault) priory, 178
Monte Gargano (Apulia) St Michael, 44
Montmajour (Bouches-du-Rhône) abbey, 179
Mont-Saint-Michel (Manche) abbey, 3, 262
'Morgan Master', 112, 114, 117, **119**, 123–27, 130, 136–39, **plates VII, IX–XI**

Nájera (La Rioja) Santa María la Real, 47, **190**, 191
Neghuts (Armenia) monastery, **90**
Neophytos of Cyprus, 83
Neuchâtal (Switzerland), St Mary, 284, **285**
New York, Cloisters Museum, 161, 168
Nicholaus, architect, 19, 21
Nicholaus, sculptor, 21, 22, 25, 27
Nîmes (Gard) Saint-Gilles, 149
Nonantola (Emilia) abbey, 15, **16**, 19, 21, **22**, 25, 28n.5–6
Nuño Pérez de Lara, 228

Oberto da Dovara, bp of Cremona, 19
Odilo, abbot of Cluny, 48, 49, 81n.10
Odo, bp of La Seu d'Urgell, 151, 153, **154**
Odo of Cluny, 145
Oleguer, abbot of Saint-Ruf, 227
Oleguer, bp of Tarragona, 205, 208
Oliba, abbot of Ripoll and bp of Vic, 39, 41, 42, 44, 45, 143, 145–47, 151, 159, 161, 164, 165, 169, 171, 203n.24
Oliba Cabreta, count of Cerdanya, 145, 159, 161
Oliva, master of Ripoll quadrivium, 143, 146
Oloron-Saint-Marie (Pyrénées Atlantiques) Saint-Croix, 89
Ordoño III, **264**, 266
Otho, 94

Paderborn (Saxony) Holy Sepulchre, 44
Palencia (Castile) San Antolin, 49

Palermo (Sicily) Martorana, 88
Pamplona (Navarre) cathedral, 47, 57, **58**, **59**
Paris, Saint-Martin-des-Champs, 267
Parma (Emilia) cathedral, 15, 19, 25
Paschal II, pope, 18, 19, 32, 57, 189, **190**, 191, 237, 238, 246
Paul, abbot of St Albans, 3, 4, 6–9
Pedret (Catalonia) Sant Quirze, 153, **155**, 169, **plate XV**
Pedro, abbot of San Millán de la Cogolla, 195
Pedro, bp of Aragon, 52, 54, 56, 57
Pedro I, king of Aragon and Pamplona, 57, 58, 189, 236–38, 266, **267**
Pedro de Rodez, bp of Pamplona, 57–59, 237
Pere, bp of Girona, 39
Pere d'Amenys, abbot of Sant Cugat del Vallès, 175
Pere de Coma, 231
Pere de Ripollet, 229
Pere de Tavertet, 179
Peter II, king of Aragon, 178, 213, 332
Peter Damian, 251
Petrus Alfonsi, 247
Philadelphia Museum of Art, 169, **170**
Piacenza (Emilia) cathedral, 19, **20**, **21**, 22, 25, 32, 33, **34–37**
Pierre Bernard, prior of Grandmont, 93, 96
Pierre d'Andouque, bp of Pamplona, 189
Pietro, bp of Lucca, 252, 256
Pietro Cadalo, bp of Parma, 19
Pietro Orseolo, doge of Venice, 159, 161, 171
Pisa (Tuscany)
   Camposanto, 27
   cathedral, 255
Placentia, queen of Pamplona, 195
Poitiers (Vienne)
   cathedral, 259, **260**
   Saint-Hilaire-le-Grand, 287n.34
Polirone *see* San Benedetto Po
Poloner, John, 86, 88
Poncio, bp of Roda, 189
Poncius de Barberano, archbp of Tarragona, 206, 210
Pons de Gualba, bp of Barcelona, 42
Pontigny (Yonne), 95
Prat de Dalt (Caldes de Montbui), 224
Precious Gospels of Bernard of Hildesheim, 186
Prudencio de Sandoval, 195, 198, 201
Puiset Bible, 120

Quarante (Hérault), 77, 78, **79**
Quarantoli (Emilia), 24
Quedlinburg (Saxony) abbey, reliquary, 242
Quintanilla de las Viñas (Castile), 73

Raimundus de Bages, 205, **206**, 207
Raimundus de Karotitulo, 205, **206**
Raimundus de Sancto Laurentio, 213, 215
Ralf d'Escures, archbp of Canterbury, 3
Ralph, sacrist of St Swithuns, Winchester, 122
Ramiro I, king of Aragon, 50
Ramon, bp of Roda da Isàvena, 151, 154
Ramon Berenguer IV, 165, 171
Ramón de Caldes, 179, 265, **266**, 327, 332, 334
Ramón de Castellterçol, archbp of Tarragona, 206, 212
Ramón de Rocaberti, archbp of Tarragona, 206, **207**, 208, 212–15
Rangerius, bp of Lucca, 252, 254–56
Raymond, abbot of Leire, 237
Raymond of Burgundy, 69, 245
Reginald of Durham, 302
Richard, abbot of Saint-Victor of Marseille, 54, 236–38, 246, 247
Richard I, king of England, 93–95, 104, 106
Richard d'Aubigny, abbot of St Albans, 3, 5, 7, 8
Richard of Ilchester, bp of Winchester, 111, 112, 121
Rikard, **298**, 306, 307

Ripoll (Catalonia) abbey, 41, 77, **78**, 143, 145, **147**, 148, 155, 156, 159, 171, 179, 203n.24, 224, 229
Ripoll Bibles, 145, 146, **148**, 159, 169, **plate XII**
Robert, prior of St Swithuns, Winchester, 122
Robert de Thurnham, 94, 95
Robert the mason, 9
Rochester (Kent)
   castle, 8
   cathedral, 8
Roda de Isábena (Catalonia), 42, 154, 189
Rodes Bible, 169, **plate XV**
Rodez (Aveyron) Saint-Pons, 237
Rome
   St Peters, 5, 44, 77, **78**, 145
   Saints Sergius and Bacchus, 179
   San Clemente, 168, 171
   San Giovanni a Porta Latina, 145
   San Paolo fuori le Mura, 145
   Santa Maria ad Martyres, 145
   Santa Maria Maggiore, 145, 161
Rouen (Seine-Maritime) Le Petit-Quevilly, St-Julien, 97, **114**

Sahagún (León) abbey, 69, 237, 239
St Albans (Hertfordshire) abbey, 2, 4–7, 9
Saint-André-de-Sorède (Pyrénées-Orientales), 143
St-Genis-des-Fontaines (Pyrénées-Orientales), 143, **144**
Saint-Gilles-du-Gard (Gard), 242
Saint-Guilhem-le-Désert (Hérault), 77, 78, **80**
Saint-Jouin-de-Marnes (Deux-Sèvres), 88
Saint-Martin-de-Fenollar (Pyrénées-Orientales), 320, **321–24**
Saint-Martin-des-Puits (Aude), 73
Saint-Pons-de-Thomières (Hérault), 52, 57, 58, 75
Saint-Sauveur-de-Casesnoves,(Pyrénées-Orientales), 321
Saint-Sever Beatus, 187
Saint-Sylvestre (Haute-Vienne), **99**
Salamanca (Castile) Santo Tomás Cantuariensis, 224
San Benedetto Po (Lombardy) abbey, 15, 17. **18**. **19**, 22, 25, 27
Sancha, countess, 262, **264**
Sancha, queen of Aragon, 109, 112, 114, 243, 332, 334n.4
Sancho, bp of Aragon, 56
Sancho, bp of Pamplona, 48, 49
Sancho III the Great, king of Pamplona, 47–49, 145
Sancho IV, king of Pamplona, 47, 195
Sancho de Larrosa, bp of Pamplona, 57
Sancho Garcés II, king of Pamplona, 47
Sancho Ramirez, king of Aragon and Pamplona, 48, 50, 52, 54, 56–58, 60, 183, 185, 189, 237
San Isidro de Dueñas (Castile), 236
San Juan de la Peña (Aragon) abbey, 49, 52, 57, 333
San-Miguel de Almazán (Castile), 89, 224, **226**
San Miguel de Villatuerta (Navarre), 47, **48**
San Millán de la Cogolla (La Rioja), 49, 187, **188**, 195, **196**, **197**, 198, **199**, **200**, 201
San Pedro of Siresa (Aragon), 52
San Salvador de Fuentes (Asturias), 269
Santa Maria del Gerri (Catalonia), 153
Santa Maria de Ujué (Navarre), 52
San Vicente de la Sierra (La Rioja), 226, 231
San Vincenzo al Volturno (Molise), 262
San Vittore alle Chiuse (Marche), 88
Sant' Antimo (Tuscany), 268, **269**
Sant Joan de les Abadesses (Catalonia), 175
Sant Marti del Canigó (Pyrénées-Orientales), 143, 146, 147, 149
Sant Miquel de Cuixà (Pyrénées-Orientales), 42, 45, 143, **144**, 145, **146**, 147, 159, **160**, 161, **162–66**, 168–71, 321
Sant Pere del Burgal (Catalonia), 78, 152, **153**, **plate XIV**
Sant Pere de Rodes (Catalonia), 41, 143, 147, 171
Santiago de Compostela (Galicia)
   Anteáltares, 64, 65, 66, 69
   cathedral, 58, 59, 63, **64–68**, 89, 168, 239, 243, 249n.74, 262

San Martin Pinario, 64
San Pelayo, 69
Santa Maria Corticela, 63, 64
Sarrians (Vaucluse), 75, 82n.15
Savigny (Manche) abbey, 179
Scolland, abbot of St Augustine's abbey, 3, 4, 7–9
Segeredo, prior of Santiago de Compostela, 68
Serrabona, (Pyrénées-Orientales) Santa Maria, 161, **162**, 163, 164, **165**
Sigena (Aragon) Santa María, **109**, **110**, **112**, **113**, 114, 130, 332
Sigüenza (Castile) cathedral, 228, 229
Sisnando I, bp of Iria Flavia, 63, 64
Small Bernward Gospel, 186
Sorbara (Emilia) Sant' Agata, 24
Soria (Castile)
   San Juan de Duero, 88
   San Nicolás, 224, 229
Spoleto (Umbria) Saints Giovanni e Paolo, 221, **222**
Stephen of Lexington, abbot of Savigny, 179
Stothard, Charles, 291
Stukeley, William, 292
Surb Nshan (Turkey), 89

Tarragona (Catalonia)
   cathedral, 205–18, **206–8**, **212–14**, 230
   St Magdalena de Bell-Lloc, 210
Taüll (Catalonia) Sant Climent, **319**
Teghenyats (Armenia) monastery, **89**
Teodemir, bp of Iria Flavia, 69
Terrassa (Catalonia), **plate I**
   cathedral, 44
   St Michael, 39, 40
   Saints Justus and Pastor chapel, 40
   Santa Maria, 39, 40, 219–33, **220–22**, **225**, **228–30**, **plate XIX**
   Sant Pere, 39, 40
Theobald, archbp of Canterbury, 130
Thibaud de Champagne, king of Navarre, 94, 96
Thomas Becket, St, 219–33, **220–23**, **225**, **228**, **229**
Tolba, 45
Toledo (Castile-La Mancha)
   Bab-al-Mardum mosque, 89
   cathedral, 69, 224, 228
   Holy Cross, 89
Toledo Bible Moralisée, 333, 334, **plate XXII**
Tolson, Richard, 298, 299
Torres del Rio (Navarre) Holy Sepulchre, 89
Toulouse (Haute-Garonne)
   Musée Saint Raymond, St-Orens sarcophagus, **236**
   Saint-Sernin, 52, 58, 237–39, 243, 247
Treviño (Burgos), 269, **271**
Tudela (Navarre), 94

Ugo da Noceto, bp of Cremona, 19
Urban II, pope, 5, 19, 57, 58, 68, 189, 238
Urgell (Catalonia)
   cathedral, 39, 42, **43**, 143, 149, 155, 229
   Holy Sepulchre, 42, **43**, 44, 45
   St Eulalia, 42, **43**, 45
   St John, 41
   Sant Miquel, 42, **43**, 45
   Sts Mary and Peter, 41, **43**, 45
   Sts Peter, Paul and Andrew, 45
Urraca, infanta, 52, 237, 239, 245–47

Urraca, queen of Castile-León, 63, 69
Urraca de Zamora, 59

Valdeblore (Alpes-Maritimes), 75
Valencia (Valencia) cathedral, 41
Velasco, bp of Pamplona, 47
Vercelli (Piedmont) Sant' Andrea, 179
Vézelay (Yonne) abbey, 261, 262
Vic (Catalonia)
   cathedral, 39–42, **43**, 44, 45, 146, 147, 155, 159, 229
   Episcopal Museum, 229, **230**
   St Felix, 41
   St John the Baptist, 41
   St Michael Archangel, 41
   St Peter's church, 40, 41, 45
   Santa Maria, 40–42, 145
   Virgin and St Peter church, 40, 41
Vierzon (Cher) St-Pierre, **265**, 266
Villelongue-dels-Monts, (Pyrénées-Orientales) Notre-Dame-del-Vilar, **320**
Vitalis, 9

WALLPAINTINGS
   Casamari, Santa Maria di Reggimento, 221
   Haute-Clauzes, Saint-Nazaire, 321
   Rouen, Le Petit-Quevilly, **114**
   Saint-Martin-de-Fenollar, 320, **321–24**, **plate XXI**
   Saint-Sauveur-de-Casesnoves, 321
   Sant Pere del Burgal. Now in Museu Nacional d'Art de Catalunya, Barcelona, 152, **153**, **154**, **plate XIV**
   Sant Quirze de Pedret. Now in Museu Nacional d'Art de Catalunya, Barcelona, **155**
   Sant Quirze de Pedret. Now in Solsona, Museu Diocesà í Comarcal, 169, **plate XV**
   Sigena Hospital. Now in Museu Nacional d'Art de Catalunya, Barcelona, **109**, **110**, **112–14**, 130
   Spoleto, Saints Giovanni and Paolo, 221, **222**
   Terrassa, Santa Maria, 219–33, **220–22**, **228–30**, **plates XIX, XXI**
   Winchester cathedral, 130
Walter de Lacy, 94, 95
Westminster abbey, 7
Westminster Palace, 9
Wido, abbot of St Augustine's abbey, 3
Wiligelmo, sculptor, 21, **22–25**, 26, 27, 28n.5
William I, king of England, 8
William II, king of England, 8
William of Corbeil, archbp of Canterbury, 3
William of Malmesbury, 5, 9
William of Volpiano, 3
Winchester (Hampshire) cathedral, 130
Winchester Bible, 109, **110**, 112, 114, 117–41, **118**, **119**, **127–29**, **plates IV–VII, XI**
Winchester Psalter, 114
Winrico, bp of Piacenzo, 19
Witham (Somerset) 99, 103, 122, 124, 125, 130
Worms (Rhineland-Palatinate)
   cathedral, 279, **280–85**
   St Martin, 287n.39
   St Paul, 287n.39

Zaragoza (Aragon) cathedral, 42, 228